Fifty years ago, Wilbur Youngman, garden editor of the old Washington Star newspaper, had a good idea. He wrote the first edition of *The Washington Star Garden Book,* plus numerous subsequent editions, thus giving to our gardening parents, grandparents, and neighbors a tradition of sound planting advice and information unique to the Washington metropolitan area. It has been my privilege to continue that tradition.

As experienced Washington gardeners know, the area's mild climate is ideal for growing an enormous range of plants. *The Washington Star Garden Book* helps to sort them out by listing plants that have proven themselves in local gardens over the years. It also provides specific advice to help you make the most of your efforts and use your time and resources wisely. Each chapter identifies public gardens in the area where you can find examples of the plants discussed in the chapter, and throughout the book, members of local plant societies, Cooperative Extension offices, and arboretums and nursery staff share their gardening expertise.

I hope the enthusiasm of these avid gardeners is infectious and that you'll join the many Washington gardening bugs who are working to make the next fifty years in our nation's capital as beautiful as the last fifty!

—Deborah Fialka

THE WASHINGTON STAR GARDEN BOOK

50th Anniversary Edition
The Washington Star
Garden Book

1944-1994

The Encyclopedia of Gardening for the District, Maryland and Virginia

by Deborah R. Fialka

Cover: Georgetown's Dumbarton Oaks
Editor: Gabe T. Adalas
Editorial Assistants: Keren R. Modrak, Raissa M. Modrak
Design Editor: G. Sturdley-Pritt
Flower Illustrations by Linda Greigg, Silver Spring, Md.
Maps and Water Garden Art by Stanley Bandong, Washington, D.C.
Composition by Gerryamanda, Washington, D.C.
Printed by Balmar Printing and Graphics, Gaithersburg, Md.
Published by The Washington Book Trading Company,
P.O. Box 1676, Arlington, Virginia 22210.
1994 Edition ISBN 0915168-50-2 $15.95
First edition published 1944.

CONTENTS

1. LANDSCAPING THE HOME GROUNDS

It is as true today as it was fifty years ago that a new house and garden require time to get acquainted. A garden is a dynamic, growing entity, and observation of the changing seasons reveals and conceals the form and structure of the plants and their foliage, flowers and fruits. There are many forces at work: orientation to the sun, exposure to the wind, and the extremes of temperature and moisture. Recording your observations is a critical first step as you begin to work on your garden.

Take up a notebook and follow in the footsteps of Thomas Jefferson. He was an enthusiastic keeper of The Garden Book in which he recorded his plantings and harvests, his ideas, and his garden successes and failures. He was constantly assessing, evaluating, and recording—to remember and learn from his experiences. Jefferson's chronological format provided a structure for keeping weather information, planting and bloom dates, and tasks completed. His record covered about sixty years. Some years it was prodigious, while in other years it fell by the wayside—but Jefferson always came back to it. More than likely you will too.

A loose-leaf notebook for recording data, scaled graph paper for drawings, and file folders are the basic materials for a garden record. File folders are useful for organizing clippings of design elements that inspire, articles and photographs of plants, and combinations noted when visiting gardens and area resources. These are invaluable resources for planning your garden.

Mapping the Existing Garden

To begin, use the plat that comes with your deed as a basis for making an enlarged scale drawing that will give the dimensions of your property and the precise location of your house on it. A usable scale (¼-inch to the foot) will enable you to locate and inventory existing plantings. It will be an hour or two well spent to show the relationships and relative size of all your garden elements on this map. The drawing will serve as a reminder of the placement of bulbs and other plants that come and go with the seasons. Make several copies to use for future planning.

Your plat has an arrow indicating north. This arrow is the key to unlocking basic information about the relationship of your site to the sun. Orientation to the sun shapes your garden by determining the plants that will succeed in a given area of the property. Garden books and nurseries frequently organize plants by their requirements for sun. A garden area in full sun is oriented to the south; in partial sun toward the west; and in partial shade toward the east.

You can flesh out your map with a series of photos of planted areas taken during the course of a day to provide a record of *sun and shade patterns*. Use a clock to show the time of each photo, and repeat the process in each season of your first year in residence.

Other environmental factors that shape the garden are *terrain*, the *exposure* to the prevailing weather patterns, and the existing *soil conditions*. The lay of the land, sloped or flat, affects the movement of the air and water on the site.

The prevailing weather patterns in the metropolitan area come from the northwest, driving the wind, rain, and snow. Soil conditions include soil structure, fertility, and drainage of surface water.

Buildings also modify and shape the garden. The house itself casts a shadow and changes the drainage of air and water. Trees and other garden elements do the same.

In an existing garden the first step is to identify what trees, shrubs, and flowering plants are already there by looking them up in field guides and garden books. In your garden notebook, jot down the pertinent facts about your plants, including their size at maturity and any desirable features or problems they present. These notes will help you evaluate the potential of existing plantings.

Here your seasonal photos from the same vantage points will help you visualize the changing aspects of any plan that exists. They will also help you identify the desirable views and any problems of your front entrance, public and private portions of the garden, and the framed views from within the house. You also need to photograph the details of any pavement and steps, as well as your patio or deck.

All this record keeping and map making may sound time consuming, but it will get you acquaint you with the garden and ultimately help you create a garden that pleases you and serves you well for years to come. Your photographs will provide you with a revealing record of your accomplishment.

Assessing the Existing Garden

Each gardener is challenged by the previous owner's garden vision. See if the information you gathered in your notes and photographs makes it possible to answer these questions.

◊ Is there an overall design concept?
◊ Does there appear to be a plan that the plants and built elements fit into?
◊ Do the built elements relate to the style of the house?
◊ Are the construction materials compatible with those of the house?
◊ Do elements serve their function?
◊ Are they accessible from the house and garden?
◊ How do the trees, shrubs, and other plants look and work?
◊ Do the plants and built elements please you?

These are questions to ask yourself and the members of your household because your answers will be essential in the development of the garden plan. The key question is whether you're happy with the garden and its function.

Your Wish List

Once you decide what you like and dislike you can make a wish list of items that address the what, where, why, when, and how of your garden. Your wish list should be a combination of fantasies and practicalities.

The Public Spaces

Gardens have public and private spaces. The public spaces have access to the street, to the drive, to the walk, and to the front door and are used by members of the household, service people, and guests. Evaluate the existing conditions particularly from the stand point of how well they serve you and your public.

◊ Is the front door obvious?
◊ Can your house number be read from the street?
◊ Is there a walk that leads directly to the door?
◊ Does the driveway have room to get out of the car on to a paved surface?
◊ Is there room to park more than one car?
◊ Is there storage for the trash and recycling bins?
◊

The Private Spaces

The private spaces are those that are used by members of the household and optimally are less open to public view. This is the area where the demands of many, for multiple uses come into play; of course, the uses may well change over time.

Space use comes in three large categories: passive uses, active uses, and work areas.

The nature of the use in large part determines the look and the design of the garden. All three categories of use vie for the same space, and elements in the design can be combined to serve different types of use and to change over time. For example, a sitting area could include a sand box that eventually could become a raised planting bed. Along with this, the following existing conditions help to define areas for different activities.

◊ How accessible is the garden, from the house, the drive, the garage?
◊ Is the door at the grade or are there steps?
◊ Is there a secluded area for sitting or dining?
◊ Is there a deck or porch?
◊ Can you see play areas from the kitchen or family room?
◊ Is the garden level or sloped?
◊ Is there sun or shade?
◊ Is there room for games and rough and tumble?
◊ Is there a place for a garden swing or hammock?

These questions and the suggested uses of space are stepping stones to compiling your wish list. Involve the members of your household in the wishing process, too. A successful garden serves everyone; if you have a rough and tumble area, you may well need and desire tranquil spaces as well. Remember that wish lists are nonjudgmental; write down all the things that come to mind even the seemingly extravagant.

If the flow of ideas dries up there are loads of resources you can turn to: collect and save clippings that show how others have addressed the use of space. During the Garden Tour season, take advantage of the many opportunities in our area to visit other people's gardens and see how they address their own situations.

The Washington metropolitan area has a wide variety of public and historic gardens, parks, and horticultural institutions accessible to the gardener. Display gardens include collections of trees and shrubs, perennials, bulbs, and wildflowers. Specialty gardens feature plant groups such as roses, herbs, and ornamental grasses. Nursery and garden center display plantings can help customers see how plants may be used. All of these resources provide the gardener with a living reference library of ideas and inspiration

Prepare Your Budget: Dollars and Time

The wish list lays out the possibilities for your garden. Now comes the reality of preparing budget of your dollars and time. To use these valuable resources wisely you will need to develop budgets for both. Dollars are essential for buying supplies, materials, and plants and for services that you cannot do yourself. However, your time and your skills can accomplish lots of items on your wish list. Tree pruning requires a professional, but you can deal with the debris. A serious drainage problem may well require a professional, but soil preparation is a gardener's pleasure. Large specimen trees and shrubs are best left to a professional.

Budgeting provides a structure for setting priorities. Probably the biggest difficulty in the budgeting process is being realistic about the amount of time you have available and determining how much time the project will take. Remember, many projects can be accomplished in phases over a period of years, thus easing the crunch on your resources. A budget and a plan go hand in hand to accomplish the garden envisioned in your wish list.

Budget Check List

Dollars/ Time		Budget Item
$___	Hrs.___	construction materials: wood, stone, bricks
$___	Hrs.___	construction of structure: decks, pools, walls
$___	Hrs.___	tree pruning and removal
$___	Hrs.___	sodding a new lawn
$___	Hrs.___	planting large trees and shrubs
$___	Hrs.___	soil preparation
$___	Hrs.___	plants and planting
$___	Hrs.___	weeding and maintenance
$___	Hrs.___	installation of paving, walks, steps
$___	Hrs.___	construction of planters, fences, trellis

Designing a Plan for the Garden

The garden combines architectural elements and plants to create an environment suitable for the activities on your wish list. Like a house, it requires a framework, and the gardens that are most successful are extensions of the house.

The concept of outdoor rooms helps to address the use of the space and informs its design. Often the most aesthetically pleasing choice results from a design that serves its function best.

The focus of this book is on the plants suitable for growing in our region (known as gardening zone 7). Consult the photographs you made and the wish list you compiled to keep the functions you want to accommodate and the focus on the problems you need to solve. Here are some tips to assist in the decisions for the built elements of the garden.

◊ The shortest distance from place to place becomes the walk.
◊ The walks for two side by side or a full wheel barrow need to be five feet wide.
◊ A durable hard surface serves best for walks, dining terrace, and a barbecue.
◊ Play equipment needs a surface that can take the wear and drain fast.
◊ Enclosures for privacy should not imprison.
◊ Some functions can share space, others are not compatible.
◊ Use materials that are similar or relate to the house.
◊ Create a focus for the views from the windows and garden paths, perhaps a bench, an arbor, or a gate.

The Roles of Plants in the Garden

In the living garden, plants serve to create the elements of an outdoor room: a hedge is an enclosure or wall, a tree creates shade and is a ceiling of sorts. Thus, plants in the garden are functional and ornamental. To work well they should fulfill both purposes.

The Functional Uses for Plants

◊ To mark the boundary
◊ To frame an entrance
◊ To mark a transition from one space to another
◊ To create privacy
◊ To screen an unattractive view
◊ To provide protection from the sun
◊ To provide a wind break

Magnolia grandiflora, a large evergreen tree at the edge of the garden can mark the boundary, screen the view, and provide a focal point; but it would not do well as a shade tree because its large leathery leaves create a very dark, dense shade, and its root system is too close to the surface to accommodate walking or paving.

A hedge is a living fence or wall: Taxus baccata, English yew, is a fine-textured needled evergreen that can be sheared to create a formal enclosure around an outdoor dining room. A more informal hedge, a row of fruit trees, can be espaliered, (trained flat and pruned to one plane) to make a fence that will also conserve space in a small garden.

The foundation plantings of the 1950s often age less gracefully than their owners, blocking light and views from the windows. A winter of heavy snowfall sends cascades of snow crashing down on mature Junipers, Rhododendrons and Azaleas, breaking their branches.

The contemporary alternative to foundation plants places them out from the walls, allowing room for growth. It is important to select plants that will not outgrow their location.

Take as an example the obvious focal point of a front door. A pair of crape myrtle, 'Natchez' planted on either side of the front walk will frame the door and shade the walk. Mugo pine 'Mops', a dwarf cultivar a Japanese pine is a slow growing conifer; its dense bristly globe is a distinctive marker for front steps. Nandina domestica, the Heavenly Bamboo of China, is an elegant evergreen shrub with lacy compound leaves on multiple upright canes about 5 feet tall. The upright panicles of white flowers ripen into clusters of bright red fruits that last all winter and into the next growing season, the kind of shrub that is perfect for viewing all year from within the home or the garden.

Ornamental Features of Plants

Ornamental characteristics include the habit of growth, the size and shape of the plant, the foliage, the flowers, the fruit, and seasonal features such as fall leaf color, winter-persistent fruit, or beautiful bark. Other considerations include rate of growth and the time and length of the flowering season.

Because urban gardens have a finite amount of space the best plants to choose have ornamental characteristics that provide interest during all seasons..

A great plant is the sum of its parts and each of the parts has a season to shine. An excellent example of this principle is the same large crape myrtle 'Natchez'. In winter its sinuous multiple trunks have cinnamon colored bark and a gracefully twiggy branch structure tipped with woody seed pods. Spring brings coppery new growth that turns rich dark green as it matures. The star season for crape myrtle is the late summer when large panicles of silky white flowers open over a period of weeks throughout the area elegant and undismayed by our persistent heat and drought.

Garden plants can be divided into large groups: woody and nonwoody (herbaceous). *Woody plants* include trees, shrubs, vines, and some ground covers with wood stems. They are further characterized by the nature or their foliage, which may be either deciduous (renewed each spring) or evergreen (renewed every couple of years or more). Evergreens foliage may consist of broad leaves, scales or needles.

Herbaceous plants die down to the ground in winter and put new growth from the crown in spring. These plants are subdivided into groups based on their life span. *Annuals* germinate their seed, grow into a flowering plant that produces seed in one growing season. *Biennials* germinate and develop a foliage plant in the first growing season; in the second year it flowers and sets seed. *Perennials* are herbaceous plants that live for several growing seasons. Each winter the plant dies back to the ground and the new growth emerges from the crown in spring.

Despite the name, perennials do not live and flourish forever; most benefit from lifting and dividing every three to four years. Ornamental grasses are considered perennial by our definition. They are in fashion in Washington; several outstanding public gardens display them. Bulbs, corms, and tubers are also perennials, and, although these plants have underground storage structures that differ from other perennials, they function in the same way.

Ornamental Characteristics of a Good Plant

Remember that English adage, "A weed is a good plant in the wrong place." The following chapters provide details of the growing conditions and ornamental characteristics of trees, shrubs, conifers, and herbaceous plants for your garden palette. The checklist below serves as a reminder of the features to look for in a good plant.

⇒ *Habit of Growth*: trunk or trunks, branch structure, bark, mature height, mature spread .

⇒ *Foliage*: size, shape, color, texture, evergreen deciduous, fall leaf color.

⇒ *Winter Interest*: bark, branch pattern, buds and twigs, fruits, pods and cones, evergreen foliage, winter flowers.

⇒ *Flowers*: fruit size, shape, color, bloom season, length of bloom season.

⇒ *Fruit*: shape-berries, pods, nuts, fleshy fruits, color, texture, winter persistence.

GETTING PROFESSIONAL HELP

To get the best value for your budget dollars you need to understand the services that landscape professionals can offer you. You will always be better served, no matter who you work with, if you ask for local references of satisfied clients. Insist on a contract that spells out costs for service, and installation and payment schedules. Express an interest in making the final choice of plant material.

Landscape architects are trained in a five-year degree program that is accredited by the American Society of Landscape Architects. They are then licensed. Their training emphasizes total design of the site and choice of plant material, with a strong emphasis on the appropriate engineering for built elements of the plan they do for you. A landscape architect will often design and recommend subcontractors to complete major phases of the work, present plans to obtain any municipal permits required, and help clients oversee subcontracted work. They will often bid on the entire job, handling and charging for the subcontracting.

As a client, you should ask to see several samples of

their residential work to determine if a signature style, or response to a particular client's need is the watchword of the firm. Since you will be charged top dollar for their services, it is wise not to ask for plan changes in mid-stream, which may require billable hours over and above the original contract estimate. As with building a house, you should always pay in increments as different portions of the work are completed, making sure to hold back as much of the 20% profit margin as you can negotiate until all the work is done.

A *garden designer* should come to the work with a primary background in horticulture, either by degree or inclination and experience. Interior designers are interested in instant effect and not in process. The garden designer's emphasis is on appropriate plant material for a site and spacing that allows plants to develop over time.

Designers often work with subcontractors who are responsible for the built elements of the plan, and will help the client obtain required permits. Charges may be hourly or by the job. Hiring a garden designer can be a good idea for a "hands on" client who wants to do the job in stages, adding and refining ideas over time with the help of an experienced eye who knows where to locate and how to plant good material.

Both designers and architects often do follow up visits for a year or two after a plan is installed. Ask for this service. Some designers employ or can recommend people to help you with the extra maintainence that new plant installations require until they are established.

Many garden designers belong to the Association of Landscape Design Professionals.

Landscape contractors build and install to a plan, though some employ designers to work up plans for a client. Most purchase their plant material through large local wholesalers and growers whose identities they guard jealously. They typically obtain construction permits if asked. Many have maintainence divisions that will follow up with a regular care program if necessary. Like full-service nurseries, landscape contractors usually offer a replacement guarantee for material that they supply and plant. Be sure that it covers a full growing year for trees and expensive shrubs. Large firms are often members of the national professional organization for landscape contractors, but reputable small firms may do high quality work. Always get references you can visit, preferably a year or two later.

Full-service nurseries may offer design services to aid the homeowner in the selection of the plant material they are selling in addition to the free gardening classes that start off each season. The advantage of being able to see and evaluate plant material at the nursery before ordering, and of working with staff to find special plants if the work is to be phased over several years, removes some of the sting of paying retail. A "good customer" discount may be offered to landscaping clients.

The cost of the design service is usually separate from the cost of delivery and installation of material, which is roughly triple the cost of plants alone. Correcting compacted subdivision fill before planting can add significant cost to a seemingly simple job.

Such nurseries are regulated members of the Associated Landscape Contractors of America, and the American Nurserymen's Association.

INSPIRATION: These are a few of the local residential gardens now open to the public. Their variety may provide ideas for your garden site:

The Old Stone House, Georgetown, 3051 M Street, NW, Washington, D.C.

Textile Museum, 2320 S Street, Washington, D.C.

McCrillis Gardens, 6910 Green Tree Road, Bethesda, Maryland.

Carlyle House Historic Park, 121 N. Fairfax Street, Alexandria, Virginia.

2. SOIL PREPARATION

Feed the soil and the garden will take care of itself is one of those truisms that is really true. The successful gardener knows that amending the structure and chemical balance of his soil to match the needs of his plants is the secret to a productive and enjoyable garden; consequently, we will start "from the ground up".

Soil analysis and improvement are the themes. You will learn how to identify your soil's structural and chemical make-up, and how to amend and improve it for your purposes. A list of tools that you will need for various garden chores ends the chapter.

Local Soil Structure
Soil is made up of *sand, silt,* and *clay,* of which clay is by far the most prevalent portion of the soil mixes for gardeners in the immediate Washington area. To the south and east sands create warmer, faster-draining gardens, while to the west and north along Piedmont river bottoms, rich loams high in organic matter are more common.

In general, sands warm quickly, provide needed oxygen for root growth where moisture is adequate, and have a loose structure that is susceptible to drought and quick loss of nutrients. Loams have the most available plant food, a high proportion of organic materials in a loose enough structure to stay moist, and to moderate temperature changes that might stress plants. Clays are rich in minerals, but so tight in texture that plant roots lack oxygen if the soil is too dry or too wet.

To test your soil's structure, put a cup of it taken from a vertical slice a shovel's blade deep, and shake it up in a closed quart jar until it liquifies. Let it stand for 24 hours and observe the result. In a balanced soil you should see 3 distinct layers of material with clay on the top and sand at the bottom. The depth of each layer will give you a rough idea of your soil's predominant structure, and how far you have to go to achieve a better ratio of its structural components. Rich, friable soil is the foundation on which your gardening plans rest; and your ability to improve it is the single most useful skill you can learn.

How To Use Compost
Composting, an old garden practice, is not used as freely as it should be by the local urban gardener. Most of the tight clays that underlie suburban gardens could benefit from the addition of some green sand for improved drainage and even

A compost pile is built-up of layers of plant material, soil and chemicals (lime, ammonium sulphate and superphosphate).

Although partial, this list of the functions of humus includes all the major reasons for its importance to your garden. In addition, the heating action of decaying plant material in a well-made compost pile destroys many pests and weed seeds, and helps the gardener recycle noxious weeds and used plant materials that would otherwise have to be sent to crowded landfills.

Composting is the process of layering plant material, lime, soil, and various fertilizers into a kind of organic cake that cooks when moistened as chemical and bacterial action decompose the plant material. Sunlight and adequate oxygen help speed this process of chemical combustion so much that a moist, well-layered compost pile set out in partial sun and aerated by forking and turning every 10 days will decompose in 4-6 weeks—while a leaf mold pile, layered with lime in the shade may take 2 years to create a rich humus.

Chopping or breaking plant material destined for the pile also hastens decomposition by exposing the raw edges to bacterial action. Bacterial starter mixtures are available to add to your plant material, but animal manures and blood and bone meals will work as well. All this can be managed in as little as a cubic yard of space. In small yards a commercial compost bin or a hand framed square of chicken wire behind a screen of shrubs constitutes equally effective ways to minimize the visual impact for you and your neighbors.

more organic matter in one of the several forms you can find it. The addition of organic matter is the best way to amend soil structure. The soil needs humus or vegetable matter for a half-dozen purposes:

◊ To hold moisture necessary for active growth.

◊ To make the soil looser so that plant roots may penetrate it in search of moisture, oxygen, and food.

◊ For the plant food released from decaying vegetable material.

◊ To boost decomposition—this produces a weak soil acid which dissolves some water insoluble soil minerals, making them available to new plants.

◊ To feed beneficial soil bacteria that cannot act without a certain amount of humus being in the soil.

◊ To make soils cooler—this moderates high temperatures in the root zone, reducing plant stress.

Adding Organic Matter

Well-rotted *animal manures*, when obtainable, should be spread and turned under with a spading fork, plow, or rototiller. They furnish nitrogen and small quantities of two

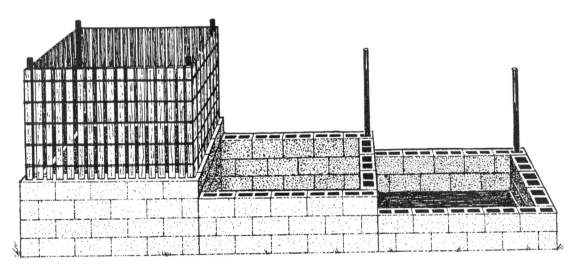

An easily constructed three section compost maker. Cement blocks and stakes or iron pipe are used in lieu of permanent construction. The large bin is for the freshly collected leaves, weeds, etc. The middle bin is less than half in size, it receives the partially rotted compost from the large bin. The third bin, the smallest, holds the finished compost until used.

Chemicals	Weight Needed per ton of Material	Volume Measure Needed per Bushel of Material ([1])
Method I:	Pounds	Cups
a. Either ammonium sulphate	80	1
or ammonium nitrate	50	½
b. Either ground dolomitic limestone ([2])	60	2/3
or woodashes ([2])	80	1½
c. Superphosphate	50	½
d. Magnesium sulfate (Epsom salts) ([3])	8	1 Tbs.
Method II:		
a. Mixed fertilizer (5-10-5)	300	3 Cups
b. Ground dolomitic limestone ([2])	60	2/3

([1]) Packed tightly with the hands.
([2]) For acid compost omit lime, limestone, and wood ashes.
([3]) Epsom salts to be added only if dolomitic limestone is unavailable and ordinary limestone is used (at the same rate).

A thin slice from the vertical surface exposed by removing a spadeful of soil is ample for a soil test.

other major plant foods, phosphate and potash (the "N," "P," and "K," respectively, of commercial fertilizer formulas), as well as humus. Dehydrated cow manure in bags is the most readily available to suburban gardeners.

Stables are also eager to give away or sell horse manure, and rabbit breeders have a ready supply of fresh product, weed-free and rich in the alfalfa by-products that make up most of the bunny food. City dwellers have recourse to "Zoo Doo," a rich mix of composted animal manures that is marketed by the Friends of the National Zoo. Fairly alkaline in composition, it is an ideal amendment for beds of roses, bulbs, many flowers, and vegetables.

The University of Maryland has championed research on the composting of recycled yard waste, processed garbage, and treated sewage sludge for 20 years. The procedures mimic home composting by blending the materials with bacteria, moisture, and air in giant windrows, sometimes under plastic tunnels, according to Dr. Francis Gouin. The finished products are processed and sold in bulk or bagged by some municipalities and commercial companies. One brand of composted sewage sludge available in local garden centers has found widespread acceptance as a top dressing for lawns and ornamental flowers. Nonetheless, says Dr. Gouin, research continues to allay public concerns about possible disease pathogens and heavy metals in sewage products.

The rate of application of composts is important, he says, noting that untreated land can take up to 3 or 4 cubic yards per 1,000 square feet, roughly equivalent to digging in a pickup truck load on a 100 foot by 100 foot garden space. Later applications should be less, as little as 1 cubic yard per 1,000 square feet for clay soils, and 2 cubic yards for very sandy soils.

Both horse and cow manure should be composted, since their pasturage often contains noxious weeds that are undigested. Correct composting subjects these seeds to 160° Fahrenheit temperatures, weakening their germination.

Green manures, often called cover crops, are planted in vegetable or annual flower beds to be plowed or spaded into the soil for its improvement.

Most often sown in early fall in areas vacated by spent plantings, the crops are grown from fall to early spring and then plowed under to decompose and improve soil texture and nutrition. Many of the recommended varieties fix nitrogen in the soil within their roots. Because these crops are more suitable for those with small farms or rototillers, information on specific cover crops can be obtained from your local Cooperative Extension agent.

Wilbur Youngman's Recipe for Compost

To make a rich, balanced plant food for general use, layer the plant material in your compost with a mixture of 45% ammonium sulphate, 40% ground limestone, and 15% superphosphate. You use 7 or 8 pounds of this mix to 100 pounds of tough oak leaves or other dry material, and 3½ or 4 pounds of mix per 100 pounds of green material. Remember to sprinkle dry layers lightly with water to keep the pile evenly moist.

When manure constitutes half the organic matter, no nitrogen is required, only phosphate and limestone. No limestone should be used, however, if the resulting compost is to be applied to blueberries, azaleas, or other acid-loving plants.

Compost should be layered, starting with a 2 inch layer of garden or woods top soil in the bottom of the pit or bin. To this, add a 6-12 inch layer of plant material sprinkled with manure or fertilizer and water. Then continue with another layer of soil followed by another layer of plant material until the pile is built. When complete, aerate the pile by poking several holes from top to bottom. Leave a slight depression in the top if the pile is exposed, so water will penetrate when it rains or is watered.

The following weight and volume measures of chemicals are given for tons or bushels of material to be composted to meet the needs of private and commercial growers. The chemical activators for your home compost pile, ammonium sulphate and superphosphate, are available in 5-pound bags from garden supply stores, where you can also buy organic manure and bone and blood meal in small

What Does pH Mean?

(Descriptive name for pH values)

	pH		pH
Extremely acid	Below 4.5	Mildly alkaline	7.4-7.8
Very strongly acid	4.5-5.0	Moderately alkaline	7.9-8.4
Strongly acid	5.1-5.5	Strongly alkaline	8.5-9.0
Medium acid	5.6-6.0	Very strongly alkaline	9.1 and
Slightly acid	6.1-6.5		higher
Neutral	6.6-7.3		

bags. Commercially composted material is available in bulk for use on landscape and ornamental gardens. Some nurseries and garden centers deliver for a price per cubic yard in the same way that they supply top soil.

Acid or Alkaline?

Unimproved soils in the metropolitan area tend to be acid as well as clay, a condition ideal for the nurturing of many forest trees, shade-loving shrubs like our flowering azaleas, cool season lawns, and some popular vegetables and fruits. Nevertheless, acid soil does restrict the range of plants that many gardeners want to grow, so it is important to know ways to test and amend the level of soil acidity so that the plants you select will be able to get the nutrients they need in your garden.

Fortunately, most plants are tolerant and will do fairly well under the general conditions that exist in this area if the soil is rich and not too dry or too wet. To get the most out of fertilizers, the soil should be at the most favorable level of acidity or alkalinity for each type of plant.

Testing for pH

Soil acidity is measured on a numerical pH scale, with 7.0 as the neutral midpoint between the acid soils with their lower numbers and the alkaline (or "sweet") soils with their higher ones. Testing your soil through the local offices of the Cooperative Extension Service usually yields readings between 4.5 and 6.8. Testing is easiest to perform in the early fall before you renew your lawn or set in landscape plants or perennial flowers for the following season. Then the state soil labs are not as crowded, and your results will arrive back in time for you to improve the areas you want to plant.

Your local Extension office can provide you with a list of locations where you can pick up soil sample boxes and forms for a small fee. You must allow almost 3 weeks for mailed results during the busy spring.

To take samples to send to soil labs, take thin slices the depth of a shovel blade from several spots in an area you have chosen for a certain use. Mix thoroughly and dry for 24 hours before sealing in a container labeled with your name, address, and the location and designated garden use. This will help the soil chemists recommend the best soil amendments.

For quicker results, simple soil testing kits are available at many garden centers and hardware stores. The kits cost from $10 to $20 and include enough chemicals for several tests of needed nutrients.

When you are in a hurry and are unfamiliar with the general characteristics of your soil, one swift way to get a reading is with pieces of red and blue litmus paper bought at the drugstore. If the blue paper turns red when placed between moist slices of soil, then the soil is acid. If red paper turns blue, the soil is sweet. If both turn purple, the soil is neutral.

Choosing Soil Improvements

The cure for excess soil acidity is lime. Some gardeners add a bit of lime to their garden plot or lawn each year, perhaps as a spring ritual. This will serve to sweeten naturally acid soils, except where heavy applications of manure or humus are made.

However, excessive quantities of lime can "lock up" needed soil minerals. Over-liming is detrimental to most vegetables, to many annuals, and to lawn grasses, most of which do best in a slightly acid soil.

Although lime is not classified as a plant food, it serves several purposes. It is a soil conditioner. It makes certain plant foods accessible, that under more acid conditions are not available. Lime loosens heavy clay, rendering its compact structure more loamy. It speeds the production of humus from decaying plant material, freeing nutrients for re-use. In more acid soils nitrogen gathering bacteria are inhibited, and lime frees them. For this reason, animal manures are dug into the soil before lime is applied, so the lime's slow action on the soil will promote gradual release of the nitrogen in the manures. Lime also locks up some harmful soil chemicals—such as aluminum sulphate.

Use of Finely Ground Limestone to Make Soil Sweeter

Change of pH	Pounds per 1,000 sq. ft.
From 3.5 to 4.5	35
4.5 to 5.5	40
5.5 to 6.5	50

Important: Light soils (sands and loamy sands) require smaller amounts while heavier soils (clays and mucks) require more than the above amounts which are for *loams*.

How To Sweeten Soils

If needed, lime should be applied in the fall. Ground dolomitic limestone or ground oystershell lime are the two preferred forms; both can be evenly distributed where you want them with a spreader. If your soil sample indicates that you are low in magnesium, you should buy dolomitic limestone to remedy the lack.

If your soil is light and sandy, it will require smaller amounts of lime than will heavier clay soils. Loamy soil of medium texture will require 4 pounds of ground limestone per hundred square feet to reduce soil acidity by one degree on the pH scale.

Manures are dug into the soil first, if needed. Then lime is spread on top where rain and snow will carry it down to the root zone. You should buy or rent a sturdy spreader that can be calibrated for the correct application. Get help from a knowledgeable garden supply store.

How To Acidify Soils

If certain areas of your soil should prove to be too alkaline for azaleas, hollies, or blueberries, the following chart will show you how to acidify soils. This is particularly likely if you are near the beach or have inherited sandy loams used to grow melons, berries or roses.

Use of Chemicals to Make Soil Acid

Change of pH	Sulphur	Aluminum sulphate
	(pounds per 100 feet)	
From 8.0 to 7.0	2.0	4.5
7.5 to 7.0	1.75	3.5
7.5 to 6.5	2.0	5.0
7.5 to 6.0	3.5	7.5
7.0 to 6.5	1.5	2.5
7.0 to 6.0	2.0	5.5
6.5 to 6.0	1.5	3.0
6.5 to 5.5	2.5	6.5
6.0 to 5.5	1.5	3.5
6.0 to 5.0	3.0	7.5
5.5 to 5.0	1.5	4.0
5.5 to 4.5	2.4	8.5

It is not considered good practice to change the soil pH reaction more than 1 pH unit in one year.

The plant food sections of large garden centers and hardware stores carry these and similar products, which include plant food labeled for use around hollies and other acid-loving shrubs. Cotton-seed meal and iron chelate are often included. In the following graph either sulphur or aluminum sulphate may be used. Amounts are listed in pounds per 100 square feet. Do not change pH more than 1 full point in any year.

How To Use Commercial Fertilizers

Applications of granulated or liquid fertilizers to the garden or lawn are not always the "magic cure-all" that many envision. They cannot change soil structure or acidity; they cannot make up for poor drainage or lack of light that may inhibit the growth of the seeds you have chosen.

What plant food can do, if prior conditions are met, is to provide a balanced formulation of the three major elements that promote plant growth in a form that fosters quick availability to the plant. *Nitrogen (N), phosphate (P), and potassium (K)* are represented by the three numbers on every commercial fertilizer bag. The most often used of these formulas for annual vegetables and flowers is 5-10-5.

This formula means that the mix contains 5% nitrogen, 10% phosphate, and 5% potassium by weight. The rest of the mix is inert material, unless necessary trace minerals are listed.

Some formulations recommended for lawns say "WIN" on the label, meaning that some of the nitrogen is in a water insoluble form that will release slowly to promote a more natural rate of growth over a longer period.

In particular, newer urea formulations release nitrogen in a form that does not burn tender foliage. They can promote a uniform rate of growth, sometimes for as long as 2 or 3 months. They do not leach out of the soil with watering before plants can benefit from them. And, though more expensive, they are used less often.

Standard mixtures of fertilizers still have their uses for the home gardener. For special forcing or supplemental

How Much Fertilizer?

Weights of Fertilizer per Acre Converted into Amounts for Smaller Areas

Acre	1000 sq. ft.	100 sq. ft.
100 lbs.	2½ pts.	½ cup
200 lbs.	5 pts.	1 cup
400 lbs.	5 quarts	1 pint
600 lbs.	7¼ quarts	1½ pints
800 lbs.	2½ gallons	2 pints
1000 lbs.	3 gallons	2½ pints
2000 lbs.	6 gallons	5 pints

The conversions in the above table are only approximate, but are close enough for practical purposes.

feeding during periods of greatest growth, they are ideal if space or lack of material precludes steady use of compost.

Nearly all the forms of nitrogen in standard mixes are quickly available and must be applied with care around plant material. Do not apply them to plants after a watering. These soluble nitrogens will burn foliage if applied to turf when it is wet.

There are a number of animal and plant by-products processed for use as fertilizers for specific purposes. Some are quite rich in major nutrients and trace minerals. Among them are kelp, cottonseed meal and bone, blood, and fish meals. They are more expensive, but often justified for special uses.

Transplant Solutions

These commercially available liquid solutions often include hormones and fertilizers to boost root growth and prevent transplant shock. The solutions are sprayed on the root balls and used to water-in all newly planted material. When planting shrubs and trees, it is best to avoid the use of dry fertilizers in the root zone for 6 months to a year.

Foliar Feeding

Foliar feeding has attracted a growing number of devotees. It consists of spraying special fertilizer compounds in non-burning solutions directly onto plant foliage. These liquid solutions are often used by indoor or pot gardeners. Foliar foods can be applied at the same time as some pesticides, a boon for ornamental rose growers. Recently, hose attachments which mix fertilizer solutions with water have made it possible to combine watering and feeding programs, a necessity if you rely on foliar feeding alone, because the material is not as long-lasting as granular fertilizers or organic plant foods that nourish the root system.

Other concentrated fertilizers are designed to be used in solution and applied to the soil when watering. These are useful for transplanting and for feeding potted plants like bonsai, orchids, and culinary herbs.

Trace Minerals

Soil tests may show that some of our gardens are deficient in trace minerals or elements. Commercial fertilizers do not provide these as a matter of course. Iron deficiency is often noted in local rose and azalea plantings that display yellowish green leaves with sharply greener veins. Sometimes the iron is present but locked in the soil until acidity can be increased by means of cotton seed meal or until iron chelate is added.

Boron and magnesium are also absent from some sandy soils. A good indicator of a deficiency of these in normally fertile soil is tasteless carrots and a sparse number of pods on lima bean vines. Boron deficient fruit often drop early or have corky brown areas in the flesh. A detailed soil test is the only sure way to confirm deficiency of trace minerals.

Dolomitic limestone may repair magnesium deficiency if the soil is sufficiently acid to require liming. Trace elements can be added easily by sprinkling powdered borax or epsom salts over the soil. These drugstore formulas of boron and magnesium sulfate are safe if you use no more than two-thirds cup of epsom salts or one-fourth cup of borax per 100 square feet to remedy the detected deficiency. Because these trace minerals are important but dangerous to plants in large doses, they should be applied in the fall and not be repeated unless symptoms reappear.

Garden Equipment

Equipment comes in two categories: tools that are absolutely essential and relatively inexpensive, and other wonderful equipment that devoted gardeners try to resist.

Most of the basics are hand tools. A good gardener likes to have enough good tools to meet every need. It is good economy to buy the best hand tools you can afford. The most frequently used tools should be the best, well-designed for ease in use, with handles that suit your height and are deeply seated in a one-piece forged socket. A well-made hand tool, properly cared for, will last a lifetime.

Many gardens are small enough to be spaded by hand, provided the gardener is not so ambitious that she tries

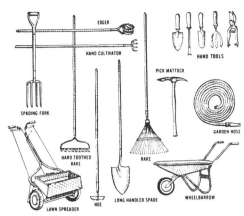

Only a few tools are essential. Keep them in good repair.

to do it all in one day. For this task, a long-handled shovel or a D-handled garden spade is as useful as a flat-bladed spading fork. Before you buy, find out what works best for you.

Every gardener will need a hard-toothed rake to remove rocks, smooth the soil, firm the soil over newly sown seed, and break up surface crust that forms days after watering.

You will want to choose from among the many patterns of garden hoes that will break clods, loosen and prepare seed beds, open furrows for seeds, and uproot weeds. An array of smaller hand tools should include two sizes of trowels for transplanting smaller seedlings, a three-tined cultivator to work in and around crowded beds, an asparagus knife to remove deep-rooted weeds, and a good scissors-action hand pruner.

One or two 50-foot lengths of garden hose are a must for adequate irrigation during our sometimes lengthy dry spells. If you are watering narrow beds or borders, you will waste less water if you use a permeable (drip) hose so that water seeps into the soil without evaporating.

A portable pump sprayer is a good buy because it can be used for foliar feeding and for insecticide and disease control solutions. Detachable hose end sprayers can also be used. A hand duster with a nozzle that allows you to direct the dust up under the leaves where many pests hide to feed is very useful.

Because planning and recordkeeping are good economy in the long run, it is wise to buy graph paper and a notebook to keep track of your planting, care, and harvest each season.

Two short stakes and string to line off rows or mark out beds are also a good idea, as is a package of bamboo or covered-wire stakes to support heavy stalks of bloom in the flower garden. An inch-thick foam pad to protect your knees, and a strong, flexible pair of garden gloves will complete your basic kit.

This is not an imposing list, nor does it represent any substantial investment; it will, however, take care of smaller gardens without taxing the gardener's budget.

Among those larger expenses the gardener may consider is an all-purpose garden cart, a well-balanced and roomy successor to the wheelbarrow—it travels on two large tires and carries everything you might need from tools to mulch. For maximum savings, this item is best bought at the end of the garden season. Its price compares to that of a lawn mower, another double duty item that can chop leaves for mulch or compost.

If you tend your own lawn, you will need a long-handled edger to keep grass from encroaching on walkways and garden beds, a sturdy lawn spreader for fertilizer and lime, the right-sized rakes for removing leaves from among your plantings, and a tarp for hauling clippings and leaves if you compost.

Those people who plan to landscape their homes will need to obtain larger pruners, a pruning saw, and a pick mattock to remove roots. Such a gardener may consider constructing or buying a cold frame, where you can safely overwinter cuttings of desirable shrubs to increase your plantings at minimum cost. Cold frames are also useful to the vegetable and annual flower gardener who wants to advance the season by protecting young plantings from the cold.

Where crop storage space is at a premium, to extend the season gardeners can purchase one of a number of translucent garden blankets that will hold soil heat into the fall while admitting sunshine and rain and discouraging air-borne insects.

BREAKING UP THE SOIL AND PLANTING IN THE GARDEN

A—Don't *begin digging* the soil when it is wet. If it packs or forms a sticky ball in your fist, then it isn't ready to be broken. Wait until it crumbles easily.

B—If you are starting a new garden plot, remove weeds, stumps, or bushes to prevent interference with the growth and care of the garden.

C—Dig *straight* down and make sure that you reach the soil at least 6 to 8 inches below the surface. Bring that underneath soil to the top.

D—Break the clods as you dig; leave the soil loose, fine and crumbly.

E—When your soil is turned over and broken up, smooth it with the back of a garden rake.

F—Rake your garden bed slightly higher in the center than at its border, to prevent finding your garden a huge puddle after a heavy rain.

G—Pound stakes at either end where you want each row; tie a string to the stakes as your guide in marking rows.

H—It is not necessary to *dig* furrows. You can make deep enough seed furrows with the end of your rake handle.

I—Space seeds in furrows as recommended for each variety.

J—Often one packet of seed of each variety is sufficient.

K—Unless soil is unusually damp, apply starter solution (see section on liquid fertilizers) directly to the seeds before replacing soil.

L—Use your seed envelope or a label as a marker at the end of row until crop is up.

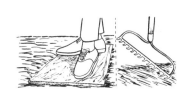

M—Firm your soil well with a plank or with the back of the rake.

N—Some sort of a border, preferably a wire or a picket fence, will greatly improve the looks of your garden and help to keep out rabbits.

To double dig a plot, first dig a furrow, and lay aside the top soil. Then, aerate and enrich the subsoil by digging in compost or needed soil amendments with a spading fork. Fill the improved trench with topsoil shoveled from the next furrow you dig, and repeat the enrichment process of the subsoil. The final improved furrow is filled with the topsoil from the first furrow. Additional compost, chopped leaves, mineral dust, or animal by-products added to the plot and dug in will result in a rich, well-drained plot 18 inches deep, ideal for long-lived plantings.

For vegetable gardens and most annual and perennial flowers and grasses, we may concentrate on enriching the top 6- to 8-inch layer after loosening the soil to a good depth with a spading fork or plow.

Fall spading is the best way to prepare soils for next season's garden. Un-rotted materials turned under in the fall decompose by spring to make plant food available. Fall-worked soil needs only to be raked or cultivated to be ready for planting in the spring since winter's freezing and thawing actions have aerated it. And fall spading will turn up many grubs and other insect pests to be killed by winter weather.

Fall soil should be left rough dug so winter rains cannot erode any slopes. Freezing and thawing will aerate the texture by spring.

Avoid spading the ground when it is either too moist or too dry. Clay soils can be ruined for the year if they are worked wet in the spring. When dry, clay soil is hard, and its clods are exceedingly difficult to break up.

To test soil for spading, take a handful and squeeze firmly. When you open your hand and tap the ball of earth gently, it will begin to crumble if it is ready to dig. Dig straight down, pushing the full blade length of the spading fork or shovel into the ground with the foot. If the soil is heavy, it is better to take a small bite, even if the digging goes slower.

In spring spading, lift each bite of dug soil and place it on top of the adjacent row. With your fork or spade knock the top litter and weed seeds into the bottom of the furrow below the level at which they can germinate—4 to 6 inches. Then the rest of the bite can be pulled back into the furrow and pulverized with the back of your implement.

Every 3 or 4 feet, further pulverize the spaded surface with a rake to smooth it and to remove any footprints from the freshly turned soil.

SOIL IMPROVEMENT RESOURCES:

Zoo Doo is sold in 5-pound bags at the National Zoo parking lots for $2.50. The Gift Shops sell 10-pound bags for $4.50 and 40-pound bags for $6.00. But the best bargain goes to the persons who load their own trucks, getting a terrific bargain at $30 to $50.Call (202) 673-4989.

A majority of the Maryland and Virginia counties in the extended metropolitan area have some form of leaf compost or mulch program in effect through their Recycling or Waste Collection offices. To find out whether free pick up or delivery at cost is available in your area, call your municipal government.

Local U.S.D.A. Cooperative Extension numbers to locate area pick up and drop off sites for soil tests are listed in the appendix. Maryland charges $5 to District and state residents for a standardized analysis that includes organic matter, pH, phosphorus, magnesium, and potash content. Nine additional tests can be ordered for extra charges ranging from $1 to $12 each. Virginia charges $6 for a standard analysis that includes nutrient levels, pH, nitrogen, phosphorus and potash, plus calcium and other trace mineral levels, with local libraries in Fairfax and some other counties serving as convenient drop off sites for samples. Tests for organic matter, soluble salts, and nitrates are $3 each.

Both Maryland and Virginia soils labs suggest that home gardeners send in their samples in the fall.

3. GOOD GARDEN CULTURE

Gardening is not an exact science; there are too many variables. Awareness of the basics, however, helps a gardener get the right plants for a given site into the ground at the right time, so that with good culture the plants will produce to their potential. The following cultural practices will give you maximum benefit with minimum effort, so that gardening will give you the rewards that it promises.

Climate and Topography
The first step is to choose permanent plantings that are suited to this climate. The greater metropolitan area straddles plant hardiness zone 7, a rating that denotes the lowest temperatures that perennials, shrubs and trees will have to endure in most years. In our case this is 0° to 10° Fahrenheit, a fact that most reputable nurseries are well aware of. Look for hardiness ratings on plants you wish to see established in your garden.

Because of the differences in topography within our region, our zone is subdivided into 7A and 7B, with the latter being warmer and lower. For example, climatic conditions in zone 7B favor the magnificent evergreen southern magnolia, while in zone 7A it struggles at the very top of its range and would need a sheltered spot to thrive

Frost Free Growing Season Varies
Topography accounts for the variations in growing season as well. Records covering the last 50 years show a variance from 157 to 218 frost-free days at different locations around our area. Although light frost does not bother some plants at all (for example peas and daffodils), other favorites (like tomatoes), will not germinate in the spring or continue to produce in the fall if temperatures fall below 60° Fahrenheit. From the wind-swept high Piedmont to the bottom land abutting the rivers that feed the Chesapeake Bay there is a diversity of climatic conditions that successful gardeners must take into account.

In general the warmest areas are low, sandy, south-facing, sheltered, and close to the rivers. Here soil temperature rises to the mid-50s by the middle of March. In higher areas north and west of Washington it could be five weeks later before the soil will sprout seeds, particularly if the soil is clay. Most annual seeds will not begin to sprout until soil temperature climbs over 60° F. in the top 2 inches.

Determining the length of the season in your area will help you choose which annual flowers and vegetables will do well in your area, and whether you can plant them for successive harvests during the season. On the other hand most deciduous trees and shrubs benefit from planting in colder soil, so their roots can become established before active top growth starts. A knowledge of your local growing season helps you plan when to buy and plant trees and shrubs during the spring and fall. You will find an area map and more information on the subject in the Appendix.

Microclimates

Your own microclimate may affect when, and even what, you may grow successfully. It pays to know your own site well. Observe how much sun each plot gets per day, whether morning or afternoon exposure, and if windswept or in a hollow prone to late frosts. These latter factors alone can create a small area unsuitable for some trees and shrubs. Consider if your garden site gets good air circulation during summer's muggy heat, or if air pollution from nearby roads could pose a problem for edibles and trees.

Factor this into your process of choosing plants for a particular purpose. Look to see what species thrive in similar settings around you. Study gardening texts to see which species match the conditions that you have to offer before you purchase.

Watering

To know how often you need to water, you need to know that after the moist soil softens seed coatings, it promotes rapid growth by putting soil nutrients into solution where new roots can find and use them. At later stages in a plant's growth cycle, the time of day and method of watering have much to do with good results.

Before you water, you should loosen the soil surface with a rake or hoe, so that water will penetrate rather than run off. After watering, wait for the soil to drain enough so that it crumbles easily, then cultivate the surface to form an evaporation barrier of air and soil.

Water in the early morning or afternoon so that any splashed foliage will dry quickly enough not to spread disease spores. Wet foliage encourages the development of molds and other bacterial diseases, so all watering should be done early enough for foliage to dry by nightfall.

Barely moistening the surface with water may have an injurious effect if it encourages the roots to grow toward the surface of the soil. Plant roots normally grow downward in search of moisture. In this condition they are less likely to suffer during a drought than if they had been encouraged to remain near the surface by frequent small waterings. When watering, the general recommendation is to let your sprinkler or hose run until the soil is moistened to a depth of 4-6 inches. It usually takes at least an hour to give soil a thorough soaking. If done this way, a watering can last a week or more.

Drip Irrigation

Although sprinklers are a favored method of applying water, especially on lawns and other large areas, more and more gardeners are using methods that allow water to reach the soil without wetting the foliage. These methods help protect plants from some diseases and reduce water costs and runoff.

Drip irrigation or soaking hoses allow thorough watering while the gardener works in an adjacent area. If a bed or border is narrow, permeable soaking hoses that ooze water along their entire length can be placed under mulch at the beginning of the season. Although this entails greater expense if you have more than one or two beds, hoses do not have to be transported back and forth, and they last longer because they are shielded from the ultraviolet radiation that reduces their useful life.

More ambitious watering systems that provide emitters working off a main water line may prove good value for wide perennial beds or shrub borders where watering closely packed foliage from above could promote summer funguses. These watering systems are best installed where cultivation of the soil is infrequent. Quick release connectors on these more expensive systems allow the gardener to use one or two outside water sources to water a number of beds in less time without dragging long lengths of hose from place to place.

Working people may find that timers to turn water on and off are also a good investment, particularly if they are trying to establish a new lawn.

Of course in many cases, watering is not essential to the success of a garden. Many farm and city gardens depend entirely on nature. Many municipalities prohibit watering a garden with city water during parts of July, August, and September. If you do not have your own well or water source, it is best to have deep root systems established, and to let cool season lawns go a little off color during a time when they would be naturally dormant.

In more vulnerable vegetable gardens cultivation and mulching may help preserve deep soil moisture. And it is well to point out again that deeply prepared seed beds, especially soils which have been improved with liberal quantities of humus, are well fortified to withstand droughts without too great a loss. This indicates that thorough soil preparation the preceding fall and spring is the first step in solving soil moisture problems.

Fertilizing: When and If To Feed

It is important to remember that all plants do not need to be fed every year. Healthy shrubs and trees will require extra pruning to keep excessive growth in check if you overfeed. Instead, look for the following hunger signs:

◊ Leaves not normal in size
◊ Yellow or chlorotic leaves
◊ Sparse foliage
◊ Dying back of branches at tips
◊ Crown full of dead branches
◊ Short annual twig growth
◊ Stunted growth

Always check for unfavorable soil structure, drainage problems, or the wrong amount of light for the species before you decide to treat for nutritional problems. Always find out the dietary needs of a particular species before you fertilize.

How Much Fertilizer?

Weights of Fertilizer per Acre Converted into Amounts for Smaller Areas

Acre	1000 sq. ft.	100 sq. ft.
100 lbs.	2½ pts.	½ cup
200 lbs.	5 pts.	1 cup
400 lbs.	5 quarts	1 pint
600 lbs.	7¼ quarts	1½ pints
800 lbs.	2½ gallons	2 pints
1000 lbs.	3 gallons	2½ pints
2000 lbs.	6 gallons	5 pints

The conversions in the above table are only approximate, but are close enough for practical purposes.

Fertilizer Program for Established Plants

Deciduous Shrubs. Apply 5 pounds of 5-10-5 fertilizer or 2½ pounds of the more concentrated 10-10-10 per 100 square feet of plantings in early spring just as growth starts.

Needle Evergreens. Apply 4 pounds of 10-6-4 or 2 pounds of 10-10-10 per 100 square feet of plantings in early spring.

Broadleaf Evergreens. Use special commercial formulas made for hollies, camellias, and other broadleaf specimens at recommended rates, and apply no more than 1 pound of iron sulphate per 100 square feet of soil at the first sign of growth, followed in a month by an application of half that amount.

Trees. Since the root systems are larger mirror images of tops, it is important to apply the fertilizers and trace minerals in a 3 foot band just outside the drip line from the outermost branches where the majority of feeder roots are growing. Newly planted trees can use a feeding the following spring or fall, of chemical fertilizers or organic material applied to the soil surface. Mature evergreens or deciduous trees can be fed the same way or with a liquid injection wand to a depth of 8-15 inches every 18 inches within the band. For trees up to 3 inches thick, use 1 pound of 10-6-4 per inch of trunk diameter; for trees over 3 inches in diameter, use 2 pounds of 10-6-4 per inch of diameter. Trees in a fertilized lawn will seldom require extra food.

Lawns. To be vigorous, local lawn grasses require an annual feeding program. For cool season grasses, bluegrass and fescue mixtures that dominate this area, feeding should begin in late summer with lawns receiving 66% of their diet in two doses before mid-November, and the other 34% in early spring.

Warm season lawns, bermuda and zoysia are fed most when they start to grow in mid-May, then fed again one month later, with a final small feeding in late summer. Special lawn formulas are sold in all garden centers and hardware stores. Most are higher in nitrogen (for leaf growth) than in phosphate or potassium. Granulated lawn fertilizers, unless their nutrients are in slow release form, should be thoroughly watered in after they are spread to prevent chemical leaf burn. In general, lawns and turf areas need 4 to 6 pounds of nitrogen and 1½ to 3 pounds each of phosphate and potassium each year per 1,000 square feet. Lawn fertilizers are often sold in various sized bags, some far too heavy for most of us to deal with, so keep in mind that it is the weight of the nitrogen in the bag that is most important, not the total weight of all the ingredients, and buy a more concentrated nitrogen product in smaller bags.

Annuals and Perennials. Early in the growing season, apply dry fertilizer at the rate of ¼ cup of 5-10-5 worked into the soil around each established perennial. Plants can be lightly fertilized thereafter at 4 week intervals if conditions merit. Nutrients are used up more quickly in light sandy soils. Finished compost is a preferred method of feeding when soils are very light or very heavy, because they improve the structure while they nourish.

Sidedressing

This is a useful technique for the row gardener, whether the plantings are vegetables or flowers. It refers to a supplementary feeding of granular fertilizer or compost to a crop just when its nutritional needs are greatest—for example, when squash and other vining crops are about to set blossoms, when sweet corn has reached more than half its height and is about to produce tassels and ears, when perennial flowers are starting to produce the current season's growth, and when annuals begin to branch before setting buds.

Just at this point the gardener should include sidedressing as part of his cultivation. To do so, open a shallow furrow just outside the root zone of the developing plants, remembering that roots often exceed top development. Into this furrow sprinkle a light application of 5-10-5 or an inch or two of finished compost before pulling the removed soil back over the row.

When annuals are one-third grown, you should apply a sidedressing, hoeing in 3 pounds of 5-10-5 fertilizer per 100 row feet or an inch of compost. This feeding can be repeated at 2 to 4 week intervals into bloom or harvest time.

A supplementary feeding for beds of annuals or perennials can be lightly scratched into the soil surface with a cultivator when it is needed. The nutrients will be carried into the root zone by rainfall or the watering schedule you have set for your garden. If you use liquid or foliar fertilizers, follow the schedule on your container.

Cultivation

Cultivation is hardly a field of activity that appeals to all gardeners, but there are solid reasons why it should be done, particularly during the early part of the growth cycle.

Cultivation helps control weeds when they are tiny, allows rainfall to be completely absorbed into the loose surface of the garden, and retards moisture loss through evaporation while enabling developing plant roots to obtain the air and water balance that they need. In all gardens, unless they are mulched beds or borders, cultivation should begin early and be repeated after each shower. By keeping the soil loose at all times, cultivation can be quickly accomplished with a rake or scuffle hoe at the soil surface. Let the soil surface become hard, baked, or weedy, and breaking it up is many times harder.

The length of time it takes for soil to be workable after a rain depends on its structure. Most good soils will be ready for a light raking within 2 or 3 days after a rain, but it is important to work it only when it crumbles easily, just as you would do if were you spading. Beginners who try to work clay soil too early run the risk of making bricks by working the air out of it.

Summer cultivations are, for the most part, shallow to avoid damaging developing root systems not far from the surface. In the perennial garden this may mean that hand cultivation with a three-prong cultivator is preferable to a wider hoe or rake. Deep cultivation also turns up too much moist soil, allowing it to dry out. In close quarters, a long-handled onion hoe may prove ideal.

Shallow cultivation, if well done, will give just as much protection against moisture loss as mulching will.

Many garden plants will cease to grow if the soil is allowed to crust to the point that plant roots are unable to get sufficient air. Sweet corn, with its band of surface roots, is often badly stunted from lack of soil aeration.

Even if mulches are employed from midsummer on, frequent cultivation in May and early June will destroy many surface weed seeds. The soil should be thoroughly stirred before applying a layer of mulch. Early applications are not advisable because they retard the warming of soil and delay the maturity of annual flower and vegetable crops. It is only after the soil is completely warmed that gardeners may safely substitute mulches for cultivation in the annual garden.

Using Mulches

Mulch provides four important benefits to the garden. It preserves soil moisture and structure, regulates soil temperature, retards competitive weed growth, and improves soil fertility.

As research shows, there are more and more values to be gained from mulching. The supply of organic material in the soil can be maintained and increased through surface application. Weed control is made easier by a thick mulch that denies light for germination to many seeds, and keeps the soil loose enough so that those weeds that do get through may be easily pulled. In decaying, mulches attract earthworms that further loosen and aerate surface soil.

Mulches also prevent rain from running off on clay soils by diffusing the force of raindrops that can churn the bare surface into a soup that seals the soil pores. Without run-off there is no soil loss to erosion.

By acting as spacers for soil particles at the surface, mulch maintains an essential air supply to plant roots. Plants do not thrive for long without an adequate mixture of moisture and air in the root zone.

Once mulched in early summer, soil temperatures rise more slowly, which is of measurable value to many plants whose roots are unable to function in hot soil. Conversely, soil under mulch maintains its warmth later in the fall. In the winter frozen soil will not thaw and heave up shallow roots if it is adequately mulched after it is frozen. And, of course, mulches retard evaporation of soil moisture.

The kinds of mulches used can vary tremendously. On open ground around vegetables and flowers, the gardener can use a number of materials that are inconspicuous and will not mat, crust, cake, or blow away. In order of preference, these include: compost, so-called pine fines of chopped pine bark, salt hay, straw, pine needles, pine bark nuggets, peat moss, chopped leaves, chopped corncobs, cocoa hulls, sawdust, and spoiled hay. Each has advantages and disadvantages.

Chopped leaves or brush can be gotten cheaply or free by contacting your municipal refuse collection agency, but leaves especially have a tendency to mat and shelter slugs on heavy clay. Compost is free if homemade, but it is so nutritious that much may be needed to smother weeds. Straw and hay are readily available; straw has no weed seeds, but it is conspicuous. Hay is less obvious, but teems with timothy and grass seeds. Spoiled hay is full of mold spores that plague allergies. Ground corncobs and pine straw made of needles are excellent, but more expensive and harder to find here. Peat moss is quite acid, as are pine bark chunks, while sawdust covers beautifully but locks up soil nitrogen.

I have not mentioned plastic and newspaper mulches for two reasons. Plastic permits no air exchange at the surface on heavy soils, although it does warm sandy soil beautifully. The lead and chemical content of newsprint can be quite high, although, like plastic, it smothers weeds well.

Around shrubs and trees many people prefer shredded hardwood, bark chunks, or chopped brush. Be sure to check the source of the wood chips to be sure that you are not ringing your young trees with chopped poison ivy or wood that has succumbed to borers or Dutch elm disease.

In display beds or borders where the contrasting textures of foliage and flowers are important, mulches of cocoa hulls, peat moss, or small stones are sometimes worth the extra expense for the way that they set off permanent plantings.

The depth to apply the mulching materials and the quantity needed vary. Peat moss, tanbark, and the mineral mulches are usually applied 1 to 2 inches deep. Coarse compost, chopped leaves and twigs, sawdust, and pulverized corncobs are applied 2 or 3 inches deep, while straw, hay, and other coarse materials need to be as deep as 3 to 6 inches.

If weeds start showing up in a mulched bed, the thickness of the mulch should be increased so that their growth is completely checked. Bermuda grass, crabgrass, and bindweed seem able to push through a greater thickness of mulch than chickweed, and other less vigorous annuals, so a real effort to remove root pieces or apply an effective preemergent is required before you mulch.

Nearly all the organic materials used as a mulch need nitrogen in some form to feed the bacteria that break them down at the soil level. Sawdust and corncobs require more nitrogen than do compost and hay. Tanbark is very slow to break down, but does not require the use of as much nitrogen.

The right time to apply mulches varies. Gardeners growing annual flowers or vegetables should wait until the soil is quite warm, then apply the mulch to speed harvests. Growers of perennials and shrubs may apply it earlier when the soil is still cool to retard moisture loss during summer's first heat waves. This will slightly delay growth, but lessen the need to water often.

Azaleas, rhododendrons, camellias, hollies, and other broadleaf evergreens with vulnerable roots need mulch at all times. Rhododendrons, however, and some junipers, when grown on our predominantly heavy soil, may be further stressed by heavy applications of mulch. Before mulching, lighten the soil mix in an extensive area around the plant or plant it in a mound of topsoil, so that rhododendron roots will drain well enough not to be subject to root rot.

There are plants that resent having a mulch closer than 3 or 4 inches to their growth centers. Delphiniums, painted daisies, and poppies are good examples among those plants subject to crown rot. Iris plants also need their rhizomes exposed to light and air.

Some gardeners think it is necessary to remove summer mulches from large garden beds during the late fall or winter. It is easier, however, to incorporate them as soil improvements during fall spading, as long as you realize they will have to be replenished the next year.

Winter mulches, on the other hand, are applied in the fall to keep soil around new plants warm enough for root growth or in winter to keep soil frozen around plants whose surface roots would be dehydrated as the soil thaws and refreezes.

Young plants or small bulbs in the top 4 inches of soil may be pushed out through frost action. To protect them, mulch should be applied when the soil is frozen to a depth of an inch or two. Unfortunately, the Washington area is prone to rapid freezing and thawing, which causes heaving of plants, and it is often hard to find a time when the soil is frozen enough so that applications of mulch will benefit. Nevertheless, gardeners may scatter a layer of pine boughs or other evergreen prunings over vulnerable beds to retard their thawing, realizing that if the boughs are put on before the ground freezes they may provide protection for field mice.

Fall-planted shrubs, particularly evergreens, are often not well enough established for their roots to function properly. In these cases, mulch will retain soil warmth and permit the roots to store food reserves for the plant into early winter.

Make your own mulch for established older plantings by simply shaking the normal leaf fall down around the base of the plant. Windrows of raked leaves through which you run a lawnmower make an even better mulch where shrubs are regularly exposed to winter winds.

Weed Control

Weeds compete with garden plants for food, moisture, and sunlight. When large, they shut off air circulation, a condition that favors the development of diseases. To control them effectively do the following:

◊ Rake the garden thoroughly just before planting.

◊ Examine rows and beds often and pull any weeds you find while they are small.

◊ Rake between plantings after every rain as soon as the soil is dry enough to work.

◊ Pull weeds more than 4 inches high by hand, grasping near the base of the plant to get all roots.

◊ Tall weeds, a foot high, will cause damage to adjacent plant roots if pulled. Use an asparagus knife to cut the plant below the soil surface.

Remember, the best time to kill weeds is when they are so small they can hardly be seen. Later on, when well rooted, considerable effort and a sharp hoe are needed to bring them under control.

Frequent cultivation is, of course, all that should be necessary to achieve rapid germination and destruction of the weed seeds in the top two inches of your garden. During the summer, however, weeds, (especially crabgrass), may take hold during prolonged periods of rainfall when the ground is too wet to work. When the wet spell ends, it often takes two cultivations, 2 or 3 days apart to stop their growth. In a large vegetable garden a shallow pass with a rototiller may speed the process. Better still, follow it with a raking out of the chopped-up weeds to prevent their re-rooting.

COMMON WEEDS

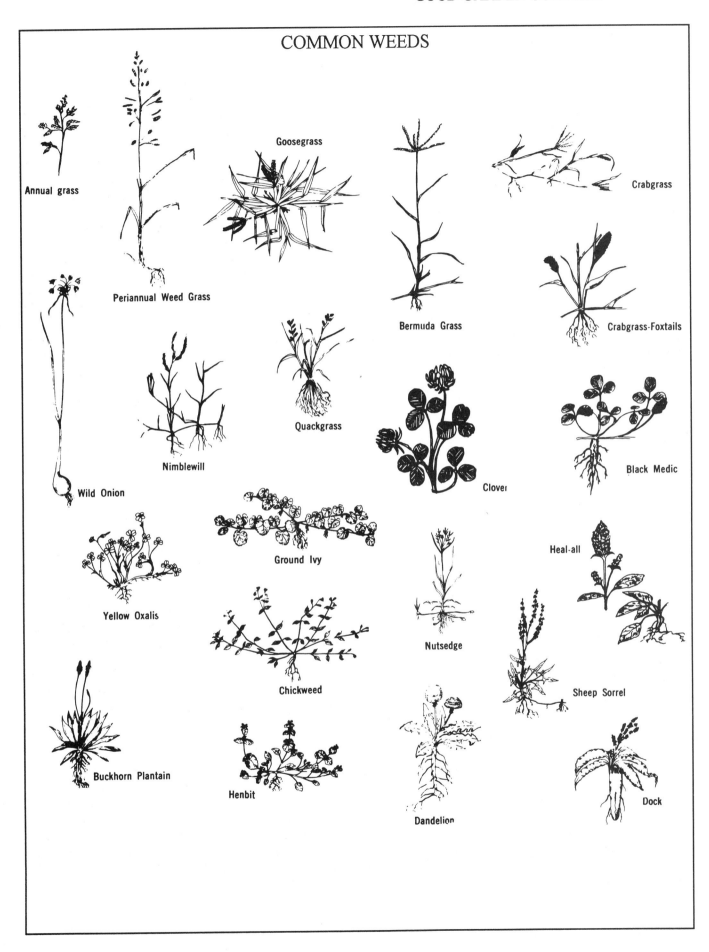

Annual grass

Periannual Weed Grass

Goosegrass

Bermuda Grass

Crabgrass

Crabgrass-Foxtails

Wild Onion

Nimblewill

Quackgrass

Clover

Black Medic

Yellow Oxalis

Ground Ivy

Heal-all

Nutsedge

Sheep Sorrel

Chickweed

Buckhorn Plantain

Henbit

Dandelion

Dock

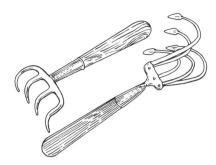

Special type tools make cultivation easier, but when weeds
get out of hand, the common hoe will be needed.

Many tools are suitable for weed control. Some gardeners do everything with a common garden hoe. When sharp and well handled, it is quick and effective. A toothed garden rake is a very good tool if it is used early and frequently up to the time that you apply mulch. It will cover much space in a short time, does not turn the soil too deeply, and tends to pull weeds out of the soil. If you have broadcast seeds in a wide row or bed, you can thin and weed at the same time with a rake when young plants are 2 or 3 inches high. Tined hand cultivators are very useful in limited spaces; the tines break up the crust and loosen weeds so they can be easily pulled. The stirrup-shaped scuffle hoe, which can be pushed and pulled through the soil surface, is very efficient with small weeds.

Once established on open ground, weeds must be chopped out using a pick mattock or an asparagus knife before they produce more seeds. This slow and laborious method seems to be the only way to bring them under control without the use of chemical weed killers that may contaminate or kill nearby plants.

The field of chemical weed control grew by leaps and bounds after World War II and has now contracted in the wake of evidence that many herbicides have long-term toxic effects on home users who do not take sufficient precautions in the use and storage of these products.

With so many young families living on today's smaller lots, it seems wise to place our emphasis here on safer methods of control. For persistent problems in the lawn or with noxious weeds like poison ivy, refer to the following chapter. Annual flower and vegetable garden plots can be treated with pre-emergent herbicides to control infestations of certain invasive grasses if this is done well before cultivation and planting.

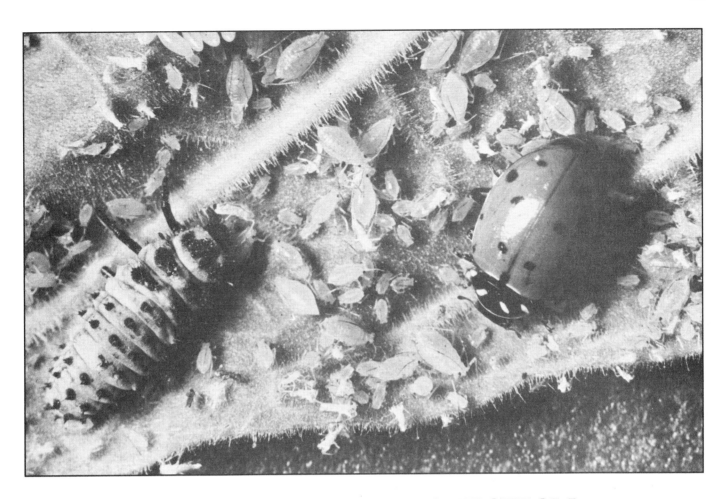

4. SAFE PLANT PROTECTION

There is a reason that this chapter appears after the one on good cultural practices. Within the last decade many gardeners have come to a new awareness that effective pest and disease control is a function of good cultural practices, alert monitoring, and a response that balances long-term effects with convenience.

Concerns about the safety to the environment and the food and water supply have led to a cautious re-evaluation of the scores of convenient chemical controls developed for weeds, plant diseases, and pests since World War II. A temptation to overuse convenient pesticides has posed its own problems. This has led to the development of strains of "super bugs" that are resistant to formerly successful controls. The Colorado potato beetle is a prime example. It is now resistant to carbaryl (Sevin), its chief control, and must be killed with the addition of 1% rotenone powder, an older botanical, to the Sevin. The small home gardener may prefer to hand pick leaves that contain egg masses or larvae.

Because new gardeners want to grow plants, not study chemistry, plant pathology, or entomology, they need convincing reasons to explore the ecosystem in their own backyard. Alternatives to chemical control may seem difficult and time-consuming. Integrated Pest Management (IPM) sounds like a way to make a housekeeping chore into a government job description.

In truth, it is very simple and consists of being as alert and curious as the average 10-year-old to get a better handle on the few problems you are likely to encounter, so you can choose controls you can live with.

Adoption of IPM practices locally was spearheaded by the National Park Service and local parks. The additional monitoring time has resulted in effective control and cost savings. Estate managers and some lawn care companies have begun to follow suit, sparked by the concerns of clients over long-term pesticide application in areas frequented by children and pets.

Accordingly, this book will place all controls within the context of Integrated Pest Management, which is a technique of monitoring the many elements that create a balance within your garden before deciding how to treat a problem. In the last 50 years research has produced a host of biological, botanical and chemical controls. Choosing them wisely can be difficult without a context that helps us balance convenience with long-term safety.

Easy biological and botanical controls will be listed ahead of conventional chemicals when they are readily available and effective. Chemicals and organic compounds with the lowest potential for toxicity to humans and beneficial organisms will be listed first.

Monitoring

Use the off-season to monitor your garden. Because the main goal of IPM is management—not total eradication of insects that destroy helpful predators along with harmful ones—regular observation is the key. This simple monitoring will give you enough information on population buildup to decide when and if to intervene.

How To Get Started

Equip yourself with a hand magnifier or a jeweler's glass, a capped pint jar, a large calendar, a handy reference, and some 3-by-5 cards. Mark out your first target areas—those parts of your yard and garden that have been damaged in the past.

What To Look For

Familiarize yourself with the excellent insect and disease identification charts that are provided by some garden chemical companies to local garden centers. Their color illustrations and descriptions are a useful adjunct to information you can glean from your local Cooperative Extension Service agent or other references prior to busier planting times. Look for the specific pests that may attack what you want to grow.   Some simple examples:

◊ In winter trees and shrubs will reveal dormant scale populations on bark, stems and the undersides of leaves.

◊ Gypsy moth egg masses will show up on tree trunks and buildings as soft chamois-colored lumps.

◊ The white speckles of adelgids will be revealed in the hemlocks.

◊ The bleached or dead foliage will point up the work of last year's most common pests: slugs, scales, tent caterpillars, aphids, gypsy moths, spider mites, bag worms, and Japanese beetles.

Mark the approximate hatch dates of all suspected pests on your calendar, so you can revisit sites to monitor population build-up.

Post the number of your local horticultural hotline and look out for the publication of location and times of your local Plant Clinic. These are often manned by the volunteer graduates of the excellent Master Gardener programs taught by local U.S.D.A. Cooperative Extension specialists in the late winter.

An Essential Skill: The Beat Test

By spring your 3 by 5 cards will come in handy. To detect the presence of active pests, tap suspected plant material over one of the cards. Even tiny critters are highly visible when they fall on white cardboard. A weekly visit to each site will detect insect population build-up in time to prevent excessive damage. If you are patient you may find that you have unexpected allies, those natural predators attracted by rising pest populations. If left alone with their favorite food, these can tip the balance in your favor before lasting damage is done.

Consult our insect charts to help analyze whether predator prey relationships are providing enough control.

Many gardeners who have changed to IPM practices did so because broad spectrum insecticides knocked out all the enemies of scale and spider mites, so that the surviving pests did far more damage than the original infestations. Nancy Bechtol, pest expert with the Maryland National Capital Parks, says that scale infestations caused by spray-created imbalances are the most common plant problem in our area.

Once your monitoring schedule is established as part of your regular garden routine, you will find that you have more time to decide which controls best fit your situation. Consult the calendar prepared by National Arboretum IPM manager Scott Akers for a year long look at the monitoring process. It helps you identify insects and diseases common to the area.

Integrated Pest Management Calendar

Integrated Pest Management is a moderate philosophy of pest management that incorporates the use of the best available combination of control methods to manage pest populations. Action is taken only when pests have been judged to reach seriously damaging levels. A few of the diverse control methods available include cultural controls, such as pruning; mechanical control, such as use of screens to exclude pests; physical control, such as hand picking pests; biological control with a natural enemy of a pest; and conventional chemical control.

January

Avoid damping-off fungi when starting plants by using only sterile fresh potting media and sterile containers. Bleach old containers with a 1% bleach solution if you want to use them again.

Look for disease resistant seeds and plants in catalogs. Keep in mind that resistance is not immunity, it only means that the resistant plant does well when attacked by a pest, not that there will be no damage from the pest the plant is resistant to.

Give houseplants a monthly rainstorm in the shower. Besides cleaning off dust, pests, like spider mites, are reduced greatly.

February

Sequester all gift plants you get on Valentine's Day. A small population of scales, mites, mealybugs, or whitefly may go unnoticed now but can infest all of your indoor plants and be very difficult to control. Within two weeks you can move them out of quarantine after carefully examining them for any pest problems.

Prune all suckers out of dogwoods now. Such pruning may prevent development of fatal Discula cankers.

Prune dead branches out of low-growing junipers. They may have been attacked by tip blight fungi and pruning will remove some of the spores.

Prune all dead branches out of Austrian, Scotch, and other two-needled pines to reduce spores of diplodia tip blight, which is often fatal to these pines. Plant resistant pines such as loblolly or scrub pine if one of your pines has succumbed to this disease.

March

Take that first warm day to carefully look around outside. Make a diagram of your landscape with all plants represented and note where you see insect or disease damage from last year. Note the severity of problems and their exact locations. You can bet that the same plants will require close attention throughout the season and you will know to take an extra hard look at these plants as you do your weekly garden walks to check for pests. You will be prepared to combat the pests before they do a lot of damage.

Check hemlocks for woolly adelgids (white fluff on the underside of branches) and scale insects (small gray-brown disks on the undersides of needles). Also check for eriophyid mite damage (branches turn off color) by tapping a branch vigorously while holding a white piece of paper under the branch. Use a magnifying glass to spot the extremely small, yellowish, carrot-shaped mites. If any one or combination of these pests occurs in large numbers, spray the tree with a 3% solution of horticultural oil when weather is going to be above freezing for two days. Make sure you spray thoroughly when using oil.

Check azalea leaves for lacebug damage, which will appear as white stippling of the leaves. Look for the shiny, tarry brown eggs on the undersides of the leaves. Note plants that have high numbers of eggs (greater than five per leaf) so that you will be prepared to treat them when they hatch.

Check apples and cherries for egg masses of the Eastern tent caterpillar. They look like black, melted styrafoam on the ends of the branches. Prune them out and destroy them.

Give roses a dormant oil spray alone or in combination with lime-sulfur to kill any overwintering insect eggs and disease spores on the canes. Make sure that you spray every cane. Pull up annual weeds such as annual bluegrass, chickweed, and cress before they have a chance to set seed.

Take back any mulch, leaves, and other debris where slugs have been a problem. Kill any slugs you find while cleaning up the garden; keeping mulch materials away from the plants until weather is warmer and drier will discourage slugs.

Cut back any remaining dead portions of perennials and ornamental grasses to remove any diseases or insects that are overwintering.

Begin cutting lawns as soon as any growth is noted to discourage annual weeds that may be attempting to set seed.

Dig out clumps of wild garlic, taking special care to get all of the small bulbs attached. In lawns, rake clumps of wild garlic vigorously to break the waxy cuticle of the leaves and improve uptake of foliar herbicides that can be used now.

April

Put up barrier bands on trees threatened with gypsy moth defoliation now. Concentrate on protecting oaks. Do not worry about protecting tulip poplars. To protect trees, attach a band of sticky tape around the circumference of the tree by mid-April. You may also attach a band of burlap above the sticky barrier, but you must remove accumulated caterpillars that appear under the burlap daily.

Plant coreopsis, cosmos, shasta daisy, and other daisy flowers to attract syrphid flies and parasitic wasps that will feed on aphids.

Begin regular fungicide treatment of roses to prevent development of black spot and powdery mildew.

Look for aphids on a wide variety of plant materials. Do nothing until aphid numbers are greater than 20 per shoot tip; if predators and parasites do not show up, treat with insecticidal soap. Repeat treatment may be needed if predators and parasites do not eventually arrive. If ants accompany the aphids, attach a sticky barrier at the base of the affect plants to prevent them from farming the aphids for honeydew and protecting them from predators.

If warm rains occur, check pears, apples, cotoneaster, and serviceberry for signs of fire blight. Prune out any diseased portions with pruning shears that are sterilized by dipping in bleach or alcohol after each cut.

Apply one treatment of a preventative fungicide to azaleas as they begin to show color to prevent the development of Ovulinia petal blight. With this treatment, flowers may last in good condition for up to three weeks and will fall off the plant when they are finished rather than sticking and drying on the plant.

May

Look for holes in leaves of cole crops and the small green caterpillars that make them. Treat infested plants with a pesticide containing the bacteria Bacillus thuringiensis.

Watch for swarms of gnat-like orange boxwood leafminer adults around boxwood now. With a systemic pesticide treat only plants that have sustained significant damage and have large numbers of adults swarming.

Start monitoring all plants for mites, especially if the weather has been warm and dry. Treat with 2% horticultural oil solution to reduce mite infestations before damage is severe. Monitor weekly by vigorously tapping a branch over a sheet of white paper. Mites will appear as small dark spots that move over the surface of the paper and leave a reddish-brown smear when the paper is wiped with the hand.

Prevent leafminer damage to spinach, beets, and chard by covering plants with a non-woven fabric to exclude the adult leafminers.

Watch peonies for the development of Botrytis blight as they finish blooming. Treat with a systemic fungicide at the first sign of blight.

Continue treating roses for black spot and powdery mildew every 7-10 days until weather is dry.

Watch for bristly rose slug sawflies on roses. They are small green caterpillars that appear on the undersides of leaves and on shoot tips. Spray them with soap if their numbers are high.

Treat paper birch with a systemic insecticide, like acephate, to prevent bronze borer, leafminer, and sawfly damage. Consider planting a 'Heritage' river birch as an alternative.

Do not be concerned with leaf blight that appears now on sycamore and ash. Treatment is seldom feasible and the trees usually withstand the disease if they are otherwise healthy. Consider planting other shade trees or resistant varieties of sycamore and ash.

Move mowing height up to between three and four inches by the middle of the month to prevent turf disease development and prevent the germination of crabgrass.

Set saucers of beer or yeast solution flush with the soil level in the garden to attract slugs. Renew the trapping solution every two days until slugs are no longer found in the saucers.

June

Look for circular notches in the new leaves of rhododendrons and azaleas after flowering has passed and new growth has begun. Heavy notching is an indication of black vine weevil feeding and larvae are present and damaging to the roots. Treat the soil under the plant with insect parasitizing nematodes or treat the top of the plant with a systemic insecticide.

Check the undersides of azalea leaves frequently for the emergence of lacebug larvae. The larvae are small, black, wingless, and spiny. This pest can be controlled with insecticidal soap, oil, or a systemic insecticide applied to the newly hatched larvae. Continue checking for larvae even after treatment since the eggs may not all hatch at the same time.

Rigorously prune any succulent sprouts emerging from the trunks of dogwoods. Foliar infections of Discula anthracnose can pass from leaves on these twigs and girdle the trunk of the tree, killing it. Consider planting a kousa dogwood or one of the resistant hybrids if you have lost a dogwood.

Continue looking for and treating mite infestations as they appear. Use a white sheet to detect mites and spot treat infestations with 2% horticultural oil spray.

Verticilium wilt will appear on maples when dry weather starts. Typical symptoms are dying back of branches from the tips and general ill health. Water the tree thoroughly if conditions are dry and prune out any dead branches. Japanese maples and Norway maples are hardest hit. If a tree succumbs to verticillium, consider replacement with a resistant maple such as paperbark maple or red maple.

Cover cucumbers with non-woven fabric to exclude the striped cucumber beetle that usually spreads fatal bacterial blight.

Plant a second crop of zucchini and other squash late in the month if your first attempt was damaged heavily by squash vine borers. The borers will have completed their life cycle and will not bother late plantings.

Look for pine needle scale crawlers now. They are bright red and about the size of a grain of sand. They can be monitored by beat testing as for mites. Treat heavily infested branches of pines with horticultural oil or insecticidal soap.

Potatoes may be heavily attacked by Colorado potato beetles now. If you have time, you can avert a chemical application by picking off adult beetles into a can of soapy water and destroying the yellow eggs that you will find in neat groups on the undersides of the leaves. Hand picking may take less time than spraying if you have a small number of plants.

Do not overfertilize your new tomato plants. High nitrogen levels now will cause localized calcium deficiency in the plants later that will result in blossom end rot.

July

Sudden death of drought-adapted plants such as lavender, santolina, lambs-ears, and sage may be due to Southern blight, a fungus that typically appears when night temperatures are high and high humidity prevents drying of foliage at the crown. Dead spots in these perennials are the result. Remove blighted shoots to the ground and dispose of them and thin these perennials to improve air circulation.

Look for stippling and bronzing of leaves of composite flowers such as calendula, black-eyed susan, and marigolds that indicates infestation of leafhoppers. Treat plants with a systemic insecticide to control these pests.

Continue to check all plants for mites; if weather is hot and humid, use a 2% solution of horticultural oil to control them.

Avoid water stress on plants now. Water trees, lawns, shrubs, and flower and vegetable gardens infrequently but deeply. If your soil is hard or clay, you may need to water an area for a short time until water begins running off and return the sprinkler to the area later. Use a shovel to check the depth of water penetration. Water should reach at least 8-10 inches below the soil level. Shallow watering will stress plants more than no watering at all; natural plant resistance to insects and disease may be weakened.

You may notice a large population of elm leaf beetles skeletonizing the foliage of your elms and zelkovas. Although the beetle larvae are present from early May on, you may want to hold off treating plants until now to see if populations develop into numbers high enough to do significant damage. Treat small trees with insecticidal soap; tolerate all but severe damage on large trees.

August

Monitor impatiens for necrotic ring spot virus. Look for tan, dead areas in the leaves that are surrounded by a purple margin as well as stunting of the plants. Remove infected plants and destroy them to avoid virus spread to other plants.

Apply a systemic insecticide, like acephate (orthene), to hollies that have been severely damaged by leaf miner. If you are planting new hollies, choose a resistant holly such as Foster holly, and try to plant them in a semi-shaded site where leaf miner is generally less of a problem.

Foliar nematode damage may appear now on hostas. Look for tan "V"-shaped or elongated spots in the foliage.

Unfortunately, there are no good sprays available for control of this pest. Remove infected leaves as damage appears.

September

If hemlock woolly adelgids are still out of control, treat trees with 3% oil solution late in the month.

Replace turf that died from drought, disease, or insect damage by seeding with a resistant turf-type tall fescue cultivar now.

As nights get cooler, be on the lookout for powdery mildew. Control powdery mildew with a solution of one tablespoon baking soda in one gallon of water with a few drops of soap to make the spray stick to foliage. If baking soda does not work, try using other fungicides; or simply cut back heavily infested foliage or tolerate damage on shrubs such as lilac. The fungus does no permanent damage to these plants.

Evaluate this year's growth on azaleas or rhododendrons for fungal problems. Individual branches that are wilted or dead signal a problem with Botryospaeria; whole plants that wilt are indicative of Phytophthora. Botryosphaeria starts as a foliar fungus at the tips of the leaves and produces bands of infected tissue. Eventually it gets into stems where it must be cut out, cutting back to white wood that is not stained with the fungus. Consider a resistant cultivar when replacing plants killed by Botryosphaeria. Phytophthora is a primarily root infecting disease, so the plant will usually wilt all at once. It is usually only a severe problem in heavy, wet soils that do not drain well. Move plants with this problem to more well drained soil or correct soil drainage where they are growing. Available fungicides do not provide lasting control for either disease.

October

Make an application of slow-release fertilizer to your lawn now. Lime if soil pH is below 6.0. Adequate nutrients and pH will ensure healthy, pest resistant turf next year.

Rigorously clean up any dogwood foliage as it falls. Compost the leaves in a hot compost heap to destroy the Discula fungus.

Bring houseplants in at the first sign of night temperatures below 45°F; but first give them a bath with a 1% horticultural oil solution to kill any insects or eggs on the plants.

Control woody and perennial weeds now with application of glyphosate (Roundup) to the foliage now. Plants are actively translocating sugars to their rootstocks now and the herbicide will be translocated as well, killing the rootstocks and eliminating the potential for re-growth.

November

Rake leaves off lawns. Continue to mow turf as long as it is actively growing. Time spent now will ensure healthier turf that is less susceptible to diseases and competition from weeds next season.

Take a good look at evergreens for signs of bagworms. Bags hang down from branch tips and are covered with chewed foliage of the tree or shrub they are found on. Remove all bags by clipping them off with scissors to control the caterpillar which may otherwise hatch in early July and defoliate many evergreens.

Cut back perennial garden foliage as it dies back to remove overwintering pests, diseases, spores, and eggs.

December

Treat your ball-and-burlap, or potted, Christmas tree with a vapor barrier to prevent excess moisture loss while it is in the house. It will have a better chance of surviving it moves out to your yard later.

Inspect poinsettias carefully for whiteflies before you purchase them. The adult insects can be seen flying around the plants; eggs appear as tiny black specks on the undersides of leaves; and larvae are small, oval, white, scale-like objects on the undersides of leaves. If you must buy plants infested with whitefly, keep them isolated from other houseplants.

Thin boxwoods by cutting small branches out all the way back to larger branches. Opening them up in this manner will prevent development of Volutella blight next season. Use the greens in holiday decorating.

Evaluate your biggest landscape pest problems and come up with a strategy that relies on more than one control method to combat the problem. For example: for black spot of roses, you may want to try using baking soda, horticultural oil, or vapor barrier instead of fungicide, along with a renewed attempt to incorporate resistant roses and a new effort to clean up fallen leaves that contain the fungus on a daily basis. A three-or four-pronged approach to control of a pest or disease is almost always more successful than control that relies only on chemical pesticides. Write out this plan to guide you in stocking up on hardware and pesticides and new plant purchases.

Carefully cut out all evidence of tip die-back caused by Diplodia fungus on Austrian and Scotch pine. This will remove spores that are splashed upward and infect higher branches the following spring.

Your Range of Pest Management Alternatives

Insect Control—Scientists who study the electrical fields and scent pheromones given off by growing plants have provocative evidence that suggests the less fit specimens are attacked more often by pests. Whether the egg or chicken comes first, a wise gardener tries to fill all his garden's cultural needs to prevent infestation. This includes the prompt removal of old crop residues when vegetables and cut flowers are spent, and good pruning and sanitation of trees that are prone to borers, scale insects, bag worms, and gypsy moths.

Biological Insect Pest Control—You may not think of planting shrubs, trees, and flowers that attract birds and butterflies as a biological control, but it often is. Many birds are quite omnivorous. Robins eat earthworms and grubs for much of the year, but gorge on dogwood berries before they migrate. Spending less money on broad spectrum insecticides and more on attractive plants is one way of assuring that your birds continue to have a healthy appetite.

Other biological controls are commercially raised insect populations that can be bought and released when the prey population is about to peak. This are usually available by mail order and require good monitoring skills so as not to waste money. Most home gardeners do better to recognize and not to eradicate their own garden helpers. This is good laissez-faire garden economics.

Botanical insect pest controls are getting renewed attention with extensive tests on substances like an extract from neem tree seeds which repels or stops development in nearly 30 common pests of ornamentals. Now available by mail order, Many of these substances are finding their way into garden centers.

Of course all botanical pesticides like pyrethrum, neem, ryania, and sabadilla should still be handled with care, since many are irritants and mildly toxic if breathed or absorbed by the skin. Others have a soap base, including some all-purpose mixes formulated separately for fruits, vegetables, ornamentals, or trees. The fatty acids in soap dehydrate many insects.

A gardener can make homemade mixtures utilizing the fatty acids in Ivory, Fels Naptha, Lux, Palmolive, or Murphy's Oil Soap, blended with garlic, pepper, and other proven insect repellants. Some gardeners even blend in the bugs they are trying to drive off.

Proportions are important. You can damage plant tissues. Rodale Press recommends a garlic spray recipe from England made by soaking 3 ounces of minced garlic in 2 tablespoons of mineral oil for 24 hours, then adding one pint of water with a quarter ounce of soap spray in it to the mixture before straining and storing in the refrigerator. Add 1 to 2 tablespoons per pint of water as a spray for aphids, cabbage loopers, squash bugs and white flies. Food plants, particularly leaf crops, should be thoroughly washed to rid plants of any lingering taste of these safe sprays.

Area Wide Solutions

Some wide spread solutions require group or municipal action, principally the Japanese beetle and the gypsy moth.

Because the gypsy moth defoliates forest and fruit

trees between April and July, and has no natural predator that prefers it, it is important to band your oak, hickory, and fruit trees in burlap to trap the distinctive blue and red dotted caterpillars. A population crash in 1989 reduced infestations. Continued vigilance will help keep them at acceptable levels. Most areas now spot spray bacillus thuriengensis (BT) based on citizen reports of egg mass infestations. BT is a safe virus strain that specifically targets the hungry caterpillars and gives them a fatal form of dysentery.

Japanese beetles, whose rising populations hatch from our lawns in July to devastate flowers, vegetables, and leaves, are best controlled with new strains of milky spore disease. This persists in the ground for two decades. Since these strong flyers travel far, whole neighborhoods should band together to seek area-wide control with the help of their local Cooperative Extension agents. In this way individual home owners will need to do only minimal spraying and trapping with pherome attractants that reduce breeding populations.

Prevention May Be Only Answer

Some previously effective but toxic chemical controls for birch and dogwood borers, root maggots, and nematodes have been removed from the home market. In many cases, there is no chemical substitute. Without diazinon there is no control for onion root maggots yet. Clandosan, made of crab shell chitin and urea nitrogen, shows promise in controlling root nematodes, but is not cleared for vegetable crops.

The Simpler Alternatives

Good drainage is the cultural preventive for onion root maggot. Rotating your crop and keeping a floating row cover over your onions during the April flights of the offending fly is your best recourse.

Spider mites on the underside of azalea, flower, and vegetable foliage can be flushed in hot weather by watering up through the leaves to dislodge these microscopic vampires before they bleach out stressed foliage. This alternative replaces regular spraying with diazinon or malathion. Commercial soap sprays and summer oils are another non-toxic alternative to wipe up the survivors.

Borers can sometimes be killed in their holes by inserting a thin wire in the tree trunks where they lurk. Peach twig borers can be pruned out of affected branch tips. But the best way to avoid trunk infestation is to wrap peach and dogwood trunks with a laminated paper and asphalt product. Do not spring prune dogwoods. The wounds are a primary entry site for borers.

Simple aluminum foil collars will protect the stems of cole crops, squash, and tomato transplants from cutworms, which feed at night, until a BT compound can be applied in your garden to eventually destroy the rest.

Toxic slug bait can be attractive to pets and children, and deadly to birds It is better to use clean cultivation methods on heavy wet soil. Avoid chopped leaf or brush mulches where slugs abound. Hoe frequently during the spring. For the first six weeks of the growing season, trap slugs at the garden's edge by setting out overturned grapefruit rinds or pie pans of beer.

Whitefly populations have become immune to many powerful chemicals. To prevent infestation, site your garden for good air circulation. Fortunately non-toxic soap sprays will dry them out and provide limited relief. So will the new summer oils, which smother pests.

Horticultural Oils—Refined Solution

An old product, refined, is getting a huge new boost for its summertime control of larval forms of scale, adelgids, bagworms, and of mites, whitefly, and aphids. The highly refined mineral oils are now light enough to spray on evergreens like hemlock, yew and azalea as well as herbaceous plants in the summer when insects and fungus are active. The oil is mixed in water with the help of a few drops of soap. National Arboretum research indicates that 2-3 ounces per gallon will achieve control without damage in most species at a wide range of temperatures.

All sprays or dusts should be applied after plants are well watered and the foliage is dry. Healthy plants can best withstand any chemical interaction that occurs.

Recommended Botanical and Chemical Insecticides

These controls are currently considered the safest for home use with the least side effects on the environment. Assess your own and your neighbors' situation when choosing products.

Ingredient (Trade Name) Controls

Ingredient (Trade Name)	Controls
Acephate (Orthene)	thrips, beetles, leaf miners, leafhopper, mites
Azadiractin (BioNeem)	larvae of many ornamental pests
Carbaryl* (Sevin)	flea beetles, corn borers, horn worms, leaf hoppers, bean and cucumber beetles, bagworms
Methoxychlor (Marlate)	coddling & Oriental fruit moth, Japanese beetle, plum curculio
Pyrethrin (Rotenone)	whitefly, aphids, thrips, mealy bugs

*undergoing EPA review: stop use 3 days before harvest.

Chemicals occur in different forms and concentrations. You will find them as wettable powder (WP), or emulsifiable concentrate (EC) or sprays or dusts. Both mixable forms will need a surfactant, i.e. a teaspoon of liquid soap, to make material cling to plants. This is one reason that various soap spray formulas have become popular.

All-Purpose Sprays

Convenient all-purpose sprays that fall within the current safety guidelines for home use are still readily available. These are specially formulated to protect fruits, vegetables, or ornamentals. Some of the newer compounds are very low in toxicity and have provided a larger data base on their relative safety. All commercial compounds should include a stomach poison or disease for chewing insects, a contact poison for sucking insects, and a fungicide or bacteriocide that protects against appropriate diseases. Read the label and observe the spray-free, pre-harvest period scrupulously.

Four-Legged Pests

Moles will eat Japanese beetles and other grubs, but the cure is worse than the disease, because your lawn and garden will look like a moonscape. Avoid poison baits or smoke bombs where possible if you have small children or pets. Try putting mothballs down their holes or trapping them—a slow process of staking out a radius of feeder tunnels that lead back to the main burrows and then setting out powerful piercing traps astride them each night. Some people claim that moth balls dropped into the main burrow will drive moles away. Employ an energetic cat to catch the voles that run in mole tunnels. The voles, mouse cousins, eat the roots that moles expose in their meanderings.

Rats will require a professional exterminator. Avoid putting kitchen scraps in the compost pile, so as not to attract them in the first place.

Rabbits and groundhogs love the tender young leaves of many garden vegetables, and can devour a whole row of plants overnight. Both may be box-trapped and relocated in the country, but repellant sprays and dusts, combined with fencing, are more convenient. Thiram is a chemical spray deterrent which must be applied every two weeks. Bordeaux mixture is also a repellant to rabbits, as are 3 ounces of epsom salts to a gallon of water sprayed on the young foliage. Tobacco dust or blood meal dusted on wet foliage also helps.

Always read the labels.

Netting and vigilance are the only proven methods of saving many fruit crops from birds and squirrels, so do not hesitate when your blueberries, cherries, or peaches near ripeness. Gather the net at the bottom of the tree or bush.

As regards deer, skunks, and raccoons, nothing works forever where populations are high, although human hair and Irish Spring soap bars near garden treasures have a good reputation. Rural gardeners will need to cage corn crops as if these were the wild animals. Better yet, get a good hound. And keep him safely flea-free, after he runs off large pests, by seeking out pet dusts that also use ground diatoms to desiccate fleas plus low amounts of improved pyrethroids.

Mosquitoes and Ticks A Garden Problem?

How much garden work is made miserable by mosquitoes in a wet season? If you have standing water or a pond, a new strain of the BT virus specific to mosquito larvae can be bought in a block form to float on the surface. BT berliner israelii provides 30 days of safe biological control. Summer oils sprays also work if you do not have a pond population of other animals and insects to consider.

If your garden is in an unmowed area or in moist woods, you can get protection from ticks, at a price. The chemical control, permethrin, is remarkably effective at killing both dog ticks and the deer ticks that carry Lyme disease. It is sold in spray form as Permanone or Permakill. Applied to clothing, it kills ticks on contact. As a synthetic form of pyrethrum, it has low toxicity, rating a CAUTION warning from the EPA. Although it costs over $20 per 8 ounce can, it sells like hot cakes to local landscapers and grounds maintainence crews.

Preventing Plant Diseases

Preventive spraying of fungicides is often necessary in our hot, muggy climate to prevent the spread of air and soil borne diseases. These will be listed with the understanding that gardeners should do their part by choosing plant varieties bred with resistance to viruses and bacterial wilts.

Built In Resistance

Your first line of defense against plant disease is genetic. When you purchase nursery stock, whether woody ornamentals like roses or your favorite tomato plant, look for disease resistant varieties. Tomatoes are a good example; look for plant labels or seed catalog descriptions to find a variety marked VFN. This stands for genetic resistance to verticilium and fusarium wilts. Some varieties also resist the mosaic virus.

Fungicides

Fungicides are the one form of plant protection that you do need to apply at suggested intervals before you see evidence of disease. After you have taken the precaution of choosing resistant varieties and growing them under optimum conditions, you will still have some plants that need this protection in our climate. Chief among them are fruit trees, roses, and flowers and vegetables prone to powdery mildew late in the growing season. Other plant diseases spread by insect hosts are more easily prevented by insecticides. All fungicides, whether dust or spray, will be more effective if applied to healthy plants after a rain and when good weather is predicted for the next several days. As with all spray mixtures, coverage will be improved if you add a surfactant to the mix, which will make it "wetter" by reducing surface tension. Soaps are surfactants.

(please turn to page 30)

Variety selection	Planting date	Crop rotation	Trapping crops	Pheromone traps	Catch traps	Common Insect Pests	Bt - B. thuringiensis	Other pathogens	Dormant oil	Safer's soap	Miscible oil	DE-Diatom. Earth	Parasites	Predators	Ryania	Sabadilla	Rotenone	Pyrethrins
						Alfalfa Caterpillar	★						★	★				
				★		Alfalfa Looper	★						★	★				
★		★			★	Aphids				★			★			★		★
						Asparagus Beetle							★	★	★		★	
						Bagworm	★											
★		★				Cabbage Butterfly	★			★								
★		★		★		Cabbage Looper	★						★			★	★	★
				★	★	Cockroaches						★					★	★
				★	★	Codling Moth	★	★	★				★	★	★	★		★
★	★					Colorado Potato Beetle							★			★	★	
★	★		★	★		Corn Earworm			★		★		★	★	★			★
★		★				Diamondback Moth	★								★			
★	★	★		★		European Corn Borer	★						★		★	★	★	
						Fall Webworm	★											
						Flea Beetles					★					★	★	★
						Fleas				★		★					★	★
★						Grasshoppers		★							★	★		
						Green Cloverworm	★											
		★				Gypsy Moth	★								★			★
	★					Hornworm	★						★	★				
				★	★	Housefly							★		★		★	★
	★			★	★	Japanese Beetle		★									★	★
					★	Leafhopper			★		★					★		
				★		Leafroller	★						★	★				
						Mealybug			★	★	★		★					
★	★		★			Mexican Bean Beetle							★				★	★
★						Mites			★	★	★		★				★	★
				★		Oriental Fruit Moth					★		★	★	★			★
						Pear Psylla			★	★	★		★			★		
						Scale			★	★	★		★					
★	★	★	★			Spotted Cucum. Beetle										★	★	★
						Spruce Budworm	★											★
	★					Stinkbugs					★					★	★	★
★	★	★	★			Striped Cucum. Beetle										★	★	★
						Tent Caterpillar	★											★
						Thrips				★			★			★		★
				★		Tomato Fruitworm/Tobacco Budworm	★						★	★	★			★
						Tussock Moth	★											★
						Velvetbean Caterpillar	★											
					★	Whitefly				★			★	★				★

Deterrent Actions | Traps

Biologicals | Minerals, oils | Bene-ficials | Botanicals

Soap spray formulas that incorporate fungicides have been on the market for some time. The formula provides a sticky base which helps prevent fungal spores from invading plant tissue. Because of their ability to prevent this invasion, new horticultural oil sprays are also being tested as fungicides. New research by Cornell University points out cases of effective control in a mix with baking soda for control of powdery mildew and black spot on roses. The mix has been tested for two years at the National Arboretum, where it has proved more effective for powdery mildew in our hotter climate. Alternation in a spray schedule with a conventional black spot control like Funginex or Daconil 2787 may be tried as a way of retaining effective disease control while cutting the use of conventional chemicals in half.

The EBDC chemicals like Mancozeb can be used on home ornamentals, but are restricted for some food crops.

Anti-desiccant sprays that some people apply to their broadleaf evergreens to prevent winter drying also show some promise as fungal disease barriers. The proper timing is crucial for all these products because most prevent rather than cure fungal diseases. One exception is streptomycin, an antibiotic used to treat dogwood anthracnose; but it is still most effective if sprayed on the buds while dormant.

The following fungicides are appropriate for home use. Many are sold under different brand names by different companies. Others are the exclusive property of one chemical company, though they may be licensed for use in other mixtures. Check labels for the common or chemical name.

Active Fungicides

Control	Diseases	Plants
Dormant oil	fungal diseases	dormant plants
Lime sulphur	overwintering pests	
Summer Oil	powdery mildew	flowers, trees
Flowable sulphur	scab, powdery mildew	fruit (not hot weather)
	leaf spot, brown rot	trees
Lime sulphur	mildew, anthracnose	peach fruit, trees
	leaf curl,	
	leaf spot, brown rot	
Fixed Copper	many fungal diseases	vegetables, fruits
(Dust or liquid flowers)		shrubs
Captan	seed decay downy	vegetables.
	mildew, anthracnose	shrubs
Bordeaux mixture	anthracnose, blight,	flowers, trees
	mildew, blackrot	fruit
Triforine	black spot, septoria	flowers
	leaf spot, downy mildew.	
	altenaria blight	
Chlorothalonil*	rusts, mildews,	flowers
	leaf blight,	early culinary herbs
	late tomato blight	vegetables
Terrachlor, Triathlon	root rot, botrytis	drench for shrubs

*Stop seven days before harvest.

Herbicides

Herbicides will kill all of the plant material that they are designed to affect, often by using a plant's own growth mechanisms against it. So it is crucial to apply them selectively. In addition, some are toxic and persistent, arguably the most dangerous of chemical controls.

Due to the danger of drift, weed control in the flower and vegetable beds is best done by cultivation, mulching, and removal of weeds before they set seed.

Families who use their lawns constantly should prevent weed invasion by planting locally adapted grasses on soil rich in organic matter, maintaining the correct pH balance, and cutting at a height no less than 2 ½ inches. An asparagus knife is the safest way to remove invading broad leaf weeds.

People who use lawn services or all-purpose weed and feed fertilizer mixes should scrupulously follow the suggested cautions to prevent exposure to active herbicides.

Herbicide sprays are most useful: as pre-emergents to control the germination of weeds and invasive grasses; when applied individually to broadleaf weeds like plantain, dandelion, and wild garlic; for clearing an old lawn prior to re-seeding; or for killing undergrowth of bamboo, cat briar, honeysuckle, or poison ivy.

Use a directed spray when spraying around ornamental shrubs. Small shallow-rooted specimens are at greater risk. Be sure that any treated grass clippings are not used for compost or mulch. Maintain a separate herbicide sprayer or be prepared to triple rinse your whole unit after each use, following all directions for safe use and storage. In short, handle and dispose of herbicides with great care. If you have any allergic reaction, discontinue use and consider hiring a licensed weed control service.

To avoid eventual recurrence and the need for more spray control, dig up the dormant root systems of vines, like poison ivy, in the fall after systemic herbicides have weakened them.

WEED CONTROL CALENDAR

The following calendar shows when to use some of the most effective herbicides. Those currently under review by the EPA are starred. Many require a surfactant for good coverage. The post-emergents work best during the period of most active growth.

Spring Only

Pre-emergents effective on annual grasses and some broadleaf weed seeds: (Balan) use twice for crabgrass, Barricade, DCPA, (Dacthal)—every 8 weeks, Basagran for nut sedge in late May, early June

Pre-emergents which do not prevent lawn grass germination: (Siduron), (Tupersan).

Summer

Post-emergents effective on all weeds and grasses (acts as a systemic to inhibit photosynthesis or displace nutrient flow): Glyphosphate, (Roundup); Poast for crabgrass and witchgrass

Post-emergents effective on weeds in lawns: *(2-4-D).

Post-emergents effective in non-crop areas on poison ivy, poison oak, willow, oak, maple, brush, etc.: Triclopyr (4 oz. per gal.)

—* under EPA review.

Always read the label carefully and follow EPA recommendations for use.

Techniques for Safe Application

For half the life of this book the Environmental Protection Agency has attempted to answer questions on the long-term effects of many chemicals through their review and special review process. As a result several products have been removed from the home-use market or re-labeled in an effort to protect consumers and their environment. But it is no secret that the most common cause of poisoning is the gardener who will not read and follow directions for the correct handling, storage, and disposal of these substances.

What Labels Mean

By law, consumers must read all the label information pertinent to their intended use. When they do, they will discover a quick way to determine the toxic potential of their choice before buying. CAUTION, WARNING and DANGER designate three escalating levels of toxicity for pest control products within the three categories of insecticides, fungicides for plant disease, and herbicides for weeds.

Therefore we will no longer recommend specific amounts of commercial pesticides in mixtures or liquid solution. Each label contains the specific concentration for the pest your target with the specific environmental conditions under which you should apply it to each species. This provides another handy use for your magnifying glass.

Pest, disease, and weed controls come in granules, powder, or liquid form to be applied as a drench, a dust, or a spray. Consumers run the greatest risk at the time of use, when mixing and applying the material. Then they can spill concentrates on the skin, breathe noxious fumes, or accidentally touch the mouth or eyes before cleaning up.

To Prevent Accidents

☐ Wear rubber gloves, a hat or scarf, long-sleeved clothes, and pants.

☐ Use a filter mask when spraying tall bushes or trees, or if you have any history of allergies.

☐ Mix material in a special container that is not used for other purposes.

☐ Apply when the air is still—to prevent drift of dust or spray particles.

☐ Thoroughly clean sprayers or dusters of extra material, and dispose of any leftover herbicides or pesticides in a closed container, particularly if you have a septic system.

☐ Change clothes and wash them separately.

☐ Wash hands and face thoroughly before eating or drinking.

Guarding Others

Children, animals, and neighbors risk ingesting toxic material on food before it is safe to harvest, skin contact with powerful herbicides or insecticides on lawns or trees, spray drift of broad spectrum herbicides that may kill adjacent plantings, and contact with spilled or improperly stored residues.

To avoid these circumstances:

☐ Do keep children and animals out of the areas sprayed with herbicides and insecticides for the time recommended by the manufacturer.

☐ Do spray or dust when the air is calm in early morning or evening.

☐ Do not spray all-purpose mixtures close to harvest time without knowing the toxic period of each component. Some are stronger, but short-lived, others weaker, but persistent. Use the longest effective period as your cut-off date.

☐ Do not use baits that mimic food to control slugs, moles, or mice if young children or pets are around.

☐ Soak up any spills with kitty litter, carefully shoveling the material into a leakproof container for disposal. Store toxic pesticides in a locked cabinet.

Safety for Plants

Plants can also suffer from improper application of materials designed to protect them. To avoid burning foliage or stunting growth:

⇒ Follow explicit directions determining the strength of a spray mixture for certain plants. Even a strong garlic and cayenne mixture in a soap solution can burn foliage. Be conservative with home brews.

⇒ Do not apply pesticides when plants are under stress from severe changes in the weather. Instead dust with wood ashes or gypsum to deter chewing and sucking insects.

⇒ Spray between 6 and 10 a.m., so foliage will dry quickly.

⇒ Use wettable powders when available rather than emulsifiable concentrates; to keep spray nozzles from clogging shake the tank every minute or two while you spray.

⇒ Keep spray nozzles 1½-2 feet from all sides of the foliage that you are covering.

⇒ Do not mix all-purpose formulas without using a recommended formula. At the wrong concentrations the components may be incompatible.

⇒ Thoroughly clean all spray equipment after each use. Ammonia and triple rinsing are recommended. Make sure nozzles are not clogged before you store or use your sprayer.

Equipment

The home gardener will need a separate applicator for herbicides, in order to prevent damage to desirable plants. Herbicides are hard to remove from closed spray equipment.

There are many types of sprayers on the market. Any you buy should be sturdily constructed and easy to clean and assemble for obvious safety reasons. You should practice with water first on any pump sprayer before mixing and using any botanical or chemical control with toxic potential.

A pump sprayer with an adjustable wand will allow you to make solutions with emulsifiable concentrates and wettable powders. These will give you complete coverage of small trees, shrubs, vegetables, flowers, and lawns. Decisions on sprayer capacity and the utility of a back-pack sprayer depend on the size and location of your garden.

If your garden is small, you may need a little vacuum pressure sprayer that attaches to a standard garden hose and nozzle. These work best with concentrated liquids which are mixed with water and expelled through the nozzle when the hose is turned on and your thumb closes the air intake. They are cheap and easy to clean. Like some lawn spreaders, they may be designed and calibrated to use only the manufacturer's products.

Container gardeners can use a spray bottle or mister to apply plant protection.

A small dusting canister may be adequate if you have a town house garden. The best results are obtained if the plant dust covers all surfaces of the plant. For this you may want a hand cranked duster equipped with a long tube and adjustable nozzle so dusts can penetrate dense foliage from the bottom up.

Measuring Is Important

In order to avoid having to dispose of excess spray solutions, you should try to estimate the number of row feet or square feet you need to cover at a given application. Contamination of local water supplies downstream from heavily populated areas and of groundwater is a real problem for which we all share responsibility.

RESOURCES:

The National Pesticide Telecommunications Network, (800) 858-7377

Bug Bulletin, (410) 857-0343

Maryland Cooperative Extension Services bulletins through local offices:

No. 2581 Recommendations for Insect Monitoring and Control

No. 294 Controlling Plant Diseases in the Home Landscape

Virginia Cooperative Extension Pest Management Guide: Home Grounds & Animals

Common Sense Pest Control, Olkowski, Daar, Olkowski; Taunton Press 1991

Chemical Free Yard & Garden, Rodale Press, 1991

IPM for Turf grasses and Ornamentals, by Ann Leslie; Lewis Press, 1993

Conversion Table

(VOLUME—NOT WEIGHT)

1 tablespoonful equals	3 teaspoonfuls equal	½ fluid ounce
2 tablespoonfuls equal	6 " "	1 " "
1 gill equals	½ cupful equals	4 " "
1 cupful "	½ pint "	8 " "
1 pint "	½ quart "	16 " "
1 quart "	¼ gallon "	32 " "
1 gallon		128 " "

VOLUME AND WEIGHT

(Cold water but not in general to spray liquids)

1 fluid ounce equals	1 ounce avoirdupois
1 gill "	4 ounces "
1 cupful "	8 " "
1 pint "	16 " "
1 quart "	32 " "
1 gallon "	128 " "

(Adopted from Bureau of Standards Miscellaneous Publication 39)

If each of us weighs our pest control decisions, and pays attention to safety in the use, storage and disposal of materials with toxic potential, our yards and gardens will give us the peace of mind they promise.

COMMON INSECTS

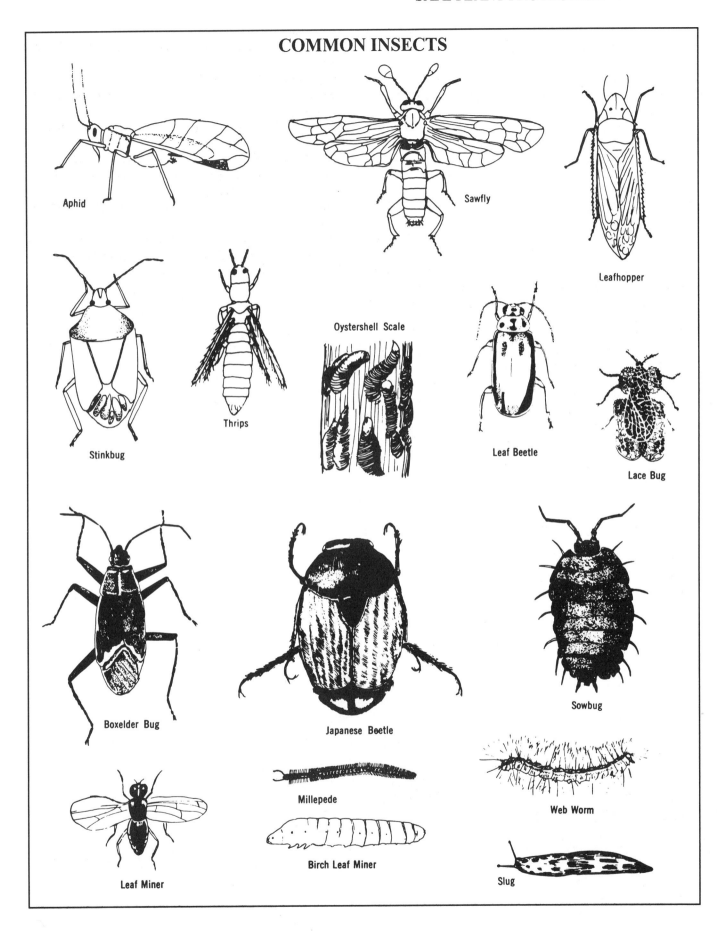

Aphid

Sawfly

Leafhopper

Stinkbug

Thrips

Oystershell Scale

Leaf Beetle

Lace Bug

Boxelder Bug

Japanese Beetle

Sowbug

Leaf Miner

Millepede

Birch Leaf Miner

Web Worm

Slug

5. PLANTS AND HOW TO CHOOSE THEM

A garden plan and plant list in hand your are ready to begin the process of choosing the trees and shrubs and herbaceous plants to make your wish list into a reality. The Botanical name is the key to getting the plant you want to create the garden you envision. Visits to garden centers and nurseries are an opportunity to get acquainted with the possibilities that are out there. Take with you a list of the types of plants you are looking for. Plants are grown to be sold in a variety of ways and you can get an idea about the sizes and how they are commonly sold; for example, a tree can be balled and burlapped (B & B), container grown, or bare-root. A garden center is rather like a one stop department store for the gardener but there are other sources for more unusual plants.

What Is In a Name

The common names for plants have a multitude of origins. They are descriptive, regional, ethnic, traditional, and even national and some names are derived from their uses. So many sources for common names lead to confusion and frequently mistaken identity. For example, if you are looking for Bluebells you would be sold Mertensia virginica, Virginia Bluebells a spring ephemeral wildflower but at a bulb nursery you would get Endymion hispanica, English Bluebells and at a perennial nursery it would be Campanula rotundifola. The following example will illustrate the importance of knowing and using the botanical name and explain the parts of the name.

Japanese cherry trees are synonymous with the spring in Washington D.C. These beautiful trees have pink buds that open white in clusters of 5-petalled flowers on bare branches. The gardener in search of the this plant needs specifics to get the same plant. There are many different flowering cherry trees native to Japan and even more cultivated in its gardens. How do you know which one you are planting?

There is a specific name for every plant. These names are written in Latin, a language internationally excepted and used by botanists and gardeners. The binomial system assigns a two part name to each plant is based on the work of the 18th century Swedish botanist Linnaeus. The plants are classified by the number and arrangement of their sexual parts; thus plants with similar flowers are in the same family. The two part botanical name is a precise, brief description of the plant.

Cherry trees are members of the genus Prunus, that describes a group plants that have the 5-petaled flowers, similar flowers, leaves and bark. Differentiating characteristics such as flower color or habit of growth identify individual species. All members of a species have the same characteristics that are reproduced when grown from seed. The white flowered Tidal Basin cherry is the species yedoensis, a latinized version of Yedo an old name for Tokyo.

Gardeners are in constant research of variations and breeding to improved plants. These "cultivated" plants come into the trade and the garden in a variety of ways and are referred to as cultivars. The recognized cultivar name follows the genus and species names and is written enclosed in inverted commas. Among the Prunus yedoensis around the Tidal Basin is a cultivar with pale pink flowers named Prunus yedoensis 'Akebono'. An important thing to note is that many cultivars like this plant do not reproduce themselves from seed and must be propagated by cuttings.

Thus, the name to look for is Prunus yedoensis, the gardener's key to finding the Japanese flowering cherry trees that create clouds of delicate white flowers and petals that flutter to the walks and grass around the Tidal Basin for a few days each spring.

How Plants are Sold

Plants come in many forms. The most basic are seeds available at the corner drugstore, in garden centers, hardware stores, and mail order catalogs. In general it is advisable to buy seeds from sources that specialize in plants because reliable seeds are their business. A mail order seed house use informative catalogs to sell seed. The seed packets have a photo, description, vegetable yields and blooms season, a drawing of the new seedling, germination and harvest times.

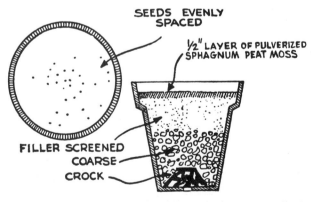

SEEDS EVENLY SPACED

½" LAYER OF PULVERIZED SPHAGNUM PEAT MOSS

FILLER SCREENED COARSE CROCK

4-to-6 inch flower pots may be used to start a supply of plants for the small garden.

Seeds are sold in dated packages; the date is on the flap of the packet; always buy seeds with the current year's date. Also check packets for quantity of seed. Do not buy seed packets with water spots or other damage; seeds are delicate and viability is easily jeopardized by water and rough treatment.

At garden centers and nurseries plants are sold in containers that come in many sizes and a wide variety of materials. There are containers with multiple cells, trays made of papier-mache and individual ones ranging from two inches pots to two feet sized tubs.

Some plants are grown from seed in the container you buy them in. These containers are called market packs; usually annuals, vegetables, and annual herbs like parsley and are sold this way. Seedlings are also grown in papier-mache trays. When making your selection look for well developed individual plants that have good color and do not appear wilted or under stress. Check to see if roots are coming out of the drainage holes plants that have become root bound will need to be cut back and will take longer to get established.

Plants grown in individual pots include perennials, larger annuals, ground cover, small shrubs and trees. Choose healthy looking plants and check for broken stems, burned leaf tips, yellowing or wilted foliage and pot bound roots.

Large trees and shrubs are field grown. They have been dug and the root ball has been wrapped in burlap that is held in place by laced twine. A very large ball is often set into a wire basket to hold it together. In the trade this practice is call balled and burlapped or B&B. These plants need careful inspection to make sure that the soil balls are firmly attached to the trunk and roots, look for cracks in the soil that expose the roots to drying out. The soil should be firm and moist. The burlap should be intact and the lacing tight enough to hold the ball together. The lacing should not have marked the bark of the trunk. Make sure to check the plant for broken branches, wilted foliage and signs of stress.

Mail order nurseries usually ship their plants bare-rooted to reduce the cost of shipping. Bare-rooted plants are dug when the growing season is over and the plants are dormant. The soil is washed away before the plants are wrapped to keep the roots from drying out and the plants are stored under controlled conditions. They are shipped between October and March. When the plants arrive, check them over to make sure that the packing has protected the roots from drying out. The root system should be well developed and the flexible roots should be free of broken roots. Shake out the roots and soak them in warm water with a liquid transplant hormone added for a few hours and then plant.

Sources of Plants for the Garden

Seeds and plants are available from mail order catalogs. There are dozens of catalogs in the trade. Many specialty growers provide mail order services; these growers specialize in unusual vegetables, iris, wildflowers, fruit trees and berries.

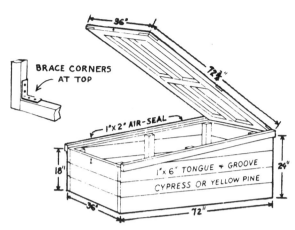

BRACE CORNERS AT TOP

1"x2" AIR-SEAL

36"

72"

18"

24"

1"x6" TONGUE + GROOVE
CYPRESS OR YELLOW PINE

36"

72"

Cold frames have many uses: Starting seeds, winter storage for tender plants and year-round propagation. Build the frames in 3x6-foot sections. Use wood or cinder blocks, which should last for several years. Treat the wood with a rot-proofing. Place the frame 6 inches into the ground and mound soil up on the outside. Use 1x2-inch strips to act as an air-seal around the top. A hook and eye will help to hold the top snugly. Cover the top with reinforced plastic; or better still, cover both sides of the top with clear plastic.

Catalogs are good reference resources and the best of them list their plants by their botanical name and include descriptive information, photographs, growing condition requirements and hardiness zone.

Because mail order houses specialize, it is often advisable to buy specialty plants such as hostas, daylilies, or bulbs from them because they have extensive varieties to choose from and offer a greater selection than that at a garden center.

A visit to a nursery or garden center can be a sensory overload because it presents so many choices— how is a gardener to find her way. A good garden center will have organized the plants into specific areas for trees, shrubs, conifers, perennials, annuals and ground covers. These large groups are sub-divided according to genera. For example the shrubs would have an area for Rhododendrons and they would be further sub-divided into the Azaleas and Rhododendrons. Each plant will have a label that includes the botanical with the cultivar name if appropriate.

Garden centers and nurseries know that plants in bloom are much more likely to sell and they stock plants during their bloom season. They install display gardens to demonstrate how plants can be used and to show interesting specimens and plant combinations. In the perennial area they have large containers planted with established plants to show the habit, foliage and flowers in season. Individual display labels or signs with a picture of the plant in bloom, the botanical and common name and information about size and growing conditions are a help to the buyer. A knowledgeable sales person is your best assistant if you make your visit when the center is not thronged with customers.

The better informed you are the more likely you are to find the right plants for your garden. Get to know the plants by visiting public gardens and going on garden tours. The following chapters focus on the plant groups and provide suggestions of those best suited to the growing conditions of the Washington area. Included in each chapter is information on planting, pruning, and general care and there are tips for special plants. At the end of each chapter, there are recommendations of public gardens to visit to see mature specimens and gardens to see unusual plantings.

TRANSPLANTING SEEDLINGS TO THE GARDEN

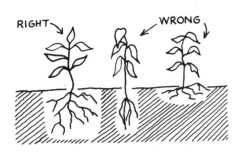

Be sure to dig the garden holes wide and deep enough to set roots in their natural position.

When you begin transplanting, dig only a few seedlings at a time and get them into the garden soil as soon as possible.

As you take the seedlings from your flats to transplant to the garden, be sure to get an ample size ball of soil with the roots.

Make hole with trowel and set in plant before removing trowel. Then add starter solution.

Then fill in with soil. Firm with your fingers but do not pack tightly.

If transplanting in July or August, it is a good idea, even though extra trouble, to put a paper bag over each plant just for a few days to protect the plants from driving wind, rain, or sun till they get started in the ground. Hold down the paper bags with a trowelful of soil.

6. THE SUSTAINABLE LAWN

A good lawn is a mark of distinction—something that every homeowner strives to have. Nowadays more and more people can achieve their goal because turf grass specialists have developed blends of cool-climate bluegrasses and disease resistant fescues that are able to stand up to the muggy summer heat of much of our area. Tougher perennial rye grasses, improved warm season bermuda grass strains, and zoysia also have their advocates. And to their credit, builders of many new subdivisions are willing to give home owners a good start by installing these lawns as turf.

Still, some problems remain. Lawn grasses installed over compacted or improperly prepared subsoil will not thrive. And lack of proper care and feeding at the right time will cause eventual lack of vigor, disease and pest problems, and the invasion of weeds.

To help solve these problems, turf management techniques now call for a new emphasis on fall fertilizing and re-seeding. This newly recommended timing for lawn care avoids the stress of early heat waves and the weeks of muggy air pollution during summer months, and also includes the periodic aeration of the soil, so it will better absorb nutrients and water. This prevents excess runoff into our watersheds, an important consideration when you think that lawns may cover more area than forest or any other crop in the greater metropolitan area.

Proper Maintenance Prevents Problems
We expect our predominantly cool season lawn grasses to stay green from early spring to late fall or early winter. A regular program of fertilization to support this growth should consist of spreading more than half of the lawn's nutrient needs after the August heat waves break, most of the rest by November to strengthen root growth and food reserves, and then adding an optional feeding during the late-February thaw prior to spring growth.

Newly popular four-step programs advocated by national lawn product companies do not really adhere to an optimum nutritional calendar because they are trying to incorporate pre-emergent controls for grasses and broadleaf weeds in their spring feedings, and to control lawn pests in their summer cycle at the risk of creating overly lush growth during our hot season. Better to take advantage of steps one and four, and apply separate controls for spring and summer problems if they are needed. It is natural for lawn growth to slow during hot weather (when we all need a vacation).

Overfertilizing with nitrogen in lawn areas is thought to cause disease and pest problems among neighboring shrubs and trees.

The usual bluegrass-fescue lawn needs about 3 to 6 pounds of nitrogen per 1,000 square feet each season to promote leaf growth. In the spring most of it can be gotten from air and rainfall at no cost to you. Turf fertilizers have such varied formulas as 10-6-4, 10-5-5, 16-8-8, and 20-10-10, where nitrogen is usually provided in complete fertilizer formulas at more than twice the amount of available phosphate or potash by weight. But these other nutrients are arguably more important here. They provide a vital boost to root development in fall and winter. And deep roots provide the best protection against drought and heat for these cool season grasses.

Fertilize Carefully

Although there are many commercially available formulas for cool and warm season grasses, the newer mixtures contain some portions of their nitrogen in slow-acting, non-burning materials. They are referred to as urea-form of water insoluble nitrogen (WIN). Unlike manures and water soluble nitrogen sources, they release this nutrient slowly through bacterial action or the dissolving of a coating by water. As a result, turf will grow at a constant rate over a large portion of the growing season without as much risk of burning the grass. This is an advantage to the homeowner, who will not have to cut as frequently during the normal rapid lawn growth of April and May. And it is an advantage to the lawn, because forcing top growth at the expense of good root development results in its diminished resistance to the inevitable drought and diseases of mid-summer.

Correct Watering Is Important

A great deal of turf grass injury is caused by improper watering during summer droughts. Cool season grasses have a tendency to go dormant in the summer. It is best to allow them to slow down and dig their roots deep in search of moisture. If a heat wave persists for 10 days, the lawn should be deeply watered in the early morning when less of the water will evaporate into the air.

Prince William County's Water Quality specialist, Marc Aveni, recommends using a tuna can as an accurate way of measuring a deep soaking that will hold any lawn for at least 2 weeks. Just place it within your sprinkler arc, and keep watering until the can is full.

New drip irrigation lines and soaker hoses are a bit harder to measure. Some can be hooked to a water timer that can be set for up to 2 hours before shutting off. In this way portions of the lawn can be watered on a rotating schedule.

A good rule of thumb is to water a lawn planted in sandy soil no more than once a week, soaking the soil 6-8 inches deep. Lawns planted on moisture retentive clay soil will need less watering, about every 10 days to 2 weeks during a drought. When metropolitan water supplies drop and rationing is threatened, water and cut the grass less frequently, allowing it to go dormant. Do not stimulate growth by feeding.

How to Prevent Trouble

Turf grass should be cut and fertilized with granulated fertilizer when it is dry. Cutting dry prevents the spread of disease organisms. Fertilizing when dry prevents strong chemical granules from clinging to wet grass blades where they will burn the plant. Fertilizers should first reach the soil before nutrients are watered in to be taken up by the roots.

Spring sunshine and rain provide enough stimulus for top growth of healthy cool season grass. As summer comes on, a proper cutting height with sharp mower blades prevents stress and disease. A trimmed height of 2½-3 inches protects the growing crowns of cool season grasses from the sun. Warm season grasses can be maintained at 2 inches. A sharp mower prevents the grass blades from being crushed or frayed, which not only looks unsightly but also promotes fungal diseases.

Problem Lawns

Two types of lawns do not respond to fertilization. The first type is in deep shade, where, without adequate photosynthesis, nutrients are not metabolized. The shady lawn needs a seed mix heavy in Chewings or Pennlawn creeping fescue. Seed it in early fall with prompt removal of all fallen leaves during the time the new lawn is becoming established. It can be fertilized sparingly with superphosphate or potash, when the leaves fall, to promote strong root development before winter dormancy. These grasses are also more tolerant of the acid soil that often accompanies shady conditions.

The second type of lawn that does not take up nutrients has an acid soil pH below 5.5; this condition locks up soil nutrients that would otherwise become available in soil with a higher and sweeter pH. To solve this problem, start with a soil test. This should indicate the amount and type of limestone to add to your grounds before undertaking additional seeding and feeding.

Lime is needed to correct soil acidity and to lock up certain harmful elements. Most gardeners make an application every year or two based on the premise that it costs very little and might help the grass. If your lawn is surrounded by an oak forest, this is probably correct. But liming can be overdone. It should always be kept away from the root zones of evergreens like azaleas, and should not be applied in ground dolomitic form if the soil is naturally high in magnesium. Additionally, neutral soils with pH 6.8 to 7.0 will favor broad-leaved weeds over many grasses, creating a new problem of weed control.

Redoing Your Lawn

In general, weed and pest control is best handled by providing turf grasses with the best opportunity to establish strong healthy roots in an adequate soil. So a soil test is also a must before planting or renewing a lawn. Ideally, soil structure should be coarse enough to provide adequate pore space for drainage and oxygen exchange plus sufficient organic matter, so that your lawn will receive most of its nutrients from the soil itself. Two inches each of compost and peat moss will lighten and improve most heavy clay soil, if the mixture is thoroughly roto-tilled into the top 6 inches of soil before planting. Adding organic matter will help very sandy soil retain moisture and will provide nutrients to a new lawn.

This is also a good time to add needed lime, because it moves slowly through a natural leaching action into the root zone, taking up to 6 months on its own in clay soils.

Once soil has been prepared and raked smooth, it should be allowed to settle for a week before being seeded. This is an excellent time to apply milky spore disease dust, at the rate of 1 teaspoon at 5 feet intervals in rows 5 feet apart. The treatment will control Japanese beetle grubs for up to twenty-five years, also protecting the roots of turf grass from destructive moles that feed on the grubs.

Buy Certified Seed

It is important to buy locally adapted mixtures with at least 3 separate varieties of certified seeds. Virginia Polytechnic Institute and the University of Maryland have cooperated to certify mixtures for specific areas. These contain standardized percentages of tough, disease resistant tall fescues mixed with some bluegrass for the metropolitan area, or bluegrass mixed with the improved cultivars of tough perennial rye grasses that are useful in the higher Piedmont elevations. The best blends are found or created by you from recommended varieties that you can find in good full-service nurseries and garden centers; and such blends will repay you for their extra cost by requiring less trouble and expense down the road.

Improved Burmuda grasses, like P-16, do well in the warmer sandy soil near the coast. Another warm season grass, Japanese zoysia, continues to appeal to some local gardeners who like its weed-free appearance and thick springy turf.

Tall fescues are the most versatile cool season grasses for our climatic conditions. Bluegrass adds good spring and fall color and grows laterally to weave a tougher turf. The best grass coverage is obtained by seeding once in one direction with a calibrated seeder, followed by a second pass at right angles to the first. A new lawn will need high quality seed at the rate of over 2 pounds per 1,000 square feet for good coverage. Renewing an established lawn will take about 1 pound per 1,000 square feet. Inexpensive hand applicators with dial settings are the best bet for the small lawn, although centrifugal seeders can be rented.

After being seeded, the lawn should be rolled or lightly firmed with a board to press the seed into good contact with the soil, and then mulched with ¼-inch seed-free chopped straw before a thorough watering. Kept evenly moist for 10 days to 2 weeks, it should germinate well through the mulch. After 2 or 3 more weeks, it is ready for a first cutting.

Laying Sod

Occasionally the homeowner will want to repair a worn patch of lawn or to renew a lawn quickly so that it can be used within the same season. This is the time for sod. Because it is much more expensive than seed, up to $1.49 per square yard (without delivery charges) insist on certified sod made up of several recommended varieties of grass, and to be sure it is freshly cut and in good condition to lay on a prepared seedbed. The roots should never be allowed to dry, so sod must be laid when the seedbed is damp and friable on fairly cool soil.

Using a broad board as a kneeler, lay the rectangles of sod in staggered rows, flipping the board to the newly completed row as you start the next to firm the roots into the bed. On a slope, work from the high side, pulling each row tight against the next. You may have to secure rows with sod staples to keep the rows from sliding until the growing roots stabilize the soil. Rake the lawn lightly to lift the grass blades when you finish, soak thoroughly, and water every 2 or 3 days for the first 3 weeks.

Warm Season Grass Needs Different Care

Both Bermuda and Japanese zoysia strains are warm season grasses. Planted as stolons or plugs of existing turf, they spread throughout a warm loamy soil to cover a yard within a season or two. Bermuda grass makes a short lawn that can take traffic and stays lushly green all summer. Zoysia is thick and resilient underfoot, but harder to cut during the growing season. Both of these warm season lawns can take our heat, but turn a golden brown in the winter.

Because their growth patterns are different from cool season grasses that go semi-dormant during July and August, they need to be fertilized in late April, June, and August. Zoysia strains also need thatching to have dead material raked out of the lawn every 3 or 4 years. This prevents a build-up of partially decayed grass that smothers new growth and harbors diseases and pests.

Keeping Up Appearances

Lawn maintenance is seasonal with most of the workload concentrated in the spring and fall. Regular cutting usually starts in early April, with intervals between cuttings decreasing until the last of May. It is wise to cut frequently enough so that you are removing no more than a third of the grass blades with each cutting. Some lawns may require mowing at 5 day intervals during the spring flush, but by June the grass will slow if you do not overfertilize, and by mid-summer a cutting every 10 days may be sufficient. People who do not enjoy this ritual will be happy to learn that turf scientists are working hard to develop dwarf fescues that are disease resistant and will not need a weekly cutting.

Many people swear by cutting a lawn on the diagonal; others with fine bladed grasses start in the center and spiral outward to throw cuttings free of the newly cut area. Many people bag their cuttings and some use them as a valuable addition to the compost pile. This practice does recycle the nutrients in the cuttings without smothering the lawn when growth is heavy. It is important to remember that many lawn fertilizers contain pre-emergent herbicides to destroy crab grass or broadleaf herbicides that interfere with growth patterns of dandelions and other lawn invaders. These contact herbicides can affect broadleaf flower and vegetable crops, if you apply finished compost to the garden. It is best to top-dress only the lawn with compost made from such treated clippings.

To lessen dependence on herbicides, if you have small children or pets, control broadleaf weeds on a small lawn with a sharpened asparagus knife. Before they begin to bloom, sever the roots 3-6 six inches beneath the surface and pull the whole plant to prevent re-seeding and recurrence later in the season.

If you do not mind a high lawn, you can inhibit crabgrass germination naturally by raising the mower blades to a summer height of 4 inches by the first hot flush of May.

The finished appearance of a lawn is enhanced by edging along walks and borders with a tool designed for this purpose. Doing so will cut encroaching turf away from the adjacent use, and should be done about every 6 weeks during the growing season.

Prince William County has begun an aggressive program to provide workshops, brochures, refrigerator stickers, and a Water Quality Lawn Care Calendar that homeowners can use to cut their expenses and learn better ways to care for their lawns. The free flyers catch attention with "Don't bag it, it's too good to waste,"on the cost benefits and landfill space savings for composters, and "Throwing money down the drain is bad for the drain" to prevent excess water, pesticides and fertilizers from entering the Occoquan Reservoir. Among the best of their seasonal tips to protect water quality is keeping fertilizer off pavements and parking pads,so that it does not flow undiluted into local sewers and streams.

Keep in mind that there are pitfalls to the control of destructive lawn insects with chemical pesticides. Some of the products that control sod webworm and cinch bugs also destroy the earthworms that help aerate and improve the soil. Good cultural practices and very selective use of pesticides are the best way around such a dilemma.

One of the most destructive bugs that live under the lawn is the Japanese beetle, which, fortunately, is most effectively controlled by neighborhood's cooperating to inject a newly improved strain of milky spore disease into the soil on an area wide basis. This selective bacteria, although harmless to humans and other insects, remains in the soil to kill continuing generations of Japanese beetle grubs for many years. One marvelous side effect of the treatment is to deprive moles of a food source that may attract them to your lawn. The only sure and safe method for mole removal is to trap and dig out these nocturnal feeders with traps, hoes, and pitchforks—a process requiring the gardener be retired and tireless, dynamite being forbidden.

The range of grasses that will grow well within portions of the Chesapeake and Potomac Region is included in the following list. The best adapted cultivars of each species are also listed so that informed consumers can ask for them from turf specialists and garden centers.

COOL SEASON GRASSES

DANISH BLUEGRASS
(Poa trivialis)

Soils: moist shady.
Height of cut: 3 inches retards weeds, forms good turf.
Uses: shady lawn in cooler parts of region.
Disadvantages: summer dormancy, susceptible to leaf spot, and hard to find.
Advantages: good color spring and fall where it is hard to grow grass.
Seeding Rate: 1 pound per 1,000 square feet.
Sowing Time: late summer.
Sowing Method: firm into top of settled seedbed.
Fertilization: 2 applications; fall: 20 pounds of 10-6-4 per 1,000 square feet, and spring: same rate with 5-10-5.
Lime: recommended amount when fall soil test shows pH below 6.0.
Mixtures: sown alone unless drier conditions call for mix with Kentucky bluegrass and Chewings fescue.

KENTUCKY BLUEGRASS
(Poa pratensis)

Soils: needs pH 6.0 to 7.0, well-drained, and fertile.
Height of cut: over 2 inches.
Uses: in turf mixtures for lateral growth, color, and fine texture.
Disadvantages: summer dormancy, needs aeration and thatching at regular intervals. Prone to leaf spot.
Advantages: good spring and fall color, heals fast.
Seeding Rate: 1½ to 2½ pounds per 1,000 square feet.
Sowing Time: late summer, re-seeding possible in March.
Sowing Method: firm into seedbed to which nitrogen and phosphate have been added at the rate of 2 pounds of nitrogen per 1,000 square feet.
Fertilization: feed in October with 1-2 pounds of nitrogen per 1,000 square feet in a high phosphate formula; supplement if needed with less than 1 pound WIN nitrogen in March.
Lime: as needed, usually 50 pounds of ground limestone per 1,000 square feet every 3-5 years.
Mixtures: lawns of bluegrass only are not suitable east of the higher Piedmont.

Sunny bluegrass lawns should contain at least 3 varieties with 65-100% made up of Adelphi, Cheri, Merit, Plush, or Ram I. Shady lawns will need the addition of 10-35% of Eclipse, Enmundi, Georgetown, Glade, Midnight, or Sydsport and at least 10% of Pennlawn creeping red fescue. If low maintainence is a reality stick with 35% of the mixture chosen from Columbia, Enmundi, Touchdown, Victa, or Pennlawn creeping red fescue.

RED FESCUE
(Festuca rubra)
Soils: needs good drainage, thrives on poor sandy soil, and is tolerant of shade and acid soils.

Height of Cut: excellent above 2 inches to control spread of crabgrass.

Uses: in shady mixtures with Kentucky bluegrass, resistant to wear.

Disadvantages: dies in poorly drained soil, bunches, susceptible to disease, and is dormant in midsummer.

Advantages: shade tolerant, good on poor, acid soil, good spring and fall color, fine-bladed, tough, and does not require frequent mowing.

Seeding Rate: alone, 2½ pounds per 1,000 square feet. In mixture, half this amount.

Sowing Time: late summer.

Sowing Method: in firm seedbed covered with ¼ inch soil.

Fertilization: two applications of lawn formula, September and March. Three pounds nitrogen per 1,000 square feet in fall and 1 pound in spring.

Lime: to maintain pH above 6.0.

Mixtures: for better performance, heavy use, and shade use creeping red fescue and Chewings fescue from 10-35% of mixture. Flyer, Pennlawn, Ilahee, Longfellow, and Victory are improved varieties.

TALL FESCUE
(Festuca eliator var. arundinacea)
Soils: tolerant, does well on poor soils, and responds to fertilization.

Height of Cut: 3 inches forms an excellent weed-free turf.

Uses: improved varieties wear well with addition of some Kentucky bluegrass.

Disadvantages: rather broad-leaved, must be mowed and fed regularly for best appearance.

Advantages: versatile, hardy, excellent wear resistance, chokes out weeds, good year-round color, and few disease problems.

Seeding Rate: 5-8 pounds per 1,000 square feet of lawn.

Sowing Time: early spring.

Sowing Method: in firm seedbed covered with scant ¼ inch fine soil.

Fertilization: spring and fall applications, each 20 pounds of 5-10-5 per 1,000 square feet, or two fall applications of 15 pounds of 5-10-5 in early September and late October and one spring application of l0 pounds per 1,000 square feet.

Lime: as needed to keep pH at 6.0 to 6.5. Sample in fall and apply in fall.

Mixtures: 90% with 10% Kentucky bluegrass for lateral growth. Amigo, Apache, Arid, Bonanza, Falcon, Houndog, Jaguar II , Olympic II, Rebel II, Shenandoah, or Winchester are improved varieties. Rebel II, Falcon, and Houndog have replaced K31 for heavy use areas. A 1994 introduction, Hubbard 87 is expected to set new standards of excellence.

PERENNIAL RYEGRASS
(Lolium perenne)
Soils: will perform on clay soils.

Height of Cut: 2½ to 3 inches protects crown of plant in summer.

Uses: at elevations over 1,000 feet in Piedmont as part of bluegrass lawn where erosion or out of season sowing is a possibility.

Disadvantages: disease prone at lower elevations.

Advantages: improves summer dormant bluegrass lawn, prevents erosion.

Seeding Rate: admixed at ¼ pound per 1,000 square feet.

Sowing Time: late summer or early spring.

Sowing Method: firm into seedbed, cover ¼ inch soil.

Fertilization: 10-12 pounds of WIN 10-6-4 per 1,000 square feet worked into soil at seeding, plus equal amount by mid-October.

Lime: maintain pH at 6.5 to 7.0, test and apply in fall.

Mixtures: less than 15% by weight when planted with bluegrass, or ¼ pound per 1,000 square feet where erosion threatens. Citation II, Blazer and Pennfine are locally recommended varieties.

WHITE CLOVER
(Trifolium repens)
Not recommended by turf specialists.
Soils: tolerant, does well on poor soils.

Height of Cut: 1-3 inches.

Uses: most standard uses except heavy shade.

Disadvantages: can be trampled out, has broad foliage, subject to herbicides, and flowers are unsuitable where bee sting allergy exists.

Advantages: thrives in wide range of soils, improves soil, provides color in lawns with summer dormant grasses, and smothers crabgrass seedlings.

Seeding Rate: 2 ounces per 1,000 square feet, 1-2 pounds per acre.

Sowing Time: early spring.

Sowing Method: firm into seed bed, cover with ¼ inch soil.

Fertilization: provides own nitrogen, uses phosphate and potash in standard lawn formulas.

Lime: tolerates acidity.

Mixtures: 5-10% with shade mixtures on acid or heavy soil.

WARM SEASON LAWNS

ZOYSIA
(Zoysia japonica)
Soils: good for wide range, except for sands.

Height of Cut: 1 inch.

Uses: as lawn for sun and light shade.

Disadvantages: must be planted as plugs or sprigs, 2 to 3 years to spread, dormant in winter, and must be thatched.

Advantages: low-growing, dense, wear-resistant, and chokes weeds.

Planting Time: May 1 to August 15.

Planting Method: 2 inch plugs set 8-12 inches apart, or 2-4 bushels of sprigs per 1,000 square feet set into prepared seedbed sowed in Kentucky bluegrass.

Fertilization: feed WIN lawn formula, May, July, September first year, and once a year in May thereafter.

Lime: as necessary in fall to keep soil pH at 6.0 to 6.5.

Mixtures: interplanted with Kentucky bluegrass that disappears a year or two after zoysia is established. Meyer, Belair and Emerald are good alternatives.

BERMUDA GRASS
(Cynodon dactylon)
Soils: adapts to many soils, but needs good fertility.

Height of Cut: ½-1 ½ inches.

Uses: lawns and playing fields subject to heavy wear in warmer and lower parts of the region.

Disadvantages: infiltrates flower beds, needs regular thatching to prevent disease, and is dormant in winter.

Advantages: rapid growth, heals quickly, easy to establish, wears well, fine leaved, takes close mowing, and resistant to diseases, insects, and weeds.

Planting Time: May.

Planting Method: plant 1-4 bushels of stolons of improved variety Tufcote per 1,000 square feet.

Fertilization: 3 applications in May, July, and September, each of 2 pounds of nitrogen per 1,000 square feet.

Lime: as needed to keep soil pH between 6.0 and 7.0.

Mixtures: none. Tufcote variety used here for athletic fields, lawns, and greens that get full sun. Midway, Tifway II and Vamont in Virginia.

Turf grass Mixtures for Local Use

Within the District a blend of 3 improved tall fescues, Falcon, Rebel II and Houndog, is mixed with Pennlawn creeping fescue as an all-purpose mixture for sun and shade with low maintenance requirements.

Broadleaf Weeds
A small infestation of broadleaf weeds is best handled in early April with an asparagus knife unless your lawn is large. Many of the commercial weed and feed formulas applied early in the spring before April 15 will control germination and emergence of undesirable weeds. Many contain pre-emergent herbicides that will also retard the germination of lawn grasses; so be sure to re-seed the lawn separately in the fall if necessary.

Close clipping may harm the lawn. Leave clippings for mulch and apply plant food in spring and fall.

CONTROL OF LAWN AND TURF INSECTS
Please note that the EPA is currently examining a cluster of 20 turf pest and disease controls for long term adverse effects. This exam may result in changed labeling requirements or removal of some chemicals for home use.

Some tall fescue mixtures that host an endophytic fungus claim impressive control over billbugs, chinch bugs, cutworms, and sod webworms that attack sod. The fungus produces alkaloids that kill insects but leaves the grass unharmed. It is sold by a mail order organic garden product company, but should not be planted close to brood mare pastures, because it has caused miscarriages.

Insect	Pesticide: Treatment
Ants	Carbaryl: Spot application.
Billbugs (Zoysia)	Prevent by thatching every 3 years
Grubs	Carbaryl: Follow label directions for each type.
Chinch bug	Carbaryl: Water lawn, apply in late May when bees are not out repeat in 2-3 weeks.
Sod Webworms	Carbaryl: Apply in evening, do not water or cut for 2-3 days.
Japanese Beetle Grubs	Milky Spore Disease: Apply in April to insecticide-free lawn. Treatment lasts many years.
Clover mite	Insecticidal soap spray: Spray band around house spring or fall when mites appear, repeat in 10-14 days.

Groundcovers Are Carefree

A home owner who wants a finished appearance without the weekly care of a lawn has a wealth of choices among groundcovers. This class of spreading foliage plants includes specimens to suit a wide range of conditions. Some are deciduous, some evergreen, and all can be used in place of a small lawn or as an easily maintained transition zone between lawns, shrub borders, and flower beds. Groundcovers fit well around the trunks of trees, where they form a mat of healthy vegetation over a shallow root zone. Even mosses have qualified as a lawn substitute in heavily wooded areas where it is not practical to attempt a lawn.

Where some erosion control or a year-round display of foliage that will discourage weeds and complement bulbs and shrubbery is needed, evergreen groundcovers are the most satisfactory. In wildflower gardens and perennial borders, deciduous groundcovers retain soil moisture during the growing season and provide some seasonal bloom.

Planting Tips

Evergreen groundcovers may be planted in early spring or fall when they are available in flats of several dozen plants. Care should be taken to see that the roots remain moist when plants are separated before planting. Although groundcovers are not picky about soil requirements, most in this area prefer moist soil with some organic matter.

Since one of the characteristics of many varieties is to spread by means of adventitious roots whenever a new stem node touches the ground, they will cover the area to be planted most quickly when the soil is well-worked. Most are planted 8 to 12 inches apart in holes sufficiently large so that the roots may be well spread out. Then the holes are filled, and the plants are watered well and lightly mulched, so that their runners can find soil in which to root. Grasses without runners are planted as far apart as they are tall.

Deciduous ground covers are planted in April using the same techniques. Most ground covers are relatively pest-free, although fungus and spider mite controls may be needed in the depths of summer.

Maintenance Needs

When groundcovers are getting established, they will need additional water to carry them through the first growing season until they have thickened enough to shade their own root systems. English ivy is the slowest to establish, and may need monitoring for two or three years. Many of the deciduous groundcovers thrive in moist shade where water is not a problem. They will still need an occasional weeding so that they can take over quickly. In the fall a bamboo rake helps keep groundcovers from being smothered or separated by heavy leaf fall. Bamboo is less likely to snag and pull up the plants while removing leaves than metal leaf rakes are wont to do.

An occasional fall feeding of sifted compost, perhaps mixed with bonemeal and ground limestone (if spring bulbs are beneath a groundcover like vinca) is all that is necessary to keep groundcovers thriving.

The following perennial groundcovers are readily available in the Washington area. With the exception of sun-loving crownvetch, most can be grown in sun or light shade. The most rampant growers can be slowed by using them in darker places, as well as by trimming, edging, and thinning out extra plants. The deciduous groundcovers, like lady's mantle, wild ginger, and sweet woodruff, need more shade. Woody, ornamental groundcovers may be found in the Evergreens chapter.

DECIDUOUS GROUNDCOVERS

Bishop's weed (aegipodium), plain and variegated forms, 4-6 in. high.
Crown vetch (coronilla varia), 6-9 in. high, pink flowers. Holds slopes.
Daylily (hemerocallis), dwarf forms to 12 in., varied colors.
Lady's mantle (alchemilla vulgaris), 3-6 in. high, dwarf and regular forms, shade-loving.
Sweet woodruff (gallium odoratum), 4 in. high, white flowers, shade.

EVERGREEN GROUNDCOVERS

Bugleweed (ajuga reptans), 3 in. high, with 6 in. flower spikes.
English ivy (hedera helix varieties), 4 in. high.
Barrenwort (epimedium varieties), 12 in. high.
Lily turf (liriope spicata, platyphylla), 10-12 in. clump.
Lambs'ears (stachys byzantina, lanata) 4 in. high, with 10 in. flower spike.
Mondo grass (ophiopogon japonicus), 4-6 in. high.
Japanese pachysandra (pachysandra terminalis), plain and variegated forms, 8-10 in. high.
Periwinkle (vinca major and minor), white, blue, or pink flowers; small form is 4-6 in. high, large form is 8-12 in. high and invasive in warm, sandy soil.
Ginger (asarum europeum), 2 in. high, moist or dry shade.
Wild strawberry (fragaria chiloensis), 2-3 in. high.
Winter creeper (euonymus fortunei), 3-5 in. high climber, with orange berries.

GROUND COVER PEST CONTROL

Plant	Pest	Treatment/Comments
Pachysandra	Scale:	Dormant oil in early April, multi-purpose spray bi-monthly from June on.
Winter Creeper (eunoymus fortunei)	Scale:	Same as for pachysandra above; malathion on crawlers mid-May and July.
	Blight:	Spray Ferbam 3 times at weekly intervals when new growth starts.
Periwinkle (vinca minor)	Blight:	Thin plants for better air circulation.
	Canker Dieback:	Spray Bordeaux mix at 10-day intervals when buds open.

INSPIRATION:
The Prince Georges and Fairfax County park systems are making the transition to sustainable lawn care. Among the promising techniques are deep aeration of soils, a new slow release fertilizer called IBDU, and a half strength Bayleton spray to prevent fungus on stressed grass. Soccer fields are the worst case test. Here are two to check out:
South Run District Park, 9501 Pohick Road, Springfield, Virginia.
Alabama Drive Park, 1100 Alabama Drive, Town of Herndon, Virginia.

LAWN CARE CALENDAR
for established bluegrass lawns

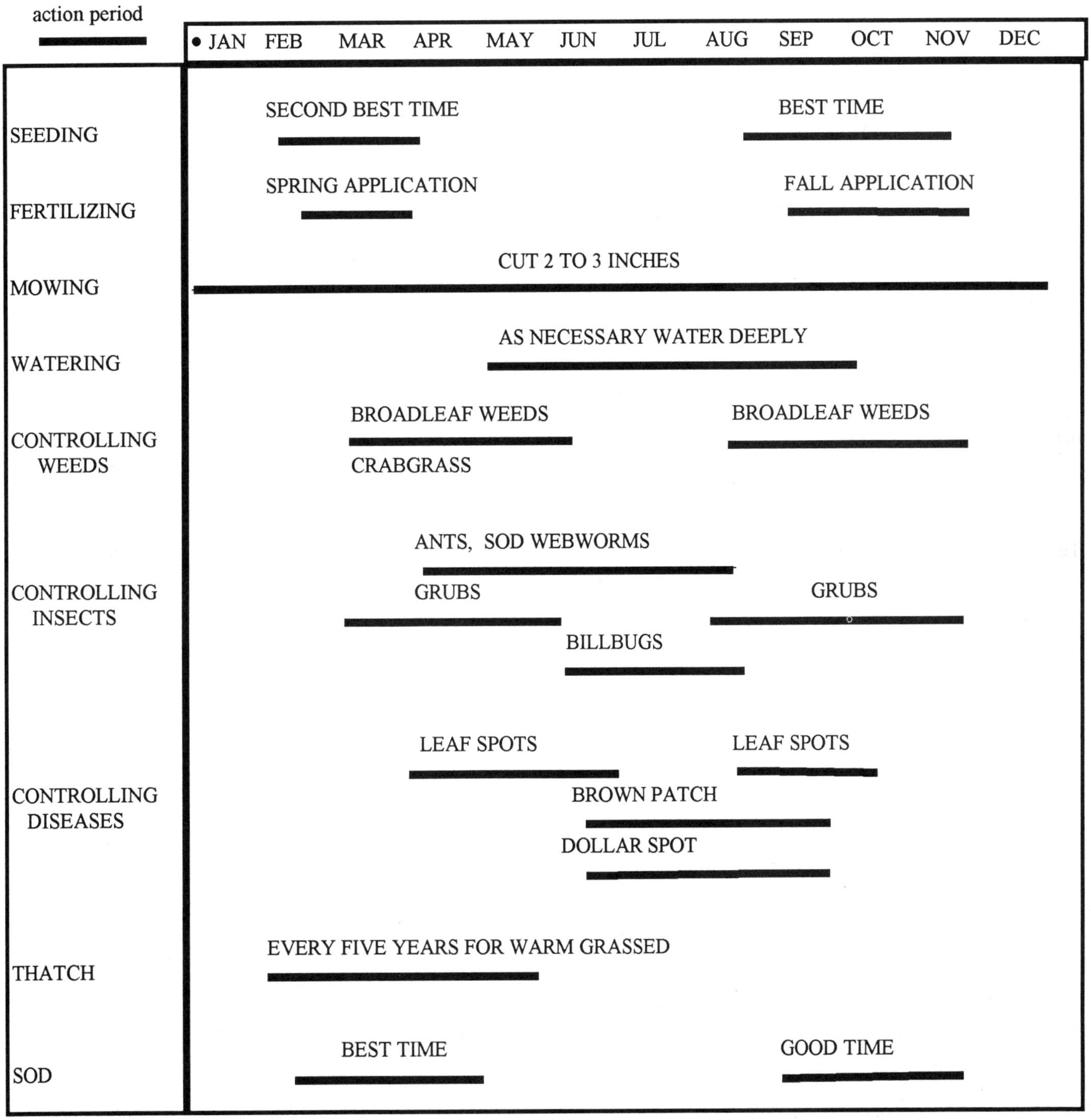

action period	JAN	FEB	MAR	APR	MAY	JUN	JUL	AUG	SEP	OCT	NOV	DEC

SEEDING
SECOND BEST TIME   BEST TIME

FERTILIZING
SPRING APPLICATION   FALL APPLICATION

MOWING
CUT 2 TO 3 INCHES

WATERING
AS NECESSARY WATER DEEPLY

CONTROLLING WEEDS
BROADLEAF WEEDS   BROADLEAF WEEDS
CRABGRASS

CONTROLLING INSECTS
ANTS, SOD WEBWORMS
GRUBS   GRUBS
BILLBUGS

CONTROLLING DISEASES
LEAF SPOTS   LEAF SPOTS
BROWN PATCH
DOLLAR SPOT

THATCH
EVERY FIVE YEARS FOR WARM GRASSED

SOD
BEST TIME   GOOD TIME

7. TREES IN THE GARDEN

The Amazonian rain forest crisis has made us aware that our forest trees are the lungs of the planet. During the process of photosynthesis trees "breathe in" carbon dioxide and "breathe out" oxygen. The hardwood forest of Rock Creek Park and other parks in the metropolitan area serve the same function. Think for a moment about a summer day—you are walking along the sidewalk and it is hot and steamy until you come to a pool of shade under a street tree, where the temperature drops and the air is refreshing.

Garden trees will shelter and shade your house and grounds from the sun. In addition they have many ornamental features that bring beauty and character to your landscape.

Trees come in many sizes, shape and type and in their native habitat each has a niche to fill and a role to play. The Eastern hardwood forest has several layers: the canopy, the understory and the ground cover. In the forest ecosystem the great trees of the forests form the canopy. They have long life spans, a hundred years or more during that they grow to great heights and girth. In the built environment forest trees are scaled to arch over city streets and frame distant vistas. Naturalistic groves and individual specimens are the essence of the urban parks designed by Frederick Law Olmstead.

Landscape Role of Trees
Is there a place for these great trees in the garden? A single specimen is likely to be the only tree there will be room for in a suburban garden. Siting it is critical because it will need plenty of room to reach its potential and not overwhelm the house and garden. The selection of a tree for the garden is one of the longest lasting choices you are likely to make and it should be considered an investment in dollars and time.

For the small residential landscape, trees from the forest understory are more suitable: Amelanchier canadensis, Serviceberry; Cornus florida, our flowering Dogwood; and Carpinus caroliniana, Hornbeam—all trees that grow at the margins of forests and under the canopy. These are trees that reach heights of 25 to 40 feet. Many of these trees have the added attractions of showier flowers and fruits and a degree of shade tolerance.

Tree Shade

The forest canopy translates into shade in the garden and shade is crucial during the summers in the Washington area. A leafy tree planted on the sunny south facing side of the house and garden provides protection from sun and heat. As the weather changes from hot to cold the bare branches of a deciduous tree admit the winter sun's light and warmth.

The quality of the shade cast by different trees varies. The orientation of the garden area to be shaded and the nature of the activity that takes place under the shade will be key when choosing suitable trees. If the site is treeless and exposed, a tree's rate of growth becomes the more important factor.

Evergreens cast a dense dark shade that is inhospitable to companion plants and may prove too dark for people also. By contrast a small-leafed deciduous tree that has compound leaves like Black Locust (Robinia pseudoacacia), or double compound leaves like Pink Mimosa (Albizzia julibrissin) create a light, sun-dappled shade. Their more open canopy, branch structure and small open leaf patterns allow other plants to grow underneath. A south or west-facing terrace or deck is going to need a leafier tree to create a comfortable place for sitting during the day. A tree well-suited for that situation and one with the added attraction of a feature for every season is Malus floribunda. This is a profusely flowered Crab Apple with red buds that open to white flowers in early May and ripen to pea-sized, rosy-red apples that persist into early winter and provide welcome food for birds. The broad spreading branches are clothed with apple green leaves that color lightly in the fall.

Screens and Focal Points

Screens serve to mask or soften a view that may be less than desirable; does the problem warrant an impervious screen or a light curtain. Magnolia grandiflora (Bull Bay Magnolia) is a perfect specimen tree to serve as an impervious screen and its grand size can do double duty as a boundary marker at the edge of the lawn.

Or use a deciduous specimen tree with an upright growth habit to provide height and a dense branch structure that will form a visual curtain even in winter. Two examples of such trees are the willow oak (Quercus phellos) and on a smaller scale the Carolina hornbeam (Carpinus caroliniana).

Another way to screen is to provide an alternative view—for example, a tree with striking features that focuses attention and distracts from the less desirable. Indian bean tree (Catalpa bignoniodes) is a tree with large panicles of white foxglove like flowers that tip the ends of every branch over large heart shaped leaves. During the summer the leaves are yellow green and in late summer they turn acid green. After the leaves fall the long green Indian bean pods are apparent and festoon the tree during the winter months.

Trees can contribute to a desired effect in a larger planting. The eye is drawn o the tree whose surrounding beds or borders hold plants deliberately chosen to emphasize certain colors or textures of the tree at different seasons.

Characteristics of Good Garden Trees

The ornamental characteristics, height and spread of the mature tree should relate to the scale of the house and garden. Additionally, the habit and rate of growth will influence the choice of trees. The term habit relates to the way the plant grows and the shape it makes in the landscape. The shape the tree branches assumes can be the upright, pyramidal, conical, round, spreading, or weeping. Good trees are defined by foresters as a single trunk with upright branches. In the garden a multiple trunk may offer a more interesting specimen and weeping branches are much more dramatic.

Equally important tree qualities are its pest and disease resistance. The right choice will insure that the tree will need the minimum of special treatment to succeed in your garden. Selecting trees that are known to be resistant is a good first step. However, a good tree is susceptible to both pests and disease if it is planted in the wrong growing conditions for that species. Consult your site plan for your growing conditions. New house sites often suffer from lack of top soil, disturbed and compacted soil and related drainage problems that need to be corrected before a tree is planted. City gardeners and those near heavily traveled roads are confronted with the added problems of air pollution and will need resistant species. Another city problem is rubble-filled soil, usually alkaline, dry and inhospitable.

Not every tree is perfect in every way and not every tree will suit every gardener. Fruit are a mixed blessing. They are the receptacles for the seed of the next generation and as such can be a nuisance because of their size, shape or method of dispersal. Some fruits attract insects; the most prolific crab apples do lure yellow jackets in late summer. Other fruits fall and need to raked up and still others germinate so readily that they produce a host of seedlings in the lawn and garden.

All deciduous trees shed their leaves, and most need to be raked up to prevent the fallen leaves from smothering other plants and the lawn beneath. Trees that have compound or double compound leaves shed both the leaves and the leaf stems that are the rachis. There are trees that shed their bark; the best shed it in small chips like mulch; while others shed in strips or large pieces.

Matching the Tree with its Site

Consult your plan to determine those characteristics that are most essential. Take into consideration the orientation of the sun, how the area under the tree will be used, the soil and other growing conditions and match these with the growing requirements of the tree, the rate of growth and size at maturity. Keep in mind the size and shape of the house, the size of the lot, and the location of all utilities above and below ground. A weeping willow is not a good neighbor for a water line and a conical shape is going to run into trouble with overhead wires. Once you have considered all these factors and matched conditions to requirements it is time to consider the ornamental qualities of the tree you are about to plant. Use the following checklist to help you get the most ornamental features for your choice of tree.

Ornamental Characteristics of a Good Tree

Shape:	*Habit:*
Round	Trunk or trunks
Pyramid	Branch structure
Conical	Twig structure
Weeping	

Winter interest:	*Foliage:*
Twigs	Evergreen
Winter buds	Deciduous
Persistent fruit	Shape and size
Bark Color/texture	Color Texture
	Fall Color

Flowers	*Fruit:*
Bloom Season	Size and shape
Length of Bloom	Pods
Size and shape	Berries
Color	Color

RECOMMENDED ORNAMENTAL & SHADE TREES

The Smaller Deciduous Trees

Many of the widely planted small trees are noted for their floral display. Of these, native American dogwood and its cultivars are deservedly one of the most popular, although they are susceptible to borers, especially in the lower, warmer areas of the region. The late-flowering Japanese and kousa dogwoods, with their pointed petals borne along the tops of the branches, are taller hardy relatives that have come into increasing favor. Nurserymen have just introduced disease-resistant hybrids of the latter to try and check the fatal dogwood anthracnose.

Because of disease and decreasing wild habitat in the last half century there is new interest in planting native trees, to help support as many of the local ecosystems as possible. Now that we are so many, over 4 million at the last census, this seems like a good neighbor policy that will pay dividends in the long run.

There are several native flowering trees that do well in light shade: among them the Virginia fringe tree, Chionanthus virginicum, and the serviceberry, Amelanchier laevis.

The redbud, Cercis canadensis, is a lovely small tree with its branches studded with purple pink before the trees leaf out, but it is subject to early die back and is short lived; C. 'Forest Pansy' is an improved form with smoky

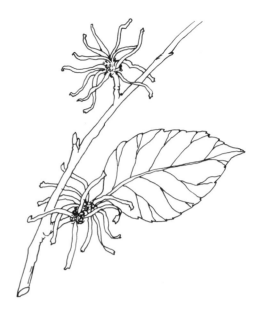

purple foliage.

Among the summer bloomers is the spectacular golden rain tree. And as tempted as they might be to recreate graceful clumps of birch on their grounds, transplanted northerners would do well to avoid them here. Only the less ornamental river birches can resist the ravages of the bronze birch bark borer.

The native American persimmon, like the gingko, has handsome foliage that colors beautifully in the fall. It is pest-free, if you do not count the possums attracted by the ripening fruit in October.

Small Trees for Special Uses

Shade: Flowering dogwood, Japanese dogwood, Oriental cherry varieties, deciduous magnolias, Japanese maple, sourwood, Japanese snowbell, Cornelian cherry, golden rain tree, improved varieties of Bradford pear, and American hornbeam.

Street: Washington hawthorn, flowering crab apples, thornless locust, Amur maple, and Bradford pear improved varieties.

Windbreak: Washington hawthorn, buckthorn, babylon willow, Amur maple, hedge maple, Japanese yew, and American hollies.

COLORFUL TREES UNDER 35 FEET

APPLE SERVICEBERRY
(Amelanchier laevis)
Height: 10-15 feet
Spread: 8-10 feet
Exposure: Sun/ high shade
Soil: Likes leaf mold
Plant: Fall, early spring

Blooms: Mid-April
Fruit: Black, attracts birds
Uses: Ornamental

 This shrubby forest understory tree can take dubious drainage and light shade while welcoming spring with a lacy net of white flowers before the foliage appears. The small fruit are very popular with birds, and the tree naturally appears in the same woodland settings as native dogwood and redbud.

BRADFORD PEAR
(Pyrus calleryana)
Height: 30 feet
Spread: 10 to 15
Exposure: Sun
Soil: Loam or rich clay
Plant: March-April/November
Blooms: Late April to May in white clusters
Fruit: Insignificant
Uses: Ornamental
The improved varieties of Bradford pear—Aristocrat, Capitol, and White House—are more conical in shape, and the branches are not prone to split off as the tree matures. These trees can take compacted soils and are immune to fire blight. Their foliage turns an interesting bronzed color in the fall. When used as street trees they should be spaced 20 to 25 feet apart.

FLOWERING CRABAPPLE
(Malus cultivars)
Height: 18 to 25 feet
Spread: 12 to 15 feet
Exposure: Sun
Soil: Loamy, moderately moist, well-drained
Plant: March or November

Blooms: May
Uses: Ornamental flowering tree

 There is always a place for such a fragrant, mounding tree with attractive flowers and fruits. The colors of these three are: American Beauty-pinkish red, Pink Perfection-clear pink, and Snow Cloud-white. All are especially noteworthy because they are resistant to cedar apple rust. Other good varieties are Sargent, a compact 8 foot tree with white flowers and red fruit, and the Japanese form M. zumi callicarpa that has fruit that persists on the tree.

 All crab apples need a regular winter pruning to remove the many suckers that obscure the branch shapes of the tree.

CRAPE MYRTLE
(Lagerstroemia indica x fauriei)
Height: 3-30
Spread: 15
Exposure: Sun/part shade
Soil: Clay loam to sandy loam
Plant: May
Blooms: July-September
Fruit: Brown pod
Uses: Specimen, mildew and drought resistant

Some choice varieties include:
L. 'Choctaw,' clear pink, exfoliating cinnamon bark, maroon fall foliage, needs little pruning, for heavier clay soils.
L. 'Tuskegee,' almost red, exfoliating gray to tan bark, orange-red fall foliage, horizontal habit to 15 feet, sun, clay loam.
L. 'Tuscarora,' dark coral pink, tan bark, orange-red fall foliage, rapid compact grower, sandy loam.
L. 'Natchez,' white flowers, dark green foliage, mottled cinnamon bark, orange to red fall foliage, tall graceful shape, tolerant of soils and high shade, best in sandy loam.

These are but four of the National Arboretum's acclaimed Indian series of 20 improved crape myrtles. These mildew resistant cultivars are beautifully adapted to our hot breathless summers, starring as flowering trees until mid-September. The filtered shade and watermelon scent of the delicate ruffled flowers invite close appreciation, making them ideal focal points for planting beds close to the house.

Crape myrtles can be trained as single trunk specimens by pruning young trees before new growth starts. The cultivars listed should be hardy in all areas of our region.

DOGWOOD
(Cornus florida, C. kousa, C.florida x kousa)
Height: 10 to 30 feet
Spread: 10 to 15 feet
Exposure: Sun/high shade
Soil: Variety of well-drained acid soils with leaf mold
Plant: Spring
Blooms: Mid April through May
Fruit: Red or scarlet, attracts birds
Uses: Specimen, understory, background, cut flowers

C.florida-Eastern dogwood, 20-25 feet, white flowers, red fruits
C. kousa chinensis, 25 feet, white, red fruits
C.mas-cornelian cherry, 25 feet, yellow, scarlet fruits
C. officinalis-Japanese cornel, 30 feet, yellow, scarlet
Cornus florida varieties: 'Cloud Nine'-white, 'Pygmy'-dwarf white, 'Rainbow Tricolor'-white with variegated foliage, and Cherokee Chief-red
Cornus florida x kousa cultivars: 'aurora,' 'Constellation,' 'Ruth Ellen,' 'Stardust,' 'Stellar Pink.'

The native dogwoods and their cultivars are most widely planted in our region on this side of the Chesapeake Bay, and they are counted upon to produce a breathtaking display of bloom from late April through May.

The other kinds that are well-adapted to this area include the early flowering Cornelian cherry and its close relative, the Japanese cornel, which bloom yellow in late March with the witch hazels. The late flowering kousa varieties appear in May after the foliage is fully developed. Their spiky fruit display is more showy than the Eastern dogwoods. A new cross between kousa and selected natives blooms between the two flowerings of its parents. These hybrids are resistant to dogwood anthracnose that has begun to severely affect our plantings.

All dogwoods are shallow-rooted, small trees that delight in an acid soil well-loaded with compost and leaf mold. Although as woodland plants they seemingly need a moist soil, they can tolerate rather dry soils at the edge of the woods. What they cannot stand is poor drainage; subsurface porosity must be good.

The dogwoods grow equally well in full sun or in high light shade. In heavy shade they are scraggly and thin. Dogwoods should be planted an inch higher than the soil line on the trunk indicates to allowing for soil to settle. It is important to keep the root area well mulched about two feet out from the trunk in order to promote acid soil conditions, retain moisture, and ward off the dogwood's chief enemy: the lawnmower. Mower wounds often lead to canker. Disease in turn encourages borers that can prove fatal to the trees. A healthy, vigorous tree is seldom troubled by borers. Leaf diseases are often fungal and can be controlled with a spring spraying of a fungicide. Prune as needed to remove dead wood.

GOLDEN-RAIN TREE
(Koelreuteria paniculata)
Height: 30 feet
Spread: 20 feet
Exposure: Sun
Soil: Varied texture, moderately moist, well-drained
Plant: March or November
Blooms: Canary yellow flowers in July and August
Fruit: Brown or yellow bladder-like fruits
Uses: Specimen

The most spectacular of the few mid- to late-summer bloomers, the golden rain tree produces large upright clusters against lacy, graceful foliage.

JAPANESE MAPLE
(Acer palmatum atropurpureum, A. palmatum dissectum, A. japonicum)
Height:10-30 feet
Spread: 10-20 feet wide
Soil: Clay loam
Plant: March, November
Blooms: Spring, fall
Fruit: Seeds
Uses: Specimen,

Aside from the dogwood, this is the most popular small specimen tree in the Washington area. Its beautifully colored foliage puts on shows in Spring and fall and its graceful slow growing form makes a dramatic focal point in the small yard or stylized garden bed.

Although expensive, the Japanese maples need little pruning once their best features have been set, and they are mostly pest-free

A. 'Bloodgood' has been the standard dark red cultivar for two decades; but there are many attractive cultivars that have interesting leaf color that changes three times during a season.

A. palmatum koreanum grows from seed. Several of the threadleaf cultivars, A. palmatum dissectum, can be used as large shrubs, as can some of the newer large leaf forms called A. japonicum. 'Full Moon.' It's worth looking for unusual foliage and color variations in these gorgeous trees. They make a dry low shade, with exposed roots as they grow older—a good reason to place them as the focal point of a bermed bed, or to grow them at forest's edge so they will assume a more vertical habit.

JAPANESE SNOW BELL
(Styrax japonica)
Height: 15 to 20 feet
Spread: 10 feet
Exposure: Light shade
Soil: Well-drained
Plant: Early April to late September
Blooms: Late May, white bell-shaped flowers
Fruit: Small green drupes
Uses: Specimen

An ideal tree for the small yard, it can be multi-stemmed, or trained to a single trunk, and has clean foliage and a neat zigzag branching habit. It is yellow in the fall and insect and disease free. As soon as they appear, pull the small seedlings that sprout from the numerous fallen drupes.

DECIDUOUS MAGNOLIA
(Magnolia soulangiana, M. stellata, M.virginia and Arboretum hybrids)
Height: 15-35 feet
Spread: 20-25 feet
Exposure: Sun/high shade
Soil: Well-drained clay loam
Plant: Spring
Blooms: Early April to mid-May
Fruit: Red in decorative husks
Uses: Specimen, background, cut flowers

M. soulangiana is the most frequently seen of the deciduous magnolias here. The great beauty of its scented chalice cups or creamy stars on bare silver branches early in April starts out a season of bloom for these species that lasts into late May. Because April frosts can turn the blooms to brown rags in a day, National Arboretum scientists have worked for 30 years developing later blooming cultivars of M. stellata crossed with M. liliflora, the so-called Girl series of large shrubs. But their latest seedling cross with M. sprengeri x M. liliflora has produced a prize-winning tree specimen, 'Galaxy,' whose rich red purple blooms are borne on an upright egg-shaped tree, 35-40 feet tall, suitable for smaller properties and median strip plantings.

The later blooming native, M. virginiana, Sweet Bay magnolia, has been crossed with another species to create a fragrant tropical looking tree, M. 'Nimbus,' with cloud-like bloom clusters borne on an open branch structure through May. These improved magnolias allow the gardener to extend the bloom season from April through July if local conditions favor the evergreen M. grandiflora.

PLUM, THUNDERCLOUD PURPLE LEAF
(Prunus cerasifera)
Height: 10 to 12 feet
Spread: 10 feet
Exposure: Sun
Soil: Well-drained garden soil
Plant: March/November
Blooms: White to pink, single blossoms in April-May

Plant several of these 15 to 20 feet apart to screen a private area of the yard for summer entertaining. The rich red-purple foliage is a standout, but it creates too dark a shade for flowers to thrive.

STEWARTIA
(Stewartia koreana, S. pseudo-camellia))

Height: 30 feet
Spread: 15 to 20 feet
Exposure: Sun/light shade
Soil: Sandy, rich in humus, moist
Plant: March and April/September
Blooms: Mid-July, camellia type blossoms
Fruit: None
Uses: Summer-blooming shade tree, specimen, town house tree

An unusual summer bloomer that does well in the sandy soils of the coastal plain.S. pseudo-camellia makes an excellent small to medium accent, with white summer flowers, orange to scarlet fall colors, and smooth exfoliating bark in winter. It needs a well-drained location and is insect and disease free.

VIRGINIA FRINGE TREE
(Chionanthus virginicus)
Height: 15-20 feet
Spread: 10 feet
Exposure: Half day sun
Soil: Well-drained
Plant: March or November
Blooms: May-June
Fruit: Insignificant drupes
Uses: Specimen

This lovely native tree is multi-stemmed, hardy, and has spicey-fragrant, feathery white flower trusses that follow the dogwoods. It has large light green leaves. The flower display is best in full sun.

THE MEDIUM SIZED TREES
The medium-sized trees include the largest flowering crab, strongest growing varieties of ornamental cherry, and the gorgeous Southern magnolia, here at the top of its range. These trees will reach 35 to 70 feet when mature, but some of practically pest-free, but they must be placed in the corner of a large yard where their exposed roots will not stub toes and wreck mower blades. A stone mulch over pockets of small early bulbs is a perfect complement for these lovely trees.

Oaks and hickories do shed nuts, with acorns leaching enough acid into the soil to thwart lawn growth over time. Acorns should be promptly raked or vacuumed each fall, and lime applied every three years to sweeten the soil.

Male Kentucky coffee trees may be preferable for those who do not want to clean up the long seed pods each fall. Exfoliating bark and ping-pong-sized seed balls are traits of all plane trees. Tall mature trees on a lot should be pruned of lower branches to provide air flow and light near the ground so that landscape plants and flowers will thrive beneath them.

TALL TREES (over 70 feet)
Shade or Specimen: tulip poplar, red maple,sugar maple, scarlet oak, willow oak, gingko, Kentucky coffee tree, 'Columbia' London plane tree hybrids, black tupelo, chestnut oak, American and copper beeches, deodar cedar, Douglas fir, and Japanese zelkova.

Street: Tulip tree, red maple, scarlet oak, willow oak, gingko, black tupelo, littleleaf linden, European linden, London plane tree, red oak, zelkova, and hybrid elms 'Columbia' and 'Liberty.'

TREES FOR SPECIAL USES
Columnar Trees for Screening
There is a considerable number of columnar growing trees that interest home owners whose space is limited. They range in mature height from 15 to 60 feet; more importantly, they may be kept to a relatively narrow width with very little pruning. There are columnar forms of the fastigiate cherry, 'Amanogawa;' the flowering crabapple, M.pyramidalis 'Strathmore;' as well as the more common shade trees. A columnar form of the English oak quercus robur fastigiata; of the birch, betula verrucosa fastigiata; and the 'Scanlon' and 'Autumn Glory' cultivars of red maple are all suitable for narrow spaces.

CONIFERS FOR THE HOME GROUNDS
Conifers are the stars of the winter landscape—trees whose subtle shades of green and silver blue remind us of persistent life in the dormant garden. they come into their own as specimens, as pungently scented windbreaks and screens, and as a backdrop to the showy branches and winter fruit of deciduous trees and shrubs.

There are columnar forms of several of the evergreens, including the Chinese Juniper, J. pyramidalis; 'Wintergreen' juniper; Incense cedar, Calocedrus decurrens 'Columnaris;'
Swiss stone pine, pinus cedrus; and white and scotch pines, P. strobus fatigiati and P. sylvestris fastigiati. Add to these the popular Leyland cypress, which can add vertical height at 3 to 4 feet each year.

Medium Tall Conifers
Chamaecyparis:

C. pisifera, Sawara retinospora	25-35'
C. plumosa aurea, Golden plume retinospora	20-25'

Juniperis:

J. chinensis 'Wintergreen,' Wintergreen juniper	15-20'
J. chinensis 'Robusta,' Robusta green juniper	18-20
J. chinensis 'Moonglow,' Moonglow juniper	15-18'

Large Conifers
Full-size conifers make excellent windbreaks or background plantings. Pines and cedars do well in the sandy soil of the coastal, with our native red cedar invading every abandoned field well into the Piedmont.

The true cedars, aristocrats among evergreens, are full-sized trees at maturity with lovely sculptural limbs and needles. Blue Atlas and Deodar cedars and Cedar of Lebanon are the most popular. The deodars have some winter die-back *(please continue on page 54)*

Tree Form and Rate of Growth

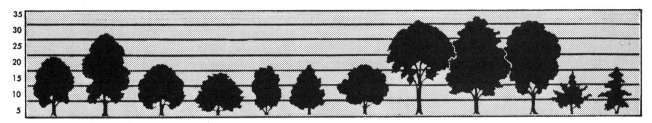

Tree growth in 10 years. Each band represents 5 feet in height. Trees in the Morton Arboretum study were 6 feet high when planted. Left to right: American ash, green ash, Amur cherry, European beech, canoe birch, buckeye, Amur cork tree, American elm, Chinese elm, Moline elm, gingko, sour gum.

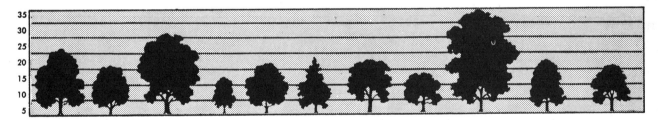

Left to right: Sweet gum, hackberry, Washington hawthorn, English hornbean, shagbark hickory, thornless honey locust, horse chestnut, Kentucky coffee tree, basswood or linden, little leaf linden, cucumber.

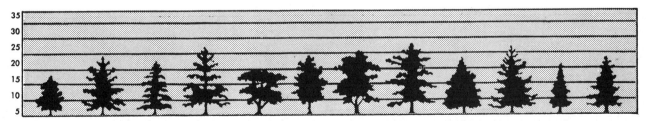

Left to right: Sugar maple, Norway maple, silver maple, bur oak, pin oak, red oak, white oak, sycamore, tulip, black walnut.

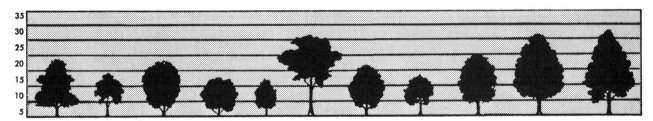

Left to right: White fir, Douglas fir, hemlock, European larch, Austrian pine, red pine, Scotch pine, white pine, Black Hills Spruce, Norway spruce, Serbian spruce, white spruce.

problems, and the hardier Kashmir type is best for colder areas. Hemlocks, Tsuga canadensis are the most shade tolerant of conifers, and therefore extremely useful as screening in older shady neighborhoods. But to look their best hemlocks need adequate space and good air circulation. They make an excellent overstory for rhododendron and mountain laurel in cooler, higher sections of this area.

White pine is also an effective screen in full sun if air pollution is not a significant factor.

Tall Conifers

Useful as specimens in the large lawn or as part of an impervious screen or windbreak.

Abies concolor, Concolor fir	70-80 ft.
Cedrus atlantica glauca, Blue Atlas Cedar	35-50 ft.
Cedrus deodara, Deodar cedar	35-50 ft.
Cedrus deodara 'Aurea', Golden Deodar	35-50 ft.
Juniperus virginiana, Virginia cedar	35-50 ft.
Picea canadensis, Black Hills spruce	50-60 ft.
Picea excelsa, Norway spruce	80-100 ft.
Picea omorika, Serbian spruce	50 ft.
Picea pungens glauca, Colorado blue spruce	60-80 ft.
Picea pungens 'Hoopsi, Hoopsi blue spruce	60-80 ft.
Pinus strobus, White pine	80-100 ft.
Tsuga canadensis, Canadian hemlock	75-90 ft.
Pseudotsuga douglasii, Douglas fir	70-100 ft.

How to Choose a Tree

☐ If you are digging up a tree to transplant on your own property, start a year ahead by root pruning it with a sharp garden spade in a circle that will correspond with the size of the eventual root ball. This will promote more compact root growth close to the tree—to minimize the transplant shock.

☐ With native trees that you transplant, small is best if you can protect them from animals, children, and mowers. They will adapt more quickly with less pruning and make rapid growth.

☐ When buying balled and burlapped trees make sure that the ball is firmly attached to the trunk, with no detectable signs of roots being torn from the plant.

☐ Check underneath the plastic trunk wraps to be sure there is no evidence of injury or disease on the bark.

☐ Fruit trees are safe to plant bare-root after they have gone dormant from late October through March, but evergreens should always be dug and transported with soil around the roots.

☐ When buying trees from a reputable nursery, always read and keep the replacement guarantee.If you lack the equipment and time to plant correctly, consider having the nursery do it to be sure that your investment is protected.

A DOZEN TREE PLANTING TIPS

• The following tips are the result of the latest research collected by the National Arboretum staff, and differ in part with previous recommendations given by American nurserymen.They are particularly useful to our area's gardeners who often must plant a variety of trees in heavy clay.

• For best results plant trees in early spring or fall several days after a rain so that there will be air spaces in the soil.

• Choose a location with adequate drainage—and reject any test hole into which water seeps.Even willow roots need oxygen mixed with water in order to extract nutrients from soil particles. Swamp trees need the least drainage.

• Dig a hole a third deeper and one foot wider in diameter than the root ball of the tree you have purchased. Thoroughly work the removed soil before it is replaced, only adding compost or leaf mold and lime if necessary.

• In heavy clay be sure to rough up the sides of the hole with a pronged weeding fork and to drive a crowbar a foot deep into several places at the bottom of the hole to ensure better drainage.

• Back fill the hole with a mound of cultivated dirt high enough to hold the tree ball an inch above the surrounding ground level. This allows for settling when the soil is filled in and watered.

• Carefully position the tree on the backfill mound, and loosen any wrapping that holds the root ball together. Remove plastic wrapping by pulling it from under the root ball. You may choose to leave burlap wrapping in the hole once the strings tying it to the trunk are removed, because it will rot.

• Water the bottom of the hole before filling in the sides around the root ball.

• Replace the soil to within an inch of the soil line where the trunk emerges, and form any extra soil into a ridge that encircles the planting hole. This shallow saucer of well worked soil will hold water to nourish the root zone.

• Mulch the entire saucer with shredded hardwood mulch to preserve soil moisture and prevent mower cuts on the young trunk.

• Wrap the trunks of young forest or fruit trees with paper, burlap, or a cut nylon stocking for the first year to prevent sun scald that will split the bark.

• Water immediately and thoroughly with a weak transplant solution. Water the first year when the soil under the covering mulch is dry to the touch an inch down.

• It is no longer considered necessary to stake newly planted trees if they are mulched out far enough to protect them from mowers. If a tree seems top heavy for its root ball size, it is better to prune it back to balance the wind stress while roots are establishing themselves.

Plant These Trees in the Spring

Nurserymen's practices have done much to reduce transplant shock. Especially is this true today when trees are root pruned in the nursery every year or two, which helps to develop a compact root mass to support top growth.

Yet even with modern practices, there are some

trees that are best transplanted in the spring. For the most part these are the species with fleshy roots—the magnolias, beech, birch, dogwood, elm, linden, red and sugar maples, sweet gum, and tulip poplar. Particularly if they are planted when dormancy has broken, after the middle of March here, they should be bought balled and burlaped to prevent the likelihood of failure.

All conifers and broadleaved evergreens should be moved for planting with a ball of soil enclosing their roots, whether planted in spring or fall.

Only the smallest trees without deep taproots are safe to buy in containers, since it is important that the roots do not circle in the pot—such trees tend to strangle themselves after they are set out to grow.

Trees dug from the wild or being moved about in the yard do not have compact root systems and, unless handled with great care, are likely to suffer considerable shock. If at all possible, such trees should be root pruned a year before moving.

Pruning for Balance and Health

Because the roots and tops of trees are roughly mirror images in size, the top of a transplanted tree will often need to be pruned back to match the root ball. The more severely the top is pruned, the more vigorous new growth will be. Of the shade trees, birch, maple, and yellowwood should only be pruned when the sap is down in early winter in order to prevent excessive bleeding. All other shade trees can be pruned in late winter or early spring.

Pruning at the time of planting is useful for correcting undesirable growth habits and structure. For example, you may remove one of a pair of top branches (called leaders) growing on opposite sides of the main trunk from the same place, to prevent a later structural weakness that could cause the tree to split. Side branches that cross or that form an acute angle with the trunk might also be removed to prevent bark injury or tearing of the branch from the trunk.

In general it is important to foster those branches that form the widest possible angle with the trunk, so that trunk growth will enclose and strengthen its hold on the branch over the years. Pruning should also follow the natural form of a particular species unless a specific formal effect is desired. Therefore, it is wise to study the mature form of a species before pruning a tree.

In a small yard it may be wise to prune the spreading lower limbs of a mature tree to protect the lawn; but this is generally not done with evergreens or beech trees with shallow roots. To ensure that trees stay healthy after pruning, gardeners should use sharp clean pruners that are sufficiently large to complete a clean cut without tearing the bark. When removing whole limbs, you should cut parallel to the trunk and just outside the bracelet of slightly wrinkled bark where the limb joins the trunk. This growth layer will

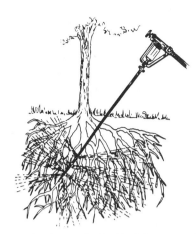

A safe and easy method for tree feeding. The injector may also be used for watering during drought periods.

can be pruned in late winter or early spring.

Pruning at the time of planting is useful for correcting undesirable growth habits and structure. For example, you may remove one of a pair of top branches (called leaders) growing on opposite sides of the main trunk from the same place, to prevent a later structural weakness that could cause the tree to split. Side branches that cross or that form an acute angle with the trunk might also be removed to prevent bark injury or tearing of the branch from the trunk.

In general it is important to foster those branches that form the widest possible angle with the trunk, so that trunk growth will enclose and strengthen its hold on the branch over the years. Pruning should also follow the natural form of a particular species unless a specific formal effect is desired. Therefore, it is wise to study the mature form of a species before pruning a tree.

In a small yard it may be wise to prune the spreading lower limbs of a mature tree to protect the lawn; but this is generally not done with evergreens or beech trees with shallow roots. To ensure that trees stay healthy after pruning, gardeners should use sharp clean pruners that are sufficiently large to complete a clean cut without tearing the bark. When removing whole limbs, you should cut parallel to the trunk and just outside the bracelet of slightly wrinkled bark where the limb joins the trunk. This growth layer will eventually cover the exposed heartwood, preventing insects or disease from invading the tree.

Some new research shows that creosote tree wound compounds do not make a real difference in tree protection; but many gardeners may want to use them on species that are disease and borer prone in this area.

PROPAGATION: HARDWOOD CUTTINGS

Hardwood cuttings are usually taken in late fall or early winter, after the shrub or tree is fully dormant. Sometimes the winters are mild enough so that cuttings taken in late February or early March give satisfactory results. The cuttings should be taken from the last season's growth.

Make cuts of material 6-8 inches long with sharp, clean pruning shears of the scissors type. Tie them in bundles of a dozen or more, label and place them in a moist but frost-free place. A peat-filled trench or a protected cold frame may serve, but it should be covered with a generous layer of leaves or straw in case temperatures drop unusually low. Place the bundles with the lower (or butt) end up, because this seems to stimulate a callus where roots will later form when the cuttings are planted.

In early March, whenever the soil is workable, prepare a propagating bed where cuttings may live undisturbed for up to two years. With a long pencil poke holes 6-10 inches apart in rows a foot apart to receive the cuttings. Carefully remove any buds on the lower part of the cutting with the tip of a sharp knife, and dip the butt end at least two growth nodes deep in a hormone rooting powder (obtainable in any hardware store or garden center). These hormones copy a natural growth hormone found in the stems at growth nodes. They are often sold in combination with a fungicide (benlate) that inhibits natural soil organisms from rotting the stems before they root. They are also available in liquid concentrate forms to be diluted and watered into the soil where cuttings are planted. The important thing for gardeners to know is to dilute all hormone formulas to the proper amount for the species you want to grow. The active ingredient is indol-butyric acid, and it can burn plant tissue at excessive concentrations.

The cuttings should be placed at least two nodes deep in their holes, and the soil firmed around each as soon as the soil is dry enough to walk on. Water your cuttings whenever rainfall is inadequate, which will depend greatly on whether you have sand or clay. The rooting zone should be kept moist and cool so infant roots can grow deep enough to support good top growth the first season. Mulches and compost can help achieve this, as well as keep down weeds without the resort to cultivation that might disturb the newly forming roots.

If you remove the plants at the beginning of the second growing season you can shorten very long roots to encourage a bushy root system in your final site. Again use clean sharp pruning shears. Do not top prune until the second season when you can pinch new growth to encourage a bushy compact appearance in shrubs. Shade and fruit trees should have their side branches pruned when dormant until they are 3-feet high.

POLLUTION RESISTANT SHADE TREES
FOR OUR AREA

Acer platanoides, Norway maple
Acer rubrum, Red maple
Amelanchier canadensis, Serviceberry
Carpinus caroliniana, American hornbeam
Celtis australis, European hackberry
Fraxinus pennsylvanica, Green ash
Gingkoaceae biloba, Gingko
Ilex opaca, American holly
Koelreutaria paniculata, Golden rain tree
Lagerstoemia indica x faurei, Crape myrtle hybrids
Liquidambar styraciflua, sweet gum
Magnolia grandiflora, Southern magnolia
Magnolia virginiana, deciduous native magnolia
Pyrus calleryana, improved Bradford pear cultivars
Quercus phellos, willow oak
Sophora japonica, Japanese pagoda tree
Tilia cordata, little leaf linden

INSPIRATION:

The National Arboretum, New York Avenue & Bladensburg Road. NE, Washington (202) 475-4815 information.
Grounds of the U.S. Capitol, Washington D.C.
Orland E. White Arboretum, Blandy Experimental Farm, off Route 50, Boyce, Virginia.

Prudent Pest Control

As with the practice of medicine, it is important to do no harm with pest control measures; so save money by monitoring and responding with chemical controls only when serious damage to your trees is threatened. Aphid populations, for example, can grow quite large without serious damage, and will attract their own predators. Elm bark beetles, bagworms, or borers, on the other hand, always spell trouble. The rule of thumb is, monitor carefully, and do as little as possible with chemicals that may destroy natural predators of your pests.

PEST MANAGEMENT CALENDAR FOR TREES

February

Prune all suckers out of dogwoods now. Such pruning may prevent development of fatal Discula cankers.

Prune all dead branches out of Austrian, Scots, and other two-needled pines to reduce spores of diplodia tip blight, which is often fatal to these pines. Plant resistant pines such as loblolly or scrub pine if one of your pines has succumbed to this disease.

March

Check apples and cherries for egg masses of the Eastern tent caterpillar. They look like black, melted styrofoam on the ends of the branches. Prune them out and destroy them.

Check hemlocks for woolly adelgids (white fluff on the underside of branches) and scale insects (small gray-brown disks on the undersides of needles). Also check for eriophyid mite damage (branches turn off color) by tapping a branch vigorously while holding a white piece of paper under the branch. Use a magnifying glass to spot the extremely small, yellowish, carrot-shaped mites. If any one or combination of these pests occurs in large numbers, spray the tree with a 3% solution of horticultural oil when weather is going to be above freezing for two days. Make sure you spray thoroughly when using oil.

April

Put up barrier bands now on trees threatened with gypsy moth defoliation. Concentrate on protecting oaks. Do not worry about protecting tulip poplars. To protect trees, attach a band of sticky tape around the circumference of the tree by mid-April. You may also attach a band of burlap above the sticky barrier, but you must remove accumulated caterpillars that appear under the burlap daily.

If warm rains occur, check pears, apples, and serviceberry for signs of fire blight. Prune out any diseased portions with pruning shears that are sterilized by dipping in bleach or alcohol after each cut.

May

Treat paper birch with a systemic insecticide like acephate to prevent bronze birch borer, leaf miner, and sawfly damage. Consider planting a 'Heritage' river birch as an alternative.

Don't be concerned with leaf blight that appears now on sycamore and ash. Treatment is seldom feasible and the trees usually withstand the disease if they are otherwise healthy. Consider planting other shade trees or resistant varieties of sycamore and ash.

Rigorously prune any succulent sprouts emerging from the trunks of dogwoods. Foliar infections of discula anthracnose can pass from leaves on these twigs and girdle the trunk of the tree, killing it. Consider planting a kousa dogwood or one of the resistant hybrids if you have lost a dogwood.

June

Verticillium wilt will appear on maples when dry weather starts. Typical symptoms are dying back of branches from the tips and general ill health. Water the tree thoroughly if conditions are dry and prune out any dead branches. Japanese maples and Norway maples are hardest hit. If a tree succumbs to verticillium, consider replacement with a resistant maple such as paperbark maple or red maple.

Look for pine needle scale crawlers now. They are bright red and about the size of a grain of sand. They can be monitored by beat testing as for mites. Treat heavily infested branches of pines with horticultural oil or insecticidal soap.

July

You may notice a large population of elm leaf beetles skeletonizing the foliage of your elms and zelkovas. Although the beetle larvae are present from early May on, you may want to hold off treating plants until now to see if populations develop into numbers high enough to do significant damage. Treat small trees with insecticidal soap; tolerate all but severe damage on large trees.

August

Apply a systemic insecticide such as acephate (Orthene) to hollies that have been severely damaged by leaf miner. If you are planting new hollies, choose a resistant holly such as Foster holly, and try to plant them in a semi-shaded site where leaf miner is generally less of a problem.

September

If hemlock woolly adelgids are still out of control, treat trees with 3% oil solution late in the month.

October

Rigorously clean up any dogwood foliage as it falls. Compost the leaves in a hot compost heap to destroy the discula fungus.

November

Take a good look at evergreens for signs of bagworms. Bags hang down from branch tips and are covered with the dead, chewed foliage of the tree. Clip off all bags to prevent a hatch in early summer that may devour new foliage.

December

Treat your ball-and-burlap or potted Christmas tree with a vapor barrier to prevent excess moisture loss while it's in the house It will have a better chance of surviving when you move it out to your yard.

DISEASE CONTROL—ORNAMENTAL AND SHADE TREES
(Virginia Polytechnic Institute)

Tree	Disease	Treatment
Catalpa	Leaf spot	Spray with Bordeaux mixture 8-8-100 when leaves unfold, when full size, and in 2 weeks.
Crabapple (Malus)	Cedar rust	Spray copper based fungicide. Delayed dormant and cover sprays when cool.
	Fireblight	Prune infected wood and burn.
	Scab	Spray Captan weekly when leaves first appear.
Elm (Ulmus)	Black leaf spot	Destroy fallen leaves spray ferbam 76% WP when leaves unfold, when full size, and 2 weeks later.
	Dutch elm disease	Cut and burn affected limbs. Call Extension agent.
Peach, Cherry (Prunus)	Leaf spot	Spray baking soda and refined oils or Captan 3 times at 2-week intervals when petals fall.
	Peach leaf curl	Spray lime sulphur on limbs before buds swell.
Sycamore(Platanus)	Anthracnose	Spray bordeaux mix 8-8-100 at bud swell, at bud break, and again 7 days later.
Willow (Salix)	Blight,black canker	Prune and destroy infected twigs. Spray bordeaux 8–8-100 when leaves are ¼-inch, and twice more at 2-week intervals.

PEST CONTROL—ORNAMENTAL AND SHADE TREES

Tree	Pest	Treatment
Deciduous Trees	Scale	Dormant strength miscible oil spray or lime sulphur.
Evergreen Trees	Scale	Superior miscible oil spray.
Ash (Fraxinum)	Borer	No approved control.
	Caterpillar	BT April on.
	Webworm	BioNeem or Diazinon late June, early July for fall webworm.
Birch (Betula)	Borer, sawfly	Acephate.
	Leaf miner	Acephate.
Catalpa	Aphids	Soap spray on migration.
	Mealy bug	Superior miscible oil or soap spray.
Crabapple(Malus)	Leafhoppers	Soap sprays from mid-May to early July at 2-week intervals.
Elm (Ulmus)	Bark beetle	Methoxychlor in early April. Cut out and burn affected branches.
	Leaf beetle	Superior oil or soap spray late May as soon as larvae are feeding.
Hawthorn	Beetles	Bioneem in late May.
(Crataegus)	Mites	Soap concentrates in May and late June.
	Tent caterpillar	BT on leaves, Sevin in tents.
Hemlock (Tsuga)	Mites	Superior oil spray in May.
	Scale	Superior oil or soap spray in May.
Linden (Tilia)	Aphids	Soap spray only if young trees are damaged.
	Bagworm	Superior oil or soap sprays,
	Bioneem	Malathion in early June to July as crawlers appear.
	Caterpillar	BT in late April or early May.
Locust (Robinia)	Borer	No approved control.
	Caterpillar	BT in late April or early May.
	Leaf miner	Acephate in mid-May.
Locust (Gleditsia)	Webworm	BT, or soap sprays when mites are active in June.
Magnolia	Caterpillar	BT in late April and early May.
Maple (Acer)	Aphids	Soap sprays if damage is heavy.
	Canker worm	Soap spray or Bioneem when larvae appear in May.
	Bladder gall	Lime sulphur spray when dormant.
	Mite	Superior oil spray as buds swell.
Mimosa (Albizzia)	Webworm	BT or insecticidal soap spray.
Oak (Quercus)	Canker worm	Superior oil or soap spray on larvae in mid-May.
	Lacebug	Bioneem or oil spray in late May and July.
	Leaf galls	No controls needed.
Pine (Pinus)	Bud worm	BT on main terminals late March.
	Mealy bug	Soap spray at 10-day intervals.
	Mites	Soap spray in April.
	Sawfly	Acephate when first seen.
Sycamore(Platanus)	Lacebug	Superior miscible oil spray in late May and July.
Tulip poplar (Liriodendron)	Aphids	Soap spray in late May if young trees.

8. SUITABLE SHRUBS

Shrubs are the stabilizing shapes of the home landscape. Well-selected woody plants whose mature size is compatible with the home give excellent and relatively permanent effect.

Shrubs have myriad uses. They can "tie" a house into its setting when they are planted along the foundation. They can soften or emphasize various features of your buildings. They can be used to lead the eye to points of interest, to divide space into areas of use, to screen an unsightly road, to mark a boundary, to act as a windbreak, or to provide a backdrop for a changing display of flowers and foliage plants. They are often themselves the star of the show, because many give a breathtaking seasonal effect of flowers, foliage or berries.

Screens and Hedges

On the edges of your property shrubs can be used as a mixed screen whose pleasing contrast of foliage, color and texture lends visual interest to the useful task of blocking an unattractive view or protecting your privacy.

Screening can be as simple as a line of vertical conifers or as intricate as a staggered planting of considerable variety where great thought is given to a play of color, texture

and foliage throughout the seasons. The trick is in fitting the site's qualities with the plant's mature size, exposure preferences (sun, wind), and moisture requirements.

To some a single species of attractive hedge plants is preferable as a screen, and the choice of material that remains healthy and attractive under constant pruning is paramount.

Green Architecture

A good hedge, a good neighbor makes but what makes a good hedge? Green architecture is an apt description of a hedge to mark a boundary, to provide an enclosure for privacy. The role of the hedge and the style are key to the selection of the plant or plants to do the job. A fine textured evergreen conifer like Taxus baccata (English Yew) sheared to create a traditional hedge is formal. This enclosure translates into privacy for a garden sitting room. A mixture of shrubs creates an informal hedge with variety of forms and textures and a tree adds height at the edge of the garden. A colorful combination would include the purple-leafed smoke bush, Cotinus coggygria plain 'Purpureus' a background for

Spiraeai x bumalda 'Gold Flame' and Hydrangea quercifolia, Oak-leafed hydrangea. Gold Flame spiraea has small golden green leaves tinged with plum color and flat flower heads of clusters of tiny pink flowers. The hydrangea has large oak-like leaves and large panicles of white flowers that fade to pink at the tips of the branches and the added attraction of wine-red fall colored leaves to highlight the persistent flowers that have faded to pink. To top off the planting a Tulip Magnolia,—Magnolia 'Galaxy', an upright cultivar with plum colored flowers in early spring.

If you choose a hedge for screening or enclosure, it requires specific planting techniques in order to thrive for years with a minimum of care.

Look carefully at the enclosed illustrations. Hedge plants should be set in 1½ to 2 feet apart in a well dug and enriched trench, making sure to choose a species that will do well if amounts of light and moisture vary sharply along the line you have chosen. In a dark area, Japanese holly and yew retain their health and vigor to an astonishing degree, while the privets grow thin and anemic.

Those people who have a useful but unsightly chain link fence set inside their property line may want to stagger hedge plantings on both sides of the fence if they can be maintained without encroachment on your neighbor. The fence disappears while its effectiveness remains. Hedge trimming to create and keep a wider profile at the bottom

How to Plant a Hedge.

during the two or three annual prunings assures you that it will remain full and attractive to the ground.

In general most hedge plants can be pruned in early June and again in mid-to late-July. After that any new growth must be allowed to harden off to prevent winter damage to the plant

The thousands of available shrubs for the home landscape may be classified for home selection purposes into three general plant categories: *conifers, broadleaf evergreens,* and *deciduous flowering shrubs*. In general terms, conifers are those evergreens with needles, like pines and junipers; broadleaf evergreens, those that retain their leafy foliage year-round, like most azaleas and hollies; while the deciduous flowering shrubs shed their leaves for the winter, like the lilac and forsythia.

Care and Feeding of Evergreens

Both conifers and broadleaf evergreens retain their leaves during winter dormancy by means of a thick cutin layer that prevents loss of moisture from the leaves or needles during sub-freezing weather. They add new leaves at the terminal growth points each spring as they shed the oldest leaves toward the interior of the plant. From this growth habit comes most of their specialized care requirements.

It is best to provide a soil reasonably well-supplied with compost or humus at the time of planting to insure good drainage and even moisture for the roots. An adequate supply of soil moisture going into the winter prevents much winter injury by allowing plants to replace moisture loss from the foliage in cold, windy weather before the soil freezes.

An evergreen's ability to protect itself can be seen most dramatically in the leaves of the native Rosebay rhododendron, which roll into tighter and tighter cylinders as temperatures drop, preventing moisture loss by reducing the exposed surface area. The slim needles of conifers are designed to minimize winter moisture loss. Gardeners can help broadleaf evergreens resist transpiration when the soil is frozen by siting the plants out of the main force of wind and sun, by mulching enough to slow soil freezing and by spraying an anti-desiccant spray, like Wilt-Pruf, on those specimens that have suffered previous winter die-back.

Feeding an established shrub that shows signs of nutrient deficiency, may be helpful. In general it is best not to stimulate excessive growth in any shrub plantings or they will outgrow the space they were selected to fill—another good reason to avoid heavy applications of nitrogen fertilizer to adjacent lawns.

If a shrub seems to lack vigor, it should be examined in March for signs of insects and disease and treated, then fed with one of the 270-day release granular formulas. For a severe nutritional deficiency, a foliar feeding with safe soluble nutrients may provide interim help before underlying questions of soil pH, fertility, drainage and appropriate location are addressed in the next planting season.

UNTRIMMED AND LOOSE   SHINGLED   CLIPPED

Evergreens should be regularly pruned to keep them compact and within bounds. However, the pruning should take the form of a shingling, rather than a formal clipping which destroys their natural appearance.

Plant the evergreen in a roomy hole. Fill the space about the balled plant with a soil mixture containing compost or peatmoss. A good soaking is the last step.

Pruning

Most landscape conifers, except spruce, deodar cedar, Blue Atlas Cedar, Cedar of Lebanon, and Douglas fir, need an annual pruning to keep them compact and youthful in appearance. Trimming is best done in the winter through the middle of March before new growth starts, and, if necessary, again in late June. Pruning done in September here may lead to new growth during a mild fall that will almost certainly winterkill. Spring pruning cuts are soon covered by new growth. It is wise to follow the growth habit and to make these cuts close to a fork or clump of growth so that stubs will not be visible. Only a formal Mediterranean, French or Japanese garden requires clipping conifers for topiary effect.

Spring pruning of flowering broadleaf evergreens differs slightly because the new growth should be cut after flowering is finished but before buds for next year's bloom are set.

Renewing Overgrown Shrubbery

When new homeowners buy an older home, they often find that the surrounding foundation shrubs or hedgerows have grown completely out of scale, or have been shaded into obscurity and ill health by a maturing canopy of trees. For reasons of economy, the question often becomes: Can this landscape be saved?

The answer often lies in the species involved. Hedges made of yew, boxwood, and Japanese hollies can take a great deal of shade. Judicious pruning up of the shade casting trees to create "high" shade, coupled with feeding and renewal pruning of the overgrown hedge material at the proper time will often produce marked improvement within one season. But privets will not thicken up unless they have at least half-day sun.

Foundation plantings are a species by species case. Among the evergreens, only yew will reliably sprout new growth from large old wood the same year. Others like plume cypress and large arborvitae grow coarse and shapeless with age, and are best removed.

Pruning of deciduous flowering shrubs by removing oldest canes to the ground and reshaping the remainder is often quite successful. The strongest growers like mockorange can often be cut down completely to regenerate new flowering growth within two years. Assess your long term goals to see which shrubs are most likely to repay efforts to reclaim them, based on their mature size, longevity, and hardiness. Then you can afford to replace poor specimens that occupy focal points in your garden with specimens that better suit the space.

Protection From Pests

For the past decade or so the principal pests for evergreens have been the bagworm, red spider mite, various scale insects, and the hemlock adelgid. It is hard for mites to get established in plantings that are well-watered and kept somewhat open to air circulation with judicious placement and pruning. A weekly water spray up through the foliage is somewhat effective. Summer oils, refined horticultural oils, provide a less toxic alternative to systemic insecticides such as acephate or cython.

The safe bacterial control, BT, has largely replaced malathion to combat bagworm crawlers in June and early July when they emerge on their principal host, the Virginia red cedar. Once their bags are constructed, the only control is to use a systemic insecticide or to handpick them off the smaller trees and shrubs. Junipers can be attacked by the juniper web worm that is controlled by applications of neem seed extract or insecticidal soap into the web early in the day during May and June. The deodar cedar seems to be vulnerable to air pollution and a drying exposure where soil is sandy, which can cause the leader to die back.

The protection of evergreens from animals, particularly dogs and cats, is necessary if they are to retain their natural shape and symmetry. Various chemical repellants are sold for this purpose, but they are volatile materials that must be regularly renewed.

Caging helps smaller evergreen plantings until they get established and has the advantage of being able to be enlarged or moved to keep pace with plant growth. Previously, spiny barberry bushes were planted around evergreen plantings to discourage animal incursions, but leash laws throughout much of the region have lessened the need for these precautions.

Basic Considerations

Because their landscape effect is year round and especially noticeable during the winter months, it is crucial to know the mature size and preferred exposure of the evergreens you may want to choose.

This is especially vital for the broadleaf evergreens, whose survival in a harsh winter is often determined by their placement out of harsh drying winds and brilliant sun.

Conifers and Their Uses

With the great variety in shapes, foliage colors and shadings, and texture (even within the same species) it is possible to create lovely effects in foundation plantings and transitional borders using evergreens as the main components in the design. Conifers, those evergreens with needles rather than leaves, are particularly useful in creating winter interest on the home grounds, particularly in exposed locations.

There are a number of so-called "dwarf" conifers suitable for foundation planting around the house. Most of them are not true dwarves but are slower growing forms of arborvitae, false cypress, yew, juniper and spruce. These varieties do not obscure a view from inside the house and create a desired effect that can last for years with minimal pruning.

Columnar forms make excellent windbreaks or hedging, while distinctively shaped species make effective focal points in a variety of beds, borders, and rock gardens.

Conifers vary. Some, like the popular junipers, arborvitae, pine, and false cypresses are sun-loving; while yews retain their health and appearance in sun or shade.

UPRIGHT CONIFERS

Threadleaf retinospora 15-20 ft. Chamaecyparis pisifera
Hinoki cypress 10-20 ft. Chamaecyparis obtusa gracilis
Hick's yew 10-20 ft. Taxus cuspidata Hicksi
Pyramidal Japanese yew 10-25 ft. Taxus cuspidata capitata

MEDIUM CONIFERS

Weeping Cedar of Lebanon 10-12 ft. Cedrus lebanyi pendula
Hollywood juniper 10-15 ft. Juniperus torrulosa 'Hollywood'
Spiny Greek juniper 10-12 ft. Juniperus excelsa stricta
Spreading Japanese yew 10-15 ft. Taxus cuspidata
Japanese umbrella pine 20-30 ft. Sciadopitys verticillata
Japanese blade pine 10-15 ft. Pinus thunbergia
Hybrid yew 12-15 ft. Taxus intermedia
Cripp's golden cypress 8-15 ft. Chamaecyparis obtusa crippsi
Emerald arborvitae 10 ft. Thuja occidentalis
Berkman's golden arborvitae 6-8 ft. Thuja orientalis aurea nana

LOW CONIFERS (3-10 feet)

Green threadbush 3 ft. Chamaecyparis pisifera 'Filifera' nana
Gold threadbush 3 ft. Chamaecyparis pisifera 'Filifera' nana aurea
Pfitzer juniper 5-6 ft. Juniperus chinensis 'Pfitzeriana'
Compact Pfitzer juniper 3-4 ft. Juniperus chinensis 'Pfitzeriana' compacta
Gold coast juniper 3-4 ft. Juniperus chinensis 'Gold Coast'
Dwarf Albert spruce 6-8 ft. Picea glauca 'Conica'
Globe blue spruce 3 ft. Picea glauca globosa
Montgomery blue spruce 3 ft. Picea pungens glauca 'Montgomery'

The principal forms of evergreens are: 1. Broad or spreading, 2. pyramidal, 3. columnar, 4. globe, 5. spreading, and 6. trailer or creeping.

Mugo pine 4-8 ft. Pinus mugo var. mugo
Dwarf white pine 3-4 ft. Pinus strobus nana
Dwarf compact blue Scotch pine 3-4 ft. Pinus sylvestris glauca nana
Densiformis yew 3-4 ft. Taxus x media densiformis
Brown Japanese yew 3-4 ft. Taxus x media Brownii
Hatfield Japanese yew 8-10 ft. Taxus x media 'Hatfieldii'
Globe arborvitae 3-4 ft. Thuja occidentalis 'Woodward'
Sargent's weeping hemlock 5 ft. Tsuga canadensis 'Sargenti'

VERY LOW CONIFERS (under 3 feet)

Dwarf Hinoki false cypress 3 ft. Chamaecyparis obtusa 'Nana'
Dwarf Maxwell spruce 2-3 ft. Picea excelsa 'Maxwellii'
Bird's nest spruce 2-3 ft. Picea abies 'Nidiformis'
San Jose juniper 2-3 ft. Juniperus chinensis san jose
Andorra juniper 2-3 ft. Juniperus horizontalis 'Plumosa'
Dwarf Japanese yew 2-3 ft. Taxus cuspidata 'Nana'
Weeping English yew 3 ft. Taxus baccata repandens
Dwarf American arborvitae 2 ft. Thuja occidentalis minima
Little Gem American arborvitae 2-3 ft. Thuja occidentalis 'Little Gem'
Dwarf Canadian hemlock 2-3 ft. Tsuga canadensis 'Bennett'; 'Jervis'
Dwarf Serbian Spruce 2 ft. Picea omorika nana

GROUND-HUGGING CONIFERS (6-18 inches)

Sargent juniper 1½ ft. Juniperus chinensis 'Sargenti'
Creeping juniper 1½ ft. Juniperus horizontalis
Waukegan juniper 1½ ft. Juniperus horizontalis 'Douglasii'
Tamariscifolia juniper 1½ ft. Juniperus sabina tamariscifolia
Blue Pacific juniper 1 ft. Juniperus conferta 'Blue Pacific'
Blue Rug juniper 5-6 in. Juniperus horizontalis 'Wiltoni'
Bar Harbor juniper 5-6 in. Juniperus horizontalis 'Bar Harbor'
Siberian carpet cypress 6-12 in. Microbiota decussata
Dwarf Japanese garden juniper 6-8 in. Juniperus procumbens nana
Buffalo juniper 6-8 in. Juniperus sabina Buffalo

Uses of Various Conifers

The junipers are perennially popular for landscape work. While some varieties host apple cedar rust that appears as red finger-like fungus, they are so well adapted to hot, dry situations, and take so well to pruning that they are one of the conifers most used as shrubs, hedging, and groundcovers. New cultivars, whose foliage turns to blue, silver, purple, and bronze with the seasons, are readily available. They survive both our winters and summers with aplomb. Our native white and red cedars are really junipers, and like all junipers should not be planted within 100 yards of crab and apple trees because they are the specific host for cedar-rust disease.

Notable Junipers:

Tall spreaders: 'Pfitzer Blue' is the standard; 'Sea Green' has rich green fountain shape.

Low spreaders: 'Andorra Compacta' has feathery texture and bright green foliage that

makes it a No.1 choice; 'San Jose' has stiff branches and gray-green color.

Medium spreaders: 'Old Gold' has the best gold color year round; 'Compact Pfitzer'

has spiny gray-green foliage.

Groundcovers: 'Blue Rug' hugs the ground, has best blue color; Dwarf Japanese Garden Juniper has blue-green color, is 6 inches tall with outstanding form.

The Useful Cypresses and Arborvitae

The Siberian carpet cypress is a beautiful, plumy, ground cover that goes maroon in the winter and greens up again each spring. It is effective planted with other evergreens and ground covers in a way that set off its winter foliage. Carpet cypress likes well-drained soil and thrives in moderate shade.

The false cypresses are an increasingly useful family of evergreens whose delicate subtlety of color and billowy forms, reminiscent of Oriental cloud forms, have made them increasingly popular. There are several dwarf forms suitable for the smaller landscape design. Chamaecyparis pisifera, the Sawara cypress, although taller, makes a stunning hedge, whose subtle variations of color create the effect of a living tapestry.

Arborvitae, formerly more popular in new and sunny subdivisions, if given adequate moisture, good sun, and regular pruning, are still a good choice. Emerald is one of the newer varieties that retain their shape at maturity. Dwarf varieties are the most useful on small lots. Although white pines are not pollution resistant, they are an attractive wind break or screen for a sunny slope. The dwarf mugo pine, however, is everywhere; it is planted in commercial landscape plans and subdivision lots alike. Its compact full appearance in dry exposed conditions endears it to many gardeners, particularly those with small spaces to fill. Other pines have specialized uses as part of Oriental gardens and in bonsai.

The dark green yews are widely employed for landscaping here. They are one of the few kinds of evergreens that are not troubled by dogs. Because they grow slowly, and have rich foliage, they deserve full use. Even fairly tall varieties can be easily pruned within bounds because yews will put out foliage again on mature wood to maintain a bushy appearance. They will thrive in shady as well as sunny situations if the soil retains moisture during dry periods. Children should be cautioned not to taste the red fleshy berries that ripen in early winter because they are mildly poisonous if eaten.

BROADLEAF EVERGREENS

AZALEA
(Ericaceae, Rhododendron species, and hybrids)
Uses: Floral, foundation, specimen
Plant: Spring/Fall
Distance: 3 to 8 ft.
Soil: Enriched with leafmold, acid, not too dry
Exposure: Shade/tolerates sun
Prune: After flowering
Species:

R. arborescens, Sweet azalea, 7-9 ft., white, deciduous.

R. calendulaceum, Flame azalea, 6-8 ft., yellow-orange-red, deciduous.

R. molle, Chinese, 4-6 ft., yellow, deciduous.

R. japonicum, Japanese, 6 ft., orange, apricot or yellow, deciduous.

R. periclymenoides, Pinxter, var. roseum, pink, 6-8 ft., deciduous.

R. roseum, Roseshell, Mayflower, 6-9 ft., bright pink, deciduous

R. vaseyi, Pinkshell azalea, 5-6 ft., soft pink, deciduous.

R. viscosum, Swamp azalea, 4-6 ft., white, fragrant, deciduous.

R. luteum (pontica), 6-8 ft., clear yellow, autumn flowering.

Knaphill hybrids (including Exburys), 2-8 ft., white, yellow, pink, orange, red, deciduous.

R. kaempferi, Torch azaleas, 4-5 ft., semi-evergreen.

R. yedoense, var. poukenensis, Korean Yodogawa, 1-3 ft., rose-purple, semi-evergreen.

R. indicum (Macrantha), 3-7 ft., orange, pink, white, semi-evergreen.

Kurume hybrids, 2-8 ft., semi-evergreen.

Glenn Dale hybrids, 2-10 ft., white, orange-red, lavender, multi-colored, semi-evergreen.

Gable hybrids, 1-6 ft., purple, pink, white, fragrant, semi-evergreen to evergreen.

Girard hybrids, 2-3 ft., pinks, full range reds, evergreen.

Harris hybrids, white through red, includes cascade forms suitable for bonsai/rockery.

Linwood hybrids, 2-3 ft., white through red, bi-color, evergreen.

Robin Hill hybrids, 2-3 ft., range of colors, evergreen.

Satsuki hybrids, includes Gumpo dwarf forms, white, pink, red, multi-colored; late, evergreen.

The azalea is probably one of the most widely planted shrubs in the Washington area, and justifiably so. Our climate and soils seem to suit them very well, and everyone enjoys their brilliant display of color and their occasional fragrance every spring. For the most part they are spring flowering shrubs with a wide range of growth habits, color, and form of flower. Although we think of most of them as evergreen, in fact many have foliage that changes or sheds in the fall, and some are completely deciduous.

Azaleas are members of the very large rhododendron family. We are blessed with nearly a dozen native American varieties, some of exceptional delicacy and fragrance. Most of those will thrive in and around Washington.

In previous years over 90 percent of the azaleas planted here were of the Kurume hybrid varieties with large flowers and evergreen foliage. Now, the efforts of local plant breeders, led by the late Dr. B.Y. Morrison, a former director of the National Arboretum, has led to an unparalleled selection for local gardeners.

The Arboretum itself contains over 1,200 species and varieties, perfect for gardeners who want to preview them before they purchase. Among their hardy and handsome newer selections are Pryored and Ben Morrison, named for their propagators at the U.S. Department of Agriculture.

Hundreds of Dr. Morrison's Glenn Dale and Back Acre hybrids have been grown here, as have other evergreen types, such as the orange-red Kaempferi or flame azaleas, the lower Gable and Girard hybrids, and the Satsuki dwarf forms, known as Gumpo. Newer choices include the Linwood and Robin Hill hybrids, many of which are not over 15 inches tall when mature.

Among deciduous azaleas, the Knaphill or Exbury selections that flower late, in a startling palette of yellows and oranges, have gained popularity, although they must be carefully sited not to clash with the cooler range of early colors. Local hybridizers have excelled here as well, with Hyatt's Yellow Cloud gaining national recognition early in the decade.

From the chart below it is easy to see that many people are engaged in hybridizing azaleas, often combining the hardier American and Asian species with more tender species adapted for the South to produce greenhouse and garden hybrids of great beauty and vigor.

It would not be possible to prepare a list of recommended varieties specifically for the Washington area without the invaluable help of the members of the Azalea Society of America and nurserymen in the area. Their experience in growing, selling, and hybridizing hundreds of azalea varieties over decades allows us to recommend some, but by no means all, of the azaleas that will thrive for you.

Among the factors considered are hardiness, vigor, purity of color, form of blossom, growth habit, size, season of bloom, and, in the case of the evergreen types, winter foliage value.

Azalea lovers face a dilemma in the Washington area as new hybrids extend the season into the heat of late spring. Many of the later bloomers are beautiful, but quickly wrecked by a combination of rain followed by hot sunshine. One solution is to choose earlier cold-hardy varieties for your main plantings, siting the late bloomers in the coolest, airiest parts of the garden.

Azaleas thrive in sun or shade, but their flowering season is longer in partial shade. They do not withstand

RECOMMENDED AZALEA VARIETIES FOR THE WASHINGTON AREA

Name	Hybrid/ Species	Bloom type	Color	Height	Season of Bloom	Foliage
Light Pinks:						
Blaauw's Pink	Blaauw	h-in-h	pink	medium	middle	evergreen
Betty Anne Voss	Robin Hill	single	pink	dwarf	late	evergreen
Coral Bells	Kurume	h-in-h	pink	low	early	evergreen
Nancy	Robin Hill	single	pink	dwarf	middle	evergreen
Rosebud	Gable	double	pink	low	middle	evergreen
Rose Pinks:						
Delos	Glenn Dale	double	rose pink	medium	middle	evergreen
Ellie Harris	Harris	h-in-h	pink	medium	middle	evergreen
Gaiety	Glenn Dale	single	pale/red	tall	middle	evergreen
Eureka	Yerkes/Pryor	h-in-h	lavender pink	medium	middle	evergreen
Salmon:						
Pink Cascade	Harris	single	yellow pink	trailing	early	evergreen
Fashion	Glenn Dale	h-in-h	salmon	medium	middle	evergreen
Louise Gable	Gable	double	salmon	low	early	evergreen
Gumpo pink	Satsuki	single	salmon	very low	late	evergreen
Linwood Salmon	Linwood	h-in-h	salmon	low	middle	evergreen
Lilac and Lavender:						
Corsage	Gable	single	fragrant	medium	middle	evergreen
Elsie Lee	Shammarello	double	lavender	low	middle	evergreen
Lilac Time	Kaempferi	double	pure lilac	medium	middle	evergreen
Linwood Lavender	Linwood	semi-double	lavender	low	middle	evergreen
Korean	Poukhanense sp.	single	purple	medium	early	evergreen
Purples:						
Purple Splendor	Gable	h-in-h	red-violet	low	early	evergreen
Sherwood Purple	Sherwood	single	red-violet	medium	early	evergreen
Herbert	Gable	h-in-h	rose-purple	medium	early	evergreen
Zulu	Glenn Dale	single	purple	medium	middle	evergreen
Kusudama	Satsuki	single	rose-purple	very low	late	evergreen
Reds and Oranges:						
Hinodegiri	Kurume	single	china rose	medium	early	evergreen
Rainfire	Harris	single	red	low	late	evergreen
Stewartsonian	Gable	single	clear red	low	early	evergreen
Gibralter	Exbury	single	orange blush	tall	late	deciduous
Buccaneer	Glenn Dale	single	orange-red	medium	middle	evergreen
Beni-Kirishima	Satsuki	double	orange-red	medium	late	evergreen
Flame	Calendulaceum sp.	single	red-or.-yell.	tall	late	deciduous
Klondyke	Exbury	single	yellow orange	tall	late	deciduous
Yellows:						
Yellow Cloud	Hyatt	single	clear yellow	medium	middle	deciduous
Florida	Austrinum sp.	single	yellows, oranges	tall	—	deciduous
Whites:						
Indica Alba	Mucronatum	single	white	med.-tall	early	evergreen
Delaware Valley White	Mucronatum	single	white	med.-tall	early	evergreen
Swamp	Viscosum sp.	single	fragrant	medium	late	deciduous
H.H.Hume	Yerkes/Pryor	h-in-h	white	medium	early	evergreen
Glacier	Glenn Dale	single	pure white	med.-tall	early	evergreen
Rose Greeley	Gable	h-in-h	w/chartreuse	low	early	evergreen
Hardy Gardenia	Linwood	double	pure white	low	middle	evergreen
White Rosebud	Kehr	double	pure white	low	middle	evergreen
Gumpo	Satsuki	single	white	very low	late	evergreen
Palestrina	Vuyk	single	white	medium	middle	evergreen
Pleasant White	—	single	white	medium	late	evergreen
Multi-Colored, Patterned:						
Dayspring	Glenn Dale	single	wh/blue pink	tall	very early	evergreen
Ben Morrison	—	single	rose/white	tall	middle	evergreen
Janet Rhea	Linwood	semi-double	red/white	low	middle	evergreen
Ho-Oden	Kurume	h-in-h	pink/white	medium	very early	evergreen
Gyokushin	Satsuki	single	white/pink	low	late	evergreen
Martha Hitchcock	Glenn Dale	single	purp/wh ctr	low	middle	evergreen
Saint James	Back Acre	single	peach/wh ctr	low	late	evergreen
Margaret Douglas	Back Acre	single	salmon/wh ctr	low	late	evergreen

Bloom Type: h-in-h, hose in hose have sepals changed into petals
Bloom Time: Early is 2nd to 4th week in April; Middle is 1st to 3rd week in May; Late is 3rd week in May to 1st week in June.

The enclosed information is the product of research conducted by members of the Azalea Society of America in the Washington area including Mr. William C. Miller, Dr. Charles H. Evans, and other hybridizers and nurserymen.

competition of shallow-rooted trees; and they do not thrive in hot, dry situations. Given a moist situation in well-drained soil that is well-supplied with peat moss or oak leaf compost, they may be counted on. Heavy mulching in the fall with hardwood bark or chopped oak leaves gives adequate protection, and the decaying leaves provide needed plant food for the next growing season while they keep the delicate root system cool and moist. They may be given a light spring application of cottonseed meal and bonemeal or Hollytone or one of the formulations for acid-loving plants, but it should be done before or after bloom, and not after the first of June.

Azaleas need a relatively acid soil, one with a pH level below 6.0. If the planting hole was not well-supplied with peat moss or located in a forested area, it may be necessary to increase the soil acidity with flowers of sulphur, or Sulfer Bright, especially around foundation plantings. This powdered form of sulphur may be scattered around the bushes to be washed down into the root zone with normal watering.

If otherwise healthy azalea foliage looks yellowed with darker veins, it usually means that an iron deficiency must be corrected, with iron chelate alone or in a fertilizer mix for these shrubs. Iron sulphate available at drug stores and larger garden centers may be sprayed on the foliage to correct this situation overnight.

Azaleas are not immune to either insects or disease. Lacebugs and spider mites are the most common pests. Several applications of soap spray or Orthene a season are required to control these pests when they appear, although a hard spray of water every day up through the foliage knocks off spider mites even as it relieves the hot dry conditions that allow them to proliferate in midsummer.

The known diseases include petal blight, which can wreck the display during warm wet springs. Kurume and indica types are most affected here, which is one good reason to search for improved hybrids developed from other species. Spray benomyl in a 50% wettable powder form at 10 to 14 day intervals on plants that have been previously affected. Avoid all overhead watering for these species in the spring. Removal and replacement of mulch beneath all affected plants after blooms have fallen will prevent the fungal spores from wintering over.

Leaf and twig blight, which gets established in July as new buds begin to form for most species, can be controlled with dust at that time.

Although these recommended varieties are hardy even in the colder regions of the Washington area, winter injury or death may occur occasionally. Very low temperatures, bright sunshine, and wind can split bark and dessicate the foliage of evergreen species, particularly if the plant has not been watered during a dry fall. Buds can be damaged by rapid changes between hot and cold weather. The best insurance against winter injury is a healthy well-planted bush, given even moisture to support its shallow roots during times of drought and mulched throughout the year.

Most species azaleas can be propagated by seed with care, but avid home gardeners with a greenhouse take early softwood cuttings of deciduous varieties and root them in flats over a heating mat under mist and lights. The evergreen and semi-evergreen varieties are easier to propagate. Semi-hardwood cuttings can be taken in midsummer, dipped in rooting hormone, and placed in a mixture of sand and peat moss in a shady situation. When they are rooted, they may be transplanted into pots or beds filled with leaf mold, peat moss, and sand. Unless the little plants are sheltered and grown through the first winter without going dormant, many will not survive; for the home gardener it may take ten cuttings to get two viable plants. The first winter they will need the protection of an oak leaf mulch or a good cold frame if kept outdoors.

Azalea Progress: 1. Well-rooted 1-year-old plant. 2. Pinched-back stocky plant. 3. Bushy 2-year-old. 4. 3-year-old in bloom.

BARBERRY
(Evergreen Berberis)
Uses: Hedge, specimen
Plant: Spring, fall
Distance: 2-4 ft.
Soil: Ordinary garden loam
Exposure: Sun, light shade
Species:
Gladynensis 'Wm. Penn Barberry', 3 ft., evergreen.
Julianae—Wintergreen, 5 ft., blue-black, evergreen.
Julianae var. nana—Dwarf wintergreen, 3 ft., blue-black, evergreen.
Verruculosa—'Warty', 2 ft., violet-black, evergreen.
Mentoriensis—'Mentor', 6 ft., evergreen.

The evergreen barberries, Julianae, Warty, Wm. Penn, and Mentor, are attractive evergreens and well adapted to a wider use. Foliage, habit of growth, yellow flowers, and abundant crops of colorful fruits give them high landscape value.

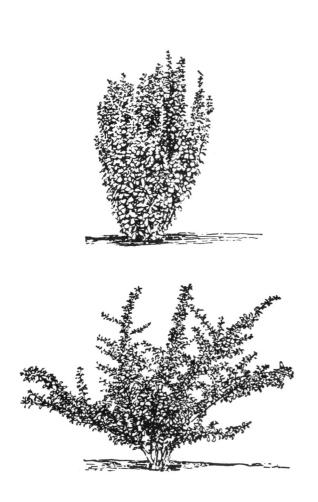

Two types of barberry: Upright, suitable for hedge; spreading, typical of Japanese barberry.

BOXWOOD
(Buxus species)

Boxwoods are looked on in this area as the aristocrats of the broadleaf evergreens, especially the slow-growing English boxwood. They give an atmosphere of graceful charm and permanence to the landscape that no other shrub can give. It might well be said that the Potomac Valley is their first home, because they were transplanted here in early Colonial times. Their rich green foliage and billowy outline mark out all the historic gardens that survive. And, when established, their hardiness and freedom from serious pests have much to do with their continuing popularity.

In much of the Middle Atlantic, box is used as the landscaping backbone in gardens of all sizes. Large specimens abound on the Washington Cathedral grounds, at the Lincoln Memorial, Mount Vernon, Arlington House, and Woodlawn Plantation. At Dumbarton Oaks there are thousands of plants of all sizes used as accent plants, dividers, and edgings.

The true dwarf boxwood, Buxus sempervirens suffruticosa, commonly known as English box, is the mainstay of all these plantings; but elsewhere the true tree form boxwood, commonly called American box, is frequently used as a hedge plant. Its botanical name is Buxus sempervirens arborescens. Further variations of foliage and growth habits that are selected out by growers are given cultivar names. A cultivar of tree form called 'Vadar Valley' has bluish leaves and is thought to be hardier than most. Others are: B. sempervirens, varieties bulata, myrtifolia, and angustifolia, as well as two cultivars with variegated foliage. The best one of these for this area is 'Elegantissima'.

In addition to English box there are the compact form from Japan, Buxus microphylla, var. japonica, and Buxus microphylla koreana, known as Korean boxwood. The latter is believed to be the hardiest of all boxwood and is a shrub of moderate size that can take below zero temperatures for a few days without suffering major damage.

Locally developed cultivars, the so-called Kingsville box, are dwarf specimens often used as hedging for formal knot gardens or as potted bonsai plants.

The boxwood are of easy culture although they do resent deep planting. They will suffer if their compact root ball is planted one inch too deeply.

Their shallow roots do their best when boxwood is planted as understory in filtered shade to protect them from drying during summer droughts. In an exposed site the foliage may redden or sunburn after a severe winter or a dry summer. Because of their shallow root system box should be cultivated with extreme care, if at all.

It is preferable to plant boxwood in October or early November, incorporating generous quantities of compost and a moderate amount of well-rotted cow manure in each planting hole. Do not use chemical fertilizers at planting time. Fertilizing is best done singly a year or two later around the drip line. Fertilize in earliest spring, so that the bushes will have the whole season to absorb nutrients and make new growth that will mature before winter. Heavy feeding should always be avoided for such a shallow rooted plant.

The goal with boxwood is slow steady growth. Such a course helps prevent exposure to the few pests and diseases that affect them.

One of the best disease control measures is proper harvest of the foliage by a process known as plucking. This can easily be done near Christmas when boxwood foliage is in demand for wreaths and kissing balls for the holidays. Small branches of the mature foliage are broken off by reaching deep into the medium-sized plant at spaced intervals. The small holes that are created promote air circulation and help blow out decayed leaves that collect in the interior crotches of the plant. Nectria, a fungus, gets its start in these leaves and its mycelium eventually penetrate the moist bark of the plant causing die back.

If annual harvesting of box branches is not sufficient

to keep the interior branches clear, collected leaves may be shaken or vacuumed from the interior of the plant before each growing season. New growth will soon conceal any noticeable holes that plucking may cause. It is more likely that no change in appearance will be noticed in the dense foliage even after plucking.

The American box, with its more open form and rapid growth, may need shearing or pruning back each year, once its desirable size is reached. This is best done in early spring in colder parts of the region so that new growth may harden adequately.

Boxwoods are not free of pests, but only a few pests are troublesome. The boxwood leaf miner and red spider mite are most common. The boxwood psylla make their presence known in early spring when new growth begins to cup or curl, but they do no lasting damage. The other two are difficult to control in the dense foliage because they feed in or on the undersides of the leaves. It is not easy to time the spraying of the miners as they emerge from the leaf in the middle of spring. However, repeated applications of Bioneem or a systemic insecticide like Orthene at the suggested intervals will control both pests. Keeping boxwood well watered during heat spells and drought will help prevent spider mite outbreaks. In the past, the boxwood nematode has appeared in damaging numbers to attack the roots of boxwood in some areas of Washington.

Slats or snow fencing laid on frames over large boxwood prevent heavy snow loads from causing splitting of branches or separation in the middle of the plant. Burlap creates a windbreak in more exposed areas that prevents wind-burning of frozen foliage.

A more serious form of winter injury stems from rapid changes in the weather. Whenever there is a mild fall followed by a sharp freeze, boxwood will sustain serious injury. Cultivating, fertilizing, and watering keeps these border plants in a softer condition and more vulnerable to winter injury. If small, these boxwood might be covered with burlap cloches laid over wire. Overgrown boxwood, like yew, can be severely cut back when dormant, and will eventually leaf out with new growth. Sheet composting in early fall, rather than fertilization, seems to provide the best rate of recovery from freeze injury. (Sheet composting: applying finished compost as a 2 inch deep mulch). But re-growth can take up to 2 years.

CAMELLIA
(Camellia japonica, sasanqua and oleifera hybrids)
Uses: Greenhouse specimen, protected foundation planting, cut flowers
Plant: Spring/early fall
Height: 3 to 10 ft.
Blooms: Spring, fall, or winter
Fruit: Not common
Distance: 3 to 6 ft.

Soil: Well-drained, acid, enriched
Exposure: Light shade. Singly after flowering or winter damage

Varieties currently recommended by growers:
C. Kumasaka—rose pink, medium rose form double to peony form. Vigorous compact upright growth. Kumasaka Variegated—rose pink blotched white.
C. Chandlerii elegans—red and white variegated.
C. Berenice Boddy—light pink with deep pink under petals, medium semi-double. Vigorous upright growth, makes a good espalier.
C. Dr. Tinsley—very pale pink at base to deeper pink at the edge with reverse side flesh pink, medium semi-double. Compact upright growth.
C. Governor Mouton—Oriental red, sometimes blotched white, medium semi-double to loose peony form. Vigorous upright growth.
C. Magnoliaflora—bluish pink, medium semi-double. Medium compact growth. Other forms: C. Peach Blossom—light pink.
C. Mathotiana—Crimson, crimson with purple cast, large to very large rose form to formal double. Vigorous compact upright growth. Rosea Superba—rose pink.
Fall blooming: C. Polar Ice—white, peony; 'Snow Flurry','Winter Snow','Winters Charm' (lavender pink), 'Winters Water Lily' (double).

No doubt there are many who think Washington is too far north for the culture of most camellias out of doors. After two decades of mild weather that saw plantings expand in the region, two disastrous winters killed 90 percent of the

existing shrubs and renewed research for hybrids that can be reliably grown in our warmer areas.

Currently the leading contenders are fall-blooming crosses between oliefera and sasanqua developed by Dr. William Ackerman of the USDA. Many other lovely varieties, some of them developed locally, are suitable for cool greenhouse culture, where their late winter bloom makes a spectacular display.

Grown outdoors, the camellia needs to make its growth early in order that the new wood will have ample time to mature before cold weather. For this reason, feeding should be done right after bloom, particularly if organic fertilizers are used. Quickly available chemical fertilizers may be safely applied up to the first of June, perhaps July, but that will depend upon the location.

The Camellia japonica does not generally withstand full sun in winter or summer. It thrives best in partial shade as provided by a northern exposure, sparse plantings, or from large trees whose branches have been removed to a height of about 20 feet. Morning sun is most harmful because during the winter it thaws out the camellias too quickly. The afternoon sun is better. Planting camellias on the northwest side of the house is preferable provided there is some wind protection.

Other winter protection need be nothing more than a good thick mulch over the root area, obtained by adding more compost or pine needles or bark mulch to the summer mulch. Protection from strong winds such as given by a burlap screen or a few pine boughs is necessary.

The beginning camellia grower has more trouble with planting than with any other phase of culture. The camellias are very sensitive to deep planting so the old saying that "one inch too deep will make them sulk and two inches too deep will cause them to die" is a good rule to keep in mind. Experienced growers prepare planting holes several weeks in

advance, filling them with a mixture of equal parts of sand, loam, and peat moss so the soil will be settled by planting time. In planting they place the root ball so that it extends at least an inch or two above the ground level, filling in and around with the same soil mixture.

Where hardpan or other factors cause poor drainage, many growers prepare a raised planting bed, placing the root ball on the surface of the ground and surrounding it with the recommended soil mixture to the top of the root ball and extending it at least three feet on all sides, edged with bricks or stones.

Once planted, the whole area is deeply mulched with coarse materials such as partially rotted leafmold, bark mulch, compost, or pine needles. Such a mulch should be maintained at all times. In the winter pieces of brush may be used to hold fallen leaves and to keep them from matting. Mulches that crust or shed water should be avoided.

The camellias seem to need less acid soil than the azalea. Because the camellia is very sensitive to soil moisture it must have good drainage; but on the other hand it cannot withstand drought, thus requiring more care as to watering.

New plants should be watered thoroughly once a week during dry spells. Established plants require less watering except in time of prolonged droughts. Sprinkling of the foliage, however, on hot summer evenings is beneficial to plant and flower bud development. Also be certain that the root zone does not dry out during our cold dry winters. Spray water on the plants only when the temperature is above freezing.

Prune to shape leggy plants, to control size, to renew vigor of older plants, or to remove weak and dead branches. Cut back to a leaf or growth bud, to a larger branch, or to the main trunk as closely as possible. Paint larger cuts (½ inch or more) with tree dressing. Heavy pruning should be done in the spring before new growth, or in the fall. Insect and disease injury so far has not proved a serious problem in this region although some growers have reported wax scale, and some have reported the peony scale on their camellias.

The varieties listed above are considered the most dependable after the recent disastrous winters. In addition to C. japonica, a number of gardeners are growing C. sasanqua, a fall bloomer that makes an attractive shrub or hedge plant for the warmer areas of the region. While a free bloomer, the sasanqua is only for garden display, as the flowers fall quickly if cut. Sasanqua and japonica culture are the same.

COTONEASTER
(Evergreen Cotoneaster)
Uses: Border, rock garden, espalier, specimen, groundcover
Plant: Spring/Fall
Height: 1-10 ft.
Blooms: Spring, inconspicuous
Fruits: Red, black—showy
Distance: 2-8 ft.

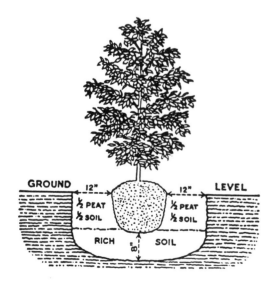

GROUND 12"   12" LEVEL
½ PEAT   ½ PEAT
½ SOIL   ½ SOIL
RICH   SOIL

Soil: Ordinary well-drained garden loam
Exposure: Sun/light shade
Prune: Spring
Species:

C. dammeri—Bearberry, semi-evergreen, fast spreader; varieties: C.'Coral Beauty', free-fruiting; C. 'Lowfast', rapid, low spreader; C. 'Skogholm', best dark green leaves; C. 'Royal Beauty', tightly branched.

C. apicultas—Cranberry, largest red berries, semi-evergreen, 3 ft. spread.

C. congestus—C. Pyrenees, evergreen, 3 ft. spread.

C. Salicifolia Repens—Willowleaf, evergreen groundcover; varieties: C. 'Emerald Green,' tightly branched; C. 'Scarlet Leader' hugs ground.

C. Microphylla—Small leaved, 3 ft. scarlet, semi-green.

The cotoneasters are useful shrubs in many situations. Their small glossy-leaved foliage, which attains attractive fall colors, and their showy fruits make them desirable. Most kinds of cotoneasters have a graceful habit of growth and several are evergreen or semi-evergreen in our area.

With few exceptions the creeping cotoneasters are the most commonly grown here. A few, such as the Spreading and Diel's, are to be found in public plantings. Most cotoneasters are planted in full sun although they will tolerate light shade.

Given average garden soil they do better than in one so rich that it stimulates excessive growth. In the case of C. horizontalis rich soil is dangerous because it produces succulent growth susceptible to destructive fire blight disease.

The bountiful supply of berries, one of the most attractive features of the cotoneasters, is enjoyed by squirrels who cut off the branches and carry them to a safe perch where they can dine in leisure.

Scale insects occasionally attack the cotoneaster and must be controlled with a dormant spray. Fire blight, infrequent in its attacks, turns foliage and terminal twigs black. Remove the infected branches by cutting 3-4 inches below the visible infection, being careful to dip the shears in a sterilizing solution between cuts and to discard the infected pieces.

Propagation is by cuttings, layers and seeds. Pot-grown plants transplant most successfully although nursery practice is for ball and burlap for large specimens.

HOLLY
(Evergreen Ilex, crenata, opaca et al)
Uses: Specimen, border, hedge, foundation planting
Plant: Spring/August-September
Height: 3-50 ft.
Blooms: Spring, inconspicuous
Fruits: Yellow, red, orange or black
Distance: 3-20 ft.
Soil: Acid, enriched with leafmold or compost, moist

Prune: As needed at Christmas or early spring
Species:

American holly (ilex opaca)—'Miss Helen', 'Jersey Knight' (male), 'Greenleaf', 'Jersey Princess', 'Wyetta.'

Japanese holly (ilex crenata)—microphylla, Helleri, Stokes, Hetzi, Compacta, repandens, Cherokee, convexa (male), fastigiata, 'Chesapeake', 'Green Luster', 'Highlander', 'Petite Point', rotundifolia.

English holly (ilex aquifolium)—Argento, marginata (variegated), Balkans, Boulder Creek, ferox aurea, Goldcoast, San Gabriel, Sparkler, Earlygold. (I. x altaclarensis), J.C. Van Tol.

Chinese holly (ilex cornuta)—Burford, Dwarf Burford, Rotunda, 'D'or', 'Dazzler', Carrisa, 'Needlepoint', 'China Girl', 'China Boy'.

Holly hybrids—'Nellie R. Stevens', 'Edward J. Stevens' (male), 'Brilliant', 'Aquipern' (male), 'Foster #2', 'San Jose', 'Sparkleberry', 'Apollo' (male), 'Blue Prince', 'Blue Princess', 'Blue Stallion', 'Blue Angel', 'Dragon Lady'.

Miscellaneous species— glabra compacta; I. glabra 'Ivory Queen'; I. pernyi; I. verticillata, Winter Green'; I. serrata; I. decidua; I. pedunculosa.

The hollies offer an almost unexpected field to the average gardener. He knows the American holly, but thinks of it as a tree, although it makes an excellent hedge plant. The dwarf forms of the Japanese holly are useful in foundation plantings. Lightly trimmed, it becomes an effective hedge plant, adapted to sun or shade. The Chinese holly has excellent foliage and makes a splendid small specimen in the protected garden. The Convexleaf variety of the Japanese holly has a much better foliage value than does the species; one of the most popular is Compacta. In recent years a number of the hollies have been selected because of superior foliage, fruiting habit, or for some other characteristic and have been propagated as named cultivars.

Hollies do best in a soil that has been well-supplied with peat moss, leafmold or acid compost. Avoid lime and use fertilizers, such as Hollytone, that are especially prepared for hollies and other acid-loving evergreens.

The Winterberry, a deciduous holly often cultivated for its berries, is adapted to the moister situations. Although lacking winter foliage, it makes a grand display of fruit all winter.

Hollies are dioecious, that is the berries are borne by the female tree, if the blossoms are fertilized by a non-berry-bearing male. For this reason gardeners desiring holly berries should purchase female plants and one male for each species or their cultivars. For female hybrids buy one of the parent males or preferably a male hybrid counterpart. This is important because some species flower at different seasons. A male tree within a block or so may serve. Otherwise it may be necessary to graft a male branch into one of the females; or during the flowering season a few branches from a male tree may be hung (in bottles of water) in the trees whose blossoms are to be fertilized.

The holly trees are not easy to transplant from the wild unless they have been root-pruned, and wild plants are usually inferior to named cultivars. Nursery-grown trees should be planted in the early spring before new growth appears, or in the fall. Container grown plants need very little pruning and can be planted here through October. The American holly should be planted on grade no deeper than they were before.

The hollies are not immune to disease or insect pest. The holly-leaf miner disfigures the foliage of the American holly, but it may be controlled by spraying with Orthene—just before and just after flowering, so as not to affect the pollinating bees. A leaf spot may attack a planting, but if detected in time, can be controlled by removing and burning infected leaves. Spraying or dusting with fermate will prevent the leaf-spot spores from entering the foliage, but will not kill spores that are already in the leaf.

Propagation is by cutting, seeds, and grafting. The new superior named cultivars are raised from cuttings or are grafted on seedlings.

MAHONIA—OREGON GRAPE HOLLY
(M. repens or aquifolium atropurpurea)
Height: 2 to 3 feet
Spread: 3 to 10 feet
Exposure: Light to moderate shade
Soil: Slightly acid, needs humus
Moisture: Moderate
Plant: April
Blooms: April-May with yellow racemes
Fruit: Oval silver-blue clusters
Uses: Foreground in shrub borders, and foundation planting

Mahonia is a perfect plant for shady places and heavy soil. Its blooms and berries are showy and long-lasting, and the evergreen foliage is attractive in all seasons.

Its common name refers to the large clusters of oval blueberry-colored fruits that last through the fall. Because the plant is so showy it can be used by an entrance or to bring out a dark corner. It tolerates temperatures down to 13° F. and can be planted bare root.

Compacta is an excellent 3 foot variety; other species include the upright M. bealei with coarse texture and large leaves, and the groundcover form, M. repens with leaves similar to M. aquifolium.

This useful low shrub spreads by suckering and benefits greatly from pruning every two or three years to promote the spread of new growth and a compact appearance. It needs mulching to protect the root zone. The atropurpurea variety of mahonia aquifolium has foliage that turns a lovely purple to bronze-red in winter.

NANDINA
(Nandina domestica—Heavenly Bamboo, Chinese Sacred Bamboo)
Height: 8 ft.
Spread: 3 ft.
Exposure: Sun, moderate shade
Moisture: Moderate
Soil: Well-drained garden loam
Plant: Spring or fall
Distance: 4-5 ft.
Blooms: July
Fruit: Conspicuous red berries, fall and winter
Uses: Accent, foundation

Nandina is an unbranched shrub related to barberry. It is most conspicuous during the fall and winter when its red berries hang in large clusters (must be in a protected situation in the suburbs).

Varieties include N. domestica compacta with its mounding form and the new 'Harbor Dwarf' that is very dense.

PHOTINIA
(Photinia serrulata, Fraseri—Evergreen Photinia)
Height: 6-25 ft.
Spread: 8 ft.
Exposure: Sun/shade
Soil: Rich in humus
Plant: March/April-September
Distance: 10-15 ft.
Blooms: May, white, flat heads
Fruit: Bright red berries
Uses: Specimen, foundation, hedge

The evergreen photinia is a rapid growing shrub or small tree with luxurious foliage; the blooms are large enough to show and the fruit display is good. It needs no protection in the city, but in the suburbs is should be planted near the house. The new foliage is a reddish bronze.

Fraseri is a desirable small form, 6-10 feet high, with lovely pink-red new foliage, and red berries in the fall.

PIERIS
(Pieris japonica, Japanese Andromeda)
Uses: Shrub border, foundation planting, specimen
Plant: Spring/fall
Height: 4-10 feet
Blooms: March-April
Fruit: Insignificant
Distance: 4 to 6 feet
Soil: Acid, slightly sandy, enriched with humus
Exposure: Partial shade, protected from wind
Prune: Little required

Species:

P. japonica compacta, 3 ft.; P. japonica 'Dorthy Wycoff', 5 ft., red buds pink flowers

P. japonica 'Red Mill', best new red growth, 6 ft., white flowers

P. japonica 'Valley Rose', 6 ft., white flowers

P. polinifolia—bog andromeda, 1 ft.

P. forestii 'Forest Flame', bright new growth, large panicles, hardy

P. japonica, smaller-sized

P. japonica variegata, gray-green foliage with creamy margins

The andromeda is an increasingly popular shrub for shady settings because of its early long-bloom period and evergreen foliage. With its mounding, upright, spreading habit, it makes a graceful backdrop for spring-flowering bulbs and is compatible with azaleas and rhododendron.

Because it is slow-growing it requires little pruning, and it is wise to obtain a variety with a size that fits your spot. Pieris appreciates a mulch of rotted oak leaves or acid pine needles.

In a dry year it may be attacked by spider mites, so keep it well-watered during a drought, as you would azaleas, and flush the spider mites with a strong blast of water up through the foliage, or use a miticide.

PORTUGUESE LAUREL
(Prunus lusitanica—Cherry-Laurel)
Height: 15-20 ft.
Spread: 6-10 ft.
Exposure: Sun/shade
Soil: Rich in humus, moist
Plant: March/April-September
Distance: 8 ft.
Blooms: May, white
Fruit: Similar to choke cherry clusters
Uses: Hedge, foliage

The cherry-laurel is a rapid growing broadleaf

evergreen, known formerly as P. laurocerasus. Sometimes used as a small tree or a clipped hedge, its glossy foliage does not winter-burn. P. 'Otto Luykens' is larger, more horizontal, with dark green foliage.

PRIVET—LIGUSTRUM
(Evergreen Ligustrum species)
Uses: Hedge, tall background
Plant: Fall/spring
Height: 5-15 ft.
Blooms: July-September
Fruits: Black, blue-purple
Distance: 1-3 ft.
Soil: Ordinary garden loam
Exposure: Sun/light shade
Prune: As needed
Species:
L. lucidum
L. vulgare—European privet, 15 ft.
L. ibolium—Ibolium, 8-10 ft.
L. amurense—Amur, 15 ft.
L. quihou—Quihou, 6 ft.
L. Japonica—Japanese, 3-15 ft. (most common)

The privets are a group of evergreen or semi-evergreen shrubs widely used for hedges, tall screens, and background plantings. They withstand unfavorable soil, shade and city conditions better than most similar types of shrubs. Some may be pruned to a narrow hedge. The small-leaved privets hold their foliage well into winter in this area and seldom suffer freeze injury. When injured, they need only to be cut back to live wood. The privets are easily transplanted either in spring or fall. For quick recovery it is well to cut them back almost to the ground.

If left untrimmed, most of the privets produce small racemes of white flowers during the summer, and these are followed in the fall by small fruits.

The Japanese and Quihou privets are considered to have exceptional landscape value here, while the Amur River species is the most cold hardy.

Privets are occasionally attacked by fungus diseases and scale insects. Both are normally controlled with a dormant strength lime-sulphur spray during the winter months after the foliage has fallen. All privets are easily propagated by hardwood cuttings.

PYRACANTHA—FIRETHORN
(Pyracantha coccinea Lalandii)
Uses: Specimen, hedge, shrub border
Plant: Spring
Height: 6-20 ft.
Blooms: May-inconspicuous
Fruits: Yellow, orange or red berries
Distance: 3-6 ft.
Soil: Well-drained, neutral

Exposure: Sun/light shade

Prune: Spring

Species:

P. coccinea lalandii 'Monrovia'—superior upright growth, orange-yellow berries;

P. coccinea 'Lowboy'—bushy to 4 ft., orange berries;

P. x 'Navajo'—compact, 4-6 ft., orange-red berries;

P. x 'Teton'—strong pyramidal growth, yellow-orange berries;

P. x 'Ruby Mound'—mounding habit, red berries;

P. x 'Mohave'—to 15 ft., orange-red berries, evergreen.

The firethorns are one of our really attractive evergreen shrubs. They are useful in the shrub border, for training against a wall, or clipped to form a hedge. Their evergreen foliage, brilliant fruits, and thorns make them especially useful. The small flowers borne in the spring are sometimes nipped by frosts destroying their fruits for that year. A good display of fruits is especially showy and catches the eye of the gardener seeking attractive, interesting shrubs long before he notes the foliage.

The firethorns should not be given a too-protected situation, one in which the wood fails to ripen early in the fall and hence is subject to freeze injury. The variety Lalandeii, long considered the most hardy, is commonly available as pot plants from the nurseries. However, there are other species that may be used in this area. The berries of all varieties usually persist into winter.

Because of the interest in red fruits, there are a number of named varieties available. Many reds are grown here, but all are subject to limited or severe damage most seasons. There is no reliable red-fruited firethorn that will withstand temperatures below 20° Fahrenheit. However, the National Arboretum has released to commercial nurseries a hardy red-fruited variety named Mohave that is resistant to fire blight and scab and comes nearest to a good red; there is also Shawnee, a 10-foot, yellow-fruited variety that is resistant to scab disease.

Firethorns sometimes suffer from fireblight (as do cotoneasters) and lacebug (as do azaleas). Treatments are described under the latter plants.

Propagation is by cuttings, layering, and grafting.

RHODODENDRON
(Rhododendron species and hybrids)

Uses: Shrub border, foundation, specimen.

Plant: Spring.

Height: 1 to 20 feet

Blooms: March-June.

Fruits: None.

Distance: 3 to 6 feet.

Soil: Enriched with leafmold, peat moss, compost.

Exposure: Shade, part sun.

Prune: Cutting flowers sufficient.

Species:

R. cariolanum—Carolina, 4-6 ft., pink, sun-light shade.

R. catawbiense—Catawba, 6-9 ft., rosy lavender, sun-shade.

R. keiski—Keisk, 2-3 ft., yellow.

R. maximum—Rosebay, 6-15 ft., white to pinkish, shade.

R. minus—Piedmont, 6-15 ft., lilac-purple, shade.

R. yakusimanum—4 ft., white-rose, sun-shade.

R. racemosum—Mayflower, 1 ft., light rose, shade.

R. smirnowii—Smirnow, 6 ft., rosy-lilac, shade.

R. macronulatum—Korean, 4-5 ft., lilac-rose, sun-shade.

R. fortunei—12 ft., lavender pink.

R. makinoi, 3-4 ft., narrow indumented leaves, pink to white.

R. Metternichii—4-6 ft., pink, indumented.

R. minus—Piedmont, 6-15 ft., lilac purple, semi-shade.

Variety	Color	Height	Hardiness
Indispensable:			
Roseum Elegans	soft rose	1	M
Best Baker's Dozen:			
Nova Zembla	dark red	2	M
Mrs. W.R. Coe	deep pink	2	M
County of York	white	2	T
Janet Blair	blush	2	T
Cadis	pale pink	2	T
Caroline	lavender pink	1	T
Scintillation	pink	2	M
Gigi	rose red	2	M
David Gable	pink	2	T
Blue Ensign	lavender blue	2	L
PJM	lavender purple	1	L
Vulcan	fiery red	3	L
Lord Robert	deep red	2	M

Also Good:

Album Elegans	white	1	T
Golden Star	yellow	3	M
A. Bedford	blue mauve	3	LM
Marybelle	peach pink	2	M
Mary Fleming	pink yellow	2	L
Windbeam	pale pink	2	L
Tom Everett	pink	2	M

Fahrenheit Hardiness Ratings: 1—down to-20°;
  2—down to-15°; 3—down to-5°.
Height: L—3-4 feet; M—4-6 feet; T—over 6 feet.
(Recommended by Donald Hyatt; Dr. Henry Skinner; Fred Coe; the late Albert Behnke; and others.)

There are some 850 known species of rhododendrons and 2,000 varieties to choose from. Those listed have the best floral characteristics and foliage value and have been grown here successfully, although at any given time some few may not be available commercially. Many of the best varieties here are Dexter hybrids, which are medium to tall plants in a full range of colors. Some of the most reliable plants for the area are the Gable hybrids developed in Pennsylvania.

Species rhododendron include many from the Far East with hardy and unusual foliage of great ornamental value. Some of these are dwarf forms suitable for the smaller garden.

Rhododendrons need cold weather for complete dormancy, and, as a group, like some shade. A few cannot withstand full sunlight. This is true of the one most commonly planted, the Rosebay, which is native to the Alleghenies, where it thrives in deep shade and moist soils. The Catawba and the Caroline types and their hybrids can withstand considerable direct sun, although they are likely to be at their best in partial or light shade. A moist, yet well-drained, soil freely supplied with leafmold or compost is needed for good growth. Avoid planting in heavy Washington clay soil unless the whole area has been so extensively or deeply dug that water cannot remain standing about the plant roots. Rhododendrons are shallow-rooted and must be planted practically on top of the soil, in raised berms. They are an understory plant and appreciate protection from strong winds.

A winter mulching of oak leaves, chopped hardwood bark, or pine needles is beneficial. The mulch should remain during the summer months to keep the soil cool. An oak leaf mulch helps to maintain the soil acidity needed for good growth.

If these ideal cultural conditions (shade, moisture, protection from injurious wind, good soil drainage, and a generous mulch are observed), there is little danger of diseases attacking the planting. Lacking in this care, there is some likelihood of soil-borne disease, and insect attack. The lace-bug, the most common pest, is controlled by spraying larvae with soap spray or orthene in the late spring and early summer. A disease of the open flowers can become a problem during the warm, moist seasons, so early flowering varieties are advisable. Control of petal blight is the same as for azaleas.

Roseum elegans is the most commonly planted variety in this area. If a gardener can provide the proper conditions so that this specimen thrives, it is a good indication that others can be successfully grown.

If a rhododendron has wilted or died, root rot is a likely culprit and so is the rhododendron borer, that attacks the roots of older plants. In either case, no further replacements should be planted in that same spot.

Propagation is not easy without special equipment. The rooting of cuttings and cloning by tissue culture are the methods employed by commercial growers. If the proper temperature and soil moisture conditions are met, the home grower can also try layering favorite specimens.

EVERGREEN GROUND COVERS

ABELIA, PROSTRATE GLOSSY
(Abelia grandiflora prostrata)
This is a prostrate form of the glossy abelia (covered in the shrub section below) that is useful as a bank cover or as the foreground in a shrub border. It has small glossy leaves that tend to get a purple cast in the winter. It is tolerant of a variety of soils and blooms from late spring until frost.

BEARBERRY
(Arctostaphylos uva-ursi)
Height: 12 to 15 inches
Spread: 3 to 4 feet
Exposure: Light shade
Soil: Improved garden loam
Moisture: Well-drained, moderate
Plant: March-April/September
Blooms: April-May
Fruit: Red
Uses: Ground cover and rock garden

A compact evergreen ideal for the shady bank, this member of the cotoneaster family is affected by few pests. The tiny white flowers are borne along the branches of attractive foliage (bronze-red in the winter) and are followed by red berries that are a great favorite with birds. It makes a lovely cascade form spilling over a wall.

DWARF JAPANESE HOLLY
(Ilex crenata helleri)
Height: 1 to 2 feet
Spread: 2 to 5 feet
Exposure: Sun, or light shade for variegated cultivars
Soil: Variable

Moisture: Can not withstand drought
Plant: March-April
Blooms: Inconspicuous
Fruit: Small black
Uses: Rock garden specimen or foreground in shrub border

This useful holly has small oval leaves, keeps its foliage color, forms a low hummock of vegetation, and is slow growing. The variegated forms with new golden foliage need richer soil and light shade to thrive.

CREEPING JUNIPER
(Juniperus horizontalis, 'Wiltonii', 'Bar Harbor' etc)
Height: 4 to 8 inches
Spread: 6 feet
Exposure Sunny
Soil: Well drained, various soils
Moisture: Moderate to dry
Plant: March-April/September
Distance: 4 to 5 feet
Uses: Ground cover

This excellent ground cover is widely planted in the Washington area to hold banks and give a tapered finished appearance to landscaped berms. These are two of a number of fine low varieties useful for covering the smaller hot dry slope. To some degree it replaces the higher Compact Andorra and Sargent junipers that are from 15 to 18 inches high. These are still useful as foreground or foundation plantings, particularly the Andorra where a silver-purple winter foliage is desirable. The Sargent juniper is bright steel blue in the winter and blue green in the summer. It is free of most of the insect pests that sometimes attack the horizontalis forms here. Take your pick.

SKIMMIA
(S. japonica)
Height: 1 to 3 feet
Spread: 1 to 3 feet
Exposure: Shade
Soil: Improved garden loam, acid
Plant: March-April/September
Blooms: Blush-pink panicles in April-May
Fruit: Shiny red clusters in fall
Uses: Low shrub border or foreground.

This excellent shrub is ideal for local acid soils. A male is need to pollinate the female plant. The blush pink flowers are lovely against dark foliage. Skimmia is hardy to 4° Fahrenheit.

HIMALAYAN SWEET BOX
(Sarcococca hookerana var. 'humilis')
Height: 6 inches to 2 feet
Spread: 12 to 18 inches
Exposure: Shade
Soil: rich in humus
Plant: March/April, September
Blooms: Early spring
Flowers: Inconspicuous
Fruit: Black
Uses: Ground cover, facing shrub

The sweet box has fragrant flowers that bloom in late winter, and shiny lance-shaped leaves. The sarcococca is an excellent ground cover in shady situations, but is tall enough for use at the front of a mixed border. It does well in a moist, rich soil, although winter mulching is advisable in this area.

The Himalayan variety recommended here is the most dwarf form. An ideal woodland garden shrub, it will not tolerate alkaline soil.

INSPIRATION:
The Gotelli Collection of Dwarf and Slow-Growing Conifers, The National Arboretum, New York Avenue and Bladensburg Road, NE, Washington, D.C. (202) 475-4815.
Orland E. White Arboretum, at Blandy Experimental Farm, off Route 50, Boyce, Virginia. Write for guided tour.

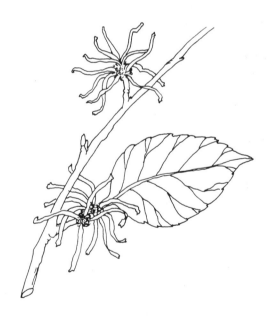

DECIDUOUS FLOWERING SHRUBS

The selection of flowering shrubs for the home grounds, foundation plantings, shrub borders, background, and specimen plantings is normally made from catalog descriptions. Seldom is the shrub viewed with a critical eye to determine its usefulness in a particular situation from the standpoint of soil, exposure, moisture, height, season of bloom, and many other relevant factors.

Is the shrub subject to numerous insects and diseases? Can it be transplanted easily? Does it have good landscape value after its season of bloom is over? What value does it have in winter? These are examples of the questions that the gardener seeking to improve the appearance of his grounds should ask about each plant under consideration.

There are hundreds of shrubs to select from. In the Baltimore-Washington region a great many northern as well as southern shrubs can be grown with a degree of success. This is the southern limit for the lilac and the northern limit for the crape myrtle and the House hydrangea. Some kinds are classed as tender in this area, but if grown under favorable conditions will survive our winters.

The shrubs described below are those generally planted. Each garden has its particular problems, and each owner should consider how well a species or variety meets them. The information listed and the brief comments are, of necessity, in general terms. Most nurserymen are more than willing to answer questions and provide more specific details than can be given within the scope of this book.

ABELIA BUSH ARBUTUS
(Abelia grandiflora)
Uses: Shrub border, specimen, hedge
Plant:: Spring/September
Distance: 3 to 6 feet.
Soil: Rich, moist
Prune: Spring
Species:
A. grandiflora, 6 feet, white, June-Fall, semi-evergreen
A. 'Francis Mason,' variegated leaves, 3 feet, white, semi-evergreen
A. 'Edward Goucher,' 2 feet, pink, June-Fall, semi-evergreen

The abelias are one of the most useful of the ornamental shrubs. They may be used as specimen plants in the deciduous or evergreen shrub border, or they may be used as a clipped hedge. They are, however, subject to winter dieback when planted in a too-protected situation.

Unlike most evergreens they do not require a highly acid soil, but will do fairly well in a sweet soil, and are tolerant of light shade. If supplied with a medium amount of moisture and plant food, they will provide abundant bloom and good foliage.

Propagation is by cuttings and seed. In warm climates they may be layered. Cuttings may be either hardwood or soft-wood; those taken in October may be rooted

in a hotbed or propagating frame protected from freezing. Young plants will need protection the following winter from freezing cold.

The abelia is comparatively free from attack by insects and disease. A prostrate form is sometimes used as a ground cover; it grows to a height of 18-24 inches.

BARBERRY
(Deciduous Berberis—B. thunbergi and species)
Uses: Hedges, specimens
Plant: Spring, fall
Distance: 2 to 4 feet
Soil: Ordinary garden loam
Exposure: Sun, light shade
Prune: Spring
Species and Varieties:
B. thunbergi—Japanese Barberry, 4-5 ft.. red-fruited, deciduous
B. thunbergi atropurpurea—Redleaf Japanese Barberry. 5 ft., deciduous .
B. thunbergi aurea—'Gold Barberry.' yellow leaves, 3 ft., deciduous .
B. thunbergi atropurpurea 'Crimson Pygmea.' red leaves, compact to 2 ft.. deciduous.

The Japanese barberry, an easily propagated shrub, may be trimmed to almost any form desired. Frequent shearing makes it so compact that it will block a dog. The small leaves and twiggy growth give the Japanese barberry landscape value as a transitional shrub to stand between evergreens and deciduous shrubs.

Barberries do not need any special care or soil, but like most plants, they will make better growth, produce more abundant crops of fruits, and attain greater vigor if fed and cared for. However, gardeners seldom have need for plants that soon outgrow their situation and this reason heavy feeding after the first year or two is unnecessary.

Insects and diseases on the barberry are comparatively rare in the Washington area. Most people look upon them as being foolproof.

New varieties of the red-leaved Japanese barberry are Crimson Pygmy and Rosey Glow.

BEAUTYBERRY
(Callicarpa americana)
Uses: Berries, shrub for border
Plant: Spring/fall
Distance: 4 to 6 feet
Soil: Ordinary, well-drained garden loam
Height: 3-6 feet
Blooms: Inconspicuous
Fruit: Violet
Exposure: Sun/light shade
Prune: Spring, to remove winter-killed twigs
Species:
C. americana—Beautyberry, French Mulberry, 6 ft., reddish violet.
C. dichotoma (purpurea)—Purple beautyberry, 4 ft., lilac-violet.
C. Japonica—Japanese beautyberry, 5 ft., violet.
C. bodinieri, var. giraldi—Girald (Chinese) beautyberry, 10 ft., violet.

The beautyberries are grown primarily for their excellent fruit display during the fall and early winter. Ordinarily the fruits, which are produced in clusters along the slender branches, are retained well into the winter.

While some gardeners will call them too tender for this area because of winter-kill, this is not a disadvantage because the beautyberry should be pruned rather severely in the early spring to promote new growth. The fruits are produced upon the new wood that heavy pruning and feeding stimulates and which is needed for the best winter display of fruits.

The American Beautyberry, a native of the South Atlantic states, is the most widely grown, but the Japanese kind is the most available in nurseries.

The beautyberries are relatively free from insects and diseases and are undemanding as to soil and exposure. Generally, they are given too much protection and suffer winter injury. In less protected situations the wood matures earlier and suffers less injury.

BUTTERFLY BUSH
(Buddleia davidii)
Uses: Shrub border, specimen, cut flowers
Plant: March-April
Height: 4-10 feet
Blooms: June-September
Fruits: None
Distance: 4-10 feet
Soil: Rich, moist
Exposure: Sun/light shade
Prune: Spring, cut back Davidi varieties severely
Species:
D. Magnifica—Oxeye, 4 ft., violet-purple
D. 'Superba,' 5 ft., violet purple
D. 'Veitchiana,' 5-6 ft., bright mauve
D. 'Royal Purple,' 6 ft., deep purple
D. 'Black Knight,' 4-5 ft., Royal blue
D. 'Daybreak,' lavender-pink
D. 'Empire Blue,' deep blue
D. 'Orchid Beauty,' 4 ft., orchid
D. 'Charming,' 7-8 ft., pink
D. 'Dubonnet,' 7-8 ft., purple
D. 'White Bouquet,' 7-8 ft., white
D. 'Petite Indigo,' 3-4 ft., lilac-blue
D. 'Petite Plum,' 3-4 ft., plum

The buddleias, or summer lilacs, are useful summer bloomers in the shrub border or as specimen plants for the lawn. The species are stronger growers than the newer improved-varieties. All are good as cut flowers, the long, pointed, terminal spikes lasting quite well indoors.

The buddleias do quite well in full sun, and if tree competition is not too severe, will grow in light shade. They do best in a rich, moist soil but seem to thrive in ordinary garden loam.

They should be cut back severely in the spring to keep them from becoming tall and leggy. The pruning also stimulates branching that most of them need; otherwise, they become too tall for the smaller yard. The newer varieties are for the most part low growing, and when well-branched make attractive shrubs.

Spent blooms should be removed often to maintain flowering during the late summer and early fall months. Also, it helps to avoid the numerous seedlings that spring up where seed is allowed to mature. Seedlings are seldom as useful as the named varieties.

Propagation of named varieties is by cuttings taken in the early fall and protected from freeze injury during the first winter.

The butterfly bushes, so named because they attract butterflies, are relatively free from insect pests and diseases.

CORALBERRY—SNOWBERRY
(Symphoricarpos)
Uses: Bank cover, winter value of fruits
Plant: Spring/fall
Height: 3-6 feet
Blooms: Inconspicuous
Fruits: Coralberry—dark red; Snowberry—snow white
Distance: 2-3 feet
Soil: Ordinary garden loam
Exposure: Shade/ sun

Prune: Spring
Species:
S. albus laevigatus— Snowberry, 5-6 ft., White hedge, 5 ft.
S. albus var. pauciflorus—Dwarf Common Snowberry. 3½ ft.
S. orbiculatus—Coralberry 4-6 ft., dark-red berries
S. chenaultii—Chenault Coralberry, 6-8 ft., pink-spotted-white

The common coralberry is the most widely grown member of this group of ornamentals, although both the foliage and the fruits are rather dull. The snowberry, particularly Mother of Pearl, has the most useful growth habit and the berries are interesting.

The common coralberry has such a spreading habit of growth that it is best restricted to banks where it is an excellent soil holder, or to the wild-flower area where its habit of taking over is not so disconcerting. The strong-growing suckers reach out and take root unless removed.

This group of plants thrives in shade or sun and is tolerant of soil and moisture conditions. If properly used it is a most valuable shrub, otherwise it may become a nuisance and a weed.

Occasionally anthracnose attacks the plants and spoils the display of fruits. A dormant lime-sulphur spray, if applied in the early spring, will control this.

DEUTZIA
(Deutzia)
Uses: Shrub border, background, cut flowers
Plant: Fall/spring
Height: 3-10 feet
Blooms: May-June
Fruits: None
Distance: 2-8 feet
Soil: Well-drained loam
Exposure: Sun/light shade
Prune: Spring (after flowering)
Species:
D. gracilis—slender, 3 ft., May, white; Nikko, 2 ft., white
D. rosea—Rosepanicle, 4 ft., May, pink
D. lemoinei—Lemoine, 4-5 ft., May, white; Boule de Neige, 4 ft., May, white
D. scabia—Fuzzy, 9-10 ft., May, white; Pride of Rochester, 9-10 ft., double white-pink

The deutzias are well known to most gardeners and are of easy culture, although they do not thrive in dry soils. A good garden loam is best for them. Normally they are grown in full sun but do best in partial shade.

The smaller growing deutzias have the greatest landscape value because the taller ones tend to be leggy and have dull foliage, hence have little landscape interest beyond their spring flowers.

The slender deutzia tends to be short-lived under neglect. The old wood should be pruned out each year—remove a fourth of the oldest canes each spring. A

highly acid soil does not produce the best growth and an occasional application of ground limestone in the spring is recommended.

The deutzias are subject to two leaf-spot diseases that, should they appear, may be controlled with Bordeaux or a metallic copper fungicide.

Propagation is by softwood arid hardwood cuttings and by layering. The slender deutzia may be divided. The Lemoine hybrids are most suitable for the smaller shrub border. There are several named varieties to choose from, varying somewhat in height, habit of growth and color. Foliage and habit of growth are especially important to landscape value.

FLOWERING QUINCE
(Chaenomeles)
Uses: Shrub border, hedge, fruits
Plant: Spring or Fall
Height: 3-10 feet
Blooms: March-April
Fruits: Greenish-yellow, large
Distance: 4-6 feet
Soil: Ordinary garden loam, deep but not rich
Exposure: Sun/light shade
Prune: Spring (after flowering)
Species:
C. japonica—Japanese flowering quince, 3 ft., March-May, brick red. Minerva—red
C. speciosa—Chinese flowering quince, 8-20 ft., May, light pink
Varieties:
 Jet Trails—white
 Texas Scarlet—scarlet
C. superba 'Cameo'—apricot pink, double
C. superba 'California Pink Beauty'—pink

The flowering quince or japonica is a popular, early spring-flowering shrub. It will often flower in late February or early March during periods of unseasonably mild weather.

The attractive foliage, low growth, and freedom of bloom, as well as ease of division, have contributed much to the popularity of this hardy shrub.

There are scores of varieties listed, mainly because of colors that range from pure white to brick red. Some varieties are lower growing than others.

The quince is of easy culture, thriving in ordinary garden loam, especially if moist. They spread by suckers that come up from the shallow growing roots, and will need to be thinned and controlled if the bush is to be kept within bounds.

Both scale and fire blight attack the quince. The scale is easily controlled with a dormant spray of lime-sulphur. The remedy for fire blight is the same as described for cotoneasters.

Propagation is by root cuttings, the lifting of suckers, and hardwood cuttings. Seedlings are easily produced from the large fruits but may vary widely from the parent plant. Named varieties may be grafted.

Fruits are generally very fragrant and while edible fresh, may be used in the making of quince jelly or the flavoring of other jellies.

FORSYTHIA
(Forsythia)
Uses: Shrub, border, banks
Plant: Spring/fall
Height: 4-10 feet
Blooms: March-April
Fruits: None
Distance: 5-10 feet
Soil: Garden loam
Exposure: Sun
Prune: After flowering
Species:
F. intermedia—Border, 6-8 ft., April-May
F. Suspensa—Weeping, 4-6 ft., March-April

All of the following varieties bloom in April-May: Showy, F. 'Spectabilis', 6-8 ft.; F. 'Lynwood Gold,' 5-7 ft.; F. 'Spring Glory,' 5-7 ft.; F. 'Arnolds Dwarf,' 3-4 ft..
The forsythias probably are as widely planted as any of the early spring-flowering plants. They are one of the earliest of the spring bloomers and are cherished as evidence of returning spring. They are of comparatively easy culture, flourishing in almost all types of soil, thriving in full sun or partial shade, and for the most part untroubled by insects or diseases. Their habit of growth as well as the landscape value of the foliage is good.

While some may say they are too commonplace, it would be difficult to find a better early spring bloomer. The foliage persists late into the fall, oftentimes turning purplish in color. They are easy to transplant.

The forsythia should not be heavily fertilized at any time because heavy feeding stimulates rank growth and the bloom is more widely spaced producing a thinner floral display.

HONEYSUCKLE
(Lonicera)
Uses: Border, background, hedge, vine
Plant: Spring/fall
Height: 4-12 feet
Bloom: April-June
Fruit: Red, yellow, blackish-purple
Distance: 2-10 feet
Soil: Ordinary garden loam
Exposure: Sun/light shade
Prune: Spring (after flowering)
Species:
L. Fragrantissima, 6-8 ft., February, white, fragrant
L. morrowi var. Xanthocarpa, 7-8 ft., May-June, white-yellow
L. tartarica—Tartarian, 10-12 ft., May-June, white-rose, red
L. bella (albida)—var. White Belle, 8-9 ft., May June, white, red
L. Korolkowi—Zabel Honeysuckle, 10-12 ft. May
L. maacki—Amur, l0-15 ft., May, white, red

The honeysuckles are a strong-growing group of shrubs that are not well adapted to the smaller yard.

Most of them are free flowering and fragrant and produce abundant crops of berries that ripen in May and June. The berries remain on the bushes for a comparatively short time as they seem to be a favorite food of several kinds of birds.

The list of honeysuckle species is a long one and in addition there are a considerable number of named varieties that differ from the species in one or more ways. The common Tartarian honeysuckle, a strong growing bush with pink and white flowers, is represented by a dozen or more varieties named because they were more dwarf (low); have yellow flowers, etc.

The honeysuckles thrive in the ordinary garden loam in full sun, or partial shade, and are tolerant of moisture conditions. They seem to be relatively free of insects and diseases.

The honeysuckles are mostly propagated by hardwood cuttings although soft-wood cuttings will be successful for some kinds. Many kinds are commercially propagated by seed.

The **Japanese honeysuckle** (Lonicera japonica) is not listed above because of its rampant invasive growth. It should be considered a dangerous nuisance that will smother plants, shrubs, and small trees. Even if kept under control, the birds scatter the seeds far and wide.

HYDRANGEA
(Hydrangea)

Uses: Specimen shrub border, hedge
Plant: Spring/fall
Height: 3-10 feet
Blooms: June-August
Fruit: None
Distance: 4-6 feet
Soil: Rich moist
Exposure: Sun/light shade
Prune: H. macrophylla after flowering; others in spring
Species:
H. macrophylla—House Hydrangea, 3-6 ft., June-July, pink/blue
H. macrophylla vars.: 'Blue Wave'—blue, sterile; 'Compacta'—soft pink, sterile; 'Mariesii'—pink, sterile; 'Merritts Beauty'—carmine red; 'Trophy'—salmon rose; 'Nikko'—blue; 'Domotoi,' 2-3 ft., double, deep pink, June
H. arborescens—'Smooth H.,' 6 ft., June, white
H. arborscens grandiflora—'Hills of Snow,' 4-5 ft., June, white
H. quercifolia—'Snow Queen', 3-5 ft., June, white/purple
H. paniculata Peegee—Grandiflora, 8-9 ft., August, pink

The hydrangeas are popular, widely planted shrubs although their foliage is rather too coarse and dull to score very highly as landscape material. The large-flowered Peegee hydrangea that flowers in August, produces huge terminal clusters that carry on into the winter. It seems to achieve its distinction because of size rather than usefulness in the shrub border.

The House hydrangea, also called Shiny-leaved, Florists, and French hydrangea, is commonly found throughout this area, although this is the northern limit for its use in the garden. North of here it is grown as a tub plant. There is a hardy variety, Nikko Blue, and also a red-flowering variety, Red Clackamas.

The Oakleaf hydrangea is a native to the South. It is hardy and of interesting leaf-form, and it will tolerate more shade than the Peegee.

Hydrangeas thrive best in a rich, moist soil because they flower on new wood and need to make strong growth each spring after pruning. The House hydrangea will not thrive and produce flowers without an adequate supply of moisture. The House hydrangea requires an acid soil if the blue flowers are desired and a sweet one for pink flowers. The acidity can be increased, and consequently the depth of color, by adding peat moss to the soil, cultivating flowers of sulphur into the soil, or watering with a solution of aluminum sulphate. The acidity is easily neutralized with ground limestone.

The hydrangeas are subject to attack by a number of diseases and insect pests, none of which seem to be serious in this area. However, the leaf spot may be controlled by Bordeaux, the insects with soap sprays or orthene.

Hydrangeas, with the exception of the House hydrangeas, should be thinned in early spring to stimulate strong growth and larger flowers. The House hydrangea is also pruned in the spring, but the pruning consists of removing the dead and weak shoots and the thinning of the remaining canes. Shortening the canes is to cut off the flower buds that form at the end of season's growth. When the terminal buds are injured by freezing or removed by pruning, the season's bloom is lost.

Hydrangeas may be propagated by cuttings, division, layering, and grafting. The named varieties, of which there are a considerable number, are usually propagated by softwood cuttings.

A climbing form clings strongly to masonry and can be expected to flower after four or five years.

LILAC
(Syringa)

Uses: Hedge, background, cut flowers
Plant: Spring or fall
Height: 3-10 feet
Blooms: April-June
Fruit: None
Distance: 3-6 feet
Soil: Well-drained
Exposure: Sun/light shade
Prune: Remove part of suckers, dead wood, oldest cane
Species:
S. microphylla 'Superba,' 5 ft., fragrant
S. persica—Persian, 8-10 ft., pale lilac, spicy fragrance
S. Meyeri, 'Palibin,' 4 ft., magenta
S. vulgaris to 15 ft., fragrant

Cultivars:
White-Single: 'Vestale,' 'Jan Van Tol'
White-Double: 'Edith Cavell,' 'Ellen Willmott'
Violet-Single: 'De Miritel,' 'Cavour'
Violet-Double: 'Marechal Lannes'
Blue-Single: 'Maurice Barres,' 'President Lincoln'
Blue-Double: 'Olivier de Serres,' 'Emile Gentil,' 'Pres. Grevy'
Lilac-Single; 'Maregno,' 'Jacques Callot'
Lilac-Double: 'Katharine Havemeyer,' 'Victor Lemoine'
Pinkish-Single: 'Lucie Baltet,' 'Esther Staley'
Pinkish-Double: 'Mme. A. Buchner,' 'Michel Buchner'
Reddish-Single: 'Marechal Foch,' 'Chas. Joly'
Reddish-Double: 'Paul Thirion,' 'Paul Deschanel'
Purple-Single: 'S. Monge', 'Ludwig Spaeth'
Purple-Double: 'Paul Hariot,' 'Congo'

Hybrids:
S. hyacinthiflora, early, single, 6-8 ft.; 'Blue Hyacinth', blue; 'Assessippi', lilac; 'Buffon,' 'Lamartine', 'Vauban': pinks; 'Pocahontas,' purple; 'Evangeline,' 'Montesquieu': reddish; 'Louvois,' violet

Lilac growing reaches nearly to its southern limit in the Washington area, although there are comparatively few gardens that do not contain one or more varieties. There is something about a lilac bush in the springtime that makes it somewhat of a must.

In spite of our location there are many varieties and species that may be grown here. The late Dr. E. A. Merritt grew many fine varieties and species, some of which are quite rare.

The common lilac, Syringa vulgaris, is probably grown more often than any other species or single variety although it has less to offer the gardener. The Persian lilac, which resembles the common in appearance, is less stiff, and flowers at a much younger age and has more and daintier blooms.

Most lilac varieties and species are rather stiff, bare-legged plants, tolerated for their bloom that is so fragrant. Because of this habit of growth, numerous suckers spring from the roots that draws somewhat upon the plant's ability to flower. Some of the suckers should be permitted to live because they may be needed to replace one or more canes should the lilac borer get in its work.

Lilacs thrive best in a neutral or sweet soil. An occasional application of ground limestone worked into the soil about the plant is needed to reduce the acidity of the soil. Wood ashes are excellent for this purpose. An annual application of compost made with limestone is another beneficial practice.

Of the numerous species of lilacs that may be grown in local gardens, the Persian and the Chinese are the more desirable. Of the more than 700 named varieties listed, only a few are adapted to this area. And few gardens can accommodate or need more than a very few. The list of varieties given here was prepared by a group of lilac specialists and includes most of those that are considered distinctive and desirable.

Lilacs are troubled with mildew in the early fall when the nights turn cool, but few consider it injurious, because the foliage matures very early. However, it can be controlled with a sulphur dust or funginex. Other diseases may appear but they are seldom encountered in local gardens. The oystershell and San Jose scales are common enemies of lilac bushes and must be controlled with a dormant spray.

Lilacs may be propagated by soft-wood and hard-wood cuttings, although they root rather poorly. Layerings are sometimes used, but budding and grafting are the more common methods. Grafting is commercially practiced on privet. It is because of this latter practice that the general recommendation is for planting varieties deeper than they grew in the nursery. In this way the plants are encouraged to develop their own roots. Shallow planting encourages the privet to develop its own top and to starve out the lilac graft.

Pruning of lilac bushes generally is limited to a thinning out of the suckers, to the removal of dead wood, and where only a few bushes are grown, to the removal of the spent blooms. Renewal pruning is recommended for lilacs. Each season remove one or more of the oldest canes, depending upon the size and number of canes.

MOCKORANGE
(Philadelphus)
Uses: Shrub border, cut flowers.
Plant: Spring/fall.
Height: 4-10 feet.
Blooms: May-August.
Fruits: None.
Distance: 5-8 feet.
Soil: Fertile loam, neutral.
Exposure: Sun/light shade.
Prune: After flowering.
Varieties:
P. 'Snowflake,' 8-10 ft., May-August, double, fragrant.
P. 'Virginal,' 8-10 ft., May-August, double, white, fragrant.
P. coronarius, 9-10 ft., May-June, single, white, sweet.

The mockorange is an old popular favorite with many gardeners because of its excellent floral display in the spring and its delightful fragrance.

Virginal is easily the best long-season variety where but one bush may be used. The flowers, largely white, are borne in clusters along the branches and the main difficulty seems to be to prune in such a way as to keep them well distributed from bottom to top of the bushes. Most gardeners neglect to prune the mockorange and the shrubs soon become bare-legged. The renewal system of pruning is needed for this reason.

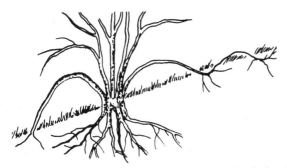

Many plants will reproduce by simply striking root from their branches. Tips may be dug into the ground, or a branch "layered" at several points. Root buds along the branch will strike root, and can then be cut and re-planted. Here is a forsythia bush with its rootings.

The mockorange is not fussy as to soil so long as it is reasonably fertile and is not too wet. They thrive in sun or light shade. By pruning after the flowering season, new growth is encouraged from the base of the plant before the formation of new buds for the following season's bloom.

The mockorange seems to be immune to most insects and diseases. Although the aphids are frequently injurious to them, they are easily controlled with nicotine sulphate or pyrethrum. The leaf miner is sometimes present and may be controlled with malathion or dimethoate spray; the latter also controls aphids.

Propagation is by soft-wood and hard-wood cuttings. Some varieties sucker freely. The seed of the species is not difficult to start.

ROSE OF SHARON—ALTHEA
(Hibiscus syriacus)
Uses: Shrub border, hedge, specimen.
Plant: Spring /fall.
Height:10-12 feet.
Blooms: July/August.
Fruit: None.
Distance: 2-6 feet.
Soil: Ordinary moist garden loam.
Exposure: Sun/shade.
Prune: Early spring.
Varieties:
Woodbridge, deep pink.
Hamabo, white with red eye.
Diana, white, July/August.

The rose of Sharon is a tall, upright-growing shrub that will tolerate almost any kind of situation, although it thrives best in a moist, loamy soil. It may be used as a specimen bush, as a hedge, or in the shrub border where its late summer bloom is often useful

There are named varieties available in single, semi-double, and double forms. Diana, a product of the National Arboretum, has much to offer—flowers up to six inches across, continuous bloom from June to September, and no seeds.

The rose of Sharon is untroubled by disease. The Japanese

beetle delights in eating the flower petals, so a protective neem dust may be needed to curb them.

Pruned in early spring to whatever form is needed; heavy pruning stimulates new growth and better flowers.

Propagation is by cuttings, although seeds germinate readily. Most seedlings, however, are lacking in form and clearness of colors.

SPIREA—BRIDALWREATH
(Spirea)
Uses: Shrub border, foundation planting, hedge, specimen.
Plant: Spring /fall.
Height: 1-9 feet.
Blooms: Marc-August.
Fruits: None.
Distance: 1-6 feet.
Soil: good garden loam.
Exposure: Sun.
Prune: Spring flowering—after flowering.
Summer flowering—spring.
Species:
S. thunberg—Thunberg's, 4-5 ft., March-April, white.
S. arguta—Garland. 5-6 ft., March-April, white.
S. prunifolia—Bridalwreath, 5-7 ft., May, white.
S. van houttei—'Van Houtte,' 6 9 ft., May, white.
S. bumalda var. 'Anthony Waterer,' 3 ft.; 'Crispa,' 2-2½ ft., June-August., rosy-crimson; var. Coccinea, 3 ft., June-August; 'Gold Flame,' 3 ft., July-August.
S. billardi—'Billard's,' 5-6 ft., June-September, rose.
S. Trilobata, 'Swan Lake,' 3-4 ft., white, May.
S. japonica alpina—'Daphne,' 1 ft., May, pink.
S. nipponica—'Snow Mound,' 3-4 ft., June, white.
S. cantoniensis lanceata, spring blooming double white.

The spireas comprise a large and varied group of deciduous shrubs that are widely used for landscape planting. They are mostly spring bloomers although there are several that flower throughout the summer.

Most spireas are tolerant of soil and exposure, although they do best in full sun in a good garden loam.

While a number of hybrids have been produced, for the most part they are listed as species. Most of them seem to be adapted to the Washington area. The most commonly grown species, Van Houtte's spirea, is a graceful spreading bush that needs considerable space.

The dwarf Anthony Waterer is very compact and useful in the foreground. The upright grower, Billard's spirea, is a vigorous grower producing rosy pink, fuzzy blooms intermittently throughout the summer. The double-flowered Bridalwreath with gracefully drooping branches (S. prunifolia) is still a favorite with many.

The twiggy Thunberg is the first to flower in the spring. In fact, it will flower in February during periods of mild weather. Arguta is an improved hybrid of thunbergi.

The spireas are easily transplanted as well as propagated. Hardwood cuttings taken in August root readily. Division of Anthony Waterer, Billard, and Bridalwreath are comparatively easy.

Diseases and insect pests are not troublesome, except for the aphids that congregate on the tender young tips in the spring.

SWEETSHRUB
(Calycanthus floridus)
Uses: Shrub border.
Plant: Spring/Fall.
Height: 4-5 feet.
Blooms: May-June.
Fruits: Interesting capsules.
Distance: 4-6 feet.
Soil: Moist. medium garden loam.
Exposure: Partial shade.
Prune: Spring.
Species:
C. floridus—Sweetshrub, fragrant, purplish-brown flowers.

The sweetshrub, an ornamental shrub of good landscape value, is grown largely for sentimental value. Its spicy fragrance is its chief charm because the chocolate-colored flowers are hardly beautiful.

The sweetshrub is easily grown in the average garden, although it does best in light shade and in not too dry a situation. There are some strains that are lacking in fragrance and should be avoided. This, of course, is not easily done since the bush must be in bloom to determine its fragrance.

Propagation is by division, soft-wood cuttings, root-cuttings, which root rather freely, and by seed. Mound layering is also practicable.

The sweetshrub seems to be comparatively free of insect pests and diseases.

VIBURNUM
(Viburnum)
Uses: Background, shrub border, specimens.
Plant: Fall/spring.
Height: 1-30 feet.
Blooms: March-June.
Fruit: Red, black, blue, yellow.
Distance: 4-15 feet.
Soil: Moist, enriched with humus, sandy loam, pH 5.5-6.5.
Exposure: Shade/sun.
Prune: Spring.

Species:
V. trilobum—American Cranberry bush, 8-12 ft., white blossoms, May, red fruit, sun/shade.
V. opulus—'Nanum' Dwarf Cranberry bush 2-3 ft., white, May, no fruit, sun/shade.
V. opulus—Compactum, 2-3 ft., creamy-white, May, red fruit, sun/shade.
V. dentatum—Arrowwood, 10-12 ft., white, June, blue-black, sun /shade.
V. rhytidophyllum—Leatherleaf, 6-15 ft., white, May, red/black, shade.
V. sieboldi—Siebold, 8-30 ft., white, May, red-black, sun.
V. sargenti—Sargeant, 12 ft., white, May, red, sun/shade.
V. carlesi—Korean spice (fragrant), 4-6 ft., pink, April, blue-black, sun/shade.
V. plicatum tomentosum—Double-file, 6-12 ft., white, May, blue-black, sun.
V. plicatum tomentosum—Mariesi, 6 12 ft., white, May, red, sun.
V. burkwoodii—Burkwood, 4-6 ft., pinkish-white. April, blue-black, shade; Mohawk, 5 ft., red buds to white with red reverse, clove fragrance.

V. plicatum (tomentosum sterile)—Japanese snowball, 10 ft., white, May, sun.

V. carlcephalum, 6 7 ft., creamy-white, April, black, sun/shade.

V. wrighti, 4-6 ft., white, May, red, sun/shade.

V. opulus Xanthocarpum. Yellow European Cranberry bush, 12 ft.. white. May, yellow, sun.

V. dilatum—Linden, 6-10 ft., cream-white, May, red, sun/shade.

V. farreri (fragrans-Fragran), 9 ft., pale-pink, March-April, red/black, sun/shade.

V. lantana—Wayfaring, 6-15 ft., cream, May, orange/black, sun.

V. prunifolium—Black Haw, 15 ft., cream-white, May, blue/black, sun, red autumn foliage.

V. setigerum—Tea, 12 ft., white, May, red, sun, shade.

V. japanicum, 4-5 ft., large flat clusters of white flowers, red fruit, light shade.

    —Dr. Donald R. Egolf, U.S. National Arboretum.

The Viburnum group is large and varied and includes a number of native shrubs of varying degree of usefulness for landscape planting. The Leatherleaf is an evergreen, and Burkwood is semi-evergreen. The American Cranberrybush and the Japanese Snowball are excellent shrubs for the tall border. The latter, V. plicatum (Tomentosum sterile) is much superior to the common snowball, (V. opulus var. roseum) which is badly troubled by aphids, but is more difficult to transplant.. Buy it B&B and in the spring.

Two new viburnums, Alleghany (10 ft.) and Mohican) are especially noteworthy in that they are resistant to bacterial leaf spot.

Most of the viburnums are too large for the ordinary city lot. The fragrant viburnum, however, is a small grower as are the Dwarf Cranberry and Compactum. The latter has fruit, the former none. Carlcephalum is of moderate size as is Wrighti.

Most of the viburnums require moist soils that are loamy with a pH of 5.5 to 6.5. There are some, such as V. acerifolium, V. dentatum, V. lantana and V. opulus, that thrive in drier situations. V. dentatum tends to form thickets in a moist situation and so is best used in a woodlands area rather than the shrub

V. Siebold, has an unpleasant odor and is best planted at some distance from the house. The foliage of the Leatherleaf is large and striking and should not be used in the smaller shrub border.

The viburnums are readily propagated by softwood cuttings. The V. carlesi is commercially propagated by root grafts and by budding that may be subject to graft blight and preference should be given to own root plants. Layering is used to multiply some species; cuttings may be used on one or two species.

The aphids are the principal insect pest on the viburnums and they are not serious except on the common Snowball. Diseases are not common.

WEIGELA
(Weigela species and hybrids)
Uses: Shrub border, specimen, cut flowers.
Plant: Fall/spring.
Height: 4 to 10 feet.
Blooms: June-September.
Fruit: None.
Distance: 6 to 10 feet.
Soil: Ordinary garden loam.
Exposure: Sun.
Prune: After flowering.

Cultivars:
W. 'Eva Rathke,' 5 ft., crimson.
W. 'Bristol Ruby,' 6-7 ft., ruby red.
W. 'Bristol Snowflake,' 6-7 ft., white, June.
W. 'Vanicek,' 6-8 ft., purplish-red, June.
W. 'Boskoop Glory,' 4-5 ft., salmon-pink.
W. Floribunda, 10 ft., dark crimson, May-June.
W. florida, 6 ft., rose-pink, May-June.
W. florida, venasta, rose-pink, May.
W. florida, Pink Princess, pink.
W florida, Java Red. violet-red, June.

The weigelas are noted for their showy displays. Masses of tubular flowers are produced each spring on the wide spreading branches. The foliage is dull and the coarse dark-colored branches offer little in the way of landscape value. It is the floral effect that is outstanding.

The weigela thrives in any good garden soil that has sufficient moisture. It is relatively untroubled by insects and diseases.

In pruning the early spring flowering shrubs, remove from ¼ to ⅓ of the oldest canes at ground.

NEW PLANTS FROM CUTTINGS

Propagating plants from cuttings is an age-old practice. Many plants must be propagated vegetatively if the varieties are to be kept true to type. Cloning prevents the genetic variation of sexual production. This asexual propagation includes cuttings, layering, grafting and budding, and division. Cuttings are used whenever possible because they take less skill and can be handled in greater numbers in a small space.

There are three main types of cuttings taken from the stems of trees and woody ornamentals: softwood, hardwood, and semi-hardwood. The softwood cuttings are taken early in the growing season while the plants are in active growth. Semi-hardwood cuttings are made in late summer. Hardwood cuttings are taken in the late fall or early winter after the wood has matured. Bud, leaf, root, and tuber cuttings are described in relevant chapters.

Stem cuttings are taken by the home gardener as well as the nurseryman in order to increase stocks of the loveliest landscape shrubs and trees that may be difficult or expensive to find. It often pays the home gardener to take ten cuttings from a favorite specimen to get two successful new plants for his garden. The healthiest specimens should always be chosen, because most cuttings will be virtual clones of the parents from which they were taken.

The most important part of successful propagation by cuttings is to get enough root and top growth the first season to allow plants to survive their first winter with growth centers intact. That in turn depends on taking the cuttings at the time most likely to lead to swift rooting and in giving them optimum growing conditions.

The best rooting time varies enormously from species to species and even within the varieties of a species, as you will see from consulting the propagation chart included at the end of this section.

Hardwood Cuttings

In general coniferous evergreens and some deciduous trees do best when cuttings are taken after they go dormant in the fall, so-called hardwood cuttings. Broadleaf, ornamental evergreens, like camellias and hollies, do best when cuttings are taken in late summer after the new growth has begun to harden; this stage provides the semi-hardwood cuttings.

A variety of other ornamentals, from azaleas to roses, takes root best when their new growth is still succulent enough to snap off easily when bent double. These softwood cuttings are taken after each growth spurt and are the easiest to propagate. The hardwood cuttings are the most difficult.

Semi-Hardwood Cuttings

Camellias, hollies, and other broadleaf evergreens are best rooted after new growth has begun to harden in late summer.

Both share a need for a warm sterile medium that roots can penetrate, constant high humidity, and lots of filtered light.

through the winter under greenhouse conditions.

The ordinary home owner can create a small propagating bench for these species by utilizing a shop lamp, flats filled with sterile rooting media, a commercial heating mat bought through a garden supply house, and a room humidifier. The more commonly used media are sharp sand, chicken grit, milled sphagnum, vermiculite, perlite, and combinations such as sphagnum and sand or perlite. Other specialists use such uncommon materials as fly ash, powdered styrofoam, fine pumice and silver sand. All have one characteristic in common: they permit air to reach the roots in spite of all the packing the gardener does to support cuttings and retain moisture. Each flat must be free from dirt and salt.

Check the requirements for each species before you root cuttings. Some cuttings root best in a non-acid medium, such as sand and perlite. Others do best in acid sphagnum. However, there is considerable leeway if the proper conditions of timing, light, warmth, and humidity are met.

Strip the lower leaves and some of the bark off of the bottom nodes of semi-hardwood cuttings before you plant and dip them in the proper concentration of rooting hormone. Knock off excess rooting powder and set the cuttings deep in the prepared flats two or three inches apart so that leaves or needles do not touch. Firm the mixture well around the stems and water gently but thoroughly to seat the cuttings. Set flats on a heating mat in a light north-facing room with a humidifier. If the light level is low, supplement it with a shop lamp that diffuses light without creating top heat. Make sure that the rooting mixture remains damp while new roots are forming.

Conifer cuttings taken in late fall are usually short side shoots that are torn off, the exception being top cuttings from upright yews. Because a small heel might cause air pockets in the medium, carefully trim it before dipping in rooting hormone. With the exception of junipers, which like clean sharp sand, conifers prefer an acid peat moss and sand mixture.

When their roots are well-developed and firmly attached, the cuttings can be removed from rooting flats and potted in two-inch pots that are then placed in another flat. At this stage the roots will be able to take up moisture, and the potting mix would be made of equal parts of loam, sand, and peat moss with a quart of dehydrated cow manure added to each bushel of mix. The newly potted plants can be watered with a soluble plant-food solution early on to boost development. It is important to keep newly rooted cuttings growing on through the first season so that they develop buds before going dormant for the winter. This reduces the chance that tiny plants will winter kill or not build food reserves that nourish buds to provide next spring growth.

Softwood Cuttings

In this case it is particularly important to take cuttings from the most vigorous specimens with desirable qualities. Softwood cuttings are taken at some special time in the plant's active growing season when they root most readily.

One good example is magnolia grandiflora, difficult to root, but possible when cuttings are taken just as new leaf buds begin to break after flowering in June. Evergreen azaleas should be cut between mid-July and mid-August when new growth will still snap when the tip is bent back toward older wood between thumb and forefinger. Deciduous azaleas are easier to root when growth is very tender. Rose cuttings may be taken when the flower on a new shoot has faded, so the modern repeat bloomers will yield cuttings several times a season.

Softwood cuttings respond favorably to mist propagation and a warm rooting medium, although hard to root species, like rhododendron and cultivars of mountain laurel, remain beyond the skill of the home owner. Gardeners can buy electric propagation mats to maintain bottom heat at a temperature of 70° to 75° F. under rooting flats, while using portable humidifiers and lights on separate timers to reproduce nursery conditions without a greenhouse. One caution is in order. Hormone concentrations vary enormously with the tenderness of the material, and should be much weaker for use on succulent growth, in order to avoid burning adventitious root cells concentrated near the growth nodes.

In taking a softwood cutting it is advisable to take a new shoot about ^-inch below a node, where most of the adventitious cells are concentrated. The top cut, if necessary, is made about ¼-inch above a node on a parallel slant with a bud or node at the tip of the cut.

The size of the cutting will vary greatly between species. A rose cutting may need to be more than 6 inches long in order to have four or five nodes where good roots and branches can grow, while dwarf azalea species may have that number of nodes in a 4 inch cutting.

Softwood cuttings must have leaves present if they are to develop roots and grow. For some years it was thought advisable to reduce leaf surface to conserve moisture, but that has been disproved. Leave all small leaves on that are above the planting depth, and cut large leaves in half. There should be two or more nodes covered by the propagating media and two or more above in most species where nodes are not very closely spaced.

Oversized Cuttings Are More Vulnerable.

In the summer temperatures may be warm enough to grow softwood cuttings in flats without electric heating mats. However, regular watering to keep the medium evenly damp during the rooting process is a must. If the flats are put outside, they should be set where there is indirect light and protection from wind and sun. A garden blanket or a cloche made of chicken wire embedded in heavy plastic sheeting can be used to filter light and to help retain moisture between waterings. A sunken cold frame in a lightly shaded spot also makes a good nursery for rooting flats and transplanted pots. All cuttings that have been potted after rooting indoors should remain indoors under lights for about two weeks before they are moved outdoors to a cold frame in filtered light. After two more weeks the plants are ready to set out in the garden. All rooted cuttings should be planted early enough in the season so they can get well-established before winter dormancy.

Azalea and rose cuttings are unique among softwoods for their need to be brought in the first winter, given regular feedings of liquid plant food, while under lights to encourage continued growth into the next season without rest. That is the way to make sure that most cuttings survive.

Simple Layering

There is one more method of plant propagation that requires little special equipment except for compost, adequate moisture, and patience. At the beginning of the growing season, many flowering shrubs and trees can be increased by scraping or girdling the lower side of a horizontal branch that is attached to the plant, dipping the wound in rooting hormone, and then bending the branch 5 or 6 inches deep into a specially prepared planting hole. It can be held down there with a small wicket and covered with enriched soil and mulch, or covered and kept in place with a rock. If necessary, stake the terminal end of the branch to keep it upright so that the tip can leaf out and grow during the time that roots are forming underground. Water frequently.

This procedure provides a margin of safety during the rooting process, for the parent plant continues to nourish the branch until roots are fully formed and can support it. Consequently, it is wise to leave plants that are layered in early spring attached until the fall or even into the next spring to be sure the plant is well started. This is essential in the case of rhododendron and magnolia, which should be layered in the early summer when they begin to leaf out. Leave these plants until the second September, making sure that a winter mulch prevents freeze-drying of the young roots that are near the surface. At the time of transplanting, dig the new plants with a sharp spade to sever the connecting branch cleanly.

Other types of layering can also be done outdoors by the experienced propagator to decrease the time necessary to grow presentable landscape plants.

Please turn page for IPM Calendar for Shrubs.

IPM CALENDAR FOR SHRUBS:

February
Prune dead branches out of low junipers to prevent possible spores of tip blight fungus from fruiting later

March
Check azalea leaves for lacebug damage that will appear as white stippling of the leaves. Look for the shiny, tarry brown eggs on the undersides of the leaves. Note plants that have high numbers of eggs (greater than 5 per leaf) so that you will be prepared to treat them when they hatch.

April
Apply one treatment of a preventative fungicide to azaleas as they begin to show color to prevent the development of Ovulinia petal blight. With this treatment, flowers may last in good condition for up to three weeks and will fall off the plant in due time rather than sticking and drying on the plant.

May
Watch for swarms of gnat-like orange boxwood leafminer adults around boxwood now. With a systemic pesticide, treat only plants that have sustained significant damage and have large numbers of adults swarming.

Start monitoring all plants for mites, especially if the weather has been warm and dry. Treat with 2% horticultural oil solution to reduce mite infestations before damage is severe. Monitor weekly by vigorously tapping a branch over a sheet of white paper. Mites will appear as small dark spots that move over the surface of the paper and leave a reddish-brown smear when the paper is wiped with the hand.

June
Look out for pine needle scale crawlers now. They are bright red and the size of a sand grain. Monitor for heavy infestation with beat test over white paper card. Treat with horticultural oil or insecticidal soap spray.

Look for circular notches in the new leaves of rhododendrons and azaleas after flowering has passed and new growth has begun. Heavy notching is an indication of black vine weevil feeding and larvae are present and damaging to the roots. Treat the soil under the plant with insect parasitizing nematodes or treat the top of the plant with a systemic insecticide.

Check the undersides of azalea leaves frequently for the emergence of lacebug larvae. The larvae are small, black, wingless, and spiny. This pest can be controlled with insecticidal soap, oil, or a systemic insecticide applied to the newly hatched larvae. Continue checking for larvae even after treatment since the eggs may not all hatch at the same time. Continue looking for and treating mite infestations as they appear. Use a white sheet to detect mites and spot treat infestations with 2% horticultural oil spray.

Spray emerging bagworm larvae with BTK (Kurstaki strain) when they emerge about a week after catalpa trees finish blooming.

July
Monitor shrubs for mites with beat test and continue to treat.

August
Apply a systemic insecticide such as acephate (Orthene) to hollies that have ben severely damaged by leaf miner. If you are planting anew this fall, choose a resistant variety such as Foster holly, and plant in a semi-shaded site to deter the pest.

September
If wooly adelgids persist on hemlock hedges, spray with 3% horticultural oil.

Evaluate this year's growth on azaleas or rhododendrons for fungal problems. Individual branches that are wilted or dead signal a problem with Botryospaeria; whole plants that wilt are indicative of Phytophthora. Botryosphaeria starts as a foliar fungus at the tips of the leaves and produces bands of infected tissue. Eventually it gets into stems where it must be cut out, cutting back to white wood that is not stained with the fungus. Consider a resistant cultivar when replacing plants killed by Botryosphaeria. Phytophthora is a primarily root infecting disease, so the plant will usually wilt all at once. It is usually only a severe problem in heavy, wet soils that do not drain well. Move plants with this problem to more well drained soil or correct soil drainage where they are growing. Available fungicides do not provide lasting control for either disease.

November
Take a good look at conifers and cotoneaster for signs of remaining bagworms. Remove bags with scissors to prevent hatch next July.

December
Thin boxwoods by cutting small branches out all the way back to larger branches. Opening them up in this manner will prevent development of Volutella blight next season. Use the greens in holiday decorating.

INSPIRATION:

The Asian Collection, Japanese Woodland, and Fern Valley, U. S. National Arboretum, New York Avenue & Bladensburg Road, NW, Washington, D.|
McCrillis Gardens, 6910 Greentree Road, Bethesda, Maryland.
Greenspring Garden Park, 4601 Greenspring Road, off Route 236 near Braddock Road, Alexandria, Virginia.

Other flowering shrubs of merit.

Campsis, Trumpet Vine, 'Madame Galen'—a summer blooming vine.

Caryopteris, Bluebeard—blue flowers in late summer.

Cornus alba siberica, Red Twig Dogwood—red bark in winter.

Clethra alinifolia, Summersweet—fragrant white flower clusters in summer.

Daphne odora variegata—March bloom, low, fragrant.

Eleagnus pungens—fall flowers, silvery foliage, fragrant.

Enkianthus—orange fall foliage, complements rhododendrons.

Fothergilla gardenii—fall color, low, early fragrance.

Hypericum, St. John's Wort—yellow spreader, resists drought.

Itea 'Henry Garnet,' summer flowers, red fall color, fragrant.

Kerria japonica pleniflora, Japanese Kerria—bright yellow doubles, April-July.

Potentilla, Cinquefoil—spreader, buttercup to white flowers.

Salix discolor, French Pussy Willow—winter catkins, spring flowers.

Vitex agnus castus, Chaste Tree—fragrant lilac-blue flowers all summer.

EARLY FLOWERING SHRUBS FOR OUR AREA

When winter has been chilling and depressing, it is pleasing to note the first blooms on spring flowers and bulbs. There are a number of shrubs and small trees that we might consider for this first bloom; some are quite fragrant. The time of flowering of those listed varies from February to early April, depending upon the weather. They are not listed according to flowering dates.

Winter Honeysuckle	Lonicera fragrantissima	6'
Chinese Witchhazel	Hamamelis mollis	30'
Cornelian Cherry	Cornus mas	20'
Japanese Cornel	Cornus officinalis	20'
Thunberg Spirea	Spiraea thunbergi	5'
Winter Jasmine	Jasminum nudiflorum	6'
Cornell Pink Rhododendron	Rhododendron mucronulatum	4'
Wintersweet	Chimonanthus praecox	6'
Early Forsythia	Forsythia ovata	8'
Spring Heath	Erica carnea	1'
February Daphne	Daphne mezereum	3'
Winter Daphne	Daphne odora	4'
Bodnant Viburnum	Viburnum bodnantense	10'
Fragrant Viburnum	Viburnum farreri	9'

9. ROSES

Now that the rose has been officially adopted as the American flower, we have a new reason to excuse local passion for a plant that, unfortunately, does not really suit the extremes of our climate. Roses are the legendary mistresses of the American garden, beautiful but demanding, and they hold millions in thrall. And, although they can be used in many ways in the medium-sized garden, not all kinds and varieties of roses may be depended on to thrive and flower profusely under our conditions.

When most gardeners think of roses, they think of hybrid teas, the type sold by florists. But there are many other kinds suited for different uses in the garden. Among the major types grown here are The Hybrid Teas, Grandifloras, Floribundas, Ramblers, Climbers, Shrub Roses, "Old Roses," and Miniature Roses. Their general characteristics and potential uses, along with specific recommended cultivars, are taken up in this chapter.

Fortunately, many of these of roses can be seen on display in the area at public gardens, like Bon Air Park in Arlington, Brookside Gardens in Wheaton, Dumbarton Oaks in Georgetown, and the National Arboretum.

When to Plant Roses
In our area fall planting of bare root rose bushes is preferred because the work may be done at leisure. The difficulty of finding plants, unless ordering from rose specialists, means that many buy their plants from local nurseries each spring. It is preferable to plant and work with all roses while they are dormant.

Look for bare root material with well-formed roots that are not cramped in too small a package, with roots and bud union that are firmly protected in packing material, and with cleanly pruned canes that are protected from damage and disease with paraffin or grafting wax.

Container grown plants are the easiest to obtain in spring. They are best planted as soon as they appear in the garden store before they have begun to grow; then, they do not have to undergo normal transplant shock while carrying a full load of new growth and flowers.

Soil Preparation Makes the Difference
Lime in the form of ground limestone, should be added to reduce the soil acidity to a pH reading of no less than 6- 6.5.

HYBRID TEAS

With all the types and classes to choose from, the majority of gardeners stick with the hybrid teas, medium size shrubs from 3 to 6 feet whose free-flowering habit, long season of bloom, and wide range of colors are enticing attractions. These modern roses have been developed from tender tea roses of southern European origin within this century. They now come in a score of hues, including whites, pinks, reds, yellows, blends, and bi-colors.

Most of the hybrid tea roses respond to our climate by producing a heavy bloom in late May and early June, flowering less abundantly in the heat of summer, and ending the season with another burst of bloom in September and early October. Individual blooms are borne on long stems.

They vary considerably in habit and size of growth, in their response to growing conditions, and in their susceptibility to our main rose diseases, black spot and powdery mildew. It is safe to say that all are vulnerable to some degree to these diseases. Freedom of bloom and form of flowers vary as well. Some have a single layer of petals, and others have so many that their opened bloom resembles a cabbage.

Some red varieties develop a blue cast in the summer sun, light colors can freckle, and petals can lack the thick creamy "substance" that helps them last longer. Others droop on stems too weak to support the open blossoms. Because so many varieties are available, it is best to see well-grown flowers in bloom before purchasing plants for the home garden.

GRANDIFLORA

This class, announced by the American Rose Society in 1954, is for tall-growing varieties intermediate between the floribunda and hybrid teas. They have smaller flowers on long stems, often appearing in clusters. Because both hybrid tea and grandiflora have medium to large blooms and make effective cut flowers they are often used interchangeably by the gardener as specimen and exhibition plants.

Hybrid Tea & Grandiflora Roses— Medium to Large Blooms with Long Stems for Cutting

Rose Name	Color	Bloom	Fragrance	Growth Habit	Comment
Pink					
Perfume Delight	medium pink	full-cupped	strong	tall, bushy	cut flowers
Sonia	coral pink	high double	some	medium bushy	arrangements
Queen Elizabeth	pink	double cupped	slight	tall, upright	easy to grow
First Prize	pink and ivory	high double	good	medium, broad	tops in shows
Tiffany	two-tone pink	high double	strong	tall, upright	soft colors
Aquarius	pink blend	high cupped	slight	medium, upright	long stems
Miss All-American Beauty	deep pink	full cupped	strong	tall, upright	big flower
Bride's Dream	light pink			upright	long stems, prolific
Duet	clear medium pink		good	vigorous	disease resistant
Great Scott	medium pink			excellent form	constant growth
White					
Crystalline	crystal white		medium	upright, vigorous	disease resistant
Honor	clear white			excellent form	best in spring & fall
Polar Star				tall good form	long stems
Pascali	creamy white	double	slight	tall, upright	long-lasting bloom
Yellow					
Gold Medal	deep yellow	double	some	tall, upright	prolific bloom
Summer Sunshine	deep yellow	double	slight	medium tall	bright color
Elegant Beauty	yellow blend	high-centered			long buds
Peace	yellow, pink edges	high, full	none	medium, broad	classic
Orange/Orange Blend					
Touch of Class	pink blend	high double	slight	medium, bushy	top show form
Tropicana	coral, orange	double cupped	spicy	leggy habit	best orange
Voodoo	orange blend	double	strong	tall, bushy	large, bright
Red/Red Blend					
Chrysler Imperial	dark red	high, full	strong	medium, upright	classic
Fragrant Cloud	coral red	double	strong	medium, bushy	lots of bloom
Mr. Lincoln	dark red	full cupped	strong	tall, upright	big, lovely
Olympiad	medium red	double	slight	medium, upright	clear, lasting color
Headliner	red blend	high double	slight	medium, upright	unique color
Double Delight	red blend	double	strong	tall, upright	has everything
Mauve					
Paradise	lavender, ruby edge	high double	slight	medium, bushy	long-lasting

FLORIBUNDA

Next to the hybrid tea roses, the cluster-flowered roses (low, bushy, hardy floribundas or polyanthas) are most widely grown. Some floribundas are compact little plants excellent for use along driveway borders or walks or in the forefront of a larger bed. Ideal for outdoor color effect, the florbunda's prolific habit of bloom comes closest to meeting the desire of many gardeners for roses throughout the season for cutting use in the home. Although they are not immune to disease, they seem to be somewhat less troubled by it.

Floribunda Roses, Small Flowers in Clusters for Cut Sprays

Rose Name	Color	Bloom	Fragrance	Growth Habit	Comment.
Evening Star	white	high double	slight	medium, bushy	superb sprays
Iceberg	white	double open	good	medium, bushy	profuse bloomer
French Lace	white	double	slight	low, bushy	exhibit clusters
Cherish	shell pink	double	strong	low, bushy	hybrid tea form
Gene Boerner	medium pink	high double	slight	medium, upright	classic form
Playgirl	pink blend	single petals			yellow stamens, big sprays
Angel Face	mauve	strong	medium	bushy	charming
Sun Sprite	butter yellow	double	strong	medium, upright	best yellow
First Edition	coral	double open	slight	medium, bushy	profuse bloomer
Redgold	red, gold	double cupped	none	medium, bushy	always in bloom
Playboy	red blend	single petals			yellow stamens nice sprays
Impatient	orange-red	semi-double	slight	medium, bushy	mass color effect
Showbiz	medium red	double	none	low, broad	profuse bloomer
Europeana	red	double rosette	slight	low, spreading	large clusters

MINIATURE ROSES

Miniature roses, which grow 10 to 25 inches tall, are often mentioned as suitable for rock gardens, window boxes and house plants. Only a few are truly suitable as house plants. All require a sheltered situation here with moderate temperatures and a proper setting in which their dainty beauty can be enjoyed. They are not rugged enough to take much hardship in the garden. While they require careful attention so as not to be stressed as container plants, they are easy to grow in the border.

Miniature Roses, Very small blooms on Small Plants.

Rose Name	Color	Bloom	Fragrance	Growth Habit	Comment
Snow Bride	white	high double	slight		exhibition blooms
Cinderella	white, flesh	double	none	compact	profuse bloomer
Irresistible	white	large blooms			of excellent form
Kingig	pink			very tall grower	top exhibition rose
Pierrine	medium pink	excellent form		compact	
Cupcake	clear pink	high double	slight	compact	long-lasting bloom
HiHo (Climber)	deep pink	full double slight		5-6 in. climber	beautiful sprays
Judy Fischer	rose pink	high double	slight	bushy	good color and form
Peaches'N Cream	pink blend	high double	slight	bushy	exhibition blooms
Minnie Pearl	pink blend	high double	slight	bushy	exhibition blooms
Mary Marshall	orange pink	high double	good	bushy	exhibition blooms
Rise'N Shine	medium yellow	high double	none	upright	exhibition blooms
Rainbow's End	yellow blend			medium height	show-stopper
Jean Kenneally	apricot blend	high double	slight	bushy	exhibition blooms
Little Jackie	orange blend	double	strong	bushy	good color and form
Dreamglo	red blend	high	slight	upright	lovely sprays
Starina	orange red	high double	slight	upright	hybrid tea form
Red Beauty	dark red	double	slight	bushy	exhibition blooms
Lavender Jewel	mauve	high	good	bushy	hybrid tea form
Magic Carousel	white and red	full double	some	bushy	picotee coloring

CLIMBING ROSES

Nothing gives such a sense of romantic profusion and luxury against a sunny wall or on an arbor, pergola, or fence as a climbing rose does. These roses combine landscape value as a backdrop, divider, or focal point with seasonal flowering. Use them anywhere you might think of using vines as long as air circulation is adequate to help them resist the summer fungal diseases that keep gardeners spraying from April to October.

Climbers are subdivided into four types—(1) ramblers; (2) large-flowered June bloomers; (3) climbing hybrid teas, and; (4) true climbers. Each requires a distinctive type of pruning.

True rambler cultivars, such as 'Dorothy Perkins' and 'Crimson Rambler', do not succeed well here because of our heat and humidity. There is one local variety, 'Chevy Chase', produced by Niels J. Hansen, which is not susceptible to mildew. Pruning a true rambler is simplicity itself. Because they bloom on new wood once a year, cut all canes to the ground after flowering is finished

Large-flowered climbers should be headed back after the June bloom, but summer rose pruning is not widely practiced here, where it is customary to remove one quarter to one third of the canes in early spring. Choose the oldest canes and cut them in small sections so as not to damage adjacent canes. Although it is a rambler, not a climber, 'Chevy Chase' is also treated in this manner.

Climbing hybrid teas, the third type, are pruned by shortening side branches on the main canes. The framework of major canes is not touched as long as the canes remain healthy. The climbing hybrid teas seldom exceed 10 feet and for this reason are commonly known as pillar roses. In general most pruning of hybrid tea forms should occur before plants leaf out because new canes begin to develop shortly after the flowering season.

The true climbers are exceedingly varied in their habit of growth. Their popularity has increased greatly in the last 50 years because most of them are repeat or recurrent bloomers. The basic principles of their pruning, however, are simple: all dead wood should be removed first, followed by additional pruning done to fit them to the space they must occupy. Very few climbers flower the first season after they are set out.

Good support is essential to the health and bloom of climbing roses. They should be securely tied to their support—trellises, arbors, fences, or pergolas— to prevent them from being whipped about by the winds. Their thorny branches can injure other canes, making entry points for cankers, diseases of the cambium layer, that damage the strength and appearance of the plant.

When possible anchor the cane with plant ties along the horizontal plane at the top of an arbor, trellis or fence to encourage the development of the most flowering growth along its length.

Climbing Roses—Repeat Bloomers If Spent Blossoms Are Removed

Rose Name	Color	Bloom	Fragrance	GrowthHabit	Comment
Handel	cream, pink edges	double cupped	good	medium tall	unique color
Sarah Van Fleet	pale pink	semi-double	slight	medium	pest-resistant
New Dawn	blush pink	double	slight	very tall	canes up to 30 feet
America	salmon pink	double	strong	tall	exhibition blooms
Golden Showers	clear yellow	flat open	good	tall	profuse bloomer
Improved Blaze	scarlet	semi-double	slight	tall	foolproof
Tempo	dark red	full double	slight	tall	eye-catcher
Don Juan	dark red	double cupped	some	medium	exhibition blooms

LANDSCAPE OR SHRUB ROSES

Among the so-called shrub roses are those that may be planted as part of a shrub border, as hedges, and as isolated specimen plants. The hardy, and vigorous Rosa rugosa are noted for their distinctive foliage, wild rose-type flowers, and their admirable ability to survive sand and salt spray without maintainence. The flowers bloom most of the summer, they have lovely scent, and the rose hips make a colorful and nutritious addition to the plant in the fall. The pink varieties in particular make a perfect foil against the sun bleached sands of a beach home.

Some modern Rugosa hybrids have a long flowering season. Most are large bushes; and some spread by underground runners and must be carefully confined if they are not to escape bounds. Rosa rugosa 'Harrison's Yellow', a disease-resistant spreading shrub, is one of the earliest to flower in the spring and is prized by many.

'Simplicity' is a beautiful clear pink hedge rose, whose ability to flower in partial shade and few thorns should encourage gardeners to plant it in the mixed border as well.

Some landscape roses that are excellent shrubs for the border are not repeat bloomers. Rosa primula (ecae) makes a large specimen shrub with interesting bark and thorns. It is covered in early May with large, single, creamy yellow flowers. Rosa 'banksia' is an old and popular variety. 'Father Hugonis', sometimes called the Golden Rose of China, is covered in May with large single yellow flowers.

Landscape roses, with foliage that is fairly resistant to molds and mildew, can be used in the ornamental border as a backdrop for flowers or as a support for summer blooming vines that do not start into active growth until the rose is ready to flower. Clematis cultivars that bloom on new growth are a good companion plant.

A subclass of trailing roses has been developed to cover banks, but few are thick enough to smother the grass and weeds that are so hard to reach beneath their thorny stems. 'Sea Foam' is a shining exception, with foliage thick enough to be considered a ground cover. It is also suitable as a hedge that forms a barrier almost three feet wide and high. It can be tied to a trellis or draped over a wall where its white fragrant blooms continue making a show throughout the summer.

The newly popular Meideiland roses, developed in France, are equally useful, although their foliage will need spray protection from black spot and powdery mildew every 10 days to keep the foliage thick enough to deter weeds when mulched. The white, pink, and red cultivars are 3 to 3½ foot mounds that can be used as low hedges and groundcover. Each will cover an area almost 25 feet square.

Landscape and Shrub Roses—Hardy Roses for Hedges, Slopes, and Screening

Rose Name	Color	Bloom	Fragrance	Growth Habit	Comment
Sea Foam	white	full double	slight	low, spreading	ground cover
The Fairy	seashell pink	small double	none	low, bushy	minimum care
Betty Prior	carmine pink	single	none	tall, broad	everblooming hedge
Carefree Beauty	pink	double open	none	broad, upright	showy, foolproof
Simplicity	medium pink	semi-double	slight	medium, upright	everblooming hedge
Bonica (meidomonac)	medium pink	double	none	medium, hedge	everblooming, pest resistant

OLD OR HISTORIC ROSES

Many of these are the parent stock of modern rose crosses, which were themselves developed centuries ago as crosses of species roses. Some are shrubs suitable for borders or as specimens. One of the hardiest is a native species, Rosa virginiana, used for landscape purposes. Rosa rugosa is technically an old rose as well.

They have a special appeal to people who cherish their associations, interesting flower forms, and their frequently wonderful scent. Only a few are repeat bloomers.

The China, Bourbon, Moss, and Cabbage rose types are found frequently in collectors' gardens. The list given here includes those species or cultivars that do the best with the least trouble in our climate. Increasingly, they are becoming available at local nurseries and garden centers.

OLD GARDEN ROSES—Species Roses or Early Crosses Prized for Form and Scent

Rose Name	Color	Bloom	Fragrance	Comment
Rosa Glauca (rubifolia)	pink-red	single	good	mauve stems, good foliage
Four Seasons (Rosa damascena)	medium pink	loose double	strong	bushy, wide early, long-blooming
Rosa Stanwell (perpetual)	white, pink	full cupped	good	well-formed, disease resistant
Rosa rugosa (alba, rubra)	white, pink	single open	strong	spreading easy, big red hips
Rosa virginiana	pink	single open	strong	trailing, hardy, landscape
Baronne Provost(1842)	pink		strong	5 ft. upright, recurrent bloom
Mme Hardy(1832)	white	exquisite form		5 ft. upright, spring bloom
Paul Neyron(1851)	pink	large	strong	6 ft. upright, recurrent
La Reine Victoria (1872)	pink	full cupped	strong	medium, upright repeat bloom
Salet (1854)	pink ruffled		petals fragrant	6 ft. spreading, recurrent, moss
Rosa Mundi (1581)	white-red			4 ft. spreading, spring bloom

Rose listings were revised with the help of Mel Albert of the Potomac Rose Society, and the Arlington Rose Foundation

R. damascena

Rambler Chevy Chase

R. chinensis
"Old Blush"

Roses are tolerant and will grow in acid soil, but in very acid soils essential nutrients are locked up and unavailable to plant roots, and harmful minerals are unlocked and attack the plants. Wait for complete soil test results before calculating the correct amount of lime to add.

Roses are customarily planted in beds or holes that have been deeply prepared to a depth of 15 to 24 inches with additions of up to 50% compost or well rotted cow manure, supplemented with a cup of superphosphate or bonemeal, to the area reserved for each rose. In the unlikely event that your only sunny area is over unimproved clay soil, double the amount of compost and add greensand to the existing soil to raise the beds by 10-12 inches. The deeper the soil is worked and enriched, the larger the root run will be and the feeding area thus provided will enable the rose plant to make correspondingly vigorous growth. Additional nutrients in the form of trace elements may be provided by the use of mineralized fertilizers. Gently mound the rose display bed and edge to define the area and to deter invasion by weeds.

Planting the Rose Bush

Rose bushes are often planted too close together to make the best growth—on the erroneous theory that the foliage should shade the ground. Studies indicate wider spacing is needed. Plants should be set so that the drip lines of adjacent plants should be at least 24 inches apart. Lower growing roses, such as floribundas, need this spacing, whereas the hybrid perpetuals and landscape roses need 3 to 5 feet of space from the center.

The planting depth of a rose bush should be determined by the bud union. After settling, the bud union should be even with the surface of the ground. This union is the point where most hybrid roses have been grafted onto strong-growing root systems to support their best top growth. If this union is buried it may produce weaker roots of its own.

Decide the depth and width of the hole by making sure that the root system may be spread out naturally over a cone of soil in the bottom. Only broken root ends should be pruned; use a clean knife or scissors action pruner.

After the bush is in place with the roots spread out, work soil gently in and around the roots to remove air pockets. When the hole is two-thirds full, it should be thoroughly trampled to firm the soil around the roots. Then fill the hole with water and allow it to soak into the soil. When this has taken place, fill the rest of the hole with soil to about an inch above the grafting union, but do not tramp or pack—it will settle to the proper depth.

If you plant in late fall, the soil should be mounded to a depth of 8 to 10 inches with a good mulch. The mounds will protect the shortened ends of the canes from drying winds during the winter. Clip the ends of newly planted roses if they protrude more than 2 or 3 inches above the mound. The next spring remove the mounds gradually over the period of a week to 10 days, preferably when it is cloudy to prevent sunburning newly exposed bark.

In an exposed site, spring planted bare root plants need this same protection, but only for 2 or 3 weeks. By the end of that time, roots should be functioning and the canes will no longer need protection from sun and wind.

If you prefer to plant the more commonly available container grown plants in the spring, you should prepare a site as you would for other roses. This can, in fact, be done the previous fall. Cut and remove the tin or plastic, but do not disturb the soil from around the roots if most of the roots have not grown through. Remove only the bottom from paper containers and slit up the sides, so the roots can spread naturally. Inspect the root ball before planting. If the roots have begun to circle in the pot, they may be root bound and will require loosening by hand so they can be spread out over the enriched soil in the bottom of the hole.

Plant the bush so that the bud union, which may be exposed on some plants, shows at ground level. Fill in with good soil, and water generously with a transplant solution. It is not necessary to mound soil around potted plants.

Packaged roses that are not in soil will need the same treatment as bare root roses, and prior soaking for 6 to 12 hours may be advisable. If such rose bushes have spindly, yellow shoots, they will need to be given heavy pruning and longer soil protection to recover from the loss of vitality from breaking dormancy too early.

Planting Pointers

♦ Neither fresh manure nor fertilizer should be in contact with the roots of the newly planted rose. Instead, soak both plant and hole with a transplant solution.

♦ Any bushes that were even slightly dry at time of receipt should be soaked for up to 12 hours before planting. If planting has to be delayed for several days, dig a trench and heel the plants in, making sure that the roots and tops are

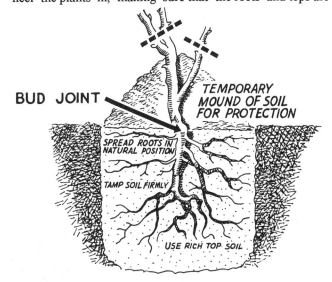

In planting the dormant rose bush spread the roots in a natural position in a hole that is large enough to accommodate them without crowding or bending.

♦ covered with damp soil or peat moss.

♦ Keep the roots and tops from drying wind during planting by keeping them in a pail of soupy mud, only removing the bush when the hole is ready for it.

♦ Fall planted roses should have their canes shortened at planting time to 6 to 8 inches. Make these cuts with clean scissors-action shears to prevent crushing. Seal with grafting wax or dressing to prevent entry of the sawfly that bores into canes.

♦ Discard any bush with lumpy knots on the roots. These root galls or nematodes will infest the soil, spreading this disease to other roses in the bed.

♦ Discard any roses with inferior root systems. They will not start off with the vigor expected of a well-grown plant.

♦ Do not plant roses where tree roots or shade will compete for nutrients and sunlight. They will probably grow, but give little satisfaction.

♦ Roses do best where they are protected from strong prevailing winds that sap vitality from newly developing canes faster than it can be replaced by the roots.

♦ Conversely, do not plant roses in a dead air pocket where they are more subject to fungal diseases and pests. Plant them where there is good, gentle air circulation and at least 6 hours of sunlight a day.

Be observant. Occasionally a shoot with 7 to 9 leaflets to the leaf appears on a hybrid tea rose. If the leaflets and the color

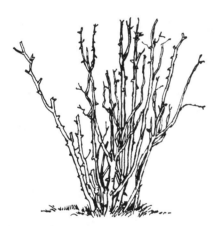

Before pruning a hybrid tea rose bush.

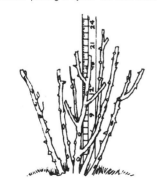

The hybrid tea rose after pruning.

of the shoot closely resemble the purchased plant, do not remove. Many Eastern and Northern bred roses are rooted on the multiflora rose, an invasive species formerly much used for livestock fencing until it escaped into the pastures it was supposed to protect. Suckers originating from below the bud union should be removed. Many Western-grown roses are on Dr. Huey root stock or its progeny, whose leaflets closely resemble the hybrid teas. Only close comparison with the leaflets and stem of the shoot with the rest of the plant will tell whether or not this is a sucker. If in doubt, it may pay to gently remove the soil down to the point of the shoot's origin to see if it comes from below the bud union.

Pruning

Pruning of hybrid teas, hybrid perpetuals, grandifloras, floribundas, and polyanthas is normally done in the early spring after danger of a killing freeze is past. When forsythia blooms is a good time to prune.

Spring pruning for bush roses is confined to removal of dead wood, weak and spindly growth, and shortening of the remaining canes. The extent of this shortening will depend on the number of blooms desired from the first flowering and the length of the stems. Current practice preaches moderation to make sure the bush has adequate foliage for best growth.

Disease can often be cut out of a plant during pruning. Observe the pith on a cane when you make a first pruning cut on a cane. If healthy, it should be white. A brown or purple patch on the cane indicates a canker that can be removed by pruning 2 or 3 inches below the area until white pith appears. Use pruners disinfected with alcohol and seal the wound with grafting wax to prevent further spread of the disease.

Pruning Climbers

Prune the large-flowered climbing roses by removing dead wood and from one-third to one-fourth of the oldest canes at the ground. These older scaly canes, which harbor disease and insect pests, should be removed after the flowering season. For heavy, thick canes, use the pruning saw or long-handled lopping shears.

The pruning of spring-flowering climbers should be postponed until after the bloom to produce the best quality flowers—produced on the new wood of last summer's growth. Of almost equal quality are roses produced on second-year wood. Older canes have lower quality bloom, and the oldest are susceptible to disease, so a regular late spring pruning is advisable.

In the late fall rose canes in exposed situations should be shortened to about 4 feet to prevent damage to other canes from excessive swaying and ice storms. In lieu of this pruning, you may mound a shovel or two of soil around the plant to hold it in place. Make sure the canes are tied in place.

Prune the large-flowered climbing roses by removing from ⅓ to ¼ of the oldest canes at the ground. The older, scaly canes, which are a home for disease and insect pests, should be removed following the flowering season.

Climbing sports, a naturally occurring mutation of hybrid tea roses that results in climbing habit, should be pruned in early spring in the same way as the bush forms. Varieties of large-flowered climbers that have repeat bloom are renewal pruned after the first bloom just like other climbers.

The pruning of landscape and shrub roses is simplicity itself. Remove the dead wood and canes that interfere with passers-by. The rugosas and hybrid rugosas need to have their canes shortened after bloom to encourage compact growth, otherwise they grow too tall and become bare-legged.

Disease and Insect Control

This is a balancing act because, for most roses, disease and insect control is a must—equal in importance with a regular feeding program. Prevention of fungal diseases and damage from sucking and chewing insects starts in late April and continues throughout each growing season.

For roses, the chief insect pests are aphids, chafers, Japanese beetles, and leafhoppers. The most prevalent fungal diseases of the leaves are black spot and powdery mildew, although rust can be a problem.

Many gardeners depend on a regular weekly program of spraying or dusting with all-purpose mixtures developed for roses. Such compounds consist of fungicides for black spot canker and mildew, as well as stomach and contact poisons to discourage chewing and sucking insects. Because of the frequency of pesticide use, there has been a real effort to use "low impact" pest control, using less toxic materials where possible. Integrated pest management, IPM, described earlier, works best against insects, where monitoring for pests and their predators, gives a better idea if, and when, it is necessary to intervene.

Ryania or neem extracts in dust or spray form, insecticidal soap, horticultural spray oil, and the chemical systemic, Orthene, are effective choices when a major invasion of chewing insects threatens buds. Contact poisons against sucking insects are not effective unless they hit the pests. Some systemic insecticides, although more toxic, allow the gardener to spray less often.

With all materials, the finer the particles of dust or mist the more effective coverage will be. Whether dusts or sprays are used does not make much difference. It is not the material, but the regularity and thoroughness of application that counts in this climate—a good reason to seek the least toxic alternative.

In the spring when growth is rapid and rain showers are frequent, you will need to apply fungicides as a preventive. When growth slows and it is drier, spraying can be reduced, although midsummer heat and humidity means that you will have to renew fungicides weekly to prevent mildew spores from multiplying.

Non-Toxic Fungicide

Rose lovers with pets and small children will want to take advantage of a non-toxic fungicide tested by the staff of Longwood Gardens and the National Arboretum. Mix 1 tablespoon baking soda and 2½ tablespoons of refined summer spray oils per gallon of water. This formula prevents powdery mildew spores from invading the leaf stomata if started before hot wet weather. Choose a dry day so the mixture will evaporate rapidly. This mix should be applied as a preventive measure every week to 10 days in the early morning, so foliage will dry by midday.

If black spot is not checked sufficiently, try alternating with Funginex and Daconil 2787 every 10-14 days, or Triathlon during heat spells.

Feeding and Watering the Rose

The feeding schedule and menu for the established rose depends somewhat on its function in the garden. But in general growers start out by giving each bush a generous handful of fertilizer (5-10-5) or a special rose food in March, and each month thereafter through July. Continued feeding in August is likely to produce late growth too soft to survive the winter, because roses are, by nature, reluctant to go dormant. The use of special rose formulas and mineralized fertilizers and foliar spray formulas give good results, although soil improvement with good quality composts is the firm foundation on which feeding should rest.

Manures can be applied in the winter after the bushes are dormant, if care is taken to see that it does not come in contact with the bark. Nutrients will leach down through the soil over the winter. An occasional reapplication of dolomitic ground limestone every few years is desirable to give trace amounts of magnesium. A soil test is recommended first, because too much may be harmful.

Roses need generous watering if regular rainfall is less than an inch a week. A rain gauge near your prize plants will tell you how often you need to supplement to help them survive the summer stress of a climate that doesn't suit them. A soaking hose will prevent excess moisture on the leaves. As with spraying, water early in the day.

Mulching and Winter Protection

Mulching of rose beds is now widely practiced here as growers realize that a heavily mulched soil gives far greater returns in growth and bloom than a well-cultivated bed. The kind of material used is relatively unimportant. The important point is to apply a mulch in the spring and keep it there until the following spring. It serves the following functions, in descending order of importance.

Keeps soil cooler, permitting better root function during hot weather.

⇒ Maintains the humus content of the soil.

⇒ Conserves moisture.

⇒ Provides better aeration of the soil.

⇒ Prevents winter exposure and heaving of roots.

⇒ Controls weeds, and.

⇒ Prevents erosion.

A relatively fine grade of chopped hardwood mulch is the most attractive and trouble-free kind of readily available mulch.

In winter, a few shovelfuls of soil can be piled over the crown of a rose bush after mulch is carefully drawn back, if you live in the upper Piedmont. Then, an inch or two can be added once the ground is frozen to prevent the thawing and refreezing effect that causes heaving and tearing of roots near the surface, although roses are not badly affected by this problem. Once the leaves fall, further wind-screening with burlap of evergreen boughs is not necessary, unless the rose bed is in a very exposed position.

Cutting Roses

The cutting of a bloom from a rose bush will affect the subsequent development of blossoms on that branch. Growers who show are very aware of the fact. When cutting roses, choose those buds with the longest stems that have just begun to unfurl. Make the cut just above the second leaf at the lower end of the flowering shoot.

Roses can be cut with sharp anvil shears, the kind that will hold the stem until the handles are released for transfer to a flat basket without fear of thorns. (Rose thorns can cause nasty infections and are always painful.)

It is good to make a second long cut on the removed stem to expose as much cambium as possible, and to put the blossoms in lukewarm water in a cool room so they can draw up as much water as possible into their stems. When arranging roses, you may keep the water fresher by removing the lower foliage and adding a combination of 1 tablespoon of Clorox and 1 cup of Sprite to a quart of water. The Clorox disinfects and the soda provides some sugars in a usable form to prolong the freshness of bloom.

Getting the Best Blooms

The cutting of a bloom from the bush may greatly affect its subsequent growth and flowering. Normally, a new shoot may appear from any leaf axil left on the branch. Such an array of new growth is seldom desirable, but this does not mean you should remove all of the shoot, which would mean all foliage.

New growth will occur from the leaf axils you left at the base of each shoot.

The removal of spent blooms from the bush does not consist of snapping off the dead flower. This leaves the maximum number of leaves, but keeps the first bud below the spent rose, and this bud seldom produces good bloom. It is far better to cut back just above the second or third leaf with 5 leaflets. These growth centers will produce better flowers.

Disbudding

To develop the largest terminal bud, pinch the 2 buds below it on alternate sides of the limb. The net effect is to send growth hormones to 2 lower leaf axils; both may send out new shoots and buds to bloom within 4 to 6 weeks.

Most varieties of hybrid tea roses produce a cluster of buds at the terminal of each new shoot. The removal of all the side buds when ¼ inch long puts all the strength of the shoot into the terminal flower for the most perfect exhibition-size bloom. Moreover a flower flanked by 1 or 2 unopened buds is not as attractive for show purposes. The competition rules of the American Rose Society disqualify hybrid tea roses that have not been disbudded. For mass garden display this practice is not necessary.

Rose Propagation

Propagation of new rose plants from your favorites by means of softwood cuttings is simplicity itself, if you remember 2 things.

(1) Take the cuttings in early September, when you can expect cooling weather, but warm soil, for the 6-7 week period before the cuttings start to grow.

(2) Use a flowering stem that is 8-12 inches long, after removal of the flowering tip. Ideally, such a cutting would have 3-4 nodes that could develop new roots.

Strip the bottom leaves from the plant, leaving just a few near the top. Dip the stems at least 3 nodes deep in rooting hormone powder; then, plant in a pot with sterile rooting medium, or in a corner of a well-prepared rose bed.

Good spraying or dusting gives complete coverage of foliage.

In cutting a rose, make the cut just above the second leaf at the lower end of the flowering shoot.

Disbud a portion of the roses, removing the side buds, thus putting all the plant's strength into the terminal bud.

Layering is an easy safe method of propagating many plants.

Because rapid root development is paramount, use peat, perlite, greensand, or triple superphosphate to make it easy for roots to form before winter. Do not fertilize with nitrogen.

Once the cutting is well watered with a transplant solution, place a half-gallon plastic milk container, with its bottom cut out, over the cutting. Growth should start in 6-7 weeks. It is always best to set out several cuttings to insure that one will survive. When new growth is noticed, unscrew the jug top to increase air circulation as the plant matures.

Over winter leave the dormant young plants in their jugs, protected from cold and wind, in a sheltered place or in the garden. In the spring, move the plants, before dormancy is broken, to their place in the garden.

ANNUAL GUIDE TO ROSE GARDEN TASKS

January
Order roses for spring planting. Transplant old bushes, weather permitting. Inventory supplies and equipment. Sharpen tools.

March
Spring pruning. Begin spraying, watering and fertilizing programs. Clean up beds. Pruning demonstration at Brookside Garden Rose Garden.

April-May
Plant roses. Continue care programs. Remove blind shoots. Monitor insects, and spray, if necessary.

June-July
Continue spraying, watering, and fertilizing programs. Remove spent blooms and blind shoots. Summer Care Clinic at Brookside Rose garden.

August-September
Continue care program but apply no nitrogen fertilizers after mid-August. Remove spent blooms.

October
Continue spray and water program until heavy frost. Order roses for fall planting. Prepare holes. Stop dead-heading and allow plants to go dormant. Prune only dead, diseased, and twiggy growth.

November
Plant fall roses. Provide winter protection for bushes after heavy frost.

December
Cut back long canes to 3-4 feet to prevent bruising and root damage from wind. Add winter mulch.
—Adapted with permission of The Potomac Rose Society

PEST CONTROL FOR ROSES

Pest	Pesticide/Treatment
Blackspot	Baking soda & summer oil, or Funginex, Daconil, or Triathlon; spray foliage 7-10 days all season
Canker	Prune and burn infected stems.
Mildew	Benomyl or summer oil spray before leaves are affected
Rose Chafer	Insecticidal soap, BT, spray buds as needed
Japanese Beetle	Ryania, neem extract, spray into flowers in early July
Leafhopper	Soap spray, ryania, neem extract, begin in late May
Aphids	Hand stripping, natural predators, or soap spray

INSPIRATION:
Brookside Gardens, 1511 Glenallen Avenue, Wheaton, Maryland.
National Herb Garden, National Arboretum, New York Avenue & Bladensburg Road NE, Washington D.C.
Dumbarton Oaks, 31st and R Streets NW, Washington, D.C.
Resources for the Future, 1616 P Street NW, D.C.
Franciscan Monastery, 1400 Quincy Street NE, Washington, D.C.
Bon Air Park, Lexington Street & Wilson Boulevard, Arlington, Virginia.
Green Spring Garden, Green Spring Road, Annandale, Virginia.
River Farm, The American Horticultural Society, East Boulevard Drive off George Washington Parkway, Alexandria, Virginia.
Resources: The Potomac Rose Society, Michael Berger, President (703)242-8263

10. BULBS FOR THE GARDEN

When bulbs are mentioned, most gardeners think of tulips and daffodils; however there are a host of so-called bulbous plants that can fill the garden. From the earliest snowdrops to the gladiolus and dahlias of summer, bulbs are prime contributors to the beauty and interest of the garden. Many produce excellent flowers for cutting.

Bulbs are undoubtedly the easiest of flowering plants to grow. Because many bulbs come from semi-arid countries with pronounced wet-dry cycles, their leaves work to store all the nutrients needed for next year's growth and flowering before the dry season causes foliage to shrivel. Then, after a set time, some, like the large autumn-flowering crocus and Colchicum, need only favorable temperatures to flower, even out of the soil. Others, such as the hyacinth, daffodil, and amaryllis, respond to a complex of the appropriate light hours, moisture, and the soil temperature.

The term "bulbs, in the general usage sense, means flowering plants, which, after blooming, use this year's growth to create food reserves for next year's bloom.
The leaves of true *bulbs* create each layer of next year's growth before dying. They are all formed like onions. In addition to the flowering onions, other examples are the tulip,

the lily, and the daffodil. Bulbs increase in size with age, while they increase their numbers by producing smaller offsets from the basal plates.

Corms are solid bodies without division or layer that contain one or more buds and the food supply. A corm lasts only one year. Most cormous plants grow a new corm on top of the old one for next year's bloom. Crocus and gladiolus grow from corms.

Tubers are enlargements of the stem or of the root where food reserves and growing centers are concentrated. Some have eyes on the enlargement, such as the potato, which is a modified stem. Others, like the dahlia and sweet potato, are enlargements of the roots and have their growth centers or eyes only on the neck. The tubers feed the plant until new roots and tops are established.

A *rhizome* is a thick, fleshy root, rather than a temporary enlargement of the root for one growing season. Rhizomes usually last for several years, whereas tubers are often absorbed during the growth process. The German (bearded) iris and the canna lily are good examples of rhizomous plants.

Tulips and daffodils are more widely grown here

than other kinds of bulbs because of their showiness and their ability to grow successfully in almost any kind of soil temporarily. Modern tulips do so at a price, however, for Washington soil is too moist and hot in the summer for most of them to persist and bloom in later years. Since both tulips and narcissus originally grew on well-drained ground, most of the species will persist, while complex hybrids are less likely to thrive over time.

Many of the small, early flowering bulbs are even more easily grown, but they have less conspicuous flowers. The crocus, grape hyacinth, and snowdrop, to mention the most frequently planted, are well suited to the home garden. All of the smaller bulbs, when planted in large clumps, will persist and even increase in the garden for years with a minimum of care.

This does not mean that bulbs will grow well in all kinds of soil, or that they do not respond to care, but rather that they give satisfying results with less required effort. Most kinds of bulbs will grow and thrive with less attention than perennials. In addition, early spring bulbs often provide the only dramatic swatches of color in shaded gardens whose palette is considerably muted once trees leaf out.

Bulbs may be divided into *hardy* and *tender* groups. The hardy ones are planted in the fall from September to December. Among these, several kinds, including the beautiful bulbous lilies, do not keep well out of the ground, unless they are protected from drying. To dry out is to lose part of their vitality. Large plump bulbs have the most vitality and produce the finest flowers.

Most gardeners in this area do not think seriously of planting hardy bulbs until October and are not too concerned if they do not get around to it until November. Experienced gardeners begin in late August with the Madonna lily, plant the earliest small crocuses and tiny bulbs in September, and continue with daffodils and tulips sometime in October. The rest of the summer lilies do not come in until November; and bulbous iris can wait until mid-December in warmer areas, lest they be tempted to put up top growth too early and thus suffer a freeze. If bulbs are gotten into the ground at the proper season, their supporting roots will develop before the ground is frozen, and the plants will be ready for the second stage of top growth and flowering that starts by February.

For the most part hardy bulbs may be left in the ground for years, particularly if the beds have been well-worked and fertilized before planting. They may stay until diminished bloom indicates that they have become crowded.

If true bulbs are transplanted, it should be done after the foliage has fully ripened so the next season's bloom is not jeopardized. To disturb a bulb before its growth is completed is to diminish its vitality. To disguise yellowing foliage, plant bulbs among clumps of perennials whose growth coincides with their demise.

When beds have been prepared with generous quantities of compost, a fertilizer formula that emphasizes superphosphate for root growth, and soil sweetening bone meal or lime, your bulbs may be replanted immediately. During

Guide to Proper Bulb Planting

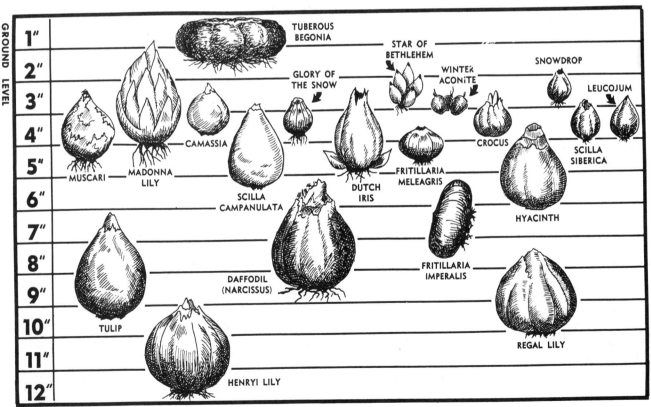

dormancy most hardy bulbs keep better in well-drained soil than in a basement or garage. In order to avoid soil-borne diseases and a build up of insect pests, it is generally sound practice to replant bulbs in a new location, if space permits it. Usually, well-grown bulbs have few problems.

Naturalizing Bulbs

If you want to plant the hardiest of the bulbs in a suitable location, hoping that they would not have to be touched for years, you should seek out naturalizing varieties of daffodils, crocuses, and many of the small early bulbs, after doing soil samples to find an area of your property that has the good drainage and sweeter soil that they prefer. The best flower display year after year comes in areas that have full sun or at least morning sun during the time that bulb foliage ripens.

Select an area where uncut grass until May or mid June will not destroy the appearance of your property. Then scatter drifts of bulbs onto the lawn or border by hand, planting them with a bulb planter set an inch deeper than the recommended depth for each species. Into each hole put a half cup of compost mixed with a teaspoon of bone meal, to give root development a boost. Then place the bulb in the hole and cover. If you must move a bulb before the foliage has yellowed and dried, dig it with a ball of earth surrounding the roots. Place such bulbs in another bed or a temporary trench where they can complete the growth cycle undisturbed before you take them up.

Beds of hardy bulbs are not often mulched in the warmer parts of the area, although they benefit from such protection. In particular, mulch is put on after the ground has frozen, to keep heaving action from tearing the roots of those closest to the surface. Often, in public plantings, these mulches are retained throughout the year to suppress weeds in the beds.

Forcing Bulbs

If your garden conditions are unsuitable for bulbs, you may still enjoy them in winter and early spring indoors, when their color and fragrance mean so much more—by forcing your favorite varieties. This can be done with bulb varieties that are marked for this purpose in your garden catalog or local garden store. Such bulbs have been chilled or warmed for the set amount of time that each species requires to begin the blooming cycle, usually from 8 to 13 weeks. The spring bulbs can then be potted, and kept watered in a cool, dark room until their roots develop well. Then they are ready to be brought out into full light for the final stages of growth and bloom. Forced warm-season bulbs do not need cool darkness for best root development.

If you order a spring bulb variety suitable for forcing, you can initiate the process yourself by giving bulbs from 2 to 3 months at temperatures below 45° Fahrenheit. Anything from a spare refrigerator to an unheated garage will do, depending on the date you start.

HARDY SUMMER- AND AUTUMN-FLOWERING BULBS

Bulbs	Blooms in	Color	Height	Planting Conditions
Acidanthera (acidanthera bicolor)	August	White with, burgundy centers	24	5 in. deep, 6 in. apart in fertile soil, sun.
Autumn Amaryllis (lycoris squamigera)	August	Lavender pink	24-30	4 in. deep, 6 in. apart, in moist soil, part shade.
Colchicum (C. autumnale) (C. speciosum)	October October	White, lilac-pink White, purple	6 6-10	5 in. deep, 9 in. apart, sun, shade, humus, in August. 4-6 in. deep, 9-12 in. apart, in midsummer.
Hardy Cyclamen (C. coum, repandum) (C. neapolitanum) (C. europaeum)	December-April August-September August-September	Pink, white Rose, white Crimson	4-5 4 4	Light shade, humus. Mulch all with pine needles. 1 in., deep, 6-10 in. apart. 2 in. deep, 6-10 in. apart. 1 in. deep, 6-10 in. apart.
Lily of the Nile (agapanthus africanus 'Mooreana')	July	Dark blue	20-24	4 in. deep, 6 in. apart, moist, warm soil, sheltered.
Lilies (lilium sp. and hybrids) Regal Tiger Turk's Cap Speciosum Auratum Hybrids	Late June July July July, August September	White-pink Orange-black centers Yellow to red White, pink To dark red	36-60 36-48 48-84 36-50 To 100	Sun, rich well-drained soil. 8 in. deep, 12 in. apart. Prone to mosaic virus. Moist, acid soil. 8 in. deep, 12 in. apart. Sun, rich well drained soil.
Lycoris, Golden and Radiata (africana) (radiata)	August June or September	Yellow Red	20 18	Sun, warmest, well-drained soil. 5 in. deep, 6 in. apart. 5 in. deep, 4 in. apart.
Peruvian Daffodil (Hymenocallis Calathina)	May-June	White	18-24	8 in. deep, 10-12 in. apart.
Sternbergia (Sternbergia lutea)	September	Yellow	6-9	5 in deep, 4 in. apart. Dry sunny soil, mulch in winter.

If such bulbs are potted in groups of three or more, kept moist, and held in a refrigerator by late September, the smaller bulbs and narcissus can be brought out into light by Thanksgiving or December 1. They will have developed roots and the tops will be poking above the soil. By watering and placing them in a sunny, but cool, window, they will flower by Christmas. Large bulbs that are potted later in October to be kept outside in a cold frame or dug trench will not be ready to come in until the holidays. They should be well-mulched to keep soil temperatures stay just above freezing, and so that you can easily retrieve them. Inspect the drainage holes for good root growth before bringing them in.

Most species will bloom within a month of being brought into light, warm conditions. They must, of course, be well watered during this crucial period and turned often so that the plants grow straight. Blooming bulbs will keep their beauty longer if they are moved out of a sunny window to a cooler room for display. A cut bamboo stake makes an unobtrusive support when green florist string secures the leggy foliage

Commercially heat-treated amaryllis bulbs will also flower in 4 to 6 weeks, if potted closely and watered around December 1. The next year, any you put out to grow in your garden can be dug by early October, held for at least 3 weeks in a warm furnace room to set the flower bud, then stored until the time you want to repot and force them. Furnace room temperatures should be above 75° Fahrenheit.

Besides the bulbs listed in this section, there are native wildflower bulbs that make a fine addition to the spring and summer garden. These are in the Wildflower Chapter.

CAMASSIA
(Camassia leichtlinii, quamash—Indian lily)
Uses: Border, bog garden.
Height: 2-3 feet.
Blooms: Late May.
Plant: September-October.
Distance: 18 inches.
Depth: 6 inches.
Soil: Rich, moist humus.
Exposure: Sun, part shade.

The Indian lily is an improved native bog plant with delicate spires of blue and white. C. quamash has a deeper blue and is a slightly smaller plant. Camassia spreads each year from offset bulbs, so that the final clumps can be up to 18 inches in diameter.
It blooms best in full sun, as long as its feet do not dry out. It is a good addition to the wildflower display garden in partial shade.

CROCUS
(Crocus species and hybrids)
Uses: Bedding, naturalizing, and forcing.
Height: 4-6 inches.
Plant: Spring-flowering, early October, autumn-flowering, late August.
Distance: 3-6 inches.
Depth: 3-4 inches.
Soil: Prepared garden loam.
Exposure: Sun, light shade.
Blooms:
Spring-flowering: 'Excelsior,' 'Remembrance,' 'Golden Goblet,' 'Queen of the Blues,' 'Purpurea Grandiflora,' 'Mammoth Yellow,' 'Imperati,' 'Cloth of Gold,' (C. susianus, C. vernum, C. moesiacus).
Autumn-flowering: Saffron (C. sativus), (C. speciosus, C. zonatus)

Crocuses are the most colorful of the early spring-flowering bulbs. They can appear in February in protected sunny situations, although they also do well in a shaded spot. They are generally planted in clumps or drifts to provide areas of vivid spring color. The many species and varieties are divided into spring-and autumn-flowering types. This latter group should not be confused with the larger flowered colchicum, a member of the lily family whose bloom resembles that of the crocus.

Crocuses are widely used as borders or edging in front of shrubbery, in the perennial bed, and for naturalizing. In reasonably well-drained soil, the corms last for many years. I have roto-tilled naturalized drifts of crocuses in the fall when redoing my lawn, only to have them come up next year better than ever because of the forced division and fertilizing. While many gardeners like to have them in the lawn, they resent the brown patches left by their dying foliage in June and the fact that the crocus patch must be left uncut while foliage matures.

Corms, like all bulbs, get their strength for next year's bloom from the ripening foliage. If this causes problems, and you can afford it, replant anew in the lawn each late summer or fall. Alternatively, confine crocuses to bed areas where they can be lifted and divided every few years without further ado.

Crocus corms are a favorite food of squirrels. It is wise to plant a little deeper if this is a problem, or to cover the newly planted corms with a sheet of one quarter inch hardware cloth before replacing the soil. This precaution is effective for years.

Autumn-flowering crocus corms may sometimes be received in July. It is best to plant them as soon as they can be obtained, because sometimes late shipments are in bloom when they arrive. These varieties flower on bare stalks: with other species, the foliage is produced in the spring.

Crocuses make the best effect when planted en masse. A group of 25 large corms planted 3 to 4 inches apart may not make a great show the first season, but its beauty will increase every year. This spacing is preferable to a closer planting that will soon exhaust the soil and deplete the corms.

The most popular crocus colors seem to be the yellows, purples, and lavender, although they come in a wide variety of shades and striped effects. Even though most gardeners buy unnamed mixed colors for mass plantings, there are over 40 species to choose from if you wish to produce definite color patterns throughout spring and fall. The named varieties are generally larger hybrid flowers.

Although seldom troubled by insects and diseases, crocuses are not immune. They can be affected by a virus that causes streaking, just as tulips are. In poorly drained soils the corms may be destroyed by a disease called fusarium rot (treatable with a fungicide).

HARDY CYLAMEN
(Cyclamen—C. coum, C. europaeum, C. hederifolium, neapolitanum)
Uses: Foreground, woods garden, under shrubs.
Height: 3-4 inches.
Bloom: Spring—coum; Summer—neopolitanum; Fall—europeum.
Plant: Late summer.
Distance: 6-8 inches.
Depth: 5 inches.
Soil: Light, woodsy humus.

These dainty small cyclamen are ideal in a north-facing door garden or raised bed where their fragrance and foliage can be appreciated. Although the flowers are small, and the tubers can take several years to create a clump of handsome variegated foliage that will make an impact, their charm is considerable. The foliage of some species often lasts through the winter.

The large tubers, which look like flattened beets, are planted no more than 5 inches deep, with the tops no more than 1 to 2 inches below the surface. Older tubers are often slightly exposed and do benefit from a light mulch of pine needles when they are not shaded by foliage. All the cyclamen like well-drained, woodsy humus.

DAFFODILS
(Narcissus species and cultivars)
Uses: Border, naturalizing, forcing, cutting.
Height: 4-24 inches.
Bloom: March-May.
Plant: September-October.
Distance: 6-10 inches apart.
Depth: 6-8 inches.
Soil: Well-drained, rich loam.
Exposure: Sun, partial shade.

(Key: *—denotes good for naturalizing, forcing, a—yellow, b—multicolored, c—white)
1. Trumpets Cultivars:
 A. *'Golden Harvest', *'Arctic Gold,' *'Aurum,' 'Ulster Prince,' *'King's Stag'.
 B. 'Content,' *'Bravoure,' 'Effective,' 'Ballygarvey,' 'Preamble,' *'Prologue,' *'Trouseau,' *'Spellbinder'.
 C. *'Mt. Hood,' 'Broughshane,' *'Cantatrice', 'Empress of Ireland,' 'Vigil,' 'Rashee'.
2. Large Cups:
 A. *'Armada', *'Camelot,' 'Carbineer,' *'Carlton', 'Fortune,' 'Galway,' *'King Alfred,' 'St. Egwin,' *'Golden Aura', 'Lemnos,' 'Tinker,' 'Home Fires'.
 B. *'Kilworth,' *'Louise de Coligny,' 'Polindra,' 'Pink Rim,' 'Interim,' 'Accent,' 'Avenger,' 'Salome,' 'Festivity,' *'Green Island,' 'Daviot,' *'Ceylon,' *'Falstaff,' *'Pinza,' 'Shining Light,' *'Chapeau,' *'Foxfire,' *'Jewel Song,' *'Rainbow,' *'Binkie'.

 C. *'Ice Follies,' *'Easter Moon,' *'Stainless', 'Canisp', 'Broomhill,' 'Early Mist,' 'Wedding Bell,' *'Daydream'.
3. Small Cups:
 A. 'Therm.', 'Chungking,' 'Jezebel,' 'Doubtful,' 'Ardour'.
 B. *'Limerick,' 'Blarney,' 'La Riante,' 'Amateur,' *'Marya', 'Perimeter,' 'Eminent,' *'Woodland Prince,' 'Rockall', *'Merlin', *'Snow Gem,' 'Enniskillen,' 'Matapan,' 'Redstart'.
 C. 'Polar Ice,' 'Mystic,' 'Chinese White,' 'Bryher,' 'Cushendall', 'Dream Castle'.
4. Doubles:
 A. *'Yellow Cheerfulness,' *'Meeting,' 'Double Event'.
 B. *'Cheerfulness,' *'Acropolis,' *'Tahiti,' *'Unique,' *'White Lion,' *'Bridal Crown'.
5. (N. Triandrus) Hybrids:
 A. 'Ruth Haller'.
 B. *'Merry Bells,' 'Lapwing'.
 C. *'Thalia,' *'Tresamble,' 'Moonshine,' 'Ice Wings'.
6. (N. cyclamineus) Hybrids:
 A. 'February Gold,' *'March Sunshine,' *'Peeping Tom,' 'Bartley,' 'Charity May'.
 B. 'Beryl,' 'Dove Wings'.
 C. *'Jenny,' *'Frostkist,' *'February Silver'.
7. (N. jonquilla) Hybrids:
 A. *'Trevithian,' *'Sweetness,' *'Quail,' *'Oregon Gold,' 'Golden Sceptre,' 'Shah'.
 B. *'Sweet Pepper,' *'Suzy,' 'Cherie,' 'Bunting,' 'Viro,' 'Finch,' 'Verdin'.
8. (N. tazetta) Hybrids:
 A. *'Martha Washington,' *'Cragford,' *'Geranium,' 'Orange Wonder,' 'Scarlet Gem'.
 B. *'Silver Chimes,' *'Scilly White'.
9. (N. poeticus) Hybrids:
 A. 'Perdita,' *'Actea,' 'Milan,' 'Sea Green,' 'Cantabile'.
10. (Narcissus) species (Miniatures):
(Narcissus bulbicodium conspicuus, N. rupicola, N. gracilis, N. watieri, N. jonquilla, N. minimus), and hybrids of all classes:
 1a. 'Little Gem,' 'Small Talk;' 1b. 'Little Beauty;' 1c. *'P. Milner;' 5b. 'April Tears,' (N. hawera), 'Arctic Morn'; 6a. *'Tete a tete,' 'Mite;' 7a. 'Pixie's Sister;' 7b. *'Bobbysoxer,' *'Lintie,' *'Sundial'.
11. Split Cups:
 b. *'Gold Collar,' 'Cassata,' 'Orangerie,' 'Valdrome,' 'Colblanc,' 'Phantom,' 'Tripartite,' 'Square Dance'.
—Recommended by the Washington Daffodil Society
Revised and updated by Delia Bankhead & Scott Bally.

The daffodils are the first spring flowers to combine beauty of form, fragrance, and graceful movement. They literally bring a garden to life.

The choice of bulbs for the home garden is not simple, for there are now hundreds of varieties. One of the

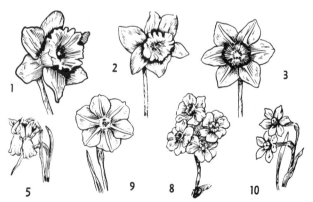

Daffodil types. 1. Trumpet. 2. Large cup. 3. Small cup. 5. Triandrus. 9. Poeticus. 8. Tazetta hybrid. 10. Species (Jonquilla). (Numbered according to classification.)

easiest and most pleasant approaches is to visit a local daffodil show and obtain the names of those varieties that appeal to you. Those given above are representative. They are about equally divided between those varieties that can be gotten readily from local nurseries and garden centers and those that must be ordered through the mail here or abroad. Some are old varieties, but all are high quality, and will stand up fairly well under the flush of early spring heat, which can wreck blooming flowers.

Beginners are often confused by the names narcissus, daffodil, and jonquil. It helps to know that Narcissus is the scientific or Latin name, and daffodil is the common English equivalent. Either may be correctly applied to all types and species. Jonquil, however, although widely used in the South to designate yellow trumpets, can only be applied correctly to hybrids of the species N. jonquilla. The species has several small fragrant flowers on a slender stem and leaves like small slender reeds.

Daffodils are widely planted, because they are not too fussy about soil or situation. Nearly all of them require good drainage. Planting them under deciduous trees and in shrub borders is satisfactory, since their flowering is complete and the foliage is well on the way to maturity by the time their woody competitors are using the same light and nutrients.

However, only a limited number, principally the small cup and poeticus varieties, may be successfully naturalized into lawns. Some older species daffodils and cultivars also do well—to the point that archaeologists can often find Colonial buildings in spring, as much by the persistent daffodil plantings as by foundation ruins. Altogether, these hardiest species will give a 3-to 4-week season of naturalized color in the lawn or lightly shaded woodland setting. The commercially available mixtures often consist of these older varieties mixed with some newer ones, which may not persist as well.

The larger, more highly bred varieties usually do best in a flower border or beds in full sun without the root competition from shrubs and trees. For the small garden it gives a better effect to plant separate clumps or drifts of a single variety. In the variety listings above, those names marked with an asterisk are suitable for the garden, naturalizing, or forcing, although not all can be used for all three. Some of the heavier doubles have trouble standing up under wind and rain in the garden. Other lovely varieties do not force well. Check specialty catalogs for specific information that will help you order wisely.

Start With Good Soil

Deep planting of daffodils is desirable for two reasons. The bulbs do not multiply as rapidly, so that they only need lifting and thinning when bloom diminishes, which could be from 5 to 10 years. Deep planting, therefore, allows the planting and cultivation of annuals that can share the ground, since the daffodil's foliage dies down in late May and June. There should be 4-6 inches of earth above the bulbs: in lighter soils, even more. In addition, they should have the same amount of well-dug soil beneath them for good root development.

The soil should be adequately prepared, as for all bulbs, with, in heavy soil, the addition of some greensand to lighten the texture and provide a slowly available form of potash. If beds are well prepared, it is not necessary to feed all daffodils every year. People with show varieties may want to do so. Such growers sometimes water in 2 tablespoons of calcium nitrite per gallon of water as buds appear; this brightens the colors of the emerging flowers. The species miniatures do not want much feeding (a bit of wood ashes is quite sufficient); what they need is excellent drainage.

Any additional fertilizer should consist of a low nitrogen formula like 2-10-10 to prevent excessive leaf growth at the expense of strong stems and flowers that hold up in rough spring weather. Apply 3 to 4 pounds per 100 square feet to beds that seem to need a boost in early fall when root growth begins. Scratch well into the surface when you are cleaning up any annuals or perennials that are planted with your daffodils. If you have missed the fall feeding, you may feed in spring just before top growth appears, but you will be nourishing next season's blooms.

Buy Healthy Bulbs

Daffodils are not seriously troubled by disease or insect pests, particularly if you are careful to buy from a reliable dealer who makes a real effort to get healthy, disease-free bulbs from his supplier. Carefully examine all the bulbs that you buy or receive from friends for signs of softness near the basal plate that grows roots, a sign of disease or of infestation by the narcissus bulb fly. Sound bulbs are plump, firm, and covered with layers of brown, dry skin that was attached to this season's dried foliage.

Take These Precautions

The next line of defense is to search out all bulbs that grow with streaked foliage, a sign of mosaic virus. These can be dug or pulled during active growth. Bag and destroy.

Most of the time you will have no disease or fly problems here, particularly if drainage is good. If you have suspicious losses (animals will not eat daffodils), dust methoxychlor deep into the crown of the growing foliage of established plantings, so that it kills any bulb fly larvae that may be trying to migrate through stems and surrounding soil to the bulb.

Central to maintaining plant vigor is the protection of the ripening foliage that produces next year's bloom. Braiding it tightly or cutting it off before it turns yellow will diminish next year's display. It is better to gently rake daffodil foliage down as it begins to sag or inter-plant it with perennials or annuals that emerge in May. These will grow as the daffodil foliage fades, gradually hiding it from view with their own display of bloom.

BULBOUS IRIS
(Iris xiphium hybrids, danfordiae, reticulata)
Uses: Varies with species, cutting, foreground, rock garden.
Height: 12-24 inches, Dutch, English (I. xiphium); 3-6 inches, I. danfordiae, I. reticulata.
Blooms: Dutch, English in May-June; others in February-March.
Plant: English and Dutch, November-December; others, September.
Distance: 2-4 inches apart.
Depth: 4-6 inches.
Soil: Well-drained loam or loamy clay.
Exposure: Sun.
Dutch—I. 'Yellow Queen,' I.White Excelsior,' I. 'Poggenbeck,' I. 'Jacob DeWet;' *English*—I. 'Wedgewood' and others; I. danfordiae—yellow; I. reticulata cv.—white, blue, purple.

The colorful Dutch iris are the most available hybrids of the bulbous groups, found everywhere year round as cut flowers. They and their English cousins are well suited to garden culture here if one can constrain them from growing foliage into the winter cold.

Due to their sparse foliage, they are best suited to the cutting garden. By siting them carefully among fuller plants in the border, use may be made of their lovely range of colors in early summer—from white to yellow, blue, and bronze. There are many varieties to choose from, most inexpensive enough so that the gardener can afford to replace them every year after cutting depletes the bulbs. The varieties listed here are popular among local gardeners.

Dutch iris do best in the light, sandy soil that best mimics the Dutch habitat where they have been developed, although they are often planted in the heavier loams and clays north and west of Washington. Since the English iris prefer slightly heavier and more acid soils, they may be preferable for long-term use in the border. Local retailers, for this reason, should be persuaded to carry more.

Late fall planting is crucial to the success of both taller species. If planted too early, the bulbs not only will root, but also send their tops above the surface of the ground into the teeth of winter, with predictable results. The Mediterranean narcissus has the same problem here, which is why it is grown as a forcing bulb.

The Dutch and English iris will thrive if planted after Thanksgiving or in early December so that their roots develop before frozen soil puts a stop to growth until spring. Dutch iris are hardy enough. It is their quick response to any warm weather that must be overcome.

The smaller danfordiae and reticulata varieties should be planted in September. They make lovely pools of color in a sheltered area by late February and are seen to best advantage close to a door or set high in a rock garden, where their light fragrance gives a whiff of spring to come. In an enriched, well-drained bed, they may persist for years, gradually spreading. If your situation is not so favorable, and soil is too heavy, iris are still inexpensive enough to renew for the special effect they give to the early spring garden.

English and Dutch iris should be lifted after the foliage has matured and stored in a cool, airy place until late fall. If most of the foliage has been cut with the flower, they

A paper cone will "pull" a hyacinth bloom up out of the foliage.

will not be worth saving, and new ones should be bought.

The smaller rock garden iris may remain in the bed year round.

FLOWERING ONIONS
(Allium species—Alliums)
Uses: Borders, dried arrangement.
Height: 10-36 inches.
Blooms: May-September.
Plant: September-October.
Distance: 8 inches apart.
Depth: 4-8 inches deep.
Soil: Sweet, well-drained, sandy loam.
Exposure: Sun, light shade.
Species: A. christophii, A.cyaneum, A. moly, A. neapolitanum, A. ostrowskianum, A. senescens.

These delightful ornamentals are undervalued in the garden, where they will thrive in a bed with good enough drainage for other bulbous plants. One mail-order nursery markets them as Cascade bells, perhaps on the assumption that no one will buy an onion except to eat.

Native to many regions of the world, these species of onions begin to bloom in May, when the white neapolitanum and the rose-pink Ostrowsky onion start to flower. Both grow about a foot tall and are a fine adjunct to the spring bed or bulb border. In June Allium moly blooms with yellow starry umbels held 18 inches high above grey-green, strap-like foliage. Then, too, bloom the largest members of the onion family, the Star of Persia (A. christophii) and A. giganteum, lilac or blue lavender with flower heads of 10 and 5 inches, respectively, held on stalks 3 to 4 feet high. They are a dramatic addition to an annual or perennial bed, particularly against evergreen foliage, and their cut stalks dry well in a warm, airy place for fall and winter arrangements. In midsummer two rarer and shorter species bloom, A. senescens (with pink flowers and twisted foliage that looks well in the rock garden) and A. cyaneum (whose blue flowers and hair-like foliage add interest to any perennial bed). In a lightly shaded, area white Chinese chives (A. tuberosum) will thrive and bloom in May or September with minimal care.

All these onions will do well throughout the region, although they prefer the light, sandy soil close to the rivers.

In the higher, colder areas they will thrive in a well-dug bed with a porous winter mulch.

The most common enemy of the onion family is the onion root maggot. Good drainage prevents most infestations. Diazinon crystals sprinkled in the planting trench will control a mild outbreak, although re-examination of its toxicity to users is now being studied.

*FRITILLARIA
(Fritilleria imperialis, F. meleagris, F. purdyii)
Uses: Border, bed, mole repellant.
Height: 1-3 feet.
Blooms: May.
Plant: October.
Distance: 4-12 inches.
Depth: 5 to 8 inches.
Soil: Moist, rich, well-drained.
Exposure: Sun, part shade.
Varieties: F. imperialis—lutea; F. meleagris—alba; purdyii

Fritillarias have one shining virtue for the bulb gardener. They repel moles. The fact that the large varieties have dramatic parasols of rich orange, red, or yellow blooms crowned with leaf tufts at the top of 3-foot stems is an added bonus. F. imperialis does appreciate deep soils for its huge bulbs. Although it can be difficult to find a spot where a clump will persist, it is worth the effort, for around it you can plant your better anemones, crocus, and chionodoxa so that voles and mice that use mole runs do not dine at your expense.

The F. imperialis prefer being planted on their sides. They can persist, without further care, for up to 5 years, when planted 8 inches deep in an improved clay soil. The bulbs can be up to 5 inches across and need planting as soon as they are bought for maximum viability. To increase your stocks without additional expense, they should be divided, and the offsets removed to grow to flowering size in a propagation bed.

Tiny F. meleagris is often called checkerboard lily or guinea-hen flower for its mottled patterning, unique in the plant world. It is a wonderful plant to naturalize in the rock garden. A mixture of color variations from brown-purple to silver-plum on the small drooping bells needs close-up viewing. If these varieties are grown with the pure white alba in light shade, the effect is quite lovely.

GLORY OF THE SNOW
(Chionodoxa species—chionodoxa)
Uses: Border, naturalizing.
Height:4-6 inches.
Blooms: March-April.
Plant: September-October.
Distance: 3-4 inches.
Depth: 2-3 inches.
Soil: Fertile, well-drained.
Exposure: Sun, shade.
Species: C. gigantea, 5 inches, lavender-blue; C. lucilae, 4 inches, blue, white; C. sardensis, 4 inches, gentian with white eye; C.tmolusi, 6 inches, blue, white.

Glory of the snow is the second earliest of the spring bulbs. Its bright blue color seems to make spring come early and planted en masse, it can have a dramatic effect in the right setting in March. For example, it is planted among the twisted roots of a lovely specimen beech on the grounds at Dumbarton Oaks in Georgetown. No one who has seen this dainty breathtaking carpet below the bare silvered shape of that tree will ever forget it.

Of easy culture, chionodoxa species deserves to be at the front of a sunny border or secluded rock garden.

The bulbs should be obtained as early in the season as possible and planted promptly. Because they are small, and members of the lily family, they rapidly lose vitality when not properly stored. They need good drainage underfoot to thrive and multiply; they make a much showier display in fertile soil. Many gardeners lift them every 3 to 4 years to rework and enrich the soil before replanting. They are hardy, however. It takes at least a dozen chionodoxa to make a visible pool of color in a small bed.

The species listed above are the kinds most commonly planted in local gardens. There are a few named varieties, as well as other species for the hobbyist.
Mice are fond of the bulbs. Wherever moles abound, mice will get to the bulbs and eat them. See the previous listing, plant them in wire cages, or employ an energetic cat.

When bulbs as small as these are naturalized in a lightly shaded lawn, it is easier to allow foliage to mature before the grass reaches an unsightly length.

GRAPE HYACINTH
(Muscari species & cultivars)
Uses: Border, naturalizing, cutting.
Height: 4-6 inches.
Blooms: March-May.
Plant: September-November.
Distance: 3-4 inches apart.
Depth: 3-4 inches.
Soil: Loamy.
Exposure: Sun, shade.
Varieties: (M. 'Heavenly Blue,' M. 'Blue Bird,' M.botryoides 'album,' M. armeniacum.

The grape hyacinth is a popular, early spring bulb. The tiny bell-shaped flowers are clustered along the length of a hyacinth-shaped spike, hence its name. Easy to grow, the

Potted bulbs need not be covered deeply. Usually they are planted in a shallow pot called a bulb pan.

grape hyacinth will naturalize in light, loamy soils where it will persist in the face of complete neglect. Planted in drifts in the lawn or in groups of 25 or more in the border, they make a very pleasing show.

Whereas the species M. botryoides, with dark blue bead-like flowers, is a very useful bulb, the named varieties that are derived from it are more showy. M. 'album' is white; M. Heavenly Blue is the largest single; M. armeniacum has flowers of cobalt blue and fall foliage.

HYACINTH
(Hyacinthus orientalis—Dutch or Roman hyacinth)
Uses: Bedding, forcing.
Height: 6-9 inches.
Blooms: April-May.
Plant: June, old bulbs; September-October, new bulbs.
Distance: 6-10 inches apart.
Depth: 4-6 inches.
Soil: Fertile, well-drained.
Exposure: Sun; part shade for Roman.
Varieties: Grande Maitre, King of Blues, L 'Innocence, Yellow Hammer, City of Harlem, Pink Pearl, Queen of Pinks, Jan Bos.

The hyacinth is deservedly popular. The massive flower heads are extremely showy and come in a wide palette of colors coupled with an intoxicating fragrance. Every color but green is represented, and the exhibition-sized bulbs make a truly stunning display when forced or staked in a bed.

For outdoor culture the smaller bedding bulbs are better adapted to the vagaries of the weather and are less likely to be blown over by spring winds and rain, although they may still need some staking.

The Roman hyacinth (H. orientalis albulus), a smaller form of the Dutch hyacinth, often throws 2 or more bloom spikes, and is good for both bedding and potting. Although some claim it is less hardy than the Dutch hyacinth, it often persists in the Washington area for years. Certainly it is less prone to basal rot. These smaller bulbs are often sold in bags by color, rather than varietal names.

Hyacinths are ideal for forcing, if they are planted in groups in a terra-cotta bulb pan or a special bulb glass that allows the roots to develop in water without rotting the bulb. They need about 2 months of cool darkness if they have not been previously prepared. Even if they have, it is important to shade the flower bud, until the leaves and spike have fully emerged, for best form.

In the garden hyacinths need a rich soil to store nutrients for such heavy bloom. This often causes losing the bulbs to disease. Dutch hyacinths are so frequently lost in heavy soils that it is worth the trouble to dig and store them in an air-conditioned room after the foliage has matured. In sandy soils it is possible to dig the bulbs when the foliage starts to yellow, so that they can be divided and replanted immediately.

Hyacinths are subject to a number of diseases and pests that may cause them to decrease from year to year. Many are bulb rots caused by heavy, moist soil. The only cure for this is to dig up the sound ones and replant them in a

better situation—after disinfecting them with flowers of sulphur or Bordeaux mix dust. The infected bulbs should be bagged and burned or put in the trash.

There is also a leaf disease called hyacinth yellows. The first symptom is water-soaked streaks in the foliage. Remove and destroy all effected bulbs to prevent the characteristic yellowing and shrinking of stem and foliage that follows.

The high nutrient requirements of hybrid hyacinths may contribute to their problems. It is wise, therefore, to use only compost, bone meal, or greensand for soil enrichment. Dutch hyacinths do not need a winter mulch, unless they are in a very exposed location. Roman hyacinths are less hardy and will need winter protection in colder areas.

LILIUM
(Lilium species, hybrids)
Uses: Border, accent, cutting.
Height: 18 inches-7 feet.
Blooms: May-August.
Plant: September, October, November.
Distance: Varies by species, 6-18 inches.
Depth: Stem rooting—bulb tip in 3-4 inches of soil.
Basal rooting—top of bulb 1 inch below surface.
Soil: High fertility, perfect drainage.
Exposure: Varies with species, sun, part shade.
Species:
Madonna, L. candidum—white, May, 3-4 feet;
Regal, L. regale—white, yellow centered, June, 3-5 feet;
Easter, L. longiflorum—white trumpet, June, 3 feet;
L. Speciosum—white, pink reflexed, July-August, 4-6 feet;
L. tigrinum—orange with black spots, July, 4-5 feet;
L. Henryi—apricot reflexed, August, 5-8 feet.
Hybrids: Enchantment—yellow, gold bicolor, June, 3 feet;
Upfacing: Mont Blanc—white to cream, June, 2½-3 feet;
Stargazer—red, edged in white, late July, 3 feet;
Black Dragon—white, burgundy reverse, July, 5-7 feet;
Trumpets: Green Magic—chartreuse, July, 5-7 feet;
Pink Perfection—pink, July, 5-7 feet;
Jamboree strain—(improved speciosum rubrum hybrid);
San Souci—pink and white, scented, August, 5-7 feet.
Aurelians, L. Henryi x Trumpets—white, pink, yellow, apricot, and orange, July, 5-7 feet.

The true lilies, not to be confused with the hardy perennial daylilies, are the showiest and most fragrant of all bulb plants. Although some species are difficult, there are many varieties that can be grown with great success in the Washington area. In recent years the development of magnificent hybrids in a wide range of colors, forms, and sizes has enabled the amateur gardener to achieve spectacular garden effects by meeting a few basic requirements.

Drainage Is Crucial

The first and most important of these requirements is perfect drainage, a nebulous state that can best be achieved in our heavy soil by planting on a slight slope and by incorporating large quantities of compost, leafmold, and possibly greensand to a depth of 2 feet. The end result will resemble a deeply dug, raised bed that can then be fertilized with 5-10-5 or any good general-purpose fertilizer.

As a further safeguard against basal rot, cautious growers may soak their newly arrived bulbs in a water suspension of benomyl, then air dry them before planting. Although most lilies will thrive in full sun, they appreciate the protection of a ground cover like vinca or a mulch over their feet to keep the soil surface cool. Some lilies, such as the lovely speciosums and speciosum-auratum crosses, the species Henri and Turkscap, and the delicately colored pink lilies, thrive in part shade. However, they will not grow straight and will have to be planted next to stakes later for support.

Bulb Planting Times

Because growers dig their bulbs in the fall, September through November are the best months for planting. If there is a danger of hard freezing before the bulbs arrive, beds should be prepared in advance and kept mulched, so the ground will stay soft enough to plant.

When properly stored under moist, cool, sanitary conditions, it is safe to buy bulbs in the spring from the best growers, but they must be planted at the correct depth immediately in early April, so that they do not break dormancy too early.

Planting Two Types of Lilies

Lilies may be divided into two classes, the stem-rooting and the basal-rooting. The first group, to which most lilies belong, must be planted deeply so that it will have plenty of soil in which to feed and to anchor the roots that support the tall stems. This variety also has basal roots, which need a very deeply prepared soil.

Some other Mediterranean lilies, including the Madonna, have roots only at the base of the bulb. These must be planted, preferably early in September, rather close to the surface of a well-prepared bed.

Large bulbs produce the finest flower displays but they may not be as practical for the home gardener, since they have a tendency to diminish after the first year. Medium-sized bulbs that are less expensive are the better buy. They will increase in size over several years, before producing offsets that should be lifted and boosted to production in pots or nursery trenches covered with a little sand.

Some of the shorter varieties good for forcing, such as Enchantment, will split several times in the pot. These clumps can be subdivided and planted out or discarded. The best quality bulbs are often more economical in the long run, because they establish themselves readily in the garden.

Cutting Lilies Carefully

When lilies flower it is hard to decide whether to cut the stalks for indoor display. This can be done every 2 or 3 years, leaving at least one third to one half the stem with foliage to nourish the plant. For all lilies the rebuilding process after flowering is best accomplished with fertilizers low in nitrogen. Phosphate and potash for strong stems and blooms are the important materials to gently scratch in around the plant.

Propagating Lilies

Lily bulbs can be reproduced from scales, from bulbils taken from the leaf axils in late summer, from bulblets produced around the existing bulb, or from seed. Usually, one removes spent flowers to ensure that the plant loses no strength to propagation. When the clump seems crowded, remove scales, bulblets, and seed from it in the early fall, plant them in sterile potting soil in flats, and then cover them with a layer of sand. Water and grow them through the winter in a sheltered cold frame, then on through the next season out of doors in the same flats in light shade. Finally, transplant the seedlings to the flower bed the second fall.

It takes from 2 to 5 years to produce a flowering bulb by this method, but flowers grown from seed are virus-free and are an inexpensive way to increase your lily collection. The Regal and Easter lilies reproduce from seed in 2 years. Speciosum rubrum, the enchanting pale cinnamon and vanilla scented lily with rosy spots, can take up to 5 years for the home grower.

Preventing Lily Diseases

The most common lily diseases are viral and fungal. The mosaic virus manifests itself by a characteristic mottling or striping of the leaves into light and dark areas. It is incurable. Keep aphids out of the garden with soap sprays, for the insects carry and spread the disease. Do not plant the old-fashioned tiger lily or Rembrandt tulips anywhere upwind or near your other lily plantings; both are notorious mosaic carriers.

Black or brown patches on the foliage indicate a fungal disease, which happily responds to spray applications of benomyl around and on the plant during the wet weather of spring and early summer. This spray will control fusarium bulb wilt, the second most common fungal disease of these plants.

You can see why it pays to buy lily bulbs from reputable dealers who handle disease-free stock in all cases. Bulbs with mosaic must be lifted and destroyed.

RESURRECTION LILY
(Lycoris squamigera, amaryllis halli—Naked Lady)
Uses: Border, woods garden.
Height: 24-30 inches.
Blooms: Lavender-pink flowers on bare stems, August.
Plant: Midsummer.
Distance: 10-12 inches.
Depth: 6 inches.
Soil: Variety of garden soils, do not allow to go dry.
Exposure: Part shade.

Resurrection lilies have long been known in parts of Maryland and Virginia as Naked Ladies, for their habit of blooming long after the foliage has sprouted and ripened in May and June. The trumpet-shaped flowers are borne three to five at a time on a bare, hollow stem that appears in a matter of days when the rest of the garden is flagging in the August heat. Its delicate pink with a fulvous overcast looks wonderful against a mature boxwood planting.

This hardy summer bloomer has no known pests or diseases and seems to thrive on a minimum of care. In the sandier soils close to the rivers, it may be planted in a lawn area, but light shade is a must so that the soil around it does not dry completely.

The flowers will last longer if the bulbs are planted about 6 inches deep in a somewhat sheltered location out of the wind and about a foot apart. The bulbs will gradually increase to fill the spaces in between.

SIBERIAN SQUILL
(Scilla sibirica—Bluebell, Siberian squill)
Uses: Border, naturalizing.
Height: 4-6 inches.
Blooms: March-April.
Plant: September-November.
Distance: 3-4 inches apart.
Depth: 4-5 inches.
Soil: Range of loamy soils.
Exposure: Sun, shade.
Species: S. sibirica alba, bifolia, tubergeniana.

The squill, or bluebell, is a dainty, early-flowering plant that shows its colors almost as soon as the bud sheath shows above ground. It is quite at home in the border, the rock garden, and when planted along a woodland path or walkway. Its intense blue makes a brave showing wherever planted that is out of proportion to its tiny size. For earliest spring bloom the Siberian squill needs a protected situation.

Their culture is very simple. They prefer a soil that is not too heavy or cold. They do equally well planted in front of shrubbery or in a grassy lawn for those gardeners who want to combine them with other early bulbs to create a "flowery mead." The bulbs should be planted in the fall in drifts of 12 to 25 for a good first-year bloom. If well situated, they will multiply and make a striking display in future years. Since they are inexpensive, it is tempting to plant more. Supplemental feeding scratched into the soil surface in the very early spring will increase the size and vigor of their bloom the same season. Squills are unaffected by most insects and diseases, although plantings should be protected from moles and voles.

SNOWDROP
(Galanthus species—Snowdrops)
Uses: Border, naturalizing, rock garden.
Height: 6-12 inches.
Blooms: January-March.
Plant: September-October.
Distance: 3-6 inches apart.
Depth: 3-4 inches.
Soil: Variety of loams.
Exposure: Sun, shade.
Varieties:
G. elwesi—Cassaba, Clawpetal, Erithrae, Globe, Snowcup;
G. nivalis—Corcyrensis (November), Maximus, Reflexus, Octobrensis (October), Flavescens (yellow).

The snowdrops are a cheerful, hardy group, as befits a bulb that is first out in January. Who has not seen them rise from frozen snowbanks looking fresh each day, after a week of freezing and thawing? Because they are so ready to bloom, most gardeners will not want to omit them from a bulb collection. Their curious little cups first open in January in more sheltered areas and may stay in bloom until late March. Some people try to spot the first one at Christmastime .

All snowdrops are easy to establish, but then difficult to move except with a large ball of earth. Most varieties have drooping, bell-like flowers tipped in green that nod from slender stems from 6 to 12 inches tall. Of the two species, elwesi is the taller and more showy. Nivalis, however, has two varieties that are fall bloomers, and one rare variety that is yellow. Snowdrops are often planted with another early bloomer, winter aconite, in a rock garden that can be seen and enjoyed from inside the house.

To protect these hardy, disease-free bulbs from bulb rots, the usual good soil drainage should be provided when bonemeal and compost are added before planting. Well-rotted manure, added as a top dressing for beds and naturalized drifts, will add any extra nutrients needed over the years.

SNOWFLAKE
(Leucojum vernum, aestivum, autumnale)
Uses: Borders, beds.
Height: 6-14 inches.
Blooms: April-June, September.
Plant: September-October.
Distance: 4-6 inches.
Depth: 8 inches.
Soil: Variety of loams.
Exposure: Sun, part shade, protected.

Snowflakes are taller, more elegant versions of the snowdrop. They have between four and eight slender bloom stalks that carry the graceful bells, and they look particularly beautiful planted with bleeding heart and as a delicate counterpoint to low azaleas. The summer snowflake is taller and blooms into June in cooler parts of the region. The pink autumn-flowering species blooms with the first fall rains in September.

Snowflakes need a deeply dug bed, because it is their peculiarity to develop 2 bulbs separated by several inches under the ground. They need room to develop and grow without disturbance. When increasing your stocks of this plant, dig with care after the foliage dies, remove the offsets that grow close to the bulb, and then replant immnediately.

The spring snowflake, vernum, needs a shaded situation to do its best. Each clump will eventually spread 4 to 6 inches. A chopped leaf mulch is perfectly adequate for winter protection and extra nutrition once snowflakes have been established.

STERNBERGIA
(S. lutea—sternbergia)
Uses: Beds, naturalizing.
Height: 6-9 inches.
Blooms: August-September.
Plant: Spring, offsets in fall.
Distance: 4-5 inches.
Depth: 5 inches deep.
Soil: Sheltered dry soil, near shrubs and trees.
Exposure: Sun.

This beautiful fall bloomer looks like a crocus that has the texture of tulip blooms. The lacquered yellow chalices are 1½inches long and appear before the foliage, which grows nearly a foot tall before it fades.

They have been growing in Israel on stony waste ground for thousands of years and are the lilies of the field of Biblical citation. It is no surprise, therefore, to find that they grow best in this area when located in sunny spots with dry soil. Until the Dutch breeders increase their cultivated stocks (instead of relying on collecting plants from the wild), these may be difficult to find. They are very effective planted next to evergreen shrubs that deplete most other bulbs. Once planted, do not disturbed them until the plants are well established. Although they are hardy in most parts of the region, they should be mulched well in a cold, exposed location.

TULIPS
(Tulipa species, varieties—tulip)
Uses: Cutting, bedding, forcing.
Height: 6-30 inches.
Blooms: April-May.
Plant: October-December.
Distance: 6-10 inches apart in groups, not lines.
Depth: 6-8 inches.
Soil: Variety of loamy soil.
Exposure: Sun, light shade.
Species: T. tarda, clusiana, sylvestris, kaufmanniana, greigii, praestans, eichleri, fosteriana, marjoletti.
Cultivars:
Single Early (12-16 inches)—Bellona, General De Wet, Mickey Mouse, Christmas Marvel, White Hawk.
Double Early (14-18 inches)—Peachblossom, Murillo, Mr. Vanderhoef, choonord.
Triumph (18-24 inches)—Apricot Beauty, Peerless Pink, Garden Party, Golden Surprise, Professor Einstein.
Darwin Hybrid (20-26 inches)—Apeldoorn, Golden Parade, Daydreamer, Jewel of Spring (picotee), Parade.
Lily Flowering (20-26 inches)—West Point, Ballade, White Triumphator,

Queen of Sheba, Mariette.
Fringed—Burgundy Lace, Maja, (mixture).
Parrot (20-26 inches)—Blue Parrot, Fantasy, Flaming Parrot, Texas Gold, White Parrot, Orange Parrot.
Single Late (20-26 inches)—Ace of Spades, Halcro, Sorbet, Mrs. John T. Scheepers, Smiling Queen.
Double Late—Mt. Takoma, May Wonder, Brilliant Fire.
—List revised by the late Col. Charles A. Thomson of the Mens' Garden Club of Montgomery County.

Tulips are one of the best loved of spring-blooming flowers, despite the fact that they diminish over the years because of our hot summer soil conditions, unless given excellent culture.

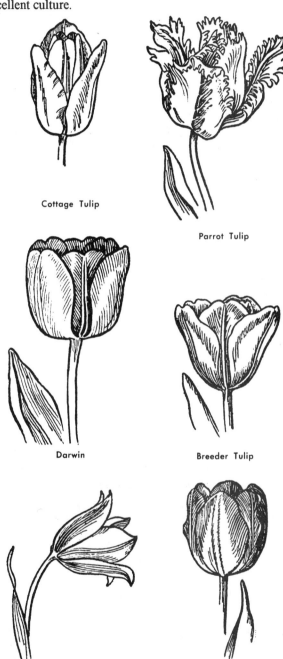

Cottage Tulip

Parrot Tulip

Darwin

Breeder Tulip

Tulipa Sylvestris

Triumph Tulip

Popular Tulip types.

DUTCH TULIP PLANTING GUIDE*

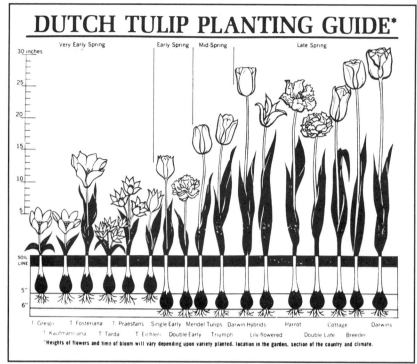

| Very Early Spring | Early Spring | Mid-Spring | Late Spring |

T Greigii   T Fosteriana   T Praestans   Single Early   Mendel Tulips   Darwin Hybrids   Parrot   Cottage   Darwins

T Kaufmanniana   T Tarda   T Eichleri   Double Early   Triumph   Lily flowered   Double Late   Breeder

*Heights of flowers and time of bloom will vary depending upon variety planted, location in the garden, section of the country and climate.

white to the blackest purple. They have stiffer stems, excellent substance, and stand up to the extremes of our May weather for long-lasting bloom.

Plenty of variety in flower shape is available. The Lily flowered have elegant pointed petals, the Fringed are conventional tulips with feathery edges, some in contrasting colors, and the Parrots are wildly extravagant in shape.

Not to be overlooked are the small, early species tulips that make excellent additions to a rock garden or small space. Tulipa clusiana, the Lady or Candlestick tulip, is a bi-color cherry rose, lined with cream. Tulipa sylvestris and tarda are other good early bloomers. T. Greigii varieties have bronzy, mottled foliage, as does T. Kaufmanniana. This so-called water lily tulip resembles a water lily, adding unusual qualities that bring a great deal to the rock garden.

When their cultural requirements are met, they are a hardy and a colorful feast for the eyes for a full month—characteristics that should ensure their popularity anywhere. The practical Dutch, by meticulous care in the production and marketing of their bulbs, start us off right with healthy and dependable bulbs certain to bloom under almost any conditions the first year.

Four centuries of culture have resulted in hundreds of varieties of tulips, which have been grouped into classes according to their flower shape and time of bloom. The classes of hybrids listed here are the most widely planted. In the Washington area's public planting displays, the Darwin hybrids are probably the most popular. Most gardeners are satisfied with the height, stamina, and good color selection of these mid-season tulips. Tulip aficionados are more likely to branch out into the species hybrids, the Rembrandt, Triumph, and multi-flowering varieties and cultivars.

Of the more popular hybrids, the first to bloom in early April are the Single and Double Early varieties, which include the Fosteriana hybrids. These are short-stemmed colossal tulips that cover beds in incandescent red, white, yellow, and orange. These early flowers are excellent for forcing. Like all tulips, they need 3 months of cool darkness after potting in order to grow a root structure to support top growth, unless previously prepared for forcing.

The next class to bloom is the Triumph. These are followed by the large-flowered Darwin Hybrids, the unusual Lily flowered, Fringed, and Parrot tulips, and the Late Doubles. These are the long-stemmed workhorses of the tulip bed. They are all May-flowering. Darwin hybrids are mostly clear, long lasting flowers of one color ranging from pure

Some of the best of the hybrids developed from these early species are T. Greigii 'Red Riding Hood' and 'Yellow Dawn,' as well as the T. Kaufmanniana 'Cherry Orchard.' Red and yellow predominate in these early tulips. Scarlet Emperor, the first great Fosteriana hybrid, now supplanted by Princeps and Fusilier, the bright red, multiple-flowered Praestans, and crimson scarlet Eichleri make strong statements against new green grass in many local gardens. These are the more commonly grown cultivars of the 40 or 50 species tulips from which modern tulips were developed. They are relatively long-lived.

Good soil preparation for tulips is rewarded with finer flowers; and it is not too much trouble to prepare the soil to a depth of 12 to 18 inches, incorporating enriched bonemeal and well-rotted compost in the bottom 6 to 10 inches. Although this seems excessive for a bulb whose base is planted 8 inches deep, the roots will reach into this layer for continued food and moisture during our hot summers. Deep planting is recommended for two reasons; first, to put the bulb down where the soil is cool, which favors the steady growth of these plants developed in a more temperate climate. The second is that deeply planted bulbs do not split as readily.

November planting is fine for deeply planted bulbs, because they will continue to develop roots well into the cold weather.

Over-feeding is to be avoided, especially with high nitrogen mixes that stimulate bulb division and excessive leaf growth. Tulips do need a balanced feeding every fall after the initial, rich, well-drained soil has been prepared. It is best to use compost coupled with an enriched bonemeal or well-balanced bulb food (4-10-0 or 6-10-8 are formulas to look for). Like most bulbs, tulips appreciate sweet soil.

Large bulbs give the best flowers for bedding or cutting, because they last longer. Except in cool moist summers, bulbs of most varieties diminish in size, split, and cease to flower regularly within 3 or 4 years, unless they are fed annually and mulched well after blooming.

Within the last decade a reputable garden mail-order firm has offered perennial tulips in red, white, and pink. These are, in fact, fine Darwin Hybrids—the white is named Jewel of Spring. They are planted very deeply in even deeper beds, and they persist longer in our climate without splitting. Some people in cooler parts of the region have gotten bloom for up to 7 years.

To dig or not to dig is a standard question among tulip growers. Here, where the subsurface soil becomes hot during many dry summers, some public gardens dig, discard, and plant anew each fall. For the home gardener, digging after the foliage has matured makes it easier to size bulbs to replant for a uniform display. They can easily be kept in onion bags in a cool, airy place. If you can settle them in a hospitable bed, they may not need to be dug for 4 or 5 years, or until bloom diminishes.

Tulips are subject to diseases. "Breaking," a virus which is found in many of the prized Rembrandt varieties with bicolor variations, is more prevalent than other diseases. Spread by aphids, it eventually weakens and destroys the bulb. Those who love Rembrandt tulips should plant them in a separate place downwind to lessen the risk to other varieties.

Its first symptom is streaking that changes the color effect of a given variety. If a diseased plant should be found in the bed, lift and destroy it before aphids spread it. Control aphids from early spring on with soap sprays.

Other tulip diseases are "fire" and "grey rot" of the bulbs. If healthy bulbs are planted in well-drained situation, the gardener will never see them.

WOOD HYACINTH
(Scilla hyacinthoides, hispanica—English or Spanish Bluebell)
Uses: Border, woodland garden, naturalizing, cutting.
Height: 8-12 inches.
Blooms: April-May.
Plant: September-November.
Distance: 6-8 inches apart.
Depth: 5-6 inches.
Soil: Well-drained loam.
Exposure: Sun, part shade.
Varieties:
S. hyacinthoides—Alba, Caerulea, Blush Queen, Rubra, Rosea.
S. hispanica—Blue Queen, Rose Queen, Excelsior, Caerulea, Rosalind.

These lovely woodland flowers, which resemble a cross between lily of the valley and hyacinths, have had more botanical names than any other bulb. The species have been known also as Endymion non-scriptus and hispanicus, Scilla non-scripta or nutans (English bluebell), and Scilla campanulata or hispanica (Spanish). It is a tribute to botanical uncertainty and continued research. However, American growers have now decided to stick to S. hyacinthoides to describe the smaller English bluebell, and S. Hispanica to describe the larger Spanish, although you may find them still in catalogs listed as any of the other names. Persevere through this confusion, for they are one of the most satisfying of flowering plants from mid to late spring.

In sandy, alkaline soil they often naturalize in the lawn quickly, forming big clumps of foliage that produce up to a dozen flower spikes without any fertilization.

They are naturally adapted to light shade, hence their common name, but they also do well in the sunny border. They can stand more moisture than most other bulbs without succumbing to disease, although best flowering is in sandy soil.

The flowers come in white, pink, and shades of blue, belying the other common name. Wood hyacinths are relatively permanent plantings, needing only to be lifted every 4 or 5 years, thinned out, and then the soil enriched before replanting. They increase rapidly by means of offsets.

When naturalized in heavier soil, the bed should be enriched in the early spring by a top dressing of well-rotted manure.

SUMMER BULBS
Tender bulbs should not be planted until the soil warms, and all danger of frost is past. This too is a general rule. However, many gardeners in warm areas, where they are used to planting in open worked ground, will begin planting their purchased gladiolus cormels into the ground in early April, because they are very slow in developing. If they can be successfully planted early, they will bloom the first season.

Tender bulbs are normally lifted in the fall after the first killing frost. However, gladiolus, Peruvian daffodils, and any South African amaryllis that have been out for the summer should be lifted before frost, and the bulbs dried in a warm place and then stored. Dahlias and cannas, on the other hand, are not mature until rather late in the season. After the first frosts their foliage may be cut back, and they can remain in the ground for a few weeks to store food reserves and cure while the ground cools.

Bulbs do not require heavy feeding each year. Manure, unless very old and well-rotted, should not come in contact with a bulb. Bone meal, compost, and greensand are the best ingredients for enriching a bed, both before and after planting.

Most gardeners believe in digging bulbs in rather deeply, particularly in warm light soil, but often they neglect to dig the nutrients down into the root zone where the plants can use them. For a thorough and lasting job that will also improve drainage, double digging is recommended. The hardy and the tender bulbs all benefit from such a practice.

WARM-SEASON BULBS

ACIDANTHERA

(A. bicolor—Abyssinian gladiola)
Uses: Border, cutting.
Height: 18-24 inches.
Blooms: August.
Plant: May.
Distance: 6 inches.
Depth: 5 inches after last frost.
Soil: Variety of soils.
Exposure: Sun.

This summer bulb is late-blooming, graceful, fragrant, and half hardy here. In a warm, protected spot with good drainage, it may not have to be taken up in the winter.

The flowers on the long stalk open from base to tip, gladiolus-like, are about half the size, and colored a crisp white with a deep burgundy throat.

The corms also resemble gladiolus corms and may be dug up with their foliage in early October when putting in spring bulbs. When the foliage is dry, it can be cut off, and the bulbs stored in a mesh bag in a garage. Kept fairly cool and dry, there will be no loss to dry rot.

Acidanthera benefit from enriched soil, but compost, bonemeal, and well-rotted manure can easily be added in the fall when digging the bulbs up. It will then be immediately available in late April or early May when all danger of frost is past. The corms take a long time to mature and may not emerge until June, so mark them when you plant.

If the soil is well-drained, acidanthera seem untroubled by most pests and diseases, although rust on the foliage should be treated if it appears with a spray.

CANNA

(C. generalis—Canna lily)
Uses: Beds, container.
Height: 4-6 feet.
Blooms: July-October.
Plant: Indoors, February-March; outdoors, May.
Distance: 18-24 inches.
Depth: 3-4 inches.
Soil: Moist, rich, well-drained.
Exposure: Sun.
Varieties: Red—The President. Yellow—Yellow King Humbert. Rose-pink—City of Portland. Grand Opera series. Dwarves—shell pink, primrose yellow, Chinese coral.

One of the showiest bedding plants is the canna, a tender tropical, that can be grown very effectively here as so many public plantings attest. The wild species bear little resemblance to the modern plant so skillfully developed by plant breeders.

Today we have cannas ranging in color from ivory and yellow to rose, salmon, and scarlet. None of them will overwinter this far north, so the rhizomes must be lifted after the first frosts and well before the ground freezes.

After curing cannas are normally stored over winter in dried peat moss to be started indoors in February and March. This gives the plants a head start so they will bloom by early July. They also can be planted outdoors in the first half of May to flower in late July. Once they begin blooming, they will persist until the October frosts.

The dormant rhizomes may be started in any warm, sunny situation where the temperature is above 70° Fahrenheit. They will grow in soil, peat moss, or sand, although most gardeners prefer a richer commercial potting mix that is sterile and not too moist. This prevents disease in the first months as the plants break dormancy indoors. As a precaution avoid heavy watering until the shoots are 2 to 4 inches high.

As soon as the danger of frost is past, the young plants should be transferred to a well-prepared bed. Incorporate liberal quantities of rotted manure or compost to a good depth the preceding fall, so that the plants or rhizomes can take off. Cannas are strong growers that need plenty of nutrients and moisture to make the dramatic display that they are capable of.

The President seems to be an outstanding scarlet-flowered plant that is widely planted here. Yellow King Humbert is another large-flowered variety whose rich yellow is speckled with orange. City of Portland is a warm rose pink. One newer series on the market is named for operas. It has new colors and larger flowers, including: Aida, gold rose; La Boheme, peach red; La Traviata, old rose; Mme. Butterfly, yellow and pink; and Rigoletto, canary yellow.

In choosing a variety, note whether or not the foliage is bronze, so that you can more accurately calculate the effect in your garden or container. Some gardeners dislike bronze foliage, while others prefer it. Most catalogs will indicate foliage color so you can choose.

After the first killing frost in the fall, remove the tops of canna lilies near the ground level and allow them to remain in the soil for a few days before digging. This is believed to improve storage quality of the large fleshy rhizomes. What is certain is that they should be dug and stored with the tops down in dry peat moss, sand, or vermiculite at 50-60° Fahrenheit. If the whole dug rhizomes are carefully packed in clear plastic bags, one is reminded to check them for signs of rot, usually from an injury, or shriveling from not enough insulation. The goal is to have them remain plump, firm, and viable.

In the spring the clumps are pulled apart, and the rhizomes divided into sections with three to five buds each. If you are sprouting them indoors for prompt replanting outside when spring bulbs fade, you may delay the division until they show signs of growth.

Japanese beetles are fond of the soft juicy flower petals and can be kept off with a dusting of malathion or carbaryl in early July. Prompt removal of faded flowers each week will encourage the plants to continue to produce fresh growth and many flowers throughout the season.

DAHLIA
(Dahlia hybrids, varieties)

Uses: Exhibition, cutting, border.
Height: 1-7 feet.
Blooms: July to frost.
Plant: May-June.
Distance: 12-36 inches.
Depth: 4-6 inches.
Soil: Rich, moist, well-drained.
Exposure: Sun.
Types: Formal decorative (FD); Informal decorative (ID); Cactus (C); Semi-cactus (SC); Incurved cactus (IC); Ball (Ba); Pompom (P); Single (S); Paeony-flowering (Pe); Orchid-flowering (O); Anemone-flowering (An); Collerette (Col).

Dahlia Sizes

Size and shape classifications are listed together in catalogs in a sometimes confusing series of letters that identifies characteristics you might want. Here are the latest initials for size listings for individual varieties, as they would appear in front of a variety name.

The letter AA signifies Giant dahlias with blooms over 10 inches across. The letter A indicates Large dahlias with blooms over 8 inches in diameter. These plants grow from 4 to 7 feet tall.

Dahlias marked B have Medium blooms over 6 to 8 inches in diameter in the same height range. BB dahlias produce small blooms over 4 to 6 inches in diameter on plants from 3 to 6 feet high.

The Ball shape dahlias used to vary widely in diameter on plants that grow from 18 inches in diameter on plants that grow from 18 inches to 4 feet tall. Collerettes, single anemone-flowering, and orchid-flowering all refer to flower shape but are usually under 4 inches across.

MB is the new classification for Miniature Ball dahlias over 2.5 to 3 inches. Pompons should be a compact 2 inches or less in diameter, with MS designating the smallest dahlias, Mignon Singles, up to 2 inches in diameter. These make fine bedding plants for the beginner.

The size classification letters will precede the flower shape code in front of each of the listed varieties.

Varieties:
White—(AAID) Walter Hardisty, (BFD) Sterling Silver, (BSC) Magic Moment, (MFD) Paulie Pal, (Ball) Brookside Snowball
Yellow—(AAID) My Doris R., (AFD) Edna C., (ASC) Kenora Sunburst, (BSC) Hamari Katrina, (BC) Jewyl Ellen, (BBC) Desert Gold, (MC) Billy, (P) Gay Willo.
Orange—(AASC) Alfred C., (AID) Sarah Jane, (BBFD) Hamilton-Lillian, (MC) Wiggles, (P) Poppet.
Pink—(AAID) Croydon Serene, (ASC) Surprise, (BFD) Cherokee Charm, (BSC) Papes Pink, (MSC) Mary Jo.
Dark Pink—(AID) Islander, (BSC) Shawnee Dream, (BBC) Brookside Sheri.
Red—(AASC) Wildman, (BBSC) Joan Baden, (MFD) Joe K., (O) Marie Schnugg.
Dark Red—(AAID) Zorro, (AASC) Dr. Les, (ASC) Tom Yano, (BC) Juanita, (P) Moor Place.
Lavender—(AAID Pennsgift, (AFD) Polyand, (AID) Lavengro, (BFD) Formby Perfection, BBFD) Camano Choice, (BBSC) The Queen, (MFD) Glow.
Purple—(AC) New Greatness, (MB) Downham Royal, (Col) Chow.
Light Blend—(AAID) Croydon Superior, (AFD) Kidd's Climax, (AC) Poetic, (ASC) Pink Jupiter, (Ball) Senior Ball, (MC) Glewbank Twinkle.
Bronze—(AAFD) Bonaventure, (AAID) Hamari Gold, (BID) Cherokee Ideal,

(Ball) Crichton Honey.
Flame—(BSC) Manor Sunset.
Variegated—(BC) Nita, (BBFD) Connecticut Dancer.
Bicolor—(BBFD) Stevie D, (BBSC) Match.
Dark Blend—(AID) Prime Minister, (BFD) Jogee, (BBFD) Southern Beauty, (MC) Ginny Johnston, (P) Winnie, (Ball) Dottie.
—Revised by Ray Struntz of the National Capital Dahlia Society.

This list of dahlias grow well locally and have won frequently on the show table. Practically all are suitable for the beginner. In all cases the more sun the plants receive, the shorter they grow—something to remember if your space is limited.

This summer-flowering, tuberous-rooted plant is so popular here that its shows are among the largest in the nation. There are shapes, sizes, and colors of flowers to appeal to almost every gardener. These sun-loving plants can be grown from seeds, from cuttings, and from tubers. This explains why new, short-bedding dahlia varieties grown from seed are also listed in this book in the chapter on annual flowers.

Nonetheless, most novice dahlia fanciers start with tubers or with plants grown from cuttings, so that they can be sure that the variety they choose is true to type. All dahlias require full sunlight at least 6 hours a day for good flower display. They will grow in any improved garden soil, but like so many bulbous plants do best in a sandy loam that offers good drainage.

The amount of trouble that they take depends on their size and whether they are used for home cutting, bed display, or exhibition. It requires a considerable amount of skill and attention if you grow heavy exhibition varieties up to 14 inches in diameter. The low-growing miniatures and dwarfs so popular in flower arranging require no staking or fertilizing, and, therefore, less attention.

Exhibition Dahlias

In preparing an area for the big dahlias, a fertilizer formula that will bring your tested soil up to a balance that favors stem

Modern Dahlia types: 1. Cactus. 2. Single. 3. Pompon. 4. Formal Decorative. 5. Informal Decorative. 6. Collarette. 7. Anenone-flowered. 8. Peony-flowered.

and flower development is a must. First, in the fall, after the soil is tested, the bed is dug and enriched with compost, bonemeal, and rotted cow manure. The next spring a formula like 5-10-10 or 4-8-12 should be broadcast at the rate of 3 to 5 pounds for every ten hills.

Prior to planting, 6-foot stakes should be firmly driven into the bed, spaced either 3 or 4 feet apart in rows that are themselves 4 feet apart. The 3-foot spacing will support single plants. The 4-foot spacing will allow you to tie 2 plants to a stake.

Dig holes close, but no closer than 3 inches to the stakes, and plant tubers or cuttings according to the texture of the soil. In heavy soil with good water-holding capacity, the tubers may not need to be more than 4 inches deep. In light, drier soil they may need to be planted as deep as 6 inches.

As soon as three to four pairs of leaves develop, the growing tip of the plant should be pinched just above the point where the stem is hollow. This forces vigorous development of six to eight side branches.

To create exhibition size blooms, A size dahlias have all but their four best branches removed. B dahlias retain six or eight branches. If frequent rainfall is lacking, these heavy feeding plants should be well-watered and cultivated frequently up to the first week in August. They should be gently tied into the stakes at 12 to 16 inch intervals with soft cloth strips or old nylons. A midsummer top dressing of their fertilizer formula at the rate of 1 to 2 tablespoons per plant at least 2 inches away from the stem will push them on.

Protect them with an insecticidal soap spray against thrips, leaf hoppers, aphids, and red spider about once a week. Then, around August, apply a wood chip or straw mulch to protect their feeder roots from further cultivation. Flower clusters (usually three buds) are likely to appear at the ends of the branches about this time.. Because these early buds do not produce the best blooms, it is a good idea to "time" the blooms by pinching out certain buds, as indicated in the sketch.

The center flower bud will bloom in about 4 weeks once it reaches pea size. A leaf bud is usually present in the center, and if the two lower side buds are removed, this will produce new leaves and another flower cluster that will bloom in 5 to 6 weeks. Other leaf buds in the axils of the first and second pairs of leaves opposite the removed buds will bloom in about 6 to 7 weeks. Pinching the buds in the lower 2 leaf axils about 4 to 5 weeks prior to a show will produce the loveliest blooms.

To aid nature in this process, about 2 to 3 weeks before show time, the ambitious gardener steps up watering to twice weekly, while feeding 2 to 3 tablespoons of 4-8-12 to each plant, followed by 2 teaspoonfuls of muriate or sulphate of potash to strengthen the stem.. When flowers appear, dust regularly with carbaryl and cover them with baskets or umbrellas tied to the plant stakes in order to preserve their best show color and form against insects and weather.

Dahlias should be cut the evening prior to a show with a slanting sharp cut and plunged immediately into cold water. If the petals begin to wilt soon after cutting, an air block has formed across the capillaries of the stem, or the bloom is not mature. Often re-cutting and plunging them into cold water again will revive the bloom.

Medium-Size Dahlias

The culture of medium-flowering dahlias is the same, except that from six to eight branches are grown per plant and the amount of fertilizing is reduced by more than half. Even although exhibition blooms are not desired, a certain amount of disbudding should be done to bring the flowers up out of the foliage where they can be seen better in the bed or flower arrangement.

Small-Flowering Dahlias

The smaller varieties should not be fertilized except for general soil improvement prior to planting. Many small blossoms are desirable. They should not be disbudded unless they are to be exhibited, and then only at the time they are picked. Low-growing varieties can be planted 4 to 6 inches deep in the perennial border without being staked and allowed to grow naturally with the average attention given

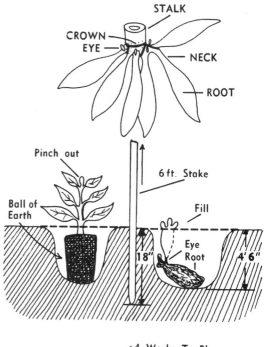

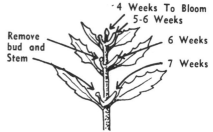

Proper method for dividing, planting and pinching dahlias.

other perennials. In a warm bed some growers cut off the flower stalks after frost and overwinter the tubers in the ground. This is somewhat risky except in sandy loam in the warmest parts of the region. Success is improved by dusting the ends of the stalks with a mixture of sulphur and Bordeaux mixture to discourage rotting. Cover the dusted stubs with a jar or plastic bag, and mulch well with earth or leaves.

In the traditional and safer storage technique, the dahlia stalks are cut off close to the ground promptly after the first killing frost. Within 2 to 3 weeks the clumps can be dug up, covered closely in cardboard boxes or sphagnum moss to prevent drying or rot, then stored in a cool place in the garage or cellar. A light sprinkling of water can be applied later in the winter if shriveling occurs. In the spring the clumps should be cut apart as shown in the planting sketch, with each root being joined to an eye or growth center on the crown.

GLADIOLUS
(Gladiolus varieties—Glad)
Uses: Cut flowers.
Height: 36-72 inches.
Blooms: 65-95 days after planting.
Distance: 4-6 inches apart.
Depth: 4-6 inches.
Soil: Rich, moist.
Exposure: Sun.

SELECTED LIST OF GLADIOLUS VARIETIES BY SIZE & COLOR

Color	Giant	Large	Medium	Small
White	Purity	Glacier	Marjorie Ann	Mighty Mite
Green	–	Lemon Lime, Green	Woodpecker	Leprechaun
Cream	Landmark	Lady Bountiful	Fresh	Domino
Yellow	–	Aurora	Chelsea	Towhead
Buff	–	Patrol	–	Jimmey Willey
Orange	Isle of Capri	Florence	Chiquita	Foxfire
Salmon	Goliath	Flying High	–	Parfait
Pink	LaFrance	Spring Song	Soft Touch	Candy Doll
Scarlet	Amazon	Victory	–	Atom
Red	Shirley Cole	Red Tornado	Red Ribbon	Dolly
Black-Red	–	Last Rose	Black Prince	–
Rose	Big Time	American Beauty	Allegro	–
Lavender	Elegance	Lavanesque	–	Masterpiece
Purple	King David	Purple Splendor	–	–
Violet	New Hope	Violet Charm	Angel Eyes	Blue Bird
Smokey	Damascus	Pompeii	–	Little Fawn

In most catalogs each gladiolus variety description has a three-figure number and the number of days. This is part of the classification system used in describing them. Take 300-75 for example. The first figure in the number relates to the size of the flower. It is based on the following size designation:

100—Miniature, florets under 2½ inches in width.
200—Small, florets 2½ to 3½ inches in width.
300—Medium, florets 3½ to 4½ inches in width.
400—Large, florets 4½ to 5½ inches in width.
500—Giant, florets wider than 5 inches. ·

The last of the two figures indicates the color class as follows:

00—white without CM*	42—pink (medium)	
01—white with CM	46—red (light)	
04—green	50—rose (light)	
10—cream	60—lavender (light)	
16—yellow (deep)	66—purple	
20—buff	70—violet (light)	
24—orange (light)	80—light rose, smokey violet	
30—salmon (light)	90—tan	
36—scarlet	96—brown	
40—pink (light) without CM		

*CM stands for conspicuous markings.

In addition to the size and color number, the catalogs may, and usually do, tell how many days the variety takes from planting to flowering. The range is quite wide at 65 to 110 days. This is crucial for the gardener who is planning his supply of cut flowers or his exhibition dates for flower shows. Here most varieties will flower a little ahead of their catalog designation, but it does depend on your elevation and exposure.

Glads are one of the most satisfactory of the summer-flowering bulbs, now that thrips are manageable. As a cut flower they are hard to beat, both for longevity of bloom in the house and for their glorious range of pastel colors.

They are of comparatively easy culture. By succession planting they will provide cut flowers from July through the summer. When brought indoors, the tall stalks with as many as twenty-five buds that open from its base to its tip will provide color for a week or more.

Gladiolus corms may be planted in warmer areas from April right up to mid June in order to provide successive flowering. The correct spacing and depth of planting are important so that tall stalks do not collapse under the weight of flowers in a storm and to prevent the corms from dividing in the hotter soil at the surface.

Gladiolus will grow and thrive in any good garden soil, but they benefit from generous feeding. It is good practice to work in 2 pounds of superphosphate to a 50-foot row at planting time. Alternatively, 5-10-5 can be spread in the bottom of a planting trench and covered with a good inch of soil before placing the corms. The corms can be planted in single row or in double rows 6 to 8 inches apart for ease in cultivation and harvesting. Leave 24 to 30 inches between such double rows.

The biggest blooms are produced when a sidedressing of 2 pounds of 5-10-5 is worked along the row just when the developing bloom spikes can be felt through the sheaf. Do not use formulas high in nitrogen or a more concentrated formula. This will weaken the plant by creating too-rapid growth that causes it to become susceptible to disease.

Water promptly and thoroughly if the bed is not getting at least an inch of rain a week; otherwise, the bloom spikes will crook when the garden gets dry. A good mulch applied as the first hot, dry weather hits will preserve soil moisture and temperatures, as well as discourage weeds. Until that time clean, shallow culture will get the plants off to a fast start. Use a scuffle hoe or resolve not to go deeper than an inch in order to save shallow feeder roots.

Some growers stake their flowers or place strong cord staked on either side of the rows to prevent wind damage and make cultivation easy.

Cutting Your Gladiolus
In cutting glads, it is desirable to harvest the spikes in the early morning just as the first florets open. Cut a minimum of

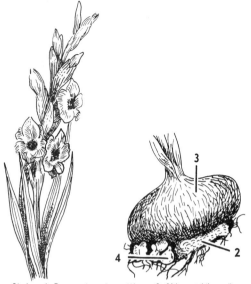

Glads: 1. Proper stage for cutting.   2. Old corm (discard).
3. New corm and 4. Cormels.

foliage so the corms will continue to store up energy for the next bloom season. Most growers leave four leaves. If this is not practical for good arrangements, buy new ones each season for the cutting garden.

How to Dig and Store
Dig up the corms 4 or 5 weeks after flowering, when they are well-grown, but before they are effected by any possible disease. Late glads may not be ready to dig until after frost. Loosen the soil on both sides of the row and gently draw out the entire plant on a bright, breezy day. Cut off the entire stalk and spread the corms to dry on screening if possible. One day in the sun and one in an airy garage help the plants cure properly before they are cleaned. If it is damp, turn a fan on the bulbs and stir occasionally to hasten the drying that prevents disease. When thoroughly dry, the old corms and dirt are removed from beneath the bulb, leaving the new corms and any small cormels on top.

Gladiolus are rather susceptible to disease and thrips that chew up emerging flowers from within. The thrips may be controlled by promptly cutting off all foliage before storage, and cleaning and drying, and by dusting them with carbaryl powder in a paper bag to catch potential overwintering larvae.

The plants can also be sprayed in the garden using insecticidal soap sprays. Discourage rusts and other diseases by buying good healthy corms and destroying any that are suspect at the time of planting, cleaning, or storage.

The cormels, if planted early in April, may sometimes flower the first season. In a well-drained soil, fall planting with a heavy mulch is satisfactory to give these new bulbs a start.
The small-and medium-sized bulbs, which do not need as much staking as the exhibition-oriented top size, get good results. Summer care and feeding often seem more important than the size of the corm to final results.

The list of recommended varieties is increased by the scores each season. Any list of recommended varieties is obsolete. Others not listed here, but whose performance has been very good are: yellow—Junior Prom, Empire Yellow; pink—Pink Prospector, Pink Performance; deep rose—Warrior, and; black red—Dark Brilliance.

LILY OF THE NILE
(Agapanthus africanus, 'Mooreana' Agapanthus)
Uses: Container, bed.
Height: 18-36 inches.
Blooms: June-July.
Distance: 12 inches.
Depth: 3-4 inches, mulched.
Soil: Rich, moist, well-drained.
Exposure: Sun, part shade, sheltered.
Varieties: Dark blue—A. mooreanus, 18 inches; inapertus 4 feet.
Light blue—A. africanus, 3 feet.
White—A. Albus, 3 feet.

This African tuberous-rooted plant is most often grown here as a tub plant that dies down in the winter and goes indoors to be brought out late in the spring. There are two varieties in dark blue, one short and one 4-feet tall. Both will survive in the garden in the warmest parts of the region.

Agapanthus is a handsome summer bloomer, well worth the mulching and coddling needed to increase the clumps. The evergreen forms are divided in the spring after 4 or 5 years. The deciduous forms are divided in the fall, after the foliage dies down. Preferring a rich, sandy soil it ought to be more widely grown in the delta areas around our rivers.

Snails sometimes bother the succulent foliage, so clean culture and good drainage, if the plants are in a tub, is very important. Check the pot drainage hole for snails and place snail bait there—a safe place where children or pets will not be harmed.

PERUVIAN DAFFODIL
(Hymenocallis or Ismene calathina—Ismene, Spider Lily)
Uses: Protected bed or border, container, forcing.
Height: 18-24 inches.
Blooms: May-June.
Distance: 12-14 inches.
Depth: 8 inches.
Soil: Rich, moist.
Exposure: Sun, part shade.

Another half hardy, summer bulb, the Peruvian daffodil has beautiful exotic blooms with fragrance. In a protected site it will live without being lifted in the fall.
Ismene is not widely planted, although this rapid grower is easily grown in well-drained soil. After planting in May, it looks well in beds just vacated by spring-flowering bulbs and helps to hide the dying foliage.

The large, white flowers are conspicuous with their fringed edges and green stripes down the midrib of each petal. They are borne on tall, naked stems before the leaves appear, like amaryllis, and have an enchanting scent.

A bed of Peruvian daffodils is somewhat ragged in

appearance when first in bloom, but rapidly developing foliage soon gives a luxuriant look.

The large bulbs that are not overwintered outdoors should be planted in spring after the danger of frost is past. Clean culture and ample moisture are important for good growth early on, as the long, drooping leaves make this difficult later in the season.

The bulbs should be dug before cold weather, although frosted foliage does not appear to effect their keeping qualities or vitality. Some gardeners do not remove the foliage until after it has dried; others cut it off as soon as digging is finished. The thick fleshy roots should not be cleaned or removed during storage.

It is easy to dry ismene bulbs near the furnace. They do not need to be boxed or wrapped, except in a very dry house.

The bulbs may be forced indoors, like amaryllis, using a pot only slightly larger that the bulb. Bring them into heat and light as soon as they are planted, and keep watered for the 10 to 14 days that they take to flower. For longer display move the pot to a cooler part of the room. After flowering the bulb should be kept nourished and growing until the weather is warm enough to plant it out of doors.

The small offsets may be removed when they are no longer firmly attached to the parent. If planted in the garden and given good culture, they will flower in 1 or 2 seasons. The larger the bulbs, the greater the number of flowers produced on each spike.

Peruvian daffodils are free from insects and disease troubles if their drainage is adequate. Snails may trouble the foliage in a damp situation.

TUBEROSE
(Polianthes tuberosa)
Uses: protected bed or border, forcing
Height: 30 inches
Blooms: July-September
Distance: 8-10 inches
Depth: 1-2 inches
Soil: light, rich, well-drained
Exposure: sun, light shade

The highly fragrant late summer flower is a relative of the Mexican agave. Most commonly available in a double-flowering form, the waxy white blossoms are borne on a terminal spire that rises from a rhizome planted in early June under an inch or two of light rich soil. The blossoms are used for perfume in Europe, which tells you how they will scent a late summer garden.

Dig up the rhizome before frost and store in a warm dry place. To force tuberoses, pot them in the fall, keep watered and at 75-80° Fahrenheit while they break dormancy. The bloom may be retarded into late November by keeping the young plant in a cool, dry place

BULBS FOR THE WASHINGTON AREA IN ORDER OF BLOOM

JANUARY-MARCH
Snowdrop—Galanthus
Winter Aconite—Eranthis hyemalis
Siberian Squill—Scilla sibirica
Crocus—species and hybrids
Iris—Danfordiae and reticulata
Glory of the Snow—Chionodoxa
Anemone—Anemone blanda
Daffodil—Narcissus species and hybrids
APRIL
Daffodil—Narcissus species and hybrids
Hardy Cyclamen—Cyclamen coum
Snowflake—Leucojum vernum
Tulips—Tulipa species, fosteriana, kaufmannia, greigii
Spring Starflower—Ipheion uniflorum
Pushkinia—Pushkinia
Checkered Lily—Fritillaria meleagris
Hyacinth—Albulus, orientalis
Grape Hyacinth—Muscari
MAY
Tulip—May-flowering hybrids
Crown Imperial—Fritillaria imperialis
Wood Hyacinth—Scilla hyacinthoides
Flowering Onion—Allium neapolitanum, ostrowsky
Dutch Iris—Iris xiphion, xiphoides
Camassia—Camassia leichtlinii
Summer Snowflake—Leucojum aestivum
Peruvian Daffodil—Ismene calathina
Madonna Lily—Lilium candidum
JUNE
Flowering Onion—Allium moly, christophii, giganteum
Easter Lily—Lilium longiflorum
Regal Lily—Lilium regale
Gladiolus—Gladiolus hybrids
JULY
Gladiolus—Gladiolus hybrids
Agapanthus—Agapanthus Mooreana
Canna Lily—Canna (until frost)
Flowering Onion—Allium senescens, cyaneum
Lilies—Lilium tigrinum, trumpet, aurelian
AUGUST
Lilies—Lilium, speciosum, Henryi, auratum
Tuberose—Polianthes p.tuberosa
Resurrection Lily—Lycoris squamigera
Hardy Cyclamen—Cyclamen neapolitanum
Golden Lycoris—Lycoris africana
SEPTEMBER—OCTOBER
Short Tube Lycoris—Lycoris radiata
Colchicum—Colchicum
Sternbergia—Sternbergia lutea
Autumn Crocus—Crocus sativus, zonatus
Autumn Snowflake—Leucojum autumnale

Deciding on Bulbs

With all the species to choose from, how does a gardener decide which bulbs would best suit his garden? One possible approach is to try and plan continuous bloom during the gardening year from bulbous plants—because so many are carefree after the initial planting.

Variations in weather patterns from year to year may cause as much as 10-14 days change in the blooming time of some species, so that occasionally some plants will bloom together that normally do not.. This uncertainty adds spice to a gardener's life—or so one would hope.

INSPIRATION:

Planting along Pennsylvania Avenue NW from 3rd to 15th Streets, Washington, D.C.

The Tulip Library, Tidal Basin at Ohio Drive, Washington D.C.

Fern Valley, The National Arboretum, New York Avenue & Bladensburg Road, NE,

Washington, D.C.

Dumbarton Oaks Gardens, 31st and R Streets NW, Washington, D.C.

Columbia Island, along George Washington Memorial Parkway, Washington, D.C.

Emily Sharp Park, Williamsburg Boulevard & Powhatan Street, Arlington, Virginia.

Waterfront Park between Prince & King Streets, Alexandria, Virginia.

Green Spring Gardens, 4601 Green Spring Rd., off Rt.236 near Braddock Road, Fairfax County, Virginia.

Brookside Gardens, 1500 Glenallan Ave., Wheaton, Maryland.

Londontown Publik House and Gardens, off Route 2 Edgewater, Maryland. Admission (410)222-1919.

Newton White Mansion, 2708 Enterprise Road, Mitchellville, Maryland.

Resources: The Washington Daffodil Society, Mary Ann Barton, Fairfax, Virginia (703)273-8641.

Chesapeake & Potomac Iris Society, Robert Hall, Oxon Hill, Md. (301)

□

notes

11. COLORFUL FLOWERS & VINES

Annual flowers are those that grow, bloom, seed and die in one season. Many of the most exquisite flowers are annuals. They are attractive in the garden—some for bedding,. some for borders, some for rock gardens, some for climbing or trailing and others for their foliage only. Many are invaluable for cutting. There are annual flowers for every purpose; all are lovely and, with proper selection, blooms may be had from early summer until frost. Annuals are widely grown and greatly enjoyed by all gardeners. There are many, many kinds, so the gardener may select those that best suit his needs.

Few annuals will tolerate more than light shade. They are members of a sun-loving group. Browallia, impatiens, larkspur, nicotiana, pansy, salvia, snapdragon, torenia, and wax begonia are tolerant of shade. Pansy, impatiens, snap-dragon, verbena, and nicotiana will tolerate the most shade. This, of course, assumes that they will not be in competition with tree roots.

Most annuals are easily grown, although the seeds of some kinds are so small that unless special attention is given them germination is apt to be poor. For this reason it is desirable to start the seed in flats or pots, preferably in sphagnum moss or vermiculite, to avoid trouble with the disease known as damping off.

Annuals often make a poor showing because they are not started early enough and are not thinned properly while small. It is a waste of time to thin after the plants have grown tall and leggy. Thin when plants are less than an inch tall.

Sweet William, snapdragons, hollyhocks, and pansies, which are included in this chapter, are normally grown as biennials; i.e., their seeds are sown in July and August, and the young plants transplanted to the flower borders in September, for flowering the following spring. With some protection thepansy, sweet william, and snapdragon will live over winter and bloom a second season.

If directly seeded in the garden, most other annuals should not be planted here until early May. Best results will be achieved by choosing those species that have the shortest maturation time.

Most annuals benefit by heavy cutting. Being annuals. they consider their mission in life completed when they have bloomed and developed seed Cutting the flowers for use indoors, or as they fade, prevents the formation of seed and plants; and this keeps the plant growing and flowering.

To produce bushy plants it is common practice among experienced gardeners to "pinch-back" most kinds of annuals as they are transplanted. Pinching-back means to remove the top of a young plant. This practice is satisfactory only when the plants are given good culture and kept growing vigorously. Frequent cultivation of the soil, weed control, fertilization and watering are needed for the best results. The results well repay the extra care in the greater vigor and better quality of bloom.

The preparation and enrichment of the soil for annuals is the same as discussed in Chapter Two. Ample quantities of compost or peat moss should be worked into the soil, Like many vegetable crops the annuals want a soil that is not too acid. Lime should be added where the acidity is lower than pH 6. Fertilizers may be added to the soil at its time of preparation and additional quantities added during the growing season to keep plants thriving. Ordinary 5-10-5 commercial mixture will serve the needs of the annuals.

Annuals afford an opportunity for color harmony in mass effect. Two or more colors may be combined, but in planning such a harmony annuals with a long-bloom-season, such as petunias and zinnias, should be selected.

Plant annuals among the bulbs as their foliage begins to die down. This serves to hide what might otherwise be an unsightly spot, and the annuals give the dormant bulbs a certain amount of protection.

AGERATUM
(Ageratum houstonianum, Floss Flower, Tassel Flower)
Uses: Low edging, rock garden, container plant.
Blooms: Throughout summer.
Color: Blues; also, white, pink.
Height/Spread: 6-24 inches, 6-12 inches.
Sun/Soil: Sun. Rich, moist, well-drained.
Seed: Indoors—February.

Ageratum is one of the most popular of edging plants. The bushy little plants produce a profusion of fluffy flowers from May to October. Thus they make excellent edging plants, but also are useful as pot plants. The taller growing varieties are excellent for cutting.

The ageratums are of easy culture but do best in a rich moist soil. They are comparatively free from insect and disease problems.

Ageratum is often used as a mass planting to provide season-long color in the border. Either short or taller growing varieties may be selected for this purpose. However, the main use of the ageratum has been as an edging plant or in the rock garden. That is why there are so many varieties in the 4 to 6 inch height range.

The blue flowered varieties are most numerous. Attention has also been given to other colors and there are white and pink varieties, too.

The plants will need a certain amount of attention if they are to remain attractive throughout the growing season. A good practice is to remove spent blossoms.

The plant commonly called Hardy Ageratum is not an ageratum, but a weedy, fall-flowering plant whose flower heads resemble the ageratum. It is known botanically as Eupatorium coelestinum. It has many common names, Mistflower is probably the most descriptive. This plant spreads both by seeds and by underground root stems, which make it objectionable in the small flower border or in the rock garden.

ALYSSUM
(Alyssum maritima—Sweet Alyssum, Sweet Alice, Heal-dog, Madwort)
Uses: Edging, rock garden.
Blooms: August to frost.
Color: White, pink, violet.
Height/Spread: 4 to 10 inches, 6 to 10 inches.
Sun/Soil: Full sun. Rich, moist loam.
Seed: Indoors—March; Out of doors—Late April.

One of the most widely grown of edging plants is sweet alyssum, a dainty little free-flowering, fragrant plant of long season blooming habit and relatively easy care. Its habit of growth is so spreading that the edging cannot be kept narrower than 6 inches. It has a comparatively uniform height of growth.

Shearing the dwarf Alyssum removes spent blossoms and encourages new growth.

The seed may be sown indoors in March or out-of-doors in April.

For the best bloom in late summer and fall, the tops of the plants should be clipped first on one side of the row and then on the other. This causes the plants to develop new branches and gives them renewed vigor. Cultivation and light feeding is desirable, although this little annual does not demand too much attention.

While the alyssum is usually called sweet, it is the tall variety, Alyssum maritimum (10 to 12 inches), that is fragrant. However, it is seldom grown as an edging plant because of its height, but it should be included in every fragrant border because of its long season of bloom.

BEGONIA
(Begonia semperflorens and hybrids)
Uses: Bedding, cut flowers.
Blooms: July to frost.
Color: White, pink, rose, scarlet.
Height/Spread: 6 to 12 inches, 6 to 8 inches.
Sun/Soil: Sun or light shade. Supplied with peat moss.
Seed: Indoors—January

The waxy-leaved begonias are only now coming into their best use—bedding. The hybrids provide vigor and uniformity that makes them one of the best bedding plants requiring very little care; they are superior to the older varieties. They do well in full sun and will take light shade. The soil should be well supplied with compost or peat moss.

They are seldom troubled by disease or insect pests.

The begonia requires little watering—they should not be watered in full sunlight. If planted in shade, they should not be watered in the evening. Too much watering and at the wrong time of day is likely to do more harm than good.

In the fall, some of the plants may be lifted and potted for indoor use.

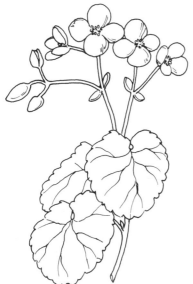

BELLS OF IRELAND
(Molucella laevis—Bells of Ireland, Molucca balm)
Uses: Cut flowers, dried arrangements,
Blooms: August-September.
Color: White
Height/Spread: 2 to 3 feet, 10 to 12 inches.
Sun/Soil: Sun. Rich, moist loam.

Bells of Ireland is an interesting and attractive, although odd, plant with large, very pale, translucent, green, shell-like calyxes, each containing a little white flower. The flower drops out as they reach maturity leaving the green calyxes or bracts that are so popular, especially in dried flower arrangements.

The seed should be started indoors in March or out-of-doors in May after the soil has lost its chill. Early seeding is important as the seed may take 4 weeks to germinate. The branching plants should be spaced about a foot apart. They will thrive in a moderately rich garden loam.

While they seemingly are immune to insects and diseases, the gardener should be prepared to protect them with an all-purpose dust or spray, because it is important to have them free from injury or markings.

BROWALLIA
(Browallia species and hybrids)
Uses: Bedding, borders, winter house culture.
Blooms: All summer outdoors. All winter indoors.
Color: Blue, white.
Height/Spread: 10-18 inches, 6 inches.
Sun/Soil: Light shade, morning sun. Well-drained.
Seed: Early spring.

If the bed is protected over winter, the plants may self-sow. If some plants are pinched back, they will branch and remain dwarfed, blooming later in the season, thus giving a long season of bloom.

Seed of Browallia speciosa should be planted in pots in the late summer for winter bloom. Treat it as a hanging basket plant for full display of blooms.

CALENDULA
(Calendula officinalis—Pot Marigold, Scotch Marigold)
Uses: Cut flowers, bedding.
Blooms: June; September-October.
Color: Yellow, orange.
Height/Spread: 18 to 24 inches, 12 to 15 inches.
Sun/Soil: Sun, very light shade. Well-enriched loam.
Seed: Indoors—February; Outdoors—July.

The gorgeous calendula is a cool weather plant that should be started early indoors for bloom before hot weather, or started in the early summer for fall bloom.

The flowers are long lasting and much desired for cutting. They are of comparatively easy culture and are not greatly troubled by insects or diseases.

The calendula is a fairly hardy annual and in some years will self-seed. The seed should be started indoors early in February so that good sized plants will be ready for planting out in April. Otherwise seed planting should be delayed until early in July. The fall flowering period is generally considered the more desirable in this area.

Space the plants a foot or more apart as they tend to sprawl. Staking is seldom practiced or needed, if the plants are well grown. This means that they should be kept growing strongly during the late summer. Fertilize once or twice and water as needed. Mulching is beneficial because they seem to thrive best under cool growing conditions. If the plants can be placed so that they are protected from the midday and afternoon sun, they seem to do much better.

The calendula does not seem to be bothered by insects or diseases in this area, except for perhaps a leaf-eater. An all-purpose dust or spray will protect them.

CALLIOPSIS
(Coreopsis tinctoria—Tickseed)
Uses: Cutting, border effect, and as an edging.
Blooms: Spring and early summer.
Color: Yellow with crimson, red or mahogany.
Height/Spread: 9 to 36 inches, 8 to 12 inches.
Sun/Soil: Sun. Good garden loam.
Seed: Sow or spring.

The calliopsis is an annual form of the Coreopsis and has much the same habit of growth. It is an excellent cut flower and does well in the sunny border. The dwarf varieties may be used as an edging.

The calliopsis is of easy culture and hardy. The seeds should be sown in the fall where they are to grow, because they do not transplant easily. For fall bloom, they may be sown in late August or early September, but this hardly seems worthwhile. Thin the seedlings to 8 to12 inches apart, with the taller growing varieties needing more space.

They seem to thrive in any good garden soil and do best if in full sun. Unless the flowers are kept cut, the season of bloom is apt to end early, but with such a profusion of flowers this can hardly be avoided.

The calliopsis is best known for its yellow flowers marked with crimson, red or mahogany. Generally, gardeners are satisfied to buy mixed colors.

The calliopsis is seldom troubled by insects or diseases. Should a disease appear, it is usually best handled by changing the area of seeding.

CELOSIA
(Celosia argenta—Cockscomb, Chinese Wool-flower)
Uses: Cut flowers, dried flowers.
Blooms: August—October.
Color: Dark red, scarlet, yellow, white.
Height/Spread: 10 to 36 inches, 12 to 18 inches.
Sun/Soil: Sun. Good garden loam.
Seed: Indoors—March; Outdoors—late April.

The Cockscomb is an old-time garden plant that achieved some popularity in recent years. Probably much of the new interest comes from the development of the plumosa varieties. The early gardeners seem to have striven for huge crested blooms that were almost grotesque. Today the emphasis is on the smaller cockscombs and plumes, which are much more useful in floral arrangements. The latter are excellent for dried flower arrangements.

The cockscombs thrive in any good garden loam in a sunny situation. They are comparatively easy to grow and do not require any special care. They are very free from insects and disease.

The colors range from dark reds through soft pinks, with gold and cream.

CHINESE FORGET-ME-NOT
(Cynoglossum wallichi, amabile)
Uses: Background, cut flowers.
Blooms: June to frost.
Color: Wide range.
Height/Spread: 18 to 30 inches, 6 to 10 inches.
Sun/Soil: Sun or light shade. Garden loam.
Seed: Indoors—March; Outdoors—April.

The Chinese Forget-me not is a biennial treated as an annual because it will bloom the first season from seed. It is a hardy plant and probably would grow just as well from seed sown in the fall as from spring-planted seed.

The modern variety, 'Firmament,' is a low-growing (15 to 18inches) fragrant plant with indigo blue flowers. The foliage is grayish green.

The Cynoglossum tends to self-seed, and, thus, should be kept under control. Young plants will live over winter with little or no protection. The Cynoglossum does not require any special care, and seems to be free from insects and diseases.

CHRYSANTHEMUM, ANNUAL
(Chrysanthemum carinatum—Annual Chrysanthemum)
Uses: Cut flowers, bedding.
Blooms: July—September.
Color: Wide range.
Height/Spread: To 3 feet, 8 to 10 inches.
Sun/Soil: Sun. Rich, moist soil.
Seed: March

The annual chrysanthemums are free flowering, summer bloomers that seem to do best in a cool climate. They have been used successfully in this area and probably deserve more attention.

Give the plants plenty of space, and keep the soil mulched from the day they are transplanted to the garden. These practices are necessary to keep the plants free from disease and nematodes that are splashed onto the leaves from the soil, if it has not been covered with a mulch.

CLEOME
(Cleome spinosa—Spider Flower)
Uses: Background, planting, cut flowers.
Blooms: June to frost.
Color: Rose, white.
Height/Spread: 4 to 5 feet, 2 to 3 feet.
Sun/Soil: Sun or very light shade. Sandy garden soil.
Seed: Outdoors in May.

The Cleome is a striking tall plant with flowers resembling small orchids. Long stamens give it a spidery appearance. The grayish green foliage is attractive, but as the plant reaches mature size, the lower leaves thin out and hence it needs growing plants in front of it. The foliage has a strong but not unpleasant odor.

The Cleome is very tolerant as to soil and location. The flowers are larger and fuller if given some attention, especially watering during drought periods.

The seed should be sown where the plants are to grow—at about the time of the last killing frost, April 20.

The variety Pink Queen is most generally planted because of its clear colors. Too often the seedlings have a muddy color. The white is well recommended, if the seed can be found. The experts do not consider the yellow to be worth planting.

One word of caution in growing the Cleome: remove the spent seed pods. Otherwise, you will be swamped with seedlings. The Cleome is seldom troubled with insects or diseases.

CORNFLOWER
(Centaurea cyanus—Bachelor's Button, Ragged Robin)
Uses: Cut flowers.
Blooms: May-June or July-August.
Color: Blue, white, red, pink.
Height/Spread: 2 to 3 feet, 12 inches.
Sun/Soil: Sun. Garden loam.
Seed: September or March

The Cornflower is a widely grown, hardy annual that will self-seed if given a chance. It is easy to grow and will produce a wealth of bloom with very little care. There are a number of named varieties, but most gardeners are content with the common mixture of double-flowered forms.

The seed of the Cornflower should be planted in the late fall, or in the early spring several weeks before the last killing frost is expected. When these planting dates are observed the plants will be taller and bushier, making a better display in the garden, and providing much more cutting material.

Ordinary garden care is adequate for this dependable, easily-grown annual. The flowers are especially long-lasting when cut.

The Cornflower is comparatively free from insects and pests. But it is sometimes troubled by rust disease of the foliage, and this may be controlled by dusting or spraying with an all-purpose mixture. The plants are subject to the aster yellows. Should this disease appear, the yellow sickly plants should be pulled and burned.

COSMOS
(Cosmos bipinnatus—Cosmos)
Uses: Background, cut flowers.
Blooms: August to November.
Color: White, rose, pink, red, yellow.
Height/Spread: 2 to 4 feet, 2 feet.
Sun/Soil: Sun of light shade. Garden loam.
Seed: Indoors—March; Outdoors—late April.

The older varieties of the Cosmos were tall, late flowering plants, excellent for background plantings. The foliage was light and graceful, although by pinching the plant back when less than 2 feet in height, branching was stimulated and the bean pole effect avoided. The colors were clear and attractive (white, rose, pink, red and yellow), but the lateness of flowering was disappointing to many, even though the Cosmos withstood light frosts.

The new hybrids are not so tall, 2-3 feet, and they tend to be bushier, with the flowers massed all over them.

Cosmos are tender annuals and the seed should be started indoors in March. However, the seed may be sown out of doors in late April after the soil has warmed. The plants transplant readily and should be pinched as they are being put in the garden to induce branching.

Cosmos need to be fertilized every month or six weeks to insure good growth and large showy flowers; water as needed. The taller varieties need staking. Insects and diseases are seldom a problem, although there is a stem blight disease. Infected plants should be pulled and burned.

CUPFLOWER
(Nierembergia—Blue Cups)
Uses: Edging, rock garden.
Blooms: July to frost.
Color: Lavender, purple.
Height/Spread: 4 to 6 inches, 6 to 10 inches.
Sun/Soil: Sun or light shade. Rich, moist.
Seed: Indoors—March; Outdoors—May.

The Cupflower is an excellent edging plant, producing a wealth of cup-like flowers throughout the season. If started indoors, bloom may start in June and continue until frost. The needle-like foliage is unnoticed because of the abundance of flowers.

The Cupflowers like a rich moist soil for best growth, but they will thrive and flower during the hottest, driest part of the summer. The color is described as a dark purple, but may be lavender and even almost white. The cupflower is considered one of the most useful dwarf edging plants for

window boxes and in flower vases. They seem to be untroubled by insects and diseases.

DAHLIA, BEDDING
(Dahlia species—Dahlia)
Uses: Cut flowers, bedding.
Blooms: July to frost.
Color: Wide range.
Height/Spread 15 to 24 inches, 12 inches.
Sun/Soil: Sun. Rich, moist.
Seed: Indoors—late March; Outdoors—May.
Growing dahlias from seed is not as common a practice as it should be. The dwarf dahlias grown from seed make excellent bedding plants. They are comparatively easy to grow and need only a fertile soil and plenty of moisture for best results.

They are not often troubled by insects or diseases, except for red spider mites.

The seeds should be started indoors in late March in order to have strong plants ready for the border as soon as the soil is warm. The young plants should be pinched at transplanting to stimulate branching.

Mulch the dahlia bed as soon as the plants are well started. Fertilize the bed at time of preparation and again just before the spreading plants make work difficult. The dahlias need lots of water, and they should be watered when rainfall is inadequate..

FOUR O'CLOCK
(Mirabilis jalapa—Marvel of Peru, Four O'Clock)
Uses: Background, border.
Blooms: June to frost.
Color: Yellow, white, red.
Height/Spread: 3 feet, 2 feet.
Sun/Soil: Sun. Garden loam.
Seed: Indoors—March; Outdoors—April.

The Four O'Clocks are tender plants that should not

planted out of doors until the soil has warmed and there is little danger of a hard frost. The plants are strong growing, well branched, and need little cultural care to insure abundant bloom. The usual form is yellow, but there are red and white in the seed mixtures.

In this area the Japanese beetles feed on the blossoms, and some people plant Four O'Clocks to attract the beetles away from roses and other flowers. The plants form tubers, somewhat like those of a dahlia, that may be dug and stored over winter for spring planting. There is no advantage in this practice except to keep a particularly desirable color.

Because the blossoms do not open until late afternoon, except on cloudy days, they are of little use for indoor decoration.

GAILLARDIA
(Gaillardia pulchella—Blanket Flower)
Uses: Cut flowers, bedding.
Blooms: June to frost.
Color: Red, yellow.
Height/Spread: 18 to 24 inches, 9 to 15 inches.
Sun/Soil: Sun. Rich, light, well-drained.
Seed: Indoors—March; Outdoors—late April.

The annual gaillardias are very useful cut flowers and they make a colorful display in the border. They tend to be less sprawling than the perennial gaillardias, and will thrive in the hottest part of the garden.

The new varieties are more colorful. They are not hardy, but their long season of bloom makes them very desirable. They will self seed under favorable conditions.
There are two forms of the gaillardia, the single and the double. The latter is more ball shaped.

The gaillardias seem to thrive in the hottest, driest weather, and for this reason mulches are not suggested. Clean cultivation, and fertilizer applied only at the time of

soil preparation, are suggested. They seem to be comparatively free of pests and disease.

GERANIUM, BEDDING
(Pelargoniums—Zonal and Regal)
Uses: Bedding, cut flowers.
Blooms: Late June to frost.
Color: White, pink, red.
Height/Spread: 18 to 24 inches, 12 to 15 inches.
Sun/Soil: Sun. Garden loam.
Seed: Indoors in January.

We have long considered the geranium as a perennial flowering plant, but of recent years growing them from seed and using them as bedding plants has expanded greatly. Not only do they have a long season of bloom, but there are a number of colors now available, and many varieties are self-branching so that pinching is not quite as generally practiced as formerly.

The geranium thrives best in full sun, but will grow in partial shade. It dislikes over-watering; in fact, does best if given very little water even in a drought period. Fertilizing should be kept to the very light side. Diseases and insect pests are not ordinarily a problem.

The summer prunings may be rooted to produce pot plants for the winter. They will make small plants to carry over winter and be ready for planting in the garden in early May.

HOLLYHOCK
(Althea rosea—Hollyhock)
Uses: Background, bedding.
Blooms: August.
Color: White, yellow, red, purple.
Height/Spread: 4 to 5 feet, 12 to 18 inches.
Sun/Soil: Sun. Rich, moist.
Seed: Indoors—February; Outdoors—Late April.

The biennial or perennial hollyhock is well known and widely grown for its stately display of large showy flowers. The annual is just as attractive, although lower-growing. They make a pleasing background for a border or for a low screen. The seeds should be started indoors in late February.

After the first bloom spike has finished flowering, it should be cut off to encourage a second blooming from side shoots that will emerge from below the point of cut. They will be smaller and not as upright, but will give a second flowering.

Hollyhocks are strong growers, but in order to get the best results from the annuals, they should be planted in a well prepared bed that has been deeply dug. Fertilizing once or twice during the growing season is helpful. Give the plants water as needed.

The hollyhocks are usually troubled with rust that can be controlled by dusting or spraying.

IMPATIENS
(Impatiens Holsti, I. sultani—Patience)
Uses: Bedding.
Blooms: June to frost.
Color: White, pink, rose, salmon, red.
Height/Spread: 10 to 15 inches, 8 to 12 inches.
Sun/Soil: Shade. High in humus, moist.
Seed: February.

For many years the Patience plant was considered a house plant, but then we learned it would bloom all season in the shade. If healthy, it would self-seed. The Impatiens is the one annual that will flower and provide color in deep shade—when not in competition with shallow-growing tree roots.

A generous supply of leafmold, compost, or peat moss should be worked into the soil both as a reservoir of moisture for the plants and as a soil improver. They do very poorly in a heavy clay soil.

Choice plants may be lifted and potted before frost for continued bloom indoors.

LARKSPUR
(Delphinium ajacis, consolida—Larkspur)
Uses: Cut flower, border display.
Blooms: June to September.
Color: Blue, white, red, pink, purple.
Height/Spread: 2½ to 5 feet, 8 to 12 inches.
Sun/Soil: Sun, light shade. Garden loam.
Seed: Fall—October; Spring—Early March.

The larkspur is one of the most useful of the early flowering hardy annuals. The seeds need only be scattered on the ground in late October to produce a mass of flowers for border display and cutting. They require little care.

Unless the plants are pulled as soon as they have finished blooming, they will self-seed and produce a new crop the next season. While the seedlings may not be as fine or tall growing as the new varieties, they will be quite useful.

Larkspur is an annual delphinium and should be used in most gardens rather than the showy perennial, which is adapted to more northern climates.

The key cultural practice is to sow the seeds either in the fall or in the very early spring so that they can germinate and start growth while the weather is cool. A light application or two of fertilizer during the growing season is beneficial. Larkspur may be transplanted in the early spring.

Larkspur are seldom troubled by diseases although there are several that are known to infect them. If diseased plants should appear in a planting, pull and burn them. A subsequent planting should be made in another part of the border.

LOBELIA
(Lobelia erinus—Lobelia)
Uses: Edging, pot plant.
Blooms: June to frost.
Color: Blue, white through wine.
Height/Spread: 4 to 6 inches, 6 to 8 inches.
Sun/Soil: Light shade, sun. Rich, moist.
Seed: Indoors—February.

The lobelia is a favorite edging plant in cool climates; its tiny compact plants flower continuously until frost. Out of their range here, they grow best in cooler parts of the area. Nevertheless, they are desirable plants because of their compact branching type of growth and freedom of bloom; they are well adapted to the narrow border.

Annual lobelias come in various shades of blue, some with a white eye. Of the two types of Lobelias, one grows erect, the other spreads and is more useful in window boxes, vases and baskets.

In this area the Lobelias are most likely to give

satisfactory results when grown in a cool situation, preferably in light shade. Oftentimes, by shearing the plants once or twice during the summer, they can be made to provide a satisfactory showing even in sun.

The Lobelias need a rich, moist soil, adequate spacing for good air circulation, and fertilization once or twice during the growing season. A mulch will help to keep the roots cool.

The lobelias are subject to disease and insect pests. If disease problems, particularly a stem rot, are persistent in your neighborhood, choose another edging flower.

MARIGOLD
(Tagetes erecta, T. patula, etc.—Marigold)
Uses: Cut flowers, bedding, background.
Bloom: June to frost.
Colors: Yellow, gold, orange.
Height/Spread: 6 inches to 3 feet, 12 to 20 inches.
Sun/Soil: Sun. Garden loam.
Seed: Indoors—March; Outdoors—Early May.

The marigolds are a large and complex group of annuals, which, because of their popularity and ease of culture, the plant breeders have been developing and improving. Others have produced new forms of flowers as well as better colors. The habit of growth varies from that of the tall, bushy American groups to the dwarf, much branched Mexican. The French groups are characterized by stocky, bushy growth and an insect-repelling scent.

In spite of the multitude of varieties, the gardener seldom buys one that is not satisfactory. This is because they thrive under our soil and climatic conditions and produce an endless number of blooms until cut down by frost.

Marigolds do not need heavy feeding, and fertilization usually promotes foliage rather than bloom. They do need watering during summer drought if they are to keep growing vigorously. The taller types need staking, otherwise, they are likely to topple in a thunderstorm. Cultivation around marigolds should be shallow to avoid injury to their roots.

Marigolds are seldom bothered by insects or disease,

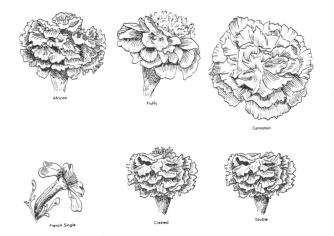

African   Fluffy   Carnation
French Single   Crested   Double

although the Japanese beetles feed in their flowers. If disease should appear pull and burn the plants.

NASTURTIUM
(Tropaeolum majus—Nasturtium)
Uses: cut flowers, bedding.
Blooms: June to frost.
Colors: White, yellow, rose, orange, scarlet, maroon.
Height/Spread: 1 to 6 feet, 1 foot.
Sun/Soil: Sun, part shade. Garden loam.
Seed: Outdoors—May 1.

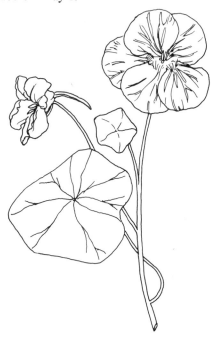

The nasturtium is one of the old-timers that is still popular, largely because it is a prolific bloomer, will grow in poor soil, and has a rather sharp fragrance. And, it will take a hot bank and poor soil as well as any annual.

Nasturtiums do not need to be fertilized; a rich soil produces a mass of leaves and few flowers. They do need to be watered because they are succulent plants. In fact, so succulent that some gardeners use the tender leaves and flowers to spice up their summer salad bowl. Do not water, however, until the leaves show signs of wilting.

The one real problem with nasturtiums is aphids that cluster about the stem. Obviously, this is a difficult place to reach with a spray. A dousing of soapy water sometimes works.

NICOTIANA
(Nicotiana alata, var. grandiflora—Flowering Tobacco)
Uses: Bedding, fragrance.
Blooms: June to frost.
Color: White, rose, red, maroon, yellow.
Height/Spread: 12 to 36 inches, 10 to 15 inches.
Sun/soil: Sun, part shade. Garden loam.
Seed: Indoors—March; Outdoors—May.

The Flowering Tobacco is a small seeded plant that is sometimes difficult to start indoors. And it is not a particularly attractive plant during the day when the flowers are limp and hang-dog. It is at night, when its starry flowers are open and its fragrance drifts across the garden, that it may be appreciated. Only the tall varieties retain their scent.

The Flowering Tobacco plants should not be heavily fertilized if a good display is desired. A well prepared seed bed in a sheltered situation is needed for best results.

The Flowering Tobacco is attractive to aphids, although many gardeners grow it without trouble.

PANSY
(Viola tricolor, var. hortensis—Pansy, Heartsease)
Uses: Cut flowers, bedding.
Blooms: March—June.
Color: Multi-colored.
Height/spread: 8 to 12 inches, 10 to 12 inches.
Sun/Soil: Sun, light shade. Rich, moist.
Seed: Mid July to Mid August.

Pansies are one of the really attractive perennials that is variously treated as biennials and annuals.

However, they are cool weather plants and should be handled to take advantage of the Washington climate. This means fall planting so that they will fill-in the first warm period in March. The production of flowers during the early spring makes an exceedingly effective border or bed.

Pansies are available in a wide range of colors. They are of easy culture and inexpensive. Most gardeners prefer to buy and use the large-flowered mixtures, although some such mixtures have too great a proportion of the darker shades and less of the yellows, lighter reds, a few whites and some of the lighter lavenders.

Pansies may be planted as edgings and as solid beds. Many people who want to have an abundance of flowers for youngsters to pick, plant some in a warm, protected sunny situation for earliest spring bloom and some in a cool shaded place for summer bloom. In the latter situation pansies frequently bloom all summer long. In the hot dry areas they will usually succumb to summer heat by mid June.

The plants should go into the border in late October or early November. They should be well mulched, but the leaves must be left uncovered. The mulch for pansies might well be a mixture of rich compost and dried cow manure. In the spring this can be supplemented with commercial garden fertilizer. A second feeding can be made in April to keep the plants growing vigorously. Do not remove the mulch in the spring because pansies like a cool moist root run.

Pansies are not immune to disease. Shift locations of the plantings every 2-3 years.

To stimulate flowering, it helps to keep the spent blooms removed, which is quite a chore, but one the children may like to perform.

PETUNIA
(Petunia hybrida—Petunia)
Uses: Bedding, edging, window boxes.
Blooms: June to frost.
Color: Wide range.
Height/spread: 6 to 24 inches, 6 to 12 inches.
Sun/Soil: Sun, light shade. Garden loam.
Seed: Indoors—March; Outdoors—May.

Next to impatiens, petunias are probably the most popular annual in America today, and no small wonder. Because of their long flowering season, their ability to take heat and drought, and their relative freedom from insects and diseases, they are especially useful.

They are most prolific of bloom. Whether used as an edging, for a mass or bed, or in window boxes and pots, they provide a continuous display throughout the season. They are available in a wide range of color, including a pale yellow.

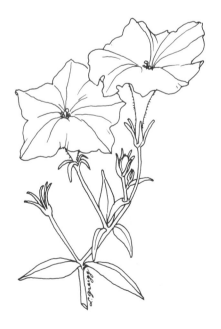

Planting to the border or to window boxes should not take place until the soil is well warmed and there is no danger of frost. Set the plants 6 to 12 inches apart. The small mound type for edgings need the most space. The balcony type can be planted fairly close, as can the bedding types.

The petunias should be planted in a soil that has been well enriched with compost, leafmold, or peat moss. Dried cow manure, or a slow-release granular fertilizer, might well be mixed at time of preparation.

If after a summer vacation the plants look a little bit tired and worn, they may be cut back to 3 or 4 inch stems, which will ensure new growth and bloom until frost.

PHLOX

(Phlox drummondi—Annual or Summer Phlox)
Uses: Cut flowers, bedding.
Blooms: July to October.
Color: White, crimson, lavender.
Height/Spread: 6 to 20 inches, 6 to 10 inches.
Sun/Soil: Sun. Light, porous, well-drained.
Seed: Indoors—March; Outdoors—late April.

The annual or bedding phlox makes a colorful display from mid-summer to frost. They are only half-hardy and should not be planted out-of-doors until danger of frost is past. In order to avoid hot weather and disease, start the plants out of doors for late development.

The bedding phlox makes its finest showing in late summer and fall. The colors of the annual phlox range from white to crimson and lavender, with many of the flowers having dark or white eyes.

The seedlings should be pinched to encourage branching. This practice also produces stockier plants that will stand up better. Removing spent flowers encourages new growth and prolongs the flowering season.

Phlox do well in an average garden soil, one that has been lightened with sand or ashes and compost suits them very well.

The red spider mite is fond of all types of phlox and must be kept under control through dusting with sulphur; which will also control mildew. Fortunately this disease is not as troublesome on the annual phlox as it is on the perennial.

PINKS

(Dianthus chinensis—Chinese Pinks)
Uses: Cut flowers.
Blooms: July to October.
Color: White, red, pink.
Height/spread: 10 to 15 inches, 6 inches.
Sun/soil: Sun. Rich, well-drained.
Seed: Indoors—March; Outdoors—April.

Pink seedlings will take severe weather, and, therefore, fall planting is a possibility in the more protected sections of the area. Actually, the Chinese pinks are short-lived perennials treated as annuals. On well drained soils the plant will live over for a second season of bloom.

The annual pinks are popular, long season flowers for the cutting bed. They are available in both single and double-flowered forms, and in a moderate range of colors. However, they are all so useful that it does not make a great deal of difference which one you plant.

They do not demand a great deal of care, nor are they often bothered by insects and diseases. They do best in a dry season.

Pine needles make an excellent mulch for the Pinks because they are airy and let moisture through. However, any material that keeps the soil moist is likely to attract slugs and snails, which like to hide under the stems.

It is commonly stated that Pinks do best in a poor, but well drained, soil. However, it is likely that most local soils will need to have both compost and ground limestone worked into them before the Pinks will thrive and produce good quality bloom.

POPPIES

(Papaver rhoeas, P. nudicale—Shirley, Iceland)
Uses: Cut flowers, bedding.
Blooms: Shirley—Fall; Iceland—Summer.
Color: Wide range.
Height/Spread: 12 to 36 inches, 6 to 10 inches.
Sun/Soil: sun. Garden loam, good drainage.
Seed: Outdoors—October-November or February-March.

The Shirley and Opium poppies are true annuals, while the Iceland is a short-lived perennial that flowers the first year from seed and is treated as an annual. The Iceland poppy is low growing, 12 to 24 inches; the others are taller, from 1½ to 3 feet, with larger flowers. The seed of the opium poppy is not offered by seedsmen.

The annual poppies are very satisfactory bloomers. Their dainty tissue-like texture and soft colors—pink, salmon, terra cotta, etc.— have made them favorites for many years in gardens everywhere. Today there are more colors, and the forms of the blossoms have even greater variation, including doubles.

However, notwithstanding these fine qualities, many gardeners do not grow them, thinking that they are difficult. Much of this is due to sowing seed too late in the spring. If planted in the fall in a well-prepared bed and covered with grass clippings or cheese cloth, or sown on the snow in February or in early March, they make a splendid showing with no other care.

For satisfactory use as cut flowers, cut poppies in the morning before the buds open. They will then last in water for several days.

Poppies do not transplant easily. Whether sown in the fall or very early spring, the plants should be thinned to 6 to 10 inches apart, depending upon the richness of the soil.

Poppies are sometimes troubled with a serious disease. It may be recognized by the black spots on stem and leaf. Pull and burn any infected plants. Aphids, too, sometimes trouble poppies.

PORTULACA
(Portulaca grandiflora—Rose Moss, Garden Portulaca)
Uses: Ground cover, edging, rock garden.
Blooms: June to October.
Color: Wide range.
Height/Spread: 4 to 6 inches, 4 inches.
Sun/Soil: Sun. Dry, open soil.
Seed: Late fall and winter.

Rose moss likes a warm sunny situation in an open or porous soil. Our heavy clays can be made suitable by mixing compost and sand into their seed bed. While the Rose moss is not considered hardy by some, it, nevertheless, must be seeded in the late fall and winter in order to obtain good germination. Spring planted seed seldom gives satisfactory results.

The portulaca is one of the best flowering covers for dry, sunny situations. The flowers open only on sunny days, which may be a disappointment to some, but their bloom continues until frost.

Other than weeding, they require practically no care during the season. They seem free from insect and disease problems.

It should be noted that the young plants of the Rose moss resemble the weed commonly called "Purslane." In fact, it is of the same family and naturally has considerable resemblance until the flowers begin to open.

RUDBECKIA
(Rudbeckia species—Coneflower)
Uses: Cut flowers, bedding.
Blooms: July until frost.
Color: Yellow, orange, brown.
Height/Spread: 1 to 4 feet, 10 to 18 inches.
Sun/Soil: Sun or shade. Garden loam.
Seed: Indoors—March; Outdoors—late April.

Most gardeners do not give much thought to the Black-Eyed Susan—yet they represent a toughie that can take our climate. The Rudbeckias withstand both heat and drought and have a long season of bloom. The modern varieties make a very pleasing show.

Rudbeckia seed may be sown indoors and transplanted to the border in early May. Or the seed may be sown out of doors a week or two before the last frost is expected in the spring. They like sun, but will take a surprising amount of shade, and make bushy plants. For best results, plant in moderately rich and moist soil.

The annuals varieties are less coarse foliaged and more in keeping with smaller gardens..

SALVIA
(Salvia splendens, S. farinacea, etc.—Ornamental)
Uses: Bedding, borders, cut flowers.
Blooms: July to frost.
Color: Red, rose, pink, salmon, white, purple.
Height/Spread: 6 to 36 inches, 10 to 15 inches.
Sun/Soil: Sun, light shade. Rich, moist garden loam.
Seed: Indoors—February.

The Scarlet sage is one of the most common bedding plants, but because of the brilliant red color should be used with caution. The red does not blend with other colors. Maybe that's why the hummingbird loves it. Recently other colors have been evolved and now there are pink, rose, salmon, wine, and white. In addition several of the blue-flowered perennial varieties may be treated as annuals. However, they have a different habit of growth and flowering. Actually, they are more useful for cutting than for bedding.

The Salvias are slow germinators so the seed should be started indoors about six weeks before the last killing frost of the spring. They are so slow in starting that it is seldom advisable to try sowing seed out of doors.

SCABIOSA
(Scabiosa atropurpurea—Pincushion flower, Mourning Bride)
Uses: Cut flowers, bedding.
Blooms: July to October.
Color: Red, white, pink, purple, blue.
Height/Spread: 18 to 36 inches, 10 to 12 inches.
Sun/Soil: Sun. Garden loam.
Seed: Indoors—March; Outdoors—April.

The Pincushion flower is an old-time favorite that has been greatly improved in recent years. They make good cut flowers and the medium tall are suitable for bedding.

The Scabiosa is not a demanding flower and will do well in the border without special attention. However, feeding and watering will keep the flowers large and attractive. Being also free from pests, they should receive more attention from gardeners who want something easy to grow.

Once established, the plants grow rapidly and begin to flower profusely. They will keep on blooming until frost cuts them down. Salvia seems to be relatively free from disease and insects.

SNAPDRAGON
(Antirrhinum majus—Snapdragon)
Uses: Cut flowers, bedding and edging.
Blooms: July-September.
Color: Wide range.
Height/Spread: 6 to 36 inches, 6 to 18 inches.
Sun/Soil: Sun, light shade. Rich garden soil.
Seed: Indoors—March; Outdoors—April.

Snapdragons are perennials that are treated as annuals; they will flower from seed the first year even when the seed is sown out of doors. They will often survive our winters if given a little protection, especially the first year plants.

Snaps were very popular with gardeners for many years until rust disease made their culture difficult. Today it would be foolish to plant other than a rust-resistant variety.

The tall-growing varieties are very attractive, but will need staking to keep them from sprawling over other plants. Unless the gardener is willing to stake them, he should grow the semi-tall varieties that are best for bedding. They are also probably the best for general garden use.

Snapdragon seed should be started indoors in February. The seed are very small and the seedlings are susceptible to damping-off disease; therefore, to avoid trouble, they should be sown in sphagnum moss, vermiculite, perlite, or sterilized soil. By using these materials to start the seed, there will be little danger of trouble with this disease. Snaps are comparatively free from other diseases and insects.

On the heavier soils snapdragons should be mulched with compost, grass clippings, sawdust, peat moss, or some similar material to keep the soil from crusting. The plants should be fertilized once a month to keep them growing

vigorously. Watering is needed whenever rainfall is insufficient to keep the soil moist.

STRAWFLOWER
(Helichrysum braecteatum—Strawflower, Everlasting,
Uses: Border, dried flowers.
Blooms: July to October.
Color: Wide range.
Height/Spread: 1 to 3 feet, 12 to 15 inches.
Sun/Soil: Sun. Garden loam.
Seed: Indoors—March; Outdoors—May.

The Strawflowers are considered to be the one of the easiest and best for drying, and they make an excellent showing in the border. The large flowers are available in single and double forms. They are easy to grow and normally reach a height of two feet or more. They will tolerate our hot dry summers exceptionally well.

Some gardeners insist that it is better to sow where the plants are to grow, but the experts recommend transplanting two or three times. The Strawflowers are not demanding as to soil, but for good growth they should be put in a soil that is moderately rich and moist.

For drying, the Strawflowers should be cut just as the flowers begin to unfold. The leaves should be stripped and the bunches hung in a dry airy place. The white strawflowers do not make an acceptable dried flower for winter arrangements.

SUNFLOWER, ANNUAL
(Helianthus—Sunflower)
Uses: Background, cut flowers.
Blooms: June to frost.
Color: Yellow, gold, red.
Height/Spread: 1½ to 6 feet; 24 to 48 inches.
Sun/Soil: Sun. Garden loam.
Seed: Outdoors—late April.

Sunflower seed should be sown out-of-doors as soon as danger of frost is past. While they withstand transplanting, seeds sown where they are to grow seem to reach flowering more quickly—so there is no advantage in starting them indoors.

Give the plants plenty of space because they branch and produce many side flowers. Plant in a soil that was enriched with both fertilizer and compost at the time of preparation. Do not mulch the plants, but keep the soil cultivated and free from grass and weeds. Water as needed.

The annual sunflowers are commonly neglected by the home gardener who may think of sunflowers in terms of the seed producer, with its huge coarse leaves and stem, and with a flower head a foot or more in diameter. However, there are a number of annual varieties with flowers much more in keeping with the ornamental border. These thrive in hot dry situations, have a very long flowering season, and seem to be free from insects and diseases.

SUNFLOWER, MEXICAN
(Tithonia rotundifolia [speciosa]—Mexican Sunflower)
Uses: Background, cut flowers.
Blooms: June-October.
Color: Red, orange.
Height/Spread: 4 to 10 feet, 2 to 3 feet.
Sun/Soil: Sun. Garden loam.
Seed: Indoors—March; Outdoors—May.

The Mexican sunflower is a tall growing and somewhat coarse-foliaged plant, but the long-stemmed flowers are most attractive. They are like small lacquer-red sunflowers.

The plant grows too strongly if given a rich moist situation (unless considerable height is desired for use as a background or screen). For the earliest bloom, the seed may be started indoors in pots or berry baskets for transplanting to the garden in early May.

The Mexican sunflower is of easy culture and undemanding, and also free from insect and disease problems.

VERBENA
(Verbena species—Verbena)
Uses: Bedding, edging, cut flowers.
Blooms: July to frost.
Color: Wide range.
Height/Spread: 6 to 18 inches, 10 to 18 inches.
Sun/Soil: Sun, light shade. Fertile, sandy loam.
Seed: Indoors—March; Outdoors—May.

Verbenas are old-time favorites that are not widely planted today except in window boxes. They make one of the most colorful low plantings for the home garden. The trailing branches are very attractive in low bowls for indoor decoration.

The new large-flowered, tall-growing mixtures are excellent for cut flowers, while the small compact plants may serve as edgings or for mass planting in the foreground. The dark green foliage makes an effective background for the solid colors of the flower heads that rise several inches above the leaves.

The seedlings should be twice transplanted if they are to have a large fibrous root system when set out of doors. The tips of the young plants should be pinched to stimulate branching, and the spent flower heads removed to encourage continued bloom.

VINCA ROSEA
(Lochnera rosea—Catharanthus roseus)
Uses: Bedding.
Bloom: July to frost.
Color: White, pink, rose.
Height/Spread: 12 to 20 inches, 6 to 12 inches.
Sun/Soil: Sun, light shade. Well drained garden soil.
Seed: Indoors—Mid February

The Vinca rosea, or Madagascar periwinkle, is a

popular bedding plant because of its long season of bloom, bright green foliage, and freedom from insect and disease. The florists have long depended upon this Vinca for use in flower boxes and for pot plants. The newer dwarf forms make a splendid showing in the smaller border.

The Vinca should not be over-watered, and then, if fertilized only occasionally, it can be depended upon to thrive in hot dry weather.

While anyone can grow this tender annual from seed, most will find that it is quite a chore to get the seed on the way in early February in order to have plants in flower in time for planting out-of-doors in mid May. Some varieties are obtainable from the plant growers.

ZINNIA
(Zinnia elegans, angustifolia—Zinnia)
Uses: Edging, bedding, cut flowers.
Blooms: June to October.
Color: Wide range.
Height/Spread: 6 to 36 inches, 6 to 18 inches.
Sun/Soil: Sun. Well-enriched moist soil.
Seed: Indoors—late March; Outdoors—April.

Zinnias are one of the most popular of the annuals because they take relatively little care, are colorful, and have a long season of bloom. They last well as cut flowers and in the border retain their color for a long period of time. They have strong stems and heavy foliage so that they present their colors in an effective setting.

There are so many types, strains, and varieties of zinnias now available that the average gardener is bewildered by the number. There are several types of the giant flowered. The Dahlia flowered is favored by some over the older flat or shallow flowers. The Fantasy type with its quilled petals is very attractive, and, while the David Burpee type is also quilled, it does not have the open center of the fantasy, but offers excellent color combinations or shadings.

The smaller flowered zinnias—variously known as lilliput, pompon, baby, or cupid zinnias—are as attractive and useful as their larger flowered relatives. They are excellent cut flowers for the smaller arrangement. In addition to those just mentioned, there are Linearis and Mexicana zinnias with somewhat different foliage and petals. They are well worth growing and are increasing in popularity.

Still other forms are the crested and double crested zinnias, which are interesting and useful variations. Not only are the forms interesting, but the colors are too. Today zinnias have clearer colors, without the fulvous overcast or lack of brilliance and depth that formerly was so common.

Zinnias benefit by rich soil and adequate supplies of moisture. They are rapid, strong growers that need plenty of food and water if they are to do their best. This means that they should be watered, when needed, and fed three or four times during the growing season. Some gardeners incorporate liberal quantities of manure in the bed at the time of soil preparation. However, a liberal supply of compost together with 2 or 3 pounds of the usual commercial fertilizer mixture per 100 square feet will serve the same purpose. This will keep the plants growing strongly for the first month; then a supplemental feeding in July, August, and again in September will ensure good growth and flowering.

Zinnias are susceptible to several insect pests and diseases. Mildew is the most common disease. It may be controlled with dusting sulphur. Persian Carpet and old Mexico varieties and the Zenith series are reportedly mildew resistant.

ANNUAL FLOWERING VINES

CANARY BIRD VINE
(Tropaeolum peregrinum—Canary Bird Vine)
Uses: Screen.
Blooms: Late June to frost.
Color: Pink, red, yellow.
Height/Spread: 10 feet, 18 inches.
Sun/Soil: Sun. Dry porous.
Seed: Indoors—March; Outdoors—late April.

The Canary Bird vine is a member of the Nasturtium group. The leaves are deeply lobed. The flowers have an interesting form from which the vine derives the common name. The flowers are not especially showy individually, but the mass of yellow bloom gives a pleasing effect.

The Canary Bird vine should be started indoors about a month before the outdoor planting date for nasturtiums. This vine requires a sunny situation. It is noted for its tolerance of dry situations.

The same aphids that trouble the Nasturtiums may be expected on the Canary Bird vine, although they should be much easier to control.

CARDINAL CLIMBER
(Quamoclit sloteri hybrida—Cardinal Climber, Starglory)
Uses: Screen, shade.
Blooms: July to October.
Color: Red.
Height/Spread: 10 to 20 feet, 6 inches apart.
Sun/Soil: Sun. Light sandy soil.
Seed: Outdoor—May.

The Cardinal vine has an attractive, finely divided foliage and cardinal-red, moming glory like flowers. The foliage is so light that the shade from the Cardinal vine is not much protection from the hot afternoon sun.

The Cardinal climber is a twiner and needs only to be started up a string or wire. Under favorable growing conditions it may reach a height of 15 to 25 feet. The seed should be notched and then soaked overnight in hot water before planting.

Seed of the Cardinal climber are frequently listed as a form of the Morning-glory (Ipomoeas).

CUP AND SAUCER VINE
(Cobaea scandens—Cup and Saucer Vine)
Uses: Screen, shade.
Blooms: Mid-summer to frost.
Color: Blue, white, mixed.
Height/Spread: 20 to 30 feet, 18 to 24 inches.
Sun/Soil: Sun, partial shade. Good garden loam, moist.
Seed: Indoors—late February; Outdoors—late April.

The Cup and Saucer vine is a tender perennial that is treated as an annual. It is a rank grower, which, under favorable conditions, reaches a height of 40 to 50 feet. The large cup-shaped flowers appear late in the summer and are followed by plum-shaped fruits.

The Cup and Saucer vine should be started in late February indoors, and the seedlings first transplanted into a 2

or 2½ inch pot, and later into a large pot. Then the husky plants will be ready to go into the garden in mid May.

The large flat seeds should be planted on edge; otherwise germination may be very poor. The vines climb by means of tendrils, so they may be trained on any rough surface or wire frame.

CYPRESS VINE
(Quamoclit pinnata—Cypress vine)
Uses: Screen.
Blooms: July to Fall.
Color: Scarlet, white.
Height/Spread: 10 to 20 feet, 6 inches apart.
Sun/soil: Sun. Garden loam.
Seed: May.

The Cypress vine, which is closely related to the Cardinal climber, has fine, fernlike, dark green foliage. Thus, it is more ornamental than shade-affording. The attractive star shaped flowers, 1 to 1½ inches in diameter, have long tubes somewhat resembling the Flowering Tobacco.

The Cypress vine is available occasionally in other than the common scarlet and white colors. The seed of the Cypress vine should be notched and soaked in hot water for a day before planting.

JAPANESE HOP VINE
(Humulus japonicus—Japanese Hop Vine)
Uses: Shade.
Blooms: Bloom inconspicuous.
Color: Green or variegated foliage.
Height/Spread: 20 to 35 feet, 12 inches apart.
Sun/Soil: Sun or shade. Rich garden loam.
Seed: May.

With more attractive foliage than the common Hop, the Japanese Hop vine is considered the best for covering trellises and large arbors—the flowers are inconspicuous. It is one of the few annuals that does well in moderate to light shade.

In May, after the soil has warmed, the seed should be sown directly in light rich soil at the base of the trellis or arbor to be covered.

The Japanese Hop vine seems to withstand both drought and heat without injury and is free from insect pests.

MOONVINE
(Calonyction aculeatum—Moonflower)
Uses: Flowers, screen.
Blooms: June to frost.
Color: White.
Height/spread: 10 to 20 feet, 18 inches apart.
Sun/Soil: Sun. Rich, moist.
Seed: May.

The Moonflower is a fragrant, large perennial from the tropics that is treated as an annual in the north. The large trumpet-shaped flowers unfold in the evening and close the following morning by noon. The Moonvine makes a showy combination with the morning-glory.

The Moonflower seed are hard-coated and should be notched and soaked in warm water before planting, so that germination will not be delayed.

The Moonflower's attractive foliage depends upon the richness of the soil and the moisture provided—given both, the heart shaped leaves form a pleasing background for the large saucer-shaped flowers.

MORNING GLORY
(Ipomoea purpurea—Morning glory)
Uses: Screen, shade, ground cover.
Blooms: June to frost.
Color: Pink, rose, crimson, purple.
Height/Spread: 10 to 15 feet, 18 inches apart.
Sun/Soil: Sun. Rich, moist.
Seed: Outdoors—late April.

The morning glories are among the most popular climbers grown in the garden. They not only produce a wealth of bloom, but their rich, dark green foliage is most useful as a screen and as a background for the large, brightly-colored trumpet-shaped flowers.

Because it grows rapidly, the morning-glory is often used to cover a low trellis or pergola, as well as fences. A natural climber, the twining vine only needs a start in the right direction—something small enough for them to wrap around.

Scarlet O'Hara is rated as the best variety for climbing; but all will climb 8 feet or more in a season, depending upon the soil and the moisture. Early Call Rose is the earliest bloomer.

The morning glories are aptly named because their flowers open in the very early morning and close about midday. Thus to be fully enjoyed, they should be where they can be

Pinch back the tops to stimulate branching and stocky growth.

observed in the morning. This also applies to the dwarf or bush form.

Morning glory seed is very hard, and to speed the germination it should be soaked overnight in water or the coat notched with a file. Because the plants can not be transplanted, the seeds must be sown where they are to grow. Someimes, plants started in pots or baskets are successfully transplanted and bloom earlier in the season. Otherwise, bloom should not be expected before late July.

They are not often troubled by insects or disease.

SCARLET RUNNER BEAN
(Phaseolus coccineus—Scarlet Runner)
Uses: Shade, ornamental, edible pods.
Blooms: June to frost.
Color: White, red, pink.
Height/Spread: 10 to 20 feet, 8 to 12 inches.
Sun/Soil: Sun. Garden soil.
Seed: Late April.

The scarlet runner bean is ordinarily grown for flowers, which are rather attractive for a member of the bean family. However, in England the edible pods are an important food crop.

There are a number of named varieties. The leaves are rather large for a bean and, of course, are rough. It is sometimes troubled by the red spider mite, which water or soap spray will help control.

The scarlet runner bean is an easy vine to grow. The seeds should be sown where they are to grow in late April or early May. String or poles should be provided for the vine to climb on. It is a twiner and does best on strings strung wherever shade is wanted.

The scarlet runner bean does not want a rich soil—the leaves would be too coarse, with the flowers less visible amid the foliage. If the pods are to be used for cooking, harvest them when young and tender.

Another popular tropical vine here is the annual Hyacinth Bean with its violet flowers and purple pods.

Dried Flowers

The gardener with limited space may want to concentrate on growing annuals that will dry to make colorful arrangements for winter use. German statice, the strawflowers and everlastings, geosporum, gomphrena, and Bells of Ireland lead the list of flowers that can be enjoyed twice. However many other species will also dry beautifully if you follow these steps.

◊ Always pick material when it is firm and stiff, but bone dry.

◊ Gather in loose bunches of 5 to 6 stems and hang upside down in a dry, warm, breezy place. Does this sound like your unfinished attic?

◊ Turn once or twice to expose all flowers equally to summer convection currents. Flowers should be thoroughly dry within 2 weeks.

◊ Store loosely in old shoe box with silica gel packs until you have enough to arrange.

◊ Using floral picks and wire to strengthen spindly stems, arrange the strongest structural elements of your design first by inserting stems into the Oasis or foam block.

◊ Fill in with daintier material, one type at a time.

Enjoy for months.

LOW MAINTAINENCE ANNUALS

Selected by the U.S. Botanic Gardens for their trial gardens. The list is not exhaustive, but does include annuals that require no staking, pinching, pest control, dead-heading, and little watering or fertilizing It assumes the planting beds are well prepared. In short if you feed the soil, these annuals will pretty much take care of themselves.

(Plants are arranged in ascending order of height).

Sweet Alyssum—repeat bloom edging, white through purple; 4-6 in.
Multiflora Petunia—'Carpet Mix,' low, assorted colors, 4-6 in.
Madagascar Periwinkle—'Cooler' series, low, pest-free, 5-7 in.
Grandiflora Petunia—'Supermagic' mix, colorful, fragrant, 6 in.
Wax Begonia—'Cocktail' mix, assorted flowers, foliage,6-8 in.
Ornamental Pepper—'Treasure Red,' white flowers, red fruit, 8 in.
Dusty Miller—persistent silvery foliage, 8 in.
Ageratum—furry white to violet flowers, rich foliage, 8-10 in.
Impatiens—'Super Elfin' mix, white through violet, 8-10 in.
Torenia—'Panda Blue,' blue purple, 8-10 in.
Globe Amaranth Gomphrena—'Buddy', purple, dries well, 10-12 in.
Sweet Basil—'Purple Ruffles', full purple foliage, scent, 10-12 in.
Madagascar Periwinkle—'Pretty' series, pinks, taller, 14 in.
Salvia farinecea species— rich blues, white, 18 in.
Globe Amaranth Gomphrena—'Strawberry Fields', red, taller 24 in.
Garden Cannas—assorted colors in short varieties, 3 ft.
Cosmos—yellows to orange, short; white to wine, tall; 3-4 ft.
Cleome—'Queen' series, white to pinks, dramatic shape, 3-5 ft.
Castor Bean—bold star shaped leaves, green to bronze, 6-8 ft.
Potato Vine—white to purple flowers, delicate foliage, 10-20 ft.
Hyacinth Bean—lovely purple flowers & pods, edible beans, 30-60 ft.

INSPIRATION:

U.S. Botanic Garden, First Street & Independence Avenue SW, Washington, D.C.

Annuals Library, Ohio Drive at the Tidal Basin, Washington, D.C.

PROVEN PERENNIALS

Perennials are plants that live for more than two years, in contrast with annuals and biennials, and, also, perennials offer a wider range of plant material than annuals. They are important to the garden because they provide a varying picture of bloom from season to season, and do not have to be replaced each season or year (although the work of maintaining them may be considerable).

The perennial border, being more or less permanent, should be well prepared before planting so that the plants will thrive and provide an attractive, healthy appearing display for many years. The incorporation of quantities of humus, bone meal, and well rotted manure is desirable in most cases, and good drainage should be provided where necessary. If the soil is a heavy clay, sand or ashes will be needed to lighten it.

The list of perennials for this area is long and there are many types and varieties of most of them to choose among. Those that are specifically adapted to this area should be given first consideration There are many that thrive in the north, such as delphinium, canterbury bells, etc., that are exceedingly difficult to grow here. But there are many attractive ones that thrive here with no coddling.

Perennials may be started from seed, although there are only a few that will bloom the first year. Many kinds come true only from divisions or cuttings. For such kinds it is better to buy a few plants and let them become established. Then, from these, others can be grown to expand the planting. To be effective, most perennials should be planted in groups of several of a kind.

Propagation

For a long time the sowing of perennial seed has been a midsummer job, even though it is more difficult because of the hot, dry weather. However, if the seed are sown in a protected bed they can receive attention as needed. If this is feasible, the seeds may be sown in March or April and the seedlings transplanted to a growing bed where they will continue their development until planting time in September. Those kinds of seeds that germinate in a relatively short time may be sown in the early fall, but they should not be transplanted until March or April.

Propagation by division of established clumps will in most cases take place in the spring for fall bloomers and in the early fall for spring bloomers. Some plants, such as iris and primroses, may be divided immediately after the flowering season, while others, like poppies are handled only during the dormant season.

Cuttings may be taken in the spring when the new shoots are 6 to 8 inches long. Some will do better if taken in late summer. This will vary, but unless unusual care is given, good results can only be obtained in the appropriate season.

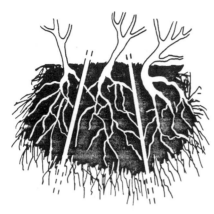

Some plants such as perennial alyssum may be divided by
cutting the mass of roots into sections.

Plant Culture

Most of the perennials are relatively free from
diseases, although they are known to be subject to them under
unfavorable conditions. Therefore, the first step in keeping
plants healthy is to keep them growing vigorously—well
cultivated, fed and watered. Where diseases do appear, the
infected plants should be removed and the others sprayed with
either Bordeaux mixture or the appropriate fungicide.

Insect pests are apt to be common. Because this area is
the meeting ground for bugs from the north with their southern
cousins, we have all the pests common to both regions.
However, there are many ways to keep them under control.

Most perennials benefit from a frequent, but shallow,
cultivation. Those with shallow roots prefer a light mulch. If
the perennial border is properly laid out, cultivation and
mulching will not be difficult. Plants that are properly spaced
have room enough about them to permit the workman to use a
hoe or larger tool.

Most perennials grow rather vigorously and flower
freely. This requires considerable moisture, so provision should
be made to supply the perennial border with the water it needs.

Only a few of the perennials require a sweet soil (flax
and dianthus are two of them). Most will thrive in a soil that is
slightly acid. The shade-loving plants, however, seem to need
a distinctly acid soil for best results. These requirements should
be observed in selecting plants for the garden.

ARTEMISIA
(Artemisia albula—Artemesia)
Uses: Foliage, cutting and background.
Height/Distance: 2 to3 feet, 18 t0 24 inches.
Blooms: Inconspicuous.
Propagate: Division—April; Cutting—May.
Plant: April-May.
Exposure/Soil: Sun. Garden loam.

Artemisia, Silver King, is a useful perennial for the
hardy border. The silvery foliage is effective in the border
because it adds contrast to the green foliage of other plants and
at the same time helps to harmonize the many colors of
surrounding flowers. Because its finely cut foliage does not
wilt readily, it is excellent for bouquets.

Artemisia is easily propagated by dividing its roots in
the spring or by taking cuttings that root readily if taken in
May. This perennial sends out strong underground shoots and
soon develops into a large clump, which needs to be kept
within bounds. Artemisia is seldom troubled by insects and
diseases.

HARDY ASTER
(Aster novae-angliae, Aster frikartii—Aster)
Uses: Cutting, background, foreground.
Height/Distance: 10 to 48 inches, 2 to 3 feet.
Blooms: September-October.
Propagate: Division in April or May.
Plant: April-May.
Exposure/Soil: Sun, partial shade. Moist, garden loam.

For fall bloom, the hardy asters are a dependable
perennial. They have been much improved over the native
wildings from which many of them have descended. They
withstand drought very well (neglecting to water them only
makes the flowers smaller).With reasonably good culture, they
produce a mass of nearly solid bloom that is very effective in
the perennial border. The tall forms make good background
material. The dwarf ones are excellent in the front of the
border. Napsbury has the longest flowering season and is a
good flower for cutting. Lassie also is recommended as a cut
flower.

Divide and replant at least every other spring,
enriching the soil while doing so. Stake the taller varieties.

Among the other notable aster species and hybrids,
A. Frikarti (2-2½ ft.) is an old favorite. Plant it in sun or light
shade. It blooms from July until frost. Two new asters, Aster
Farreri-Berggarten (18-24 in.); and Aster Yunnanensis-
Napsbury (2 ft.) and Aster alpelhis—Triumph, which bloom
from July to August, are good blues.

The hardy asters are relatively free from insect and
disease troubles. Mildew and such other leaf diseases as may
appear are easily controlled with a good all-purpose dust.

BABY'S BREATH
(Gypsophila paniculata—Baby's Breath)
Uses: Cut flowers, border.
Height/Distance: 24-36 inches, 4 feet.
Blooms: June-September.
Plant: April or September.
Propagate: Seed, division, cuttings—early spring or fall.
Exposure/Soil: Sun. Dry, rather poor soil.

Gypsophila is a popular cut flower especially useful
in bouquets with other flowers. The small, dainty foliage and
tiny single or double flowers are most effective. Because of its
ease of culture and long season of bloom, most gardens should
have one or more plants for cutting sprays as needed.

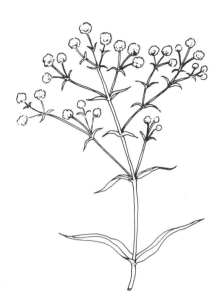

The hardy Gypsophila thrives in a rather poor dry soil that is loose; thus cultivation is important. The plants may be divided or set out in the early spring or in September.

There are some very attractive double forms of the Gypsophila, but they may be propagated only by grafting. The single-flowered forms are inferior from seed, but the old plants may be divided; or cuttings may be taken in August and rooted in peat moss.

Repens, a 4 to 6-inch dwarf, is excellent for the rock garden, where its dainty white flowers in June and July make a pleasing display.

There is a new creeping form with pale pink flowers, Rosy Veil, that bloom in the early summer. It is a good ground cover in sunny places.

BALLOON FLOWER
(Platycodon grandiflorus—Chinese Bellflower, Balloon Flower)
Uses: Cut flowers, border, rockery.
Height/Distance: 12 to 36 inches, 8 to 12 inches.
Blooms: June-October.
Propagates: Seed—March, August.
Plant: April, September.
Exposure/Soil: Sun, part shade. Medium, well-drained, sandy loam.

The balloon flowers are an excellent substitute for the bell flowers in this area. These hardy perennials may be grown from seed sown in early March and will flower the first season. The species P. grandiflorus album is a white form and a double. P. grandiflorus mariesii is dwarf and suited to the rock garden.

The balloon flower makes a strong bushy plant that seldom needs staking. If well grown, they are most attractive in the hardy border.

A deep, rich sandy soil that is well-drained suits them best. They are grown most easily from seed as the fleshy roots

are difficult to divide. The crown should be about an inch below the surface of the soil. Because it is so close to the surface, care should be used to avoid injury to the crown when removing the dead bloom stalks in the fall.

CANDYTUFT
(Iberis saxatilis, sempervirens—Candytuft)
Uses: Edging, rockery, bedding.
Height/Distance: 6 to 12 inches, 15-24 inches.
Blooms: April-June.
Propagate: Cuttings or division—September; Seed—August.
Plant: September-April.
Exposure/Soil: Sun, light shade. Moist, moderately rich.

The perennial candytuft, one of the best of the edging plants, is really a small shrub. It is very useful in a rock garden. It is of easy culture and may be grown from seed, although it takes 2 years to produce compact plants.

The plants form a dense mat of foliage and when once established should not be disturbed. They are all relatively low growing.

Because it is evergreen, the candytuft is useful where its rich green foliage shows up well during the winter. Purity is a free bloomer and compact. The dwarf forms do best in this area.

Prune candytuft stems after flowering to prevent bare foliage holes from developing in the center of the plant.

CHRYSANTHEMUM
(Chrysanthemum indicum, morifolium, sibirium—Mums)
Uses: Cut flowers, bedding.
Height/Distance: 1 to 5 feet, 12 to 18 inches.
Blooms: August-November.
Propagate: Division, cuttings—April to June.
Plant: April to July 15.
Exposure/Soil: Sun. Rich, moist garden loam.

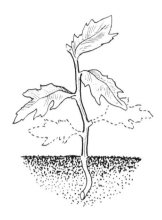

A chrysanthemum shoot stripped for rooting.

Cushions—12-18 inches

Variety	Color	Type	Height	Bloom Date
Yellow Cloud 9	yellow	incurved	low	September 20
Sea Urchin	chartreuse	quill	low	September 25
West Point	yellow	button	very low	September 28
Troubador	yellow	decorative	low	October 5
Yellow Supreme	yellow	decorative	low	October 5
Chiquita's Rival	bright yellow	button pom	low	October 5
Yellow Starlet	primrose	single	low-medium	October 5
Cloud 9	ivory-white	incurved	low	September 20
Baby Tears	white	pompom	very low	September 25
Powder River	white	decorative	low	September 25
Pearls	pure white	white pompom	low	September 30
Ballerina	purewhite	quill	low	October 5
Marbletop	white	anemone	low	October 15
Corsage Cushion	white	lancinated	low	October 15
Cameo	pink	decorative	very low	August
Jewel Box	lilac rose	pompom	low	September 20
Autumn Royal	fuschia pink	decorative	low	September 25
Small Wonder	rose fuschia	decorative	low	October 1
Chiffon	clear pink	decorative	low	October 1
Grandchild	orchid, red eye	decorative	low	October 1
Ann Ladygo	pale pink	anemone	low	October 15
Mango	red-purple	anemone	low	October 15
Gypsy Wine	claret purple	pompom	low	September 25
Seminole	lavender	single spoon	low	September 30
Desert Sunset	terracotta	decorative	low	September 20
Triumph	pastel bronze	decorative	low	September 20
Festive Cushion	red bronze	decorative	low-medium	September 20
Tiger	gold bronze	button pom	low	September 25
Ironsides	orange-bronze	decorative	low	October 1
Spunky	bronze	button	low	October 5
Newgo	bronze	anemone	low	October 10
Red Hot	molten copper	decorative	low	September 20
Ruby Mound	burgundy	decorative	low	September 25
Drummer Boy	scarlet	pompom	low	October 5
Red Mischief	red	single	low	October 15
Fireside Cushion	bright red	single	low	October 25

Garden Hardies—18-36 inches

Variety	Color	Type	Height	Bloom Date
Festive Queen	primrose yellow	decorative	medium	September 15
Hunter's Moon	yellow	pompom	medium	September 25
Sombrero	lemon yellow	decorative	medium	October 1
Cheerleader	deep gold	incurve	tall	October 5
Acacia	soft yellow	incurve	tall	October 10
Gianna D'Angelo	yellow	spoon	medium	October 15
Ruby Breithaupt	primrose yellow	decorative reflex	low	October 15
Happiness	yellow	single	tall	October 25
Autumn Bride	white	quill-anemone	tall	September 20
French Vanilla	cream white	decorative	medium	September 25
Raggedy Ann	snow white	carnation	medium	September 25
Ostosa	white	decorative	low	October 5
Jessamine Williams	white	quill	medium	October 5
Blizzard	white	pompom	tall	October 15

Variety	Color	Type	Height	Bloom Date
Confetti	strawberry	carnation	tall	September 25
Waltz Time	pink	decorative	medium	September 25
Quarterback	bright pink	incurve	medium tall	September 25
Spinning Wheel	lavender pink	quill-anemone	medium	September 25
Lancer	lavender pink	quill	low	October 1
Raspberry Ice	fuschia pink	decorative	medium	October 15
Pink Dot	pink	pompom	medium	October 25
Carrousel	aster purple	quilled	medium	October 1
Purple Waters	deep purple	decorative	low	October 5
Autumn Fire	fiery bronze	decorative	tall	September 15
Ginger	bronze tones	decorative	medium	September 23
Fine Feathers	peach-bronze	spoon	tall	October 1
Dolli-ette	bronze	quill	medium	October 5
Bronze Giant	bronze tones	decorative	tall	October 5
Orbit	bronze	spoon	medium	October 15
Dazzler	orange bronze	semi-double	tall	October 25
Soldier Bold	cardinal red	reflex	medium	September 15
Daredevil	deep red	pompom	medium	September 25
Red Climax	ruby red	decorative	tall	September 25
Fireworks	holly red	decorative	tall	October 1
Volunteer	red	decorative	medium	October 10
Remembrance	red	decorative	tall	October 20

Bloom in the following varieties can be triggered by shading for 14 hours a day to produce buds. Bloom dates listed are the amount of time from bud to flower.

Disbuds—pinched for exhibition

Variety	Color	Type	Height	Bloom Date
Derek Bircumshaw	yellow	incurve	medium	8 weeks
Gold Lode	yellow	reflex	low	9 weeks
Golden Nob Hill	yellow	irregular incurve	tall	10 weeks
Cymbals	butterscotch	single	medium	10 weeks
Super Yellow	lemon yellow	quill	tall	10 weeks
Yellow Knight	clear yellow	spider	tall	10 weeks
Winter Carnival	icy white	decorative	tall	9 weeks
Silver Sheen	white	incurve	medium	9 weeks
Sophisticate	white	semi-double	tall	9 weeks
Free Spirit	white	anemone	medium	9 weeks
Cloudbank	white	anemone	tall	9 weeks
Silver Strand	white	spider	medium	9 weeks
Nob Hill	pure white	irregular incurve	tall	10 weeks
Donlopes White	white	spider	tall	10 weeks
Quarterback Pink	pink	incurve	low	6 weeks
Major Bowes	pink	incurve	medium	8 weeks
Dark Parasol	deep pink	spoon	medium	8 weeks
Deep Hot Pink	luminous pink	reflex	medium	9 weeks
Westland Pink	light pink	quill	medium	9 weeks
Peacock	deep pink	decorative	medium	10 weeks
Streamer	lavender pink	spider	tall	10 weeks
Black Magic	deep purple	reflex	tall	8 weeks
Lili Gallon	wine/silver	reflex	medium	9 weeks
Frolic	vibrant purple	pompom	medium	9 weeks
Stadium Queen	bronze	incurve	medium	6 weeks
Wildfire	intense orange	decorative	medium	9 weeks
Onward	red bronze	incurve	tall	9 weeks
Dark Dramatic	bronze	semi-double	medium	9 weeks
Evening Glow	salmon	spider	tall	9 weeks
Honey	light bronze	quill	medium	10 weeks
Copper Ann	bright bronze	decorative	medium	10 weeks
Indianapolis Bronze	bronze	irregular incurve	tall	10 weeks
Red Headline	ox-blood	decorative	medium	6 weeks
Stoplight	bright red	single	medium	9 weeks
John Riley	crimson	reflex	medium	8 weeks
Matador	deep red	decorative	short	9 weeks
Oberlin	red tones	quill	short	9 weeks
Symbol	orange	reflex	tall	10 weeks
Alberta	red	spider	tall	10 weeks

Harvest Giants—may be grown as disbuds or garden hardies

Variety	Color	Type	Height	Bloom Date
Silver Song	white	reflex	medium	September 15
September Song	pink	reflex	medium	September 15
Bronze Song	bronze	decorative	medium	September 15
Pumpkin	bronze	reflex	short	September 20
Autumn Leaves	orange	reflex	tall	September 25
Touchdown	pink	reflex	tall	October 15
Full Moon	white	incurve	tall	October 15
Yellow Moon	yellow	incurve	tall	October 15
Indian Summer	red	reflex	tall	October 20
Redskin	red	decorative	tall	October 20

Revised with the help of members of the Potomac Chrysanthemum Society.

The chrysanthemum have long been the mainstay of the fall perennial border. In recent years hybridizers have brought us many early-blooming varieties in many types and colors, and most escape the first frost.

The flowering season for this area is divided into early (late August 5 to October 5), midseason (October 5 to 25), and late (October 25 to November 5). The color range varies from pure white through the yellows, pinks, bronze, purple and reds. We have low-growing, medium height, and tall mums.

The chrysanthemum fanciers now speak of the different varieties according to the bloom structure. The 2 visible characteristics are identified by a difference in the outer petals and center or disk petals. Some of the major classes of the modern chrysanthemum are singles, anemones, pompons, incurves, decorative reflexes, spoons, quills, and spiders.

Most gardeners use the bush-type plants listed above for mass effect in landscaping. If these varieties are grown to single blooms, they are very small. Those gardeners interested in exhibition blooms may grow the large standards or disbuds. Disbuds suggested as proven varieties for this area are Silver Sheen, Mrs. Roy, Major Bowes, Southern Comfort, Miss Oakland, Marguerita, Edwin Pointer, Super Chief, Indianapolis Group, Princess Ann, Symbol, Lamont, Bess Witt, Nightingale, Donolopes White, Yellow Knight, Bunbu, Silver Strand, Coronation Pink, Honey, World's Fair, Miss Olympia and Lillian Doty.

Each year in the spring chrysanthemums may be propagated by division of the clumps A still better method involves rooting cuttings taken from the top 3 inches of the new shoots when they are at least 8 inches high. Placed in a moist mixture of sand and peat moss, they will root in about 2 weeks.

When the plants have roots ¼ to ½ inch in length, they are ready for transplanting into pots or beds.

The cultural requirement for the growing of chrysanthemums can be condensed to three points:

(1) Mulch to keep the roots cool and functioning, to conserve moisture, to avoid laborious cultivating, and to keep nematodes from splashing up from the soil to the foliage.

(2) Keep the plants growing continuously by watering as needed and feeding lightly every 2 to 3 weeks until the buds begin to show color.

(3) To control aphids and slugs, use soap spray, orthene and snail pellets at the base of the garden plants. Ferbam or captan will protect the plant from diseases and fungus.

For good bushy growth of the hardy garden types, the young plants should be pinched when established and again about every 2 weeks until the first week of July. Pinching of other types and forms varies markedly from that given the garden hardies. Remove only the tip. Do not pinch the cushion mums.

The standards or exhibition varieties should be grown to not more than 3 stems by removing all side shoots after the first pinch. Since the latter type will grow tall, it is suggested they be supported. However, they are only expected to produce 2 to 4 flowers per plant, whereas the hardy garden types are expected to produce several sprays and many blooms per plant.

Staking is desirable for all except the cushions.

Chrysanthemums bloom according to the length of the night. that is why the greenhouse gardener with his shading cloth (black sateen) and electric light can produce blooming plants any time of year. Twelve to fourteen hours of shading per day are necessary to start the budding process in controlled blooming.

Cushion mums, those early blooming mounds of color mentioned above, make an excellent edging for the later blooming decoratives and pompoms. They seemingly need only to be well watered and fed to produce a mass of bloom from late August to October. Because of their habit of growth, they do not need pinching to produce a mass of blooms.

When chrysanthemums have finished blooming, cut the plants off at 4 to 6 inches from the ground and destroy the cut-off tops. Mulch them with a loose airy material such as pine straw after the ground is frozen to prevent repeated freezing and thawing. If the plants do not have good drainage, lift them with a large clump of dirt, set them on the ground in a well-drained location, and mulch them. Loosen mulch if snow packs around the plants.

A cold frame that is kept cool and well ventilated is a fine place to over-winter varieties. Spray them with an insecticide and a fungicide in March. As the weather becomes warm in March and April, side dress the plants with fertilizer and gradually remove the mulch to assure healthy shoots for propagation.

In preparing the soil, it is a good idea to dig in superphosphate (at the rate of 3 pounds per 100 square feet) to promote strong stem growth.

If your space is limited, use mums as annuals for color, discarding them after rooting cuttings of your favorites in the cold frame for next year.

Diane Roe of the Old Dominion Chrysanthemum Society suggests that to protect your show mums from cucumber beetles, dust each opening bloom with Sevin powder from a nylon knee sock; and, if earwigs are a problem, remove all the mulch where they hide.

COLUMBINE
(Aquilegia species, hybrids—Columbine)
Uses: Cut flowers, border.
Height/Distance 12 to 36 inches, 9 to 18 inches.
Blooms: April-June.
Propagate: Seed—June; division—September.
Plant: Early spring, September.
Exposure/Soil: Light shade, sun. Light, warm, moist.

The columbine is a loverly dainty perennial for the early spring border. The newer types with their long spurred flowers are attractive and now available in a wide range of colors suitable both for cutting and border display. They need protection from the hot midday sun.

The native species all do well here and add interest to the border. A. canadensis (18 inches) with reddish orange flowers, A. longissima (18 inches), pale yellow flowers with exceedingly long spurs, and A. caerulea (24 inches), the famous Rocky Mountain blue columbine are all native species.

With the exception of the named varieties, columbines are usually propagated from seed which should be sown either in the early spring or late summer. They will not grow well during the heat of summer. Established plants of desirable color may be lifted and divided in the early fall.

Columbines are frequently troubled by leaf miner, which is not serious except for disfiguring the foliage and is easily controlled with acephate. Crown rot is troublesome on the heavier soils; frequent lifting and dividing may avoid it. Most gardeners sow seed each spring or in August, thus ensuring young plants for flowering the following spring.

COREOPSIS
(Coreopsis grandiflora—Coreopsis)
Uses: cutting, bedding.
Height/Distance: 1 to feet, 12 to 18 inches.
Blooms: June-October.
Propagate: Seed—March or July; Division—April-May

Plant: April-May.
Distance: 12 to 18 inches.
Exposure/Soil: Sun. Rich, moist.

The coreopsis, or tick-seed, is one of the most dependable yellow flowered perennials. With a relatively long season of bloom, they make a colorful spot in the flower border as well as a useful cut flower. They are of easy culture, being grown either from seed or from division—the doubles only by division. If the seed are sown in the early spring, the plants will flower the first season.

C. verticillata 'Zagreb' and 'Moonbeam' are tops for pest free flower production all summer. There is also a dainty species, Auriculata nana (15inches), which blooms all summer.

The coreopsis is occasionally troubled by a beetle which may be controlled by Orthene.

DAYLILY
(Hemerocallis—Daylily)
Uses: Border and bedding.
Height/Distance: 1 to 4 feet, 3 to 5 feet.
Blooms: May-September.
Propagate: Seed—November; Division—April and immediately flowering.
Plant: April to September.
Exposure/Soil: Sun or light shade. Garden loam, ample humus.
Varieties:

Early: 'Berti Ferris,' 20 in.. orange ruffled; 'Stella D'Oro,' 13 in., gold with green throat, reblooms.

Early to midseason: 'June Bug,'24 in., gold with maroon eye, green zone.

Midseason: 'Pardon Me,' 18 in., cream; 'Francis Fay,' 24 in., melon; 'Love That Pink,' 30 in., clear pink; 'Buddha,' 32 in., dark red; 'Jubilee Pink,' 36 in., clear, deep

pink; 'Mary Todd,' 36 in., orange and cinnamon; 'Winning Ways,' 32 in., pale greenish yellow, large; 'Clarence Simon,' 30 in., large pink and creamy melon; 'Shady Lady,' 30 in., yellow with wine eye; 'Hope Diamond,' 30 in., light creamy yellow; 'Green Glitter,' 30 in., large, lemon yellow; 'Mary Mae Simon,' 32 in. creamy yellow and pink.

Late midseason: 'Joey Langdon,' 30 in., bright red, heat resistant; 'Jamie Douglas,' 26 in., yellow; 'Purple Bounty," 30 in., red purple; 'Bengal Tiger,' 30 in., green and cinnamon-dusted; 'Smiling Jack,' 34 in., ruffled gold.

Late season: 'Hyperion,' 38 in., clear yellow; 'Catherine Woodberry,' 30 in. pastel lavender.

In addition to the varieties listed above, there are a considerable number of other new tetraploid and diploid hybrids. There are double-flowered daylillies, miniatures for the smaller garden, later flowering varieties to extend the season, and evening blooming varieties. Some of these latter even last for two days instead of one, and some are fragrant. Also there are reblooming and continuous blooming, as well as many variations in flower, coloring, and form—saucers, spiders, recurves, and flat plate shapes.

The daylillies are one of the most dependable lily-like flowers of all perennials. They are hardy, tolerant, free blooming, and immune to most insects and diseases. They require little in the way of culture, and little or no fertilizer. Water is needed while flowering. By a careful selection of varieties, flowers may be had from May until September.

Some varieties are rather dwarf, while others are tall—up to 4 feet. They do best in sun or light shade, and they will not flower in heavy shade.

The colors until the last few years, have been mostly shades of yellow. Now pinks and reds and burgundies, and bicolors with darker eyes, are being offered. Before selecting varieties, it is wise to see them in flower, especially those having red in them, for they may have an unattractive fulvous overcast.

GAILLARDIA
(Gaillardia aristata—Blanketflower)
Uses: Cutting, bedding.
Height/Distance: 18 to 24 inches, 12 to 18 inches.
Blooms: June-October.
Propagate: Seed—July; Division—April; Stem cuttings—August-September; Root cuttings—October.
Plant: April, May or September.
Exposure/Soil: Sun. Sandy garden loam.

The Gailllardia is a very satisfactory perennial with a long season of bloom. It is not too particular in its requirements, although it repays good culture. It is useful for cutting and makes a colorful showing in the perennial border. It is relatively free from insects and diseases.

Burgundy is the reddest gaillardia, with shining wine red petals tipped with yellow. Dazzler has bright golden yellow petals with a maroon center. Sunset and Tangerine are more nearly yellow than are most varieties. The Portola hybrids are bronze-scarlet tipped with yellow.

The gaillardia may be readily propagated by division and by cutting, as well as grown from seed. The named varieties can be reproduced only by dividing and cutting. For this reason, many gardeners prefer to buy a mixture and propagate by division those colors they like. Occasionally, an old clump grows well but does not flower; this usually can be corrected by lifting and dividing it in the early spring.

The gaillardia does best in full sun in soil that is not too heavy. They tend to sprawl over nearby plants; this can be prevented by staking or pruning, or by growing the so-called upright strains that are available. Because the upright forms do not grow as tall, they may be a more satisfactory choice for smaller borders.

For indoor use, the flowers should be cut while they are still cup-shaped, before they are fully opened.

HOSTA
(Hosta species and hybrids—Plantainlily)
Uses: Edging, border, specimen planting.
HeightDistance: 10 to 30 inches, 9 to 24 inches.
Bloom: July-September.
Propagate: Seed—April; Division—September: Cuttings—September.
Plant: March-April.
Exposure/Soil: Light to full shade; may tolerate sun. Medium rich, moist, but well-drained.
Species and Varieties:
H. Plantaginea, 2½ ft., white, very fragrant, August.
H coerulea, 2½, ft., blue flowers, July.
H. lancifolia, 2 ft., pale lilac flowers, August-September.
H. sieboldiana, 2½ ft., white flowers, July.
Honeybells, 3 ft., lavender-blue, July-August.
Ventricosa, 3 ft., purple, July-August.
Royal Standard, white, sun-tolerant.
Variegata, 18 in., violet-blue, July.
Francis Williams, 8 in., silver edged, lavender, September.

Hostas, sometimes called Plantainlily, are frequently grown for their foliage effects although all have attractive flowers. The summer-blooming H. plantaginea is noteworthy in that it flowers during a period when few perennials are in bloom; it has large ribbed, glossy leaves that are most attractive. Hostas are of easy culture and thrive in shady situations. Some tolerate sun and can be used in the perennial border. The best of these is the new variety Royal Standard.

When hostas are used in foundation plantings and other unfavorable plant locations, the soil should be carefully and deeply prepared. Quantities of manure or compost should be worked into a subsoil to increase the water-holding capacity of the soil.

Hostas may be grown from seed, but most gardeners depend upon division. In poorly drained soils, crown-rot may ruin a planting. When this occurs, the plants should be lifted and destroyed and the soil sterilized with a corrosive sublimate solution.

IRIS
(Iris germanica—Bearded Iris)

Uses: Cut flowers

Height/Distance: 4 to 48 inches, 6 to 15 inches.

Blooms: April-June.

Propagate: Division—after flowering.

Plant: June-August.

Exposure/Soil: Sun, shade according to species. Moderately rich, well-drained.

Tall-bearded varieties:

'Arctic Fury,' white ruffled; 'Babbling Brook,' light blue; 'Blue Sapphire,' magnesium blue; 'Camelot Rose,' orchid and burgundy: 'Curtain Call,' pink plicata; 'Debbie Riardon,' white-yellow amoena; 'Frontier Marshal,' large red; 'Grand Waltz,' ruffled lavender; 'Glazed Orange,' orange; 'Lord Baltimore,' purple and white amoena; 'Lady of Loudon,' pale blue and white; 'Night Owl,' blue-black; 'Pink Taffeta,' pink; 'Royal Touch,' pansy violet.

Iris breeders have provided gardeners with a wonderful selection of the "Rainbow" flower from which to choose almost any color, height, or flowering season. The bearded iris begins its blooming season with the dwarf. in April followed by the intermediates, and then the tall-bearded varieties extend the season into early June.

In the culture of bearded iris, two important requirements are: sunshine and good drainage. The first is easily arranged, except in gardens that are shaded. If an open area is not available, the plants should be set where they will receive sunshine for a half day. The second presents little or no difficulty in light soils, but in heavy loam and clay, drainage must be considered. If the soil is in good tilth, as found in a good garden, adequate drainage may be provided by raising the bed a few inches. A heavy loam or clay soil may be lightened by adding organic matter, such as decayed leaves, rotted manure, or composted materials. Blue chip, kelp bonemeal, cottonseed meal, or pulverized phosphate rock may be added. All material should be thoroughly mixed with the soil and allowed to settle before planting begins.

For good growth, avoid using fertilizers high in nitrogen content, and do not over-fertilize. Lush growth may be produced, which renders the rhizome more susceptible to the rot organisms always present in the soil. Dolomite, a calcium magnesium carbonate, may be used to neutralize excess acidity caused by decaying organic matter. The fertilizer may be worked into the soil either at the time the bed is prepared or shortly before planting.

The best time to plant iris is from late June to early August, which will allow time for the plants to become fully established. Later plantings may be made, but precaution should be taken to prevent heaving—use a mulch of coarse materials such as pine boughs or salt hay put on the bed after the ground is frozen.

The plants should be set with the rhizome slightly exposed or barely covered with soil. The slender roots should be spread out and downward and the soil firmed about them. Do not plant deeply. The plants may be set 8 to 24 inches apart. If a more immediate effect is desired, plant more closely or in groups of 3 or more plants 4 inches apart. Thin or move iris when they become crowded. It is a good idea to remake the bed about every 3 years. Newly set plants should be watered, if the ground is dry, and a thorough watering should be given in dry weather.

The cultivation of iris should be shallow to avoid disturbing the roots. Keep the beds free from weeds and do not permit encroachment by other plants. Remove outer leaves as they turn brown. At all times, keep old iris leaves, grass, etc., away from the rhizomes. Clean cultivation is a good preventive for rhizome rots.

If rot should appear, scrape out all infected tissue and expose to the sun for several days; after this the rhizome may be dusted with a copper compound, such as Bordeaux mixture, and reset.

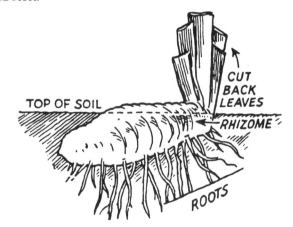

For bearded iris, prepare entire bed, then plant singly in holes ample enough to permit proper spread of roots. Leave top of rhizome exposed.

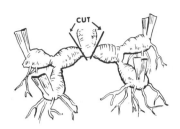

Don't make the iris divisions too small—it delays blooming a year.

The iris borer is a pest but there are sprays and dusts available which are effective when used according to directions on the package. Local growers have experienced good results with either a 5% carbaryl dust or 50% carbaryl wettable spray. There is also an emulsion, carbaryl #2 Aqua, which is very convenient for spraying. Acephate sprayed on the foliage when it is 6 to 8 inches high or saturating the bed has proved effective.

Before dusting or spraying, beds should be cleaned and all old foliage and debris burned. Borers hatch in April and May from eggs in the old foliage and travel overland to the new growth. Control—3 times at 10-day intervals—should start when new growth is 6 to 10 inches tall. The adjacent ground as well as the rhizomes must be sprayed. Wet saw-tooth edges on new growth indicate borer presence and a systemic spray is effective as a last resort, where available. Leaf spot can be controlled by adding a fungicide to the spray or dust.

Dwarf bearded iris, like native cristata or tectorum, are beautiful at the front of the bed or as a shady ground cover. Their care and culture are described in the wildflower section. Consideration of the numerous beardless iris is limited by space, but Siberian iris have proved to be effective, trouble-free border plants that require less care than the bearded varieties. The flowers come in blues, purples and whites and are a third to half the size of the bearded iris, but very numerous on each plant. They bloom here in June. The plant clumps grow so vigorously that weeds have trouble competing. They are easily propagated by division and by self-seeding, if given room, and they make good cut flowers.

The native sweet flag, I. pseudocorus, a tall, yellow iris found on stream banks shares a love of moist, rich sites with the shorter Japanese older cultivars that thrive here. The Japanese iris bloom somewhat later and their charming flattened flowers allow you to enjoy the intricate structure of each petal and sepal. But for elusive heavenly scent, the German iris still have no equal.

PACHYSANDRA
(Pachysandra terminalis—Pachysandra, Japanese Spurge)
Uses: Ground cover.
Height/Distance: 6 to 8 inches, 12 inches.
Blooms: Inconspicuous.
Propagate:Division—April,September;Cuttings—July-August.

Plant: April, September.
Exposure/Soil: Shade. Well-drained garden loam.

Pachysandra is one of the more important shade-loving ground covers. It will thrive in even less favorable situations than periwinkle and English ivy. It may also be used in partial shade or where it receives only the morning sun.

The rooted cuttings may be planted 12 inches apart, but for a quicker effect may be as close as 6 inches. The soil should be carefully prepared with considerable compost or well-rotted manure incorporated before planting. A top-dressing with compost should be made after planting to keep the soil cool.

The cuttings may be pinched back the following season (a year after planting) to force new growth to spring from the roots.

PAINTED DAISY—PYRETHRUM
(Chrysanthemum coccineum—Painted Daisy, Pyrethrum)
Uses: Cut flowers.
HeightDistance: 18 to 24 inches, 12 inches.
Blooms: May-June.
Plant: April, September.
Propagate: Division, seed.
Exposure/Soil: Sun, light shade. Rich garden soil.

The painted daisy, or pyrethrum, is a spring flowering chrysanthemum that is a garden favorite with many because it is such an excellent cut flower. The long-stemmed flowers, pink and red, have excellent keeping qualities when cut, and the foliage is of value after the flowers are gone.

Painted daisies are not demanding in their cultural requirements, although they do best in a well-enriched loamy soil. Drainage is important to their health, and summer moisture seems to injure them. Very little summer watering is needed; avoid wetting the foliage. They can withstand severe drought. If the tops are sheared immediately after flowering, a

second crop of blooms may be expected in late summer.

Propagation is by division or seed. The clumps may be divided in early spring (April) and in the fall (September). This should be done every second or third year to maintain health and vigor. Plants grown from seed are likely to contain some undesirable colors, but, of course, they can be discarded. The doubles do not come true from seed, and, if named varieties are wanted, they must be obtained from a plant grower. However, many gardeners are satisfied to buy seed mixture and then propagate the plants they like.

The painted daisy is subject to about the same pests and disease as is the hardy chrysanthemum, and the treatments are the same. Most gardeners consider them to be remarkably free from troubles when well-fed in a properly prepared bed.

Pyrethrum has a reputation as an insect repelling flower, but the commercial product with its somewhat similar name, pyrethrin, is actually made from a related species.

PENSTEMON
(P. torreyi—Beardtongue)
Uses: Border.
Height/Distance: 2 to 4 feet, 1 foot.
Blooms: June-August.
Propagate: Seed—March; Division or cuttings—September.
Plant: Early spring.
Exposure/Soil: Light shade. Light, well-drained garden loam.

The penstemon is an easily grown, long-season perennial for the hardy border. It is free flowering with attractive dark green foliage. It will do best in light shade in a well-drained but not-too-dry loam. The addition of sand and compost is necessary if it is to thrive in a clay soil.

They are comparatively easily grown from seed, oftentimes blooming the first season from early-sown seeds. Divisions may be made in the fall.

There are a number of species of the perennial penstemons, but barbatus, torreyi, digitalis and grandiflorus are most commonly grown.

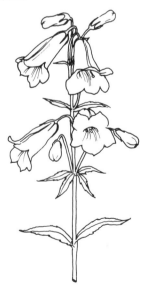

PEONY
(Paeonia officinalis, suffruticose—Peony)
Uses: Cut flowers, border, bedding.
Height/Distance: 18 to 36 inches, 3 feet.
Blooms: May-June.
Propagate: Division—August-September.
Plant: September.
Exposure/Soil: Sun, part shade. Heavy, well-fertilized loam.

From top: Single, Double, Semi double, Anemone, Japanese

Peonies are one of the oldest, most widely planted of the spring-flowering perennials. They thrive in the border where their huge blooms make a splendid showing. They are popular as a cut flower, although their blooms are rather large for most uses.

Peonies last for many years, hence the planting site should be deeply and well prepared before they are set out. Set the roots with the eye not over 1 to 2 inches below the ground level. Planting deeper than this is apt to result in failure to bloom.

Peonies need supplemental feeding and clean culture for best results. Bonemeal and well-decayed manure worked into the soil around the crown in the late summer will aid materially in keeping them vigorous. The larger flowered varieties should be staked.

Peonies are not greatly troubled by insects or diseases. A bud-rot may appear but this may be controlled by keeping aphids and ants off, and by removing and burning the old foliage in the fall.

There are a number of types of peonies besides the commonly planted "bomb." The single, the Japanese, the semi-double, the crown, and the rose are other attractive

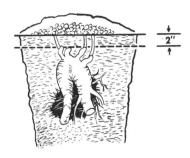

Plant peony roots with the eyes only an inch or two below the surface or they may fail to bloom.

useful types. This is especially true for home decoration where the bombs are apt to be too large and heavy.

The early maturing species and varieties are most likely to prove satisfactory in our area. Tree peonies, unlike the herbaceous ones, need light shade, and may be safely planted 4 to 6 inches deep. Both types need good drainage to thrive. The tree peonies retain their above ground stems which are brittle and easily broken, thus protection may be needed.

The National Arboretum has an excellent collection which might well be used to select varieties.

PHLOX
(Phlox paniculata, divaricata, etc.—Phlox, Moss Pink)
Uses: Cut flowers, bedding, edging, rock garden.
Height/Distance: From creeper to 3 feet, 10 to 18 inches.
Blooms: April to September.
Propagate: Cuttings, division.
Plant: April, September.
Exposure/Soil: Sun, light shade. Well-drained, rich.
Varieties:
P. divaricata—12 to16 in., blue April.
P. stolonifera—6 to 10 in., blue pink, white, April.

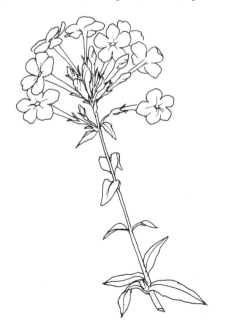

P. subulata—creeper, white, red, pink, purple April blooms.
P. carolina—20 to 36 in., white June-September blooms.
P paniculata—20 to 36 in., white, pink, blue, June-September blooms.

A well-grown plant of the hardy garden phlox is a thrilling sight, especially in late summer when there are so few perennials in bloom. The large trusses off brightly colored flowers make a commanding sight. However, the early spring blooming Phlox subulata, moss pink, is a welcome sight, for, if planted on a sunny slope or in a rock garden, it puts on a showy display in early April.

Plant breeders have produced a large number of varieties. The color range includes pure whites, whites having variously colored eyes, pinks, reds, and shades of violet and purple. Their heights range from 2 inches to 4 feet. The varieties may be subdivided according to season of bloom—early, mid, and late season.

The new phlox stolonifera, 'Sherwood Purple,' a dwarf, blooms in April along with divaricata and subulata. It is excellent for light shade and will tolerate sun. The moss pink is of the easiest culture. It will grow into a large mat, if the soil is well drained and the plants enjoy full sun throughout the summer. The new English variety, nivalis 'Camla,' is similar to subulata but less rampant.

The hardy garden phlox, as distinguished from the annual Phlox drummondi, is a summer bloomer. In the north, where the cool, moist growing conditions enable it to thrive, it is the mainstay of the garden. In this area, if we want its marvelous display, we must be prepared to meet certain requirements. Phlox require a deeply prepared soil—one in which quantities of compost or rotted manure have been incorporate—to provide the cool root run needed as well as the plant food essential for vigorous growth.

The plants should be well-spaced so that air circulation is good, one step in the control of mildew and the red spider mite. A light airy mulch is needed to keep the roots cool if the ground is not fully shaded by the plan. Ground corn cobs make a better mulch than does peat moss which is highly acid. Coarse compost is good.

The plants should be lifted and divided at least every third year and replanted in well-enriched soil. Each spring the weaker should be removed before the flowering season. It may also pay to thin out the remaining stems to insure the production of larger, though fewer, blooms.

As soon as the florets have faded, the bloom head should be removed. This prevents the growth of muddy-colored seedlings, which will crowd out the choice cultivars, and to retain the plant's strength for the formation of more bloom..

Disease and insect control can easily be accomplished with an all-purpose dust or spray program. The red spider mite, rust, and mildew are nearly always encountered wherever phlox are grown. However, vigorous growing plants seem to be less difficult to protect than plants struggling under poor culture.

PHYSOSTEGIA

(Physostegia virginiana—Obedient Plant, False-Dragon-Head)

Uses: Cut flowers, bedding.
Height/Distance: 18 to 60 inches, 8 to 15 inches.
Blooms: August-September.
Propagate: Division—spring or fall. Seeds.
Exposure/Soil: Sun or light shade. Rich, moist
Exposure: Sun or light shade.

Physostegia, sometimes called false-dragon-head or obedient plant, is a little-appreciated hardy perennial. It is easily grown, but more importantly it is a later summer bloomer. The taller varieties flower in August. The dwarf P. virginiana and its cultivar, Vivid (vivid pink), bloom in September and October.

The physostegia should be lifted and reset in good soil each spring for best results. They are such strong growers that they soon exhaust the soil. If not thinned out they grow too thickly and the blooms lack quality. This is especially true of Vivid.

PINKS

(Dianthus species and hybrids—Pinks)

Uses: Cut flowers, border, bedding.
Height/Distance: 6 to 18 inches, 9 to 24 inches.
Blooms: May-September.
Propagate: Seed—April; Division—April; Cuttings—June; Layers—Summer.
Plant: April, September.
Exposure/Soil: Sun. Warm, moderately rich garden loam. Sweet.
Species:
Allwoodii—A hybrid resembling, a carnation.

D. plumarius—grass pink, 18 inches.
D. gratianopolitanus—cheddar pink, 4-10 inches.
D. arenarius—sand pink, 6-15 inches.
D. deltoides—Maiden pink, creeper.
D. alpinus—Alpine pink, 4 inches.

The Dianthus, or pink family, is a large and complex one, with many desirable hardy species and numerous cultivars; some of which closely resemble a hardy carnation. It includes low-growing, prostrate plants and tall, stately ones, most of which are fragrant.

The pinks like a warm, loose soil well supplied with lime. A soil that tends to become wet causes the prostrate forms to rot. Whenever the clumps become large and crowded, they should be lifted and divided.

There are a number of diseases and insects affecting this group of plants, but if planted in a suitable location little trouble may be expected.

PLUMBAGO

(Ceratostigma plumbaginoides—Leadwort)

Uses: Ground cover.
Height/Distance: 6 to 12 inches, 12 inches.
Blooms: August-October.
Propagate: Division—April-May.
Plant: April-May.
Exposure/Soil: Sun. Garden loam.

The plumbago or leadwort is a desirable late season flower. Because the blue flowers persist until freezing weather, it is especially valuable for the sunny rock garden and as a sunny place ground cover.

The plumbago is not fussy as to soil so long as it is well-drained. It starts into growth so late in the spring that it may be injured if left unmarked. An annual variety, P. auriculata, has a white form.

POPPY

(Papaver orientale—Oriental Poppy)

Uses: Border, cutting.
Height/Distance: 18 to 36 inches, 15 to 18 inches.
Blooms: May-June.
Propagate: Division or root cuttings—August-September;
Plant: August-September.
Exposure/Soil: Sun. Moderately rich, deep, well-drained.

The oriental poppy is one of the most vividly colored perennials that can be grown in the late spring flower garden. Their huge flowers and striking colors command attention. They are easily grown and handled if taken at the right season of the year—August and September.

The oriental poppies start into growth in the early fall and retain their leaves during much of the winter. In spring they make rapid growth and throw up many flower stems which bear huge cup-like flowers in May and June.

When the plants go dormant in July and August, it is wise to fill the holes left by the dying stems with light soil to avoid water standing around the root. Do not irrigate them.

The oriental poppies may be lifted and divided in August or September. One method is to cut the roots with a spade and lift the clump out, then fill the hole with soil leaving the roots in place. Each piece of root left in the ground will become a new plant, and a season later there will be a number of well-started plants to be lifted and reset..

The oriental poppies seem to be relatively free from pest and disease in this area, although there are a number known to attack them. The bacterial blight cannot be prevented and infected plants should be destroyed.

PRIMROSE
(Primula species and hybrids—Primrose)
Uses: Edging, bedding, cutting.
Height/Distance: 4 to 12 inches, 6 to 9 inches.
Blooms: April-June.
Propagate: Division—September; Seed—March or August.
Plant: April, September.
Exposure/Soil: Medium shade. Moist, well-drained.
Varieties: P. veris (cowslip), P. elatior (oxlip), P. polyanthus (polyantha), P. auricula.

Primroses are colorful perennials for use along paths or nooks in the woods or near the house—they are distinctly shade-loving. However, too often the spot selected for them is too dry because of tree roots. If grown under a tree, it is essential to incorporate quantities of peat moss or compost into the soil to insure sufficient supplies of moisture for them.

Formerly, primroses were available principally as strains, such as the Pacific hybrids. Today we have a considerable number of named varieties on the market. P. Auricula 'Giant,' P. Acaulis 'Blue,' 'Julius-Edstein,' and P. Veris-'Colossus' are varieties now listed in the catalogs.

Primroses are best started from seed in a coldframe in March or out of doors in April or May. Some gardeners wait

until July, but they are apt to run into difficulties because of hot weather.

Divide established plants in the spring immediately after flowering; the early fall is even more satisfactory.

Primroses are troubled by red spider mites and the primrose flea beetle. The red spider mite may be controlled by water spray; it is usually necessary to use soap spray for the beetle.

There are a number of other primrose species that are hardy, but more exacting in their requirements. The modern hybrids are best grown in the cooler, protected parts of our area. Or you can treat them as spring bedding annuals.

SCABIOSA
(Scabiosa caucasica—Pincushion Flower, Blue Bonnet)
Uses: Cutting border.
Height/Distance: 24 to 36 inches, 10 to 12 inches.
Blooms: June-September.
Propagate: Seed, division.
Plant: Spring, mid summer.
Exposure/Soil: Well-drained sweet.

The scabiosa is an easily grown, although short-lived, sun-loving perennial. There have been a number of named varieties introduced, but they have been largely displaced by the (Isaac) House Mixture.

The seed may be started in the early spring or in July. The latter date is preferred since spring-sown plants may not bloom the first season.

The seedlings should be pinched to produce well-branched plants. They are sun lovers and do best in a sweet soil, 6.5-7.0 pH.

In cutting the flowers of the perennial scabiosa, it is good practice to leave the foliage—this is the opposite of the cutting practice for the annual scabiosa. The plants are at their best for three years.

SHASTA DAISY
(Chrysanthemum maximum—Shasta Daisy)
Uses: Cut flowers, bedding.
Height/Distance: 12 to 24 inches, 12 to 18 inches.
Blooms: June-August.
Propagate: Division—April, September.
Plant: April-May.
Exposure/Soil: Sun. Deep, rich, moist.

Shasta daisies are a popular garden flower, a member of the chrysanthemum family. Their large flowers on long stems make them ideal for cutting. The single-flowered varieties are more vigorous growers than the double-flowered. Some of the newer varieties flower nearly all summer. However, Marconi seedlings are the most dependable.

Shasta daisies need a well-prepared soil. They should be lifted and reset every other year. If neglected, they tend to run out and become weak and unattractive.

The various varieties have different flowering

seasons, so for a long period of cutting, several varieties should be planted. Keeping the plants watered and fed and the spent flowers removed will also help to prolong the flowering season.

Occasionally the Shasta daisy is troubled with leaf blotch. This disease may be controlled by spraying with Bordeaux mixture. Removal of dead leaves and stems in the early spring will help to keep the planting free of disease.

The Japanese oxeye or Nippon daisy resembles the Shasta and is a fall bloomer with lush shrub-like foliage. C. Weyrichi is a dwarf fall bloomer with neat foliage and large white and pink blossoms.

SUNFLOWERS, PERENNIAL
(Helianthus decapetalus, orgyalis, mollis, etc.)
(Heliopsis helianthoides, scabra)
Uses: Cut flowers, background.
Height/Distance: 2 to 5 feet, 18 to 24 inches.
Blooms: June-September.
Propagate: Seed division cuttings.
Plant: Seed in March; plants in April.
Exposure/Soil: Sun. Garden loam.

The perennial sunflowers are valuable plants for the sunny border, producing a long season of bloom and making a pleasing display in the garden over much of the summer. The flowers are useful for cutting. There are both single and double varieties that are long-lasting.

The perennial sunflower is seldom considered for the flower border, perhaps because it is associated wrongly with the huge annual (Helianthus annuus), which is commonly grown for bird seed. The names are the same but the performance is far different. The perennial is a much lower growing plant, from 2 to 4 feet in height, with clear yellows, buttercup, and golden yellows available. The garden varieties are much branched and the flowers seldom exceed 3 inches in diameter.

The perennial sunflower is of the easy to grow, requiring only a sunny border. It may be safely transplanted with a ball of soil about its roots at almost any season. Only a few insects and diseases trouble it. A fungicide may be desirable to control rust in the summer and mildew in the fall.

Some varieties of the perennial sunflower, those arising from Heliopsis helianthoides, have leaves that are quite smooth. Those developed from Heliopsis scabra have rougher foliage.

VERONICA
(V. maritima, spicata, incana, etc.—Speedwell)
Uses: Cut flowers.
Height/Distance: 18 to 24 inches, 6 to 12 inches.
Blooms: June-August.
Propagate: Division—April; Seed—March or August.
Plant: April, September.
Exposure/Soil: Sun, light shade. Moderately rich garden loam.

The veronica family has a number of very useful garden subjects. Their clear blue flowers and dark green foliage are a desirable addition to the hardy border. The taller growing species (V. maritima) are good for cutting. V. longifolia subsessils is one of the best for this area.

Veronica prefer a moist soil for best results, although it should have good drainage. They may be planted in the early spring or fall, and are not demanding. They are seldom troubled by insects or diseases.

The veronica may be grown from seed or they are easily divided in the spring or late summer.

VINCA MINOR
(Vinca. minor—Periwinkle, Running Myrtle)
Uses: Ground cover.
Height/Distance: 6 to 8 inches, 12 inches.
Blooms: April-May.
Propagate: Division, cuttings—April or September.
Plant: April or September.
Exposure/Soil: Shade or sun. Garden loam.

Vinca minor is one of the most useful of the ground covers. It is evergreen and the stems root so that it is a useful plant for shady slopes. It will tolerate sun but is slower growing under such conditions.

The flowers make a colorful showing in early spring. Vinca major has both larger leaves and flowers but is not as hardy; Bowles is a deeper shade of blue, and there is a white form, not too commonly grown.

Plants may be set out in the early spring or in the early fall. Spaced a foot apart, they will in the course of 2 or 3 years form a solid mat that will last for years. When used for an evergreen edging, the runners should be pinned into place and unneeded shoots kept trimmed off.

PERENNIAL VINES

With the demise of lots large enough to conceal an annual vegetable garden behind a screen of annual vines, the perennial vines, which can make permanent use of vertical walls for decorative effect, have come into their own.

Vines can be grown in a confined root space, between a walkway and a wall for example, if attention is given to the correct soil pH, soil tilth, and drainage requirements. In fact these conditions may cut down on the pruning necessary to hold most species in check. Some vines, like the lovely wisterias can be let go to climb a strong tree where they will bloom for years among the bare branches in its crown before the tree leafs out each spring. Others will be quite happy on a trellis in a large sturdy tub on a patio.

BOSTON IVY
(Parthenocissus tricuspidata)
Uses: Wall covering, fall color.
Blooms: Insignificant, berries—blue to black.
Height: 30 feet.
Seed: Fall.
Plant: From cuttings in late spring, seeds in fall.
Exposure/Soil: Sun, light shade. Wide variety of fertile, slightly acid soil.
Prune: Fall.

Boston Ivy is a true climber that comes equipped with little suction cups to help it on its way. It is wonderful when used to cloak a brick wall that serves as a soil-warming heat trap in the winter, because it drops its leaves just when the soil needs the wall's thermal mass. Conversely when the wall is heating up the soil too hot for spring bulbs, Boston ivy leafs out and prolongs your bulb season.

The leaves turn a shiny variegated mixture of red, yellow, and plum in the fall before they drop. Like all vines, Boston Ivy can be invasive, and should be pruned a foot below eaves troughs once it is thoroughly established on a house. Fortunately it is less tenacious than English ivy and can be cut near the ground and pulled from a wall or structure after the leaves fall.

It can be rooted fairly easily in the fall by pushing torn strips of vine that include some old wood into moist, well-worked soil at the foot of a wall. Make sure it is lightly mulched so the soil does not dry out the first winter. When the young plant makes some new growth the next year, it should be pruned in September to 2 or 3 well-spaced branches about 8 to 12 inches up the wall. The next year it will begin to spread in earnest.

Occasionally Japanese beetles infest an ivy planting, shredding the foliage. If beetles are that numerous in your area, it is time to think about neighborhood applications of milky spore disease. Otherwise, Boston ivy gives no trouble provides beautiful effect after 3 or 4 years.

CLEMATIS
(Clematis paniculata, jackmanii, etc.—Clematis)
Uses: Trellis, wall, or trailing cover for other shrubs.
Bloom: May through September, according to species.
Height: 10 to 30 feet.
Plant: 2-year old plants in October or in spring.
Exposure/Soil: Sun, filtered sun. Moist, cool and sweet.
Prune: Varies by species (see below).
Species and Varieties:
Spring flowering—Montana species, jackmanii, Nelly Moser, Duchess of Edinburgh (double).
 Summer and fall blooming—Orientalis, tangutica (yellow-flowered), paniculata, (Viticella hybrids, jackmanii hybrid, Elsa Spaeth, Gipsy Queen, Madame Baron Veillard, Will Kennett.

Clematis are thin woody vines that twist their paired leaves around a support to climb, so they need adequate netting or a trellis to help them get a purchase on a wall or other solid structure.

They like cool, moist feet and need to be planted with the crown of the plant 2 inches below ground while the top of the vine seeks filtered sunlight. They should not be planted within 4 or 5 feet of an intensively worked bed because the roots are as fragile as the stems appear.

Where winters are severe, they need some soil and mulch over the root zone even in a sheltered spot. And the sometimes tatty tangle of deciduous vines that they produce must be pruned at just the right time for each species in order to save a season's bloom.

But they are worth all the trouble they take when they bloom, because a well grown clematis can produce hundreds of palm-sized blossoms that float against the delicate foliage

in a gorgeous palette of colors that includes whites, yellows, pinks and on through the deepest purple. They are ideal for a lightly shaded garden sheltered from the wind where they can drape themselves as they please over compatible shrubs and low walls with the aid of a few plant clips.

To make the slightly alkaline or neutral soil which they prefer, add up to 5 pounds of ground limestone per 100 square feet of area where you site them. Keep the soil evenly moist through the year with a 2 to 3 inch mulch of peat moss or leaf mold mixed with a cup of ground limestone. Young plants are sometimes marked by placing a brick flat side down on the sunny side of the root zone, which helps to retain soil moisture in the summer.

Easiest to grow is the native sweet autumn clematis, which bears a profusion of white starry miniatures here in late August. If kept well-watered, it is virtually pest free and will rejuvenate year after year, even if cut to the ground. Like all clematis the seed pods are a spidery whorl that is quite attractive into the fall.

Most of the hybrids derived from clematis species grow 8 to 12 feet tall. Those that bloom in the spring on wood of the previous year should rarely be pruned. After some of these varieties flower, if seed heads are removed, they may have a second bloom on new growth late in the summer. Wait until after first flowering to do any necessary pruning or shaping. This applies mainly to the older jackmanii types (alba, rubra, Superba), the montanas, and some patens and florida hybrids.

If it is necessary to thin or retrain any of the late blooming species that flower on new wood, do it in late winter before growth starts. In general this applies to the newer jackmanii hybrids, paniculata, the lanuginosa and viticella hybrids, orientalis, tangutica, and the tenderer, native taxensis.

It definitely pays to read the species and varietal labels on clematis cultivars and to record them for future reference.

CLIMBING HYDRANGEA
(Hydrangea anomala petiolaris)
Uses: Brick or stone wall cover, background for border.
Blooms: June.
Height: Up to 75.
Plant: Spring or fall. Can be grown from seed.
Soil: Rich in humus, well-drained.
Exposure: Sun or partial shade.
Prune: Fall or early spring.

A mature petiolaris is a beautiful feature in the estate garden; but it can be pruned to suit the needs of smaller gardens as well.

These hydrangeas are true climbers and cling with suction feet to a wall surface. They should be set about a foot out from a soundly mortared wall in early fall or spring in rich moist soil. It will take 2 or 3 years of slower growth for them to get established, and it is important that the roots are not subject to drought conditions during this time. After they take off, they are hardy and pest free.

Petiolaris blooms from the base of the plant which gives the effect of lacy white skirts against tall richly green growth. The large white umbels with lacy centers are borne as much as 3 feet from the main plant.

Being deciduous, the vine can be pruned best in late autumn or early spring when the stem structure can be clearly seen and cut to the pattern and size you prefer.

HONEYSUCKLE
(Lonicera henryii, flava, heckrottii)
Uses: Twining vine, fragrance, groundcover.
Blooms: June through frost.
Height/Distance:To 12 feet with pruning. Groundcover, 3 feet.
Plant: Spring or fall.
Exposure/Soil: Sun or part shade. Moist, prepared soil.
Prune: Annually or more as needed. Late fall or early spring.
Varieties: Henryii (white to cream), flava (native yellow), Heckrottii (coral and yellow).

With important reservations: namely, do not grow any other varieties that are more vigorous than these recommended here, you can enjoy honeysuckle. These twining vines can be kept within bounds by pruning, or training to a trellis or a bank, or by digging out the volunteers in early summer.

Henryii is semi-evergreen and lends itself to erosion control. Flava is a lovely yellow native and like heckrottii can grace an outdoor lamp post or a trellis close to porch, patio, or deck where the delightful scent can be enjoyed from June into the fall. Hummingbirds like the scarlet varieties best.

Honeysuckle needs no special care, and no fertilizer, but it requires vigilance. Prune trellis specimens vigorously in the late fall to 2 or 3 healthy stems that will provide next season's growth.

Plants or collected seeds can be set out in the fall or spring. These plants are ideal for the confined root zone between walk and wall or porch. Varieties grown from stratified seed have the disadvantage of varying from the habits of parent stock. Root cuttings taken in early spring might be surer. Keep the ground evenly moist until plants attain enough size to shade themselves.

SILVER LACE VINE
(Polygonum aubertii—Silver Fleece)
Uses: Trellis, arbor, wall top.
Blooms: Late-summer.
Height: 15 to 30 feet.
Plant From divisions, stem cuttings or seed.
Exposure/Soil: Sun or part shade. Variety of soils.
Prune: Annually; hard in fall or late winter.

As one of the fastest growing, drought-resistant, and pest free perennial vines, silver lace or China silver fleece, deserves to be more widely grown here than it is. From mid summer it is covered with billows of lacy blossoms borne in 6 inch upright clusters on the tops of the lance-shaped leaves.

The vine requires strong supports because of its twining habit and rapid growth which can result in collapsed tangles if young plants are not carefully trained. If grown on a wall it might be well to provide sturdy trellising or wire set in with masonry nails to give the plant a leg up.

Because silver lace vine flowers on new wood, it should be rigorously pruned out and thinned in late fall or winter. Sometimes during a cold winter the vine will die back to the ground, but an adequate mulch will usually preserve the roots, and it will take off again the next year.

WISTERIA
(Wisteria floribunda, sinensis)
Uses: Porches, walls, trees, specimen, tub.
Blooms: May.
Height: 25 to 75 feet.
Plant: Pot grown plants in early spring.
Soil: Rich in leaf mold or humus, well-drained.
Exposure: Protected from wind. Sun/part shade.
Prune: Summer and winter, if at all.
Varieties: Floribunda—alba, longissima, rosea, 'Royal Purple'; Sinensis—alba.

These mysterious and beautiful climbers flower extravagantly if they are given the proper space and time to develop.

The Japanese species, floribunda, is smaller, hardier, and has more varieties with a rich characteristic fragrance, so it is preferable if you must confine wisteria to a container or a small space. Left without pruning, as some experts recommend, it will twine from right to left around the supports provided and bloom in 7 to 8 years in good soil. It should be well-watered and mulched the first year and have half a pound of superphosphate scratched into the soil around its roots each fall.

To stimulate earlier flowering or to create a standard, some growers root prune around a 4-to 5-year-old plant,

digging a circular trench almost 2 feet deep out at least a yard from the main stem. They combine this with winter pruning of any side shoots that might draw strength from the supported main trunk plus winter and summer pruning back of new top growth to half its length. Other growers argue against this practice in the garden and prefer to confine heavily-pruned standards or tree-form wisteria to large tubs.

It is important to train wisteria to the shape that suits you while they are young, whether it be espaliered against a wall or trellis or trained to run on top, because the stem goes thick and woody with age. It is one plant that repays early care with decades of bloom.

In late July and in February, mature plants may be kept in abundant bloom by heavy cutting of all new shoots to within 6 buds of branches joining with the stem. The winter pruning should include removal of all weak or dead wood.

The most fragrant Japanese hybrids are the white and pink forms, alba and rosea, although individual species plants of floribunda may be beautifully scented. 'Royal Purple,' longissima, and macrobotrys have the deepest color and long racemes that flower gradually from base to tip. All Japanese wisteria flower later in the season than the Chinese species.

Sinensis flowers open all at once on bare wood as early as late April in warmer parts of the region. The species color is a blue-violet, although there is a white form. Left unpruned it will climb over 50 feet into the branches of a strong tree, like an oak, where it will bloom before the tree leafs out. It is slightly less hardy and requires a protected situation, but like all wisteria it blooms more profusely when grown in the sun.

The furry seed pods turn from green to brown in the fall, making a most attractive display. But warn small children of the lima bean-like seeds within. From early personal experience, I can attest that they are poisonous.

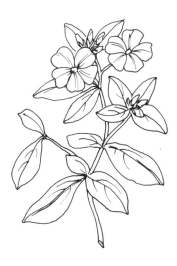

PLUMBAGO

ORNAMENTAL GRASSES

In recent years there has been a revival of interest in the ornamental grasses so popular as accents in Victorian gardens. Although the plume, or pampas grasses, are familiar to older residents, this revived interest has brought to light many other species. Their sizes, textures, and colors are a real addition to landscaping values in a variety of situations.

One local landscape architect has made a national reputation with his use of grasses in the public gardens that he has done for the U.S. Department of Agriculture, as well as in his striking arrangements that bring to life the tiniest, city patio garden.

Chosen and sited with care, the following grasses will need neither weekly cutting nor fertilizing. Many are hardy natives whose foliage persists through the winter with minimal protection. Due to the range in height, color, and texture, they can be used as pools of color to separate or complement perennials, as focal points in a border or bed, and either as background or cover.

For immediate effect it is probably better to buy or get divisions of ornamental grasses in early spring, setting them in slightly enriched, sweet soil to the same depth they were growing. Cut any tangled old growth back to 4 to 6 inches before new foliage appears, and keep the clumps lightly mulched for the first two winters. Fertilize lightly in early June. If you are unsure how quickly a particular genus may spread, harvest its seed heads before they ripen and scatter the first year, and in a cold frame plant some seeds that you save out of the dried arrangements.

Most of the varieties listed here grow in tufts or clumps that spread slowly from the center. Nevertheless, thorough digging of invasive large specimens should be combined with bagging and trashing of the unwanted root clump, lest it invade your compost pile and be recycled back into parts of your garden where it will be a nuisance.

Most ornamental grasses thrive in full sun and moderate amounts of soil moisture, although some specimens can take some drought and shade, as indicated below.

ORNAMENTAL GRASSES

Common and Botanical Name	Height	Flowers	Foliage and Uses
Sedges (carex conica variegata, carex morrowii aurea variegata sylvatica)	6-12 in.		Range of color and variegation. Shady area ground cover.
Blue Fescue (festuca ovina var. glauca)	9 in.	June	Silver-blue to late winter. Foreground.
Hair Grass (deschampsia caespitosa)	18 in.	July	Into late winter. Takes drought.
Ribbon Grass (phalaris arundinacea) 'Picta'	18 in.	Through December. Very hardy.	
Blue Oat Grass (helictotrichon sempervivens)	2 ft.		Blue sprays into December. Dense.
Pennisetum (P. alapecoroides, P. orientale, P.caudatum)	2-4 ft.	Aug.-Sep.	Into December. Mass affect. Winter display. Cut plumes.
Feather Grass (calamagrostis)	3-6 ft.	Summer.	Into December. Cut plumes.
Northern Sea Oats (chasmanthium uniola latifolia)	3 ft.	September	Late winter. Some shade.
Purple Moor Grass (molinia altissima)	4-6 ft.	August	Dried seed heads. Late winter. Blooms dry well.
Miscanthus (M. purpurescens, M. gracillimus, M. sinensis 'Zebrinus')	4-6 ft.	September	All winter. Red foliage, striped blades. Cut plumes.
Floridulus Giganteus	10 ft.	August	Into winter. Good screen. Accent. Dried blooms
Plume Grass (erianthus Ravennae)	14 ft.	August	Mid-winter. Accent. Dried blooms.

Pest and Disease Control for Perennial Vines

Plant	Pest	Pesticide/Treatment
Honeysuckle	whitefly	Summer oil spray. mid May to mid July.
	leafroller	Summer oil. begin late May. Difficult.
Clematis	borer	Marlate. spray in July to kill moth.
	leaf spot	Ferbam as preventive.
Ivy. Boston or English	scale	Summer oil. at 2-week intervals. June & July.
	mildew	Summer oil or sulphur spray. begin in July.

Resources:

Old Dominion Chrysanthemum Society, Diane Roe (703) 534-6569.
Chesapeake Chrysanthemum Society, Pat Buffington (410) 964-2479.
Potomac Chrysanthemum Society, Jessie Clarke (202) 726-0819.
National Capital Daylily Club, Margo Reed (301) 424-6392.
Potomac Hosta Club, Debbie Bochnek (703) 281-9244.
Chesapeake and Potomac Iris Society, Sara Marley (703) 338-7594.
Potomac Lily Society, Robert Janner (703) 548-9682.

Plant	Pest	Pesticide and Treatment	Other Controls and Comments
AGERATUM	Whitefly	Pyrethrum or soap sprays at 5 day intervals.	Air circulation between plants.
CHRYSANTHEMUM	Leafspots Mildew	Chlorothalonil or benomyl after wet weather.	Remove infected leaves in fall.
	Rust	Ferbam, spray when first noticed	Remove and burn infected foliage.
	Beetles	Acephate spray as necessary.	
	Plant bugs	Acephate or neem as needed.	Soap sprays.
COCKSCOMB	Leafspots	Bordeaux mixture after wet weather.	Pick off and burn badly infected leaves.
COLUMBINE	Leaf miner	Pick off and burn infected leaves. Spray when leaves are half open. Acephate as directed.	
DAHLIA	Mildew Beetles and borers	Chlorothalonil spray as directed. Malathion and carbaryl.	
	Leafhoppers Thrips	Acephate spray as needed. Acephate as flowers begin to open.	
DAYLILIES	Thrips	Acephate as flower buds begin to form, 2 or 3 times at 10-day intervals.	
HOLLYHOCK	Anthracnose	Bordeaux mixture; spray after wet weather.	
	Rust	Ferbam, chlorothalonil, sulphur as directed. Remove dead leaves in fall.	
	Leafhoppers	Neem extract.	
	Beetles	Sevin, spray as needed.	
HYDRANGEA	Leafspots Mildew	Chlorothalonil or benomyl after each wet period. Benomyl when mildew first appears.	
	Leaf tier	Acephate as directed.	Pick off rolled leaves.
IRIS	Leafspots	Balan at start of new growth in spring and 14 days later.	Remove and burn infected foliage in fall or winter.
	Borers	Remove infected bulbs	
	Soft rot	Cut out infected parts	
LILIES	Virus	Soap spray for aphids that spread disease.	Dig and burn plants, replant later.
NASTURTIUM	Tarnished plant bug	Acephate, apply as needed. Soap spray at 5-day intervals.	
PEONY	Anthracnose	No chemical control.	
	Botrytis	Benomyl, chlorothalonil, ferbam—spray as directed. Start when shoots emerge.	Remove and burn foliage from infected plants in mid-September.
	Leafspots	Bordeaux mixture or chlorothalonil several times early in season.	
	Thrips	Acephate when in bloom if troubled.	
	Japanese beetles	Traps, milky sport.	
POPPY	Bacterial blight	No chemical control.	Remove and burn.
	Leafhoppers	Acephate spray as needed.	
SHASTA DAISY	Leafspots	Bordeaux or chlorothalonil spray as directed.	
	Beetles	Acephate spray as needed.	
SNAPDRAGON	Rust	Ferbam at 10-day intervals.	Grow resistant varieties.
	Mildew	Benomyl when needed.	
SWEET ALYSSUM	Leafhoppers	Malathion as needed.	
VERBENA	Plant bugs Leaf miner	Acephate in June and July	
ZINNIA	Mildew	Benomyl or chlorothalonil spray at first sign.	Destroy foliage.
	Japanese beetles	Acephate or malathion as needed.	
	Leafspots	Bordeaux mixture or folpet spray at first sign.	

12. GARDENING IN THE SHADE

—This chapter is vintage Wilbur Youngman, the original author of this book. It is as timely and comprehensive now as it was in the 1950s when first written—and as useful for the new owner of a woodland lot as for the gardener needing a makeover of a yard grown shady by maturing trees.

A shaded area on a part of the home grounds is both pleasant and desirable, but to convert it into a garden may present some special problems. The use and development of such an area is desirable, since, if allowed to remain undeveloped, it may become an eyesore. Whether the area is large or small is not as important as that it be made to contribute to the family's pleasure.

Shade is a relative term. Normally, we think of shade as dense, medium, or light. Shade on the north side of a building or under a low spreading tree is likely to be dense. Under a spreading tree, such as an ash, the shade is probably medium dense. Under a dogwood, birch, or pruned apple tree, the shade is light.

There are plants which will thrive in each situation, although the flowering plants and shrubs adapted to dense shade are comparatively few. By removing the lower tree limbs, many more kinds of plants and shrubs may be grown, since well-trimmed trees permit more light and air, and thus are more favorable to plant growth.

Shaded areas, whether on a slope or on the level, may be developed into gardens and outdoor recreation areas through the use of many kinds of plants, provided the plants are placed in favorable growing conditions. The problem of the right soil is basic. However, when there is a surface wash problem, its solution takes precedence over any soil improvement.

Control of surface wash from higher areas usually involves some form of diversion program to carry water to one side or the other of the garden. The easiest solution is a shallow ditch dug across the top of the bank or at the edge of the shaded area. If the flow of water cannot be diverted by a ditch, it may be necessary to erect a retaining wall pierced with a drain to carry the water away. This method requires more construction than the other, but it is worth the effort since it is essential that no large volume of water flows over the garden, washes away the topsoil, and floods plant beds.

If the shaded area is covered with roots from shallow rooted trees, the problem of preparing for shade-loving plants is difficult and restrictive. Areas filled with tree roots are best handled by creating pockets in which plants are placed and given some protection from the greedy roots. The smaller bulbs and other early spring-flowering plants are more likely to survive under such competition and to provide most of the bloom.

Under deep-rooted trees the problem is one of preparing the soil for the desired kinds of shrubs and plants. First, however, it should be noted that few plants will thrive under any black walnut—its roots are toxic to many kinds of plants and shrubs, especially members of the rhododendron family. Under the oak and hickory, in areas between the major roots, the soil should be enriched to a depth of 12 inches with compost. Leaves often are a problem in such a yard, but if composted they will serve this purpose very well, the only expense being the labor of layering the leaves onto the pile with other nutrients and then spading the partially rotted humus into the soil.

One seldom needs to add lime to the shade areas, unless one is trying to grow grass, since practically all shade-loving plants thrive in an acid soil. However, most of the soils in this area lack phosphate. Because this nutrient travels very slowly through the soil, phosphate should be added in some form at the time of preparation, if a soil test indicates this need. Bonemeal or greensand mixed into the soil at the same time as the compost will provide a source of phosphate, as well as some calcium.

Other variations in soil preparations may be needed to take care of special plant groups. Some may need a lighter soil and the addition of sand. Others may thrive in a moist soil, and the moisture-holding capacity of peat moss may be needed. These requirements will be noted in the discussion of groups of shade-loving plants.

Planting the Shady Garden

Most of the early spring-flowering bulbs thrive in a shady situation and may be depended upon for a fine floral display in late March and April. Perennials, bulbs, shrubs, and ferns will furnish most of the plant materials for the shady garden. The range in size, cultural requirements, and season of bloom is considerable, and a careful selection of these should be made so that the shady garden will provide the color and enjoyment desired. To be effective it should be as carefully planned as any perennial border. Height of plants, flowering season, and foliage values are important in making the plan.

Planting time for a shady garden will necessarily be spread over a considerable period because many plants are not dormant at any one season. Dormancy is a requirement for the safe transplanting of many species, including the wildflowers. This is why so many collected woodland species (usually dug while in bloom) die. However, if you order the plants from your nursery, they will be on hand at the proper time and will be of the right size and with a good compact root system to insure a strong start.

Most shady gardens in this area will depend on andromedas, hollies, rhododendrons, azaleas, mahonia, laurels,

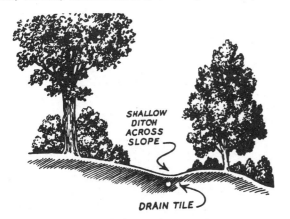

The shady garden on a slope should be protected from the "wash" from adjacent areas. A shallow ditch across the top of the slope above the garden area may suffice, but if necessary it may be supplemented with a tile drain to carry the run-off away.

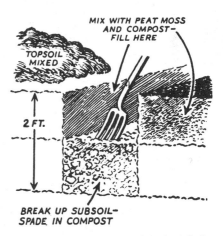

Mixing compost, and where necessary, sand into the soil, is an essential soil improvement practice for the shady garden.

leucothoe, and the dogwoods to provide the background. These plants will thrive in shade, although some varieties do better in a lighter shade than do others of the same species. All need an acid soil, one that is well-supplied with humus, preferably a mixture of peat moss and oakleaf compost. These plants are normally set out in the early spring or fall. Transplant the smaller sizes of dogwood, since they do not suffer as much shock and are therefore not as susceptible to attack by the flatheaded apple borer or the dogwood borer.

Blueberries might be added to the list, but because the squirrels and birds love the fruit, little should be expected on the breakfast table. In the shady wildflower garden blueberries are grown for their foliage.

The azaleas are of great value in the shady garden, coming as they do with flowering seasons from late March to mid-June and in all heights. There are low-growing evergreen azaleas for beds and foreground planting. The varieties of the tall deciduous species blend well with background shrubbery. The earlier ones yield pink to purple blooms, while the later-blooming run to warmer shades from yellow to orange and coral. Only a few azaleas will tolerate wet feet; of these Rhododendron viscosum (swamp azalea) is the most commonly available.

Most of the hollies (American, English, Chinese, and Japanese) thrive in medium to light shade, in a soil well-supplied with compost. A male pollen parent is required for berry production for all but the Japanese and a few varieties of English holly. They all require medium moisture and will fail in dry soils or soggy low spots. The only exception is Winterberry (Ilex verticillata), which thrives in rather moist places.

The summersweet (Clethra alnifolia) is a summer-flowering shrub that will grow in moist soils in light shade, but it reaches a height of 6 to 8 feet and cannot be used in the small garden. Various viburnums have beautiful foliage, sweet-scented blooms, and berries for the birds to boot.

The cotoneasters thrive in shade, and their glossy foliage, neat habit of growth, and shining fruits make them desirable. The squirrels are not satisfied to harvest the berries, but cut off whole branches laden with fruit and carry them to a convenient storage place before the feast.

Perennials for the Shady Garden

The list of perennials that will thrive in shade is surprisingly long and includes spring bloomers, as well as a few summer-flowering kinds. Of the early spring bloomers the species primulas might well have a prominent place beside shady paths, though more recent hybrids seem to need more sun. Virginia bluebells do well in the lighter soils. The wild wood phlox (P. divericata and related cultivars), the astilbes, coral bells (Heuchera), various columbines, shooting star (Dodecatheon), the bleeding hearts, and many violets will also proliferate.

The Christmas rose is the earliest of spring bloomers, oftentimes holding its bloom above the snow.

Summer- and fall-flowering plants include the many varieties of plantain lilies (Hosta), Japanese anemone, liatris, goatsbeard, snakeroot (Cimicifuga), geum, ligularia, and bellflower (Platycodon). The Christmas and the Lenten roses often bloom from late winter through April. Frostflowers (Eupatorium) will bloom in shade but are invasive. There are hundreds of varieties of daylilies that will bloom beautifully in succession from June through September in light shade. However, they will not flower too well in medium shade, and not at all in deep shade.

Bulbs

Almost all kinds of hardy bulbs will flower in the shady garden, but tulips are least likely to be successful, unless planted in beds where they may receive special care. Some sturdy varieties of narcissus can be counted on year after year in light to moderate shade under trees that leaf out late. Small early bulbs make the best show.

The trilliums do unusually well here, as do the western trout lilies (Erythronium) if planted in a well-drained, loamy soil. Even the Turk's-cap lily, sometimes called the swamp lily, may be counted on to thrive and multiply in light shade.

Ferns

There are some 40 species of ferns native to the Washington area and many of them are invaluable in the shady garden. Some are inclined to be weedy and should be used with care. Others, such as the cliff brake, require a sweet soil and some sun. The delightful, little walking fern is best used in a rockery. The Christmas fern, which is evergreen, is especially useful, with its silvery new fronds reaching up from the flattened green rosette of last year's growth. The showy royal fern can not be counted on unless its feet are close to running water.

Ground Covers

Occasionally there is a part of the shady garden that needs a carpet of evergreen to protect it from erosion and to prevent weeds from becoming established. The most commonly used groundcovers are myrtle (Vinca minor), pachysandra, bishops' weed (Aegopodium), wintercreeper (Euonymus fortunei), ajuga, and in a place where shallow roots compete, English ivy.

Some of the wild gingers make handsome evergreen ground covers in fairly dry woodland, as does crowsfoot. Ground ivy (Nepeta hederacea) is so successful a ground cover it is now considered a weed. The variegata form has pink or white leaf margins. Mazus is a tiny creeping plant that is lovely in a small rock garden, though sometimes hard to find. Hardy begonia, Begonia evansiana, and the many lovely impatiens varieties are often used as an annual groundcover where soil is moist and loamy. Both these plants will self-seed once established.

Growing grass in the shade is a thankless, but not impossible, task. Chewings fescue and some of the newer creeping fescues are adapted to drier soils where there is light shade and no competition from shallow-rooted trees.

Danish bluegrass thrives in moist soil and light to medium shade. Some lawn care specialists recommend fall seeding for the shady lawn, taking care not to overfeed the grass, and keeping leaves raked or vacuumed regularly. This gives the grass a chance to become established while there is adequate light and the ground is not frozen.

The omission of summer flowering annuals from the table below is intentional. Almost without exception they are not shade lovers. A few, such as pansies, nicotiana, balsam, snapdragon, sweet alyssum, salvia, and verbena will tolerate light shade provided they get adequate plant food and moisture. Impatiens, except for the New Guinea hybrids, are unexcelled for deeper shade. The following plant lists suggest the variety of plants available for the shady garden, and their season of bloom as well as height at maturity.

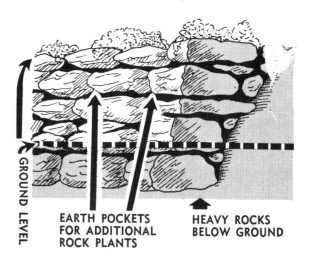

GROUND LEVEL

EARTH POCKETS FOR ADDITIONAL ROCK PLANTS

HEAVY ROCKS BELOW GROUND

Very often a rock wall is desired in the shady garden. The wall, to be stable and attractive, should be deeply laid to avoid dislocation by freezing and thawing, and should slope towards the bank.

Plants for the Shady Garden

Kind of Plant	Shade	Height	Space	Blooms	Color	Soil	Moisture	Fruit
FLOWERING TREES (Height and Space in Feet)								
Dogwood	L	15-25	15	April	white/pink	M	Medium	Red
Fringetree	L	10-20	15	May	white	L	Dry	blue
Redbud	L	15-25	20	April	mauve	M	Medium	--
Sourwood	L	25-30	15	June	white	M	Moderate	--
American Holly	M	15-40	15-20	May	yellow	M	Medium	red
English Holly	M	25-40	15-20	May	yellow	M	Medium	red
LARGE SHRUBS (Height and Space in Feet)								
Mockorange	L	10-12	8-10	May	white	M	Medium	--
Firethorn	L	8-12	4-8	May	white	M	Medium	orange,red
Burning bush	L	6-9	8-10	October	redleaf	M	Medium	--
Jetbead	L	6-10	6-8	May	white	M	Medium	black
Chinese holly	L	10-15	8-10	May	white	M	Medium	red
Japanese holly	L	6-12	6-8	--	--	M	Medium	--
Camellia	L	6-12	3-6	March	white/red	L	Moderate	--
Witch Hazel	M	8-10	8-10	March	yellow	M	Moist	--
Five-Leaf Aralia	M	6-10	6-10	--	--	M	Moist	--
Rhododendron (maximus)	D	10-15	10-12	June	white	M	Moist	pink
Summersweet	L	8-10	6-8	July	white	M	Moist	--
MEDIUM SHRUBS (Height and Space in Feet)								
Abelia	L	6-8	6-8	Summer	pink	M	Medium	--
Andromeda, Japanese	M	6-8	4-5	March	white	M	Medium	--
Andromeda, Mountain	M	5-6	6	April	white	M	Dry	--
Mahonia	L	5-6	5-6	May	yellow	M	Medium	blue
Azalea, flame	M	6-8	6	June	yellow	M	Moderate	--
Azalea, Exbury	L	4-8	4-6	June	orange	M	Medium	yellow
Barberry, Juliana	L	4-6	3	May	yellow	M	Medium	blue
Hydrangea, oakleaf	L/M	6-8	5-6	June	white/purple	M	Medium	--
Sarcococca	L	6	4-6	May	white	M	Medium	scarlet
Viburnum cassinoides	M	4-6	6-8	July	white	M	Moist	red/yellow
LOW SHRUBS (Height and Space in Feet)								
Tree Peony	L	2-4	3	May	various	R	medium	--
Azalea, Gable	L	3-6	4-6	May	various	M	Medium	--
Azalea, Girard	L	3-6	4-6	April	various	M	Medium	--
Azalea, Lynnwood	L	3-6	4-6	May	various	M	Medium	--
Azalea, Gumpo	L	1-2	3	May	various	M	Medium	--
Azalea, Viscosum	M	2-3	3	June	white	M	Moist	--
Leucothoe	M	2-3	3	May	white	M	Moist	--
Mountain Laurel	M	3-6	3	May	white	M	Moist	--
Rhododendron	M	2-10	4-10	May-June	various	L	Moist	--
Boxwood	L	2-6	2-3	--	--	M	Moderate	--
Skimmia, Reeves	L	1-2	2-3	June	cream	M	Moderate	scarlet
PERENNIALS (Height and Space in Inches)								
Lily of the Valley	M	8-10	10	May	white/pink	R	Moist	--
Primroses	M	6-12	12	April-June	various	R	Moist	--
Hosta	M	10-30	10-30	April-August	purple/white	M	Medium	--
Lungwort	L	6-8	12-18	April	pink-blue	R	Medium	--
Columbine	L	24-30	10-15	May-June	various	M	Medium	--
Shooting Star	M	12-15	8-10	April	lilac	R	Medium	--
Globeflower	L	12-18	8-10	April-June	gold	R	Medium	--
Bugbane	M	36-60	12-18	July	white	M	Medium	--
Astilbe	L	24-36	12-18	May-July	various	R	Medium	--
Monkshood	L	24-60	12-18	May-September	various	R	Moist	--
Goatsbeard	M	36-60	24-36	June-July	white	R	Medium	--
Lady Slipper	D	12-18	12-15	May	pink	R	Medium	--
Jacob's Ladder	L	12-15	12-15	May-July	blue/white	M	Medium	--
Bleeding heart	M	18-30	18-24	April-May	pink	R	Medium	--
Fringed	L	10-15	10-12	May-September	rose	R	Medium	--
Christmas rose	D	10-18	12-18	January-March	white	R	Medium	--
Lenten rose	D	12-18	12-18	February-March	purple	R	Medium	--
Daylilies	L	10-36	12-36	May-September	various	R	Medium	--
English daisy	L	6-8	6-8	April-May	white/red	R	Medium	--
Crested iris, cristata	L	6-8	8-10	May	lilac	R	Dry	--
Crested iris, verna	L	8-10	8-10	April	blue	R	Dry	--
Wood phlox	L	10-15	6-8	May	purple	R	Medium	--
Harebell	L	10-15	15-18	June-September	blue	R	Dry	--
Chinese bellflower	L	18-24	24-30	May-October	white/violet	R	Dry	--
Virginia bluebell	M	12-15	10-12	April-May	blue-pink	L	Moist	--
Mayapple	M	15-20	10-12	May	white	M	Medium	--
Epimedium	M	10-15	18-24	April	white/yellow	M	Medium	--
Japanese iris	L	24-36	24-30	May-June	various	M	Moist	--
Japanese anemone	L	30-48	30-40	September	white/pink	M	Moist	--
Foamflower	M	6-12	10-12	April-June	white	R	Moist	--

Plants for the Shady Garden

Kind of Plant	Shade	Height	Space	Blooms	Color	Soil	Moisture	Fruit
HARDY BULBS (Height and Space in Inches)								
Narcissus	M	6-18	6-10	March-May	various	M	Dry	--
Camassia	L	15-30	10-12	May-June	whitelavender	M	Dry	--
Begonia, Hardy	M	10-15	8-10	June-September	white/pink	M	Medium	--
Cyclamen, Hardy	L	3-6	8-10	March/September	pink	L	Medium	--
Troutlily	M	6-12	6-8	April-June	white/yellow	L	Dry	--
Wood Hyacinth	M	10-15	6-8	May	white/pink	M	Medium	--
Grape Hyacinth	M	4-6	6	May	white/blue	M	Medium	--
Star of Bethlehem	M	10-15	10-12	May	white	M	Medium	--
Turk's Cap Lily	L	18-30	10-15	June	orange	M	Moist	--
Sternbergia	L	3-4	4-6	September	yellow	M	Medium	--
Lycoris, squamigera	M	24-30	10-12	August	lilac/pink	M	Medium	--
Crocus	L	2-4	4-6	March/September	various	M	Medium	--
Allium	L	12-15	4-6	May/September	white	M	Medium	--
Spring Beauty	M	2-4	4-6	April	pale pink	L	Medium	--
Trillium	M	4-6	4-6	April	white/red	M	Medium	--
Snowdrop	M	4-6	2-4	Febrary-March	white	M	Medium	--
Chionodoxa	M	3-5	2-4	March-April	blue	M	Medium	--
Scilla	M	3-5	2-4	March-April	blue	M	Medium	--
Snowflake	M	12-15	8-12	April-June	white	M	Medium	--
TENDER BULBS (Height and Space in Inches)								
Begonia, Tuberose	M-D	10-15	12-15	June-October	various	R	Moist	--
Agapanthus	L	24-36	12	July	blue/white	R	Medium	--
Acidenthera	L	24-36	8-10	August	white/plum	M	Medium	--

Keys: Shade: L—light; M—medium; D—dark   Soil: L—light; M—garden loam; R—rich

13. CONTAINER GARDENING

Containers, whether used indoors or out, give the gardener an opportunity to create a total environment for plant growth. By adjusting planting media, light, temperature, and the material in the container, you can create small ecosystems as disparate as a desert or a jungle.

Specialist gardeners exploit the mobility of hanging baskets and portable pots to move orchids, tropicals, succulents, and miniaturized bonsai indoors and out with the changing seasons.

On the small balconies and townhouse patios that many new home owners have to work with, containers make possible the production of useful herbs and salad vegetables, or a splash of flowering annuals or vines during the summer. And in most backyards planters can also enliven and decorate the patio, the deck or the odd blank wall.

Tender perennials, water garden plants, and woody ornamentals will all thrive in tubs when ground space is impossible to get. And bulb pans allow us to bring outdoor flowers, like narcissus and hyacinths, to bloom indoors for a welcome preview of spring. Variety is, indeed, the spice of life for the container gardener.

Choose the Pot for the Plant

The first principle of container gardening is to regard the container as essential to the plant's success. Many materials are suitable and durable. Terra cotta and other unglazed clay and stoneware pots, and trays, and flue liners are good containers for plants that need excellent drainage and that benefit from drier conditions between waterings. All the desert plants, geraniums, and Mediterranean herbs will look and do well in such pots with a compatible, light soil mix. Unglazed pots should always be soaked before filling to avoid wicking moisture away from the root systems of transplants.

Cast concrete planters are suitable for annuals, summer bulbs, perennial vines, and trees that are not acid-loving. (Remember, when choosing plants, that the lime content of cast concrete causes the pH of the soil to rise). These containers should be permanently sited before they are planted, unless they are quite small, because of the great difficulty in moving them later. As with all large containers they should be bought with a particular plant and location in mind.

Treated or rot resistant wooden planters and soy or whiskey barrels all keep the soil from heating too quickly. They are excellent containers for small shrubs and trees, collections of bulbs and vines, and other plantings that require cooler soil temperatures and even moisture levels.

Newer cast fiber glass planters and window boxes have the same thermal advantages as wood, but are not porous. Although expensive, fiber glass is lighter to handle and transport and does not react chemically with the soil mixtures, as soy or whiskey containers can if they are not steam-cleaned and aired.

Inexpensive plastic pots and hanging baskets are often just what is needed. They can be easily cleaned, transported, and grouped unobtrusively so that foliage hides their decorative deficits. Plastics help retain soil moisture, although the amount of exposed surface soil will affect the rate of evaporation. They can be used to give indoor plants a summer's outing—by digging them into a garden bed up to the rim or hiding them in a decorative cache pot of glazed pottery on a deck or patio.

Indoor gardeners can use something as grand as a closed glass display case or as simple as a fish bowl covered with plastic wrap to create climate controlled displays of compatible plants.

Within this range of choices, one can spend as little or as much as one pleases. But no matter what the shape, color, texture or material that you choose to complement your planting, be certain that it will drain, for your plant's appearance and health depend on it.

The principal for a unique bonsai tray or a dime store cactus container is the same. Make sure that it can be set up a little bit off the surface to promote good drainage. Round pots come with saucers to catch and evaporate watering overflow. Outside planters can be raised up slightly on wooden shims or bits of slate; inside planters can be set in a humidifying pebble tray.

Potting Mixtures

The first thing that goes in any pot is a wire screen or some broken shards of crockery to cover the obligatory drainage hole. This discourages roots from following the dissolved nutrients in the water out of the pot, and it prevents slugs from getting in.

There are many commercial potting mixes on the market, most of which can be modified to meet the drainage and nutritional needs of a wide variety of plants. If you have a storage area, mixes can be purchased for less in large bales from wholesalers or garden centers and reconstituted with water in the bag before potting up a large number of plants.

The medium that fills any pot should be sterile, particularly if the plant is to be grown indoors where lower ultraviolet radiation does not retard the rapid growth of the soil fungus diseases that can attack your plants. Most commercial potting mixes advertise this fact. Look for it.

It's best to sterilize home garden soil to prevent the transfer of soil borne pests and fungal diseases to your transplants.

Put the soil in pans set on racks in a closed water bath or crab steamer until it has been at 180° Fahrenheit for 10 minutes. Use a kitchen fan to disperse any odor. Soil steamed in this fashion can be mixed and used as soon as it is cooled.

The mixes for all container gardens should be predominantly light and porous to prevent soil compaction which, in a confined space, would squeeze out the air spaces vital to roots. Many specialty soil mixes are now available. For the self-sufficient we include several home-made formulas that can be used to pot different types of plants.

POTTING MIXTURES USING GARDEN SOIL

No.1—A standard mixture for general use.
2 parts of good garden loam
1 part peat moss or leaf mold
1 part builder's sand
or
3 parts of screened compost
½ part builder's sand
½ part peat moss

No.2—For cactus and succulents.
To the standard mixture above add:
¼ by volume of chicken grit, gravel mixture, or similar materials
plus 1 quart of ground limestone per bushel.

No.3—For begonias, ferns, African violets, etc.
To the standard mixture add:
¼ by volume of peat moss, compost, or leaf mold.

No.4—For azaleas and other acid-loving plants.
To the standard mixture add:
¼ by volume of oak leaf mold or oak leaf compost.
Any of the above mixtures may be enriched through the addition of two quarts of pulverized cow manure per bushel of mixture. Ground bonemeal may be added as a source of phosphate at the rate of 1 quart per bushel to each of mixtures No.1 and 2.

No. 5—For Water Garden Plants
Commercial mixes are heavy clay with organic matter. Gardeners with heavy clay soil should mix one part with two parts rich loam and one part well-rotted horse manure compost. This should be mixed and moistened to create a muck before planting water or bog plants.

Here are some equivalents and additions to commercial mixes for various specialty plantings.
No.6—For Epiphytic Orchids and Bromeliads
Standard commercial mix is made from
80% medium chunks fir bark
10-15% medium charcoal
5% osmunda fibre or perlite

No.7—For Bonsai (National Arboretum formula)
1 part chicken grit
1 part sieved ProMix or ground sequoia bark
1 part Turf Ace

Most home growers can't water once or twice a day, so a commercial mix of fast draining grit and peat moss can be amended as follows:
Indoor Tropical Bonsai
2 parts commercial bonsai mix
1 part potting soil
Outdoor Bonsai
2 parts commercial bonsai mix
1 part topsoil

Starting seed Indoors
Start annual seeds no more than 4 to 6 weeks ahead of a time when soil temperatures are likely to be 65° Fahrenheit, so they don't linger indoors, growing too lanky and tender to survive.

Without a greenhouse, growing sturdy seedlings indoors is a bit of a challenge, but it can be done. An unheated garage with regular lighting plus a shop lamp on a timer is a good place to set up shop. Provide 5-8 hours of bright natural light or 16 hours of lighting that can be adjusted above a rack or bench with temperatures around 60° Fahrenheit. Promote good air circulation by running a small fan when temperatures are highest.

Peat pellets that swell with water to make sterile containers for seeds are readily available at garden supply centers. For easier tranplanting later, the peat pellets can go in a flat with drainage holes.

A sterile seed sprouting mixture or a sterile potting mixture are excellent mediums that resist damping off fungus.

Moisten the mix so that it is damp and fluffy, then fill the flat containers two inches deep with it. Smooth and firm it with a wooden block. Press with the edge of the block to make furrows in it that are two inches apart. Sow your seed singly and cover with sand, pulverized compost, milled sphagnum, or fine vermiculite.

Water the seed well after planting by lowering the flat into a starter solution high in phosphorus to encourage root development. Place it somewhere with even bottom heat. The top of a refrigerator is ideal if you can remember to check morning and evening for soil moisture and sprouting. Mist it with a small water sprayer to keep the surface moist without displacing seeds, or cover it with plastic wrap aerated with a few holes.

The seeds do not need light until they have germinated. Be sure to identify all the seeds in your rows by marking the date and variety on a plastic label or popsicle stick at the end of each row. After they have sprouted be sure that they are directly under your light source and no more than 4-6 inches below it in order to encourage short sturdy seedlings.

As plants develop their first sets of true leaves, you should increase water gradually to match increased transpiration. You will get best results for seedlings if you gradually raise the shop lamp to keep the same light intensity on the growing leaves.

Transplant to your chosen spot when the plants are 3-4 inches tall after they have been hardened off with increasing exposure to sunlight and outdoor temperatures for four or five days, perhaps in a cold frame or under floating row cover. Extras can go in 4 inch pots for spares or giveaways to friends.

How to Re-pot a Plant
Pot-grown plants that you buy will need to be re-potted into a larger container. For a while, perhaps years, you will be able to maintain the size of your foliage plant by pruning, and its health by scratching in an inch or two of the correct medium with a few flakes of charcoal at the beginning of each active growing season. But eventually the soil will need replenishing and the plant's root system will want room to stretch. Keep the plant fairly dry before re-potting so that the root ball will slide out of the pot when you turn it upside down and tap the side.

If you wish the plant to grow vigorously, score the bottom of the root ball into quarters with a sharp knife. Cut off matted roots from the bottom of the ball and comb out roots on the side. Separate the scored sections enough to fit over a cone of soil mixture laid into the new pot over an inch or two of crocking or clean gravel to promote drainage. Put at least an inch of new soil mixture between the sides of the pot and the root ball and three times that depth between the crocking and the plant.

If you are re-potting any plant with high moisture needs in heavy soil, add a tablespoon full of charcoal pieces to each quart of mix to prevent souring of the mix over time. The plant's crown where it emerges from the earth should be an inch below the rim of the container when the soil is firmed and watered. Water thoroughly with a transplant solution, and set the plant in a sheltered spot for a day or two before returning to its place.

If you want to control the size and health of your plant, re-pot it in the same size container, and shave up to an inch off the entire root ball with a sharp knife after pruning the top a corresponding amount.

Epiphytic orchids, bromeliads and most palms are an exception to the rule. Orchids and bromeliads should be anchored by their roots in a bark medium which allows daily moisture and nutrients to be absorbed quickly by the whole plant without the medium staying soggy. Young plants are anchored in the pots by pounding the bark mixture down among the roots, and supporting the top heavy growth with bamboo or metal stakes clamped to the pots. It is worth taking a class to learn to do this right because you are approximating conditions at the top of the forest canopy.

Though desert palms need all their fibrous compact root system to survive, they grow too slowly under most home conditions to be a concern. Top off the soil yearly when active growth begins with 1-2 inches of fresh Mixture No.2.

Outdoor Container Culture

Cultural practices will differ among your various outdoor container plants depending on your goals. For outdoor containers of herbs, vegetables, or annual flowers, which are meant to grow quickly for full production within one growing season, generous amounts of water, nutrients, and, if possible, full sunlight are the practice. For woody ornamentals, perennial vines, and naturally or artificially dwarfed trees grown outdoors, where the goal is steady, controlled growth for longevity within a fixed environment; the soils, exposure, and fertilizing frequency are adjusted accordingly.

In the most demanding example of controlled growth, bonsai plants are root pruned to match top pruning, planted in a quick draining, gravelly medium low in nutrients, watered frequently, and fed just often enough to permit some dwarfed growth. They are placed in filtered light during the summer and well-wrapped and protected during the winter to prevent damage from extreme temperature swings.

For less demanding trees, shrubs, and vines, watering just enough to prevent any stress from drought, occasional fertilization at the beginning of the growth cycle, and careful pinching and pruning of plants in order to maintain the proper size and shape are enough during the growing season.

Winter Care Outdoors

Even hardy outdoor plants are more vulnerable to winter damage in a container. Plants whose roots or tops are likely to freeze may need to be grouped in a more sheltered area, shielded with burlap or bubble plastic with the top open, or sprayed with a commercial spray that prevents transpiration.

Some container plants, large rosemary bushes or bonsai, for example, do beautifully in a protected cold frame. Others too awkward to move, must be wrapped or sheltered with wind screens where they stand.

Indoor Care Cycles

Indoors, controlled growth is the norm. The goals are slow growth, health, hardened foliage, and a long bloom period during the darker days of the growing year, which can be achieved by regulating light, water, plant food, and temperature.

Some plants that come indoors after a summer vacation undergo an acclimatization process that reduces their intake of light, water, and nutrients for the winter dormancy period.

First, they are placed in a bright area of the house that is free from drafts and fluctuations of temperature. Then, the time periods between watering and feeding are gradually extended.

Some succulents and cactus actually need to be dry during the dormancy period that normally would precede the winter rains and will not flower if this dormancy is not initiated. The South African bulb, Hippeastrum 'Amaryllis', will not flower unless it has several weeks of warm, dry conditions after it is moved indoors in mid-September. Many other plants that derive from areas of the world like South Africa with pronounced wet-dry seasons behave this way. Cacti, succulents, bromeliads, epiphytic orchids and the euphorbias like poinsettia will flower in the home if gardeners will remember when a little time out is needed. Grouping plants with similar seasonal needs together is an easy way to grow them successfully.

To be aware of these natural cycles is to prevent the most common cause of disease and death among indoor plants—overwatering during a natural rest period.

Correct Watering

A gardener can easily experiment with the water requirements of his indoor plants by marking a funnel with 1, 2, or 3 cup designations prior to sticking it into a plant container and filling it until water begins to run out the drainage holes. Record the amount for that plant and wait to see how long it takes to lose its firm appearance before watering again. This time will vary somewhat with the plant's response to seasonal changes and interior light and humidity.

Knowing the geographic origins of your plants will aid you. Most plants from desert or dry-warm Mediterranean climates need soil to become dry between waterings even when flowering, while plants from temperate or jungle climates tend to prefer even soil moisture.

Container gardeners with many plants may want to invest in a water meter to check soil moisture deep in the pot until they are adept at recognizing when plants need water by observing their physical appearance.

When indoor gardeners vacation, soil additives can extend the period of time that soil remains adequately moist. These powdery gels are mixed with the potting soil. They work by attracting, then slowly releasing, moisture, which extends the required time between waterings by up to a week. The gels are particularly effective for tropicals, like Spathiphyllum, that usually need daily watering.

Fertilizing

Many container gardeners feed very dilute solutions of a complete water soluble fertilizer to their flowering plants at every watering. It is easy to remember, but unnecessary.

Many jungle foliage plants grow slowly but continuously under indoor conditions with scant extra nutrients. Some flowering plants like African violets, begonia, and gloxinia will do so if fed monthly, although they might normally take seasonal breaks.

The simpler method for many container plants is to fertilize once a year with a slow release formula good for 180 or 270 days, so that normal watering provides minute but constant amounts of nutrients as it moves through the soil. This should be timed to coincide with the onset of active growth if a plant is one that has a dormancy period.

Liquid solutions provide better absorption of nutrients for orchids and many epiphytes that feed through air roots and their foliage. Directions for the proper dilution and timing appear on all commercial specialty plant formulas.

Indoor Humidity Control

Most newer homes are now provided with internal humidifiers connected to the heating system, so hot dry air indoors is becoming a thing of the past. Those plants that require extra air humidity (usually they are from cool, moist habitats or are tender tropicals) can be helped without your living in dank conditions. The simplest way to create a moist microclimate is by grouping these specimens on a pebble tray where pea gravel, white quartz, or smooth black river stones hold the pots just out of a small amount of water. African violets and hanging basket specimens requiring extra humidity can be lightly misted with a special sprayer when conditions warrant.

Bonsai grown outdoors will need such misting up to twice a day when temperatures are over 80° Fahrenheit because of their reduced ability to pull moisture from the soil.

Keeping Hanging Baskets Cool

If you are planting a hanging basket outdoors, you might use an open basket lined with sphagnum moss. Smithsonian Institution gardeners fill large baskets with sterile potting mixture and add in bedding plants and variegated ivies. Watering the whole well provides some soil cooling through

evaporation of the moss, and drips will not matter on deck or patio. If carefully monitored, such a basket can function in dry, hot weather by controlling the soil temperature naturally through evaporation while humidifying the plants. This works best when the local humidity is fairly low and the plants in questions are protected from afternoon sun.

Providing Light

The sun's rays outdoors provide more than enough radiant energy to provoke flowering and good growth, even in those shade loving plants that never seem to have more than an hour or two of direct sunlight. Plants develop evenly outdoors because the sun moves each day, lighting them on all sides. Indoors all plants placed in a single exposure need to be turned regularly to develop well.

In our homes the vast majority of houseplants are erstwhile tropical jungle inhabitants that are used to lower light conditions. But some flowering plants, most notably the orchid species that grow well up in the tree canopy, and flowering perennials, have special light requirements which must be met with supplemental lighting.

Those people with south-facing windows, deciduous trees, and controlled humidity in the house may have room to set up plant displays of flowering cactus or orchids, which come into their own after leaves fall. Most of us, with less ideal conditions or other claimants in our families for those warm bright spaces, do not. But there are alternatives short of building a greenhouse: Use your air space.

The greatest amount of light entering a house is found near the tops of windows, an ideal place to fill hanging baskets with those plants that need extra light. Bay windows on different sides of the house are excellent light traps. Baskets or glass shelves give more growing room.

Different plants should go in these bays. Cool season

bloomers like Gardenia, Cineraria, Streptocarpus, primrose, and ferns prefer north or east light, which does not heat the bay unduly during the day. Semi-tropical bloomers can use the more sheltered western and southern exposures, although care must be taken to place the plants so that the foliage does not bleach or burn. Bright western and southern exposures are best for desert dwellers which can take heat and dry conditions during the day.

Those plants that need high light and high humidity will often thrive as hanging plants in a bright bathroom or kitchen window. Orchids and coleus are good candidates here. There are many microclimates in the average home. Explore the possibilities for your plants.

Gardening Under Lights

When light and available space conditions do not coincide, artificial lighting can provide as much radiant energy as sunlight can in a given location.

The simplest of these devices is a cool phase fluorescent shop lamp in conjunction with incandescent light sources to increase the available light into the 75-1,000 foot-candles range needed to grow different plants. Research has shown that the most successful formula is four standard fluorescent tubes to 300 watts of incandescent light.

Start by measuring the available room light with a light meter, preferably one that measures artificial light rather than photographic conditions. If the room has natural daylight, on a sunny day take several measurements parallel to the surface to be used. If it does not, take measurements with the room lights on. Then calculate how much total light will be needed to grow the plants you want, keeping in mind the following designations.

◊ *Low light requirements* are from 25-100 footcandles, with optimum light conditions between 75-100.
◊ *Medium light requirements* are from 75-500 footcandles, with optimum conditions between 200-500.
◊ *High light requirements* are from 200-500 footcandles, with optimum conditions at 500.
◊ *Very high light requirements* are from 1,000 footcandles and up, with optimum conditions over 1,000.

Before purchasing the bulbs you want, you may subtract the available light from the total that you need to buy bulbs for. Your lighting salesman can translate these figures into the required wattages, but you still must measure the final results with a light meter, because lamps often vary from specifications.

You should be able to raise and lower the finished lamp in order to adjust its height over either seedlings or mature plants so that their foliage is not burned by heat from the bulb or metal housing. These fluorescent lamps can also be purchased as light sticks to be plugged in under cabinets, counters, or shelves, if you wish to turn unused counters or

shelf space into plant display cases. When a particular specimen's light needs are met, you can bring it into another room in the house for a short term display and enjoyment.

The following selection of plants has light requirements that may be difficult to meet in the average home without supplementary lighting for 8-12 hours a day. Keep in mind that some seasonal species like poinsettia will need unbroken darkness for 13 hours a day by October in order to set buds for Christmas bloom.

Keeping track of light requirements for your favorite plants is easier if you grow those with similar requirements together, and set the supplemental lighting to go on and off at the proper hours with a timer. Remember that houses in wooded areas have far more available daylight in winter than summer, thus allowing the gardener to cut down on supplemental lighting then.

Botanical Name & Common Name—Moisture
Need Very High Light: 700-1000 footcandles
  Aloe vera, aloe—dry
  Begonia tuberosa, tuberose Begonia—moist
  Gardenia jasminoides 'Veitchi' gardenia—moist
  Hibiscus rosa, sinensis hibiscus—moist
  Rosa miniature, roses—wet
Need High Light: 200-700 footcandles
  Ananas comosus, pineapple—moist
  Browallia, browallia—moist
  Caladium, caladium—moist/drier when dormant
  Cyclamen, cyclamen—moist/drier when dormant
  Eriobotrya japonica, loquat—moist
  Lantana, lantana—dry
  Primula sieboldi, primrose—moist
  Streptocarpus, streptocarpus—moist

Propagation

Those who have time may want to experiment with propagating their own favorites, always an interesting process because plants reproduce in so many different ways.

Some of the most popular flowering houseplants like African violets can be cloned from leaf material by laying a callused leaf cutting into rooting hormone powder, and then into a small pot filled with sterile potting mix or sand and vermiculite. By watering with dilute transplant solution from the bottom, misting and securing a clean plastic bag over the top of the pot, you create a mini-greenhouse in which this and similar plants will produce rooted offspring. The medium and the light conditions can be adjusted for various species. Cleanliness, even humidity, and appropriate light conditions are the keys to success. Most woody material can be propagated from cuttings under the same controlled conditions.

If you lack a controlled environment to grow the small offshoots of plants like orchids or bromeliads, leave them attached to the parent plant until they are fully established before detaching and potting.

Whenever root material appears on infant plantlets, those babies are safe to pot up—one of the reasons that Anthericum (spider plant) and Kalenchoe retain their popularity. Pinning a spider plantlet at the end of its runner into an adjacent pot will promote rapid root growth. Collecting the minute plants on the leaf margins of Kalenchoe pinnata, (the airplant), is tedious but rewarding. One plant can yield hundreds of plantlets when set out in a sandy cactus and succulent mixture and nurtured with a dilute transplant solution until the roots take hold.

Some succulents like cactus offsets need to be detached with a sterile knife, air callused, planted in a sterile Mixture No. 2 and treated in the same manner. To prevent overwatering, try creating a mini-greenhouse of clear plastic with a few holes poked in it for better aeration for the first month.

Air Layering Jungle Plants

Air-layering the tops will provide new bushy plants from old leggy ones in a couple of months. Large leafed foliage plants, like Dracaena fragrans massangeana (Corn plant) and Dieffenbachia (Dumb cane), can be scored with a clean knife a foot below the crown of foliage, the cuts in the bark coated with rooting hormone, and then covered with a sterile compress made of handfuls of damp sphagnum moss soaked in transplant solution and secured inside a sheet of plastic. The compress should extend 6 inches above and below the cuts to give adequate space for a good root system and be fastened at top and bottom with elastic or string to retain moisture. When you can see the new roots pushing through the sphagnum, the new plant can be carefully detached with sharp clean shears.

Corn plant and Dumb cane are so easy to propagate that one can callus and root the top cuttings directly in new pots if they are misted daily and kept on a pebble tray.

In general, it is best to re-pot or propagate plants after they flower and near the beginning of a season of active growth.

Container Garden Care

Most plants should be watered thoroughly from the top. Watering from the top is needed to flush out the chemical salt accumulation left behind by evaporation. Pour off any excess water in the saucer after an hour or two. Do not water again until the surface of the soil becomes almost dry to the touch. Syringe the leaves of glossy foliage plants. Even African violets, gloxinia, and velvet plant, which are watered by placing the pot in a shallow sink, may be gently syringed with tepid water to remove the dust, but care must be taken to see that the leaves are dry before moving the plants into sunlight.

Fertilizing once a month is a general rule unless you use slow release pellets. Usually the period when plants are forming flower buds is a good time to feed them more. During the dormant period for each species no feeding should be the rule. Regardless of the plant's need for fertilizer, the manufacturer's directions should be followed.

Keep the plants free from insect pests and diseases. There are safe general purpose mixtures now available for use on house plants, including some insecticidal soap sprays. Often a thorough syringing will remedy the ill.

A brief session in the shower bath is another method of thoroughly soaking the soil in the pots. In addition, the shower helps to flush out accumulated salts, and removes sucking insects. A cold shower is the best insect shocker.

Re-potting, as far as practicable should be taken care of at the time plants move out-of-doors, rather than in the fall when they are being brought indoors.

Many houseplants may be set outside during the summer months. Sink the pots up to their rims in a sunny or shaded spot in the garden according to the need of each species. Water and feed as necessary. In the fall, bring them into their accustomed places in the house in a gradual manner, allowing them to slowly adjust to the change in air and humidity.

Before bringing the plants indoors, they should be thoroughly sprayed three times at weekly intervals to remove all insects. Give the plants fresh air but avoid drafts. Its especially important to move plants back inside while fresh air is still circulating through the house.

The following sample of flowering plants is by no means exhaustive. You will find dozens of species and hundreds of cultivars at your local nursery. The atriums and lobbies of good hotels and office buildings abound with attractive specimens you might want to consider for your home.

Among cacti and succulents alone, there are at least 30 species readily available to the home hobbyist. Rather these choices serve to indicate the range of species available. The selections are grouped by their light requirements.

FLOWERING CONTAINER PLANTS:

Botanical & CommonName	Temp.	Mix	Active Growth	Water	Propagate/Comments
Medium Light—75 to 500 footcandles					
Achmea fasciata, Bromeliad	65-75°	1	Winter	keep cups filled	root offshoots
Clivia miniata, Clivia	60-70°	1	Winter	little when dormant	separation
Episcia, Flame violet	65-75°	3	year round	moist	leaves, cuttings, plantlets
Fuschia, Fuschia	50-65°	1	Winter-Summer	moist in bloom	cuttings
Impatiens holsti, Impatiens	60-65°	1	year-round	moist	cuttings, seed
Spathiphyllum, Spathiphyllum	60-70°	3	year-round	wet	division
High Light—200 to 700 footcandles					
Saint pauli, African violet	65-70	3	year-round	moist	leaf-cuttings
Begonia coccinea, Angel wing	60-70	3	year-round	dry between waterings	cuttings
Begonia semperflorans, Wax	65-75	3	year-round	dry between waterings	cuttings, seeds
Sinningia speciosa, gloxinia	65-75	3	year-round	moderate	leaves or division
Kalenchoe blossfeldiana, kalenchoe	55-65	2	early spring	stop after bloom	leaf cuttings, seeds
Orchidacae oncidium, orchids	55-65	O	Fall-winter	daily	division, plantlets
O. phalaenopsis, orchids	55-65	O	Fall-winter	daily	division, plantlets
O. dendrobium, orchids	55-65	O	Fall-winter	daily	division, plantlets
Schlumbergera, Christmas cactus	62-70	2	Fall-winter	while flowering	cuttings
Aphelandra squarrosa, zebra plant	65-85	3	Fall-winter	moist	cuttings
Very High Light—1000 footcandles+					
Cactaceae opuntia, cactus	65-70	2	Winter	withhold when dormant	
C. mamillarias, etc., cactus	65-70	2	Winter	withhold when dormant	
Pelargonium, geranium	45-65	1	year-round	dry between waterings	cuttings
Euphorbia pulcherrima, poinsettia	65-70	1	Fall-winter	drier when dormant,	stem cuttings July
Citrus taitensis, ornamental orange	60-70	1	Spring-Fall	dry between waterings	seed

FOLIAGE PLANTS

Foliage plants have gained a great deal of attention since the advent of planter boxes in contemporary homes. Plantsmen for the last 50 years have imported and improved many new species from jungles and savannas around the world. Most of these shrubs, vines and herbaceous perennials are of interest because they will grow without direct sunlight and in areas where few, if any, flowering plants will thrive. Many of them will grow in parts of the room far from windows.

However there are a few foliage plants renowned for their brilliant foliage or occasional flowering that do need seasonal sunlight to bring out their best. Such plants can be rotated between sunny areas and light shade. Light requirements of container plants will be clearly indicated on the labels in the houseplant section of any reputable nursery. When in doubt, ask.

Soil

Since most of these plants are from the tropics, they need a soil rich in humus. The exceptions are the palms, sansevieria, and pandanus which require more sand and less peat for drainage. They also need additional calcium so the pH levels are near neutral (6.8-7). In general a high moisture requirement means that plants can take a higher proportion of loam and peat in the mix. Commercial potting mixtures for houseplants generally strike a good balance between moisture retention and drainage in a sterile medium that inhibits soil fungus if the gardener does not overwater. These are preferable for indoor container plants that do not have the benefit of ultraviolet radiation and fresh air to discourage soil fungus diseases.

Temperature

Most of our listed plants thrive in daytime temperatures in the low 70s. The nighttime temperatures should be 5-10 degrees lower. Those few plants that need a warmer situation are indicated, and will be happier in a south window or solarium. Though our rooms are now kept cooler night and day, these plants will prove hardy. Crotons and poinsettia dislike chilling and should be placed where drafts from open doors will not stress them.

Watering

Requirements of the foliage plants vary greatly between the species. Most of the tropicals want a moist but not waterlogged soil. During the dormant season of species used to a wet dry cycle, watering should be reduced sharply. Do not let water sit in the saucers of any foliage plants. It is safer to

FOLIAGE CONTAINER PLANTS

Botanical & Common Name	Soil Mix	Active Growth	Water	Propagate/Features
Low Light—25 to 100 footcandles				
Aglaonema, Chinese evergreen	1	year round	moist	cuttings
Aspidistra elatoir, Aspidistra	2	year round	tolerant	divide
Dracaena fragrans, Corn plant	1	year round	tolerant	cuttings
Pandanus veitchii, Screw pine	2	winter	moist if active	offsets
Philodendron, philodendron	1	year round	moist	
Maranta leuconeura, Prayer Plant	2	summer	moist	division
Sanseveria, Sansevieria	1	year round	tolerant	division
Syngonium, African arrowhead	3	year round	moist	division
Medium Light—75 to 500 footcandles				
Pilea cardierei, Aluminum Plant	3	year round	moist	pinch frequently
Aucuba japonica Aucuba	1	spring to fall	drier if dormant	division, splashy foliage patterns
Mephrolepsis etc., Dallas fern	3	year round	moist	full compact form
Dieffenbachia amoena	3	year round	moist	air layer, likes warm rooms
Dizygotheca, Thread leaf	Pro	year round	moist	filtered light
Fatshedra lizea, Fatshedra	1	year round	tolerant	strong upright grower
Ficus benjamina etc., Figs	1	Spring-Fall	moist if active	interesting shapes, easy care
Monstera delicosa, Monstera	1	year round	moist	prune frequently
Chamaedora elegans, Parlor palm	1	year round	tolerant	
Tolmiea, Piggy Back plant	3	year round	dry	plantlets
Scindapsus aureus, Pothos	1	year round	dry	prune frequently
Schleffera brassia, Schleffera	3	year round	tolerant	distinctive foliage
Chlorophytum etc., Spider plant	1	year round	moist	plantlets
High Light—200 to 700 footcandles				
Asparagus etc., Asparagus fern	1	year round		division hanging baskets
Auracaria etc., Norfolk Island pine	1	year round	dry out	feed 1 time
Coleus blumei verschaffelti	1	year round		cuttings, gorgeous colors
Crassula argentea etc. Jade plant	2	Spring-fall	drier if dormant	interesting species
Codiaeum variegatum, Croton	1	year round	moist	feed 1 time, brilliant foliage
Fatsia japonica, Fatsia	1	year round	dry out	large leaves
Podocarpus macrophyllus 'Maki'	1	Spring-fall	moist	feed 2 times
Gynura etc., Purple Passion Vine	1 or 3	year round	moist	cuttings
Saxifraga etc., Strawberry begonia	2	year round	when dry	cuttings, hanging baskets

group plants with similar microclimate needs on a pebble tray so any excess water will contribute to ambient humidity rather than rotted roots. An occasional drying between waterings will help to keep roots healthy.

Fertilizing

Fertilize sparingly. You will just end up pruning more on most foliage plants. Once or twice a year with a slow release pelletized fertilizer at the beginning of active growth is quite sufficient. A sickly but prized plant might need a foliar feeding, but it is often just as easy to prune and repot in fresh soil, or clone your favorite. Vines like philodendrons should be kept on a diet in enough light to encourage short spaces between leaf nodes. Lanky stringy specimens give house plants a bad name. Usually it is good practice to keep most of the foliage plants "pot-bound." Never go up more than the next sized pot, or your more vigorous specimens will soon outgrow their usefulness as decorative accents.

Sanitation

Sanitation is the best pest control. Soap sprays have revolutionized indoor pest control. They are a new old idea. But prevention is still cheaper. All house plants need to have their foliage washed free of dust every few weeks. A cool shower or syringing in place will have the additional benefit of curbing sucking insects and helping you monitor the situation. Mealybugs on plants that can't take cold water can be controlled by touching them with a swab dipped in alcohol.

12 EASY FOLIAGE PLANTS FOR THE BEGINNER
Selected by Dr. Henry M. Cathey

Common and Botanical name	Light level/Moisture	
False Aralia		
(Dizygotheca elegantissima)	medium	moist
Corn plant		
(Dracaena fragrans)	low	wet
Neanthe bella palm		
(Chamaedorea elegans)	low	moist
Pewter plant		
(Aglaonema roebelinii)	low	moist
Bromeliad		
(Achmea fasciata)	medium	moist
Boston fern		
(Mephrolepsis exalta bostoniensis 'Dallas')	medium	moist
Dumb cane		
(Dieffenbachia amoena)	medium	dry
Fatsia		
(Fatsia Japonica)	medium	moist
Podocarpus		
(P. macrophyllus 'Maki')	high	moist
Prayer plant		
(Maranta leuconeura)	medium	moist
Schleffera		
(Brassaia actinophylla)	medium	dry
Wax plant		
(Hoya carnosa)	medium	dry

INSPIRATION:

Conservatories at the following locations:

Brookside Botanic Gardens; 1500 Glenallan Avenue, Wheaton, Maryland.

U.S. Botanic Gardens, 1st & Independence Avenues SW, Washington, D.C.

The Pan American Union, 17th Street & Constitution Avenue NW, Washington, D.C.

Amazonia Exhibit, The National Zoo, Connecticut Avenue & Woodley Road NW Washington, D.C.

Green Spring Farm Park, 4603 Green Spring Road, Annandale, Virginia.

BONSAI—LIVING SCULPTURE

Bonsai appeal to gardeners who long to create something that will last beyond their own time. These miniaturized plants have boomed in local popularity since a world class collection of Japanese, Chinese, and American specimens have taken up residence in their own pavilion at The National Arboretum.

All of the training, pruning, and growing techniques are bent toward the creation on a small scale of a plant that embodies the wisdom and character gained from dealing with life's adversities.

Garden centers and specialty nurseries offer beginner bonsai for the indoor and outdoor grower, both of them available in the attractive pots that add so much to the sense of balanced beauty essential to their appeal.

Indoors most of the plants are woody tropical shrubs, fast growing hardy plants that can take the frequent pruning, training wires, and diluted nutrients that shape and restrict new growth. Because of the rapid drainage of the soil mixes around the limited root structure, daily watering is a necessity.

Indoor bonsai are perfect candidates for grouping on a pebble or gravel tray so that the moisture that transpires from below will prevent the leaves or needles from drying between waterings. They are a good choice for the gardener with indoor plant experience who wants to assess the appeal of these miniaturized and long-lived plants. Indoor plants should be moved outdoors to a protected area during the warm season, taking the usual precautions for tropicals.

Most outdoor bonsai work takes place in early March just before plants break dormancy.

Home growers of bonsai who have taken National Arboretum curator Robert Dreschler's acclaimed classes use a rooting mixture composed of equal parts of chicken grit, sieved ProMix or chopped sequoia bark, and Turf Ace, with the sifted "fines" discarded and the coarser material saved the mix. The roots are carefully pruned to fit the size and shape of the container you have chosen; then the moistened soil mix is carefully worked down and around the root system with the blunt end of a chopstick to anchor the plant and eliminate any air pockets.

Home growers who are not able to water every day can create the heavier mix (described earlier in this chapter); but their plants may require more pruning.

Next, prune to remove branches that obscure the basic shape suggested by the plant, and then wind your copper wire around selected branches to enhance and refine the shape you are seeking during the coming period of growth.

After watering with a dilute transplant solution, place the plant in a protected area where it will not be exposed

to climactic extremes while its growth resumes.

Give the plants a dilute liquid feeding every 7-10 days with their regular daily watering. The entire maintainence process is meant to mimic the harsh conditions that form the many bonsai plants collected in rocky areas where their natural struggles to survive have produced distinctive plant specimens.

Root Cuttings

With a little practice and a cold frame, bonsai enthusiasts can collect or propagate their own outdoor specimens from the wild with root cuttings from certain kinds of trees and shrubs. Bonsai practitioners often seek surface root material of beech, sweet gum, maple, and pine in order to create miniature groves of trees in containers.

All root cuttings are taken in the fall after the trees are dormant. It is customary to expose the roots on one side of a tree or shrub until enough large roots are uncovered for your needs. Roots approximately as large in diameter as a thin lead pencil should be taken. They may be cut in 2-4 inch lengths, with the butt end square cut and the tip end slanting. Tie in bundles and store in damp peat moss in a frost free trench or cold frame like hardwood cuttings. By late March the cuttings should be callused and ready to plant 6-10 inches apart in a shallow trench.

The cuttings may be placed slanting or horizontal and are covered with about 2 inches of friable loam or compost. Soils that crust should be avoided. As soon as the new growth breaks the ground, the soil should be well mulched to prevent weeds and to retain moisture during the growing season.

If rainfall is not adequate, water to keep the ground damp and feed with a liquid plant food several times during the season. Always feed when soil is already moist. Early the second spring the plants can be lifted and prepared for

training in a bonsai container that will complement the effect you hope to achieve.

To people with an artistic bent and enough gardening experience to appreciate their growth cycles and requirements, bonsai are worth all the effort. For the small garden they make beautiful focal points that with age increase in beauty to create an aura that transcends their size. That they can be carried from home to home gives them even more appeal.

Bonsai For Beginners
Indoor Plants:
  Ficus retusa, Rubber Plant
  Ficus benjamina, Weeping Fig
  Serissa, Serissa (more cold tolerant)
  Carmona microphylla, Fukian Tea
  Segeretia theezans, Chinese Sweet Plum
Outdoor Plants:
  Juniperus chinensis sargentii, 'San Jose', Sargent's Juniper;
  Ulmus chinensis, Chinese Elm;
  Acer buergerianum, Trident Maple.

INSPIRATION:
The National Arboretum Bonsai Collection, Washington, D.C.
Resources:
The Essentials of Bonsai, Timber Press,
The Potomac Bonsai Society, Jay Spencer (301) 871-5768

MINIATURE WATER GARDENS

A water feature has always been an essential part of great gardens throughout the world. Even the famous Japanese temple gardens approximate the effect of water, surrounding isolated stones with gentle curves of raked pebbles that seem to lap against island shores.

Formerly water gardening in our area might consist of a few bog plantings or iris sited by a stream that ran through the yard when a property happened to include a stream. Concerns for water quality in the watershed are leading developers to pay stricter attention to buffer zones that will protect against excess nutrients and siltation. Streams are more likely to be part of a naturalized common area, instead of an individual lot.

But water features are more popular than ever, thanks to beautiful public examples and the presence of a major water garden company in Buckeystown, Maryland. Suddenly it seems that a water garden is a viable option for any container gardener in the smallest townhouse or patio apartment. Though larger ponds are balanced ecosystems beyond the scope of this chapter, container or tub culture can provide a watery retreat that has an impact out of all proportion to its size.

Diverse molded plastic containers, halved barrels and watering troughs are all potential water features provided

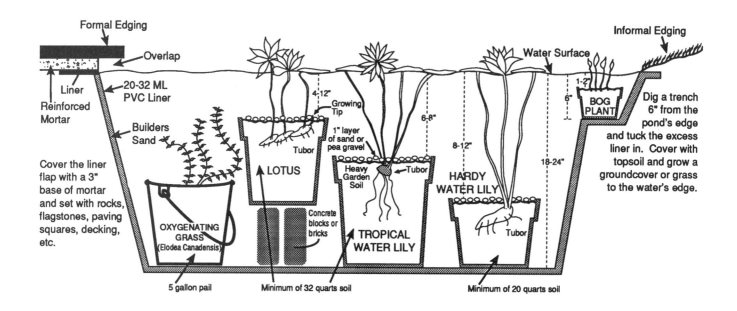

that the depth is at least 14 inches and that the container holds at least 30 gallons of water. This ensures that the water temperature does not rise and fall too rapidly to sustain plants, algae eaters, and any fish you might need to dispel mosquitoes. Whiskey barrels should be free of any residue or lined with pool liner if you are not sure of their safety.

To further control temperatures in this small volume of water, it is wise to site your container where there is shade protection during the hottest hours of the day, even though sunlight is necessary for good bloom.

With those basics observed, you could create the simplest garden by adding a water garden soil mix of heavy clay mixed with rich loam and well aged horse manure in the bottom six inches, soaking it as you mix, and then allowing it sit for half a day. Next, set in your chosen plant material, perhaps one small hardy lily, or the smaller water poppy or parrots feather, for surface foliage or bloom, and one vertical accent plant in a taller sunken pot, perhaps a water iris, papyrus, pickerel weed, or arrow arum. Finish the planting by strewing a half inch layer of pea gravel or black river stones over the soil surface, and filling the pot with a slow trickle of water down the side of the container to minimize sedimentation.

If your municipal water system uses chloramine instead of straight chlorine, you will have to add one of a number of commercial neutralizers you can find in any aquarium supply store before adding any algae eaters or fish. Straight chlorine will evaporate in two or three days while any sedimentation clears.

If you wish, you could add one algae eater and one or two gambusia to control mosquito larvae, following release directions to prevent undue shock to the fish. If you do not want fish, float a compressed block of the israelii strain of the natural control Bacillus thuriengensis to kill mosquito larvae for 30 days.

If you prefer greater water depth, omit soil in the container. Plant all water plants in pots that match the container color at the proper depth for each species. A black container will give the illusion of greater depth and provide a viewing background for flowers and fish. In this situation a tropical plant, like water hyacinth, can safely provide water filtration and bloom until fall. It floats (and spreads) while the roots cleanse the water. Bunches of submerged plants also serve this purpose. These feathery plants filter pond water and provide extra food and shelter for small fish. Because they are edible the plants are often protected with small mesh wire cages to keep fish from nipping new growth in the bud.

Shading of the water surface with plants moderates temperature and prevents the bloom of excess algae. Since air exchange at the surface is also important, remove old leaves or plant sections regularly so no more than two thirds of the water surface is covered. Fertilize water lilies monthly with a lily formula tablet for best bloom.

The first temperature drop near freezing will damage tropical plants, so they must be moved indoors and kept moist through the winter. Hardy native plants will go dormant beneath the surface when their pots are lowered to the bottom.

Unless the tub is in a very warm sheltered area, icing over will smother the one or two fish such a mini-garden can support. Clearing the surface during a cold spell or installing a small deicer unit will allow members of the carp family to survive. Others should take a winter vacation indoors in an aquarium. (Prepared with the help of Rob DeFeo, National Capital Parks, NPS).

Recommended Water Plants

Vertical Bog Plants:
Iris fulva, I.. versicolor (red, blue natives) to 6 in. deep;
Pseudocorus (yellow water iris) to 4 in. deep;
Siberica (Siberian iris) to 2 in. deep;
Peltandra virginica, (water arum) to 6 in. deep;
Pontederia cordata, (pickerel weed) to 12 in. deep;
Equisetum hyemale, (horsetail) to 6 in. deep;
Lobelia cardinalis, (cardinal flower) to 3 in. deep;
Cyperus haspans, (dwarf papyrus) to 4 in. deep;
Typha minima, (dwarf cattail) to 12 in. deep.

Floating Water Plants:
Nymphoides peltata (floating heart) 4-12 in. deep;
Nymphoides cristata, (water snowflake) 3-12 in. deep;
Hydroclets nymphoides, (water poppy) 4-12 in. deep;
Eichornia crassipes, (water hyacinth) floats;
Nymphaea 'Dauben' and 'Fabiola,' small blue, pink hardy lilies that bloom in partial shade.

Submerged Plants:
Cabomba caroliniana, (Cabomba);
Sagittaria subulata, (Dwarf Sagittaria).

Terrarium Gardens

If humidity and space are chronic problems in your home, a terrarium may be an attractive, viable solution. It will allow you to enjoy greenery that is virtually self-sustaining, a carefully arranged collection of small plants in a closed glass house that recycles its own oxygen and carbon dioxide and maintains its own humidity through the normal process of photosynthesis and evaporation.

Bottles, fish bowls, and aquarium tanks are the perfect places to build one of these small worlds (children love to help) according to Dr. Henry Cathey's U.S.D.A. booklet, the source for the following information.

To start a jungle environment, spread a ½-¾ inch layer of dry, coarse sphagnum moss on the bottom of a clean, dry container. Add about ¾ inch dry, pasteurized potting mix, and firm into the moss with the large end of a chopstick.

Next, bring your group of small pot plants together alongside the bottle and group them into an attractive arrangement that faces primarily in one direction. Choose compatible species with the same culture requirements. Possible choices are small woodland plants, cacti and other succulents, or the smallest tropical plants.

When you are satisfied by the contrast in color, texture, and height, remove most of the potting soil around the plants and trim their roots to 2 to 3 inches with scissors. Pinch out all dead or diseased foliage.

Work the roots gently into place in the bottle, keeping them evenly spread for better support. Sift more dry potting mix over the roots to cover them, firming out any air pockets with your chopstick and gently shaking the mix down among the leaves by tapping the container.

When the root structures are secure and the tops are harmoniously grouped so that the top of the tallest species comes two-thirds of the way up the sides of the container, slide thin pieces of live moss around the plant stems to cover the mix. Tamp down gently. You should be able to tip the container, which you may need to do to remove excess water after the next step.

Water by filling a clean squeeze bottle and allowing water to flow gently down the side of the container until the soil, but not the leaves, is well-moistened. Go slow and you will not have to drain off any excess. Allow to dry uncovered in a cool place until all leaf and container surfaces are dry, but soil is slightly moist, usually several days.

Remove any imperfect foliage and cover with a clear top or plastic wrap with holes. Cover loosely because air exchange is essential for healthy plants. Water only when lower sphagnum layer begins to lighten.

After nine months fertilize only with one-quarter strength house plant solution to control growth.

Terrariums are perfect for a counter top under a light stick. For contrast, try a desert version. Display on a counter or table with good light from outside or from above.

Plan to keep about a year, perhaps controlling top growth by swabbing the growing points with a drop of rubbing alcohol on a Q-tip.

INSPIRATION

Kenilworth Aquatic Gardens, Kenilworth Avenue & Douglas Street NE south of New York Avenue Washington, D.C.
U.S. Botanical Gardens, Independence Avenue & 1st Street NW, Washington, D.C..
Bolivar Pool, Department of Interior, between 19th and 21st Streets at D Street NW, Washington D.C.

WHAT TO DO FOR YOUR SICK PLANTS

Cause	Symptoms	What To Do
CULTURAL PRACTICES		
1. Too little humidity.	Edges of leaves brown and crisp.	Place plants on top of pan filled with gravel and water. Water should not touch pot. For large pots, place tins of water on top of soil.
2. Too much water.	Entire plant wilts. Dark brown blotches or yellowing on leaves; soggy soil.	Decrease watering, check drainage. Improve soil texture with perlite to improve drainage.
3. Not enough water or too much heat.	Leaves turn yellow with brown spots; leaf edges brown and crisp; leaves may also appear limp and wilt between waterings.	Find best temperature for plant. Water thoroughly.
4. Too much light.	Yellow, brown or silvery spots appear on leaves. Leaves closest to light sources most affected.	Move plants farther from window. Under artificial light, move plant farther from bulb.
5. Not enough light.	Plants do not flower, stems stretch toward light source, become long and spindly.	Provide more light or artificial light. If already growing under artificial light, increase wattage or move plant closer to bulb.
6. Too much fertilizer.	Plants do not flower; new growth is weak. Salts may build up on clay pot or soil.	Do not fertilize as much and/or as often.
7. Not enough fertilizer.	Leaves discolor and fade. Growth slows down. Bottom leaves yellow.	Use greater concentration of fertilizer or fertilize more often. This is especially important during plant's growing season. (Some plants are always in their growing season and do not go dormant.)
8. Temperature variation.	Yellow spots on leaves, leaves turn yellow and fall off.	Avoid using icy cold water; symptoms may also be caused by hot sun shining on wet leaves; drafts from air conditioners, heat vents, opening doors to outside, etc.
9. Overcrowded plant too big for pot.	Plant more than three times higher than diameter of pot. Roots push through drainage hole and plant may wilt between waterings.	Repot in larger container or divide.
10. New foliage is yellow.	May be lack of acidity for acid-loving plants.	Water plant with solution of iron sulphate.
11. Bruising of plant.	Tips of leaves may turn brown; leaves are crushed or broken.	Prune off bruised plant parts and also move to more protected location (especially ferns).
INSECTS		
1. Aphids	Sucks juices. Leaves discolor. Secreted juices are host to sooty mold.	Wash leaves with warm, soapy water, rinse with clear water. If severe, spray with insecticidal soap sprays.
2. Spider mites	Barely visible to naked eye. Damage appears as a speckling of leaves. Tiny webs on underside of leaves.	Wash leaves with tepid, soapy water. For chemical control, spray commercial soap spray.
3. Gnats	Adult gnats do not harm plant, but the maggots are known to damage plant roots.	Regular insecticidal soap spray for prevention. Repot and wash roots or destroy if maggots appear.
4. Mealy bugs	Covered with waxy powder and leave cottony residue on plants. Are also sucking insects.	If not severe, touch each bug with a Q-tip dipped in alcohol, or use correct soap formula.
5. Scales	Spray outdoors with BT or neem at crawler stage (late June-July). Use soap spray before bringing plants inside in the fall.	Spray outdoors with malathion at crawler stage (usually May-July). Use soap spray before bringing plants inside in the fall.
6. Whiteflies	Adult whiteflies, sucking insects, fly when disturbed. Leaves turn yellow and drop off. May eventually kill plant.	Wash new plants with tepid, soapy water. Rinse with clear water before adding to collection. Do not crowd. Prevent with regular soap spray. Use yellow panel to attract stragglers.

14. THE VEGETABLE & FRUIT GARDEN

Growing your own food gives the beginning gardener almost instant feedback. For that reason it is the most popular form of gardening for the novice gardener who decides to move beyond basic property maintainence.

Aside from beginner's luck, which does occur fairly regularly, a successful experience hinges on 3 principles:
◊ Choosing your best site for the food you want to grow.
◊ Planning your garden in advance.
◊ Doing thorough soil preparation and maintainence.

To take these essentials in order, you need to look for a well-drained site on your property or in a community garden that has at least 6 hours of direct sunlight a day. More is even better. Some leaf crops and snap beans will mature with less light, but it will take them much longer. Shade often implies competition from nearby planting, so the garden will be less suitable for double or triple cropping in the same space.

The amount of light will determine the site. Your family size, available time, and the amount of produce you want to grow will determine the size and nature of your garden. Here, a plan is invaluable. With it you can determine what you want to grow, how much you will need, and the space and length of time necessary to accomplish your goals.

Most vegetables are annuals that take a specific amount of time to mature. A plan must note the length of the growing season in your area (i.e. the time between the last frost of the spring and the first frost of fall). Check the season length for your general area and modify with observations in your own neighborhood. There can be a week to 10 days difference in the last frost date between a walled sunny garden and an exposed low field two blocks away.

If your growing season is 150 days and you wish to grow warm season vegetables that occupy the garden most of the summer, it will take careful siting to fit in salad lettuces and cool season crops at the beginning or end of the garden cycle. You may need to seed your own transplants indoors in February to have plants ready when your garden is. Two crops in the same space in a season may be possible. Three may not.

If your growing season is close to 200 days, as it will be in warmer, sandy areas close to the Bay, you may be able to grow cool season crops from March to May, following them with heat lovers that take from 55 to 90 days to mature, and still get in more cool season crops that will mature from late September through October.

Here seed catalogs are invaluable, because they give variety characteristics, including the average time it takes a plant to mature from the time it germinates. If quantity of produce per given space is most important to you, look for and choose the heavy producing varieties in your catalogs. On the other hand, if delicious taste unavailable in commercially grown varieties is paramount, use your catalog to order these varieties—for example, the King of the Garden lima bean, an

Planting Calendar

For the Washington Area

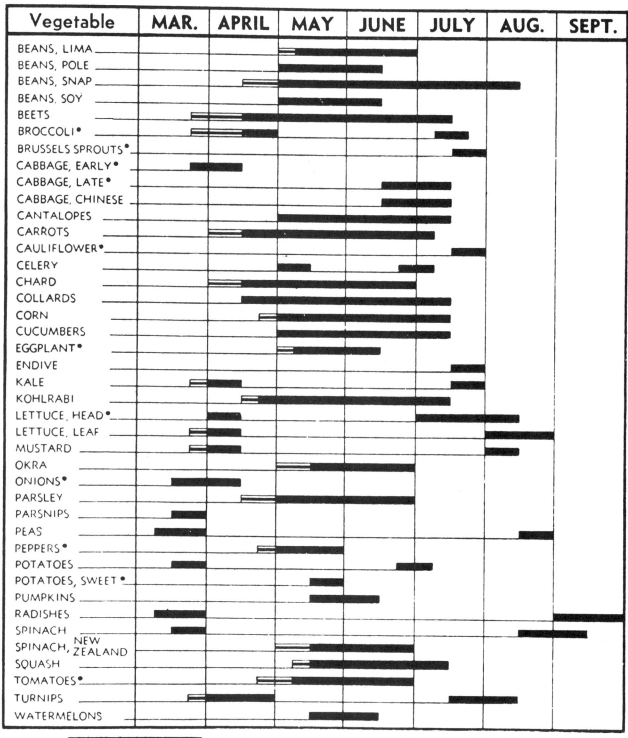

Vegetable	MAR.	APRIL	MAY	JUNE	JULY	AUG.	SEPT.
BEANS, LIMA							
BEANS, POLE							
BEANS, SNAP							
BEANS, SOY							
BEETS							
BROCCOLI•							
BRUSSELS SPROUTS•							
CABBAGE, EARLY•							
CABBAGE, LATE•							
CABBAGE, CHINESE							
CANTALOPES							
CARROTS							
CAULIFLOWER•							
CELERY							
CHARD							
COLLARDS							
CORN							
CUCUMBERS							
EGGPLANT•							
ENDIVE							
KALE							
KOHLRABI							
LETTUCE, HEAD•							
LETTUCE, LEAF							
MUSTARD							
OKRA							
ONIONS•							
PARSLEY							
PARSNIPS							
PEAS							
PEPPERS•							
POTATOES							
POTATOES, SWEET•							
PUMPKINS							
RADISHES							
SPINACH							
SPINACH, NEW ZEALAND							
SQUASH							
TOMATOES•							
TURNIPS							
WATERMELONS							

Normal planting period

Advance planting period
in protected sections of city

• Dots indicate PLANTS or SETS

old vining variety still unexcelled in tenderness, size, and taste. It hogs the ground the whole season, requires very sturdy supports, must be planted in very warm soil or it rots, will not set blossoms in very hot weather, and yet is still worth every sacrifice the gardener must make.

The choices that you make about these annual crops will depend on the kinds that your family will eat and, therefore, will enjoy caring for. Also, to some degree, it depends on the amount of space that you can spare.

Different Plots, Different Crops

Here we come to the dilemma imposed by the shrinking lot sizes of homes throughout the metropolitan area. Where most homeowners a generation ago considered a quarter-acre lot to be the norm and a half-acre not unusual, this is not the case today; many home sites are much smaller. Finding enough open space to grow fruits and vegetables to meet the fresh produce needs for a small family has meant a vast change in garden planning and planting. We are fast changing from row culture to so-called "square foot" or intensive garden culture. These methods are adaptations of techniques developed by French market gardeners with small land holdings over the last 2 centuries. Intensive cultivation, close spacing, and successive replantings of crops in the same space are combined with the use of special portable materials to control soil and air temperatures in order to stretch the growing season in both directions. These vegetable factories depend entirely on excellent soil preparation and renewal in order to support heavier production.

Contents of the Large Garden

In more conventional row gardening, your choice of vegetables is entirely dependent on the space that you have. In gardens over 1,000 square feet, a full selection of 20-30 edible crops is possible. There is room for onions, early and late cole crops like cabbage and broccoli, several plantings of salad greens and beans, 2 plantings of peas, carrots, and beets, or some early potatoes followed by those vegetables. One 30-foot row can accommodate warm weather crops like peppers, eggplant, and okra for the entire season. All this could be done on 600 square feet, leaving another 400 square feet for vining crops like tomatoes, squashes, melons, or cucumbers, and a 10-by-10 foot block of sweet corn. Fall and winter greens like kale and turnips or spinach could follow the corn crop, while a May-harvested lettuce row could support the herbs and a full-season green like swiss chard. Two rows at the edge of the garden might be devoted to fruit, such as strawberries or raspberries. Such a garden could provide all of the fresh produce for a family of four from May through October, with some left over for entertaining and preservation. The question is who would be there to tend it in today's two-income families?

Thinking Smaller

A garden half that size, 500 square feet, would be able to accommodate everything but large beds of sprawling vines, potatoes, and corn. Tomatoes, which produce more expansively per plant than any other, would still be possible, because six well-tended tomato plants in cages can provide a family of four enough fresh eating for a season. Cucumbers on a trellis or fence slightly shaded by the tomatoes would still be possible. A careful choice of the shortest season varieties would be necessary to ensure 2 or 3 harvests to each row devoted to lettuces, peas, beans, beets, and carrots.

A conventionally planted garden under 200 square feet might well be confined to salad crops, a double row of peas followed by beans, a few eggplants, and peppers to complement six tomatoes, four hills of bush-type summer squash, half a dozen broccoli planted in early spring and mid-July, and a row of carrots and beets, followed by more bush beans planted to ripen in September. With careful planning one end of the garden might be freed in time to broadcast mixed winter greens over a 4-by-10 foot bed in early September. Most of the fresh produce that a family of four would eat could be grown.

To do this kind of planning, you may calculate yields for set row lengths using our Vegetable Planting Guide.

Intensive Gardening

The smallest garden spaces are those areas that have seen the greatest revolution in technique within the last 15 years. Dug deeper, enriched more, planted wider and thicker, and watered by soaking hoses, small spaces can produce 2 or 3 times the yield of row gardening with 25 to 30% more seed and a little less labor.

Dick Raymond, a nationally known advocate of what he calls "wide row" gardening, has calculated that he can grow 144 onion sets in 2 square feet by harvesting two-thirds of them in the first 6 weeks as scallion, eating half the rest as young boiling onions, and leaving the rest evenly spaced to mature to storage size by August. Other crops, peas, broccoli, beans, and carrots also benefit from cooler soil and less weed competition.

For those with access to railroad or landscape ties, raised bed gardening is probably a better choice if space is at a premium. These small beds are easy to work and weed from all sides and can be solidly planted with no loss from soil compaction.

The following suggestions will maximize yield in any type of garden.

◊ Arrange rows or beds so that all crops get maximum sunlight. For example, running rows north to south, or planting the lowest crops the furthest south in the garden.

◊ Choose the driest and warmest part of the site for early spring crops, to be followed by heat-loving summer vegetables in May.

◊ Decide which short-season crops you can grow twice and where there will be space to fit them for successive planting, based on maturity dates for main crops. This is when you will look for varieties of each crop that fit the length of your growing season.

◊ Adjust the width of the rows for different size gardens as well as for different crops. In general the smaller the plot, the more desirable it is to plant a series of wide rows or raised beds to increase yields without wasting space on long paths.

◊ Choose companion crops that can occupy the same areas because of compatible cultural requirements and differences in growth rates. Radishes and carrots are a good example. Radishes mark late germinating carrot rows. They are harvested before carrots need all the sunlight, and pulling them up loosens the soil, so the carrots grow faster.

◊ Arrange the most efficient irrigation plan that fits your schedule and soil requirement. This may require burying a soaker hose under areas with heavy feeding crops, for example, melons, tomatoes, cucumbers, squashes, and corn.

◊ Set aside an area for composting crop residues and/or a cold frame to propagate new bedding plants if space permits.

◊ Order seeds early if you wish to propagate cole crops and other transplants indoors under lights in February and March.

◊ In the spring. plan to improve your soil the first moment you can dig and work your garden. Then, in the fall, ensure each following year's success by sheet composting and rough digging the plot.

Fine Tuning Your Plan

Once the general outline of your plan is set, you might fine tune it with the aid of the species and varietal recommendations in the garden catalogs that arrive in January or by those given in the back of this chapter. Try and save one space for something you have never grown or eaten. Variety is the spice of life. The following hints may help.

Look for species and varieties that are high in essential vitamins and minerals. The leaf crops are especially important in this regard. They take little space and mature rapidly. You could plan to have 1 or 2 available at all times. Carrots, squashes, and tomatoes, with higher levels of vitamin A, are also available.

Avoid those species that do not thrive here. A well-grown artichoke, with our short growing season and heavy soil, will not be worth the effort expended.

Avoid overplanting at any time. Consult the enclosed graphs for approximate yields. Although these are based on row planting, you can figure that wide rows will use 25% more seed and produce plants at 2 to 3 times the rate as a similar length of single row. A conventional 5-foot row of radishes will provide enough for a small family for 2 weeks, about the limit for harvesting the tender, juicy roots. The same amount could be scattered instead among carrots and melons as row markers that provide some insect protection.

Gardeners should never have to eat overripe produce from the home garden. Vegetables at the peak of perfection are the goal. No small family will need more than 4 to 5 hills of summer squash if they want young, tender specimens for the table. Many crops are at their peak for only 2 or 3 weeks. Stagger plantings so new rows ripen as older ones fade. Lettuces, spinach, snap beans, peas, beets, and corn are other good examples.

If you have time to freeze and can, you may plant correspondingly more in the first or main crop planting, except for snap beans, peas, and broccoli, whose fall harvest is often the best of the year. If space to do all you want still eludes you, consider other alternatives.

The Mini-Garden (less than 100 square feet)

A mini-garden usually occupies a few containers, planters, window boxes, or a strip between a patio and a wall. Because of the shallow soil or narrow plots often found in these places, the shallow-rooted salad plants do best here in the spring. Shallow planters warm more quickly in the sun and can often be planted by March 1 in a sheltered spot.

A variety of lettuces and spinach interspersed with spring onion sets and radishes will begin to produce salads in 1 month to 5 weeks. The radishes and spring onions can be pulled first, leaving room for head and leaf lettuces. Leaf lettuces last longer if outer leaves are harvested first, but head lettuces, like buttercrunch, should be harvested whole. By May 1 these first planted spaces will be ready for summer vegetables. In-ground strips may be improved to receive cane fruits, an herb garden, or a few caged tomato plants. Remember that six well-grown tomato plants will provide a family of four with all the salad tomatoes and slicers that they can possibly eat in a season.

Dwarf varieties of other vegetables will be more satisfactory for container mini-gardens. There are at least half a dozen varieties of tomato suitable for the mini-garden, such as Patio, Sugar Lump, Tiny Tim, Tom Thumb. New interest in tiny vegetables for use in gourmet cooking has also resulted in dwarf carrots, cucumbers, cabbages, and smaller squashes and melons. The chief factors for success are well-drained, fertile growing mediums and a watering schedule that matches the evaporation rate of soil in the container. The soil mixes recommended for perennial and annual flowers in the Container Gardening chapter of this book are suitable for growing vegetables. The U.S. Department of Agriculture Garden Bulletin No. 163 contains a lot of specific information about growing edible plants in containers. Small as they are, with the proper care, dwarf vegetables will provide tasty food as well as a fun supplement to your regular shopping.

Landscaping With Food Plants

With today's smaller properties and constraints on time, an efficient use of space will provide you with the most satisfaction. It is sensible to think of permanent plantings of those delicacies that give a sense of luxury and variety to the table.

A grapevine against an unused wall of the house will provide grapes in September and grape leaves for cooking all summer as well as a landscape accent. Raspberries, which bear fruit in spring and fall, are as good a hedge plant as other prickly shrubs and infinitely more delicious. A sunny out-of-the-way spot makes a better asparagus bed than it does a place to store wood. And a dwarf fruit tree is just as lovely as a landscape dogwood, and it pays its keep for the extra trouble that it takes.

A patio planter is an excellent spot to plant enough herbs for year-round use if you harvest to dry and store them when you prune. Strawberries or different color lettuces make an excellent ground cover or edging in the right bed or border. Rhubarb is a striking accent plant in the perennial garden.

And a home owner can extend the fall flowering season by interplanting chrysanthemum beds with large rosettes or annual flowering kale, whose lavender, silver, cream, and green heads last well into winter. The leaves taste as nice in salads as they look.

Start With Your Soil

Once your plan is on graph paper and in your mind, turn your attention to improving your soil. Soil may not always be perfect, but fortunately it can be modified to suit the gardener's needs. Heavy soils can be lightened by mixing in quantities of sand, ashes, peat moss, chopped leaves, spoiled hay, compost, or dehydrated cow manure. Porous sandy or gravelly soils can be made to hold onto nutrients through the addition of the organic ingredients. Wet spots can be raised and drained.

The pH range, which is the measure of soil acidity or alkalinity, can be brought to an optimum slightly acid 6.8 with the addition of ground limestone to sweeten it or the addition of sulphur and peat moss to acidify alkaline soils. All this can be done as the result of soil testing in the late fall when soil is still warm and nutrients can be deeply dug in with a spading fork or a rototiller. Adequate soil test kits are available for under $20.00 from garden centers and hardware stores. They tell you how to take and dry samples of soil from several places in your designated plot prior to testing. By testing yourself you will save from 3 to 4 weeks waiting on results from state soil labs.

Aim to work in up to 6 inches of the organic soil improvements, which is equivalent to one-third, by volume of the top foot of soil.

Over the winter frost action will aerate the soil while the additions are slowly being incorporated by bacterial action. Adding these ingredients will also help to raise the level of the vegetable plot if your sunny area is in a low spot.

Fall is also the time to hoe any raised beds that your want to use for extra early crops that require deep soils with good drainage.

Adequate soil preparation is so central to a gardener's success that you should not attempt to plant without it, even if the idea of having a garden doesn't strike you until late April. Use well-rotted manures and broadcast 10-10-10 over the entire plot before final cultivation to add the nitrogen necessary to help digest the additions into a form which is usable by new plant roots. Then you will be ready to plant according to your garden plan with a realistic hope of success.

The Right Tools for the Job

As pointed out in Chapter 1, there is no substitute for top quality, light hand tools. The ones you are most likely to return to again and again in your vegetable garden are a good garden spade of the shape and size that best fits you, a straight-toothed garden rake, 1 or 2 sharp hoes whose inner edges have been tapered, a trowel, and a set of planting stakes and string with which to line off rows or beds. Add a pair of good gloves, knee pads, a well-designed wheelbarrow or cart, stakes or fencing to support vining crops, a sprayer or duster, and good hoses that will reach all corners of your garden, and you will be set for this and many other seasons.

Intensive Gardening—Space Stretcher

Now is the time to more fully explain intensive gardening techniques, for they can increase yields in any size garden, although they are most useful where space is severely limited.

As the Japanese and French market gardeners have proved, even a 10-by-10 foot plot can be designed and used to produce 2 or even 3 crops from each space over the course of a 6-month season. In-ground storage capacity and careful choice of crops like winter-hardy spinach will stretch the harvest from March up into December.

In general, intensive gardening requires soils prepared 18 inches deep, even though most plants will use only the top 12 inches. In such a garden, seeds are broadcast over a row that is at least as wide as a rake head—16 inches. Rows for bedding transplants can be as wide as 24 inches.

The broadcast seedlings are thinned once when they are about 2 inches high, and then the remaining plants are allowed to grow to cover the surface. The growing plants shade the entire bed, keeping the surface cool and smothering weeds. Larger plants are harvested first, loosening the soil and leaving spaces for the smaller to fill.

In conventional row planting, seedlings are thinned once when they are about 2 inches tall so that the sturdiest specimens are evenly spaced at a recommended growing distances. This important step allows rapid, even growth without undue competition for available nutrients in the root zone.

Onions, peas, and beans are all suitable for this intensive method of broadcast seeding and thinning. So are the leaf crops, everything from lettuces to swiss chard, kale, and

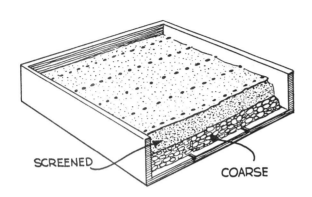

SCREENED

COARSE

The seed flat is used to grow plants for the large garden.
Keep in a cool, sunny window.

spinach. Carrots and beets particularly appreciate raised, wide beds with deeper soils, since the usual unimproved soil is high in clay, and they need sandy loam for rapid, tender growth. It is best to add a little extra sand and humus in the section you save for these. The flavor, shape, and texture will all be better, and onion crops will enjoy these sites another season.

Transplanted vegetables like peppers, eggplant, leeks, broccoli, and cabbage are staggered in the wide rows so that their mature foliage will completely fill the beds.

Potatoes, corn, tomatoes, and any of the other vining crops still produce best when planted in single rows or hills and allowed to cover a bed up to 3 feet in width. Corn, for example, is a heavy feeder which should be planted in rows 12 to 14 inches apart (to form a block at least 5 or 6 feet square), in order for good pollination to occur.

Any vining crop that can be grown with vertical supports is fine for an intensive garden, as long as it can be staked or trained on cages or a trellis. Each heavy feeding transplant is set into the soil with a cupful of compost or has a spoonful of fertilizer scattered an inch beneath the bottom of its planting hole for use by the expanding root system. Liquid foliar feeding or granular superphosphate provides a further boost as fruiting plants begin their flowering. Some people have good luck planting four tomatoes, melons, or cucumbers 1 foot in from each corner of a 3-foot square after the center portion has been further enriched with a large bucket of well-rotted manure. When a large funnel to direct water into the center is in place, the growing plants are tied onto the outside of a large cage of wire placed around the central "feeding station." All the plants are watered centrally by drip irrigation into the funnel throughout the growing season. The foliage remains dry, and it is easy to inspect the plants and to reach the huge harvest.

Plant Support

The small garden needs to make the best use of all available space if it is to provide a bountiful harvest. One way to accomplish this is through the use of supports for many vining and sprawling plants. By growing leggy plants with suitable supports, you can take advantage of vertical space, including walls that may border your garden.

In a few cases metal stakes, wooden fence posts, or trellises should be set up before planting to make a permanent location for grapes, climbing roses, perennial vines, or lima beans which might benefit from being planted in the same place each year. These should be sunk at least 2 feet in the ground into a poured concrete base for stability before stringing the horizontal wire or mesh to support the plants.

Other forms of support are bamboo or sapling poles to make tents for pole beans; brush cuttings for rows of peas or flowers that need delicate but thorough support; and sections of framed fencing or wire cages to hold up tomatoes, squash, or cucumbers. These can be set up just before the plants begin to stretch out and need support.

Fruiting vines do particularly well against a boundary fence where old nylons can be looped under heavy melons or squash and tied to the supporting fence. Hog fencing, available at farm cooperative stores, is particularly useful for all vine cages since the squares are smaller at the bottom, thus allowing young vine tendrils to attach firmly. They are much stronger than commercial tomato cages.

Chicken wire from farm supply or hardware stores can be framed into panels to support a variety of annual vines. Newer plastic netting is available, but may tear when spent vines are removed at the end of each season.

Stakes to support a heavily laden tomato plant, or a tall show-dahlia, should be 2-by-2 inches square and driven 15 to 18 inches deep into the soil next to the plant, before its root system is large enough to damage. South of the city, tobacco stakes are often in abundant supply, as farmers abandon this traditional cash crop.

If you plan to clear your garden each winter to work the soil, you will need to select plant support materials with an eye to the amount of space you have available to store them.

Soil in the intensive garden is always fertilized after each crop is harvested (and its residues removed for composting), then it is immediately replanted or reseeded.

Garden Blankets & Row Covers

By using cloches or garden blankets to break the wind or hold in soil warmth, you extend the growing season in both directions. Gardeners in this area can get active growth from March 1 into November over much of the region.

In the winter the intensive garden soil is tested and renewed. It may take from 3 to 5 pounds of ground limestone per 100 square feet to restore pH to an optimum 6.8 to 7 and as much compost and other organic material as can be dug in or seeded to restore it over the winter.

Such a garden is a veritable vegetable factory, and its compact nature is an advantage, for it is easy to lay out irrigation hoses for the season in or beneath the rows and to work and weed its smaller surface by hand in a short time. Everything is easy to observe and keep track of by spending a relaxing hour after the day's work 3 or 4 times a week.

Cultural Notes

All the basic gardening techniques of transplanting, watering, cultivating, sidedressing, and mulching are thoroughly explained in previous chapters. Because most vegetables are annuals, the planting of seeds is covered thoroughly in the sections on Annuals and Container Gardening.

To permit root expansion in heavy soils, fill a deep (4") furrow with compost before sowing seed.

Thinning

Thinning as a basic technique is worth explanation here. Each type of plant needs a certain amount of space for its root system to gather enough nutrients for rapid unimpeded growth, which produces the fastest and tastiest food. Most direct seeding will produce three or four times more plants than are needed, which is why you can grow an entire bed of transplants in a flat the size of a paper napkin.

You must be willing to remove three out of four of these new seedlings so that the rest will thrive. A vigorous, shallow raking to destroy extra plants and germinated weed seeds works well. So does using nail scissors to cut tiny hairlike seedlings like carrots, lettuces, and onions at the correct intervals.

Corn, beets, tomatoes, and extra vining crops planted in hills should be pulled out by hand. Some large seeds like beans and peas are usually planted at the correct distance and need no further thinning, unless extra has been planted for persistent crows or rodents.

When transplanting young plants, it helps to make a planting board, notched on one long side at 2-inch intervals, to place them evenly at the proper distance from each other.

What Grows Best When

It is worth noting that some vegetables grow better at certain times of the year and should be planted at these times for best results. You already know that lettuces, peas, scallions, leeks, spinach, the root crops like beets and carrots, all the cole crops including cauliflower, and the so-called fall greens like kale, mustard, rape, and turnips prefer cool soil. All are usually planted to ripen when conditions are favorable.

Leeks and onions, for example, take a long time to mature. Onions are planted early in the season, so they can be harvested when thin and mild for salads, eaten later as boiled vegetables with new peas, and left to mature in late summer, so they can be used dry during the winter.

The many kinds of lettuce and spinach will flourish as long as the weather is cool, and then will bolt within the week in which temperatures climb over 85° Fahrenheit. They are planted in early spring, therefore, and replanted again late in the summer when they can sprout quickly and mature slowly as it cools.

Broccoli and cauliflower also bolt and spring crops should be planned to harvest in early June.

Many of the warm season crops do not do well when it cools. Only lima and snap beans, and members of the solanum family (eggplants, peppers, and tomatoes) will go on producing into late September. The cucurbits (cucumbers, vining squashes, and particularly melons) all need to set fruit before mid-summer for maximum production and flavor. For this reason most of them are planted once, although some gardeners stagger their summer squash plantings in case the first crop is diminished by squash borers in late July.

Beans and corn are also planted successively from late April to mid July, so that the last crop ripens by mid September.

With crops that are not replanted, it is very important to harvest frequently so that the plants continue to try and reproduce themselves. Cucumbers and squash should be harvested when small and firm with immature seeds.

Since melons are not delicious until their seeds are ripe, the vines "turn off" early and stop producing after the first fruits mature.

Legumes will continue to produce well for 3 or 4 weeks if they are picked frequently.

Some plants (for example, peppers, lima beans, and eggplants), will not set flowers at temperatures much over 90° Fahrenheit. They will resume when the heat wave is over.

Planting the Fall Garden

If you want to grow crops up until frost and beyond, you must start planning the fall garden by the middle of June when your first crops are being harvested. The list of fall crops is long. Chinese cabbage, savoy and red cabbages, brussels sprouts, broccoli, cauliflowers, collard, and kale are only a few. Mustard greens, turnips, radishes, peas and spinach, late carrots, beets, and snap beans are other possibilities. Fall broccoli and snap beans are usually best because their chief insect pests, the cabbage looper and the Mexican bean beetles, have population explosions in late June that stress these crops. Fall broccoli is seeded when the spring crop comes in June, but not transplanted to the garden until late July. Planted at the same time, beets and carrots will ripen and keep in the ground well into winter.

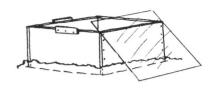

Crop Rotation

Here we should mention the principles of crop rotation, which will do so much to prevent problems with soil deficiencies, disease, and insect build-up in your garden in future years. Crop rotation means that you should alternate crops, depending upon the nutrients they take from the soil. For example, leafy greens that need high nitrogen should be followed by plants such as beans and other legumes, which fix nitrogen in nodes on their roots and are ideal to follow leaf crops. In turn, because they improve the soil, you might want to cut off the spent plants and plant a heavy feeding crop like corn in the same spot the next year.

Each of these 3 species attracts entirely different pests, so a population build-up of any one sort is prevented.

At this point, the garden plan becomes a good planning tool for the next season.

Keeping Soil Moist

The biggest problem is getting fall crops to germinate well in hot, dry soil, and the solution is simple. In spring you plant seeds on warm ridges when the soil is cold, in summer you plant deeper in trenches to conserve soil moisture. Trampling freshly sown seed firmly into the soil is good practice for summer sowing.

Keeping the soil evenly moist in the middle of summer is the key to continued production. If the rains fail, your summer garden will need an inch a week, whether by sprinkler or drip irrigation.

A good rule of thumb is to water in the morning before 10 AM, so foliage will dry thoroughly, and work the soil in the evening. To measure a thorough watering once a week, set out a tuna can within the sprinkler arc. When it is at least half full, that area is watered. Soaking hoses will take about 2 hours to release an inch of water along their length.

Protecting Your Plants

In protecting edible plants it is crucial to consider the safety of the eater as well as the eaten. Please read the chapter on pesticides for specific recommendations on those pesticides you can safely use, and when you purchase them read the labels again to be sure of the solution strength and length of time that should expire between application and the harvest. Prevention should always be your first line of defense.

The insects you are most likely to encounter are, in order of their appearance: root maggots, leaf hoppers, potato bugs, aphids, cabbage loopers, cut worms, Mexican bean beetles, cucumber beetles, stink bugs, squash borers, tomato hornworms, corn ear worms, and red spider mites.

Root maggots attack the roots of onions and radishes. These pests can be prevented by planting the vegetables in light, well-drained soil. A sprinkling of cayenne pepper at the base of plants in mid-April also inhibits the fly that uses the onion crops to lay its eggs.

A sprinkling of woodashes, soap, or horticultural oil sprays help deter chewing insects, which are the caterpillars, leafhoppers, beetle larvae, ear worms, and squash borer,; and some sucking insects like aphids. Mineral oil applied inside the tips of corn ears after the silk has emerged will deter corn ear worms from entering.

Parasitic wasps that control tomato hornworm, and clutches of voracious lady beetles and lace wing larvae, are available by mail order in the spring. They are of more help to the experienced gardener familiar with the appearance times of pests in his or her plot, because the ordered insects will not remain in the garden if food is unavailable to keep them there. The best natural control is Bacillus thurengiensis, a caterpillar-specific bacteria that safely paralyzes their gut when they eat sprayed foliage. This will not work on cut worms or borers, which live below ground and emerge at night to feed. To thwart the worms, small collars of newsprint or foil can be wrapped around the stems of transplants to extend 2 inches above and below the soil line. Sprinkling flour on foliage is a reasonably effective and safe way to deter swift leaf hoppers and flea beetles in addition to interplanting pyrethrum daisies. Insecticidal soap and refined oil sprays also give nontoxic control by drying or smothering many mites, aphids, and scales.

Arguably, the most important insects to control are aphids and cucumber beetles, because they spread sooty mildews and fungal wilts that affect cucumbers and other vining crops. Planting radish seeds on squash and cucumber hills does repel some beetles. Regular spraying of preventive fungicides like benomyl are necessary in this climate to supplement insect control on these crops; of course, the purchase of varieties resistant to verticilium and fusarium wilts is crucial.

Some Helpful Hints

Look for VFN and mosaic and rust resistance in the descriptions of crops before you buy. The more resistance, the less damage from infection.

To prevent spreading fungal spores from one

Trampling the freshly sown seed firmly into the soil is good practice for summer sowings.

planting to another, don't work the garden if foliage is wet.

If bean beetles have riddled an entire planting of snap beans, carefully remove all plant residues from the soil to remove eggs and larvae before replanting.

Always rotate your crops as much to discourage buildups of a particular insect pest in one spot as to avoid depleting the soil of particular nutrients that one crop may require.

If you follow sound cultural practices and prevent weather conditions from unduly stressing your garden, most of these pests will do minimal damage to your crops.

The following table indicates approximate planting time for specific fall harvesting dates of 13 popular vegetables. Some, like spinach, could last through the winter to make the first crop of the next spring. The plantings are timed to allow harvest of the more tender vegetables 2 weeks before the first expected frost date in outlying areas. When planting for a late garden, it is important to allow a little extra time to maturity, because the day length gradually decreases after mid summer.

VEGETABLE PLANTING GUIDE

Vegetable	Sow Seed	Set Plant	Harvest
Broccoli*	June 15	July 15	September 25
Brussels Sprouts*	June 1	July 1	October 15
Cabbage*	June 15	July 15	October 1
Cauliflower*	July 1	August 15	October 15
Collards*	July 15	August 20	October 15
Endive*	August 1	—	September 15-November 1
Kale!	August 1-30	—	October 15
Lettuces	August 15-September 1	—	October 1
Peas	August 15-September 1	—	October 15
Winter Radishes	August 15-30	—	October 15
Spinach!	August 15-September 15	—	September 25-November 15
Turnips	August 15-30	—	October 15-30

*—Start in seed bed and transplant
!—Improved or unaffected by frost

VEGETABLE CROPS

Here is a list of vegetable crops and their individual cultural requirements. The latest varietal recommendations are by John Edwards of the Men's Garden Club of Montgomery County and Adrienne Cook of The Washington Post. They have been successfully planted by club members and other area gardeners.

ASPARAGUS
When to Plant: Late March to mid-April, October-November.
Roots: 1 year old, set 6-8 inches deep, 18 inches apart. Rows are 3 feet apart.
Soil: Rich, sandy, fertile.
Plant: 24 crowns for average family of four.
Variety: Mary Washington rust resistant, Jersey Knight all male hybrid.

Asparagus is a perennial vegetable that produces for so many years that it requires a permanent site at the edge of the garden. Ordinarily the roots are planted in an open trench that has been deeply dug and heavily improved with well-rotted manure or compost and bonemeal below the planting level. To do this you should open up a trench 2 feet wide, removing the top 8 inches. Fork manure and compost thoroughly into the subsoil, packing it down slightly and adding an inch of the topsoil before fanning out the roots of the 1-year-old crowns in a diamond pattern onto the surface. In other words, stagger the plantings, starting 6 inches from each edge of the trench to fit 10 roots in a 10-foot row.

Carefully add 2 inches of improved topsoil from the side of the trench to just cover the crowns. As the new shoots grow, gradually fill the trench, until you finish with a wide mounded row. Mounding is advisable, because it helps to keep the bed well-drained. Standing water and a sunken bed keeps the soil cold and retards early spring growth.

Asparagus should not be harvested the first season. It should not be cut heavily the second. Just take the large spears. The lush top growth is necessary to promote stronger root development that will provide 20 years or more of heavy cropping. When it matures for full harvesting in 3 years, 24 row feet, or 24 crowns, ought to provide 6 weeks worth of fresh eating, at least 10 bunches weighing 1½ pound apiece.

Asparagus surfaces early. Late in April fat spears will begin to poke up. Using an asparagus knife, they should be cut when the tips are still tight, or snapped above the surface of the ground, to avoid injuring other shoots. Stop cutting by June when the stalks begin to be thinner and more fibrous. Protect the resulting lacy foliage from the larvae of the common asparagus beetle by spraying with Bacillus Thuringiensis (Dipel, Thuricide) or insecticidal soap. These gray insignificant worms can strip the cambium off the slender stalks in a week or two.

The productivity of an established bed depends

Pre-planting soil preparation is important to the life and productivity of the asparagus bed.

entirely on your keeping the bed clear of competing weeds and grass and on annual heavy feeding. In the fall give a good top dressing of 2 or 3 inches of well-rotted manure. In the first dry spell of March broadcast a quart of 10-10-10 for every 5 feet of row after you cut the dry stalks and remove weeds. A shallow cultivation at that time will help warm the soil surface and speed the harvest. Weed and straw mulch the bed after harvest to deter competition.

Growing asparagus plants from seed is usually considered too time-consuming for the home gardener. The new all male hybrid roots now coming onto the market are much more prolific. Strains of Jersey Knight, Jersey Giant, and others should be increasingly available. A more productive French strain , *larac*, may be obtained from specialty growers.

BUSH BEANS & POLE BEANS

When to Plant: Bush/pole beans: late April until early August, every 3 weeks; limas, May to mid-June. Shell beans same as limas.

Seed: Bush/pole beans: plant 3 to 4 inches apart is wide row or in straight rows 18 inches apart. Sow 1 inch deep in spring, 2 inches deep in hot weather.

Soil: Improved garden soil.

Yield: Bushel equals 24 pounds, 40 pints frozen, 16 quarts canned; Limas equals 32 pounds, 14 pints frozen, 8 quarts canned.

Species: Green snap beans, wax beans, broad beans, bush limas, shell beans.

Bush Bean Cultivars:

Green Snap—Topcrop (50 days), Tendercrop (54 days), white-seeded Provider (55 days), Blue Lake 274 (55 days), Bountiful Stringless (50 days), Derby (57 days).

Yellow Wax—Cherokee (52 days), Goldcrop (65 days).

Broad Beans—Roma II (59 days).

Bush Limas—Henderson (65 days), Fordhook 242 (75 days) stands heat.

Shell Beans—Edible soybeans, Prize (85 days) late crop, Envy (75 days).

Pole Bean Cultivars:

Green Snap—Blue Lake Stringless (60 days), Fortex (60 days), Kentucky Wonder (65 days), Scarlet Runner (70 days), Yard Long Beans (80 days).

Yellow Snap—Burpee's Golden (60 days).

Broad Beans—Romano (60 days), Early Riser(45 days).

Lima Beans—Sieva (78 days), King of the Garden (88 days).

Shell Beans—Jacob's Cattle Bean, or any of a number of long-season drying varieties. Limas can also be dried. Appropriate for the large garden.

Beans are the backbone of the garden. They thrive most of the season if they can be protected from bean beetles and drought. They ripen swiftly and continuously over a 3 or 4 week season, necessitating harvest every 3 or 4 days. For that reason, you should plant as much as you can handle comfortably at any one time. Beans do not wait.

If you want to eat or preserve 25 pounds of bush beans in a 4-week period, you should plant no more than 20 to 25 row feet. If space is tight, a 16-inch-wide row 10 to 12 feet long is more than adequate.

A better choice might be to plant successive plots or longer lasting planting of pole beans or limas. In general green and yellow pole beans can be counted on for a full month or more, while limas mature late and keep going until October.

Beans are a warm weather crop that should not be planted before late April or early May. Limas require even warmer soil and may rot before they germinate, unless the soil is over 65° Fahrenheit. Mid-May is early enough in colder areas. Soak lima seeds in warm water for quick germination if you want beans by early August.

Legume innoculants are often sold with bean seeds to ensure that beans germinate well in new ground. After a plot has been through several crop rotations, they are probably not necessary. Limas, however, are well-known to love being planted in the same row, so it may be worth setting up permanent poles at the north end of the garden so these tall plants do not shade other vegetables. Limas also love a little boron. One tablespoon of borax added to a sprinkling can of water before flowering will treat a 50-foot row and increase yields.

Some beans have both pole and bush forms, so you can decide what best suits you. The choice between pole and bush depends largely on the effort required to provide support. Most pole varieties require a week longer to produce, although Burpee's Golden Wax produces in 50 days. Most pole beans will outyield bush beans and bear longer.

A simple support for pole beans may be made from a few stout stakes, guide wires at top and bottom, and laced garden twine. Anchor firmly as protection against summer winds; bean vines are heavy.

Gardeners can avoid rust problems on bean foliage by working around the crop when leaves are dry and examining the undersides of leaves often for the yellow egg cases of the Mexican bean beetle. To control this pest, a

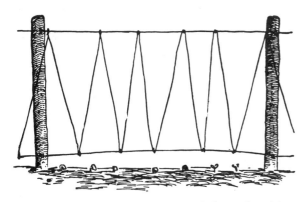

A simple support for pole beans may be made from a few stakes, some wire and string. Anchor firmly as protection against summer winds.

duster with an extension tube is used applied up through the foliage when the air is calm. Spray at 10 to 14 day intervals up to a week before harvest.

Mosaic and anthracnose will not be a problem if you buy resistant varieties and have a garden plot with good air circulation.

Beans should be harvested continuously when snap beans are tender and stringless, and when limas have just plumped out their furry pods. Shell beans, of course, should be left to mature on the vines. Edible soy beans are ready when the pods turn brown, although they may be harvested earlier for cooking fresh.

All bush beans should be cut from the row when the harvest is over, leaving the roots with their fixed nitrogen to be used by the next crop. Rake up dried leaves from the row to get rid of any insects and compost if foliage is healthy.

BEETS
When to Plant: Late February in cold frame for early crop, April-May for summer crop, mid-July for fall crop.
Seed: 1 inch deep, 2 inches apart. Rows, 15 inches apart or broadcast in wide row and thinned for greens.
Soil: Rich, sandy, moist.
Yield: 1 bushel equals 52 pounds, 35-40 pints frozen, 20 quarts canned, equals 10-15 pounds greens, 10-15 pints frozen.
Varieties: Pacemaker III (50 days), Ruby Queen (56 days), Warrior (57 days), Cylindra (60 days), Lutz Winter Keeper (80 days).

Beets are thought of as difficult in this area, although they grow beautifully on the sandy Eastern Shore. They are so tasty and sweet when well-grown, with the added bonus of fresh green leaves for cooking, that it is worth digging in sand and compost in a couple of places to make them happy. Besides, your carrots and gourmet onion crops will also be overjoyed in these same spots.

Beets have multiple seeds, which explains why 1 ounce yields nearly 75 pounds of beets and greens. They need even soil moisture to germinate, and can be overplanted with

a sprinkling of radish seeds to help break the surface, so the beets can follow. Do not bother to transplant them, as you will be unhappy with the results, however, they may be grown in an unused cold frame for a late April harvest. Beets profit from an application of 5-10-10 or woodashes worked into the soil before planting to stimulate root growth. Since they do not keep their tenderness and quality for long in hot weather, it is best to make several small plantings for continuous harvest. The last planting should be Lutz Winter Keeper, an old variety with delicious flavor, large roots, and low fiber that stores for a month or two in mulched ground.

Beets, thankfully, have few enemies, except for leafhoppers that may chew some of the leaves. Again, a sprinkle of soil-sweetening woodashes or a light soap spray usually takes care of the problem. You may begin to harvest them when they are 2 inches in diameter after thinning them to that spacing when they are about 2 inches high.

BROCCOLI
When to Plant: Set out transplants in late March for spring crop, mid-July for fall crop. Allow 4 weeks to grow transplants from seed.
Plants: Set in 18 inches to 2 feet apart in conventional row, 12 inches apart in staggered formation on a 24-inch wide row bed. Interplant with leaf lettuce.
Soil: Rich, moist, well-drained for best results.
Cultivars: Green Comet (55 days), Goliath (55 days), Green Duke (60 days), Calabrese, sprouting type (65 days).

Broccoli is an increasingly popular garden vegetable, even though spring crops are stressed by our early heat waves and despite its popularity with aphids and cabbage loopers.

If insects are regularly controlled with Bacillus Thurengiensis or soap sprays, this excellent vegetable will make good spring growth in the cooler parts of the region.

In warmer areas it makes a delicious fall crop that produces well until late October. Look for a cross with cauliflower that gives a taste of that vegetable without the blanching problems caused by hot weather.

To prevent soil-borne diseases it is important to plant all cole crops in a spot that was not used to grow them the previous year.

Broccoli transplants are easy to obtain now, so they can be planted in early April, but they are just as easy to grow in a sunny, cool window or under lights. Allow about 5 weeks to ready them for the garden after planting them individually in Jiffy peat pots.

Set them into well-fertilized soil after they have hardened off for a week in a cold frame or an unheated light garage. Plants will benefit from a half cup of compost at the bottom of each planting hole and a paper cutworm collar that extends 2 inches below the surface when the hole is filled. Pinch off half of the young leaves when you transplant to prevent stress on the roots as they take off and protect them

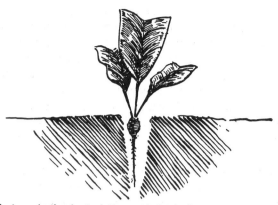

In transplanting beets, lettuce and chard, disturb the roots as little as possible, remove from a third to a half of the leaf area and shade for a few days.

from frost and cabbage loopers with a translucent garden blanket.

Broccoli need side-dressing with 5-10-5 scratched within 6 inches of the stem every 3 weeks as heads form. These should be harvested with a sharp knife while the buds are tight and blue-green. Heading varieties like Green Comet and Goliath will have one main crop followed by sprouts that form further down in the leaf axils. Sprouting varieties produce many smaller heads along the stem.

You can grow your own transplants for fall broccoli, either in a cooler portion of the garden shaded by taller plants, or in a cold frame with the top removed. Late season transplants are not always as easy to find.

BRUSSELS SPROUTS
When to Plant: Sow seed in June, set out plants August 1.
Seed: ¼ inch deep in propagation bed, transplant to 18 inches apart in the row.
Soil: Well-enriched garden loam.
Yield: ½ to 1 quart per plant.
Varieties: Jade Cross E (95 days), Long Island Improved (90 days), Captain Marvel (63 days).

Removal of lower leaves from time to time aids "sprout" formation. Harvest sprouts before outer leaves begin to turn yellow with age.

Brussels sprouts are not dependable in the warmer parts of the area where August and September are too hot for good growth. But the fine flavor and hardiness of the plant make it a desirable winter vegetable.

This member of the cabbage family has a delicate distinctive flavor of its own, particularly if it is quickly stir-fried or steamed until it is barely tender. The plant is not injured by hard frosts and will continue to grow and develop until the ground freezes.

Requiring a long season to reach maturity, the seeds should be sown in a prepared bed that has some shade in the afternoon. They will be ready to transplant if necessary by August 1, or they can be thinned to grow on in their original location. If transplanted, the lower leaves should be removed to lessen the strain on the root system and plants should be well watered and shaded the first few days. An occasional side dressing at 3-week intervals of nitrate or ammonium sulphate at the rate of 1 pound per 100 row feet will boost development. Clean cultivation and regular watering are necessary for good growth. Straw mulch can help retain soil moisture during August and early September and soil warmth after that.

The same insects and diseases that attack broccoli and cabbage are common to brussels sprouts, and woodashes, soap spray, and Dipel or Thuricide are equally effective.

Removal of lower leaves from time to time aids sprout formation up the stalk.

Sprouts should be harvested when they are 1 to 1½ inches across but before the outer leaves turn yellow.

CABBAGES
When to Plant: Set out in late March for the early crop. Seed from June 15 to July 15 for fall crop.
Plant: 10 to 20 inches apart in single or staggered 36-inch wide row.
Soil: Fertile sweet soil, moist, high in nitrogen.
Yield: 15 cabbages from an 8-foot row, 20 Chinese type.
Varieties:
Green—Stonehead (75 days), Emerald Cross (68 days);
Red—Ruby Perfection (85 days), Ruby Ball (65);
Savoy—Savoy Ace (85 days), Chieftain (85 days);
Chinese—Jade Pagoda-Michichli cross, spring (60 days), Monument, fall (70 days);
Napa Type—Two Seasons, spring, fall (62 days);
Pak Choy (60 days), Prize Choy (50 days).

Because it is essentially a cool weather crop, most gardeners should include a few head cabbages in their early plantings. Cool, moist weather and well-enriched garden soil are necessary for it to make rapid succulent growth. It is a good spring crop in the cooler parts of this area, although it seems to do better in the fall for gardeners who have warm, sandy soil if they irrigate. Some of the trouble people have with this crop can be traced to our hot, dry summers and failure to seek out "yellows"-resistant varieties. It is also important that soil be well limed with a pH around 6.8.

Cabbage seed should be started early enough indoors so that stocky transplants are hardened off by late March or early April. Allow 5 weeks. The more common green varieties will be available in flats at many garden centers. Late crop plantings may be gotten from seeds sown out doors in June.

In setting the plants it is essential that the roots be kept covered and the soil on them disturbed as little as possible. Therefore, they are good candidates to be grown in compressed peat pellets before transplanting. Water with a little ground limestone in it will meet the seedlings' need for sweet soil.

Set the plants deeper than they came from flat or bed with a little cutworm collar of paper around the seedlings. Remove all but the top 2 or 3 leaves and shade for several days if it is bright and windy.

Of the numerous cabbage pests that trouble these succulent plants, all, except for the cabbage maggot, eat the leaves. The leaf eaters are easily controlled with Dipel or Thuricide. If cabbage maggots have been in your garden in the past, a small square of tar paper may be slit to slide around the stem of the plant, so that creosote fumes will repel the maggots.

Except for the yellows, cabbage diseases are best controlled through rotating the crop. Do not plant cabbages in the same spot more often than once in 3 years. The soil under cabbages can be drenched in commercial copper solutions to control seed-borne diseases.

Use a fertilizer high in nitrogen for good leaf development. One or two side dressings of sulphate of ammonia or chicken manure will supplement a standard fertilizer mixture like 5-10-5.

The fall crop needs to be planted early enough to mature before freezing weather, although heading cabbage can take light frost. Transplanting in late June is the best idea

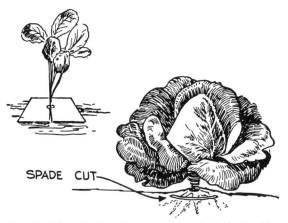

In soils infested with cabbage maggot protect plants with squares of tarred paper. Cutting roots on one side with a spade will stop splitting.

(from seeds sown outdoors on to a peat pellet in late May). Heading cabbages can be mulched heavily with straw well into November. To prevent large specimens from splitting, root prune one side of the roots with a spade. Later in the winter, cabbages can be stored upside down in a shallow trench or cold frame, and covered with a few inches of soil.

Gardeners with small plots ought to plant 2 or 3 different types of cabbage to prolong the harvest season. The looser Chinese cabbages, Napa and Pak Choy, mature faster. These so-called Oriental cabbages are more closely related to mustard, but they are often planted and grown in the same manner as the other cabbages. Most are planted in mid-July for early fall harvest. Several varieties, however, may be planted in the spring as well, though, for best flavor, they should be harvested as soon as possible before hot weather sets in. They are spaced closer because their growth habit is more upright.

Chewing insects can be controlled with an insecticidal soap spray, which should be thoroughly rinsed off before use in cooking or salads. Many people who cannot tolerate the sulphur content of regular cabbages can eat Chinese cabbage, without distress, which is one reason why this class of oriental green is receiving more attention from home gardeners.

CARROTS

When to Plant: From early April at 3- to 4-week intervals until July 15.

Seed: Broadcast ¼ inch deep with radishes after soaking in water overnight and rinsing.

Soil: Light, sandy loam.

Yield: ½ ounce seed equals 2 bushels, 75 pints frozen.

Varieties: Royal Chantenay (68 days), Danvers Half Long (70 days), Thumbelina (60 days), A Plus Hybrid, high vitamin A, (71 days).

As a crop for the home garden, carrots have almost as many uses as tomatoes. They are high in vitamins A, B, and C, and now they have been discovered to be one of the vegetables, along with broccoli and kale, whose consumption may inhibit cancers of the digestive tract.

But carrots are not easy to grow in heavy soils. Where there are clods or stones, roots may be small, deformed, and lacking in sweetness.

Compost, coal ashes, and sand may all be worked into the soil a foot deep to help it become loose and friable as these root crops like it. A cup of mixed bonemeal and superphosphate for each 10-foot row is also helpful for a high pH and swift root development.

Contrary to legend, carrot seeds are easy to germinate if you soak them overnight and rinse well before planting. The old trick of pouring boiling water on the row once it was planted accomplished the same purpose, namely washing off a chemical germination inhibitor.

Once the tiny seeds germinate (all you will need for a 2-by-4 foot bed is a heaping teaspoon of seed), you should thin with a rake to about 1 inch apart. Other thinning of "carettes" for early eating will provide room for larger roots.

Once the ground can be worked, it is desirable to plant every 3 or 4 weeks until mid-summer. For this reason most plantings should be small so carrots can be used at the peak of flavor, although you may wish to increase the last one in July to provide enough for winter storage. In this climate, carrots can be mulched in the row to last well into the winter. All the listed varieties are suitable for planting in heavy soils.

If insects or disease should attack the crop, dust or spray with BT, insecticidal soap, or neem oil. Raised beds and good drainage will prevent outbreaks of root maggots or nematodes.

Most carrots are harvested and eaten fresh, but pit storage is satisfactory in the worst part of the winter, if the pit is dug below the frost line in well-drained soil, filled with fresh sand, and if the carrots are pointed down with their tops removed. Alternatively, they may be stored in boxes filled with clean damp sand or peat moss in an unheated garage.

CHARD
When to Plant: Early April.
Seed: ½ inch deep, thin to 12 inches apart.
Soil: Variety of improved garden soils.
Yield: 1 bunch equals 12 to 14 pounds over the season.
Varieties: Lucullus, green (50 days), Rhubarb Chard, red (60 days), Fordhook Giant (60 days).

Chard is the most productive of the summer leafy greens. It may be harvested from early summer until frost. It is a good source of vitamin A, with fair amounts of C and riboflavin and good quantities of essential minerals like iron.

Frequently known as swiss chard, this tall, handsome green resembles beet greens. Its handsomest form is rhubarb chard, which is often found in ornamental annual plantings as well as in the garden.

Sow the seeds no more than ½ inch deep in mid-

Discard old chard leaves, use tender young leaves. Careful cutting does not interfere with new growth.

April. Since the seeds germinate in clusters, seedlings will need to be thinned to a final distance of 10 to 12 inches. These thinnings can be transplanted if the tops are reduced by one-third.

Because the flavor and tenderness of the stalks depend on rapid succulent growth, rich soil is desirable. One or two sidedressings with 5-10-5 or compost will keep the growth vigorous. Frequent shallow cultivation and feeding with liquid manure every 2 or 3 weeks will maximize yields.

Harvesting is done by removing the outer leaves as needed. Overmature, stringy leaves should be discarded; tender, newer growth is more desirable. Since the vegetable is high in iron, and its taste grows more pronounced with long cooking, it is best quickly stir-fried or steamed.
It is delicious as a mild curry stir-fried in olive oil with peanuts and raisins. The leaves may be used alone, as may the stems, or both may be chopped for cooking.

COLLARDS
When to Plant: Early April, early August.
Seed: Plant in rows 2 inches apart, thin to 6 inches apart.
Soil: Sandy loam.
Yield: 2 pounds per row foot.
Variety: Hicrop Hybrid (75 days).

Collards are the other summer green, famous in soul food cookery. The leaves take to long simmering and have a smoky distinctive flavor. Best of all, the crop is hardy, heat resistant and nearly pest free. Side dressing with nitrogen or compost when plants are 6 inches high will help speed growth of the large tender leaves.

Leaves are cut from the outer portions of the tall plants as needed and cut free of the center rib before boiling with bacon or a ham hock.

Control flea beetles with insecticidal soap spray or neem oil and cabbage loopers with BT.

CORN
When to Plant: Every 2 weeks from late April or early May until mid-July.
Seed: 1 inch deep, 14 inches apart in minimum 5-foot square blocks. Separate extra sweet varieties so they do not cross pollinate with less sweet ones.
Soil: Fertile garden loam.
Yield: 1 to 2 ears per stalk, 8-ounce seed yields 80-90 plants.
Varieties, In order of maturity:
Early Extra Sweet, Butter Fruit (68 days); Butter and Sugar (73 days); Honey and Pearl (76 days); Silverado (83 days); How Sweet It Is (80 days); Silver Queen (92 days). Isolate all of these varieties from each other.

Although sweet corn takes too much space even by the standards of 20 years ago, gardeners enjoy it so much that they will be tempted to stretch a point and grow a block.

A block is recommended because it has been proved more efficient for good pollination to grow corn in a prepared bed at least 5-by-5 feet square. Commercial growers plant corn 14 inches apart, knowing they will never have to get in to work the crop until harvest. The home gardener must plant blocks that he or she can reach into with a narrow hoe to weed and sidedress. A 6-foot width is about the largest planting you can manage by hand. By planting small blocks often, a small but continuous harvest is ensured from the middle of July until early September. Most corn remains in top condition only a few days, so this strategy also ensures quality.

The varieties mentioned here are all the newer varieties, some of which are super sweet hybrids and hold their sweetness for up to 48 hours when picked. Some people still subscribe to putting the kettle on to boil before running to the garden, but it is increasingly unnecessary.

Corn is sidedressed twice with 10-10-10, the first time when the soil is pulled up around each 3- to 4-inch tall seedling to smother young weeds. You can sprinkle 1 cup of granulated fertilizer for every 10 feet of row or about 2 cups for a 5-by-5 foot block just before you cultivate to uproot weeds. During cultivation snug extra soil from between the plants up around each stem to give it support. Corn appreciates clean cultivation and the lack of competition.

A second feeding of the same amount of fertilizer is sprinkled over the bed when the corn is at the tassel stage, and it is gently scratched in with a narrow onion hoe so as not to cut the shallow corn roots.

Gardeners no longer sucker corn (that is, pull extra small stalks away from the base of larger plants). But they must be vigilant to spot the ravages of the corn earworm, which eats the kernels at the tips of ears. The cheapest and best prevention is to put drops of mineral oil at the base of the silks while they are pollinating.

Rotenone may be dusted on plants that are young in mid-July to deter Japanese beetles. The Kurstaki strain of BT will control European corn borer, which goes in through the husk if you forget to remove half of the corn tassels before the pollen shed.

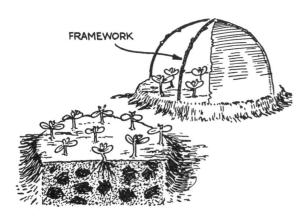

FRAMEWORK

The spadeful of manure under the soil makes the cucumber "hill."

You will know your corn is ripe when the silk begins to turn dark brown and dry, and the ear feels plump and filled out to the tip. Some people prefer corn that is a little immature for its delicate crunchiness. An overripe ear has a doughy and waxy taste and texture, familiar to anyone who has ordered corn from a fast food place.

Once you have grown your own, you will never be satisfied with commercially raised corn again.

CUCUMBERS
When to Plant: Late April to early July.
Seed: Plant in hills 3 to 6 feet apart or one 4-by-4 foot bed, enclosed by a supporting fence.
Soil: Rich, sandy loam.
Yield: 10 pounds per hill.
Varieties: Victory (60 days), Sweet Slice (62 days), Sweet Success (58 days), Liberty, for pickles (55 days); Wilt Resistant—Gemini (52 days), Supersett, double hybrid.

Cucumbers have few nutritional virtues, and they suffer here from wilts and viruses, but everybody loves them, so they are worth trying to grow well. Nothing says summer so well as a big bowl of slicers in vinegar or yoghurt, garlic, and mint.

Unless they are grown in cages or on framed chicken wire panels, conventional varieties require considerable space and are not recommended for the smaller garden.

Their successful culture here depends on rich, sandy soil, which is well-drained, so they are usually planted in hills or raised beds deeply enriched with manure when the soil warms in May. Each hill gets 5 seeds and a few interplanted radish seeds to repel the striped cucumber beetles that spread bacterial and fungal wilts.

Some highly productive varieties must be planted with a pollinator to fertilize the all-female plants. This seed should be marked with a row marker and not thinned.

Set any trellis or support next to the hills when the plants are quite small so as not to compact or disturb the roots.

When the seedlings appear, they are thinned to the 2 strongest in each hill and the surface is worked regularly to keep the loose, light soil that promotes rapid growth.

Cucumbers do appreciate a light covering like a translucent garden blanket and this may help to prevent infestation until the developing blossoms need pollination. They have also been known to do better when planted to the north or east of tomato plants so that they can receive some afternoon shade.

As the vines expand they should be gently guided onto their supports so tendrils will take hold. Cultivation should be reduced to hand weeding so as not to disturb plants on the ground, and a straw mulch can be applied at this time to keep soil cool and moist and to control weeds.

Regular spraying with Bioneem to foil beetles is advisable until blossoms show; Sevin is toxic to the bees, that help to pollinate the vines. Start a preventive spray schedule with summer oil spray or benomyl, to prevent infection of the vines through harvest.

Cucumbers will produce well for 3 to 4 weeks if they are well irrigated. This is one crop that appreciates regular drip irrigation with soaking hose, which has the added bonus of keeping the foliage dry.

Harvest frequently and thoroughly to promote high production, being sure you get all the fruit off the vine. As with all fruiting crops, maturing seeds "turn off" the production mechanism of the plant. Cut the young cucumbers off the vine. This will prevent tearing the vines, particularly those that are vertical. Harvest in the evening when fruits are firm and foliage is dry.

For continuous harvest, you may want to plant a second time, perhaps replacing a bed of peas with cucumbers in late June. If soil is hotter, the seeds may be planted ¼ inch deeper and the surface sprinkled with sand, so it does not crust before plants come through. Completely remove all old or diseased vine foliage from the garden. Only disease-free foliage should be composted.

New burpless cucumber varieties are the preferred choice of those people who find older varieties indigestible. Sweet Slice and Sweet Success are newer burpless hybrids.

EGGPLANT
When to Plant: Sow seeds in flats under lights, March 15; transplant in mid-May when soil warms.
Seed: Cover ¼ to ½ inch deep in flats or compressed peat pellets. Set regular transplants 3 feet apart; smaller Japanese eggplant 2 feet apart in the garden.
Soil: Enriched, fairly acid soil.
Yield: 10-20 fruits per plant.
Varieties: Dusky (56 days), Black Bell (80 days), Classic (76 days), Japanese Long and Ichiban hybrid (61 days), Ping Tung Long (65 days).

Eggplant thrives under the same cultural conditions as tomatoes and should not be planted outdoors until the end of the first or second week in May. It is a full season crop that can occupy the ground until frost.

Four to six well-grown plants should provide enough for the average family. They can be started under lights by the gardener or purchased as transplants from garden centers and nurseries.

People who find eggplant too acidic may well enjoy the milder Oriental varieties, which are long and slender. Ichiban is one of a number of cultivars that are locally available. Although each fruit is smaller, there are many more produced throughout the season.

The transplants should be sited in well-enriched, moist soil from 2 to 4 feet apart, because the larger varieties tend to sprawl as they carry the weight of maturing fruit.

Eggplants are heavy feeders and they appreciate 2 or 3 sidedressings of 5-10-5 worked within a foot of the stems several times during the season. Clean culture is desirable and a mulch can be applied to conserve soil moisture after the ground is thoroughly warmed in June.

The flea beetle and the lacebug both feed on eggplant foliage and can reduce it to lace if plants are not covered with a garden blanket. Otherwise, they must be dusted or sprayed with pyrethrum, rotenone, or neem oil regularly. Keeping eggplants away from potato plantings and the possibility of Colorado potato beetles is recommended. The principle disease that troubles eggplant is a soil-borne wilt. It can be prevented by rotating eggplant crops to new locations in the garden each year.

The fruits are ready to harvest as soon as they become deep in color, firm, and glossy. When they dull, they are past their peak of flavor and the seeds have hardened inside. Eggplant freezes well when sliced and brushed with olive oil to prevent oxidation. In this form it is suitable for cooking in casseroles and stews.

ENDIVE
When to Plant: July 15 to August 1.
Seed: ¼ inch deep in seed flat or cold frame, covered; transplant 12 inches apart in row or bed.
Soil: Fertile, moist, well-drained.
Yield: 1 pound rosette from each plant in late fall.
Varieties: Green Curled (65 days), Deep Heart (71 days), Full Heart Batavian (90 days).

Endive is representative of the increasingly popular bitter salad plants that are grown here in the fall. Others include the Italian chicories like the red and cream radicchio, Agusto (70 days), arugula, and romaines like Parris Island (68 days). Some are grown into the fall and blanched at the heart by tying up the outer leaves while the plants are still in the ground. Endive and radicchio can be harvested by digging the roots and replanting them in a barrel in cool darkness for winter forcing. Broad-leaved Belgian endive or witloof is forced in this fashion.

Like many of the other salad greens, endive ranks high in vitamins A, B1, riboflavin, and C. It should be tender and crisp to be fully enjoyed, which is dependent on its rapid,

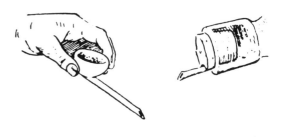

Two devices for sowing small seeds—the one from the store, the other home made.

succulent growth. In a well-fertilized, moist soil, these conditions are fulfilled.

Start the small seeds in a flat where they can be well-watered and cared for before transplanting to the garden in about 3 weeks. To balance the effects of summer heat, cut off all but 1 or 2 leaves from the transplants, and keep shaded until they take off.

Clean culture is recommended, although some growers mulch with straw to help keep the leaves clean. As soon as the plants are large, and only in cool weather, the outer leaves may be tied over the hearts to blanch them. Frost does not injure endive, which may be left in the ground until December.

This crop is practically free of pests and diseases. Rabbits, however, may feast on mature plantings. Spraying the plants with an epsom salt solution will prevent most rabbit injury.

KALE

When to Plant: August 1 to September 1.
Seed: ½ inch deep after broadcasting on prepared covered bed, thin to 6 to 10 inches as plants mature.
Soil: Enriched garden loam.
Yield: 1 packet gives 2 bushels packed.
Varieties: Vates Dwarf Blue Curled Scotch (54 days), Siberian (65 days).

This most nutritious of all the fall greens is rich in calcium, hardy as iron, and is improved in flavor by a light frost. It is therefore a very desirable crop that has a much longer season than most spinach varieties, and it can be harvested through the winter if it has an adequate snow cover.

Kale, to be succulent, tender, and of good flavor, should make rapid growth, sometimes a problem in the dry heat of late August. When it is planted, it should be given an occasional boost with a high nitrogen fertilizer and kept well-watered when necessary.

The best planting method is to broadcast the seeds over the surface of an enriched, wide row, perhaps in combination with mustard and turnip varieties with edible foliage. The resulting seedlings can be raked once to thin, and then allowed to cover the soil surface, shading their own roots. Additional hand thinning will provide a first harvest before frost although full flavor develops in cooler weather.

Kale is not ordinarily bothered by disease, but cabbage worms and aphids are serious pests. The late hatch of the green worms are controlled by 1 or 2 sprayings with Dipel or Thuricide. Aphids may be regularly contained with insecticidal soap spray up to a week before harvest.

If you shear the plants 3 inches high when they mature or harvest the outer leaves, the plants will continue to produce through the winter.

LEEKS

When to Plant: March in flats, April in garden as transplants.
Seed: Broadcast ¼ inch deep in flats set in cool, sunny window.
Soil: Rich, moist, sweet, well-drained.
Yield: 6 pounds per square foot.
Varieties: Broad London (100 days), Titan (110 days).

Leeks are the largest of the mild gourmet onions, just as shallots are the smallest. Both are planted in March as early as a bed can be prepared. Leeks are started indoors under lights, so the small seedlings can go in the garden by mid-April at the latest. They make their best growth in cool weather.

Shallots are started from sets planted 2 inches apart. But leek seedlings need twice as much room to attain the truly impressive size that make them stretch in soups and braising dishes. Plant them in a raised bed 4 inches apart, after enriching the soil with a generous sprinkle of bonemeal or superphosphate.

Snug them in 3 to 4 inches down and leaving 6 inches of soil all around so you can regularly hill up to bury and blanch the swelling stems.

About a month later fertilize the bed again with a sprinkling of 10-10-10 or compost just before a regular hilling. The leeks grown this way will be large and tender by late July or early August. They will hold in the ground through a mild winter if the green tops are shortened in November.

The chief enemy of the leek is the onion maggot, and good drainage is the cheapest non-toxic prevention.

LETTUCES

When to Plant: Early: March to mid-April; late: August to September.
Seed: ½ inch deep.
Soil: Rich, sweet, moist.
Yield: 25-50 pounds from a packet of leaf or head lettuce.
Varieties: Crisphead—Mission, spring only (70 days); Butterhead—Buttercrunch (55 days), Merveille des Quatre Saisons, cut and come again (54 days); Loosehead—Green Ice (45 days), Black Seeded Simpson (46 days), Salad Bowl (45 days), Red Sails (45 days), Oak Leaf (42 days), Mesclun mix (40-50 days); Cos: Parris Island (75 days).

Lettuce is the most widely grown of the salad crops. Because it is a cool weather crop, our heat makes crisp head lettuce problematic later in the season.

To be of the highest quality, it needs rich, moist soil. To get the best variety, start planting rows 8 feet long or beds 4 feet long as soon as the lettuce leafs, and start head lettuce in the cold frame to move to its garden bed in late March.

There it can be staggered in a wide row spaced 12 inches apart. Leaf lettuces should be thinned to 2 or 3 inches apart after 2 weeks in the row.

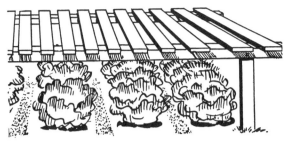

Hot weather checks growth of lettuce and makes leaves bitter.
A portable shade prolongs the "season."

Head lettuces benefit from some shade in the afternoon, so they can be planted next to taller crops or in the shadiest edge of the garden. If there is no shade, a lathe screen set up on cider block may help them to head up or extend the crop in hot weather.

Hot weather checks the growth of lettuce and makes its leaves bitter. A portable shade prolongs the season.

Leaf lettuces will quickly bolt and grow bitter in the late spring heat, so succession plantings are recommended. Stop in the summer, but resume in the coolest part of the garden in mid-August. Late lettuce often sprouts well when planted a little deeper under dampened burlap.

Foliar feeding with high nitrogen formula is a good way to speed production, but it should be applied halfway to final harvest.

Because the leaves of salad plants are eaten raw, do not spray for aphids or other pests except with insecticidal soaps, and rinse thoroughly before eating. If slugs are a problem, sprinkle a belt of woodashes on the soil around plantings; this will discourage the slugs, and the lettuce will use the woodash lime.

Some lettuces may be sheared about an inch high. These cut-and-come-again varieties will produce another crop with good flavor if it is not too hot.

MELONS AND CANTELOUPES

When to Plant: May.
Seed: Covered ½ inch deep, in hills 5 to 6 feet apart.
Soil: Rich, light, sandy soil, ample moisture.
Yield: 1 or 2 melons per vine.
Varieties:
Canteloupe—Saticoy (80 days), Ambrosia (86 days), Heart of Gold (90 days), Earlisweet (72 days), Gold Star (87 days).
Watermelon—Sugar Baby (82 days), Bush Charleston Gray (90 days).

Melons in this area have been a snare and a delusion because of our heavy soils. What they love is the Eastern Shore's sandy, sweet soils and scorching summer heat.
But for those who love the taste of home-grown melons, there is hope. Intensive gardening, with its emphasis on soil preparation and raised beds creates a better environment for all melons. In turn, smaller bush-type watermelons enable

the gardener with a 3-by-10 foot plot to put in two hills of melons for a possible yield of four watermelons or up to eight canteloupes. For some people, that will do.

In heavier soils it is a good idea to dig in a generous quantity of sand and well-rotted manure or compost into the center of each hill or bed. Roots will grow down into the nutrients as the vines develop.

To combat the low sugar content of melons grown on heavier soils, water in a tablespoon of Epsom salts and a half tablespoon of borax for each 50 feet of row before planting.

Melons are a hot weather crop and should not be planted here until May 7 or later. Like cucumber seeds they are attacked by black fly, and the seedlings are attractive to the striped cucumber beetles, which carry bacterial wilts. Cover the plant row with a floating row cover until blossoms are ready to pollinate. The best control is regular dusting or spraying with insecticidal soap or Bioneem up through the undersides of the leaves, where it will also reach aphids. A preventive fungicidal spray, like benomyl, should be started before the plants flower

Melons should grow rapidly, so they set fruit before midsummer. It takes most canteloupes and melons 6 weeks to set blossoms. The new bush type Charleston Gray watermelon is supposed to spread 5 feet instead of the usual 12. Stop cultivating the bed when vines begin to cover it, so as not to disturb the infant fruit.

You must harvest canteloupes and watermelon when ripe. Canteloupes are at their peak for a 24-hour period, which is even shorter in very hot weather. Look for a slight crack where the stem is attached to the melon and gently press the blossom end of the fruit. If ripe it will give just slightly and that end of the plant will have a pronounced melon odor.

Watermelons are trickier. Look at the vine leading to the melon. When the tendril closest to the melon between the fruit and the hill is brown and dry, the melon is usually ready. It then feels somewhat heavier for size than an unripe neighbor. Each plant will yield 1 or 2 fruit.

A shallow frame filled with manure may be employed when growing melons and cucumbers on heavy soils. A pail of water poured over the manure every few days is part of the scheme.

MUSTARD GREENS

When to Plant: March, August 1-15.
Seed: ¼ inch deep, thin to 6 inches.
Soil: Rich, moist garden loam.
Yield: 1 packet of seed equals 50 to 90 pounds.
Varieties: Tendergreen (28 days), Green Wave (42 days), Southern Giant Curled (45 days).

Somewhat resembling Chinese cabbage, and related to it, the mustard green is seldom grown in local gardens. High in vitamins, this cool weather green should be given greater attention.

Tendergreen, an improved variety, is fairly tolerant of hot weather and is the best variety for spring sowing. Other varieties may be planted very early or late, as they are not bothered by a frost.

All greens like a rich, moist soil. A sidedressing of high nitrogen fertilizer half way to maturity will promote fast, tender growth.

Mustard greens are attacked by all the cabbage pests, and the controls employed are the same. A greater emphasis on nontoxic controls is wise for this leaf vegetable.

OKRA

When to Plant: May.
Seed: ½ inch of soil, covered, 6 inches apart. Thin to 12 to 18 inches apart when 2 inches high.
Soil: Enriched garden loam.
Yield: 1 pound per standard plant over the season.
Varieties: Annie Oakley (50 days), Clemson Spineless (56 days), Burgundy (60 days).

Okra is commonly thought of as a Southern crop, that thrives in warm weather. Its large mallow-type flowers are a handsome addition to the garden, and its pods are good french-fried, sauteed, steamed, and pickled.

There are several different types of this woody, branching plant. All must be planted directly in the row after the soil is warm. Okra may be grown anywhere tomatoes and cucumbers will thrive. In heavy soil, it may benefit from 1 or 2 inches of compost put into the bottom of the furrow before planting.

Some okra are dwarf plants. Others grow 4 to 6 feet high, so you can choose a variety to fit your space.

Since pods get woody more quickly when conditions are dry, it is important to keep plants well-watered and to sidedress once or twice a season with 5-10-5.

The pods should be harvested 3 or 4 days after the flowers droop and fade, since the pods quickly turn woody after they attain full size. Cut off all pods at the base with a sharp knife to promote continued growth and flowering. Woody old pods can be dried, since okra seed saves well in a dry, cool area.

ONIONS

When to Plant: Mid-March.
Seed: Plant seeds in flats by late February for transplanting first week in April.
Sets: 1 inch apart in a bed for scallions, 2 inches apart for boiling onions, 3 inches for storage onions.
Soil: Light, rich, sweet soil.
Yield: 50 feet row equals 200 dry onions, 500 shallots.
Varieties:
From sets—Stuttgarter, White Silverskin, Yellow Globe (60-90 days), Dutch Yellow for shallots.
From seeds—Granex Hybrid, Sweet Spanish, Sweet Sandwich, improves in storage (80-120 days).
Bunching—Evergreen Long White, Beltsville Bunching, Japanese Bunching.

Onions are the first thing in the garden, and one of the most prolific and healthful of vegetables. They require sweet, well-drained soil which should be thoroughly limed the previous fall to bring the pH up to 6.8.

Growing onions from sets is simplicity itself in the proper soil. The sets, whether of shallots, onion, or garlic are pushed into the soil 1 to 3 inches apart until the tips just show. It is even easier to plant the varieties that can be used as scallions and boiling onions 1 inch apart, because harvesting through the season will thin the final crop of storage onions, and none of the row will be wasted.

In growing the bulbs it is good to remember that those produced from sets are fairly good keepers, but those produced from seed are better. Bulbs grown from the plants that are available in the spring from Southern growers do not make good storage onion, although they are fine salad types.

Multiplier or potato onions are a perennial form that may be planted in the fall like garlic cloves. But these onions are grown from top sets. They are hardy and produce an early spring crop, while garlic does not mature until late June.

The most commonly grown perennial onions are the Egyptian or Multiplier and Welsh onion. Another good variety is Japanese Bunching, which has whiter stems. Plantings of perennial onions last for years, increasing from top sets and starting into growth in the fall just as chives die down.

Two other members of the onion family are of local interest to good cooks. A Falls Church restaurant owner has begun to grow a giant Chinese scallion of sweet, mild flavor, which may yet find its way into local garden centers. And more people are planting sets of the warm subtle shallots, the indispensable onion of French cooking.

Onions need a good supply of nitrogen during the growing season, and benefit from a watering with liquid manure, which can be made by steeping dehydrated cow manure in water for 24 hours. A narrow onion hoe is by far the best tool to keep the soil loose and friable. Close planting in a wide row and pulling every other one loosens the soil through the season.

It is important to pinch out any flowering stalk that emerges from the top when it is small. That bulb will be much lower in quality.

Harvesting storage onions, shallots, and garlic begins in July when the tops begin to fall over. Brush over the collapsing foliage a few days before the onions are pulled from the row.

Choose a dry bright day and spread the harvest on the ground or on screening in the sun. Remove all but a 1-inch stub of the tops as they dry, unless you plan to braid and store your crop in a dry, warm place where you can check it frequently. Unbraided onions should be stored loosely in crates or string bags in an airy place.

In the home garden, onions are seldom troubled by disease if the soil is not infested with onion maggots. Crop rotation is the best prevention. Any aphid infestation can be quelled with soap sprays.

PARSNIPS

When to Plant: Late March to April.
Seed: 3 inches apart in rows 18 to 24 inches apart.
Soil: Light, rich garden loam.
Yield: 2 by 6 foot row gives ½ bushel.
Varieties: Harris' Model (95 days), All America (100 days), Improved Hollow Crown (105 days).

Parsnips are grown in the garden to provide roots for winter and early spring use. They are a delicious occasional vegetable that complements the rich flavor of pork and game, but their nutritive value is dubious for frequent consumption.

They are not at their best until the soil is cold; indeed, many growers claim that freezing improves the flavor. At least a portion of the crop should be left in the bed under a light straw mulch for spring use.

The plants have a 100-day maturity time and could be planted in May if the soil were not already too warm and dry for good germination in warmer parts of the region. Where it stays cooler, this is the preferred planting time for most tender roots. Close to the city and to the south and east, they should be seeded in late March and April to take advantage of good soil moisture.

A deep, finely pulverized seedbed is recommended for these root crops. They often grow 12 inches long.

Compost, coal ashes, and sand should be dug in at least 12 inches deep, because there is frequently a lot of clay in the soils in this area. Open a deep furrow and fill it with compost to act as a planting bed.

Root crops need space for the root to form. It helps to cover the seed with no more than ½ inch of sifted compost, peat moss, or sand. Place 2 or 3 seeds in each hill, since they are poor germinators. Parsnip seed is short-lived and should be gotten fresh each spring.

A light overcast of fast sprouting radish seeds will keep the soil from crusting and provide another crop from an area that would otherwise be taken up for the entire season.

Dig parsnips with a potato fork 2 or 3 inches away from the row or bed to avoid piercing them with a tine.

GARDEN AND EDIBLE POD PEAS

When to Plant: As early as ground can be worked in spring.
Seed: Broadcast on surface of a row 24 to 36 inches wide or plant 2 inches apart in double rows 6 inches apart. Allow 18 to 24 inches between double rows for cultivation and harvest. Push in 2-3 inches deep and cover.
Soil: Sweet, well-drained garden loam.
Yield: 1 pound plants 100 feet of row, ½ pound plants a 3-by-10 foot row. 1 pound yields 1 bushel.
Varieties:
Early Garden Peas, for shelling—Daybreak (55 days), Knight (62 days), Frosty (64 days).
Edible Pod Peas, Oriental types—Oregon Sugarpod, medium, (68 days); T Multi Star (75 days).
Sugar Snap Peas, short vines—Sugar Ann (56 days), Novella (64 days).
Sugar Snap Peas, medium vines, prolific, long season—SugarBon (58 days), Super Sugar Mel (68 days), Sugar Daddy (74 days).
Sugar Snap Peas, tall, 6-8 feet—Sugar Snap (62 days), Snappy.
Southern Peas—Extra Early Blackeye, Brown Crowder, Mississippi Silver (85-90 days).

You might ask, why would anyone grow a vegetable that takes so much space in a small garden? The usual answer is, where else can you get decent peas?

Within the last 15 years peas have been genetically redesigned for the great benefit of the home gardener. The

Root crops need space for the root to form.

Sow seeds as thinly as possible. Thin out all surplus plants.

English garden pea is a good cool weather crop that can go in as soon as the ground is workable. It is harvested in early June.

The only enemy of the English garden pea is hot weather which promotes wilts and mildew. This makes early harvest in spring essential.

They come in several heights, the shortest of which is planted in wide beds supported by pea brush to prevent matting and collapse in late spring storms. Dwarf peas benefit by a support, and it is essential for tall varieties. The tallest are grown like lima beans on wires and garden twine anchored against the wind by sturdy 6-foot poles.

The wrinkle-seeded varieties, like Laxton's Progress, are conceded to be sweeter, and early maturing varieties like Knight ripen in May, thereby missing disease problems. The yield from a 50-foot double row is about 1 to 2 bushels. After shelling a crop, you get about a dozen quarts of peas.

Oriental edible pod varieties for steaming and stir fry have always been delicious; unfortunately, they do not yield heavily in our June heat.

Sugar snaps, an American invention, have the sweetness of English garden peas extended to the juicy edible pod. After stringing, the entire crop may be eaten fresh or quickly steamed, producing an increase in yield from quarts to bushels for the same amount of space and less labor. The original sugar snap will produce into July if you have the space to spare. New cultivars are shorter, earlier, and nearly stringless.

All these peas still have their advocates, but the following general cultural requirements must be met, for success in growing them here.

◊ Plant all your varieties at the same time in spring. If you have space vacated by an early corn crop, you might try fall plantings of short season varieties. These you may vary by a week or more. You will need to begin planting by August 1; plant in a trench to preserve soil moisture. Baby them through the month, until the cool weather. Trench planting keeps the roots of fall peas cool. Fill gradually from the sides as the seedlings grow.

◊ Two 3-by-10 foot plantings will give enough for a small family to eat fresh. Taller varieties will produce more on vertical supports, but you will need walking space between rows. The vacated spring pea patch can be used by bush beans, summer squashes, or other heavy feeding vegetables later.

◊ Legume innoculants can provide better germination. Alternatively, soak the seed, then dry for an hour before planting. Peas do not require heavy feeding. Soil limed and enriched in the fall ought to be adequate for good growth when sprinkled with a little all-purpose fertilizer at planting time. Good drainage is important.

◊ Even dwarf peas in a wide bed may need some support to prevent mildew. After planting the seeds, push trimmed bamboo tops or small pruned branches into the soil of the bed to provide pea brush for the vines to climb on. This prevents collapse onto wet ground under the weight of the harvest.

◊ Light, shallow cultivation will keep soil loose and weed-free until the young plants start to vine. Avoid getting too close to roots of tall varieties.

◊ Promptly remove all trash from the trellis or bed when harvest is finished, but leave the roots—they fix nitrogen for leaf or vining crops that follow.

So-called Southern peas stand up well to our hot summers. These include crowder peas and black-eyed peas, both of them delicious shelled from the long pods and cooked fresh. They may be planted in late April or early May and will take from 65 to 85 days to mature. The long pods will produce about 10 to 15 pounds of shelled peas for each 4 ounces of seed that you plant 3 inches apart. That is enough for a 50-foot row. Most of the Southern peas are tall. The pods can also be allowed to dry on the vines and the peas shelled and stored for winter use.

PEPPERS
When to Plant: Set out transplants second week in May.
Seed: In compressed peat pellets, end of March under light.
Plants: 18 inches apart, standard plants; 12 inches, dwarf, hot peppers.
Soil: Well-drained garden loam.
Yield: 40-60 fruits from 6 plants over the season, more from small-fruited varieties.
Varieties:
Sweet—Gypsy (62 days), Cubanelle (65 days), Golden Bell (68 days), Purple Beauty (70 days), Bell Captain (71 days), Camelot (74 days).
Hot—Hungarian Wax, Hot Portugal, Ancho 'Poblano' (65 days), Anaheim, Jalapeno, Big Jim, Serrano (75 days), Long Red Cayenne (72 days), Havana, Thai Hot (70 days).

Peppers are increasingly popular, as testified by the prices people are willing to pay for Dutch golden and chocolate sweet peppers in the market. Different varieties are

Dwarf peas benefit by a support; it is essential for tall varieties.

essential seasoning ingredients in South East Asian and Latin American cuisines. Why not grow a variety of your own, for use fresh and dried?

Sweet peppers are a useful crop in the garden, beginning to bear in July after plants are set out in May and continuing to set fruit into late September. They are tender plants that should be set out (when the soil is thoroughly warm) into moist, rich, slightly acid soil. They will need cutworm collars that extend 2 inches above and below the soil surface after planting. It is good garden practice to shelter them for a few days from the sun with bottomless plastic milk cartons with the caps off.

Peppers should not be fertilized until they bloom. Each plant can then be sidedressed with 1 teaspoon of granulated 5-10-10. A high nitrogen formula will increase leaves at the expense of fruit. Better fruit set can be achieved by spraying a solution of 1 teaspoon of Epsom Salts in a window spray bottle of water on plants when they are blooming.

Do not be alarmed when blossoms drop off: mulch instead. Often peppers will not set fruit when the night air temperature is much above 85° Fahrenheit. You can reduce stress on the plant and prevent a rot at the blossom end of the fruit by making sure that the soil does not dry rapidly during a heat wave.

If the potato flea beetle attacks your peppers, or another solanin family member, sprinkle flour on foliage after each watering or spray with neem or pyrethrin product. In hot, wet weather, a copper-based fungicide will prevent anthracnose, which leaves gray, rotted spots on the fruits. Other bacterial diseases can be prevented by crop rotation. Hot peppers seem less affected by dry soil and insect pests, but they should also be well nourished for maximum production.

Harvest peppers with a sharp knife even though many break easily from the stem. If you are growing large fruited peppers, you may want to stake and tie the main branches with soft cloth strips to prevent them from splitting under the weight of fruit.

In the fall, before frost, pull the plants and store them upside down in an airy garage. All but the smallest fruits will continue to ripen, so they can be dried, frozen, or used fresh.

POTATO

When to Plant: March (plant seed under lights in mid-January.

Seed: Cut sections of tuber with growth eyes, set 2 to 4 inches deep and 18 inches apart in wide trenches.

Yield: A quarter peck of seed potatoes yields 1 bushel mature potatoes.

Varieties: Pontiac (100 days), Irish Cobbler (110 days), Bliss Triumph, Kennebec (112 days), Russett Norkotah (140 days), Homestead Hybrid (135 days from seed).

Work fertilizer and compost into bottom of furrow, cover lightly before placing seed, and "ridge" soil. After a week or two, depending upon date of planting, the ridge is leveled off.

The yield on potatoes does not justify their use in a small garden. Nevertheless, the delicious and almost unobtainable new potatoes the size of golf balls may sway some people to folly. These small potatoes can be harvested in mid-June and the vines pulled from the patch to make room for more productive crops.

Fall potatoes do not do well in warmer sections of the region, but might be attempted in a large garden in the Piedmont for a fresh winter crop.

Spring crops should be planted here between St. Patrick's Day and April 1. They are not fussy about soil preparation; indeed, they have been used as a first crop on heavy soils. They do produce larger, better shaped potatoes in sandy soil, so many people plant shallow and cover with straw. It is well to avoid adding manures or high nitrogen fertilizers in soil preparation. Compost and a high phosphate formula are better, although 5-10-10 will do fine. In that way you will avoid scab that roughens the potato skin, and the plant will produce tubers rather than foliage.

Obtain certified seed potatoes from your garden supplier to be sure of a disease-free product with viable eyes. Many supermarket potatoes have been treated with an anti-sprouting chemical. Cut potatoes into pieces that have 1 or 2 eyes and allow them to air dry or callous in a cool, dry room for a day before planting. Small potato buds and seed are available through major garden catalogs for those who want to compare results.

The most efficient use of space is to dig a shallow trench 3 feet wide and lay the potatoes inside 12 inches apart. Then replace 2 inches of soil over potatoes and cover the whole bed with 4 inches of clean straw mulch. Although the ground cannot be cultivated, weeds are smothered, and the new foliage is supported by the mulch. Later in spring up to 4 more inches of straw should be added to keep light and weeds from getting to the bed. To stave off two generations of the voracious Colorado potato beetle, rotate crop areas, cover your emerging plants with floating row covers for the first 6 weeks, inspect for egg masses under the leaves, and use neem or pyrethrin products weekly if beneficial insects do not provide enough control. These white and black striped insects hatch pale beige larvae that devastate foliage. Spray or dust up through the leaves with a trombone sprayer, or hand pick the larvae in the early morning when they are cold and slow. Spray any late crop with a fungicide to prevent a common leaf blight. Benlate and Bravo are effective.

A narrow trench is used for row planting. Cover compost and fertilizer at bottom of furrow with 1 inch of soil. Add potatoes and ridge soil over the trench for a week or two, then level until foliage appears. As plants grow soil is pulled up around them again for support and increased root production.

Mature potatoes may be dug as soon as the vines begin to die, but they store better if left in the ground for a week or more because the sugars are turned to starch. New potatoes must be harvested when the vines are still green by digging into the side of the patch to extract potatoes, and then re-firming the soil around the plants for further growth.

Irish Cobbler is a productive spring crop but does not keep well. Katahdin, Kennebec, and the red boiling potato, Pontiac, keep well into the winter in a dark storage place that stays close to 50° Fahrenheit. The curious may want to order some of the tasty newly available potatoes like Cherries Jubilee or Yukon Gold from specialty growers.

SWEET POTATOES
When to Plant: May.
Seed: In a flat with compost in a sunny window in March.
Set: Plants 3 to 4 inches deep, 12 to 15 inches apart.
Soil: Rich, sandy, acid soil with good drainage.
Yield: 1 bushel per 30-40 plants.
Varieties: Nemagold, Centennial, Redmar, Jewel.

Sweet potatoes and yams are altogether better suited to our hot summers, and if they are planted in a raised bed to which sand has been added, they are very productive and relatively pest free.

Sweet potato plants are set in a ridge. Use fertilizers low in nitrogen, but high in phosphate and potash.

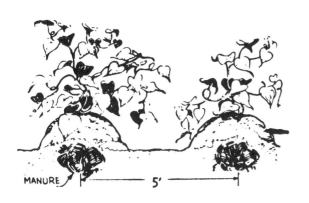

Sweet potato plants are set in a "ridge." Use fertilizers low in nitrogen but high in phosphate and potash.

The sweet potato has beautiful vining foliage, which figures as prominent vegetable in South East Asian cuisine.

It is simplicity itself to grow enough slips from one large sweet potato indoors. It will root in a large, clear jar if one tip of the potato is submerged in water. Or it may be split and placed (flat sides down) in a shallow tray of compost. Youngsters may find it interesting to monitor the plant's progress over the 2 months that you keep the compost moist for maximum slip production. Harden them off outdoors a week before planting.

The slips are planted in May up to their leaf tips in deeply worked soil, to which 5-10-10 fertilizer has been added to boost root production (the bed will need 1 pound for every 10 feet of row). The plants should be protected from sun and wind for the first week with hot caps or translucent milk cartons.

Keep pruning the vining tips of the plants when they get 2 or 3 feet long, lifting the vines off the soil regularly to prevent them from rooting at the nodes. This will force growth to the developing tubers and provide you with an unusual leaf vegetable.

Sweet potatoes may be harvested at any time close to the first frost. If you have not harvested by then, promptly cut off all the vines, so that frost damage does not translocate to the tubers underground.

Dig sweet potatoes with great care to avoid bruising the skins. Such bruises will inevitably rot. The tubers must be cured for winter storage by holding them for 12 days in a room where it is a moist 85 degrees, so it is better to harvest in early September when the weather is still hot. They are then cooled gradually to about 55 degrees, where they will keep for several months. Potatoes can also be harvested and used fresh, but they will not keep more than a few weeks.

In the home garden, if crops are rotated, and disease-free slips are obtained, sweet potatoes are seldom affected by pests or diseases.

RADISHES
When to Plant: Every 2 weeks from March to mid-May for continuous harvest; winter radishes, August 15.
Seed: ½ inch deep, 1 inch apart in rows 12 to 15 inches apart, or broadcast and thin out.
Soil: Well-drained garden loam.
Varieties:
Summer—Cherry Belle, Champion, Comet, Icicle, Easter Egg Collection (25-28 days).
Fall—Daikon, Black Spanish (30-45 days).

Radishes are quick, tasty, and useful to the gardener. Small varieties mature in less than a month, and can be used as row markers for slower crops, as they can break through the soil more easily.

In our hot spring weather, they rapidly lose their crispness and delicate bite to become pithy and harsh, but even in this condition they have their uses—for the volatile compounds they exude are credited by organic gardeners with repelling cucumber beetles from vulnerable cucumbers and summer squash vines.

For best flavor in the spring, grow the tiny red and white ball varieties; keep the soil cool and moist to promote succulent growth.

If the ground is low, raise your rows or beds to avoid attracting onion maggots to your radish crops. If they appear, you can sprinkle a layer of diatomaceous earth when soil surface is dry. Replace after each rain and do not grow root crops in the same space. Sprinkle flour on radish foliage after each rain to deter flea beetles.

Cultivate radishes to keep soil loose around their rapidly developing roots.

Some of the longer varieties are better grown in September when the air and ground start to cool. Icicle holds its flavor and texture better at this time, and the giant Japanese daikon radish is at its best in cool weather, its mild coarse texture holding for weeks under a straw mulch. These deeper roots require deeply prepared soils, and should probably not be attempted where root maggots are a problem.

RHUBARB

When to Plant: Late fall, early spring.
Seed: Plant roots deep enough so growth "eyes" are 4 inches below surface, 3 feet apart.
Soil: Cool, rich, manured, shaded from afternoon sun.
Yield: 9 or 10 stalks per plant each season; 4 stalks equals 1 pie filling or 1 quart sauce.
Varieties: Valentine, McDonald, Victoria (green).

Many gardeners look forward to having rhubarb pie and rhubarb sauce each spring, although the plant does not seem well adapted to the warm climate of this area. It was formerly grown commercially in Prince Georges County. The pie plant requires a well-drained soil rich in humus, particularly manure. It seems to thrive best in the colder, higher elevations where the ground freezes solid, perhaps destroying some of the soil fungi that attack the cut surfaces of plants at lower elevations.

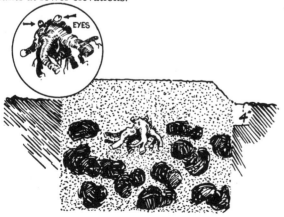

Rhubarb needs a rich soil and protection from the hot sun.

Rhubarb needs a rich soil and requires shade from the fiercest rays of the sun, so it should be sited in front of an eastern or northern wall to give it some relief.

When planting roots, make sure that the soil is well firmed around their irregular shape and that the eyes that produce new stalks are 4 inches below the surface. Careful shallow cultivation is necessary to keep weeds down while the plants are becoming established. Mulch the soil in summer to retain moisture, but clear the site of mulch and any old foliage in winter, so the ground can freeze.

You may begin to sparingly harvest rhubarb the second spring it is in the ground, until the third year, then you may pull up to late June.

Gently pull and twist the stalks from the plant to avoid damaging any nearby shoots. Remove and do not eat the leaves, which contain concentrations of oxalic acid that are damaging to the kidneys. Cut the central seed stalk when it appears, so it does not deplete stalk production.

Soapy water may control any attacks by aphids on the plant. You will never have to worry about root or crown rot if you choose a spot with excellent drainage.

SPINACH

When to Plant: Mid March.
Seed: ½ inch deep, covered, and 1 inch apart, thin to 4 inches.
Soil: Well-drained, sweet garden loam.
Yield: ½ ounce seed yields 3 bushels in one 100-foot row. ¼ ounce yields 2 bushels interplanted with scallions in a wide 3-by-15 foot row.
Varieties: Melody (42 days), Tyee (40 days), Bloomsdale Long Standing (42 days), Savoy Supreme (40 days).

Spinach is rich in vitamins and minerals including iron, but in recent years it has been learned that it makes calcium unavailable to the body, which may be why generations of milk-loving children have actively resisted it.

Nonetheless, it is delicious vegetable, as good raw in salads as it is cooked. In this area, generally fall-sown seeds provide the first green harvest of the spring. Those seeds are sown in August and September.

Spring sowings are done as soon as the ground can be worked, because spinach is a cool season vegetable that needs 6 or 7 weeks to mature before hot weather makes it bolt.

To be tender and flavorsome it needs soil that is well-limed and full of humus, and it benefits from deeply dug manure. Any additional nitrogen may be supplied by a sprinkle of ammonium sulphate or 10-10-10 fertilizer worked in at planting time. Keep soil surface loosely worked before plants cover the bed.

The first harvest is made up of thinnings from thickly sown seed, but cutting can begin at 6 to 7 weeks.

Spinach is bothered by few insect pests and should not be sprayed with any toxic poison. If leaf miner or anthracnose disfigures the crop, hand pick the affected leaves.

SQUASH

When to Plant: May and early June for succession planting of summer squash, May for winter squash.

Seed: 3 to 5 seed ½ inch deep, covered in hills or beds 4 feet wide.

Soil: Rich garden loam.

Yield: ½ ounce plants 50 feet, yields 100-300 fruits.

Varieties:

Summer Squash: Zucchine—Aristocrat (50 days), Zuccini Elite (48 days), Goldrush, Raven (45 days). Yellow Crookneck—Supersett (52 days), Multipik—Early Prolific Straightneck, Goldbar (50 days). Scallop—Peter Pan (49 days), Scallopini (50 days), Sunburst. Kuta Hybrid (48 days), Gourmet Globe Hybrid (45 days), Butter Blossom (85 days) for blossoms, courgettes.

Winter Squash: Buttercup (95 days), Sweet Mama (85 days), Table King (85 days), Waltham Butternut (85 days), Hercules (88 days), Blue Hubbard (115 days).

Summer squashes are usually overplanted by new gardeners who cannot imagine just how prolific they can be when well-grown. Small families need no more than 4 hills of summer squash of different varieties. A slightly later planting of 2 or 3 plants is an insurance policy should you fail to see the small pile of "frass" drilled out of the vine stems near ground level when the borer enters.

To begin, all squash are planted in the same manner, in hills or wide raised beds full of enriched garden loam. The seeds are planted as soon as the danger of frost is past and the soil is warm. This is from late April to late May. For the earliest harvest (and to foil borers), start seeds indoors and transplant seedlings in mid-April into hills warmed under black plastic. Plants can be protected for 2 to 3 weeks inside a circle of plastic freezer bags filled with water to moderate air temperature in warmer areas.

Three to five seeds are planted in a circle 5 inches apart. When they germinate and get their second set of true leaves, thin them to the strongest 2 plants in each hill. Winter squash will spend the whole season developing 2 or 3 squash per vine. They will require a sidedressing of 5-10-10, like cucumbers and other melons, just as they start to spread. Summer squash, if frequently harvested, may

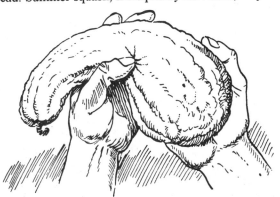

If skin of a squash is easily pierced with a finger nail it is tender and ready for harvest.

produce a dozen fruit apiece. They should be sidedressed when the plants begin to blossom. The fruits are best when very small, but are good as long as a thumbnail sinks easily into thin succulent skin.

Since squash literally grow overnight, you should check your plants each day after the first flush of sterile male blossoms. Squash blossoms are also quite edible and make a delightful casing for stuffing and steaming—a tasty way to control some of the squash's production.

Because of this heavy production, soil under squash should be very enriched before planting. This also helps if you have to reroot a vine that has been attacked by borers.

If borers are present, it is possible to slit the stem with the grain from the point of entry and kill the intruder with pyrethrin dust in a plastic squeeze dispenser. After air drying the wound for an hour or two, young tendrils further out should be mounded with rich soil over a leaf node to encourage new root formation to support the damaged plant. Keep the "patient" well watered while new roots form.

Borers emerge at night; when you spot them, cover the row with a translucent row cover by late June to prevent the moth parents from laying eggs in early July. Blossom pollination should not be much affected.

Squash just do not freeze well at home and they are indifferent canned, so plan on growing only enough of them for your enjoyment fresh.

Winter squash are tougher characters, and they do not suffer as much from pests and diseases. Like some varieties of summer squash, some have been developed for the smaller garden, so the vines will not hog needed space. These bush squash have fruits that are close in size and texture to those of the larger vines, but row in a space half the size. Some vining winter squash like Butternut are suitable for growing on supporting cages. They require the same planting and culture as summer squash.

TOMATOES

When to Plant: Early May, determinate transplants for early July harvest.

Seeds: In row for late crop in mid-May, cover ¼ inch deep. Thin to 2 inches apart 6 weeks ahead of transplanting time for late crop.

Plants: 3 feet apart, staggering 6 plants in a 3-by-10 foot row.

Soil: Rich, slightly acid garden loam.

Yield: 6 plants yield 4 to 5 bushels over the season.

Varieties:

Indeterminate—Park's Whopper (70 days), Jet Star (72 days), Big Girl, Supersonic (78 days), Beef Master (80 days), Homestead.

Determinate—Celebrity (70 days), Floramerica (75 days), Roma VF (62 days), Viva Italia (72 days), Pixie Hybrid II patio (78 days). Yellow: Lemon Boy (72 days), Husky Gold (70 days). Small-Fruited: Sweet Chelsea, Sweet Million (65 days), Sugarlump (68 days), Garden Delite (75 days). Plum and pear types.

Advocates of this type of support for tomatoes say that yields are greatly increased, and that no pruning is necessary. If the vines are mulched at planting time, the only care needed is an occasional feeding, watering if rainfall is inadequate, and tucking stray shoots inside of the cylinder. The openings in the reinforced wire are 6 x 6 inches.

Tomatoes are the queens of the garden. People are truly mad about them, and small wonder. They are one of the most versatile of all our vegetables. An excellent source of vitamins and minerals, they can be used raw or cooked in a hundred ways. They are relatively easy to grow and give a big yield for the space occupied.

It is commonly said that anyone can grow tomatoes, because these hardy vines do not require special care; they do, however, repay good cultural conditions with abundance. Seasoned gardeners go to considerable lengths to see that their tomato plants are well and carefully planted. Young plants put into warmed ground in early May will continue to produce until frost stops their growth in October. A well-grown plant should produce more than half a bushel of fruit over the season.

When choosing varieties, it is wise to plant several types for different purposes. A main crop tomato like the older reliable Marglobe or Rutgers is fine for eating and canning. The popular beefsteak slicers listed here are best for eating fresh, and come red, orange, pink, yellow, tart, and mild. Small cherry and plum tomatoes are perfect for salads and are borne on unbelievably prolific and hardy plants. All these tomatoes are indeterminate, meaning that they continue to set fruit until frost.

Determinate varieties include the wonderful Italian paste and sauce types, which also make firm canning tomatoes for winter salads, and appealing medium-size tomatoes like Floramerica and Celebrity. These tomatoes set fruit and ripen within a short period. Of the so-called patio tomatoes, most are determinate, retaining a compact size and shape, so the gardener is well advised to plan several plantings.

Careful planting technique has much to do with this success. It is no secret that tomatoes left to sprawl on the ground are the most productive, and the reason is that they will root at growth nodes given any encouragement by moist soil to increase the "feeding" capacity of the plant.

A gardener can take advantage of this fact in a smaller space and get an earlier harvest by removing all the leaves except the top cluster from tall disease-resistant transplants that he buys or grows. Allow the stems to air dry while digging long trenches or holes 3 feet apart. Dust the stems lightly with rooting powder and lay the moist root ball and the whole length of the stem in the richly prepared soil. Put a paper cutworm collar around the top 4 inches of the stem. Cover with 6 inches of soil and compost, leaving the top knot exposed to mark the row. If space is a consideration, staggered plantings in a 3-foot-wide row will allow you enough room for the troughs in which you plant the stems. Alternate the ends of the trough at which the leaves emerge.

When the tops get over a foot tall it is time to stake or surround them with tomato cages. If you are staking, place them 18 inches deep next to the tomato when you plant so as not to injure the root system. Use old nylons or strips of sheeting to form soft loops for the limbs that are tied tight only to the support. Stakes should be 6 feet tall for a standard slicing tomato. Determinate varieties and cherry tomatoes will be fine on a 4-foot stake, and they can also be planted a little closer.

Attach staked tomatoes with loose loops of cloth. Lightly prune extra suckers that develop in the leaf axils for more vertical growth, leaving some to shade the plant so fruit does not sun-scald.

Cages can be put in place later because the weight of the vines growing through the supporting wire will hold them in place. If caged tomatoes are mulched at planting time and receive their supplemental feeding in a liquid form, they need no further care but an occasional watering to insure a good harvest. The cage should be 6 feet high for large standard varieties with the openings in the reinforced wire 6-by-6 inches to allow extraction of the fruit.

Tomatoes will need one good sidedressing of 5-10-10 or superphosphate (a table spoon per plant), or some compost (a cup per plant) at blossom time, lightly worked into

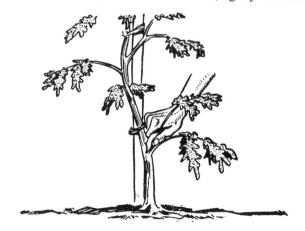

Prune tomatoes by removing the shoots that emerge from the leaf axils to get fewer but better fruits.

the area where you buried the stems. By that point, there should be a solid root system along the length of each trench.

Tomatoes planted in this way will start to bear low on the plant, so you might mulch with 2 or 3 inches of clean wheat straw to keep the fruit clean and to preserve soil moisture. Even soil moisture prevents blossom end rot in the first fruits. This mulch will also keep down weeds, so that an occasional volunteer is all you will need to pull from the soft soil beneath. Be sure that the soil is well worked before you apply mulch.

The chief tomato pest is the hornworm, a truly ferocious-looking character which is slow and can be hand picked with gloves. Leave those worms that appear to have white growths on their bodies; this signals the presence of larvae that will hatch, kill the worms, and look for new victims. Flea beetles may attack young foliage but can be deterred with soap spray or a little Sevin early in the season.

Early and late blight, however, and some bacterial wilts, are a problem for gardens where tomatoes have been grown regularly. Always buy resistant strains. Clean up all garden residues at the end of each season before working the soil, and spray tomato plants regularly with a fungicide like Bravo.

Occasionally tomato leaves curl in tightly, although they do not loose their color. This is a temporary circulation problem and often does not affect fruit production.

Water tomato plants generously when rains fail to provide even soil moisture. Soaking hoses are an excellent way of getting water to the plants during the heat of summer since they can be laid under straw mulch.

In the fall when cold nights threaten, you should pinch back new flowering tips on the indeterminate vines so that all the plants' efforts will go into ripening existing fruit. At the end of the season whole plants can be pulled and stored upside down in a basement or garage where the fruits can ripen. You may also harvest all fruits and store those that are perfect after removing the stems. Put the fruit stem-end down in a shallow box covered with a layer of newspaper. Tomatoes ripen from the blossom end, and you will be able to check their progress at a glance.

TURNIPS

When to Plant: July 15 to mid-August for fall crop.
Seed: Broadcast, sprinkle dirt over. Place with other fall greens in bed 3 feet wide, thin with rake when 2 inches high.
Soil: Good, acid, garden loam.
Yield: 20 pounds of turnips and greens to a 10-foot row.
Varieties:
Tokyo Cross (35 days), Purple Top White Globe (57 days).
Turnip greens—Shogoin (70 days), Seven Top.

Turnips are essentially a cool weather crop, needing moisture and low temperatures for good growth. The fastest growing varieties, therefore, should be sown later in the season. In milder areas they may be left in the ground into November for continued harvest along with kale. They do not store as well indoors as the rutabaga or yellow turnip, but they do not take quite as much space either. Turnips for greens may be seeded between the plantings of the latest sweet corn so that they receive a little shade in late August.

Because turnips need to make rapid growth to be succulent, some gardeners broadcast fertilizer and mix in the bed before planting. Others work in a little when they thin the young seedlings with a rake. A bed will need 2 to 3 pounds of 5-10-5 per hundred square feet.

Turnips attract the same pests as cabbages. Soap sprays and Dipel or Thuricide are the recommended controls, because foliage is often eaten. Follow the usual crop rotation practice to avoid any soil-borne pathogens in future years.

Sources of Supply

There are a wealth of seed suppliers in this country. The five major seed houses that serve the Eastern seaboard are supplemented by a host of specialty growers set up for mail order service.

The larger growers have the advantage of zoned choices of vegetables, often marked to denote that they are especially suitable for our regional growing conditions. The specialty growers extend your choices. It is always wise to read maturity dates and other disease resistance features carefully before ordering.

It also benefits the gardener to order before mid February so that he may receive in a timely manner those seeds to be started indoors and transplanted later. In-ground gardening can often begin here by mid March for those people with the foresight and time in the fall to prepare their soil.

Catalogs of fruit trees and berry fruit are sent at times of the year when it is best to ship bare root or live stock. Local berry and fruit growers on the Eastern Shore often ship live plants within 24 hours of receipt of your order, so it is wise to have sites prepared for the plantings in advance. Strawberry plants can be kept for a day or two in the crisper drawer of your refrigerator.

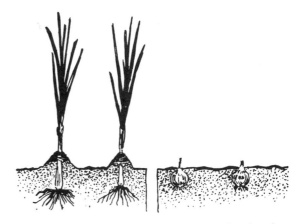

Shallow planting of onion sets produces better bulbs than deep planting. The same applies to onion plants.

VEGETABLE PLANTING GUIDE
Planting Calendar

Kinds	Seed for 50 Ft. Ounces	Distance Apart		Depth to Cover	Crop Matures in	Yield
		Rows Feet	In Row Inches	Inches	Days	
Asparagus	33*	3 feet	1-1 ½ feet	4-6	!	13 Bunches
Bush Beans	4-8 ounces	1-1 ½ feet	4-6 inches	1-2 inches	50-75	36 Pounds
Pole Beans	8 ounces	2-3 inches	6 inches	1 inch	50-90	37-60 Pounds
Beets	½ ounce	1-1 ½ feet	2 inches	½-1 inch	55-80	40-60 Pounds
Broccoli	25*	3 feet	2 feet	¼-½ inch	100	25-40 Heads
Brussels Sprouts	30*	3 feet	1-1 ½ feet	¼-½ inch	120	30-40 Pounds
Cabbage	25-30*	2-2 ½ feet	1 ½-2 feet	¼ inch	98-120	50-150 Pounds
Carrot	⅛ ounce	1-1 ½ feet	1-2 inches	¼ inch	75-110	50-100 Pounds
Cauliflower	25*	2-2 ½ feet	1-1 ½ feet	¼-½ inch	120-140	25 Heads
Chard	½ ounce	2 feet	1 foot	½ inch	50-60	25-40 Pounds
Chinese Greens	¼ ounce	2 feet	1 foot	¼-½ inch	65-75	35-50 Heads
Collards	¼ ounce	2-3 feet	1-1 ½ feet	½ inch	80	50-60 Pounds
Cucumber	¼ ounce	3-6 feet	3 feet	¾ inch	60-80	17-35 Pounds
Eggplant	20*	3 feet	2-3 feet	¼ inch	100-120	60-100 Fruit
Endive	⅛ ounce	2 feet	1 foot	⅛ inch	60-80	50 Heads
Fennel	⅛ ounce	18 inches	1 foot	¼ inch	60-70	50 Heads
Kale	4 ounces	2 feet	8-10 inches	⅛ inch	50	50 Heads
Kohlrabi	⅛ ounce	1-½ feet	4-6 inches	½ inch	65	40 Pounds
Lettuce, Leaf	⅛ ounce	15 inches	10 inches	¼ inch	45-60	25 Pounds
Lettuce, Head	50*	15 inches	1 foot	¼ inch	80	50 Heads
Melons	¼ ounce	4-6 inches	3-5 feet	½ inch	80-90	60-120 Pounds
Mustard Greens	⅛ ounce	1-1 ½ feet	6 inches	¼ inch	28-40	25-45 Pounds
Okra	½ ounce	2-2 ½ feet	1-1 ½ feet	¼ inch	50-60	45 Pounds
Onion Sets	1 pint*	15 inches	3 inches	—	30-60	30 Bunches
Onion Plants	200	15 inches	2inches	—	60-100	3 Bushels
Parsnips	¼ ounce	18 inches	2 inches	½ inch	100	2 Bushels
Peas, .Garden and Sugar Snap	16 ounces	1-1 ½ feet	1-2 inches	½ inch	60-90	20-40 Pounds
Peas, Southern	4 ounces	2-2 ½ feet	3 inches	1 inch	68-85	10-15 Pounds
Peppers, Sweet	35*	2-2 ½ feet	1-1 ½ feet	—	60-70	250 Fruits
Peppers, Hot	35*	2-2 ½ feet	1-1 ½ feet	—	70	300 Fruits
Potato, White	60*	2-2 ½ feet	8-10 inches	4 inches	110-140	60 Pounds
Potato, Sweet	35-50*	5 feet	12-15 inches	5-6 inches	100-130	1 Bushel
Pumpkin	¼ ounce	6 feet	6 feet	1 inch	100-120	40-50 Fruit
Radish	½ ounce	1 foot	1 inch	½ inch	25-60	50 Pounds
Rhubarb	17*	5 feet	3 feet	4 inches	/	150 Stalks
Salsify	¼ ounce	1-1 ½ feet	2 inches	½ inch	100	30 Pounds
Spinach	¼ ounce	1 feet	4 inches	¼ inch	40	25 Pounds
Squash, Summer	¼ ounce	3-4 feet	3 feet	½ inch	120-160	30-50 Fruits
Squash, Winter	¼ ounce	4-6 feet	4-5 feet	½ inch	120-160	30-50 Fruits
SweetCorn	#	14 inches	14 inches	1 inch	70-100	200 Ears
Tomato	20-25*	3 feet	2-4 feet	to tops	65-80	8-15 Bushels
Turnips	⅛ ounce	1-1 ½ feet	2 inches	⅛ inch	40-60	60 Pounds

!—first harvest in 2 years; T2*—planted as seedlings, sets or rooted cuttings;/—outer stalks of rhubarb first pulled in 2 years; #—recommend block planting at least 5 ft. by 5 feet, 14 inches apart for good pollination.
Revised and updated Maryland Leaflet 15.

IPM CALENDAR FOR EDIBLES

January

Look for disease resistance when selecting seeds and plants from catalogs. Resistance is not immunity; it means the plant will do well when attacked by a disease, not that there will be no damage.

March

Check apples and cherries for the egg masses of Eastern tent caterpillars. They look like black melted styrofoam on the end of branches. Prune them out and destroy.

Pull up annual weeds, such as annual bluegrass, chickweed and cress, before they have a chance to set seed.

Take back any mulch, leaves and garden debris and kill the slugs, where they were a problem. Wait to apply fresh mulch until the soil's warmth and dryness will discourage their return.

May

Along the leaves of cole crops look for holes caused by small green cabbage loopers. Treat with a pesticide containing BT.

Prevent leaf miner damage to spinach, beets and chard by covering the plants with a non-woven fabric to exclude the adult leaf miners.

Set saucers of beer or yeast solution flush with the soil level to attract slugs in the garden. Renew every two days until slugs no longer appear.

June

Cover cucumbers with non-woven fabric to exclude the striped cucumber beetle that spreads a fatal bacterial wilt.

Potatoes may be heavily infest with Colorado potato beetles now. In the cool of the morning, hand pick the adults and any small clusters of yellow eggs on the undersides of the leaves and drop them in soapy water to kill them; this may take less time than spraying if you have only a small planting.

Plant a second crop of zucchini and other squash late in the month if your first was attacked by vine borers. The borers have completed their life cycle and will not attack the late planting..

Do not over-fertilize your new tomato plants. Sidedressing with compost is better than a jolt of nitrogen, which can produce localized calcium deficiency that causes blossom end rot.

July

Avoid water stress on plants now. Water all your plantings infrequently but deeply. If your soil is stiff clay, you may need to water once until the water runs off, wait, then return and water again. Use a shovel to check the depth of water penetration, which should be 8 to 10 inches into the soil. Shallow watering stresses plants more than no watering.

NUTS, FRUITS, AND BERRIES

Fruits are a worthwhile addition to the home garden. If wisely selected, they do not take too much space. However, like all succulent plants, they must be protected from insects and diseases. In most cases, the same equipment and materials used to protect roses will be adequate for the home fruit garden. Tree fruit pest control formulas are sold commercially, but ryania or neem extract sprays show promise as less toxic insect controls.

Although some gardeners think fruits are too slow in reaching productive size, there are some varieties that bear fruit the second year, chief among them fall planted strawberries. Bramble fruits, raspberries, blackberries, and wineberries also produce the second year. Apples, peaches, pears, and grapes are slower, but some dwarf fruit bears early.

A medium-size suburban lot may well include a few of the bush fruits to supplement the vegetable crops. Some of the less vigorous blackberries, like Raben and Ranger, and the newer thornless varieties, are now better suited to the home garden than in the past.

NUTS

Some varieties of nut trees do well in this area, and they can, as well, be counted on for shade. The following kinds and varieties are recommended for the Washington area.

American Chestnut hybrids, Dunstan.
Chinese Chestnuts: Nanking, Meiling, Orrin, Crane.
Hazelnut: Royal & Barcelona for pollination.
Hickory: Shaul, Glowver, Lingenfelter.
Pecan: Major, Pereuque, Sweeney, Duvall.
Black Walnuts: Ohio (disease resistant), Myers.
English Walnut (Persian): Broadview, Hansin.
—Selected by USDA and University of Maryland specialists.

Filberts or hazelnuts should be planted on a north slope lest the bloom be destroyed by frost. Harvested in September and eaten fresh, they are deliciously different from the roasted varieties.

Hickories and pecans must be purchased very small, because they are hard to transplant, having deep tap roots.

Nut trees require the same planting and care as shade trees. Annual fall feeding by vertical mulching is recommended for rapid growth while young. Vertical mulching consists of using an auger to drill 6-inch deep holes, two feet apart, around and just outside the drip line of the young tree. The holes are then filled with a mixture of compost and pine fines.

Little pruning is needed except to remove weak or crossing branches; but young trees benefit from a stiff plastic spiral tape that will protect the trunk from sun-scald and animal damage for 2 or 3 years.

BLUEBERRIES

When to Plant: March, November.

Plants: 4 feet apart, rows 6 feet apart, edge of woods.

Soil: Rich, cool, acid, well-drained.

Varieties, in order of ripening: Earliblue, Blueray, Berkeley, Herbert, Darrow, Jersey.

Blueberries, a tidy bush fruit, are well-adapted to this area. Many local gardeners plant the newer varieties, which require the acid soil common in this area. Low-growing ornamental bushes, they will grow well in light shade, and a soil enriched with oak leaf compost or peat moss. In summer and winter they benefit from a heavy mulching with wood chips or well-rotted compost.

The newer varieties have much larger fruit than native wildlings. You must plant at least two varieties for good cross-pollination.

After the plants reach fruit-bearing size in 3 years, some regular feeding is needed. A rhododendron or azalea formula will suffice or you might try mixing superphosphate and cotton seed meal with the compost for mulch. Maintain a pH of 4.5 to 5.5, as they prefer acid soil. The phosphate in commercial fertilizer formulas locks up iron, so additional iron chelate may be needed every season or two to keep the plants in good condition.

A quarter to half a pound of ammonium sulphate, ammonium nitrate, or urea may be used to supply nitrogen to each bush in lieu of commercial formulas. If a soil test shows the soils are magnesium deficient, ¾-pound of magnesium sulphate may be applied to the soil around each bush.

Jersey, a small-fruited variety, is well-adapted to our conditions, hardy and disease free. Half soil and half oak leaf compost makes good planting for blueberries. Mulch with half-rotted oak leaves in early summer and in late fall.

RASPBERRIES

When to Plant: Late March, early April.

Plants: 3 feet apart in rows 6 feet apart.

Soil: Slightly moist with well-rotted compost or manure.

Varieties:

Red—Reville, September Sentry, Southland.

Black—Cumberland, Bristol.

Purple—Sodus.

The newer varieties of raspberries bearing in both spring and fall are good choices for small gardeners. The first crop appears in June and the second in early September.

Two-year-old raspberry plants will bear the first year, although it is generally agreed to be a good gardening practice to remove the fruiting canes when they are first transplanted. Commonly, one-year-old canes are readily available for spring planting from large garden centers and mail-order houses.

Raspberries do prefer light, moist soil; heavier clays can be improved by the addition of humus so these brambles will thrive and bear. They will not thrive in heavy shade or in a hot, dry situation. Dewberries, the large native cousins of the raspberry, need full sun.

The common practice of letting as many red raspberry canes develop as the plant will produce reduces yields. Experienced growers thin out the shoots that spring up from the crown to 5 to 7 of the strongest. The remaining canes are shortened to 3 or 4 feet, so they are upright in the row. The home gardener wanting first-class fruit should thin the canes, fertilize, and mulch the beds in late March. One pound of 10-10-10 may be applied to each 100 square feet of the beds. The selected canes may be loosely tied to stakes. The older canes that have fruited should be promptly pruned out as soon as the fruiting season is over.

Black raspberries and purple raspberries do not throw up as many suckers as the redcaps, but they need to have their long willowy canes shortened and tied to stakes in the home garden. If new plants are desired, however, the tips of plants should be fastened to the ground in the desired spot with a peg and covered with soil. In one year a new plant will have fully developed.

It is best for home gardeners to grow red or black raspberries, but not both because of their susceptibility to viral diseases carried by the other species. It is most important for the grower to look for certified virus-free plants from good sources of supply. County Extension offices can be of help locating these.

Disease may be controlled by a dormant spray and by controlling aphids that spread the virus with soap sprays.

Southland, a new red raspberry, is relatively virus-free, because aphids do not like to feed on it. Also, it is well adapted to our climactic conditions.

In addition there are now some huge, fruited crosses of blackberries and European Tayberries that are being grown commercially in Virginia. Some of these hybrids may soon be available to the home grower. Experience has shown that drip-irrigated bramble fruits have a longer, more productive season than those grown in a conventional manner.

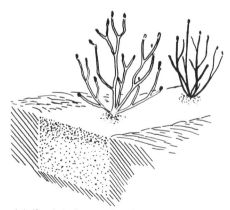

Half soil and half oak leaf compost makes good planting for blueberries. Mulch with half-rotted oak leaves in early summer and in late fall.

WINEBERRY

The Japanese wineberry is a solution for those who want a completely trouble-free cane fruit. It bears on second-year wood, and the plants are not troubled by pests or diseases. Like blueberries, this naturalized exotic grows very well at the edge of woods, does not require heavy feeding or care, and will produce larger and larger crops of jewel-like berries with a tart pleasing flavor. Wineberries bear in July, after the spring raspberry crop, and before blackberries. They can sometimes be found in farmers markets, although plants can easily be identified and transplanted from the wild. The canes are red and furry rather than sharply thorned, and the underside of the hairy leaves are a distinct silver. Wineberries can be located in July when their fruit can be sampled, and in September plants can be dug, and pruned back for transplanting.

STRAWBERRIES

When to Plant: March, April, September.
Plants: Space plants 1 foot apart in 3-foot-wide raised beds. Stagger plants, using 75 to 100 plants for a 30-foot row.
Soil: Well-enriched, well-drained, sandy loam.
Varieties, early to late: Earliglow, Sunrise, All Star, Delite, Jersey Belle, Marlate.

Few fruit crops are so well adapted to the space and resources of the home gardener. This luscious home-grown fruit is far superior to all but the choicest commercial varieties.

The secret to early production here is fall planting. We are fortunate to be within a hundred miles of three of the largest commercial producers of these plants in the country. In many cases, plants come from these Eastern Shore shippers within the week ordered.

It is, therefore, wise to prepare in early September before you order. Make a planting bed rich in well-rotted manure and compost. Choose a site in full sun, and raise the beds with additions of compost and greensand if your soil is heavy.

Lay in a good supply of clean, weed-free straw to mulch the plants through the winter. Just before the plants arrive, thoroughly cultivate the soil surface to uproot any weed seedlings. Strawberries cannot compete with grass and weeds.

Strawberries planted in the fall usually set heavy blossoms the following spring. It is hard, however, to get the plants shipped when they are not dormant.

If you must plant in spring, be sure to remove all the blossoms the first season, so the strength of the plant goes into good root and crown development.

Whereas deeply set plants are subject to crown rot, shallowly set plants will dry out. Therefore, next to planting in rich soil, the most important step is to set the crowns level with the soil surface, with the roots fanned out for support when they are firmed in. This ensures their health and vigor.

When placing the plants in the bed, strive to put about one plant in each 10-inch square of bed. This apparently sparse spacing will soon fill in because strawberries send runners in all directions that root to produce new plants that bear the second season. For this reason, some commercial growers plant down the middle of a wide row, and mow the center flat the third year to give space for new plants on the side to send back fresh runners for longer production. The original plant will bloom the second year, reach peak production the third year, and then decline.

To renew the beds after the third year, spade in the straw mulch and remove the oldest plants, those with long exposed crowns. This will give room to reset the younger plants 6 inches apart for a bountiful harvest.

Mulch thoroughly in December after the ground is frozen to prevent these shallow-rooted plants from damage due to heaving when ground freezes and thaws.

Some straw can be raked off the rows in March or out of the bed, but leave some around the plants to help keep berries clean and dry when they ripen.

Give a supplemental feeding with 10-6-4 granulated fertilizer in mid-August at the rate of 3 to 4 pounds per 100 square feet.

If red stele disease is a problem in your immediate area, you should grow resistant varieties like Surecrop and Midway.

If your space does not permit a full-fledged strawberry bed, you may prefer Alpine strawberries. These neat small plants do not set runners, but they do bloom all summer long, producing a small crop of delicate berries, the *fraises des bois* of French cuisine. These make an excellent border for a perennial or annual cutting bed, and they are quite winter hardy with some mulch. The varieties Reugen Improved and Charles VII can be gotten as plants or by mail order. There is also a yellow-fruited variety.

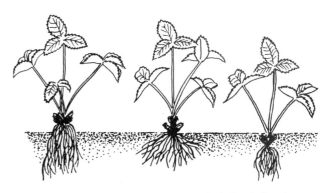

Deeply set plants are subject to crown rot; shallowly set, dry out—
Place crown at soil level.

DWARF FRUIT TREES

When to Plant: Late fall, early spring.

Soil: Any well-drained, moderately rich, garden loam. Full sun in a not too windy situation. Do not plant in a hollow where frosts linger.

Varieties:

Apples—Lodi, Quinte Beacon, Gala, Golden Delicious, Granny Smith, Grimes Golden, Summer Rambo, Paragon, Stayman, Winesap.

Pears—Seckel, Moonglow, Maxine, Stark's Delicious.

Peaches—Redskin, Red Haven, Marland, Belle of Georgia, white.

Many gardens are too small for standard fruit trees, and so gardeners give up all hope of enjoying fruit, shade, and flowers from their own trees.

This need not be, because today there are productive trees grafted onto dwarfing stocks: they have roots that support themselves but do not permit normal size. Nurseries using a Malling understock create a very dwarf tree about the size of a large spirea, a medium dwarf tree that is about the size of a large lilac and hardier, and some half standard sizes.

This gives a wide range of choices for different size yards and is a boon for pruning and management.

Fruit trees are as ornamental as any shrub. In formal gardens they are often espaliered to make living fences or striking patterns against a wall, producing in very limited space.

They are as easily grown as any other tree if adequate attention is paid to fertilization, pruning, and pest control.

Planting differs for dwarf trees in that it is essential that the graft union be kept above ground, so it does not root and overwhelm the understock that controls size. Their limited root system also means that such trees must not be allowed to go dry during a drought. Fertilization should occur when young in the fall with a handful of commercial fertilizer worked in around the drip line to promote vigorous growth.

It is best to order small 1-year-old trees of peach varieties, so they can be pruned to 3 or 4 well-spaced branches that stick out as straight as possible from the trunk. This main frame is the basis for the open vase-shape that allows peaches to soak up the sun as they ripen.

Fall is a good time to plant fruit trees of all types. Most species require at least 2 varieties to ensure good pollination. Catalogs are helpful, but local orchardists and truck farmers are the best source of information on varieties that do well in your area. Consult them when you visit a farmer's market or pick your own operation. This allows you to choose varieties after tasting.

In October most trees are entering dormancy, but if bought balled in burlap, they will make a month of root growth before winter. They should be pruned according to planting directions, as soon as they are safely dormant. Trees can be planted bare root through the winter if large holes have been dug in advance and filled with leaves to prevent deep freezing of the soil.

Dwarf varieties usually start to bear the second year after planting and are in full production within 4 or 5 years. The gardener can help this process by thinning the young fruit annually after the tree thins itself during the "June drop." Space the fruit 3 to 6 inches apart, even if this means removing more than half the fruit from the tree. You will get larger, healthier fruit and more even annual harvests.

Continue to prune during dormancy, keeping the center of the trees open to admit sunlight and the sprays that you will need to protect your crop from a host of fungal diseases and insect pests. Remove about half of the new growth each year. There is some evidence that summer pruning of young peach trees during the second and fourth July promotes better development.

Most stone fruits require 10 sprayings from the bud swell in March right through to harvest. They require most of the same pesticides as roses, with the addition of some dormant lime sulphur spray to kill disease spores on the bark. The spraying schedule varies a little for each species. Peaches are by far the most vulnerable species of fruit tree. They are also subject to two borers. The peach twig borer can be pruned off the top 6 inches of twigs in March; harder to control is the peach borer, because lindane, its control, is a highly toxic chemical. Scrupulous attention and clean culture are your best bets.

Flowable sulphur sprays at 2-week intervals are still the only effective means of controlling brown rot on peaches. If possible, buy resistant cultivars of all stone fruit.

Fire blight is a fungal disease of pears. The only cure is drastic pruning and streptomycin sprays. It is best to plant them away from quince, pyracantha, crabapple, and cotoneaster.

Maryland and Virginia both put out detailed spray charts for Home Fruit Production that you will find invaluable. All-purpose fruit spray mixtures can be purchased at garden centers.

Cherries, plums and prunes, and apricots can be grown in this area. The chief competition for cherries is birds and squirrels, so dwarf trees that can be completely wrapped in netting from mid-June through harvest are advisable. Plums and prunes suffer, as peaches do, from brown rot at the core, unless regularly sprayed. Damson Plum and Shropshire are more resistant. Methley has good quality eating fruit.

Some gardeners may want to try Oriental persimmons. These handsome trees produce fruits in September that are 10 times as large as the small native persimmon. The fruits are ripe when frost neutralizes a natural alum in the flesh. You will know they are ripe if you see glowing eyes in your trees on frosty nights—possums and raccoons love the fruit.

GRAPES

When to Plant: Early spring, late fall.

Plants: Set roots 8 inches deep and 8 feet apart.

Soil: Well-drained, light, flinty.

Varieties:

Dessert Type: Blue—Concord, Fredonia, Van Buren.

Dessert Type: Red—Dunkirk, Vergennes, Red Flame Seedless.

Dessert Type: White—Niagara, Seneca, Brocton, Himrod White Seedless.

Maryland Wine Grapes: White—Seyve Villard 5276, 12-375, Seibel 256; Red—Seibel 7053, Johannes Seyve 26205, Seyve Villard 18315.

Virginia Wine Grapes: White—Seibel 5279 (Aurora), Seyve Villard 5276 (Seyval), Seibel 4986 (Rayon D'O); Red—Kuhlmann 188-2 (Foch), Seibel 13053, Baco I (Baco Noir), Seibel 9549 (De Chaunac), Seibel 1000 (Rosette), Seibel 5898 (Rougeon).

Grapes are adaptable to smaller yards, where they can be grown on a trellis, atop a low wall, or tied to a fence.

Their culture is comparatively simple, although like most heavily productive plants they repay good care with an abundant harvest.

They are said to be best grown in a medium loam, but can thrive on many types of soils, as long as there is good subsurface drainage. For best fruit production they should have full sun, but most will tolerate shade for part of the day.

Wine grapes do demand full sun and a deep soil. They also require a thorough spray program for insects, mainly Japanese beetles, and diseases, mostly fungal. The European varieties are far more susceptible to downy and powdery mildews, anthracnose, and black rot than are the American dessert grapes. They should, therefore, be grown in as dry and airy a site as can be found. It is important to select varieties that can stand this area's fluctuating temperatures. Former County agent Bill Geiser, who tested many grape varieties in Calvert County, has identified those that can be grown north and south of Washington.

Wine grapes may be grown on the same sturdy wire trellis as those usually used for table grapes. If space permits, the gardener may want to grow several varieties in order to have a harvest spread over a number of weeks. Grapes begin to ripen in late August. A mature vine should produce over 20 pounds of fruit. Normal yield is 3 gallons of wine from a 48-pound bushel of grapes.

In planting the vines, dig holes wide enough for the roots to spread out without crowding. Set the vines 2 inches deeper than they grew in the nursery. Buy either 1- or 2-year-old vines; they take about the same time to mature. After planting, which takes place in early March, prune back the tops to 2 or 3 strong buds.

In subsequent years, correct pruning will determine the quality of the harvest. In general it is important to prune by early March before the sap starts to flow, so the cuts can

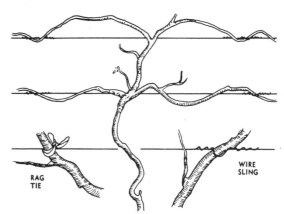

The 4-arm Kniffen system is common method of training grapes on an inexpensive support.

by early March before the sap starts to flow, so the cuts can callous. And it helps to know that grapes bear their fruit on new wood (that is, wood from buds on the old wood). You should cut back radically, leaving no more than 2 buds on each major cane. On a mature vine, you should leave no more than 40 to 60 buds in order to ensure good fruiting.

Keep the soil around vines open and well cultivated. This can be done first in the spring at the same time that you give a light sprinkling of a fertilizer low in nitrogen. You want to encourage fruiting, not foliage.

A Dormant spray of lime sulphur, followed by a spray program of Bordeaux mixture and lime sulphur will help control problems with black rot. Japanese beetles dislike hydrated lime or woodashes on the foliage, although ryania is effective without killing bees. Wrapping the pollinated fruit clusters in white paper bags keeps wasps and other pests from destroying fruit before you are ready to harvest. As with all fruit, pick it at the peak of perfection.

Fruit Calendar

Fruit species bear in this rough order:

MAY: Strawberries.

JUNE: Strawberries, Raspberries, Cherries, Plums, Peaches.

JULY: Wineberries, Apricots, Peaches, July Apples.

AUGUST: Blackberries, Peaches, Nectarines, Grapes.

SEPTEMBER: Raspberries Grapes, Pears, Apples.

OCTOBER: Apples, Pears, Persimmons.

INSPIRATION;

Green Spring Farm Park, Green Spring Road, Annandale, Virginia.

Mount Vernon Kitchen Garden, George Washington Memorial Parkway, Mount Vernon, Virginia.

GROW Urban Garden, Independence Avenue & 6th Street SW, Washington, D.C.

National Park Service Community Garden, 9th & Peabody Streets NW, Washington, D.C.

15. ENJOYING HERBS

In the last two decades herb growing has attained real popularity even as building lots and gardens have grown smaller. It is a tribute to their rich variety and versatility.

In backyards and on historic properties gardeners often fit herbs into the permanent borders for their ornamental value as well as for their fragrance. Container gardeners find their taste and beauty can often survive winter in an indoor setting. Meanwhile, the culinary uses of herbs have grown rapidly as more and more cuisines join the American melting pot.

Despite the many satisfactions of herb gardening, beginners should be forewarned that our mid-Atlantic climate poses some restrictions that should shape your choice of plants, soil preparation, and planting times. Many favored culinary herbs are adapted to the milder, moister European weather, and others thrive in dry, sandy soil under intense sun. It may be necessary to seek a favorable situation for certain plants, or even to create the microclimate and soil conditions under which a wide variety of your favorites may be reasonably expected to thrive.

Fortunately, many of our most popular herbs are native species, and some are scarcely improved over all these years of cultivation—because they are useful, hardy, and attractive just as they are.

Choosing a Site

The vast majority of culinary and fragrance herbs need 6 to 8 hours of sunlight a day during the growing season if they are to develop full taste or aroma. The major exceptions are the mints, lemon balm, chives, burnet, and chervil, which can get by with 3 to 4 hours a day. Good drainage is also important. When you want to devote an entire bed to herbs, seek a site that is naturally well drained. Since some herbs suffer from fungus diseases during our muggy heat waves, it is wise to site a herbal bed so that one portion has some afternoon shade and all of it has good air circulation. Keep the bed small enough to work in from without.

In today's smaller gardens it is easy to fit herbs into an existing perennial or vegetable garden by planting the annual herbs next to vegetables and using the perennials as foliage or flower accents in the perennial border. Culinary herbs are perfect in a sunny spot close to the kitchen door or near an outdoor terrace where you entertain. Mints were traditionally planted there because they repel invading flies. The half-hardy perennials benefit from a sheltered spot that will catch sun late into the fall. Some low-creeping herbs do well between the flagstones of a garden path or as a patch of flowering lawn. Creeping thyme, English pennyroyal, and perennial chamomile are three possibilities for a sheltered garden. Remember that herbs cannot compete with tree or shrubbery roots.

Soil Conditioning

If your soil is not normally light, rich, and well-drained, you should get busy and make it that way, digging between 15 and 24 inches down to aerate the soil and then adding about 6 inches of compost, leaf mold, or shredded sphagnum to the top 12 inches of soil.

Gardeners with heavy clay soil should definitely improve the drainage. At the National Arboretum former herb collection curator Holly Shimazu successfully lightened the heavy clay soil that predominates in Piedmont Maryland and Virginia by digging in several inches of coarse ground quartz. Sold as chicken grit in area farm supply stores, this material discourages root rot during our hot summers.

You might add fine sand, compost, and sphagnum to a section devoted to Mediterranean and desert plants since they like lighter soil. For these plants you should dig in ground limestone to sweeten the soil if your soil analysis indicates a pH below 6-6.5. Lavender, for example, needs neutral or alkaline soil between 6.8 and 8 pH. In general, only the moisture-loving plants like more acid soil. Bonemeal sweetens soil while cottonseed meal acidifies, however both add fertility. Well-rotted cow manure or a complete slow-release fertilizer can be dug in as added nutrition. The result should be a raised fluffy bed, which can then be bordered with stone, pressure-treated wood, or other edging material.

Planting

Herbs that grow here are varied plants that come from every part of the temperate zone around the world. Culinary herbs that thrive in the damp coolness of northern Europe do best here if they are planted in early spring and again in the fall. Among these are the annuals chervil, coriander, and dill. These plants appreciate some shade during the hottest part of summer and definitely need adequate moisture. Annuals coriander and dill will self-seed in rich soil and produce a more bountiful crop in the fall. So will the perennials sweet cicely and chives, with chives becoming invasive in the garden if most flower heads are not gathered.

Many perennial or biennial herbs do well if planted either in the spring or fall. Perennial and annual seeds are planted in the spring, with most of the annual herbs needing the warmer soil of early May for good germination. A few like chervil can be planted in late fall. Parsley needs soaking and rinsing to get rid of chemicals that inhibit germination. Still other seeds must germinate in fine sand in the light.

Because their rapid tender growth has been fostered under greenhouse conditions, all plants that you purchase in the spring should be carefully hardened off for 4 or 5 days before you plant them in the garden. They may be placed in a coldframe with its door propped open during the day, or merely introduced gradually to cooler air and sunlight during the day for 2 or 3 days, then finally left out on a mild night before planting. Water with a dilute transplant solution as soon as you plant and protect the seedlings on cold nights with paper hot caps, bottomless milk cartons, or a garden blanket.

For easier culture it is best to segregate the annuals so that you do not disturb young perennial roots when you are pulling and discarding spent annuals in the fall.

Perennial herbs, like their flowering counterparts, should be set far enough apart so the plants will still have good air circulation when they mature. Knowing the potential size of each variety will save the labor of dealing with crowding and disease problems in years to come.

Pest and Disease Control

There are only a few pests and diseases that affect herbs in the garden. Aphids and spittlebugs occasionally attack new growth. Leaf miners and spider mites can take hold during late spring or the hot dry days, respectively. But most herbal plants, by virtue of their aromatic properties, have better than average resistance to pests. If you are growing culinary herbs, you should not spray too close to harvest.

Fungal problems like root rot show themselves when mature foliage at the base of the plant begins to die. Here the cheapest solution is often to yank the plant and turn the soil over to bake in the sun, then put a replacement plant in a different spot.

Feeding Herb Plants

Many young herb plants, particularly those harvested often during the season should be given a liquid feeding every month during the growing season. Some tender perennials that will survive during the winter in pots should be fed in early spring as they begin to break dormancy. Use complete fertilizer formulas, some of which include vitamins and growth hormones, to help develop sturdy root systems.

Herbs from hotter climates develop their best intensity of aroma and flavor if the soil is fertilized once at the beginning of the season with a complete, slow-release granular formula. Herbs that demand sweet soil should get a little ground limestone worked into the bed every two years if the surrounding soil is acid.

Harvest and Preservation

Some herbs have foliage or flowers that may be cut or gathered only once a season, while others can be harvested at intervals from June through September.

The harvesting of most kinds of leaf herbs begins before the flowering season while the growing tips are young and tender. The leaves and tips should be harvested in mid-morning after the dew has dried, but before the heat of the day.

Culinary herbs are at their peak when used fresh. Then they can be used as sprigs in marinades or on the grill. Stripped from their stems, the leaves and flowers are delicious in sauces, salads, herb butters, and vinegars. They are also delicious when chopped and frozen with a little water in ice cube trays, then double-bagged in plastic to be stored in the freezer. In this form, they should be added to sauces, soups and stews without thawing.

To preserve surplus culinary herbs or to prepare fragrance herbs for use in a potpourri, spread the leaves on sheets or trays in a dry, shady situation, or hang them upside down in loose bunches where air circulation is good. Flower petals should be spread on clean sheets of paper. A dehydrator is perfect, a clean attic with a draw fan is next best, and a 140° oven for 3-6 hours will do in a pinch. Turn the drying leaves frequently if they are lying on a solid surface. When they are thoroughly dry, strip the leaves from the stems and store them in a glass container.

The colors of herbal flowers, such as lavender sticks, can be preserved in silica gel crystals or a mixture of clean sand and borax stored inside an opaque box or tin so that light does not fade their colors.

Herbal seeds are harvested as the heads begin to change color. To avoid their shattering, clip the seed heads in the morning shortly after the dew has dried. Spread them to dry on sheets or pillowcases. When thoroughly dry, rub the seeds out. They will need a week or more of additional air-drying before storing. All dried herb products store best in glass jars in a cool dark place. Most lose half their fragrance and savor within a year. So give them as gifts or use them early and often until your next crop comes in.

Seasonal Care

Moisture-loving herb plants in heavy soil need no special protection summer or winter; however, many of our favorites (thyme, sage, rosemary, and lavender, for instance) are Mediterranean plants whose shallow roots need light soil. In winter the hardiest of these species must be protected from freeze drying with a mulch of the smallest size pine bark chunks you can find, as is done at the National Arboretum. Another light, though acid, mulch is baled pine needles.

All those varieties of Mediterranean herbs which are not reliably hardy in zone 7 should be grown as tender perennials: to be potted and brought indoors just before frost if you do not have an especially sheltered spot for them. The one hardy variety of rosemary, Rosemarinus Arp, should have its foliage wrapped in bubble plastic to prevent transpiration when the root zone is frozen. The soil should not be mulched.

Herbal Usage

There are hundreds of plants, from annuals to common trees, that have been used as herbs; that is, they are grown for one or a number of culinary, dyeing, fragrance, or medicinal uses. Listed are those readily available plants most likely to grow well in the our area. Reputed medicinal uses should be thoroughly researched and checked with a pharmacist before the home gardener tries any form of self-medication, including herbal teas using ingredients not found in commercial mixtures. Of course, this does not preclude growing medicinal herbs for their beauty and landscape value.

Some herb plants can make the transition from garden to container each winter to give added pleasure indoors. They will be listed. Take particular note of their cultural requirements to be sure that you can meet most of them indoors. In a separate list, species are grouped by the growing conditions they favor, which will enable you to choose herbs to match your specific sun and soil.

CULINARY HERBS

The letter key that follows each plant's name denotes its various uses: Culinary, C; Dyeing, D; Fragrance, E; Pest Repellant, PR; Medicinal, M; Indoor, I, and species that have high ornamental value are marked with an O.

ANGELICA
Angelica archangelica) C, O.
Soil: fertile, well-drained.
Exposure: sun/part shade.
Propagate: self-seed, or refrigerate fresh seed, then sow on surface of flats in cold frame in December.
Height/Distance: 4 feet; 2 feet apart.
Harvest & Use: young leaves for steaming fish, stalks cooked as condiment, candy, liqueur flavoring.
Plants needed: 1 or 2 as background plants.

BASIL
(Ocimum basilicum) Italian or American green and purple varieties. C.
Soil: fertile, well-drained.
Exposure: sun, sheltered.
Propagate: seed or transplant when soil is 65° F.
Height/Spread: 8 to 24 inches; 12 to 14 inches apart.
Harvest & Use: cut back to 2 sets of leaves on each stem just before bloom. Use fresh, frozen, or in pesto. Fertilize for repeat harvest at 3 to 4 week intervals. Italian bush basil is a

small mounded variety that is perfect for edging or pot culture, while other varieties yield far more per plant.
Plants needed: 2 to 8 depending on variety.

BORAGE
(Borago officinalis) C.
Soil: light to average in nutrients, well-drained.
Exposure: sun.
Propagate: seed in May.
Height/Distance: 3 feet; 12 to 18 inches apart.
Harvest & Use: young leaves. Chop leaves to flavor Pimm's Cup with cucumber, blue flowers to candy, or put in salad and fritters.

BURNET
(Poterium sanguisorba) C.
Soil: light, well-drained.
Exposure: sun/part shade.
Propagate: self sow, or seed in May.
Height/Distance: 2 feet; 1 foot apart.
Harvest & Use: leaves in spring and summer. Use for salads and cold drinks needing cucumber taste. Cut bloom stalks in May to encourage leaf growth.

CHERVIL
(Anthriscus cerefolium) C.
Soil: light, well-drained.
Exposure: partial shade.
Propagate: seed in early April or transplants in October.
Height/Distance: 18 to 24 inches; thin to 9 inches apart.
Harvest & Use: tender leaves with delicate parsley flavor from outside of plant. Use for salads 6 to 10 weeks from sowing.

CHIVES
(Allium schoenoprasum, A. tuberosum) C, O.
Soil: good garden loam.
Exposure: sun/part shade.
Propagate: seed in March and April, ¼ inch deep; transplants easily.
Height/Distance: 10 to 12 inches; 1 inch apart.
Harvest & Use: tender spears, flowers. Use tender spears for the onion flavor, flower stalks for fresh and dry arrangements. Garlic chives, A. tuberosum, have light garlic flavor.
Plants needed: 3 to 6 for flavor, more for ornamental use.

CORIANDER
(Coriandrum sativum) C.
Soil: rich, sandy, well-drained.
Exposure: sun/part shade.
Propagate: seed in early April, September.
Height/Distance: 3 feet in flower; 4 inches apart.
Harvest & Use: leaves from outside of plants in spring and

fall. Use tender leaves for Chinese and Latin cooking, seeds when plant matures.
Plants needed: 10-foot row of pot herbs.

DILL
(Anethum graveolens) C.
Soil: rich, sandy, well-drained.
Exposure: sun, protected.
Propagate: sow seeds ¼ inch deep in April, self-seed in late summer.
Height/Distance: 2 to 3 feet; thin to 6 inches apart.
Harvest & Use: outer foliage. Use dill for seasoning fish, potatoes. Leave a few seed heads for re-seeding a thicker fall crop.
Plants needed: 4-foot row.

FENNEL
(Foeniculum vulgaris, F. rubrum, F. dulce) C, O.
Perennial/Annual.
Soil: rich, well-drained.
Exposure: sun.
Propagate: seed in early April, or transplant.
Height/Distance: 5 feet; 4 to 6 inches apart as background.
Harvest & Use: outer stems. Use to throw on the grill as a bed for fish. Bronze fennel is a handsome feathery accent in the garden. Bulb fennel is a salad plant with a hint of licorice flavor that's harvested in early fall, reputedly a good digestive.
Plants needed: 6 to 8.

GARLIC
(Allium sativum, A. ampeloprasum) C, PR.
Soil: rich, loose, well-drained.
Exposure: sun.
Propagate: cloves in late September.
Height/Distance: 2 feet; 8 to 10 inches apart.
Harvest: June-July
Plants needed: 2 dozen
This rewarding crop enjoys sweet rich soil during the winter. Snap off the center bloom spike when it first appears for largest size bulbs. Side dress elephant garlic and mulch in early April and May for baseball sized bulbs that will keep through the next winter. Dig, wash clean, and air cure in a warm, dry area out of the sun as soon as the foliage begins to yellow.

GOOD KING HENRY
(Chenopodium bonus henricus) C, P.
Perennial/Annual.
Soil: rich, well-drained soil.
Exposure: sun/part shade.
Propagate: transplant or self-sow.
Height/Distance: 2 to 4 feet when flowering; 4 to 6 inches apart.

Harvest & Use: outer leaves of Good King Henry are a good cooked pot herb in May and June. Chenopodium album, the related American annual weed, lamb's quarters, is also delicious when gathered under 6 inches high. Both are nutritious vegetables.
Plants needed: 2 dozen.

HOREHOUND
(Marrubium vulgare) C, M.
Soil: light, well-drained.
Exposure: sun/shade.
Propagate: seeds, divisions in spring.
Height/Distance: 6 to 12 inches.
Harvest & Use: leaves and stems for candy flavoring and cough syrup.
Plants needed: 1 or 2.

HORSERADISH
(Armoracia lapathifolia) C.
Soil: rich, moist.
Exposure: sun/part shade.
Propagate: pencil thick roots planted 3 to 5 inches deep on a slant.
Height/Distance: 2 feet; 8 to 10 inches apart.
Harvest & Use: grate roots for fresh condiment.
Plants needed: one, since plant is invasive.

LOVAGE
(Levisticum officinale) C, O.
Soil: rich, moist, well-drained.
Exposure: sun/shade.
Propagate: sow seed in previous fall, transplant from pots in spring. Hard to move bare root.
Height/Distance: 4 to 6 feet; 2 feet apart.
Harvest & Use: leaves and stems as needed for strong celery flavor in tea or cookery; ground seeds or flowers flavor candy.

MINT
(Mentha piperata, M. pulegium, M. spicata, etc.) C, O, PR.
Soil: moist garden loam.
Exposure: sun/shade.
Propagate: from tip or root cuttings spring or fall.
Height/Distance: 10 to 24 inches; confine each plant to vertical flue liner set in garden, unless you have a separate mint bed.
Harvest & Use: shear new growth of mint plants as needed for seasoning, flavoring, or dried for teas and sachets. The variety of color, foliage, taste, and hardiness make them a must for the herb bed. Often planted near a door to repel flies. Choose among fruit and spice scents, as well as tea mints and traditional flavors. Vigorous growers.
Plants needed: 5 or 6 in a 3-foot-square bed.

OREGANO
(Oreganum majorana, O. compacta, O. vulgare ssp. hirtum, onites, etc.)
Tender perennial.
Soil: light, well-drained.
Exposure: sun for best flavor.
Propagate: indoors in sand late March except sterile Italian oregano which is divided spring or fall.
Height/Distance: 1 to 2 feet; 18 inches apart.
Harvest & Use: shear plants before flowers open in June, or pinch back new growth as needed. The oregano family includes sweet marjoram, the most delicate and popular of these related herbs. Potted it can be wintered over indoors. Other oreganos vary in strength and hardiness here with O. vulgare being the most cold proof. Greek oregano (O. onites) and mountain oregano (O. vulgare) are the most pungent. Like the thymes, oreganos germinate well on a sandy surface in the light.
Plants needed: 2 or 3.

PARSLEY
(Petroselinum crispum neapolitanum, P. crispum and Crytotaenia japonica) C.
Biennial/perennial.
Soil: rich garden soil.
Exposure: sun/part shade.
Propagate: soak and rinse seed for 24 hours or pour boiling water on row after April planting for quicker germination. Japanese parsley is an unrelated perennial, which may be transplanted spring or fall.
Height/Distance: 10 to 18 inches; 1 foot apart.
Harvest & Use: outer leaves midsummer and following spring before plants set seed. Japanese parsley is mild and can be harvested every year.
Plants needed: 3 to 12.

ROSEMARY
(Rosemarinus officinalis vars.) C, O, F.
Tender perennial.
Soil: light, well-drained.
Exposure: sun.
Propagate: from cuttings taken in April or layered branches.
Height/Distance: 2 to 5 feet in warmer parts of region; 2 to 4 feet.
Harvest & Use: cut back fresh branches as needed or prune whole plant in April and July for dried leaves. More than 2 dozen varieties are available with subtly different growth habits and fragrance. They make lovely pot plants, best wintered over in a greenhouse or cold frame north or west of the city. Just one, Rosemarinus officinalis 'Arp', is reliably hardy here—if the foliage is wrapped in bubble plastic from January through March. Its roots should not be mulched. Other of these handsome pungent shrubs may survive in a sheltered sandy garden.
Plants needed: 1 for cooking, more for ornamental use.

SAGE
(Salvia officinalis) Broadleaf, purple, dwarf, tricolor, variegated, pineapple varieties. C, O.
Perennial/tender perennial.
Soil: light, well-drained, sweet.
Exposure: sun.
Propagate: seed, layering, root; transplants easily.
Height/Distance: 1-5 feet; 1 to 3 feet apart.
Harvest & Use: prune back in early spring to encourage new branching, to keep plant open, and to ward off fungus diseases. Strip leaves for drying or fresh use. The variegated sages, Tricolor and S. icterina, as well as the Pineapple sage are less cold hardy. The trade-off is spectacular effect in the garden, with pineapple sage growing 5 feet high with red flowers in the fall as well as having leaves that are fruity and delicious to flavor summer punches.

SORREL
(Rumex acetosa) C.
Soil: rich garden loam.
Exposure: sun/shade.
Propagate: seed or divide and transplant in early April.
Height/Distance: 2 feet; 1 foot apart.
Harvest & Use: leaves as needed through season for salads, soups, and sauces. Cut center seed stalk for continued leaf production.

SWEET BAY
(Laurus nobilis) C, O, I.
Tender perennial: excellent in tub.
Soil: light, well-drained.
Exposure: sun.
Propagate: seed or from rooted cuttings taken in early fall. Difficult.
Height: 4 to 5 feet when grown and pruned as tub plant.
Harvest & Use: when pruning back branches in winter and again in early summer to shape the plant. Leaves may be stripped from cut branches or the cut branches formed into a herb wreath for kitchen use; use plant for topiary affect indoors or on patio.

SWEET WOODRUFF
(Galium odoratum) C, O.
Soil: moist, acid soil.
Exposure: shade.
Propagate: transplant divisions spring or fall, root cuttings in the spring.
Height/Distance: 6 inches; 4 to 6 inches apart
Harvest & Use: flower umbrels and new leaves for May wine.
Plants needed: as many pots as needed for herbaceous ground cover.

TARRAGON
(Artemesia dranunculus) C.
Soil: rich, warm, well-drained.
Exposure: sun/part shade.
Propagate: by tip cuttings or division in spring or early fall.
Height/Distance: 24 inches; 12 to 18 inches apart.
Harvest & Use: fresh as needed, dry in midsummer. This herb is unexcelled for fresh salad dressings, marinades, and vinegars with its delicate yet pungent flavor. To help save the plants from fungus diseases, site the plants for good air circulation, harvest frequently, and cut the stems in late fall. Do not mulch.

THYME
(Thymus) Common French, English, creeping, variegated silver or golden, lemon, wooly, camphor and Cretan varieties. C, O.
Perennial/tender perennial.
Soil: light, well-drained.
Exposure: sun.
Propagate: seed on top of clean moist sand in spring, root division from natural layering spring and fall.
Height/Distance: 13 to 15 inches; 12 to 18 inches.
Harvest & Use: shear back half in late spring and late summer. Dry and strip branches or soak for use in grilling. Creeping thyme is used as a fragrant groundcover between stones and is not harvested.
Plants needed: 4 for cooking; use 6 plants as groundcover for every 6 feet of walkway.

WINTER SAVORY
(Satureja montana, S. glabella) C.
Soil: moderately rich, dry.
Exposure: sun/part shade.
Propagate: seeds, cuttings, or layering in spring.
Height/Distance: 2 to 15 inches; 6 to 8 inches.
Harvest & Use: fresh as needed for seasoning soups, stews, and salad dressings; cut in midsummer to dry. S. glabella is a prostrate form that is very aromatic when trod upon.

HERBS FOR FRAGRANCE, ORNAMENT, PEST CONTROL, AND DYES

ANISE HYSSOP
(Agastache foeniculum) F, O.
Soil: rich garden loam.
Exposure: sun/shade in summer.
Propagate: by division in spring or fall.
Height/Distance: 3 to 4 feet; 10 to 12 inches apart.
Harvest & Use: violet flower spikes in June, leaves for potpourri.

ARTEMESIA
(Abrotanum pontica, A. schmidtiana) F, PR, O.
Soil: light, well-drained.
Exposure: sun.
Propagate: divisions for recurring pontica and Schmidtiana; cuttings in spring for southernwood (abrotanum).
Height/Distance: 4 to 48 inches; plant 1 to 3 feet apart with good air circulation.
Harvest & Uses: southernwood foliage as sachet material and moth repellant. A. pontica is, feathery blue green ornamental, used to flavor vermouth; the silvery A. schmidtiana and A. nana varieties are medium-and small-size mounds suitable for perennial bed and rock garden.

BOX, DWARF
(Buxus microphylla compacta, Kingsville hybrids) O.
Soil: average garden loam.
Exposure: sun/part shade.
Propagate: by cuttings in March.
Height/Distance: 1 foot; 1 foot apart.
Harvest & Use: Unexcelled as evergreen edging for formal herb gardens.

CATNIP
(Nepeta mussinii) F, PR.
Soil: light, well-drained.
Exposure: sun/shade.
Propagate: seeds, division, cuttings.
Height/distance: 18 to 24 inches; 1 foot.
Harvest & Use: cats love fresh foliage. New growth in midsummer can be dried or steeped to make a spray which will repel ants and flea beetles on garden plants.

CHAMOMILE
(Chaemaemelum nobile) O, M.
Soil: ordinary garden loam.
Exposure: sun/light shade.
Propagate: set out plants of Roman chamomile in the spring in a weed-free lawn that is well-watered. Mow often the first year to encourage spreading.
Height/Distance: 1 foot; 1 foot apart.
Harvest & Use: from untrampled part of lawn, use flowers in August for tea or hair rinse.

COMFREY
(Symphytum caucasicum) O, M.
Soil: rich, sweet.
Exposure: sun/part shade.
Propagate: from seeds or divisions, invasive.
Height/Distance: 3 feet; 1 to 2 feet.
Harvest & Use: crushed leaves steamed make a poultice for sprains and bruises; pink and blue flowers are decorative in garden from June through August. Chopped plants make good compost. Very invasive.

CURRY PLANT
(Helicrysum angustifolium) O, F, C.
Tender perennial.
Soil: light, well drained in buried pot.
Exposure: sun.
Propagate: tip cuttings in spring.
Height/Distance: 2 to 3 feet; 2 feet apart in the garden.
Harvet & Use: yellow flower spikes in May for dried arrangements, leaf cuttings for potpourri or seasoning for cold dishes. This plant is a member of the everlasting family.

ENGLISH PENNYROYAL
(Mentha pulegium) P, O.
Soil: moist, rich.
Exposure: shade/part sun.
Propagate: by division in spring.
Height/Distance: 2 to 3 inches; 1 foot apart.
Harvest & Use: leaves and fresh runners to dry and repel moths and fleas. The plants make a good groundcover in a moist shady corner of the garden.

FEVERFEW
(Chrysanthemum parthenium) O, PR.
Soil: any garden soil.
Exposure: sun.
Propagate: seeds, division in spring or fall.
Height/Distance: 1 foot apart.
Harvest & Use: in June and July for white or yellow rayed flowers to use in dried arrangements. Whole plant repels insects from nearby crops.

FOXGLOVE
(Digitalis, D. purpurea, Excelsior hybrids, Mertonensis ambigua) O, M.
Biennial.
Soil: rich, well-drained.
Exposure: partial shade.
Propagate: seed in May or August for bloom following year.
Height/Distance: 3 to 4 feet; 1 foot apart.
Harvest & Use: flower spikes in various colors June and July. Leaves of D. purpurea used by druggists for heart stimulant, not for home use.

GERMANDER
(Teucrium chamaedrys, T. canadensis) O.
Perennial: semi-evergreen shrub.
Soil: average garden soil.
Exposure: sun.
Propagate: from cuttings.
Height/Distance: 15 inches; 10 to 15 inches apart.
Harvest & Use: as a border for herbal knot gardens, this shrub will have rosy blooms in July if not trimmed earlier.

LAVENDER
(Lavendula angustifolia, L. intermedia) F, O, I.
Perennial/tender perennial.
Soil: light, rich, sweet (6.8 to 8 pH).
Exposure: full sun for best fragrance.
Propagate: cuttings in August or September.
Height/Distance: 18 to 30 inches; 2 feet apart.
Harvest & Use: June and July, or June and larger bloom in September for varieties that bloom two times a year. These splendid flower spikes in pink to purple shades hold their scent for years when dried. For healthiest plants, prune several times the first year to develop strong roots and crown. Fertilize all lavenders with a liquid feeding once a month during the first growing season. Tender varieties make good pot plants.

LEMON BALM
(Melissa officinalis) F, O, C.
Soil: good garden loam.
Exposure: sun/shade.
Propagate: readily by seed, division, or cutting.
Height/Distance: 18 inches; 1 foot apart.
Harvest & Use: shear leaves 3 or 4 times a season before bloom to dry for pungent citrus-like potpourri, or use fresh in teas and other recipes.

MONKSHOOD
(Aconitum napellus, A. henryi and A. wilsonii) O, M
Perennial: does not like to be moved.
Soil: rich, moist.
Exposure: light shade.
Propagate: self seed, or transplant from pot early in spring.
Height: 4 to 8 feet.
Harvest & Use: white, violet, or dark blue flower spikes in late summer or early fall. Napellus supplies aconite for medicine, not for home use.

POMEGRANATE, DWARF
(Punica granatum nana) O, D, C.
Tender perennial, root hardy in the warmer lower areas like the Eastern Shore.
Soil: light, rich.
Exposure: sun.
Propagate: seeds, cuttings in summer.
Height/distance: to 6 feet in tub; 2 feet apart.
Harvest & Use: orange flowers and dwarf fruit for red dye, fruit for salads and sauces. This is a handsome deciduous shrub even if it did not flower in June, and give fruit whose tart jeweled seeds spark Middle-Eastern cooking.

RUE
(Ruta graveolens) O, P.
Soil: light, well-drained.
Exposure: sun/shade.
Propagate: cuttings, seed in May.

Height/Distance: 3 feet; 6 inches apart.
Harvest & Use: blue green leaves by cutting back plant to shape in spring. They are used in flea repellant solutions and in flavoring some cheeses and brandy. Some skin allergies have been reported from handling rue.

SAFFLOWER
(Carthanus tinctorius) D, O.
Soil: light, poor.
Exposure: sun.
Propagate: seed in May.
Height/Distance: 2 to 3 feet; 6 inches apart.
Harvest & Use: flowers from July on for dried arrangements or making rose-red dyes for cloth.

SANTOLINA
(Santolina chamaecyparis, S. virens and S. incana) F, O, PR.
Perennial: reliably hardy in warmer parts of region.
Soil: light, well-drained.
Exposure: sun.
Propagate: cuttings in spring.
Height/Distance: 1 to 2 feet; 1 foot apart.
Harvest & Use: green or gray foliage and stems for moth repellant, button flowers in midsummer for drying. Cheese-like pungent aroma is strongest in the bright green S. virens. Both green and silver varieties make very ornamental borders for herb beds if pruned. Airy site prevents fungus.

SCENTED-LEAF GERANIUM
(Pelargonium) F, O.
Tender perennials.
Soil: light, sandy, sweet.
Exposure: sun.
Propagate: 4-inch cuttings in March dried for 2 to 3 hours after dipping in hormone powder and rooted in damp sterile perlite. Grow under lights until ready to move outdoors.
Height/Distance: 1 to 2 feet; 1 to 2 feet apart in garden as annuals or grow in pots or tubs to move indoors in winter.
Harvest & Use: flower and spice-scented leaves for potpourri or culinary use. Fresh, the geraniums give off their scent when planted near the radiated heat of a stone or brick patio.

SWEET CICELY
(Myrrhis odorata) F, C.
Soil: moist, rich.
Exposure: high shade.
Propagate: self-sow sparingly in woodsy garden; seed in fall, thin to 1 foot apart.
Height/Distance: 18 to 30 inches; 1 foot apart.
Harvest & Use: ferny foliage for salads, strewing. Seeds are borne straight up on the umbrels and give characteristic sweet licorice flavor to salads when green; when black they are dried for cooking or potpourri.

VALERIAN
(Valeriana officinalis) F, O, M.
Soil: good garden loam.
Exposure: sun/part shade.
Propagate: seed and division.
Height/distance: 4 feet; 2 feet apart, invasive.
Harvest & Use: fragrant flowers of white to pink purple in late July and August smell like heliotrope. Rhizome was used by druggists as a nerve sedative, not for home use.

YARROW
(Achillea) O, PR.
Soil; light, well-drained.
Exposure: sun.
Propagate: seed on surface of sand; division in spring.
Height/Distance: 4 to 48 inches; 1 foot apart, move every few years.
Harvest & Use: white, red and yellow flower heads for dried arrangements, whole plant quickly dried. These beautifully lacy plants are unexcelled for dry arrangements, and reputedly increase the flavor and aroma of herbs growing nearby, which may explain their reputation as an insect repellant. Tomentosa aurea, a dwarf golden yarrow is a valued rock garden plant for its low aromatic foliage with dense clusters of golden flowers.

Successful Herb Gardening
◊ The most important thing for success with herbs is good soil. This to the contrary of all the misinformation that Mediterranean herbs thrive in poor soil. Given our damp heat and unimproved clay, poor soil is a recipe for root rot.
◊ Dig in generous quantities of compost and shredded sphagnum moss.
◊ Frequent use of young perennial herbs the first season results in healthier plants with a better shape. Cutting the stems makes them branch more rapidly.
◊ Woody perennial herbs that lose most of their leaves during our winters should be cut back in early spring to renew them. Thyme, savory, hyssops, lavenders, and winter savory all benefit from removing one-third to one-half the stem length.
—*Thomas DeBaggio, Herb-grower, Arlington, Va.*

INSPIRATION: The National Herb Garden, The National Arboretum, Washington, D.C.
Meadowlark Gardens, Beulah Road off Route 7, Vienna Virginia.
River Farm, American Horticulture Society, off Mt. Vernon Parkway, Alexandria, Virginia.
Medicinal Herb Garden, National Institutes of Health, off Cedar Lane, Bethesda, Maryland.

Resources: The Herb Society of America, Potomac Unit, Jo Sellers (703) 451-7037.

SUN & SOIL PREFERENCES OF HERBS

Light Soil with Full Sun

Perennials	Annuals
	Lamb's Quarters
	Nasturtiums
	Safflower

Light, Sweet Soil with Full Sun

Perennials	Annuals
Anise Hyssop	Borage
Artemesia	
Curry Plant	
Dwarf Pomegranate	
Scented-leaf Geraniums	
Lavender	
Myrtles	
Lemon Verbena	
Rosemary	
Sage	
Santolina	
Sweet Bay	
Thyme	
Winter Savory	

Rich Soil with Full Sun

Perennials	Annuals
Comfrey	Basil
Fennel	French Marigold
	Good King Henry

Light Soil with Part Shade

Perennials	Annuals
Catnip	
Horehound	
Rue	

Rich, Moist Soil with Part Shade

Perennials	Annuals
Angelica	Chervil
Bee Balm	Dill
Burnet	Coriander
Chives	Foxglove
Lovage	Pot marigold
Mint Monkshood	
Parsley	
Pennyroyal	
Sorrel	
Sweet Cicely	
Sweet Woodruff	

16. GARDENING WITH CHILDREN

Gardening with children is so much fun and will so increase a gardener's pleasure that I could not leave this revision without sharing some techniques that have worked for me over the last fifteen years. I am deeply indebted to Alice Skelsey's wonderful book, *Growing Up Green,* which has confirmed my own experiences.

The ideal situation is for the gardener to work with a group of children at school. What child does not want to get out of the classroom and do something more physically active? Together the class can achieve some really impressive gardens, because many hands make for light work, and perhaps nurture a lasting interest in botany, biology, and horticulture.

But the pleasures can be just as great at home with the small child, for whom it is the greatest of treats to do something grown-up with a parent or family friend. This period does not last long. And these days as we rush ourselves and children through their childhood, your window of opportunity will be lost if you wait much past a child's sixth birthday. They will be off to practices and lessons galore, and

you will be stuck on the sidelines as the chauffeur. Seize the day. Gardening is something you can do together with a mutual feeling of accomplishment. It will keep you both off the streets.

And you will find that your small gardener's short stature and passion for dirt is a great advantage to you, for he will see things that you miss—things worth seeing, like worms, bugs, the first green sprouted seed, and perhaps its root as well.

No great preparation is required in order to garden with children. It can and should be relaxing for you both. But there are a few guidelines that seem to work very well, and a few types of gardening that are especially appealing to children.

General Guidelines
Garden in the morning after breakfast when small children are fresh. Harvest near lunch time. Share a snack when you finish your work so you can talk over your discoveries.

Save a spot at the edge of your garden and make your

special garden there for you and the children. Then you will not be jittery about small feet wandering into your favorite plantings on the way to and from your special place. Save a small piece of this as a "just for you" spot that a child can reach and tend easily on his own.

In an outdoor garden, prepare the ground ahead without counting on the child's participation at first. If you have small rows and beds with clear walkways, it's easier for a child to concentrate on the planting process.

Buy big seeds in packages with nice clear labels. Peas and beans and onion sets are ideal. Stick to radishes, carrots, and lettuce for little seeds, with perhaps a pack of cherry tomatoes.

Always let your gardening partner do the planting and covering, and most of the harvesting. Don't take over. Even two- and three-year-olds can get it pretty straight; and their feeling of accomplishment is enormous.

Get a magnifying glass so you can tell weeds from plants. (This may take years, as adult gardeners can tell you). Better yet, get a 50 cent bug box made of lucite with a magnifying lid. After all, you may need the help to see insects clearly.

Mark rows clearly with large labels, with name on one side, picture on the other, courtesy of your resident artist. This is a good rainy day project to build anticipation. But don't make too big of a deal of gardening beforehand. It's more fun to go out and get started.

If you buy the children a small tool, make it a trowel, so they can dig, or a sturdy rake, so then can weed and thin.

Rely on hand weeding and removal for pest control when working with the child in the garden until they are six years old. Second choice is soap sprays.

Don't spend over half an hour at a session unless your little friend is completely absorbed.

Eat what you harvest the same day. You may be growing a vegetable lover. But don't make a big deal out of that either. When did you first like beets? On the other hand, a few strawberry plants might prove to be instructive, fun, and irresistible.

Flowers

As you can see, I believe children like to grow vegetables for starters. There's the immediate feedback. But many do love flowers. One of the best and sturdiest is dwarf marigolds. They are almost pest-free and bloom to frost. They can easily be broken off the plant.

When you're at the garden center, do let the children choose a plant to put in their own special spot. But steer them to the ranks of the sturdiest and easiest plants before you suggest it.

Bulbs

You will discover that children make the most enthusiastic bulb gardeners. In the fall they will happily plant bulbs outdoors in beds you prepare without the least understanding of what is to come up in the spring.

You can help make it real for them by buying forcing varieties of these same bulbs for blooms indoors in the winter. They do well in shallow terra cotta bulb pans and smell as wonderful in a child's room as they do in the rest of the house. Make sure you let the children know that bulbs can't be eaten, if your children are dedicated tasters. Some bulbs are poisonous. But there is little danger, if they are safely planted and stored in a dark place that only you know about, until you bring them out with green shoots and their roots showing. Then both of you will be raring to go when the seed catalogs arrive in January.

The Last Word

Bill Hash, director of the Washington Youth Gardens, who has helped thousands of area children grow their own vegetables and flowers, offers these tips:

Be sure to force some paper narcissus or amaryllis in winter. They are so beautiful and fast growing that children find them irresistible.

Chives are a great favorite in a salad garden row. Children are charmed by the flowers and will pluck them to nibble as they go about the garden.

Every child wants to grow carrots; but carrots take forever in a child's time frame. So make sure that the salad row has lettuce, scallions, and several types of radishes, so they can pull a surprise from the ground within a month. It will help make the longer wait for carrots bearable.

INSPIRATION:

Children's Gardens at:

American Horticultural Society, River Farm, off George Washington Memorial Parkway south of Alexandria, Va.
Twin Oaks Youth Garden Center, 14th & Taylor Streets, NW, Washington D.C.

17. THE WILDFLOWER GARDEN

The growing of wildflowers in the home garden is a natural desire, usually beginning during childhood. This desire persists with many gardeners all through their gardening days.

Some of this interest in wildflowers undoubtedly stems from their earliness. Others think of them because of their natural habitat in the woods. Perhaps we might add a third point of interest—they are native to this area. Also, most of them are comparatively free from insect and disease problems.

The metropolitan area's list of native flowers and ferns is very extensive. More than 50 kinds of ferns, for example, are to be found in this vicinity. Several kinds of violets, as well as the trillium, gentians, and other wildflowers, may be seen in our parks, at the nature trail at Great Falls, and in the Fern Valley section of the National Arboretum. The latter includes, of course, many wildflowers from areas distant from Washington.

Conservation Lists

Some of our native plants are being sadly thinned through thoughtless mutilation of the plants by those who want a pretty bouquet or who destroy them by careless handling. To publicize the importance of pres-ervation, conservation groups both in Maryland and Virginia have prepared lists of those which should be protected. In addition, the garden clubs have provided lists of our wildflowers which are not permissible in flower shows or other exhibitions unless they are grown on the gardener's property.

Native Plant Protection List

For the District of Columbia and Nearby
Maryland and Virginia
Prepared by
Conrad B. Link and Russell G. Brown
University of Maryland

This list has been prepared for the National Capital Area Federation of Garden Clubs as a guide for garden clubs and others interested in the use and preservation of native plants. It has been adapted for this area using the "Wild Flower Protection List" by P. L. Ricker, published by the Wild Flower Preservation Society, as a guide.

The preservation of our native plants is an important interest of garden clubs and others concerned with the preservation of our natural beauty and resources. One desire of such groups is the intelligent use of native plants in garden plantings, in the home, as well as in flower shows. The following list has been divided into two sections. The first part includes those native plants that are satisfactory as garden plants, many of which are propagated and sold commercially, and that are also found in this area in the wild. The second part includes those kinds that are less commonly found and are in danger of becoming extinct in this area, yet they may be abundant in other sections of the country. These native plants should not be ruthlessly destroyed and efforts should be made to protect them. Some would be adaptable for garden use whereas others are more difficult to grow because of some specialized soil or cultural condition that is necessary.

Gardeners are cautioned in the general collection of native plants. Permission should be obtained from the land owner. Certainly when fields and woods are being destroyed for construction of buildings and roads, there should be no restriction on the part of the gardeners to try and collect such plants for transplanting to a garden. Where a species grows in great profusion, with hundreds of thousands of individuals present, the taking of a plant for propagation is not likely to do serious harm. The digging of a large number of plants is to be discouraged.

Part I

These native plants are in need of protection in this area. However, since they are often propagated and grown as garden plants, they may be cut and used in flower shows. Careful picking so as not to destroy the plant is practical. In the case of woody plants, careful cutting becomes a form of pruning and not injurious.

Azalea—see Rhododendron
Bloodroot—Sanguinaria canadensis
Bittersweet—Celastrus scandens
Bluebell—Mertensia virginica
Columbine—Aquilegia canadensis
Dogwood—Cornus florida
Fringetree—Chionanthus virginicus
Holly—ilex opaca
Loosestrife—Lythrum
Lily—Lilium (native species)
Mountain Laurel—Kalmia latifolia
Phlox—native species. P. ovata
                   P. maculata
                   P. divaricata
                   P. subulata
Shadbush—Amelanchier canadensis
Sheep Laurel (Lambskill)—Kalmia angustifolia
Stonecrop—Sedum (native specie
Redbud—Cercis canadensis
Rhododendron—Rhododendron nudiflorum
    (Pinxterflower)
Rhododendron maximum—Roseboy
Rhododendron viscosum—Swamp Azalea

Part II

These native plants are less commonly found in this area and thus are in need of protection and preservation. Some of these are not readily adapted to garden culture. Many could be picked as cut flowers if the roots are not disturbed and if sufficient foliage and flowers are left for continued growth and reproduction.

Anemone—Anemone species
Baneberry—Actaea
Bellflower—Campanula (native species)
Bellwort—Uvularia species
Blue Cohosh—Caulophyllum thalictroides
Blue-eyed-Mary—Collinsia verna
Cardinalflower—Lobelia cardinalis
Celandine—Chelidonium majus
Checkerberry Wintergreen—Gaultheria procumbens
Clubmoss—Lycopodium
Columbine—Aquilegia canadensis (native species)
Cohosh—See Baneberry
Coralroot—Corallorrhiza
Dutchman's-Breeches—Dicentra cucullaria
False Solomonseal—Smilacina stellata; S. racemosa
Ferns—especially Walking Fern
Fetterbush—Leucothoe racemosa
Thimbleberry—Rubus odoratus
Gentians—Native species
Goldstargrass—Hypoxis hirsuta
Golden Groundsel—Senecio aureus
Groundnut—Apios americana tuberosa
Hepatica—Hepatica americana; H. acutiloba
Horsegentian—Triosteum perfoliatum
Indianpipe—Monotropa uniflora
Iris, vernal—Iris verna
     crested—Iris cristata
Jackinthepulpit—Arisaema triphyllum
Jacob's Ladder—Polemonium
Ladyslipper—Cypripedium
Larkspur, wild—Delphinium tricorne
Lobelia—Lobelia siphilitica (Giant Lobelia)
    Lobelia cardinalis (Cardinal Flower)
Marshmarigold—Caltha palustris
Willowleaf spirea—Spirea salicifolia
Milkwort—Polygala paucifolia (Fringed polygala)
Mistletoe—Phoradendron
Miterwort—Mitella (Bishopscap)
Jerseytea—Ceanothus armeicanus
Orchids—all native species
Paintedcup—Castilleja
Pasqueflower—Anemone patens
Peatpink—Silene caroliniana
Phacelia—Phacelia
Phlox—Native species
Pinesap—Monotropa hypopitys
Pitcherplant—Sarracenia purpurea
Poorrobins-Plaintain—Erigeron pulchellus
Puttyroot—Aplectrum
Rosegentian—Sabatia angularis
Rue-Anemone—Anemonella thalictroides
Ruellia—Ruellia carolenensis
Saxifrage-Saxifraga—native species
Shinleaf—Pyrola elliptica
Shootingstar—Dodecatheon meadia
Solomonseal—Polygonatum biflorum: P. canaliculatum
Squirrelcorn—Dicentra canadensis
Staggerbush—Lyonia mariana
Stargrass—Aletris or Hypoxis
Sundew—Drosera species
Rosegentian—Sabatia species
Toothwort—Dentaria laciniata
Turtlehead—Chelone species
Trailing-Arbutus—Epigaea repens
Trillium (Wake Robin)—all species
Twinleaf—Jeffersonia diphylla
Violet Woodsorrel Oxalis—Oxalis violacea
Waterleaf—Hydrophyllum
Walkingfern—Camptosorus rhizophyllus
Wildbergamot—Monarda fistulosa
Wild Calla—Calla palustris
Wild Geranium (Cranesbill)—Geranium maculatum
Wildginger—Asarum canadense
Wintergreen—Pyrola species

There is an exception to the above rules. Because of the spread of real estate developments into suburban areas, it is recommended that gardeners seeking wildflowers precede the bulldozer and rescue all they can. This is in the hope that by careful handling, plants, that would otherwise be destroyed, will be saved. In this connection, it should be noted that though the bulldozer may not uproot them, the thinning of the trees and the change in the flow of soil moisture is just as fatal to our natives as is their being uprooted.

To insure success in handling our wildflowers, one should begin by noting their environment and trying to duplicate it as far as possible in the home garden. In most cases, this is a shady garden. Secondly, there are usually certain periods which are better for transplanting than are others. This, of course, cannot always be observed. Third, it is important to lift the plants with a minimum of disturbance to their root system. Next, they should be wrapped in a sheet of plastic to prevent any drying out during the trip from native habitat to garden. In planting them in the wildflower garden, it is well to incorporate generous quantities of sphagnum peat moss or leafmold into the planting area. A generous mulch of leaves to which they are accustomed is usually very beneficial, and lastly, there are some plants which are so difficult to transplant that it is seldom worth the effort. In this category, we might well include the Trailing Arbutus and the Pink Ladyslipper. The latter seems to require a layer of well-rotted leaves in which its roots will thrive. Lacking in this, it does not persist more than one or two years. The Butterfly milkweed is another example. Unless it can be dug in August when it is dormant, it is very difficult to transplant. Our beautiful Royal ferns have a very high moisture requirement, and unless this can be satisfied, they should not be disturbed.

Which of the Wildflowers Are Adapted to Our Gardens?

In the metropolitan area, we will find wildflowers growing in almost every situation—sun, shade, moist, dry, and in bogs and along stream banks. Not all these conditions can be duplicated in any one garden; therefore, it is important to select those kinds which are best adapted to the gardeners' areas. Also, it is wise to refrain from planting those which are gross spreaders. Examples of this latter point are the Common Woods Violet, the Mistflower, the Blackeyedsusan, the New England aster, and perhaps the Goldenrod. This point is particularly important where one has a mixture of the dainty small springflowering kinds and the taller more vigorous growing summer-flowering plants. The Springbeauty, for example, would soon be crowded out by the Common Woods Violet. Some kinds are more at home in a rock garden type of planting than others. In such situations, they show off to better advantage and thus give more satisfaction.

Some kinds go together effectively. The Virginia Bluebells and the Fawnlily, for example, are good companions and thrive in the same situation.

Collect or Buy?

Whether we should go into the woods and fields to collect our wildflowers or buy them from a reputable nursery is a much debated point. In the first place, most states have a restriction or prohibition against taking plants from public lands. Most land owners resent wanton stripping of their property. Therefore, the plant collector should make certain to obtain the owner's permission before engaging in any plant collecting operations. Secondly, we should recognize that most plants move best at certain seasons of the year, and sometimes this is not at the season when most gardeners enjoy a trip through the woods or fields. Another point, usually wildflowers are growing in competition with weeds, grass and tree roots; consequently, their root systems are rather straggly and oftentimes difficult to lift intact. Thus, the securing of the desired kinds from reputable specialists has several advantages. They can provide the roots of the Butterfly milkweed at the proper season of the year. At digging time there is nothing to indicate their location unless it be a seed stalk. The showy Trilliums are nearly extinct in this area, and one should have at least a dozen of the root stocks for planting in order to have a good show of bloom. Those allergic to poison ivy might well find it to their advantage to buy rather than hunt.

Preparing the Soil

In the shady garden, it is desirable to prepare the new home as early as possible. First this involves the removing of competing tree roots and, if possible, preparing a barricade to keep them out of the planting area. The hole should be dug fairly deeply and filled with native soil whenever possible, although sphagnum peat is an excellent substitute. For the Virginia Bluebells, the soil should be made as light as possible through the addition of sand or perlite. The Fawnlily (Dogtooth violet) has a very long tuber, and the soil might well be prepared to a depth of a foot or more.

Since the wild root systems are likely to be rather straggly, it is desirable to take small plants rather than large ones. Oftentimes, the strays that are outside the patch are more likely to move successfully than are plants taken from the crowded area.

Even with small plants, it is desirable to take a fairly large ball of earth to avoid damaging the roots and to reduce the shock of transplanting. Thus, it is better to make several trips rather than try to do everything at one time. Be sure to cover the containers with plastic or some other material to prevent their drying while being transported.

Generally, the best time to take most of our wildflowers is in the early spring while they are dormant or just as new growth is starting. This is especially important of our native shrubs and trees. Of course, there are exceptions to this rule. The native azaleas can be moved when in bloom. Many others may be moved successfully if the above guides are followed. Ferns, for example, may be moved at any time, but as the new fronds begin to unroll, they are very brittle and easily broken.

It is important to plant the wildlings at the same depth as they grew in their native habitat. An exception to this rule is the hemlock and possibly the American holly. The soil should be level or slightly depressed about them so that moisture will drain into the root area rather than away from it. (This would be fatal in a soil that is lacking in subsurface drainage.) With the plant properly placed in the planting hole, the soil should be worked in and around the roots and then settled with water to eliminate air pockets. Small plants can and might well have leafmold over the planting area as a mulch. In addition, and especially for sun-loving plants, it is well to shade them for a period while they are becoming re-established. The trunks of dogwoods, redbuds, and others that are to be planted in a sunny situation should be wrapped the first season to prevent sunscald of the bark. Discarded nylons are especially well suited for this purpose.

During the first season after planting, it is important to water them whenever rainfall is inadequate. This is especially important in the shady garden since the tree leaves above oftentimes absorb a considerable portion of the rainfall.

If these plants are taken in the fall, it is well to mulch them rather heavily with leaves; however, in order to avoid the leaves matting down, it is usually desirable to first scatter brush over the area. When planted at other seasons, a fall mulch may or may not be necessary depending on whether the fallen leaves will stay in place. In a windswept situation, it is usually advisable to scatter brush to hold the leaves.

Most wildlings will suffer some root shock which is difficult to avoid unless the plants are small. If large plants are taken, a portion of the top should be removed. This practice is exceedingly important when moving woody plants such as dogwood, redbud, American holly and others. The tops of perennial plants, where they have several stems, might well be thinned.

It is seldom advisable to use commercial fertilizer or manure on any of the natives. Usually, the leaf mulch will provide enough plant food to take care of their needs. After they have once been established, an acid-forming type of fertilizer might be safely used, or perhaps dehydrated cow manure, but no inorganic fertilizer.

Spring Ephemerals

BLOODROOT

(Sanguinaria canadensis—perennial)

Height:	6-10 inches.
Flower:	White 1 to 1½ inches, borne on solitary stems, single and double flowers to be found in wild. Early spring-flowering.
Exposure:	Light shade.
Soil:	Moist woodsy, moderately acid.
Transplant:	Early spring.
Uses:	Rock gardens, rock walls.
Improved varieties:	No.
Propagate:	Division in fall, self-seeds, seed sown as soon as ripe.
Conservation list:	On conservation list I.

The Bloodroot is an excellent plant for the wildflower garden. The showy white blooms above gray-green foliage are attractive. They are not difficult to grow, thriving in rich woodsy soil. The rhizomes spread and an appreciable clump soon develops.

The Bloodroot's showy flowers have their petals spread out wide in the morning; they are erect at noon and close at dusk. The flowers last for several days, the doubles longer.

The plant derives its common name from the juice of the stem and roots which is red.

One might well intersperse Bloodroot plants among the rhododendrons and other acid-soil loving plants in shady situations. They are quite showy in the shady rock garden and rock walls, wherever attractive foliage and bloom are desired.

Plant the thick root, about one-inch deep, in soil that has been enriched with leafmold, compost or peatmoss. The older the root the larger number of flowers a single plant will produce.

BLUEBELLS, VIRGINIA

(Mertensia virginica—perennial)

Height:	10-24 inches.
Flower:	Light blue, buds a pink, terminal clusters, early spring.
Exposure:	Semi-shade.
Soil:	Sandy, enriched with leafmold, moist, moderately acid.
Transplant:	Early spring or while dormant in summer or fall. 4-inches deep.
Uses:	Near stream banks, rock garden, companion to daffodils, primroses.
Improved varieties:	No.
Conservation list:	On conservation list I.

The Virginia Bluebell, also known as Virginia Cowslip, is an early spring bloomer, usually found near a creek bank where the soil is sandy and always moist. The bright blue of the flowers is quite showy.

The bright blue color makes them excellent companions for the daffodils and the primroses which bloom at the same season. They also make an interesting combination with the Western Fawnlily since both need the same type of soil and shade.

The Bluebells should be transplanted in the early spring or in the summer and fall while they are dor-

mant. The clumps may be divided. Once happily established, they will self-seed.

The one objection to this charming native is that it dies down in the summer leaving a bare space in the wildflower garden. For this reason it is well to have them interplanted with the Rue-anemone or other plants which retain their foliage throughout the season.

Old clumps that have become too crowded for good growth may be lifted after flowering and divided. This is about the only care needed once they are well established.

BLUETS (Quaker Ladies)

(Houstonia caerulea—perennial)

Height:	6-8 inches.
Flower:	Pale blue, star-shaped, on long stalks, early to mid-spring.
Exposure:	Sun or light shade.
Soil:	Moist, woodsy, acid.
Transplant:	Anytime.
Uses:	Ground cover.
Improved varieties:	No.
Propagate:	Self-sow, divide in early spring or fall.
Conservation list:	Not on conservation list.

The tiny Bluets do not seem to be much when viewed as a single plant, but a carpet of them over an open space is effective. If in suitable surroundings they will self-seed and spread.

They will grow in a sunny situation provided the soil has been enriched with leafmold, compost, or peatmoss. Otherwise they seem happier in light shade, although here too they need an enriched soil.

The Bluets are easily transplanted at anytime and there is seldom need to propagate for they will quickly seed an area if it is to their liking.

If space is limited the Bluets make a better showing in a rock garden than when lost among a host of other wildlings. The flowers are tiny, averaging less than ½-inch in diameter. It is a carpet of them that produces the dainty effect. A large clump in the rock garden or in some area in the shady garden is effective.

FAIRYBELLS

(Disporum lanuginosum—perennial)

Height:	1-2 feet.
Flower:	Creamy bells, red fruited, solitary/pairs at tip of stems, spring.
Exposure:	Light shade.
Soil:	Enriched woodland, moist, acid.
Transplant:	Spring, fall.
Uses:	Background, filler plants.
Improved varieties:	No.
Propagate:	Division early spring, fall; seed (depulp before sowing).
Conservation list:	Not on list.

The Fairybells are dainty little flowers that thrive in light shade in a woodsy soil that is not too dry. They are tolerant of acidity and will thrive among azaleas and rhododendrons. The fruits turn red in the fall and are long lasting.

The Fairybells are often mistaken for a Solomon-plume (False Solomonseal) to which they are related—as well as to the true Solomonseal, Twisted Stalk and Bead Lily. It is well to note the difference in the flowers if the other characteristics are not known. The name Fairybells is descriptive and they appear either singly or in pairs at the tip of each stem.

The plants transplant best in early spring or fall. Large clumps may be divided, and they are easy to raise from seed. Seeds should be depulped before sowing in the fall.

The Fairybells with their creamy white or green-tinged flowers which hang down may not be showy enough for some. However, they are easy to establish and are attractive both in flower and fruit.

FAWNLILY

(Erythronium Spps.—perennial)

Height:	8-12 inches.
Flower:	Lily-like of various colors—spring.
Exposure:	Light shade.
Soil:	Sandy, enriched with peatmoss, leafmold, acid, well-drained.
Transplant:	Difficult, best buy bulbs in fall.
Uses:	In wildflower border, rock garden.
Improved varieties:	No.
Propagate:	By offsets.
Conservation list:	Not on lists.

The Fawnlily is its accepted common name, but in this area they are known as the Dogtooth Violet, Adder's-Tongue, etc. In the west, where they are common, they are called Troutlily, Fawnlily, Glacierlily, etc.

The common Eastern Fawnlily usually grows so thickly in our woods that it seldom flowers freely. Also, the stems are short and the flowers not too showy. The Western Fawnlilies are taller growing, have larger flowers, and are more dependable.

The corm or bulb of the Fawnlily is long and slender, and is very brittle. Consequently it must be well packed

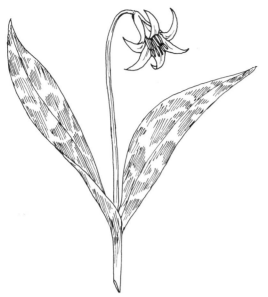

to prevent damage in shipping and in planting. Because of its form the digging of the corms in the wild is seldom satisfactory except in sandy soils.

The Fawnlilies make a very pleasing combination with the Virginia Bluebells in the wildflower garden, blooming at the same season and requiring about the same kind of soil and moisture. Both disappear in early summer and the space might well be used for the planting of summer-flowering annuals.

The Glacierlily of the northwest has bright yellow flowers; the Fawnlily (E. californicum) has creamy white flowers E. hendersoni of Southern Oregon has pale lavender flowers with purple throats. These are only a few of the many kinds of Fawnlilies.

JACOB'S-LADDER

(Polemonium reptans—perennial)

Height:	9-12 inches.
Flower:	Light violet, bell shaped, terminal clusters, spring.
Exposure:	Sun, light shade.
Soil:	Woodsy, rich humus, moist, neutral to moderately acid.
Transplant:	Spring, fall.
Uses:	Rock garden, among azaleas, front of shady border.
Improved varieties:	No.
Propagate:	Divide after flowering, self-sow.
Conservation list:	On list II.

There is some confusion as to the botanical species of the Jacob's-Ladder. Our native is Polemonium reptans. There is an introduced species, P. caeruleum, which is quite similar. Collected plants are likely to be the P. reptans, while the purchased ones may be P. caeruleum. The latter has undoubtedly escaped in some areas since it has found conditions here to its liking.

The other common names for the Jacob's-Ladder are Greek Valerian and Spring Polemonium. The name Jacob's-Ladder undoubtedly derives from the alternate arrangement of the leaves, ladder-like in appearance.

An attractive plant with lacy leaves and pleasing clusters of flowers at the tips of the upper branches, it needs only a rich woodsy soil to thrive in a rock garden, or along the paths in the wildflower garden. It will take either sun or light shade; the latter gives better results in this area except where both soil and moisture are adequate. The Jacob's-Ladder does not persist for long in a droughty soil either in sun or shade.

This plant should take away some of the bareness of the Rhododendron planting with its lacy foliage.

It is best transplanted in the early spring or in the fall. Divide old clumps after they have flowered. However, in a suitable situation they will self-seed freely.

MAYAPPLE

(Podophyllum peltatum—perennial)

Height:	12-15 inches.
Flower:	Hidden by foliage, 1½-2 inches, fragrant, white, spring.
Exposure:	Light shade.
Soil:	Enriched, moist, acid.
Transplant:	Anytime, early spring best.
Uses:	Carpets open woodlands, is a spreader.
Improved varieties:	No.
Propagate:	Division.
Conservation list:	No.

The Mayapple is a familiar spring-flowering plant in open woodlands. The wide-spreading, umbrella form of foliage usually hides the fragrant white flower below. There is only one flower on a plant and appears in the axle of the two leaf stems. It may be 1½ to 2 inches wide.

The Mayapple may be transplanted at any time, but early spring is less of a shock to the plant.

A moist soil well enriched with leafmold, peatmoss or compost is suitable for this flower. However, it is a spreader and should not be planted in the smaller wildflower garden. Certainly, an ideal soil favors the rapid growth of the spreading rhizomes.

The fruit, when ripe, is edible, but green fruit, roots and foliage are poisonous. They contain a bitter resinous substance that is sometimes used as a purgative. The rootstock may cause severe dermatitis on some.

The Mayapple is also known as Mandrake which alludes to its flowering season, but the name properly belongs to a European plant.

PHLOX, SWEETWILLIAM

(Phlox divaricata—perennial)

Height:	8-12 inches.
Flower:	Lilac to lavender, showy terminal clusters, early to mid-spring.
Exposure:	Light shade.
Soil:	Rich leafmold, moist, acid.
Transplant:	Anytime, early spring best.
Uses:	Cultivated borders, naturalize in wildflower garden.
Improved varieties:	Yes—alba, laphami.
Propagate:	Division, root cuttings, seed.
Conservation list:	On list I.

The Sweetwilliam Phlox, also called Wild Wood's phlox, Blue phlox, etc., is of the easiest culture and will spread by seed. However, it dies down early in the summer and thus this habit can hardly be called a fault. The color display in the wildflower garden or in an open woodland is excellent.

The Sweetwilliam is easily divided if a special form is desired. It also may be propagated by root-cuttings. However, most gardeners will enjoy the ordinary form and let it spread naturally.

Give the Blue Phlox a soil that has been enriched with leafmold, sphagnum moss or compost. This will make the soil acid and hold the moisture.

There are many other kinds of phlox native to this area. The P. maculata, which is also called Sweetwilliam, is also desirable. It has about the same size of plant and flowers, but the flowers are pink or purple. The stems are purple-spotted.

Another native is the Wild Pink Phlox, P. ovata, which has larger flowers, and are rose-pink. The stems are a bit shorter. It flowers in late spring. Creeping Phlox, P. stolonifera, usually grows about 6 inches high, has mauve-pink flowers and is useful as a ground cover in woodland areas.

The Mountain Pink, Moss Phlox, or Moss-Pink, P. subulata, which is so commonly sold by merchants in the early spring, is also native in this area. Unlike the others it is a sun-lover. However, all want a soil that has been generously enriched with peatmoss. The Moss Phlox will tolerate a drier soil and loves to sprawl over a large rock.

RUE ANEMONE

(Anemonella thalictroides—perennial)

Height:	6-9 inches.
Flower:	Clusters of 1-inch flowers at tips of stems, mid-spring.
Exposure:	Light to dense shade.
Soil:	Rich, humusy, moist, acid.
Transplant:	Late spring.
Improved varieties:	No.
Propagate:	Divide late spring (tubers), fall.
Conservation list:	In list II.

The dainty little Rue-anemone is considered excellent for the shady wildflower garden, although its small stature would indicate it might be lost among taller growing plants. Perhaps it is best used in the rock garden.

The gray-green leaves are quite similar to those of the Meadowrue and the Columbine.

This wildflower seems to thrive in shade in a deep woodsy soil that is moist but well-drained.

Each clump has many tiny tubers which may be divided in late spring. The plant is completely dormant by early summer. While this plant may seem to be delicate, actually it is a sturdy wildflower and is easily established in a shady garden.

SPRINGBEAUTY, CAROLINA

(Claytonia caroliniana—perennial)

Height:	5-10 inches.
Flower:	White or rose tinted, deeper rose veins, clusters. spring.
Exposure:	Light shade, sun.
Soil:	Moist, rich woodsy, acid.
Transplant:	Spring, fall, or after flowering.
Uses:	With Virginia Bluebells, carpet woodland.
Improved varieties:	No.
Propagate:	Division spring or fall, seed.
Conservation list:	No.

The Carolina Springbeauty is a dainty little flower that will carpet the ground under favorable conditions. Its early spring display is always desirable. When picked, the flowers soon wilt, but they are so attractive that every child wants to pick them.

This wildflower thrives in light shade in a moist soil that has been enriched with peatmoss or other humus. In such a situation it soon spreads by seed to carpet the area.

It is not difficult to transplant. The tubers should be covered with about 2 inches of soil. The plants disappear by mid-summer.

The Springbeauty may be planted in special soil pockets in the rock garden, it is also attractive when planted among the Virginia Bluebells. They may also be potted up for forcing.

The Carolina Springbeauty is smaller flowered than the Common Springbeauty (C. virginica) which is also native to this area. The latter is also called Mayflower, Grass-Flower, and Good-Morning-Spring.

STAR-OF-BETHLEHEM

(Ornithogalum umbellatum—perennial)

Height:	5-10 inches.
Flower:	White in flat-topped clusters—spring.
Exposure:	Sun, light shade.
Soil:	Rich, woodsy, moist but well drained.
Transplant:	Anytime.
Uses:	Rock garden, border for woodland paths.
Improved varieties:	Yes.
Propagate:	Division of bulbs in late fall.
Conservation list:	No.

The Star-of-Bethlehem is a dainty little bulbous flower that has found eastern North America a suitable home and has become widely naturalized. In the areas where naturalized many of the clumps have so impoverished the soil that they are poor bloomers. However, if lifted and separated, they should soon regain their normal flower display.

The Star-of-Bethlehem thrives in a rich woodsy soil, one that has been enriched by the addition of peatmoss, leafmold or compost. It does best in light shade.

The bulbs may be lifted in the late summer or early fall, divided and reset in enriched soil.

This plant which dies down in the summer leaving a bare spot in the wildflower garden or rock garden may be followed with summer-flowering plants.

The flowers are showy. There may be 15 or 20 on 10- to 12-inch stems. Dainty and star-shaped, but more especially happy in our climate, as well as tough and enduring they should not be overlooked for the wildflower garden.

VIOLET, BIRDSFOOT

(Viola pedata—perennial)

Height:	5-10 inches.
Flower:	Upper petals lilac, lower ones dark purple-black; spring.
Exposure:	Sun, light shade.
Soil:	Well-drained, rich in humus, acid.
Transplant:	Anytime.
Uses:	Sunny rock garden, border.
Improved Varieties:	No.
Propagate:	Seed, division.
Conservation list:	No.

The Birdsfoot Violet is one of the better violets to grow. It may be short-lived in a soil that is lacking in acidity. It is often to be found along the roadside, sometimes on high banks.

There are many forms of the Birdsfoot Violet to be found in most parts of the United States. Some seem to be thriving in soils that are lacking in the acidity of the Eastern States. This has been interpreted by some to indicate that in time these violets build up a toxicity from which they eventually perish. To demonstrate this theory, they dig up the plants every few years and re-plant in fresh soil.

The Birdsfoot Violet gets its name from the deeply divided leaves which are thought to resemble a bird's foot, having 3 or more segments. The flowers are quite large and showy when grown under favorable conditions.

The Birdsfoot Violet is not aggressive and hence is not objectionable in the wildflower garden while the common woods violet soon becomes a weed crowding out other plants.

The foliage dies down in the summer leaving a bare area where summer-flowering annuals might well be planted.

Under favorable conditions this violet self-seeds and hence division is seldom practiced. It may be safely transplanted at anytime if kept moist during transportation. The flowers are fragrant and long-lasting.

Persistent Flowers or Foliage

ALUMROOT

(Heuchera americana—perennial)

Height:	1-2 feet.
Flowers:	Slender branched spike, dull brown or bronze, June-Sept.
Exposure:	Light shade.
Soil:	Average garden loam, tolerant of acidity.
Transplant:	Any time.
Uses:	Low mounds of foliage suitable for rock garden or border in the shady garden.
Improved varieties:	Yes.
Propagate:	Seed, division in spring or fall, leaf cuttings.
Conservation list:	No.

The Alumroot, often mistakenly called Coralbells (the name properly belongs to a western species), is an attractive and easily grown wildflower. The compact mounds of evergreen foliage are surmounted by tall stems of airy flowers. The usual wildling has dull and inconspicuous blooms, but there are a number of improved varieties of Coralbells whose flowers are larger and much more showy.

The Alumroot delight in light shade and are tolerant of soil and acidity; however, they thrive best in a soil that has been enriched with leafmold, compost or peatmoss. They do not tolerate wet feet.

The excellent mounds of foliage resembling geranium leaves are useful in the shady rock garden, and along walks they give a well-defined pattern topped by spikes of bloom from June to September. They are a desirable addition to any wildflower garden.

The plants transplant easily, preferably before the tall flower spikes unfold. Propagation is mainly by division and seed, although selected specimens may be propagated by leaf cuttings.

The common species, Heuchera americana, is our native, but most of the wildflower nurseries offer the Coralbells H. sanguinea, in its improved forms. The flowers are much showier. One caring only for the foliage might well use our native, but if color and show is desired, the Coralbells or its improved varieties should be ordered.

BERGAMOT, SCARLET WILD

(Monarda didyma—perennial)

Height:	3-5 feet.
Flowers:	Red, shaggy flower heads, summer-fall.
Exposure:	Sun, light shade.
Soil:	Tolerant as to soil but should be moist, moderately acid.
Transplant:	Any time.
Uses:	Background, naturalizing, cutflowers.
Improved varieties:	Yes.
Propagate:	Division in spring or fall.
Conservation list:	No.

The bergamot is an oldtime favorite and has many common names such as Oswego-Tea, Bee-balm, Horse-Mint, etc. The shaggy flowers which protrude from the flower head are attractive in flower arrangements and long lasting. In the garden, they are host to the hummingbirds which add to their interest.

There are considerable variations in the flower color, and one might well have clumps of the various ones to meet the needs of color arrangements.

The bergamot is quite tolerant of soil as long as it is moist. Too rich a soil encourages or speeds the spread of a clump so that it may be too much for the location. In the fields, this is an advantage since it crowds out weaker plants and makes for a more effective show. However, this characteristic makes it useful to hold

stream banks and other areas subject to erosion.

It is easily moved at almost any time. To increase the number of clumps, one may divide in the spring or in the fall. They also may be increased by saving seed.

BLACK-EYED SUSAN

(Rudbeckia hirta—annual, biennial)

Height:	2-3 feet.
Flower:	Orange-yellow with blackish-brown cone, terminal clusters, summer and fall.
Exposure:	Sun or shade.
Soil:	Poor dry to rich moist, slightly acid.
Transplant:	Easy, anytime.
Uses:	Cutflowers, mass color.
Improved varieties:	Yes.
Propagate:	Seed self-sow, division.
Conservation list:	No.

The Black-eyed susan is a hardy vigorous growing annual or biennial that thrives under varying conditions. The coarse foliage is the one feature generally criticized. The showy yellow flowers are long-lasting and the plants flower over a long period in summer and fall.

The Black-eyed susan will grow equally well in full sun or light shade and is tolerant of soil. It is normally planted in ordinary garden soil and there seems to be no especially favorable season for transplanting. It may be found growing in quite acid soils, in moist situations and in dry thin soils.

Because the flowers are long-lasting it is useful as a cutflower. It may be planted as a background for other wildflowers, in waste areas, and in fence rows.

The Black-eyed susan has been used in hybridizing and there are new kinds of varieties which make use of some of its better characteristics.

Since the Black-eyed susan is a prolific seeder, it may not be desirable to plant it in the smaller wildflower garden unless the gardener is prepared to remove the spent blooms before seed is formed. This is much easier than pulling up countless unwanted seedlings.

BUTTERCUP, SWAMP

(Ranunclus septentrionalis—perennial)

Height:	2-3 feet.
Flower:	Bright yellow, 1-1½ inch in dia., long stalk, late spring, and early summer.
Exposure:	Sun and light shade.
Soil:	Moist grassland, tolerant, acid.
Transplant:	Spring.
Uses:	Carpet wetlands, cutflowers.
Improved varieties:	No.
Conservation list:	No.

The Swamp buttercups are pretty much the same—they have excellent foliage, bright yellow flowers and they grow like mad. Unless one has a fairly large area to be devoted to them, they should be by-passed. They like a moist situation such as other plants will not tolerate, and that is their major contribution.

They are tolerant of exposure and soil as long as it is very moist. While they stand upright in the spring, once the flowering season is past, and it is a long one, the stems spread out over the ground and root at the nodes much the same way as crabgrass does. These rooted stems may be cut apart and a considerable number of plants obtained.

COLUMBINE, WILD

(Aquilegia canadensis—perennial)

Height:	1-4 feet.
Flower:	Red and yellow, slender stalks, long-spurred, spring.
Exposure:	Sun, light shade.
Soil:	Tolerant of soil and acidity, grows on banks and along roadsides.
Transplant:	Early spring.
Uses:	Rock garden, slopes, border.
Improved varieties:	No.
Propagate:	Seed, division, self-sow.
Conservation list:	On conservation list I

The Wild Columbine, also called American Columbine and Eastern Columbine, is a dainty grower that may be seen along the roadsides, on banks, and in moist meadows. It is colorful and attractive. However, it should not be called American Columbine since there are a number of native species.

The columbine is tolerant of soils and acidity, but responds to enriched soils that are well drained. It will grow in full sun but does best in light shade. It is excellent for the rock garden, where its foliage (if free of the miner) is attractive all season.

The clumps of Columbine are easy to divide, but generally it is easier to let them self-seed. Transplant the seedlings to new locations in the early spring.

BLEEDINGHEART, Fringed

(Dicentra eximia—perennial)

Height:	12-18 inches.
Flower:	Reddish pink, heart-shaped on long racemes, all summer.
Exposure:	Sun or light shade.
Soil:	Tolerant but prefers moist woodsy.
Transplant:	Spring or fall.
Uses:	Ground cover, massed in border, etc.
Improved varieties:	Yes.
Propagate:	Divide clumps in early spring, self-seeds.
Conservation list:	No.

The Fringed Bleedingheart is also called Plumy Bleedingheart, Wild Bleedingheart, etc. It is not as widely planted as it might be because most gardeners do not know where to find it and lack knowledge of its attractive foliage and long season of bloom.

The Fringed Bleedingheart is tolerant but thrives best in moist woodsy soil. It will grow in full sun or in light shade. It is a compact grower topped by racemes of pink, heart-shaped blooms. It will self-seed in favorable situations and is much easier to grow than its relatives, Squirrel-corn and Dutchman's-breeches. As it remains in flower all season long, its usefulness and interest might well be called outstanding. There is an improved variety.

The Fringed Bleedingheart may be transplanted at any season although spring and fall are considered the better times.

The clumps may be divided in the early spring. It also will self-seed in favorable situations.

Mention above was given that it is sometimes called Wild Bleedingheart. This is because the Showy Bleedingheart which is so often grown in the wildflower garden is an introduced plant from Japan. We grow the Showy Bleedingheart oftentimes in the wildflower garden in rather shady situations and they do have heart-shaped flowers, but that is where the comparison ends. The Showy flowers in the spring and then dies down. The Fringed blooms throughout the season. It has compact ferny foliage, while the Showy is a tall-grower with bold foliage.

COHOSH BUGBANE (FAIRYCANDLES)

(Cimicifuga racemosa—perennial)

Height:	4-6 feet.
Flower:	Tall stalks covered with tiny white flowers, summer.
Exposure:	Light shade.
Soil:	Rich, deep woodsy, moderately acid.
Transplant:	Early spring.
Uses:	Background, accent when in clumps.
Improved varieties:	No.
Propagate:	Divide crowns early spring, fall, seed.
Conservation list:	No.

The Fairycandles, so named because of their shape, are also known as Black Snakeroot, Black Cohosh, and Bugbane. They are especially noticeable in late

summer in open woodlands. Under favorable conditions they will reach 6 feet in height. The tall cylindrical flower spike stands well above the attractive foliage.

It is important to plant the Fairycandles in deeply enriched soil, incorporating generous quantities of leafmold, compost, or peat moss into the soil. They like a moist soil but not wet—good drainage is important. However, they will soon fail in a poor, dry soil.

Because of the season of bloom and their height, the Fairycandles might well be included in the background of the shady flower border as well as in the wildflower garden.

A well established clump will consist of a number of crowns which may be separated in the early spring or late fall. Like other wildflowers they will self-seed in time.

BUTTERCUP, TALL

(Ranunculus acris—perennial)

Height:	2-3 feet.
Flower:	Bright yellow, 1 inch in diameter, on tall branched stems, spring and early summer.
Exposure:	Sun or shade.
Soil:	Rich moist soils, acid.
Transplant:	Anytime.
Uses:	Ground cover, cutflowers.
Propagate:	Seed, divisions.
Conservation list:	No.

The Buttercups are showy plants with their bright green foliage and rich yellow cup-like blooms. They make their best showing in the sun, but will grow in shade if the soil is rich and moist.

There is something symbolic about a buttercup and gardeners usually transplant them from the wild only to

find that they are spreaders and will take over vacant spots in their garden if the soil is suitably prepared.

In many cases they are most useful as a ground cover in situations that are too moist for other plants. If the soil is boggy, the species R. septentrionalis, the Swamp buttercup, is probably better adapted. The Tall buttercup, for ordinary moist conditions, is a better flower for cutting and its matted growth will serve to hold a bank.

CRANESBILL (WILD GERANIUM)

(Geranium maculatum—perennial)

Height:	1-2 feet.
Flower:	Magenta to lavender pink, terminal clusters, spring and summer.
Exposure:	Light shade.
Soil:	Dry to moist, not too rich, tolerant of acidity.
Transplant:	Anytime.
Uses:	For extensive areas, among ferns, etc.
Improved varieties:	No.
Propagate:	Free seeder, clumps may be divided spring and fall.
Conservation list:	On list II.

The Wild Geranium makes a colorful display in the shady garden, but it is a free seeder and may become weedy under favorable conditions. The flowers are showy and produce over a long season, but wilt quickly if cut.

The seed pod is shaped like the crane's bill, hence one of the common names. However, it is a true geranium and thus is always of interest although lacking in some desirable features.

The plants may be transplanted at any time, and desirable clumps may be divided in spring or fall.

The Wild Geranium is useful among ferns, where it provides color, and in wooded areas that are not devoted to dainty wildings.

FERN, CHRISTMAS

(Polystichum acrostichoides—perennial)

Height:	2-3 feet.
Flower:	————.
Exposure:	Light shade.
Soil:	Deep gravelly, enriched, moist, acid.
Transplant:	Early spring.
Uses:	Ground cover, border, background for small wild-flower bed.
Improved varieties:	Good named forms available.
Propagate:	Division in early spring.
Conservation list:	On list II.

The Christmas Fern is a popular evergreen for shady gardens in this area. It is tolerant of soils, although thriving in a gravelly well-drained one. However, the soil should be enriched with leafmold, compost, or peat moss to insure moisture.

This fern transplants best in the early spring but care should be taken not to injure the brittle fronds which are unfurling. It should be planted in a shady situation, will thrive even on the north side of a building.

The Christmasfern may be grown among evergreen shrubs such as azaleas and rhododendrons as it is not a rampant spreader.

This fern is somewhat variable in color and growth and consequently there are a number of named forms offered by wildflower nurseries. They may be perferable to collected specimens for the more personal wildflower garden or shady border. The common collected specimens should be adequate for a ground cover in a woodsy garden.

Established clumps may be divided in the early spring.

Like most of our native ferns, they are on the recommended conservation list. This means that collectors might well clean out woods that are being staked for bull-dozer action. Otherwise it is well to remember that the wildflower nurseries have desirable forms.

FERN, COMMON POLYPODY

(Polypodium vulgar virginianum—perennial)

Height:	10-12 inches.
Flower:	————.
Exposure:	Light shade.
Soil:	Loose woodland, moist.
Transplant:	Spring, early fall, space 2 feet.
Uses:	Evergreen ground cover.
Improved varieties:	None.
Propagate:	Division early spring.
Conservation list:	On list II.

The Common Polypody is an attractive evergreen fern with neat growth habits. The fronds are about 2 inches in width and 10 to 12 inches in length.

The fern grows in light shade in a moist woodland soil, but will tolerate short dry periods. The clumps should be spaced about 2 feet apart for good cover.

The Common Polypody is a hardy fern and like the rhododendron curls its fronds in cold weather.

It is a slow spreader and thus is considered one of the better ferns for use in the shady garden.

This fern may be moved at anytime, but like all ferns, it is not easy to handle without damage to the fronds when they are beginning to uncurl.

FERN, MAIDENHAIR

(Adiantum pedatum—perennial)

Height:	12-14 inches.
Flower:	————.
Exposure:	Light shade.
Soil:	Rich with humus, well drained but moist at all times, acid.
Transplant:	Early fall best, but anytime.
Uses:	Delicate ground cover, for foliage in arrangements.
Improved varieties:	No.
Propagate:	Division.
Conservation list:	On list II.

The dainty Maidenhair fern is considered one of the best for the shady garden. It is delicate and a slow spreader.

It will thrive in a deep woodsy soil that is always moist. Hence it is most commonly found along stream banks and near springs. However, it will not tolerate wet feet, thus, there is a desirable balance between soil moisture and drainage.

The Maidenhair fern is a slow spreader and will not usurp a large area in the garden. In the wild it is commonly found in isolated patches. In the wildflower garden it is often used to hide areas left bare by dying foliage of such plants as the Virginia Bluebells. They may be grown among the Rhododendrons and other broadleaved evergreens.

Propagation is by division in the early spring. However, it takes keen observation to note the slowly rising croziers which are earth-colored. The best time to divide is just as they begin to show.

FERN, ROYAL

(Osmunda regalis var. spectablis—perennial)

Height:	1-5 feet.
Flower:	———.
Exposure:	Light shade.
Soil:	Deep, rich, moist but not wet feet, acid.
Transplant:	Early spring before the fronds begin to unfurl.
Uses:	Ideal for along stream banks.
Improved varieties:	No.
Propagate:	Division in early spring or fall.
Conservation list:	On list II.

The Royal fern is looked upon as one of the most stately of ferns. It is especially attractive when growing along some small stream where its roots are always moist but not in wet soil. In other words, the roots can adjust to their moisture needs. This fern cannot take dry soils.

It is only suited to the larger garden where streams, springs, or pools provide suitable growing conditions. Also, because of its tall growth under favorable conditions, it is likely to be too tall for many situations.

This fern is deciduous—it dies down in the fall as does the Maidenhair; the other two included are evergreen. It is best divided in the early spring before the fronds begin to unfurl or in the fall. If divided in the fall the newly planted divisions should be well mulched to prevent heaving.

HEPATICA, LIVERLEAF

(Hepatica acutiloba—perennial)

Height:	6-8 inches.
Flower:	White to pink, single on stems, early spring.
Exposure:	Light shade.
Soil:	Moist rich woodland soil, moderately acid.
Transplant:	Anytime, even while in flower.
Uses:	Rock gardens, rock walls.
Improved varieties:	No.
Propagate:	Division after flowering or in fall, self-sow.
Conservation list:	On list II.

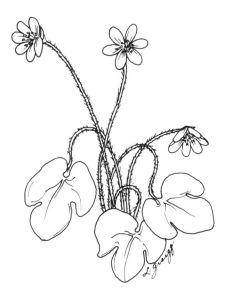

The dainty little Hepaticas, in spite of their common name, Liverleaf, are considered very choice wildflowers for the shady garden. While small and shown to best advantage in a rock garden, they may be used in other spaces. The flowers are borne on willowy stems above the foliage and show to advantage.

There are two native Hepaticas, the Sharplobe and the Roundlobe. The Sharplobe is more commonly found in this area, and is not as demanding for high acidity as the Roundlobe.

They are easily transplanted, even while in flower. Propagation, if desired, consists of pulling the crown apart after flowering or in the fall. Usually, in favorable situations they self-sow freely and division is not necessary. This is preferable since the older and larger plants make the best displays.

In planting the Liverleafs, it is well to use generous quantities of woods soil in the planting hole, lacking this use compost or peatmoss.

They should not be allowed to dry out during droughts. They are evergreen and the bronzy foliage is attractive during the winter. A mulch of leaves is helpful but do not cover the foliage.

IRIS, CRESTED

(Iris cristata—perennial)

Height:	4-6 inches.
Flower:	Pale lavender blue, short stalks, spring.
Exposure:	Shade.
Soil:	Well-drained and enriched with leafmold, compost, moderately acid.
Transplant:	Anytime, best after flowering.
Uses:	Rock garden and in wildflower garden where low growth may be seen.
Improved varieties:	Yes.
Propagate:	Divide after flowering.
Conservation list:	On list II.

The dainty little Crested Iris are considered one of the better wildflowers for the shady garden. They do not withstand competition with weeds and coarse growing wildflowers, hence are more likely to thrive in the rock garden. However, a bed of them near the pathway can be equally interesting.

They may be moved at anytime, but in the spring before flowering it is well to lift them with a ball of earth on the roots. After flowering they may be moved bare-root without injury. After flowering is the time to divide the rhizomes and to replant in soil that has been enriched with leafmold, compost or peatmoss. Do not attempt to cover the rhizomes with more than a half inch of soil. They will work to the top of this once the roots have become established.

The Crested Iris is a shade lover and will not thrive in full sun.

Protect the planting from injury; they are so small that many may not notice them. Walking upon the Crested Iris is not considered beneficial, nor should animals be allowed to romp over them.

IRIS, VERNAL

(Iris verna—perennial)

Height:	6-8 inches.
Flower:	Lavender-blue to white, on short stalks, spring.
Exposure:	Light shade.
Soil:	Rich in humus, moist, sandy, acid.
Transplant:	Anytime.
Uses:	Rock garden, small beds.
Improved varieties:	No.
Propagate:	Division after flowering.
Conservation list:	On list II.

The dainty little Vernal Iris is a bit larger grower than the Crested Iris. They are sometimes found in the same general area, but usually in different localities. Both are shade lovers and need a soil that has been enriched with leafmold, compost or peatmoss. Both need a moist situation but will not tolerate wet feet.

The Vernal Iris may be moved at any time, but if moved before flowering should be lifted with the roots in a ball of soil. After flowering they may be moved bare-root.

The rhizomes should be separated after flowering. Plant in a slightly raised bed and barely cover the rhizomes. Once the divisions are established the rhizomes will be on top of the soil.

The Vernal Iris like the Crested, makes a pleasing show in the shady rock garden, or on top of a rock wall. Beds beside the walk in the wildflower garden are showy but may be in danger of being stepped upon unless protected.

JACK-IN-THE-PULPIT, WOODLAND

(Arisaema triphyllum—perennial)

Height:	1-2 feet.
Flower:	The white Jack is beneath a green canopy stripped purple-brown, green or white. In late summer the Jack may become a cluster of red berries.
Exposure:	Light shade.
Soil:	Tolerant, but thrives best in deep rich soil that is moist, acid.
Transplant:	Anytime, spring, fall, dig deep enough to include the "indian turnip."
Uses:	Accent plant in the wildflower garden.
Improved varieties:	No.
Propagate:	Division, seed.
Conservation list:	On list II.

The stately Jack-in-the-pulpit is an accent plant in any wildflower garden. While related to the Skunk Cabbage, they are much easier to grow and are more interesting. The Jack-in-the-pulpit will attain good size and foliage if planted in a soil that is moist and has been deeply enriched with woods soil, compost, or peatmoss.

The Jack-in-the-pulpit may be transplanted at anytime but this is best done in the early spring or in the fall. Since the Indian Turnip, the corm from which the plant grows, is deep down it is well to dig deeply so as not to disturb the roots below the turnip.

EASTERN PENSTEMON (BEARD-TONGUE)

(Penstemon hirsutus—perennial)

Height:	1-2 feet.
Flower:	Purple or violet with lighter colored lip, panicles, spring.
Exposure:	Sun, light shade.
Soil:	Well-drained, gravelly or sandy, moderately acid.
Transplant:	Anytime.
Uses:	Sunny border, rock garden, cutting.
Improved varieties:	Yes.
Propagate:	Division early spring, seed.
Conservation list:	Not on list.

The Beard-Tongues are easily grown, useful plants. The flowers, which are borne in panicles, are small but numerous. However, the foliage is attractive throughout the season.

The Eastern Beard-Tongue may be transplanted at any time, but if to be divided this is best done in the early spring. The Beard-Tongues seed freely and this may not be desirable in a rock garden.

The Mid-Land Penstemon, also called the Foxglove Penstemon (P. barbatus), has spread into the eastern states and this may cause some confusion. However, its flowers are large, white with purple lines, and it is a taller grower. It may be more attractive to some than the Eastern Penstemon.

The Penstemons are easily raised from seed. However, the Western Penstemons, which are more showy than those mentioned above, are often available but unfortunately do not always like our climate.

RATTLESNAKE-PLANTAIN, DOWNY

(Goodyear pubescens—perennial)

Height:	Plants 3-6 inches, flower stalk 12-16 inches.
Flower:	White, helmet shaped, many on stalk, late spring, summer.
Exposure:	Light shade, sun.
Soil:	Woodsy, acid, moist but well-drained.
Transplant:	Anytime.
Uses:	Rock gardens, terrariums.
Improved varieties:	No.
Propagate:	Division spring and fall by separating rhizomes.
Conservation list:	Not on list.

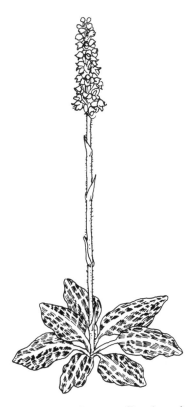

The curious little Downy Rattlesnake plantain, a member of the orchid family, is of most interest for use in terrariums, although it is also useful in the rock garden. The main interest seems to be in the curiously marked leaves, which some believe to resemble snakeskin.

The plant may be lifted at anytime, but this should be with a minimum disturbance to the roots.

The Rattlesnake-plantain thrives in woodsy, acid soil. It should be moist but well drained.

The mat of rhizomes may be divided if additional plants are needed. This is best done in the spring or fall.

The flowers of the Rattlesnake-plantain are not showy, and many would not recognize it by them. It is the white veined green leaves that are of interest.

SOLOMONPLUME, FALSE SOLOMONSEAL

(Smilacina racemosa—perennial)

Height:	2-3 feet.
Flower:	Feathery white panicles at the tip of the branches, late spring.
Exposure:	Light shade.
Soil:	Woodsy, moderately acid, moist.
Transplant:	Spring or fall.
Uses:	Companion plant for Solomonseal, ferns, etc.
Improved varieties:	No.
Propagate:	Division, seeds.
Conservation list:	On list II.

The False Solomonseal is a showy wildflower both in the spring and in the fall when the dark-red fruits appear. However, the birds seem to favor the berries and once ripe they quickly disappear.

This wildflower is a good companion for the ferns. In the wild it is frequently to be found among them. It does well in light to moderate shade.

Propagation is by dividing the rhizome, this is best done in the fall, although it may also be done after flowering.

The soil needs to be enriched by the addition of peatmoss, compost or leafmold. It should be moderately acid and moist.

The foliage of the False Solomonseal resembles that of Solomonseal in quality as well as in veining.

Some consider the False Solomonseal to be a spreader because of the rhizome root, but this is slow and not objectionable.

SOLOMONSEAL

(Polygonatum biflorum—perennial)

Height:	2-3 feet.
Flower:	Bell-like yellow-green hanging from each node, late spring.
Exposure:	Light shade, sun.
Soil:	Rich, moist, acid.
Transplant:	Early spring.
Uses:	Shady wildflower garden.
Improved varieties:	No.
Propagate:	Seeds.
Conservation list:	On list II.

The Solomonseal is a popular plant for the wildflower garden. The many bell-like flowers hanging from the leafnodes are followed by green berry-like fruits which turn dark blue in the fall. The foliage is attractive and may be useful in the background of the smaller wildflower border.

The Solomonseal will thrive either in sun or shade if planted in a soil that has been enriched by the addition of peatmoss, compost, or leafmold. It should be moist and acid.

This plant is not easily divided and so propagation is usually by seed.

The Solomonseal makes a good companion plant for Rhododendrons and other broad-leaved evergreens in shady situations.

TRILLIUM

(Trilliuam grandiflorum—perennial)

Height:	10-15 inches.
Flower:	2-3 inch white blossoms.
Exposure:	Light shade.
Soil:	Enriched with peatmoss, leafmold or compost, moderately acid.
Transplant:	Anytime, preferably in the fall after the bulbs have matured.
Uses:	In moist shaded woodlands, moist situation in rock garden.
Improved varieties:	No.
Conservation list:	On list II.

may be found in heavy shade, but generally they do best in light shade.

The bulbs should be planted in the fall, preferably in clumps of ten or a dozen since they do not multiply rapidly. They may be lifted after flowering and the bulbs replanted then or stored until fall.

The Trillium bulbs need protection from rodents which may be supplied by surrounding them with hardware cloth. A covering is also desirable since the bulbs are given only a 2-inch covering with soil.

The White Trillium is the most showy and easiest to grow, but there is also the Nodding Trillium, the Red Trillium, the Painted Trillium, etc. The latter is usually considered more demanding and requires an acid soil, considerable moisture, a cool situation in summer, and a soil that is generously enriched with some form of humus.

GINGER, WILD

(Asarum canadense—perennial)

Height:	8-10 inches.
Flower:	Small jug like, brown-purple, very early in spring.
Exposure:	Shady.
Soil:	Rich with humus, well drained, moderately acid.
Transplant:	Spring, fall.
Uses:	Ground cover, under rhododendrons, etc.
Improved varieties:	No.
Propagate:	Division spring, fall.
Conservation list:	On list II.

There are many areas along the Eastern seaboard where the Wild Gingers may be found. They thrive in any woodland where there is moderate moisture and a deep rich soil. They may be found on loamy slopes in soils that are neutral to moderately acid.

In the garden the Wild Ginger is useful as a low-growing ground cover and it is at home beneath a

Rhododendron or similar tall growing shrub.

This native should be handled in the early spring or fall to avoid checking its growth.

The Wild Ginger is a slow spreader and thus is adapted to the smaller wildflower garden.

The small jug-like flower is hidden by the large round leaves and is seldom noticed. Its color is a brownish purple and is roughly an inch in diameter.

Sun Lovers

BUTTERFLY MILKWEED

(Asclepias tuberosa—perennial)

Height:	1-2 feet.
Flower:	Orange-yellow, clusters, summer-flowering.
Exposure:	Sun.
Soil:	Gravelly, moderately acid.
Transplant:	August, September.
Uses:	Cut flowers, summer color in border.
Improved varieties:	No.
Propagate:	Seed-fall, root cuttings in May.
Conservation list:	No.

The Butterfly milkweed is always attractive with its showy, orange-yellow colored bloom clusters in June. The nectar-laden blooms attract butterflies; hence its common name.

This flower thrives in hot dry situations although it does best in a gravelly soil. It is quite tolerant of acidity but seems to thrive best in a slightly acid, well-drained soil.

The plant dies down after flowering, and unless the spot is marked, is seldom located for digging while dormant. August or September is usually considered the best time to dig them. However, because the roots are large and brittle, it is usually safer to dig a small plant or to buy them from a grower.

The Butterfly milkweed may be propagated by digging a portion of the root in May, and cutting it into one- or two-inch sections which may be planted shallowly in a sandy soil. Seeds may be collected in the fall and sown in late fall, or they can be sown in the spring.

The flowers last well in arrangements. It is important to leave some of the foliage so that the root will continue to grow and develop for another season's bloom.

The Butterfly milkweed lasts for many years in a well-drained situation, and is particularly effective when placed in front of evergreens. It is not a spreader, but clumps will increase in size and a well-established one may have 10 or 12 flower stalks in bloom at a time. This is one of the reasons why it is such a desirable wildflower.

The attractive blooms are followed by beaked pods three or four inches long which are useful in flower arrangements either before or after opening.

The Butterfly milkweed is one of the most attractive of all the milkweeds. Certainly, it is much less a spreader, and for this reason is a good garden subject. However, for a moist situation, one might also wish to try the Swamp milkweed. The Purple milkweed and the Blunt-leaved milkweed are other possibilities.

CACTUS, PRICKLY PEAR

(Optunia compressa—perennial)

Height:	4-6 inches.
Flower:	Yellow, 2-3 in. dia., summer.
Exposure:	Sun, will tolerate light shade.
Soil:	Dry, poor, neutral to moderately acid.
Transplant:	Spring.
Uses:	Rock gardening, seashore gardens.
Improved varieties:	No.
Propagate:	Break off pads in spring and insert in sandy soil.
Conservation list:	No.

The Prickly-pear Cactus is a native to the eastern states, the only member of the cactus family which is. It will thrive in poor gravelly soil in full sunlight. Its habit of growth is such that it is best planted on banks. It will tolerate salt air and sandy soils.

The sprawly habit of growth requires considerable space for a wilding, and the sharp spines make it repulsive to some. Children soon learn to stay clear of it.

The fruits are edible but have tufts of bristles on them which may discourage use.

In spite of these unfavorable points, the cactus is more than an exotic plant. The wax-like texture of the flowers give them a richness of color that is unmatched by other plants.

DAISY, FIELD

(Chrysanthemum leucanthemum—perennial)

Height:	1-2 feet.
Flower:	White daisy-like on long stems, summer.
Exposure:	Sun.
Soil:	Tolerant of soils, meadowlands, neutral to moderately acid.
Transplant:	Anytime.
Uses:	Border, cutflowers.
Improved varieties:	No.
Propagate:	Seed, division in spring, fall.
Conservation list:	No.

The Field Daisy, or Ox-eye Daisy as it is often called, is an introduced plant that has made itself at home. It is to be found along the roadsides, in meadows, and in gardens where its vigor and tolerance make it adaptable.

Because of its free seeding it can be weedy, and unwanted seedlings should be promptly removed.

The Field Daisy is a productive bloomer and is well worth cultivating as a cutflower. The individual blooms range from 1 to 2 in. in diameter.

GOLDENROD, PLUME

(Solidago juncea—perennial)

Height:	1-5 feet.
Flower:	Large fluffy flower masses, curving at the top, golden-yellow June to November.
Exposure:	Sun.
Soil:	Tolerant, moderately enriched with compost, leafmold; moderate to strongly acid, medium moist.
Transplant:	Spring.
Uses:	Mass effect, cutflowers.
Improved varieties:	Yes.
Propagate:	Divide, self-seed freely.
Conservation list:	Not on list.

There are a large number of native goldenrods in the U.S., and the east is not without its share of these late-summer and fall-bloomers. They range from small flat-topped species to tall willowy kinds with interesting curves to the racemes. Some have dainty foliage, other coarse, rough leaves that may be too large for good appearance. Thus it is important in selecting a native to choose plants which have the more desirable characteristics.

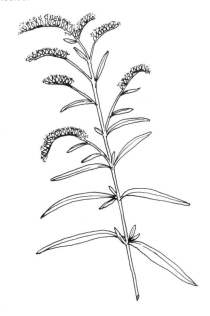

The Plume Goldenrod is considered by many to be one of the best in this area. It thrives in open sun and in dappled shade in meadowlands, and along the roadsides. Its height and flower display will be affected by the soil and moisture where growing. It may be recognized by the smooth reddish stems. Also, in this species there are small leaves growing in the axils of the larger leaves.

Most goldenrods are too strong growing for the smaller garden, but there are some that grow only a foot in height that may be used if the spent blooms are removed before they drop their seeds.

A desirable plant may be increased through division of the root mat in the spring. Thus, it is best to choose carefully and take only a suitable plant and do the propagation the next spring.

Goldenrods are quite tolerant of soil and moisture but should have full sun if they are to give the display wanted. The richer the soil, the taller and the larger they will grow. But of course, the foliage will be larger and coarser too.

QUEEN-ANNE'S LACE

(Daucus carota—biennial)

Height:	2-4 feet.
Flower:	White in large flat umbels, summer.
Exposure:	Sun.
Soil:	Grasslands.
Transplant:	Spring (small roots).
Uses:	Cutflowers, dried flowers.
Improved varieties:	No.
Propagate:	Seeds.
Conservation list:	Not on list.

The Queen-Anne's Lace is so widespread and often considered a weed, that it is a surprise to many that it is an introduced plant. Also, it is the wild species from which our common vegetable, carrots, have been developed.

The Queen-Anne's Lace is useful both as a cutflower and for dried flower arrangements. The plants are so commonly available in roadside and meadow that it is doubtful one would want to raise them. Especially so since the seed have to be sown one season, live over winter as small plants (roots) and then produce the flower stalk the next season. If plants are grown the gardener should prevent the formation of seed. For drying the flowers are cut just as they open and before seed formation begins.

To transplant Queen-Anne's Lace it is well to dig the small roots in the early spring. They may also be dug in the late fall.

Queen-Anne's Lace flourishes in any good garden soil in full sun.

ROSEMALLOW

(Hibiscus palustris—perennial)

Height:	3-5 feet.
Flower:	White, pink, some have a red eye, summer.
Exposure:	Sun, light shade.
Soil:	Deep, rich, moist—tolerant of moisture and will grow in usual garden soil.
Transplant:	Early spring.
Uses:	Background, mass color.
Improved varieties:	Yes, many hybrids offered.
Propagate:	Seed.
Conservation list:	No.

The Rosemallow, Swamp Mallow, and sometimes called Hibiscus, is normally found along streams and moist situations. The huge flowers are most showy.

The large fleshy roots are difficult to handle except while dormant. Since the plants are easily grown from seed, there is little point in trying to dig them except for some special color or form. However, most flower seed merchants unually offer selections or hybrids and for this reason it may not even be advisable to collect seed in the wild.

The Rosemallow is supposed to thrive in deep moist soils but apparently will do almost as well in the usual garden soil. It will grow in full sun but the colors and flowers seem brighter in light shade.

During the height of the Japanese beetle invasion the flowers were badly damaged since the Rosemallows were in bloom when the beetles were flying. Since the beetles are seldom troublesome now, the Rosemallow may be worth growing for its mass color effects.

YUCCA

(Yucca filamentosa—perennial)

Height:	4-6 feet.
Flower:	On tall stalks with a large cluster of waxy-white blooms—summer.
Exposure:	Sun.
Soil:	Dry, tolerant of acidity.
Transplant:	Early spring taking small rosettes.
Uses:	In dry, sunny border.
Improved varieties:	No.
Propagate:	Divide taking smaller rosettes, self-seeds.
Conservation list:	Not on list.

The stately Yucca makes an appreciable showing in the sunny border in mid-summer. The tall spikes with many flowers, which may be 2 inches in length and almost as much in diameter, bloom in June or July.

This plant, which is normally associated with the West, actually is a native from south Delaware and one of the few Yuccas that will tolerate the wet soils of the east.

The Yucca thrives best in full sun in a poor gravelly soil. The hotter and drier, the better. It is tolerant of soil acidity but most gardeners avoid the use of peatmoss or other acidifying materials.

The tall flower stalks should be removed after flowering and before the seeds fall. Otherwise the gardener may find many seedlings to be removed or transplanted.

The Yucca is a long-lasting perennial that produces many rosettes which may be dug and new plants established. Seed may take 4 or 5 years to attain flowering size, the rosettes usually in 2 or 3 years.

The Yucca is often called Spanish Bayonet and Adam's Needle. These names derive from the long sharp pointed leaves that grow from the main root in rosette form.

Late Bloomers

ASTER, New England

(Aster novae-angliae—perennial)

Height:	2-5 feet.
Flowers:	Violet to pink, branched flower head, late summer.
Exposure:	Sun, light shade.
Soil:	Moist, not too rich, neutral to slightly acid.
Transplant:	Spring (and in bloom).
Uses:	Informal border, background.
Improved varieties:	Yes.
Propagate:	Self-sows, divide clumps in spring.
Conservation list:	No.

The tall showy asters always command attention in the fall. They are common along our country roads, in the edges of grasslands, and in the edges of woodlands. There is considerable variation in their color. This species and other American natives were exported to Europe where the plant breeders did much to make them more attractive and useful.

The aster does well in ordinary garden soil but will repay any improvement in it with stronger growth and better blooms heads. They need a moist soil since they are late summer bloomers.

The plants may be transplanted at any time, even while in bloom. The root system is quite fibrous and holds the soil fairly well.

Propagation is by division in the spring. Named varieties usually are lifted and divided every few years. The clumps reach large size and produce many flower stems. Normally, numerous seedlings appear, and it is well to remove them before the planting becomes unmanageable.

There are many wild asters in our fields and woodlands, some of which are fully as attractive as the New England aster. One could have quite a garden just of asters.

The flower heads of the New England aster contain a great many buds. There are always some that are about to open, some open, and some that are past. For this reason, they should be cut for indoor use just as the first flowers open. The faded flowers detract from the appearance.

In exposed situations, the tall stems should be staked before they are borne to the ground by fall rains.

CARDINAL FLOWER

(Lobelia cardinalis—perennial)

Height:	2-5 feet.
Flower:	Bright red on tall stalks or racemes, late summer and fall.
Exposure:	Light shade, sun if in moist situation.
Soil:	Rich humus-filled, moist, acid.
Transplant:	Spring.
Uses:	Accent near pools, along streams.
Improved varieties:	No.
Propagate:	Divide in spring, will self-seed.
Conservation list:	On list II.

The Cardinal flower is bright red and commands attention wherever it may be. The best show is provided by a clump near a pool or against a boulder.

The Cardinal flower grows best in rich, moist woodland soil, but will tolerate full sun if the soil and moisture conditions are favorable.

The late summer-flowering of this plant makes it useful in maintaining color in the wildflower garden. Some say the Cardinal flower is temperamental and will die out. This may be due to the soil becoming too dry, more likely it is not acid enough.

The flower spikes should be cut off to prevent seeding and to encourage the growth of perennial basal shoots. In this way large clumps are formed. Without this care the Cardinal flower tends to have only one or two flower stalks per plant.

LILY, TURKSCAP

(Lilium superbum—perennial)

Height:	2-8 feet.
Flower:	Orange-red spotted purple, recurved petals, late summer.
Exposure:	Light shade, sun.
Soil:	Moist, sandy-peat, meadow—enriched.
Transplant:	Early spring, late fall.
Uses:	Shady flower border.
Improved varieties:	No.
Propagate:	Seed, division, scales.
Conservation list:	On list I.

The Turkscap lily is a native of this area and is to be found in moist woodland soils near creeks; also in meadows near a stream bank. It thrives in a sandy soil that has been enriched with leafmold, peatmoss, or compost. The soil should be acid. In a suitable soil it will thrive in full sun and attain a height of 6 to 8 feet.

The bulbs should be lifted in the early spring or in late fall.

Propagation is from seed, separation of the bulbs which are on a long angular rhizome, or a special form might well be propagated by the scaling method.

The flowers are so fully recurved that this lily may well be viewed from any angle. It adds color to the border in late summer.

It is on the Conservation list I, hence unless being rescued from a development area, might well be obtained from a lily grower or from a wild-flower specialist. It is easy to grow. Its height suggests planting among shrubs.

This lily is base-rooting, hence does not require deep planting. In the wild the bulbs may be found with only a couple of inches of soil over them. However, 4 to 5 inches is the recommended depth in a well enriched sandy soil.

MEADOWRUE, TALL

(Thalictrum polygamum—perennial)

Height:	3-6 feet.
Flower:	White, large feathery clusters, summer and early fall.
Exposure:	Sun, light shade.
Soil:	Soil should be moist and rich.
Transplant:	Spring or fall.
Uses:	Background for lower-growing plants in light shade.
Improved varieties:	No.
Propagate:	Division early spring or after flowering.
Conservation list:	No.

There are a number of the Meadowrues in this area. This species is known both as tall and as fall Meadowrue. The foliage somewhat resembles that of the Columbine.

It is an easy plant to grow, but prefers a moist, rich soil. It will grow fully as well in sun as in light shade if the soil is favorable.

The early Meadowrue (T. dioicum) is a lower grower (2 ft.), flowering in the spring. The flowers are a green-yellow and borne in panicles.

The Purple Meadowrue (T. dasycarpum) differs from the tall in that its stems are purple and the flowers are both white and purple. The showy clusters appearing in summer.

MISTFLOWER, HARDY AGERATUM

(Eupatorium coelestinum—perennial)

Height:	1-2 feet.
Flower:	Azure blue, fluffy terminal clusters, Aug.-Oct.
Exposure:	Sun, light shade.
Soil:	Rich, moist, moderately acid.
Transplant:	Anytime, spring preferred.
Uses:	Sunny border, cutflower.
Improved varieties:	No.
Propagate:	Division, in spring, seed.
Conservation list:	No.

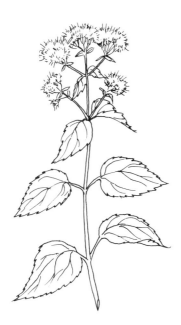

The Hardy Ageratum, Mistflower, or Eupatorium as it is variously called is a showy fall bloomer. The blue flowers are fully as attractive as the true ageratum. It is of easy culture.

The one bad fault, and it is a bad one, is that it spreads rapidly both by underground stolons and by seed. It is almost impossible to eradicate once it gets into a rock garden. The foliage is rather coarse for the smaller wildflower garden.

The flowers are much sought after for flower arrangements in the fall. It might be useful to prevent erosion on a moist sunny slope.

The Other Wildlings

Mention of a number of other wildflowers and plants has been omitted for several reasons. For example, the Trailing-Arbutus is only happy when it can be planted on a slope. It is not often easily transplanted. The Chelone is a native that is better bought from a nursery than collected, largely because it moves best when dormant or very early in the spring. The commercial nurseries ship it in the spring or fall. The wild orchids, such as the Pink Ladyslipper and the Yellow Ladyslipper, are not easily transplanted because of their stringy root system. The pink is particularly difficult to move. The same is to be said of the ground cover commonly called Crowfoot to Ground Pine. It prefers the area beneath pine trees if it is not to die. The Teasel is an interesting prickly, tall growing biennial that is popular in flower arrangements. Undoubtedly some will want to grow it. Interestingly enough, it is an introduced plant that likes our climate and soils and is to be found growing wild in many places.

Another well-known wildflower, Chickory, is such an invasive weed that although we love its chickory-blue flowers we should not plant it in the garden unless we can build a retaining wall around it. Another common wildflower, sometimes called Butter-and-Eggs and Yellow Bedstraw, is so fragile and transitory that most people lose interest. The Pitcher Plant is adapted to bog conditions which are seldom feasible in the garden. It is no more than a curiosity.

Collecting Seeds

Most of these wildflowers seed rather freely, and if the seed is collected when mature and sown immediately in a suitable bed, it is quite possible to produce new plants. Oftentimes, they will seed naturally, and these seedings should be lifted and transplanted to a suitable area until large enough to be incorporated in the planting. Such plants, of course, are of interest to other gardeners, and the surplus is usually easily disposed of.

Propagation

Many of these wildflowers may be propagated by division, a few by root cuttings, and a very few by rooting of stems in suitable propagating media. Generally, however, this is the work of the specialist, although many gardeners find it an interesting and rewarding practice. Certainly those who have sizable shady gardens will have need for many plants of each kind. Specific mention of methods was made above in the case of plants which I have grown.

Meadow Gardening

One easy alternative for wildflower gardeners is meadow gardening using a small portion of open lawn. Here the soil can be dug and prepared for early fall planting with a selected collection of wildflower seeds suitable for this area. Seeds are broadcast in early September (rampant spreaders are preferable) and are raked and pressed into the surface. Then they are lightly mulched with chopped straw and salt hay. After overwintering a variety of perennials and self-seeding annuals will begin to provide color throughout the following season. Mowing such a meadow is delayed until the following fall to allow seeds to mature. Seeds for meadow gardens that are made up of Eastern wildflowers are available commercially and solve many of the problems of collecting.

GROWING TO SHOW AND SHARE

Should you want to follow up an enthusiasm for some aspect of gardening that appeals to you, challenges you, or just makes you feel that you want to know more about it, there are wonderful resources and good friends to be made in the 135 local chapters of the National Capital Federation of Garden Clubs. And there are other established garden organizations in Virginia and Maryland as well, notably those that sponsor the annual House and Garden tours that are such an enjoyable way to experience different outlying counties.

Some of these organizations are national in scope, but all exist to help area gardeners. To this end they sponsor garden shows for members, teach classes in flower arranging and judging, and play an active role in starting and maintaining the many public gardens local residents enjoy.

In addition there are local plant societies whose members share a common passion for some gardening specialty. These groups' interests range from modern roses to a love of wildflowers—with stops in between for a score of horticultural specialties. Through them much of the information in this book is kept updated, which will surprise no one, for gardeners are the most generous of people in sharing their experience.

LOCAL GARDENING ORGANIZATIONS
With the gracious permission of *The Capital Gardener*, the publication of the National Capital Federation of Garden Clubs, we list the current addresses and phone numbers by which you may reach these groups.

National Capital Federation of Garden Clubs
District One—The District and close-in Montgomery and Prince Georges Counties.
Director: Mrs. Ralph Guarino (301) 843-5406
Assistant Director: Ellen Fields Utley (301) 552-1052

District Two—Alexandria, southwest Fairfax County and Prince William County.
Director: Mrs. Dean Moser (703) 569-4382
Assistant Director: Mrs. Raymond Peterson (703) 221-3980

District Three—Northwest Fairfax County and Loudon County.
Director: Mrs. Michael Alden (703)-273-3730
Assistant Director: Mrs. David Spencer (703) 759-7733

District Four—Montgomery County.
Director: Mrs. Thomas Carter (301) 762-5682
Assistant Director: Mary Corley (301) 340-0148

Plant Societies

All Hallows Guild, Washington Cathedral
Mrs. Guy T. Steuart III (301) 656-6351

Azalea Society of America:
Brookside Gardens Chapter: William Johnson (301) 946-2908
Northern Virginia Chapter—David Raden (703) 273 8094

Potomac Bonsai Association
Chris Yeaponis (703) 591-0864

National Capital Cactus & Succulent Society
Walter Weyres (301) 350-3537

Camellia Society of the Potomac Valley
Arthur Maryott (301) 654-5727

Chesapeake Chrysanthemum Society
Pat Buffington (410) 964-2479

Old Dominion Chrysanthemum Society
Diane Roe (703) 534-6569

Potomac Chrysanthemum Society
Jessie Clarke (202) 726-0819

Washington Daffodil Society
Mary Ann Barton (703) 273-8641

Dahlia Society
Mary Partridge (703) 356-7738

National Capital Daylily Club
Margo Reed (301) 424-6392

Herb Society of America
Potomac Unit, Jo Sellers (703) 451-7037

Potomac Hosta Club
Debbie Bochnek (703) 281-9244

Chesapeake and Potomac Iris Society.
Sara Marley (703) 338-7594

Potomac Lily Society
Robert Tanner (703) 548-9682

Maryland Native Plant Society.
Barbara Medina (301) 622-3289

Potowmack Native Plant Society
Anne Hayes, P.O. Box 161, McLean Virginia 22101

National Capital Orchid Society
Gordon Slaymaker (703) 644-7958

Potomac Rose Society
Bob Aldie (301) 460-4716

Flower Arranging
Floralia Club
Betty Giles (703) 338-7594

Ikebana International, Washington Chapter
Jennie Berg (301) 644-1534

General Interest
Hyattsville Horticultural society
Harold Stevens (301) 935-6096

Men's Garden Club of Montgomery County
Bernard Chew (301) 340-1556

Takoma Horticultural Club
Helen Hoggarth (301) 588-4917

GARDENING ADVICE

The Cooperative Extension Service has qualified horticultural agents to answer gardening questions. Addresses and phone numbers are listed below.

Extension Service Offices

District of Columbia
Garden questions: (202) 282-3069.
Soil sample drop-offs: 901 Newton Street NE, 9-4:30 weekdays.

Maryland
Home & Garden Information Center: (800) 342-2507
Anne Arundel County (410) 220-6759
Baltimore City
Baltimore County
Calvert County 535-3662
Caroline County
Carroll County 848-4611
Charles County 934-5403
Frederick County 694-1594
Harford County
Howard County 313-2707
Montgomery County 590-9638
Prince Georges County 868-8738
Queen Anne County 758-0390
St. Mary's County 4750448
Bookside Botanic Gardens Hot Line 949-8230 x3

Virginia
State Office, VPI, Blacksburg Virginia (703) 231-9892
Alexandria 838-0960
Arlington County 358-6407
Chesterfield County 751-4401
Culpeper County 825-2233
Fairfax County 222-9760
Fauquier County 347-8650
Frederick County 665-5699
Henrico County 672-5160
Loudon County 777-1262
Prince William County 792-6285
Richmond City 786-4150
Rappahannock County 675-3619
Spotsylvania County 582-7096
Stafford County 899-4020
Green Spring Garden 642-5173

Local Climatic Conditions Washington Metropolitan Area

The greater National Capital Region lies within Zone 7, which has been further divided into zones 7A and 7B, with Zone 7B being slightly more temperate. Roughly, counties in our region to the north and west of a line running from Annapolis to Washington to Richmond are in Zone 7A, and areas to the south and east of this line are in Zone 7B. In the immediate Washington area, the District, Arlington, Alexandria, the parts of Prince Georges and Stafford Counties near the Potomac, and all of Charles, St. Mary's, and Caroline Counties are in Zone 7B. Your Cooperative Extension Agent can provide you with full information, and a county-by-county map on the opposite page.

As a general rule, which must be amended by local topographical features and conditions, Washington's spring and fall frost records for the past 60 years show:
⇒ In the spring, the last frost occurs after April 20 in areas to the north and west of the city, and before April 20 in areas to the south and east of the city.
⇒ In the fall, frost appears before October 20 in areas to the north and west of the city, and after October 20 in areas to the south and east of the city.

The chart below is arranged in order of the elevations of the places listed. As expected, the highest elevations have the shortest growing seasons, but there are some interesting variances from this rule (for instance, parts of Laurel are high but warm, while parts of nearby Glenn Dale are low but cold).
⇒ Average annual rainfall is from 37 to 43 inches throughout the region.
⇒ Where the average annual growing season data is used, gardeners should figure on the growing season for warm weather crops being about 10 to 12 days less than the average and the season for cool weather crops that can stand light frost being about 10 days longer.

Average Length of Growing Season

(Revised and updated for Maryland and Virginia within 40 miles of the District.)

Area/Elevation	Last Frost	Growing Season	First Frost
Lincoln VA—500 ft.	April 17	186 days	October 21
Laurel MD—400 ft.	April 9	204 days	October 31
Rockville MD—320 ft.	April 24	176 days	October 10
Loudon County VA—313 ft.	May 10	154 days	October 10
Dulles Airport VA—290 ft.	May 11	169 days	September 24
Glenn Dale MD—150 ft.	April 29	163 days	October 10
BWI Airport MD—140 ft.	April 17	194 days	October 27
LaPlata MD—140 ft.	April 24	179 days	October 21
Owings Ferry MD—120 ft.	April 15	190 days	October 25
College Park MD—90 ft.	April 18	186 days	October 21
Fredericksburg VA—50 ft.	April 20	175 days	October 20
Annapolis MD—40 ft.	March 30	232 days	November 17
Quantico VA—12 ft.	April 23	187 days	October 21
National Airport DC—10 ft.	March 25	199 days	November 14

Approximate Equivalent-Volume Measures of Materials to Use in the Row and Per Plant at Various Rates Per 100 Square Feet.

Rates per 100 Sq. Ft.	Rates per 10 feet, rows Spaced—				Rates per Plant, Spaced—	
	3 ft.	2 ft.	1 ft.	5x5 ft.	2¼x2¼ ft.	2x1½ ft.
10 Pints	3 Pints	2 Pints	1 Pint	2½ Pts.	1 Cup	½ Cup
6 "	3½ Cups	2½ Cups	1¼ Cups	3 Cups	½ " (h)	¼ " (h)
5 "	3 "	2 "	1 "	2½ "	½ "	¼ "
4 "	2½ "	1½ "	¾ "	2 "	6½ Tbs.	3 Tbs. (h)
3 "	1¾ "	1¼ "	½ " (h)	1½ "	5 "	2½ "
2½ "	1½ "	1 "	½ "	1¼ "	4 "	2 "
2 "	1¼ "	¾ "	6½ Tbs.	1 "	3¼ "	1½ "
1½ "	¾ " (h)	½ " (h)	5 "	¾ "	2½ "	1 " (h)
1 "	½ "	6 Tbs.	3¼ "	½ "	1½ "	2½ Tsp.
1½ Cups	½ "	5 "	2½ "	6 Tbs.	1 "	1½ "
1 "	5 Tbs.	3¼ "	1½ "	4 "	2½ Tsp.	¾ "
½ "	2½ "	1½ "	¾ "	2 "	1¼ "	½ "
4 Tablespoons	1¼ "	2½ Tsp.	1¼ Tsp.	1 "	½ "	¼ "
1 "	1 Tsp.	½ " (h)	⅓ "	¼ "	1/6 "	1/12 "
2 Bushels	½ Bus. (h)	1½ Peck	6 Qts.	½ Bush.	3 Qts.	1½ Qts.
1 "	1 Peck (h)	1 " (s)	3 "	1 Peck	1½ "	¾ "

Tbs.—tablespoon; Tsp—teaspoon; (h) heaping; (s) scant.

Note: Pint of water weighs 1.046 pounds; Acre contains 43,560 sq. ft.; Pint=2 cups=32 tablespoons=96 teaspoons. Measures given are level-full except as noted.

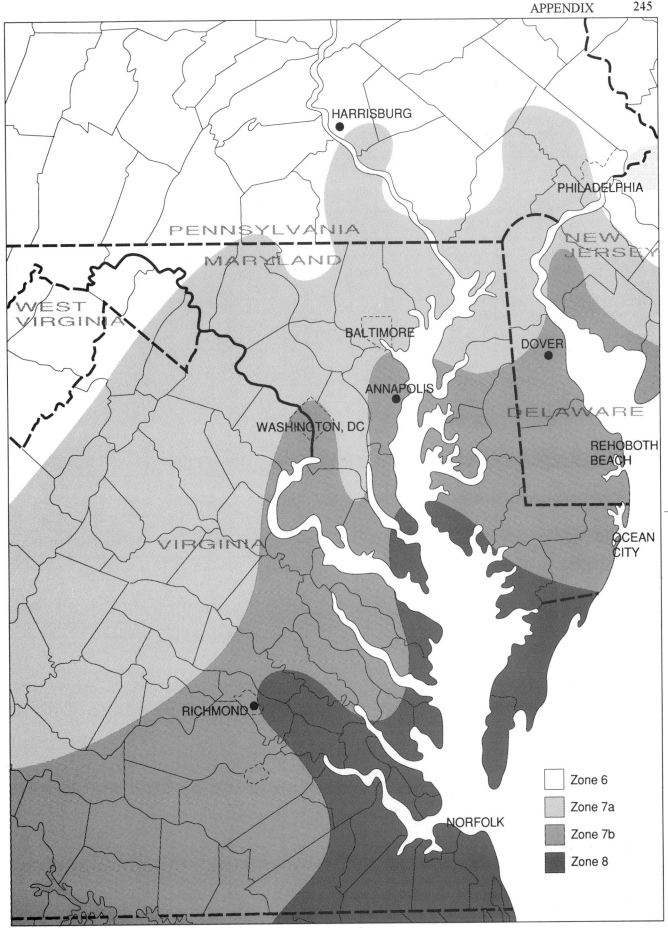

HARRISBURG

PENNSYLVANIA

PHILADELPHIA

NEW JERSEY

MARYLAND

WEST VIRGINIA

BALTIMORE

DOVER

ANNAPOLIS

DELAWARE

WASHINGTON, DC

REHOBOTH BEACH

VIRGINIA

OCEAN CITY

RICHMOND

NORFOLK

	Zone 6
	Zone 7a
	Zone 7b
	Zone 8

CONVERSION TABLE

For Converting Tons or Pounds Per Acre Into Pints, Cups, Tablespoons, or Teaspoons Per Row or Plant.

From Agriculture Department Tables

Weights of various fertilizing materials per acre, per 1,000 square feet, and per 100 square feet and the approximate equivalent-volume measures for 100 square feet, grouped according to weight in comparison with that of water.

Materials	Acre	Weights specified per— 1,000 Sq. ft.	100 Sq. ft.	Volume measure for 100 Sq. ft.
	Pounds	Units	Units	Units
Weight about the same as that of water	1,300	30 Pounds	3 Pounds	3 Pints
	870	20 "	2 "	2 "
(Ex. Cal-Nitro, A-N-L)	435	10 "	1 "	1 "
	220	5 "	½ "	1 Cup
	110	2½ "	¼ "	½ "
Weight about 1.3 that of water	5,660	130 "	13 "	10 Pints
	3,485	80 "	8 "	6 "
(Ex. Ground limestone, ground dolomitic limestone, granular sodium	870	20 "	2 "	1½ "
nitrate potassium sulfate.)	565	13 "	21 Ounces	1 "
	280	6½ "	11 "	1 Cup
Weight about 9/10 that of water.	1,960	45 "	4½ Pounds	5 Pints
	1,650	38 "	3¾ "	4 "
(Ex. ammonium phosphate, super-phosphate, 5-10-5, 4-8-4, etc.	1,220	28 "	2¾ "	3 "
muriate of potash.)	1,000	23 "	2¼ "	2½ "
	785	18 "	30 Ounces	2 "
	610	14 "	21 "	1½ "
	390	9 "	15 "	1 "
	300	7 "	11 "	1½ Cups
	200	4⅜ "	7½ "	1 "
	100	2¼ "	3½ "	¼ "
	50	18 Ounces	2 "	4 Tbs.
	11	5 "	½ "	1 "
Weight about 8/10 that of water.	1,740	40 Pounds	4 Pounds	5 Pints
	650	15 "	1½ "	2 "
(Ex. Epsom salts, bonemeal.)	175	4 "	6½ Ounces	1 Cup
	44	1 "	1½ "	4 Tbs.
Weight about 7/10 that of water.	1,740	40 Pounds	4 Pounds	6 Pints
	1,525	35 "	3½ "	5 "
(Ex. Sewage sludge, Uramon, Ammonium sulfate, granular ammonium	650	15 "	1½ "	2 "
nitrate, aluminum sulfate, granular borax.)	300	7 "	11 Ounces	1 "
	150	3½ "	5½ "	1 Cup
	44	1 "	1½ "	4 Tbs.
	11	5 Ounces	½ "	1 "
Weight about 6/10 that of water.	1,300	30 Pounds	3 Pounds	5 Pints
	545	12½ "	1¼ "	2 "
(Ex. Cottonseed meal, sulfur, fish scrap.)	260	6 "	10 Ounces	1 "
	130	3 "	5 "	1 Cup
Weight about 5/10 that of water.	1,100	25 "	2½ Pounds	5 Pints
	435	10 "	1 "	2 "
(Ex. Hydrated lime.)	220	5 "	8 Ounces	1 "
	110	2½ "	4 "	1 Cup
Manure (moist):				
Loose	13 Tons	600 Pounds	60 Pounds	2 Bushels
Packed	13 "	600 "	60 "	1 "
Dry straw or leaves packed tightly with hands.	5 "	250 "	25 "	2 "